NEW FUNDAMENTAL TECHNOLOGIES IN DATA MINING

Edited by **Kimito Funatsu**
and **Kiyoshi Hasegawa**

New Fundamental Technologies in Data Mining
Edited by Kimito Funatsu and Kiyoshi Hasegawa

Published by InTech
Janeza Trdine 9, 51000 Rijeka, Croatia

Publishing Process Manager Ana Nikolic

Technical Editor Teodora Smiljanic

Cover Designer InTech Design Team

Additional hard copies can be obtained from orders@intechopen.com

New Fundamental Technologies in Data Mining, Edited by Kimito Funatsu and Kiyoshi Hasegawa
p. cm.
ISBN 978-953-307-547-1

For EU product safety concerns:
IN TECH d.o.o., Prolaz Marije Krucifikse Kozulić 3, 51000 Rijeka, Croatia,
info@intechopen.com or visit our website at intechopen.com.

Meet the editors

Prof. Kimito Funatsu was born on December 3, 1955 in Japan. He received his Doctor degree (Dr. Sci.; physical organic chemistry) from Kyushu University which is one of the oldest imperial universities (1983) and joined Prof. Shin-ichi Sasaki's group, Toyohashi University of Technology (1984) as research-associate. During researching in Prof. Sasaki's group he worked on chemoinformatics field, i.e., Structure elucidation system CHEMICS, organic synthesis design system AIPHOS, molecular design. In 1990 he took the post of associate-professor. In 2004 he moved to The University of Tokyo as full Professor to continue the same research work. Recently he is trying material design and soft sensor. He is a chair of division of chemical information and computer sciences, Chemical Society of Japan.

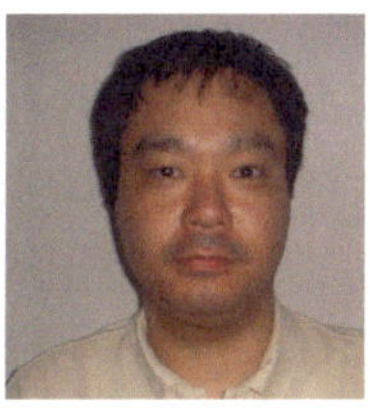

Dr. Kiyoshi Hasegawa was born on August 18, 1963 in Kanazawa, Japan. He received his Ph.D. from Toyohashi University of Technology (1995) and worked at Biostructure group in Chugai Pharmaceutical Company in Japan. While working in Chugai, he spent three months at Swiss Basel Research Center in Roche for developing new de novo design program (2003). He is now principal scientist in his group and is involved in many SBDD projects. He is also the Roche data mining working group member and the secretary general of Japan Chemical Information Science. His interests are de novo design, Chemogenomics, data mining and web application.

Contents

Preface

Data mining, a branch of computer science and artificial intelligence, is the process of extracting patterns from data. Data mining is seen as an increasingly important tool to transform a huge amount of data into a knowledge form giving an informational advantage. Reflecting this conceptualization, people consider data mining to be just one step in a larger process known as knowledge discovery in databases (KDD). Data mining is currently used in a wide range of practices from business to scientific discovery.

The progress of data mining technology and large public popularity establish a need for a comprehensive text on the subject. The series of books entitled by 'Data Mining' address the need by presenting in-depth description of novel mining algorithms and many useful applications.

The first book (New Fundamental Technologies in Data Mining) is organized into two parts. The first part presents database management systems (DBMS). Before data mining algorithms can be used, a target data set must be assembled. As data mining can only uncover patterns already present in the data, the target dataset must be large enough to contain these patterns. For this purpose, some unique DBMS have been developed over past decades. They consist of software that operates databases, providing storage, access, security, backup and other facilities. DBMS can be categorized according to the database model that they support, such as relational or XML, the types of computer they support, such as a server cluster or a mobile phone, the query languages that access the database, such as SQL or XQuery, performance trade-offs, such as maximum scale or maximum speed or others.

The second part is based on explaining new data analysis techniques. Data mining involves the use of sophisticated data analysis techniques to discover relationships in large data sets. In general, they commonly involve four classes of tasks: (1) Clustering is the task of discovering groups and structures in the data that are in some way or another "similar" without using known structures in the data. Data visualization tools are followed after making clustering operations. (2) Classification is the task of generalizing known structure to apply to new data. (3) Regression attempts to find a function which models the data with the least error. (4) Association rule searches for relationships between variables.

The second book (Knowledge-Oriented Applications in Data Mining) is based on introducing several scientific applications using data mining. Data mining is used for a variety of purposes in both private and public sectors. Industries such as banking, insurance, medicine, and retailing use data mining to reduce costs, enhance research, and increase sales. For example, pharmaceutical companies use data mining of chemical compounds and genetic material to help guide research on new treatments for diseases. In the public sector, data mining applications were initially used as a means to detect fraud and waste, but they have grown also to be used for purposes such as measuring and improving program performance. It has been reported that data mining has helped the federal government recover millions of dollars in fraudulent Medicare payments.

In data mining, there are implementation and oversight issues that can influence the success of an application. One issue is data quality, which refers to the accuracy and completeness of the data. The second issue is the interoperability of the data mining techniques and databases being used by different people. The third issue is mission creep, or the use of data for purposes other than for which the data were originally collected. The fourth issue is privacy. Questions that may be considered include the degree to which government agencies should use and mix commercial data with government data, whether data sources are being used for purposes other than those for which they were originally designed.

In addition to understanding each part deeply, the two books present useful hints and strategies to solving problems in the following chapters. The contributing authors have highlighted many future research directions that will foster multi-disciplinary collaborations and hence will lead to significant development in the field of data mining.

January, 2011

Kimito Funatsu
The University of Tokyo, Department of Chemical System Engineering,
Japan

Kiyoshi Hasegawa
Chugai Pharmaceutical Company, Kamakura Research Laboratories,
Japan

Part 1

Database Management Systems

1

Service-Oriented Data Mining

Derya Birant
Dokuz Eylul University,
Turkey

1. Introduction

A *service* is a software building block capable of fulfilling a given task or a distinct business function through a well-defined interface, loosely-coupled interface. Services are like "black boxes", since they operate independently within the system, external components are not aware of how they perform their function, they only care that they return the expected result.

The *Service Oriented Architecture* (SOA) is a flexible set of design principles used for building flexible, modular, and interoperable software applications. SOA represents a standard model for resource sharing in distributed systems and offers a generic framework towards the integration of diverse systems. Thus, information technology strategy is turning to SOA in order to make better use of current resources, adapt to more rapidly changes and larger development. Another principle of SOA is the reusable software components within different applications and processes.

A *Web Service* (WS) is a collection of functions that are packaged as a single entity and published to the network for use by other applications through a standard protocol. It offers the possibility of transparent integration between heterogeneous platforms and applications. The popularity of web services is mainly due to the availability of web service standards and the adoption of universally accepted technologies, including XML, SOAP, WSDL and UDDI.

The most important implementation of SOA is represented by web services. *Web service-based SOAs* are now widely accepted for on-demand computing as well as for developing more interoperable systems. They provide integration of computational services that can communicate and coordinate with each other to perform goal-directed activities.

Among intelligent systems, *Data Mining* (DM) has been the center of much attention, because it focuses on extracting useful information from large volumes of data. However, building scalable, extensible, interoperable, modular and easy-to-use data mining systems has proved to be difficult. In response, we propose SOMiner (Service Oriented Miner), a service-oriented architecture for data mining that relies on web services to achieve extensibility and interoperability, offers simple abstractions for users, provides scalability by cutting down overhead on the number of web services ported to the platform and supports computationally intensive processing on large amounts of data.

This chapter proposes SOMiner, a flexible service-oriented data mining architecture that incorporates the main phases of knowledge discovery process: data preprocessing, data mining (model construction), result filtering, model validation and model visualization. This architecture is composed of generic and specific web services that provide a large collection of machine learning algorithms written for knowledge discovery tasks such as classification, clustering, and association rules, which can be invoked through a common GUI. We developed a platform-independent interface that users are able to browse the available data mining methods provided, and generate models using the chosen method via this interface. SOMiner is designed to handle large volumes of data, high computational demands, and to be able to serve a very high user population.

The main purpose of this chapter is to resolve the problems that appear widely in the current data mining applications, such as low level of resource sharing, difficult to use data mining algorithms one after another and so on. It explores the advantages of service-oriented data mining and proposes a novel system named SOMiner. SOMiner offers the necessary support for the implementation of knowledge discovery workflows and has a workflow engine to enable users to compose KDD services for the solution of a particular problem. One important characteristic separates the SOMiner from its predecessors: it also proposes Semantic Web Services for building a comprehensive high-level framework for distributed knowledge discovery in SOA models.

In this chapter, proposed system has also been illustrated with a case study that data mining algorithms have been used in a service-based architecture by utilizing web services and a knowledge workflow has been constructed to represent potentially repeatable sequences of data mining steps. On the basis of the experimental results, we can conclude that a service-oriented data mining architecture can be effectively used to develop KDD applications.

The remainder of the chapter is organized as follows. Section 2 reviews the literature, discusses the results in the context of related work, presents a background about SOA+Data Mining approach and describes how related work supports the integrated process. Section 3 presents a detailed description of our system, its features and components, then, describes how a client interface interacts with the designed services and specifies the advantages of the new system. Section 4 demonstrates how the proposed model can be used to analyze a real world data, illustrates all levels of system design in details based on a case study and presents the results obtained from experimental studies. Furthermore, it also describes an evaluation of the system based on the case study and discusses preliminary considerations regarding system implementation and performance. Finally, Section 5 provides a short summary, some concluding remarks and possible future works.

2. Background

2.1 Related work

The Web is not the only area that has been mentioned by the SOA paradigm. Also the Grid can provide a framework whereby a great number of services can be dynamically located, managed and securely executed according to the principles of on-demand computing. Since Grids proved effective as platforms for data-intensive computing, some grid-based data mining systems have been proposed such as DataMiningGrid (Stankovski et al., 2008), KnowledgeGrid (K-Grid) (Congiusta et al., 2007), Data Mining Grid Architecture (DMGA) (Perez et al., 2007), GridMiner (Brezany et al., 2005), and Federated Analysis Environment for Heterogeneous Intelligent Mining (FAEHIM) (Ali et al., 2005). A significant difference of these systems from our system (SOMiner) is that they use grid-based solutions and focus on grid-related topics and grid-based aspects such as resource brokering, resource discovery, resource selection, job scheduling and grid security.

Another grid-based and service-based data mining approaches are ChinaGrid (Wu et al., 2009) and Weka4WS (Talia and Trunfio, 2007). A grid middleware ChinaGrid consists of services (data management service, storage resource management service, replication management service, etc.) to offers the fundamental support for data mining applications. Another framework Weka4WS extends the Weka toolkit for supporting distributed data mining on grid environments and for supporting mobile data mining services. Weka4WS adopts the emerging Web Services Resource Framework (WSRF) for accessing remote data mining algorithms and managing distributed computations. In comparison, SOMiner tackles scalability and extensibility problems with availability of web services, without using a grid platform.

Some systems distribute the execution within grid computing environments based on the resource allocation and management provided by a resource broker. For example, Congiusta et al. (2008) introduced a general approach for exploiting grid computing to support distributed data mining by using grids as decentralized high performance platforms where to execute data mining tasks and knowledge discovery algorithms and applications. Talia 2009 discussed a strategy based on the use of services for the design of open distributed knowledge discovery tasks and applications on grids and distributed systems. On the contrary, SOMiner exposes all its functionalities as Web Services, which enable important benefits, such as dynamic service discovery and composition, standard support for authorization and cryptography, and so on.

A few research frameworks currently exist for deploying specific data mining applications on application-specific data. For example, Swain et al. (2010) proposed a distributed system (P-found) that allows scientists to share large volume of protein data i.e. consisting of terabytes and to perform distributed data mining on this dataset. Another example, Jackson et al. (2007) described the development of a Virtual Organisation (VO) to support distributed diagnostics and to address the complex data mining challenges in the condition health monitoring applications. Similarly, Yamany et al. (2010) proposed services (for providing intelligent security), which use three different data mining techniques: the association rules, which helps to predict security attacks, the OnLine Analytical Processing (OLAP) cube, for authorization, and clustering algorithms, which facilitate access control rights representation and automation. However, differently from SOMiner, these works include application-specific services i.e. related to protein folding simulations or condition health monitoring or security attacks.

Research projects such as the Anteater (Guedes et al., 2006) and the DisDaMin (Distributed Data Mining) (Olejnik et al., 2009) have built distributed data mining environments, mainly focusing on parallelism. Anteater uses parallel algorithms for data mining such as parallel implementations of Apriori (for frequent item set mining), ID3 (for building classifiers) and K-Means (for clustering). DisDaMin project was addressed distributed discovery and knowledge discovery through parallelization of data mining tasks. However it is difficult to implement the parallel versions of some data mining algorithms. Thus, SOMiner provides parallelism through the execution of traditional data mining algorithms in parallel with different web services on different nodes.

Several studies mainly related to the implementation details of data mining services on different software development platforms. For example, Du et al. (2008) presented a way to set up a framework for designing the data mining system based on SOA by the use of WCF (Windows Communication Foundation). Similarly, Chen et al. (2006) presented architecture for data mining metadata web services based on Java Data Ming (JDM) in a grid environment.

Several previous works proposed a service-oriented computing model for data mining by providing a markup language. For example, Discovery Net (Sairafi et al., 2003) provided a Discovery Process Markup Language (DPML) which is an XML-based representation of the workflows. Tsai & Tsai (2005) introduced a Dynamic Data Mining Process (DDMP) system in which web services are dynamically linked using Business Process Execution Language for Web Service (BPEL4WS) to construct a desired data mining process. Their model was described by Predictive Model Markup Language (PMML) for data analysis.

A few works have been done in developing service-based data mining systems for general purposes. On the other side, Ari et al., 2008 integrated data mining models with business services using a SOA to provide real-time Business Intelligence (BI), instead of traditional BI. They accessed and used data mining model predictions via web services from their platform. Their purposes were managing data mining models and making business-critical decisions. While some existing systems such as (Chen et al., 2003) only provide the specialized data mining functionality, SOMiner includes functionality for designing complete knowledge discovery processes such as data preprocessing, pattern evaluation, result filtering and visualization.

Our approach is not similar in many aspects to other studies that provided a service-based middleware for data mining. First, SOMiner has no any restriction with regard to data mining domains, applications, techniques or technology. It supports a simple interface and a service composition mechanism to realize customized data mining processes and to execute a multi-step data mining application, while some systems seem to lack a proper workflow editing and management facility. SOMiner tackles scalability and extensibility problems with availability of web services, without using a grid platform. Besides data mining services, SOMiner provides services implementing the main steps of a KDD process such as data preprocessing, pattern evaluation, result filtering and visualization. Most existing systems don't adequately address all these concerns together.

To the best of our knowledge, none of the existing systems makes use of Semantic Web Services as a technology. Therefore, SOMiner is the first system leveraging Semantic Web Services for building a comprehensive high-level framework for distributed knowledge discovery in SOA models, supporting also the integration of data mining algorithms exposed through an interface that abstracts the technical details of data mining algorithms.

2.2 SOA + data mining

Simple client-server data mining solutions have scalability limitations that are obvious when we consider both multiple large databases and large numbers of users. Furthermore, these solutions require significant computational resources, which might not be widely available. For these reasons, in this study, we propose service-oriented data mining solutions to be able to expand the computing capacity simply and transparently, by just advertising new services through an interface.

On the other side, while traditional Grid systems are rather monolithic, characterized by a rigid structure; the SOA offers a generic approach towards the integration of diverse systems. Additional features of SOA, such as interoperability, self-containment of services, and stateless services, bring more value than a grid-based solution.

In SOA+Data Mining model, SOA enables the assembly of web services through parts of the data mining applications, regardless of their implementation details, deployment location, and initial objective of their development. In other words, SOA can be viewed as architecture that provides the ability to build data mining applications that can be composed at runtime using already existing web services which can be invoked over a network.

3. Mining in a service-oriented architecture

3.1 SOMiner architecture

This chapter proposes a new system SOMiner (Service Oriented Miner) that offers to users high-level abstractions and a set of web services by which it is possible to integrate resources in a SOA model to support all phases of the knowledge discovery process such as data management, data mining, and knowledge representation. SOMiner is easily extensible due to its use of web services and the natural structure of SOA - just adding new resources (data sets, servers, interfaces and algorithms) by simply advertising them to the application servers.

The SOMiner architecture is based on the standard life cycle of knowledge discovery process. In short, users of the system can be able to understand what data is in which database as well as their meaning, select the data on which they want to work, choose and apply data mining algorithms to the data, have the patterns represented in an intuitive way, receive the evaluation results of patterns mined, and possibly return to any of the previous steps for new tries.

SOMiner is composed of six layers: data layer, application layer, user layer, data mining service layer, semantic layer and complementary service layer. A high speed enterprise service bus integrates all these layers, including data warehouses, web services, users, and business applications.

The SOMiner architecture is depicted in the diagram of Fig. 1. It is an execution environment that is designed and implemented according to a multi-layer structure. All interaction during the processing of a user request happens over the Web, based on a user interface that controls access to the individual services. An example knowledge discovery workflow is as follows: when the *business application* gets a request from a *user*, it firstly calls *data preparation web service* to make dataset ready for data mining task(s), and then related *data mining service(s)* is activated for analyzing data. After that, *evaluation service* is invoked as a complementary service to validate data mining results. Finally, *presentation service* is called to represent knowledge in a manner (i.e. drawing conclusions) as to facilitate inference from data mining results.

<u>Data Layer</u>: The *Data Layer (DL)* is responsible for the publication and searching of data to be mined (data sources), as well as handling metadata describing data sources. In other words, they are responsible for the access interface to data sets and all associated metadata. The metadata are in XML and describes each attribute's type, whether they represent continuous or categorized entities, and other things.

DL includes services: *Data Access Service (DAS), Data Replication Service (DRS),* and *Data Discovery Service (DDS).* Additional specific services can also be defined for the data management without changes in the rest of the framework. The *DAS* can retrieve descriptions of the data, transfer bases from one node to another, and execute SQL-based queries on the data. Data can be fed into the DAS from existing data warehouses or from other sources (flat files, data marts, web documents etc.) when it has already been preprocessed, cleaned, and organized. The *DRS* deals with data replication task which is one important aspect related to SOA model. *DDS* improves the discovery phase in SOA for mining applications.

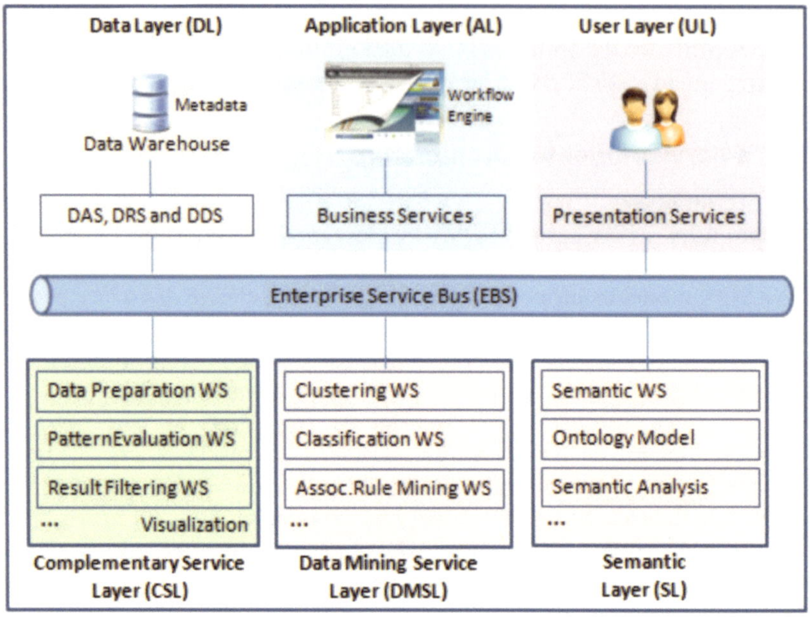

Fig. 1. SOMiner: a service-oriented architecture (SOA) for data mining

<u>Application Layer</u>: *Application Layer (AL)* is responsible for business services related to the application. Users don't interact directly with all services or servers - that's also the responsibility of the AL. It controls user interaction and returns the results to any user action. When a user starts building a data mining application, the AL looks for available data warehouses, queries them about their data and presents that information back to the user along with metadata. The user then selects a dataset, perhaps even further defines data preprocessing operations according to certain criteria. The AL then identifies which data mining services are available, along with their algorithms. When the user chooses the data mining algorithm and defines the arguments of it, the task is then ready to be processed. For the latter task, the AL informs the result filtering, pattern evaluation and visualization services. Complementary service layer builds these operations and sends the results back to the AL for presentation. SOMiner saves all these tasks to the user's list from which it can be scheduled for execution, edited for updates, or selected for visualization again.

<u>User Layer</u>: *User Layer (UL)* provides the user interaction with the system. The *Results Presentation Services (RPS)* offer facilities for presenting and visualizing the extracted knowledge models (e.g., association rules, classification rules, and clustering models). As mentioned before, a user can publish and search resources and services, design and submit data mining applications, and visualize results. Such users may want to make specific choices in terms of defining and configuring a data mining process such as algorithm selection, parameter setting, and preference specification for web services used to execute a particular data mining application. However, with the transparency advantage, end users have limited knowledge of the underlying data mining and web service technologies.

<u>Data Mining Service Layer</u>: *Data Mining Service Layer (DMSL)* is the fundamental layer in the SOMiner system. This layer is composed of generic and specific web services that provide a large collection of machine learning algorithms written for knowledge discovery tasks. In DMSL, each web service provides a different data mining task such as classification,

clustering and association rule mining (ARM). They can be published, searched and invoked separately or consecutively through a common GUI. Enabling these web services for running on large-scale SOA systems facilitates the development of flexible, scalable and distributed data mining applications.

This layer processes datasets and produces data mining results as output. To handle very huge datasets and the associated computational costs, the DMSL can be distributed over more than one node. The drawback related to this layer, however, is that it is now necessary to implement a web service for each data mining algorithm. This is a time consuming process, and requires the scientist to have some understanding of web services.

Complementary Service Layer: *Complementary Service Layer (CSL)* provides knowledge discovery processes such as data preparation, pattern evaluation, result filtering, visualization, except data mining process. *Data Preparation Service* provides data preprocessing operations such as data collection, data integration, data cleaning, data transformation, and data reduction. *Pattern Evaluation Service* performs the validation of data mining results to ensure the correctness of the output and the accuracy of the model. This service provides validation methods such as Simple Validation, Cross Validation, n-Fold Cross Validation, Sum of Square Errors (SSE), Mean Square Error (MSE), Entropy and Purity. If validation results are not satisfactory, data mining services can be re-executed with different parameters more than one times until finding an accurate model and result set. *Result Filtering Service* allows users to consider only some part of results set in visualization or to highlight particular subsets of patterns mined. Users may use this service to find the most interesting rules in the set or to indicate rules that have a given item in the rule consequent. Similarly, in ARM, users may want to observe only association rules with k-itemsets, where *k* is number of items provided by user. *Visualization* is often seen as a key component within many data mining applications. An important aspect of SOMiner is its visualization capability, which helps users from other areas of expertise easily understand the output of data mining algorithms. For example, a graph can be plotted using an appropriate visualize for displaying clustering results or a tree can be plotted to visualize classification (decision tree) results. Visualization capability can be provided by using different drawing libraries.

Semantic Layer: On the basis of those previous experiences we argue that it is necessary to design and implement semantic web services that will be provided by the *Semantic Layer (SL)*, i.e. ontology model, to offer the semantic description of the functionalities.

Enterprise Service Bus: The *Enterprise Service Bus (ESB)* is a middleware technology providing the necessary characteristics in order to support SOA. ESB can be sometimes considered as being the seventh layer of the architecture. The ESB layer offers the necessary support for transport interconnections. Translation specifications are provided to the ESB in a standard format and the ESB provides translation facilities. In other words, the ESB is used as a means to integrate and deploy a dynamic workbench for the web service collaboration. With the help of the ESB, services are exposed in a uniform manner, such that any user, who is able to consume web services over a generic or specific transport, is able to access them. The ESB keeps a registry of all connected parts, and routes messages between these parts. Since the ESB is solving all integration issues, each layer only focuses on its own functionalities.

SOMiner is easily extensible, as such; administrators easily add new servers or web services or databases as long as they have an interface; they can increase computing power by adding services or databases to independent mining servers or nodes. Similarly, end users can use any server or service for their task, as long as the application server allows it.

3.2 Application modeling and representation

SOMiner has the capability of composition of services, that is, the ability to create workflows, which allows several services to be scheduled in a flexible manner to build a solution for a problem. As shown in Fig. 2, a service composition can be made in three ways: horizontal, vertical and hybrid. *Horizontal composition* refers to a chain-like combination of different functional services; typically the output of one service corresponds to the input of another service, and so on. One common example of horizontal composition is the combination of pre-processing, data mining and post-processing functions for completing KDD process. In *vertical composition*, several services, which carry out the same or different functionalities, can be executed at the same time on different datasets or on different data portions. By using vertical composition, it is possible to improve the performance in a parallel way. *Hybrid composition* combines horizontal and vertical compositions, and provides one-to-many cardinality, typically the output of one service corresponds to the input of more than one services or vice versa.

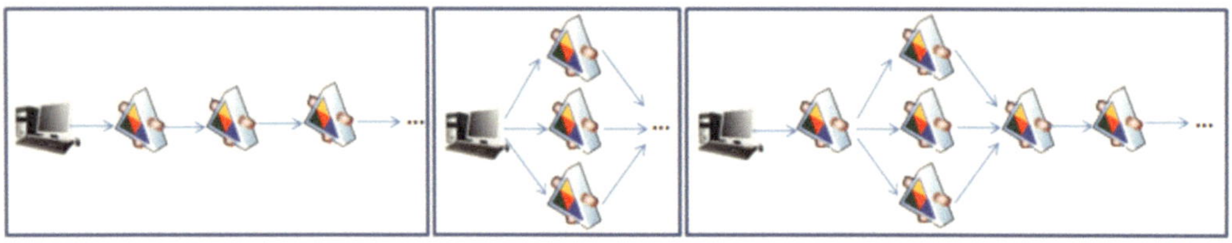

Fig. 2. Workflow types: horizontal composition, vertical composition, and hybrid

A workflow in SOMiner consists of a set of KDD services exposed via an *interface* and a *toolbox* which contains set of tools to interact with web services. The *interface* provides the users a simple way to design and execute complex data mining applications by exploiting the advantages coming from a SOA environment. In particular, it offers a set of facilities to design data mining applications starting from a view of available data, web services, and data mining algorithms to different steps for displaying results. A user needs only a browser to access SOMiner resources. The *toolbox* lets users choose from different visual components to perform KDD tasks, reducing the need for training users in data mining specifics, since many details of the application, such as the data mining algorithms, are hidden behind this visual notation.

Designing and executing a data mining application over the SOMiner is a multi-step task that involves interactions and information flows between services at the different levels of the architecture. We designed toolbox as a set of components that offer services through well defined interfaces, so that users can employ them as needed to meet the application needs. SOMiners's components are based on major points of the KDD problem that the architecture should address, such as accessing to a database, executing a mining task(s), and visualizing the results.

Fig. 3 shows a screenshot from the interface which allows the construction of knowledge discovery flows in SOMiner. While, on the left hand side, the user is provided with a collection of tools (toolbox) to perform KDD tasks, on the right hand side, the user is provided with workspace for composing services to build an application. Tasks are visual components that can be graphically connected to create a particular knowledge workflow. The connection between tasks is made by dragging an arrow from the output node of the sending task to the input node of the receiving task. Sample workflow in Fig. 3 was composed of seven services: data preparation, clustering, evaluation of clustering results,

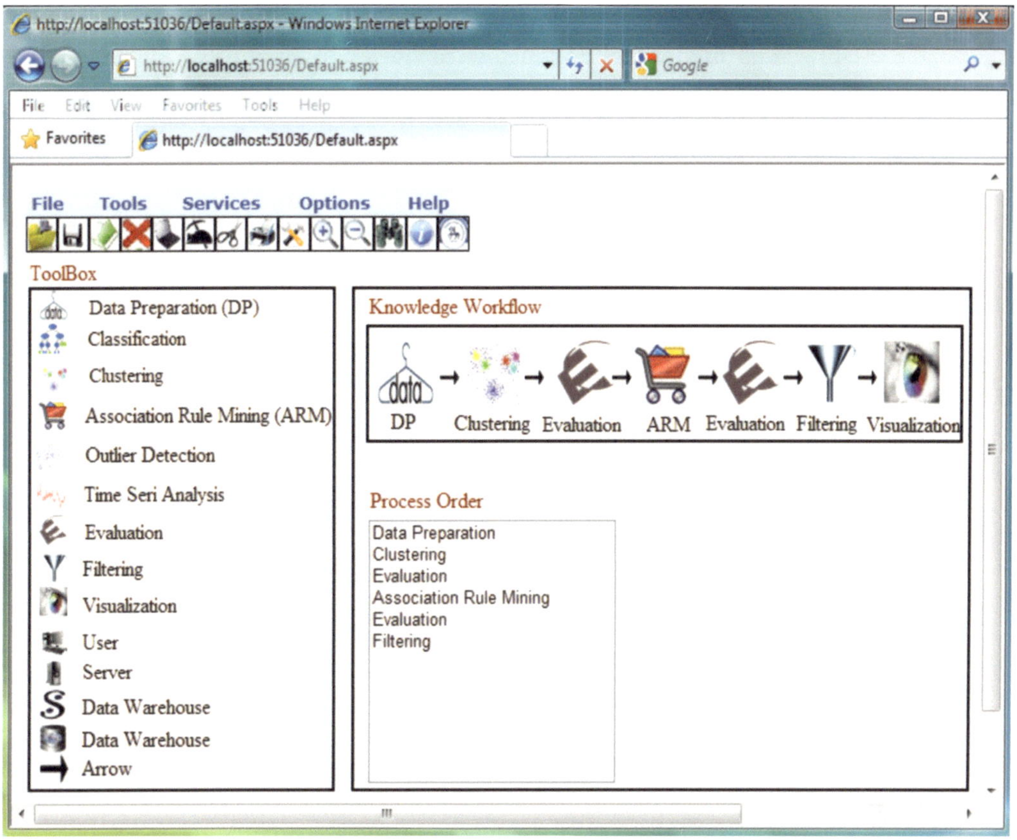

Fig. 3. Screenshot from the interface used for the construction of knowledge workflows

ARM, evaluation of association rules, filtering results according to user requests, and visualization.

Interaction between the workflow engine and each web service instance is supported through pre-defined SOAP messages. If a user chooses a particular web service from the place on the composition area, a URL specifying the location of the WSDL document can be seen, along with the data types that are necessary to invoke the particular web service.

3.3 Advantages of service-oriented data mining

Adopting SOA for data mining has at least three advantages: (i) implementing data mining services without having to deal with interfacing details such as the messaging protocol, (ii) extending and modifying data mining applications by simply creating or discovering new services, and (iii) focusing on business or science problems without having to worry about data mining implementations. (Cheung et al., 2006)

Some key advantages of service-oriented data mining system (SOMiner) include the following:

1. *Transparency*: End-users can be able to carry out the data mining tasks without needing to understand detailed aspects of the underlying data mining algorithms. Furthermore, end-users can be able to concentrate on the knowledge discovery application they must develop, without worrying about the SOA infrastructure and its low-level details.

2. *Application development support*: Developers of data mining solutions can be able to enable existing data mining applications, techniques and resources with little or no intervention in existing application code.
3. *Interoperability*: The system will be based on widely used web service technology. As a key feature, web services are the elementary facilitators of interoperability in the case of SOAs.
4. *Extensibility*: System provides extensibility by allowing existing systems to integrate with new tasks, just adding new resources (data sets, servers, interfaces and algorithms) by simply advertising them to the system.
5. *Parallelism*: System supports processing on large amounts of data through parallelism. Different parts of the computation are executed in parallel on different nodes, taking advantage at the same time of data distribution and web service distribution.
6. *Workflow capabilities*: The system facilitates the construction of knowledge discovery workflows. Thus, users can reuse some parts of the previously composed service flows to further strengthen the data mining application development's agility.
7. *Maintainability*: System provides maintainability by allowing existing systems to change only a partial task(s) and thus to adapt more rapidly to changing in data mining applications.
8. *Visual abilities*: An important aspect of the system is its visual components, since many details of the application are hidden behind this visual notation.
9. *Fault tolerance:* The application can continue to operation without interruption in the presence of partial network failures, or failures of the some software components, taking advantage of data distribution and web service distribution.
10. *Collaborative*: A number of science and engineering projects can be performed in collaborative mode with physically distributed participants.

A significant advantage of SOMiner over previous systems is that SOMiner is intended for using semantic web services to the semantic level, i.e. ontology model and offer the semantic description of the functionalities. For example, it allows integration of data mining tasks with ontology information available from the web.

Overall, we believe the collection of advantages and features of SOMiner make it a unique and competitive contender for developing new data mining applications on service-oriented computing environments.

4. Case study

4.1 SOMiner at work

In this section, we describe a case study and experimental results obtained by the construction of a knowledge workflow in which data in a data warehouse was analyzed by using clustering and ARM algorithms, with the goal of evaluating the performance of the system. In the case study, interface within the SOMiner framework has been used to implement a data mining application related to dried fruit industry, and obtained significant results in terms of performance. The analyzed data provided by a dried fruits company in Turkey consists of about three years of sales data collected within the period January 2005 and April 2008. The complete data that consists of five tables (customers, products, sales, sales details, and branches) included about 56,000 customers, 325 products, 721,000 sales and 3,420,000 sales details. Fig. 4 shows the star schema of the data warehouse that consists of a fact table with many dimensions.

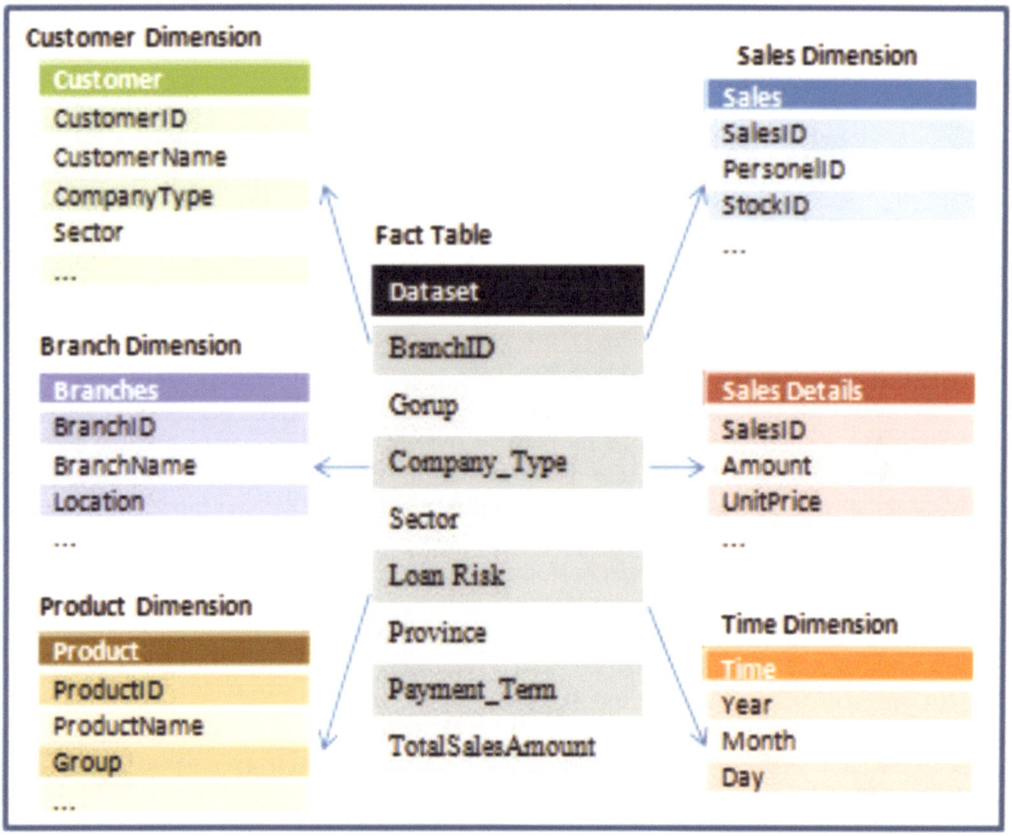

Fig. 4. Star schema of the data warehouse used in the case study

In the case study, once clustering task was used to find customer segments with similar profiles, and then association rule mining was carried out to the each customer segment for product recommendation. The main advantage of this application is to be able to adopt different product recommendations for different customer segments. Based on our service-based data mining architecture, Fig. 5 shows the knowledge discovery workflow constructed in this case study, which represents pre-processing steps, potentially repeatable sequences of data mining tasks and post-preprocessing steps. So, we defined a data mining application as an executable software program that performs two data mining tasks and some complementary tasks.

In the scenario, first, (1) the client sends a business request and then (2) this request is sent to application server for invoking data preparation service. After data-preprocessing, (3) data warehouse is generated, (4) clustering service is invoked to segment customers, and then (5) clustering results are evaluated to ensure the quality of clusters. After this step, (6) more than one ARM web services are executed in parallel for discovering association rules for different customer segments. (7) After the evaluation of ARM results by using Lift and Loevinger thresholds, (8) the results are filtered according to user-defined parameters to highlight particular subsets of patterns mined. For example, users may want to observe only association rules with k-itemsets, where *k* is number of items provided by user. Finally, (9) visualization service is invoked to plot a graph for displaying results.

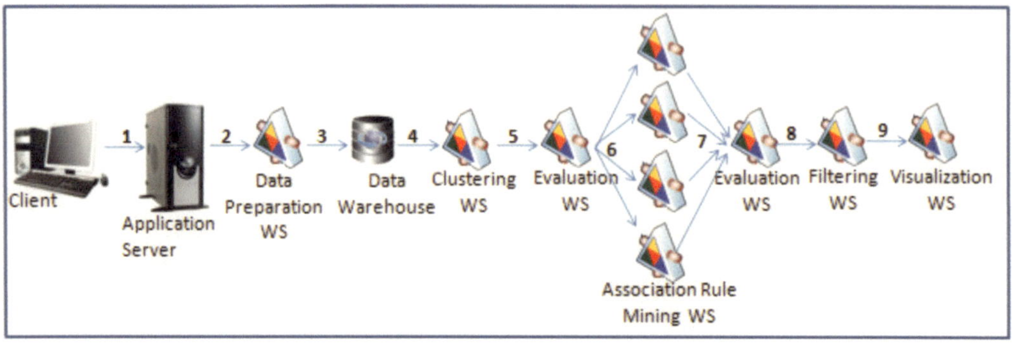

Fig. 5. An example knowledge discovery workflow

Given the design and implementation benefits discussed in section 3.3, another key aspect in evaluating the system is related to its performance in supporting data mining services execution. In order to evaluate the performance of the system, we performed some experiments to measure execution times of the different steps. The data mining application described above has been tested on deployments composed from 4 association rule mining (ARM) web services; in other words, customers are firstly divided into 4 groups (customer segments), and then 4 ARM web services are executed in parallel for different customer segments (clusters). Each node was a 2.4 GHz Centrino with 4 GB main memory and network connection speed was 100.0 Mbps. We performed all experiments with a minimum support value of 0.2 percent. In the experiments, we used different datasets with sizes ranging from 5Mbytes to 20Mbytes.

While in the clustering experiments we used the customer and their transactions (sales) data available at the data warehouse, in the ARM, we used products and transaction details (sales details) data. Expectation-Maximization (EM) algorithm for clustering task and Apriori algorithm for ARM were implemented as two separate web services. The execution times have been shown in Table 1. It reports the times needed to complete the different phases: file transfer, data preparation, task submission (invoking the services), data mining (clustering and ARM), and results notification (result evaluation and visualization).

Values reported in the Table 1 refer to the execution times obtained for different dataset sizes. The table shows that the data mining phase takes averagely 81.1% of the total execution time, while the file transfer phase fluctuate around 12.8%. The overhead due to the other operations - data preparation, task submission, result evaluation and visualization - is very low with respect to the overall execution time, decreasing from 6.5% to 5.4% with the growth of the dataset size. The results also show that we achieved efficiencies greater than 73 percent, when we execute 4 web services in parallel, instead of one web service.

Dataset Size	File Transfer	Data Prepar.	Task Submission	Data Mining			Results Notification
				EM	Apriori	Total	
5 MB	3,640	1,820	212	7,110	29,156	36,266	691
10 MB	5,437	1,995	253	13,251	24,031	37,282	720
15 MB	8,287	2,064	248	18,343	23,477	41,820	862
20 MB	11,071	2,218	264	34,528	23,233	57,761	1,485

Table 1. Execution times (in milliseconds) needed to complete the different phases

The *file transfer* and *data mining* execution times changed because of the different dataset sizes and algorithm complexity. In particular, the *file transfer* execution time ranged from 3,640 ms for the dataset of 5MB to 11,071 ms for the dataset of 20MB, while the *data mining* execution time ranged from 36,266 ms for the dataset 5 MB to 57,761 ms for 20MB.
In general, it can be observed that the overhead introduced by the SOA model is not critical with respect to the duration of the service-specific operations. This is particularly true in typical KDD applications, in which data mining algorithms working on large datasets are expected to take a long processing time. On the basis of our experimental results, we conclude that SOA model can be effectively used to develop services for KDD applications.

4.2 Discussion and evaluation

The case study has been useful for evaluating the overall system under different aspects, including its performance. Given these basic results, we can conclude that SOMiner is suitable to be exploited for developing services and knowledge discovery applications in SOA.
In order to improve the performance moreover, the following proposals should be considered:

1. To avoid delays due to data transfers during computation, every mining server should have an associated local data server, in which data is kept before the mining task executes.
2. To reduce computational costs, data mining algorithms should be implemented in more than one web services which are located over different nodes. This allows the execution of the data mining components in the knowledge flow on different web services.
3. To reduce computational costs, the same web services should be located over more than one node. In this way, the overall execution time can be significantly reduced because different parts of the computation are executed in parallel on different nodes, taking advantage at the same time of data distribution.
4. To get results faster, if the server is busy with another task, it should send the user an identifier to use in any further communication regarding that task. A number of idle workstations should be used to execute data mining web services, the availability of scalable algorithms is key to effectively using the resources.

Overall we believe the collection of features of SOMiner make it a unique and competitive contender for developing new data mining applications on service-oriented computing environments.

5. Conclusion

Data mining services in SOA are key elements for practitioners who need to develop knowledge discovery applications that use large and remotely dispersed datasets and/or computers to get results in reasonable times and improve their competitiveness. In this chapter, we address the definition and composition of services for implementing knowledge discovery applications on SOA model. We propose a new system, SOMiner that supports knowledge discovery on SOA model by providing mechanisms and higher level services for composing existing data mining services as structured, compound services and interface to allow users to design, store, share, and re-execute their applications, as well as manage their output results.

SOMiner allows miners to create and manage complex knowledge discovery applications composed as workflows that integrate data sets and mining tools provided as services in SOA. Critical features of the system include flexibility, extensibility, scalability, conceptual simplicity and ease of use. One of the goals with SOMiner was to create a data mining system that doesn't require users to know details about the algorithms and their related concepts. To achieve that, we designed an interface and toolkit, handling most of the technical details transparently, so that results would be shown in a simple way. Furthermore, this is the first time that a service-oriented data mining architecture proposes a solution with semantic web services. In experimental studies, the system has been evaluated on the basis of a case study related to marketing. According to the experimental results, we conclude that SOA model can be effectively used to develop services for knowledge discovery applications.

Some further works can be added to make the system perform better. First, security problems (authorization, authentication, etc.) related to the adoption of web services can be solved. Second, a tool can be developed to automatically transfer the current traditional data mining applications to the service-oriented data mining framework.

6. References

Ali, A.S.; Rana, O. & Taylor, I. (2005). Web services composition for distributed data mining, *Proceedings of the 2005 IEEE International Conference on Parallel Processing Workshops, ICPPW'05*, pp. 11-18, ISBN: 0-7695-2381-1, Oslo, Norway, June 2005, IEEE Computer Society, Washington, DC, USA.

Ari, I.; Li, J.; Kozlov, A. & Dekhil, M. (2008). Data mining model management to support real-time business intelligence in service-oriented architectures, *HP Software University Association Workshop*, White papers, Morocco, June 2008, Hewlett-Packard.

Brezany, P.; Janciak, I. & Tjoa, A.M. (2005). GridMiner: A fundamental infrastructure for building intelligent grid systems, *Proceedings of the 2005 IEEE/WIC/ACM International Conference on Web Intelligence (WI'05)*, pp. 150-156, ISBN: 0-7695-2415-x, Compiegne, France, September 2005, IEEE Computer Society.

Chen, N.; Marques, N.C. & Bolloju, N. (2003). A Web Service-based approach for data mining in distributed environments, *Proceedings of the 1st Workshop on Web Services: Modeling, Architecture and Infrastructure* (WSMAI-2003), pp. 74-81, ISBN 972-98816-4-2, Angers, France, April 2003, ICEIS Press 2003.

Chen, P.; Wang, B.; Xu, L.; Wu, B. & Zhou, G. (2006). The design of data mining metadata web service architecture based on JDM in grid environment, *Proceedings of First International Symposium on Pervasive Computing and Applications*, pp. 684-689, ISBN: 1-4244-0326-x, Urumqi, China, August 2006, IEEE.

Cheung, W.K.; Zhang, X-F.; Wong, H-F.; Liu, J.; Luo, Z-W. & Tong, F.C.H., (2006). Service-oriented distributed data mining, *IEEE Internet Computing*, Vol. 10, No. 4, (July/August 2006) pp. 44-54, ISSN:1089-7801.

Congiusta, A.; Talia, D. & Trunfio, P. (2007). Distributed data mining services leveraging WSRF, *Future Generation Computer Systems*, Vol. 23, No. 1, (January 2007) 34–41, ISSN: 0167-739X.

Congiusta, A.; Talia, D. & Trunfio, P. (2008). Service-oriented middleware for distributed data mining on the grid, *Journal of Parallel and Distributed Computing, Vol.* 68, No. 1, (January 2008) 3-15, ISSN: 0743-7315.

Du, H.; Zhang, B. & Chen, D. (2008). Design and actualization of SOA-based data mining system, *Proceedings of 9th International Conference on Computer-Aided Industrial Design and Conceptual Design (CAID/CD)*, pp. 338–342, ISBN: 978-1-4244-3290-5, Kunming, November 2008.

Guedes, D.; Meira, W.J. & Ferreira, R. (2006). Anteater: A service-oriented architecture for high-performance data mining, *IEEE Internet Computing*, Vol. 10, No. 4, (July/August 2006) 36–43, ISSN: 1089-7801.

Jackson, T.; Jessop, M.; Fletcher, M. & Austin, J. (2007). A virtual organisation deployed on a service orientated architecture for distributed data mining applications, *Grid-Based Problem Solving Environments*, Vol. 239, Gaffney, P.W.; Pool, J.C.T. (Eds.), pp. 155-170, Springer Boston, ISSN: 1571-5736.

Olejnik, R.; Fortiş, T.-F. & Toursel, B. (2009) Web services oriented data mining in knowledge architecture, *Future Generation Computer Systems*, Vol. 25, No. 4, (April 2009) 436-443, ISSN: 0167-739X.

Perez, M.; Sanchez, A.; Robles, V.; Herrero, P. & Pena, J.M. (2007). Design and implementation of a data mining grid-aware architecture, *Future Generation Computer Systems*, Vol. 23, No. 1, (January 2007) 42–47, ISSN: 0167-739X.

Sairafi, S.A.; Emmanouil, F.S.; Ghanem, M.; Giannadakis, N.; Guo, Y.; Kalaitzopolous, D.; Osmond, M.; Rowe, A.; Syed, J. & Wendel, P. (2003). The design of discovery net: Towards open grid services for knowledge discovery, *International Journal of High Performance Computing Applications*, Vol. 17, No. 3, (August 2003) 297–315, ISSN: 1094-3420.

Stankovski, V.; Swain, M.; Kravtsov, V.; Niessen, T.; Wegener, D.; Kindermann, J. & Dubitzky, W. (2008). Grid-enabling data mining applications with DataMiningGrid: An architectural perspective, *Future Generation Computer Systems*, Vol. 24, No. 4, (April 2008) 259–279, ISSN: 0167-739X.

Swain, M.; Silva, C.G.; Loureiro-Ferreira, N.; Ostropytskyy, V.; Brito, J.; Riche, O.; Stahl, F.; Dubitzky, W. & Brito, R.M.M. (2009). P-found: Grid-enabling distributed repositories of protein folding and unfolding simulations for data mining, *Future Generation Computer Systems*, Vol. 26, No. 3, (March 2010) 424-433, ISSN: 0167-739X.

Talia, D. (2009). Distributed data mining tasks and patterns as services, *Euro-Par 2008 Workshops - Parallel Processing, Lecture Notes in Computer Science*, pp. 415-422, Springer Berlin / Heidelberg, ISSN: 0302-9743.

Talia D. & Trunfio, P. (2007). How distributed data mining tasks can thrive as services on grids, *National Science Foundation Symposium on Next Generation of Data Mining and Cyber-Enabled Discovery for Innovation (NGDM'07)*, Baltimore, USA, October 2007.

Tsai, C.-Y. & Tsai, M.-H. (2005). A dynamic web service based data mining process system, *Proceedings of the 2005 The Fifth International Conference on Computer and Information Technology (CIT'05)*, pp. 1033-1039, IEEE Computer Society, Washington, DC, USA.

Wu, S.; Wang, W.; Xiong, M. & Jin, H. (2009). Data management services in ChinaGrid for data mining applications, *Emerging Technologies in Knowledge Discovery and Data Mining*, pp. 421-432, Springer Berlin / Heidelberg, ISSN: 0302-9743.

Yamany, H.F.; Capretz, M. & Alliso, D.S. (2010). Intelligent security and access control framework for service-oriented architecture, *Information and Software Technology*, Vol. 52, No. 2, (February 2010) 220-236, ISSN: 0950-5849.

2

Database Marketing Process Supported by Ontologies: A Data Mining System Architecture Proposal

Filipe Mota Pinto[1] and Teresa Guarda[2]
[1]Polytechnic Institute of Leiria,
[2]Superior Institute of Languages and Administration of Leiria,
Portugal

1. Introduction

Marketing departments handles with a great volume of data which are normally task or marketing activity dependent. This requires the use of certain, and perhaps unique, specific knowledge background and framework approach.
Database marketing provides in depth analysis of marketing databases. Knowledge discovery in database techniques is one of the most prominent approaches to support some of the database marketing process phases. However, in many cases, the benefits of these tools are not fully exploited by marketers. Complexity and amount of data constitute two major factors limiting the application of knowledge discovery techniques in marketing activities. Here, ontologies may play an important role in the marketing discipline.
Motivated by its success in the area of artificial intelligence, we propose an ontology-supported database marketing approach. The approach aims to enhance database marketing process supported by a data mining system architecture proposal which provides detailed step-phase specific information.
From a data mining framework, issues raised in this work both respond and contribute to calls for a database marketing process improvement. Our work was evaluated throughout a relationship marketing program database. The findings of this study not only advance the state of database marketing research but also shed light on future research directions using a data mining approach. Therefore we propose a framework supported by ontologies and knowledge extraction from databases techniques. Thus, this paper has two purposes: to integrate the ontological approach into Database Marketing and to make use of a domain ontology - a knowledge base that will enhance the entire process at both levels, marketing and knowledge extraction techniques.

2. Motivation

Knowledge discovery in databases is a well accepted definition for related methods, tasks and approaches for knowledge extraction activities (Brezany et al., 2008) (Nigro et al., 2008). Knowledge extraction or Data Mining (DM) is also referred as a set of procedures that cover all work ranging from data collection to algorithms execution and model evaluation. In each of the development phases, practitioners employ specific methods and tools that support them in fulfilling their tasks. The development of methods and tasks for the different disciplines have been established and used for a long time (Domingos, 2003) (Cimiano et al., 2004) (Michalewicz et al., 2006). Until recently, there was no need to integrate them in a structured manner (Tudorache, 2006). However, with the wide use of this approach, engineers were faced with a new challenge: They had to deal with a multitude of heterogeneous problems originating from different approaches and had to make sure that in the end all models offered a coherent business domain output. There are no mature processes and tools that enable the exchange of models between the different parallel developments at different contexts (Jarrar, 2005). Indeed, there is a gap in the KDD process knowledge sharing in order to promote its reuse.

The Internet and open connectivity environments created a strong demand for the sharing of data semantics (Jarrar, 2005). Emerging ontologies are increasingly becoming essential for computer science applications. Organizations are beginning to view them as useful machine-processable semantics for many application areas. Hence, ontologies have been developed in artificial intelligence to facilitate knowledge sharing and reuse. They are a popular research topic in various communities, such as knowledge engineering (Borst et al., 1997) (Bellandi et al., 2006), cooperative information systems (Diamantini et al., 2006b), information integration (Bolloju et al., 2002) (Perez-Rey et al., 2006), software agents (Bombardier et al., 2007), and knowledge management (Bernstein et al., 2005) (Cardoso and Lytras, 2009). In general, ontologies provide (Fensel et al., 2000): a shared and common understanding of a domain which can be communicated amongst people and across application systems; and, an explicit conceptualization (i.e., meta information) that describes the semantics of the data.

Nevertheless, ontological development is mainly dedicated to a community (e.g., genetics, cancer or networks) and, therefore, is almost unavailable to others outside it. Indeed the new knowledge produced from reused and shared ontologies is still very limited (Guarino, 1998) (Blanco et al., 2008) (Coulet et al., 2008) (Sharma and Osei-Bryson, 2008) (Cardoso and Lytras, 2009).

To the best of our knowledge, in spite of successful ontology approaches to solve some KDD related problems, such as, algorithms optimization (Kopanas et al., 2002) (Nogueira et al., 2007), data pre-processing tasks definition (Bouquet et al., 2002) (Zairate et al., 2006) or data mining evaluation models (Cannataro and Comito, 2003) (Brezany et al., 2008), the research to the ontological KDD process assistance is sparse and spare. Moreover, mostly of the ontology development focusing the KDD area focuses only a part of the problem, intending only to modulate data tasks (Borges et al., 2009), algorithms (Nigro et al., 2008), or evaluation models (Euler and Scholz, 2004) (Domingues and Rezende, 2005). Also, the use of KDD in marketing field has been largely ignored (with a few exceptions (Zhou et al., 2006) (El-Ansary, 2006) (Cellini et al., 2007)). Indeed, many of these works provide only single specific ontologies that quickly become unmanageable and therefore without the sharable and reusable characteristic. Such research direction may became innocuous, requiring tremendous patience and an expert understanding of the ontology domain, terminology, and semantics.

Contrary to this existing research trend, we feel that since the knowledge extraction techniques are critical to the success of database use procedures, researchers are interested

in addressing the problem of knowledge share and reuse. We must address and emphasize the knowledge conceptualization and specification through ontologies.
Therefore, this research promises interesting results in different levels, such as:
- Regarding information systems and technologies, focusing the introduction and integration of the ontology to assist and improve the DM process, through inference tasks in each phase;
- In the ontology area this investigation represents an initial approach step on the way for real portability and knowledge sharing of the system towards other similar DBM process supported by the DM. It could effectively be employed to address the general problem of model-construction in problems similar to the one of marketing (generalization), on the other side it is possible to instantiate/adapt the ontology to the specific configuration of a DBM case and to automatically assist, suggest and validate specific approaches or models DM process (specification);
- Lastly, for data analyst practitioners this research may improve their ability to develop the DBM process, supported by DM. Since knowledge extraction work depended in large scale on the user background, the proposed methodology may be very useful when dealing with complex marketing database problems. Therefore the introduction of an ontological layer in DBM project allows: more efficient and stable marketing database exploration process through an ontology-guided knowledge extraction process; and, portability and knowledge share among DBM practitioners and computer science researchers.

3. Background

3.1 Database marketing

Much of the advanced practice in Database Marketing (DBM) is performed within private organizations (Zwick and Dholakia, 2004) (Marsh, 2005). This may partly explain the lack of articles published in the academic literature that study DBM issue (Bohling et al., 2006) (Frankland, 2007) (Lin and Hong, 2008).
However, DBM is nowadays an essential part of marketing in many organizations. Indeed, as the main DBM principle, most organizations should communicate as much as possible with their customers on a direct basis (DeTienne and Thompson, 1996). Such objective has contributed to the expressive grown of all DBM discipline. In spite of such evolution and development, DBM has growth without the expected maturity (Fletcher et al., 1996) (Verhoef and Hoekstra, 1999).
In some organizations, DBM systems work only as a system for inserting and updating data, just like a production system (Sen and Tuzhiln, 1998). In others, they are used only as a tool for data analysis (Bean, 1999). In addition, there are corporations that use DBM systems for both operational and analytical purposes (Arndt and Gersten, 2001). Currently DBM is mainly approached by classical statistical inference, which may fail when complex, multi-dimensional, and incomplete data is available (Santos et al., 2005).
One of most cited origins of DBM is the retailers' catalogue based in the USA selling directly to customers. The main means used was direct mail, and mailing of new catalogues usually took place to the whole database of customers (DeTienne and Thompson, 1996). Mailings result analysis has led to the adoption of techniques to improve targeting, such as CHAID (Chi-Squared Automated Interaction Detection) and logistic regression (DeTienne and

Thompson, 1996) (Schoenbachler et al., 1997). Lately, the addition of centralized call centers and the Internet to the DBM mix has introduced the elements of interactivity and personalization. Thereafter, during the 1990s, the data-mining boom popularized such techniques as artificial neural networks, market basket analysis, Bayesian networks and decision trees (Pearce et al., 2002) (Drozdenko and Perry, 2002).

3.1.1 Definition

DBM refers to the use of database technology for supporting marketing activities (Leary et al., 2004) (Wehmeyer, 2005) (Pinto et al., 2009). Therefore, it is a marketing process driven by information (Coviello et al., 2001) (Brookes et al., 2004) (Coviello et al., 2006) and managed by database technology (Carson et al., 2004) (Drozdenko and Perry, 2002). It allows marketing professionals to develop and to implement better marketing programs and strategies (Shepard, 1998) (Ozimek, 2004).

There are different definitions of DBM with distinct perspectives or approaches denoting some evolution an evolution along the concepts (Zwick and Dholakia, 2004). From the marketing perspective, DBM is an interactive approach to marketing communication. It uses addressable communications media (Drozdenko and Perry, 2002) (Shepard, 1998), or a strategy that is based on the premise that not all customers or prospects are alike. By gathering, maintaining and analyzing detailed information about customers or prospects, marketers can modify their marketing strategies accordingly (Tao and Yeh, 2003). Then, some statistical approaches were introduced and DBM was presented as the application of statistical analysis and modeling techniques to computerized individual level data sets (Sen and Tuzhiln, 1998) (Rebelo et al., 2006) focusing some type of data. Here, DBM simply involves the collection of information about past, current and potential customers to build a database to improve the marketing effort. The information includes: demographic profiles; consumer likes and dislikes; taste; purchase behavior and lifestyle (Seller and Gray, 1999) (Pearce et al., 2002).

As information technologies improved their capabilities such as processing speed, archiving space or, data flow in organizations that have grown exponentially different approaches to DBM have been suggested: generally, it is the art of using data you've already gathered to generate new money-making ideas (Gronroos, 1994) (Pearce et al., 2002); stores this response and adds other customer information (lifestyles, transaction history, etc.) on an electronic database memory and uses it as basis for longer term customer loyalty programs, to facilitate future contacts, and to enable planning of all marketing. (Fletcher et al., 1996) (Frankland, 2007); or, DBM can be defined as gathering, saving and using the maximum amount of useful knowledge about your customers and prospects...to their benefit and organizations' profit. (McClymont and Jocumsen, 2003) (Pearce et al., 2002). Lately some authors has referred DBM as a tool database-driven marketing tool which is increasingly aking centre stage in organizations strategies (Pinto, 2006) (Lin and Hong, 2008).

In common all definition share a main idea: DBM is a process that uses data stored in marketing databases in order to extract relevant information to support marketing decision and activities through customer knowledge, which will allow satisfy their needs and anticipate their desires.

3.1.2 Database marketing process

During the DBM process it is possible to consider three phases (DeTienne and Thompson, 1996) (Shepard, 1998) (Drozdenko and Perry, 2002): data collection, data processing (modeling) and results evaluation.

The Figure 1 presents a simple model of how customer data are collected through internal or external structures that are closer to customers and the market, how customer data is transformed into information and how customer information is used to shape marketing strategies and decisions that later turn into marketing activities. The first, Marketing data, consists in data collection phase, which will conduct to marketing database creation with as much customer information as possible (e.g., behavioral, psychographic or demographic information) and related market data (e.g., share of market or competitors information's). During the next phase, information, the marketing database is analyzed under a marketing information perspective throughout activities such as, information organization (e.g., according organization structure, or campaign or product relative); information codification (e.g., techniques that associates information to a subject) or data summarization (e.g., cross data tabulations). The DBM development process concludes with marketing knowledge, which is the marketer interpretation of marketing information in actionable form. In this phase there has to be relevant information to support marketing activities decision.

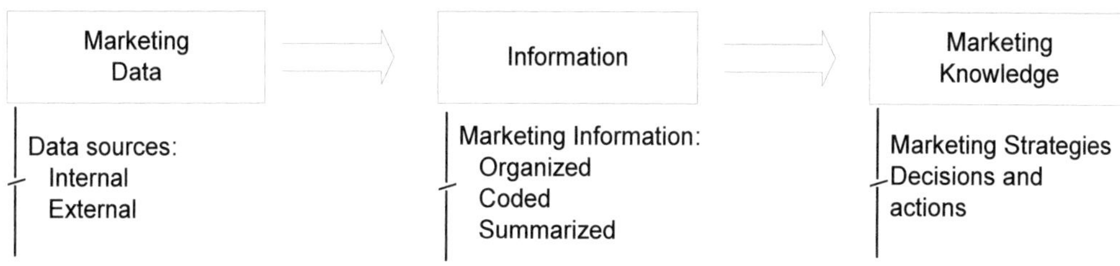

Fig. 1. Database marketing general overall process

Technology based marketing is almost a marketing science imperative (Brookes et al., 2004) (Zineldin and Vasicheva, 2008). As much as marketing research is improving and embracing new challenges its dependence on technology is also growing (Carson et al., 2004). Currently, almost every organization has its own marketing information system, from single customer data records to huge data warehouses (Brito, 2000). Nowadays, DBM is one of the most well succeed marketing technology employment (Frankland, 2007) (Lin and Hong, 2008) (Pinto et al., 2009).

3.1.3 DBM process with KDD

Database marketing is a capacious term related to the way of thinking and acting which contains the application of tools and methods in studies, their structure and internal organization so that they could achieve success on a fluctuating and difficult to predict consumer market (Lixiang, 2001).

For the present purpose we assume that, database marketing can be defined as a method of analyzing customer data to look for hidden, useful and actionable knowledge for marketing purposes. To do so, several different problem specifications may be referred. These include market segmentation (Brito et al., 2004), cross-sell prediction, response modeling, customer valuation (Brito and Hammond, 2007) and market basket analysis (Buckinx and den Poel, 2005) (Burez and Poel, 2007). Building successful solutions for these tasks requires the application of advanced DM and machine learning techniques to obtain relationships and patterns in marketing databases data and using this knowledge to predict each prospect's reaction to future situations.

In literature there are some examples about KDD usage in DBM projects usage for customers' response modeling whereas the goal was to use past transaction data of customers, personal characteristics and their response behavior to determine whether these clients were good or not (Coviello and Brodie, 1998) e.g., for mailing prospects during the next period (Pearce et al., 2002) (den Poel and Buckinx, 2005). At these examples different analytical approaches were used: statistical techniques (e.g., discriminate analysis, logistic regression, CART and CHAID), machine learning methods (e.g., C4.5, SOM) mathematical programming (e.g., linear programming classification) and neural networks to model this customer's response problem.

Other KDD related application in DBM projects is customer retention activities. The retention of its customers is very important for a commercial entity, e.g., a bank or a oil distribution company. Whenever a client decides to change to another company, it usually implies some financial losses for this organization. Therefore, organizations are very interested in identifying some mechanisms behind such decisions and determining which clients are about to leave them. As an example one approach to find such potential customers is to analyze the historical data which describe customer behavior in the past (den Poel and Buckinx, 2005) (Buckinx and den Poel, 2005) (Rebelo et al., 2006) (Burez and Poel, 2007) (Buckinx et al., 2007).

3.2 Ontologies

Currently we live at a web-based information society. Such society has a high-level automatic data processing which requires a machine-understandable of representation of information's semantics. This semantics need is not provided by HTML or XML-based languages themselves. Ontologies fill the gap, providing a sharable structure and semantics of a given domain, and therefore they play a key role in such research areas such as knowledge management, electronic commerce, decision support or agent communication (Ceccaroni, 2001).

Ontologies are used to study the existence of all kinds of entities (abstract or concrete) that constitute the world (Sowa, 2000). Ontologies use the existential quantifier $\exists$ as a notation for asserting that something exists, in contrast to logic vocabulary, which doesn't have vocabulary for describing the things that exist.

They are also used for data-source integration in global information systems and for in-house communication. In recent years, there has been a considerable progress in developing the conceptual bases for building ontologies. They allow reuse and sharing of knowledge components, and are, in general, concerned with static domain-knowledge.

Ontologies can be used as complementary reusable components to construct knowledge-based systems (van Heijst et al., 1997). Moreover, ontologies provide a shared and common understanding of a domain and describe the reasoning process of a knowledge-based system, in a domain and independent implementation fashion.

3.2.1 Ontologies definition

From the philosophy perspective, ontology is the theory or study of being, i.e., of the basic characteristics of all reality. Though the term was first coined in the 17th century, ontology is synonymous with metaphysics or first philosophy as defined by Aristotle in the 4th century BC (Guarino, 1995). Ontology is a part of metaphysics (Newell and level, 1982): it is the science of the existence which investigates the structure of being in general, rather than analyzing the characteristics of particular beings.

To answer the question *"but what is being?"* it was proposed a famous criterion but which did not say anything about what actually exists:*"To be is to be the value of a quantified variable"*(Quine, 1992). Those who object to it would prefer some guidelines for the kinds of legal statements. In general, furt her analysis is necessary to give the knowledge engineer some guidelines about what to say and how to say it.
From artificial intelligence literature there is a wide range of different definitions of the term ontology. Each community seems to adopt its own interpretation according to the use and purposes that the ontologies are intended to serve within that community. The following list enumerates some of the most important contributions:

- One of the early definitions is: 'An ontology defines the basic terms and relations comprising the vocabulary of a topic area as well as the rules for combining terms and relations to define extensions to the vocabulary.' (Neches et al., 1991);
- A widely used definition is: 'An ontology is an explicit specification of a conceptualization´ (Gruber, 1993);
- An analysis of a number of interpretations of the word ontology (as an informal conceptual system, as a formal semantic account, as a specification of a conceptualization, as a representation of a conceptual system via a logical theory, as the vocabulary used by a logical theory and as a specification of a logical theory) and a clarification of the terminology used by several other authors is in Guarino and Giaretta work (Guarino, 1995).
- From Gruber's definition and more elaborated is: 'Ontologies are defined as a formal specification of a shared conceptualization.'(Borst et al., 1997);
- 'An ontology is a hierarchically structured set of terms for describing a domain that can be used as a skeletal foundation for a knowledge base.' (Swartout et al., 1996);
- A definition with an explanation of the terms also used in early definitions, states: 'conceptualization refers to an abstract model of some phenomenon in the world by having identified the relevant concepts of that phenomenon. Explicit means that the type of concepts used and the constraints on their use are explicitly defined. Formal refers to the fact that the ontology should be machine-readable. Shared refers to the notion that an ontology captures consensual knowledge, that is, it is not primitive to some individual, but accepted by a group (Staab and Studer, 2004);
- An interesting working definition is: Ontology may take a variety of forms, but necessarily it will include a vocabulary of terms, and some specification of their meaning. This includes definitions and explicitly designates how concepts are interrelated which collectively impose a structure on the domain and constrain the possible interpretations of terms. Moreover, ontology is virtually always the manifestation of a shared understanding of a domain that is agreed between communities. Such agreement facilitates accurate and effective communication of meaning, which in turn, leads to other benefits such as inter-operability, reuse and sharing. (Jasper and Uschold, 1999);
- More recently, a broad definition has been given: 'ontologies to be domain theories that specify a domain-specific vocabulary of entities, classes, properties, predicates, and functions, and to be a set of relationships that necessarily hold among those vocabulary terms. Ontologies provide a vocabulary for representing knowledge about a domain and for de scribing specific situations in a domain.' (Farquhar et al., 1997) (Smith and Farquhar, 2008).

For this research, we have adopted as ontology definition: *A formal and explicit specification of a shared conceptualization, which is usable by a system in actionable forms.* Conceptualization refers to an abstract model of some phenomenon in some world, obtained by the identification of the relevant concepts of that phenomenon. Shared reflects the fact that an ontology captures consensual knowledge and is accepted by a relevant part of the scientific community. Formal refers to the fact that ontology is an abstract, theoretical organization of terms and relationships that is used as a tool for the analysis of the concepts of a domain. Explicit refers to the type of concepts used and the constraints on their use (Gruber, 1993) (Jurisica et al., 1999). Therefore, ontology provides a set of well-founded constructs that can be leveraged to build meaningful higher level knowledge. Hence, we consider that ontology is usable through systems in order to accomplish our objective: assistance work throughout actionable forms.

3.2.2 Reasons to use ontologies

Ontology building deals with modeling the world with shareable knowledge structures (Gruber, 1993). With the emergence of the Semantic Web, the development of ontologies and ontology integration has become very important (Fox and Gruninger, 1997) (Guarino, 1998) (Berners-Lee et al., 2001). The SemanticWeb is a vision, for a next generation Web and is described in a Figure 7 called the "layer cake" of the Semantic Web (Berners-Lee, 2003) and presented in the Ontology languages section.

The current Web has shown that string matching by itself is often not sufficient for finding specific concepts. Rather, special programs are needed to search the Web for the concepts specified by a user. Such programs, which are activated once and traverse the Web without further supervision, are called agent programs (Zhou et al., 2006). Successful agent programs will search for concepts as opposed to words. Due to the well known homonym and synonym problems, it is difficult to select from among different concepts expressed by the same word (e.g., Jaguar the animal, or Jaguar the car). However, having additional information about a concept, such as which concepts are related to it, makes it easier to solve this matching problem. For example, if that Jaguar IS-A car is desired, then the agent knows which of the meanings to look for.

Ontologies provide a repository of this kind of relationship information. To make the creation of the Semantic Web easier, Web page authors will derive the terms of their pages from existing ontologies, or develop new ontologies for the Semantic Web.

Many technical problems remain for ontology developers, e.g. scalability. Yet, it is obvious that the Semantic Web will never become a reality if ontologies cannot be developed to the point of functionality, availability and reliability comparable to the existing components of the Web (Blanco et al., 2008) (Cardoso and Lytras, 2009).

Some ontologies are used to represent the general world or word knowledge. Other ontologies have been used in a number of specialized areas, such as, medicine (Jurisica et al., 1999) (CeSpivova et al., 2004) (Perez-Rey et al., 2006) (Kasabov et al., 2007), engineering (Tudorache, 2006) (Weng and Chang, 2008), knowledge management (Welty and Murdock, 2006), or business (Borges et al., 2009) (Cheng et al., 2009).

Ontologies have been playing an important role in knowledge sharing and reuse and are useful for (Noy and McGuinness, 2003):

- *Sharing common understanding* of the structure of information among people or software agents is one of the more common goals in developing ontologies (Gruber, 1993), e.g., when several different Web sites contain marketing information o r provide tools and techniques for marketing activities. If these Web sites share and publish the same underlying ontology of the terms they all use, then computer agents can extract and aggregate information from these different sites. The agents can use this aggregated information to answer user queries or as input data to other applications;

- *Enabling reuse of domain knowledge* was one of the driving forces behind recent surge in ontology research, e.g., models for many different domains need to represent the value. This representation includes social classes, income scales among others. If one group of researchers develops such an ontology in detail, others can simply reuse it for their domains. Additionally, if we need to build a large ontology, we can integrate several existing ontologies describing portions of the large domain;
- Making *explicit domain assumptions* underlying an implementation makes it possible to change these programming-language codes making these assumptions not only hard to find and understand but also hard to change, in particular for someone without programming expertise. In addition, explicit specifications of domain knowledge are useful for new users who must learn what terms in the domain mean;
- *Separating the domain knowledge from the operational knowledge* is another common use of ontologies, e.g., regarding computers hardware components, it is possible to describe a task of configuring a product from its components according to a required specification and implement a program that does this configuration independent of the products and components themselves. Then, it is possible develop an ontology of *PCcomponents* and apply the algorithm to configure made-to-order PCs. We can also use the same algorithm to configure elevators if we "feed" it an elevator component ontology (Rothenfluh et al., 1996);
- *Analyzing domain knowledge* is possible once a declarative specification of the terms is available. Formal analysis of terms is extremely valuable when both attempting to reuse existing ontologies and extending them.

Often ontology of the domain is not a goal in itself. Developing an ontology is akin to defining a set of data and their structure for other programs to use. Problem-solving methods, domain-independent applications, and software agents use ontologies and knowledge bases built from ontologies as data (van Heijst et al., 1997) (Gottgtroy et al., 2004). Within this work we have develop an DBM ontology and appropriate KDD combinations of tasks and tools with expected marketing results. This ontology can then be used as a basis for some applications in a suite of marketing-managing tools: One application could create marketing activities suggestions for data analyst or answer queries of the marketing practitioners. Another application could analyze an inventory list of a data used and suggest which marketing activities could be developed with such available resource.

3.2.3 Ontologies main concepts

Here we use ontologies to provide the shared and common domain structures which are required for semantic integration of information sources. Even if it is still difficult to find consensus among ontology developers and users, some agreement about protocols, languages and frameworks exists. In this section we clarify the terminology which we will use throughout the thesis:

- *Axioms* are the elements which permit the detailed modeling of the domain. There are two kinds of axioms that are important for this thesis: defining axioms and related axioms. Defining axioms are defined as relations multi valued (as opposed to a function) that maps any object in the domain of discourse to sentence related to that object. A defining axiom for a constant (e.g., a symbol) is a sentence that helps defining the constant. An object is not necessarily a symbol. It is usually a class, or relation or instance of a class. If not otherwise specified, with the term axiom we refer to a related axiom;

- A *class* or *type* is a set of objects. Each one of the objects in a class is said to be an instance of the class. In some frameworks an object can be an instance of multiple classes. A class can be an instance of another class. A class which has instances that are themselves classes is called a meta-class. The top classes employed by a well developed ontology derive from the root class object, or thing, and they themselves are objects, or things. Each of them corresponds to the traditional concept of being or entity. A class, or concept in description logic, can be defined intentionally in terms of descriptions that specify the properties that objects must satisfy to belong to the class. These descriptions are expressed using a language that allows the construction of composite descriptions, including restrictions on the binary relationships connecting objects. A class can also be defined extensionally by enumerating its instances. Classes are the basis of knowledge representation in ontologies. Class hierarchies might be represented by a tree: branches represent classes and the leaves represent individuals.
- *Individuals*: objects that are not classes. Thus, the domain of discourse consists of individuals and classes, which are generically referred to as objects. Individuals are objects which cannot be divided without losing their structural and functional characteristics. They are grouped into classes and have slots. Even concepts like group or process can be individuals of some class.
- *Inheritance* through the class hierarchy means that the value of a slot for an individual or class can be inherited from its super class.
- *Unique identifier*: every class and every individual has a unique identifier, or name. The name may be a string or an integer and is not intended to be human readable. Following the assumption of anti-atomicity, objects, or entities are always complex objects. This assumption entails a number of important consequences. The only one concerning this thesis is that every object is a whole with parts (both as components and as functional parts). Additionally, because whatever exists in space-time has temporal and spatial extension, processes and objects are equivalent.
- *Relationships:* relations that operate among the various objects populating an ontology. In fact, it could be said that the glue of any articulated ontology is provided by the network of dependency of relations among its objects. The class-membership relation that holds between an instance and a class is a binary relation that maps objects to classes. The *type-of* relation is defined as the inverse of *instance-of* relation. If *A* is an *instance-of B*, then *B* is a *type-of A*. The *subclass-of* (or *is-a*) relation for classes is defined in terms of the relation *instance-of*, as follows: a class *C* is a *subclass-of* class *T* if and only if all instances of *C* are also instances of *T*. The *superclass-of* relation is defined as the inverse of the *subclass-of* relation.
- *Role*: different users or any single user may define multiple ontologies within a single domain, representing different aspects of the domain or different tasks that might be carried out within it. Each of these ontologies is known as a role. In our approach we do not need to use roles since we only deal with a single ontology. Roles can be shared, or

they can be represented separately in approaches without integration facilities. Moreover, roles can overlap in the sense that the same individuals can be classified in many different roles, but the class membership of an individual, its inherited slots and the values of those slots may vary from role to role. A representation of the similarities and differences between two or more roles is known as a comparison.

- *Slots* (values that properties can assume). Objects have associated with them a set of own slots and each own slot of an object has associated with it a set of objects called slot values. Slots can hold many different kinds of values and can hold many at the same time. They are used to store information, such as name and description, which uniquely define a class or an individual. Classes have associated with them a collection of template slots that describe own slot values considered to hold for each instance of the class. The values of template slots are said to inherit to the subclasses and to the instances of a class. The values of a template slot are inherited to subclasses as values of the same template slot and to instances as values of the corresponding own slot. For example, the assertion that the gender of all *female* persons is *female* could be represented by the template slot *Gender* of class *Female-Person* having the value *Female*. If we create an instance of *Female-Person* called *Linda*, then *Female* would be the value of the own slot *Gender* of *Linda*. Own slots of an object have associated with them a set of own facets, and each own facet of a slot of a frame has associated with it a set of objects called facet values, e.g., the assertion that *Francisco* favorite foods must be *sweet food* can be represented by the facet Value-Type of the *Favorite-Food* slot of the *Francisco* frame having the value *Sweet-Food*. Template slots of a class have associated with them a collection of template facets that describe own facet values considered to hold for the corresponding own slot of each instance of the class. As with the values of template slots, the values of template facets are said to inherit to the subclasses and instances of a class. Thus, the values of a template facet are inherited to subclasses as values of the same template facet and to instances as values of the corresponding own facet.
- A *taxonomy* is a set of concepts, which are arranged hierarchically. A taxonomy does not define attributes of these concepts. It usually defines only the is-a relationship between the concepts. In addition to the basic is-a relation, the part-of relation may also be used;
- A *type* is an ontological category in artificial intelligence (in which it is synonymous of class) and in logic;
- A *vocabulary* is a language dependent set of words with explanations/documentation. It seeks universality and formality in a local context (for example a marketing domain).

Focusing on ontology reuse capability (one of the most important aspect in many research projects), we attain to assist the end user in new DBM and KDD projects through knowledge base instantiation and inference.

4. Research approach

Through an exhaustive literature review we have achieve a set of domain concepts and relations between them to describe KDD process.
Follo wing METHONTOLOGY (Lopez et al., 1999) we had constructed our ontology in terms of process assistance role. This methodology for ontology construction has five (Gomez-Perez et al., 2004) main steps: specification, conceptualization, formalization, implementation and maintenance (Figure 2).

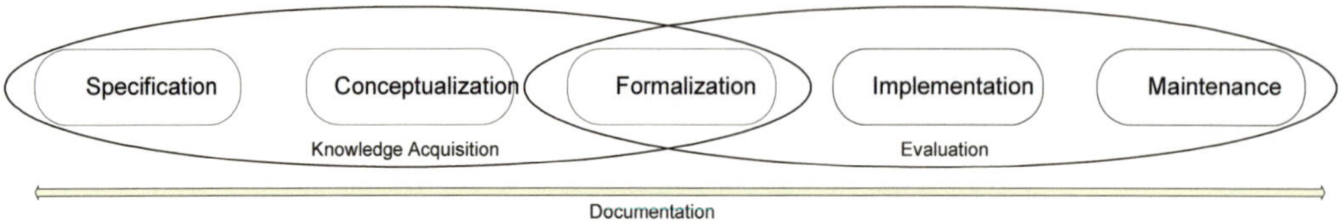

Fig. 2. Methontology framework (adapted from (Lopez *et al.*1999))

Nevertheless, domain concepts and relations were introduced according some literature directives (Smith and Farquhar2008). Moreover, in order to formalize all related knowledge we have used some relevant scientific KDD (Quinlan1986) (Fayyad *et al.*1996) and ontologies (Phillips and Buchanan2001)(Nigro *et al.*2008) published works. However, whenever some vocabulary is missing it is possible to develop a research method in order to achieve such a domain knowledge thesaurus.
At the end of the first step of methontology methodology we have identified the following main classes (Figure 3):

Fig. 3. KDD ontology class taxonomy (partial view)

Our KDD ontology has three major classes: *Resource, ProcessPhase* and *ResultModel*. ProcessPhase is the central class which uses resources (Resource class) and has some results (ResultModel class). The former Resource class relates all resources needed to carry the extraction process, namely algorithms and data.

The *ResultModel* has in charge to relate all KDD instance process describing all resources used, all tasks performed and results achieved in terms of model evaluation and domain evaluation. This class is use to ensure the KDD knowledge share and reuse.

Regarding KDD process we have considered four main concepts below the *ProcessPhase* concept (OWL class):

Data Understand focuses all data understanding work from simple acknowledge attribute mean to exhaustive attribute data description or even translation, to more natural language;

Data Preprocessing: concerns all data pre-processing tasks like data transformation, new attribute derivation or missing values processing;

Modeling: Modeling phase has in charge to produce models. It is frequent to appear as data mining phase (DM), since it is the most well known KDD phase. Discovery systems produce models that are valuable for prediction or description, but also they produce models that have been stated in some declarative format, that can be communicated clearly and precisely in order to become useful. Modeling holds all DM work from KDD process. Here we consider all subjects regarding the DM tasks, e.g., algorithm selection or concerns relations between algorithm and data used (data selection). In order to optimize efforts we have introduced some tested concepts from other data mining ontology (DMO) [Nigro *et al.*2008], which has similar knowledge base taxonomy. Here we take advantage of an explicit ontology of data mining and standards using the OWL concepts to describe an abstract semantic service for DM and its main operations. Settings are built through enumeration of algorithm properties and characterization of their input parameters. Based on the concrete Java interfaces, as presented in the Weka software API (Witten and Frank2000) and Protégé OWL, it was constructed a set of OWL classes and their instances that handle input parameters of the algorithms. All these concepts are not strictly separated but are rather used in conjunction forming a consistent ontology;

Evaluation and Deployment phase refers all concepts and operations (relations) performed to evaluate resulting DM model and KDD knowledge respectively.

Then, we have represented above concept hierarchy in OWL language, using protégé OWL software.

```
<?xml version="1.0"?>
<rdf:RDF
  xmlns:owl2xml="http://www.w3.org/2006/12/owl2-xml#"
  xmlns:rdf="http://www.w3.org/1999/02/22-rdf-syntax-ns#"
xml:base="http://www.semanticweb.org/ontologies/2009/5/DBMiPhDfpinto.owl">
 <owl:Class rdf:ID="InformationType">
  <rdfs:subClassOf>
   <owl:Class rdf:ID="Data"/>
  </rdfs:subClassOf>
 <owl:Class rdf:ID="Personal">
  <rdfs:subClassOf>
   <owl:Class rdf:ID="InformationType"/>
```

```
  </rdfs:subClassOf>
</owl:Class>
</owl:Class>
<owl:Class rdf:ID="Demographics">
  <rdfs:subClassOf>
    <owl:Class rdf:ID="Personal"/>
  </rdfs:subClassOf>
</owl:Class>
<owl:Class rdf:about="http://www.w3.org/2002/07/owl#Thing"/>
<owl:Class rdf:about="#InformationType">
  <rdfs:subClassOf rdf:resource="#Data"/>
</owl:Class>
```

Following Methontology, the next step is to create domain-specific core ontology, focusing knowledge acquisition. To this end we had performed some data processing tasks, data mining operations and also performed some models evaluations.

Each class belongs to a hierarchy (Figure 4). Moreover, each class may have relations between other classes (e.g., *PersonalType* is-a *InformationType* subclass). In order to formalize such schema we have defined OWL properties in regarding class' relationships, generally represented as:

Modeling^ has Algorithm (algorithm)

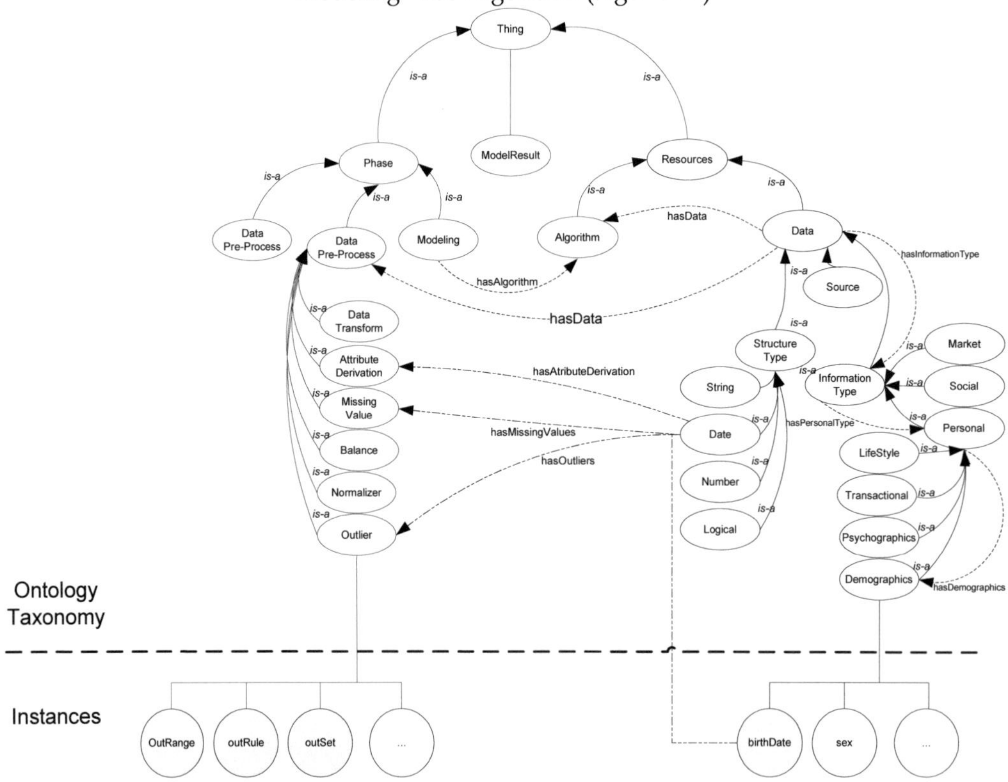

Fig. 4. KDD class/property/instance relation example ilustration

In OWL code:

```
<owl:Class rdf:ID="AlgorithmSelection">
  <rdfs:subClassOf>
   <owl:Restriction>
    <owl:someValuesFrom rdf:resource="#Algorithms"/>
    <owl:onProperty>
     <owl:ObjectProperty rdf:ID="hasAlgorithm"/>
    </owl:onProperty>
   </owl:Restriction>
  </rdfs:subClassOf>
  <rdfs:subClassOf>
   <owl:Class rdf:ID="Modeling"/>
  </rdfs:subClassOf>
 </owl:Class>
```

The ontology knowledge acquisition, firstly, happens through direct classes, relationships and instances load. Then through the KDD instantiation, the ontology acts according to the semantic structure.

Each new attribute is presented to the ontology, it is evaluated in terms of attribute class hierarchy, and related properties that acts according it.

In our ontology Attribute is defined by a set of three descriptive items: *Information Type*, *Structure Type* and allocated *Source*. Therefore it is possible to infer that, Attribute is a subclass of *Thing* and is described as a union of *InformationType*, *StructureType* and *Source*.

At other level, considering that, data property links a class to another class (subclass) or links a class with an individual, we have in our ontology the example:

StructureType(Date)
→ *hasMissingValueTask*
→ *hasOutliersTask*
→ *hasAttributeDerive*

Attribute InformationType (Personal) & Attribute PersonalType(Demographics)
→ hasCheckConsistency

As example, considering the *birthDate* attribute, ontology will act as:

```
? Attribute hasDataSource
        attribute hasDataSource (CustomerTable).
? Attribute hasInformationType:
        attribute hasInformationType (Personal) then:
        attribute hasPersonalType(Demographics)
? Attribute hasStructureType
        attribute hasStructureType (Date).
        : attribute hasStructureType(Date) AND
PersonalType(Demographics) then:
        : attribute (Demographics; Date) hasDataPreparation
        : attribute (Demographics; Date) hasDataPreProcessing
AND Check missing values
AND Check outliers
AND Check consistency
AND deriveNewAttribute
```

In above example, the inference process is executed on reasoner for description logic (Pellet). It acts along both class hierarchy (e.g., *Personal or Demographics*) and defined data properties (e.g., *hasStructureType* or *hasDataPreparation*). In above example the attribute belongs at two classes: *Date* and *Demographics*. Through class membership, the *birthDate*, attribute inherits related data properties, such as *hasDataPreparation* or *hasDataPre-Processing*

5. Ontology leaning cycle

Ontology assistance to KDD aims the improvement of the process allowing both better performance and extracted knowledge results.Since KDD process is the core competency of database use, it is the centre focus of our work.

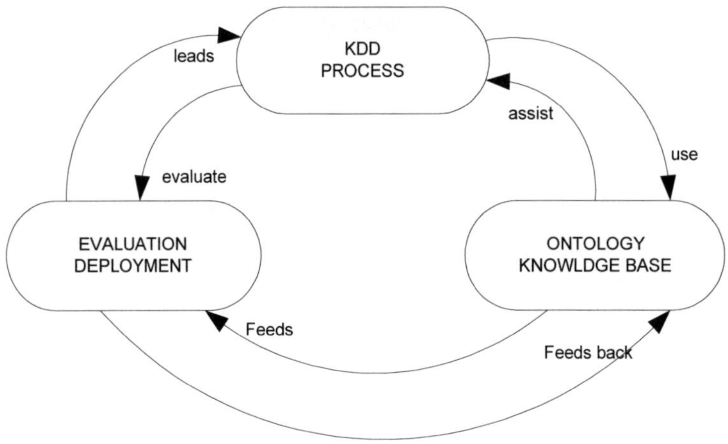

Fig. 5. Ontology learning cycle

As depicted in Figure 5, KDD process is located at the centre of our system. Therefore, data analyst uses knowledge during the process execution; knowledge feeds performance for higher achievement, and performance leads measures performance through evaluation and deployment methods; performance feeds back knowledge (ontology update) for later use of that knowledge. Also knowledge drives the process to improve further operations.
Since the KDD process generates as output models, it was considered useful to represent them in a computable way. Such representation works as a general description of all options taken during the process. Based on PMML descriptive DM model we have introduced an OWL class in our ontology named *ResultModel* which holds instances with general form:

ResultModel {
domain Objective Type;
algorithm;
algorithmTasks;
algorithmParameters;
workingAlgorithmDataSet;
EvaluationValue;
DeploymentValue
}

Moreover, our ontology has the learning capability mutually assigned to aforementioned model the ontology structure. Then it is possible both: so suggest (e.g., algorithm) and rank each suggestion (e.g., accuracy). Such approach may lead in a future to the development of an automatic learning capability and is depicted in figure 6.

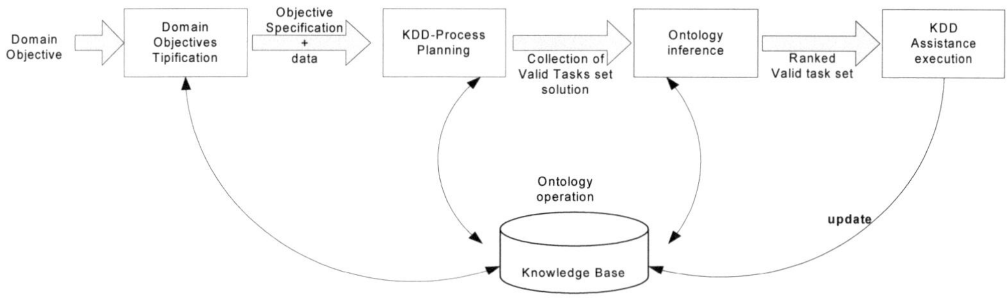

Fig. 6. Database Marketing ontology knowledge base operations

Data analyst is guided through the entire process supported by knowledge base. Such support is carried by domain objectives specification, KDD process planning, ontology inference or KDD assistant execution.

6. Results

As results we have achieved an explicit KDD ontology which integrates background and practical knowledge (Figure 7).
The KDD structure has two main distinct classes: resources and phase, as depicted in Figure 7. The former, holds and refers to all assets used at KDD process, like data repositories or algorithms; the latter, refers to the practical development of KDD process phases, like data preparation or modeling. Each super class has its own subclass hierarchy. Moreover, there are relationships between each class (e.g., *hasData* or *hasAlgorithm*).

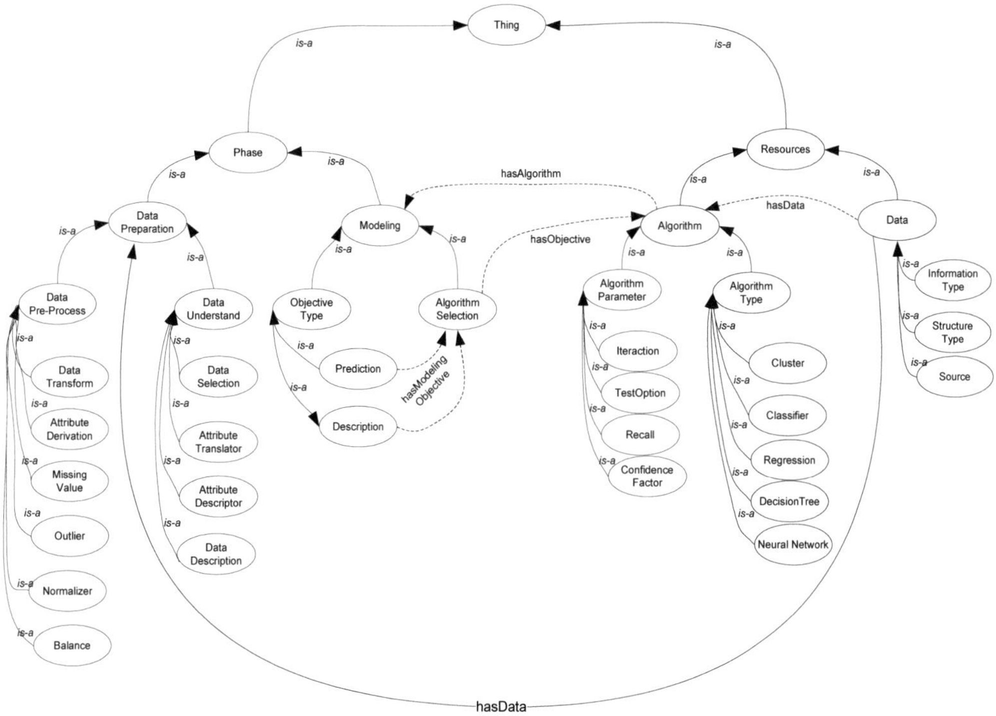

Fig. 7. KDD ontology class-properties hierarchy general view

7. Conclusions

During this work we have introduced process oriented ontology for database marketing knowledge based on Data Mining system architecture. Instead of imposing a fixed order for the DBM process, we have proposed a solution based on the ontologies and the knowledge extraction process. This approach is useful since it is used for end user assistance in the entire process development.

The proposed architecture defines, at different levels, a connection between ontology engineering and KDD process. It also defines a hybrid life cycle for the DBM process, based on both approaches. This life cycle that effectively assists the end-user, is composed by the knowledge extraction process phases and other specific marketing domain activities. Each phase is divided in tasks, directly or indirectly, related to ontology engineering, marketing and KDD.

This ontology is meant to be a subcomponent in the overall KDD process. Its usage of knowledge obtained from prior examples makes it applicable when several related databases are used.

Further work can be done in a variety of ways: this can be used for more specific knowledge extraction process or for more business oriented objectives. We believe that this approach convincingly addresses a pressing KDD need.

8. References

Arndt, D. and Gersten, W. (2001). Data management in analytical customer relationship management. In ECML/PKDD 2001 Workshop Proceedings. Data Mining For Marketing Applications.

Bean, R. (1999). Building a foundation for database marketing success. Technical report, DM Review Magazine.

Bellandi, A., Furletti, B., Grossi, V., and Romei, A. (2006). Ontology-driven association rule extraction: A case study. Contexts and Ontologies: Representation and reasoning in 16th European Conference on Artificial Intelligence, 1:1–10.

Berners-Lee, T., H., and J., Lassila, O. (2001). The semantic web. Scientific American, 284:34–43.

Berners-Lee, T. (2003). Www past and future. Technical report, W3C.

Bernstein, A., Provost, F., and Hill, S. (2005). Toward intelligent assistance for a data mining process: An ontology-based approach for cost-sensitive classification. IEEE Transactions on knowledge and data engineering, 17(4).

Blanco, I. J., Vila, M. A., and Martinez-Cruz, C. (2008). The use of ontologies for representing database schemas of fuzzy information. International Journal of intelligent Systems, 23:419–445.

Borges, A. M., Corniel, M., Gil, R., Contreras, L., and Borges, R. (2009). Towards a study opportunities recommender system in ontological principles-based on semantic web environment. WSEAS Transactions on Computers, 8(2):279–291.

Borst, P., Akkermans, H., and Top, J. (1997). Engineering ontologies. The International Journal of Human Computer Studies. In Special Issue: Using explicit ontologies in knowledge-based system development, Vol. 2/3 pp.365-406., 46(2-3):365–406.

Bolloju, N., Khalifa, M., and Turban, E. (2002). Integrating knowledge management into enterprise environments for the next generation decision support. Journal of Decision Support Systems, 33(2):163–176.

Bombardier, V., Mazaud, C., Lhoste, P., and Vogrig, R. (2007). Contribution of fuzzy reasoning method to knowledge integration in a defect recognition system. Journal of computers in industry, 58(4):355–366.

Bohling, T., Bowman, D., LaValle, S., Mittal, V., Narayandas, D., Ramani, G., and Varadarajan, R. (2006). Crm implementation: Effectiveness issues and insights. Journal of Service Research, 9(2):184–194.

Brezany, P., Janciak, I., and Tjoa, A. M. (2008). Data Mining with Ontologies: Implementations, Findings, and Frameworks, chapter Ontology-Based Construction of Grid Data Mining Workflows, pages 182–210. Information Science Reference - IGI Global.

Brito, P. Q. (2000). Como Fazer Promocao de Vendas. Mc Graw-Hill.

Brito, P. Q. and Hammond, K. (2007). Strategic versus tactical nature of sales promotions. Journal of Marketing Communications, 13(2):131–148.

Brito, P. Q., Jorge, A., and McGoldrick, P. J. (2004). The relationship between stores and shopping centers: Artificial intelligence and multivariate approach assessement. In Proceedings of Annual Conference of IABE 2004, Las Vegas, USA.

Buckinx, W. and den Poel, D. V. (2005). Customer base analysis: Partial defection of behaviorally-loyal clients in a non-contractual fmcg retail setting. European Journal of Operational Research, 164 (1):252–268.

Buckinx, W., Verstraeten, G., and den Poel, D. V. (2007). Predicting customer loyalty using the internal transactional database. Expert Systems with Applications, 32:125–134.

Brookes, R. W., Brodie, R. J., Coviello, N. E., and Palmer, R. A. (2004). How managers perceive the impacts of information technologies on contemporary marketing practices: Reinforcing, enhancing or transforming? Journal of Relationship Marketing, 3(4):7–26.

Cannataro, M. and Comito, C. (2003). A data mining ontology for grid programming. In First International Workshop on Semantics in Peer-to-Peer and Grid Computing, in conjunction with WWW2003, pages 113–134.

Cardoso, J. and Lytras, M. (2009). Semantic Web Engineering in the Knowledge Society. Information Science Reference - IGI Global, New York.

Carson, D., Gilmore, A., and Walsh, S. (2004). Balancing transaction and relationship marketing in retail banking. Journal of Marketing Management, 20:431–455.

Ceccaroni, L. (2001). Ontoweeds - An ontology-based environmental decision-support system for the management of wastewater treatment plants. PhD thesis, Universitat Politecnica de Catalunya, Barcelona.

CeSpivova, H., Rauch, J., Svatek, V., and Kejkula, M. (2004). Roles of medical ontology in association mining crisp-dm cycle. In Knowledge Discovery and Ontologies.

Cellini, J., Diamantini, C., and Potena, D. (2007). Kddbroker: Description and discovery of kdd services. In 15th Italian symposium on Advanced Database Systems.

Cheng, H., Lu, Y.-C., and Sheu, C. (2009). Automated optimal equity portfolios discovery in a financial knowledge management system. Expert Systems with Applications, 36(2):3614–3622.

Cimiano, P., Hotho, A., Stumme, G., and Tane, J. (2004). Conceptual knowledge processing with formal concept analysis and ontologies. In ICFCA - Second International Conference on Formal Concept Analysis.

Coviello, N., Milley, R., and Marcolin, B. (2001). Understanding it-enabled interactivity in contemporary marketing. Journal of Interactive Marketing, 15(4):18–33.

Coviello, N., Winklhofer, H., and Hamilton, K. (2006). Marketing practices and performance of small service firms - an examination in the tourism accommodation sector. Journal of Service Research, 9(1):38–58.

Coviello, N. and Brodie, J. (1998). From transaction to relationship marketing: an investigation of managerial perceptions and practices. Journal of Strategic Marketing, 6(3):171–186.

Coulet, A., Smail-Tabbone, M., Benlian, P., Napoli, A., and Devignes, M.-D. (2008). Ontology-guided data preparation for discovering genotype-phenotype relationships. Journal of BMC Bioinformatics, 9:1–9.

den Poel, D. V. and Buckinx, W. (2005). Predicting online-purchasing behaviour. European Journal of Operational Research Dirk Van den Poel and Wouter Buckinx, 166(2):557–575.

DeTienne, K. B. and Thompson, J. A. (1996). Database marketing and organizational learning theory: toward a research agenda. Journal of Consumer Marketing, 13(5):12–34.

Diamantini, C., Panti, M., and Potena, D. (2004). Services for knowledge discovery in databases. In In Int. Symposium of Santa Caterina on Challanges in the Internet and Interdisciplinary Research SSCCII-04, volume 1.

Diamantini, C., Potena, D., and Cellini, J. (2006a). Uddi registry for knowledge discovery in databases services. In Proc. of AAAI Fall Symposium on Semantic Web for Collaborative Knowledge Acquisition, pages 94–97, Arlington, VA, USA.

Diamantini, C., Potena, D., and Smari, W. (2006b). Collaborative knowledge discovery in databases: A knowledge exchange perspective. In Fall Symposium on Semantic Web for Collaborative Knowledge Acquisition, pages 24–31, Arlington, VA, USA. AAAI, AAAI.

Domingos, P. (2003). Prospects and challenges for multi-relational data mining. SIGKDD Explorer Newsletter, 5(1):80–83.

Drozdenko, R. and Perry, D. (2002). Optimal Database Marketing. SAGE Publications, Thousand Oaks, USA.

El-Ansary, A. I. (2006). Marketing strategy: taxonomy and frameworks. European Business Review, 18:266–293.

Euler, T. and Scholz, M. (2004). Using ontologies in a kdd workbench. In ECAI-2004 Workshop on Ontology Learning and Population.

Farquhar, A., Fikes, R., and Rice, J. (1997). Tools for assembling modular ontologies in ontolingua. In In Proceedings of Association for the Advancement of Artificial Intelligence 97, pages 436–441. AAAI Press.

Fayyad, U., Piatetsky-Shapiro, G., and Smyth, P. (1996). From data mining to knowledge discovery in databases. In Magazine, A., editor, AI Magazine, volume 17, pages 37–54, Univ Calif Irvine, Dept Comp & Informat Sci, Irvine, Ca, 92717 Gte Labs Inc, Knowledge Discovery Databases Kdd Project, Tech Staff, Waltham, Ma, 02254. American Association for Artificial Intelligence.

Fensel, D., Horrocks, Harmelen, V., Decker, S., Erdmann, M., and Klein1, M. (2000). Oil in a nutshell. Proceedings of the 12th European Workshop on Knowledge Acquisition,

Modeling, and Management - EKAW'00 Lecture Notes in Artificial Intelligence, 1937:1–16.

Fletcher, K., Wright, G., and Desai, C. (1996). The role of organizational factors in the adoption and sophistication of database marketing in the uk financial services industry. Journal of Direct Marketing, 10:10–21.

Fox, M. and Gruninger, M. (1997). On ontologies and enterprise modelling. In Springer-Verlag, editor, Proceedings of International Conference on Enterprise Integration Modelling Technology. Springer- Verlag.

Frankland, D. (2007). How firms use database marketing services. Technical report with user interview data, ForresterResearch Inc.

Gronroos, C. (1994). From marketing mix to relationship marketing:towards a paradigm shift in marketing. Management Decision, 32(2):4–20.

Gomez-Perez, A., Fernandez-Lopez, M., and Corcho, O. (2004). Ontological engineering. Springer, 2nd edition.

Gruber, T. R. (1993). A translation approach to portable ontology specifications. Knowledge Acquisition, 5:199–220.

Guarino, N. (1995). Formal ontology, conceptual analysis and knowledge representation. International Journal of Human and Computer Studies, 43:625–640.

Guarino, N. (1998). Formal ontology and information systems. In Guarino, N., editor, FOIS'98 Formal Ontology in Information systems, pages 3–15, Amsterdam. IOS Press.

Jarrar, M. (2005). Towards Methodological Principles for Ontology Engineering. PhD thesis, Vrije Universiteit Brussel, Faculty of science.

Jasper, R. and Uschold, M. (1999). A framework for understanding and classifying ontology applications. In IJCAI 99 Ontology Workshop, pages 16–21.

Jurisica, I., Mylopoulos, J., and Yu, E. (1999). Ontologies for knowledge management: An information systems perspective. In for Information Sciences, A. S., editor, Proceedings of the Annual Conference of the American Society for Information Sciences (ASISâ€™99). American Society for Information Sciences.

Kasabov, N., Jain, V., Gottgtroy, P., Benuskova, L., Wysoski, S., and Joseph, F. (2007). Evolving brain-gene ontology system (ebgos): Towards integrating bioinformatics and neuroinformatics data to facilitate discoveries. In IEEE, editor, International Joint Conference on Neural Networks, Orlando - US.

Kopanas, I., Avouris, N. M., and Daskalaki, S. (2002). The Role of Domain Knowledge in a Large Scale Data Mining Project, volume 2308 of Lecture Notes in Computer Science, chapter Methods and Applications of Artificial Intelligence, pages 288–299. Springer Berlin / Heidelberg.

Leary, C. O., Rao, S., and Perry, C. (2004). Improving customer relationship management through database/internet marketing. European Journal of Marketing, 38(3/4):338–354.

Lin, C. and Hong, C. (2008). Using customer knowledge in designing electronic catalog. Expert systems with Applications, 34:119–127.

Lixiang, S. (2001). Data mining thechniques based on rough set theory. PhD thesis, National University of Singapore.

Lopez, M. F., Gomez-Perez, A., Sierra, J. P., and Sierra, A. P. (1999). Building a chemical ontology using methontology and the ontology design environment. IEEE Intelligent Systems Journal, 1:37-46.

Marsh, R. (2005). Drowning in dirty data. Database Marketing & Customer Strategy Management, 12(2):105-112.

McClymont, H. and Jocumsen, G. (2003). How to implement marketing strategies using database approaches. The Journal of Database Marketing & Customer Strategy Management, 11(2):135-148.

Michalewicz, Z., Schmidt, M., Michalewicz, M., and Chiriac, C. (2006). Adaptive Business Intelligence. Springer.

(Newell and level, 1982) Newell, A. and level, T. (1982). The knowledge level. Artificial Intelligence, 18:87-127.

(Neches et al., 1991) Neches, R., Fikes, R., Finin, T., Gruber, T., Patil, R., Senator, T., and Swartout, W. R. (1991). Enabling technology for knowledge sharing. Artificial Intelligence Magazine, 12(3):36-56.

(Nigro et al., 2008) Nigro, H. O., Cisaro, S. G., and Xodo, D. (2008). Data Mining with Ontologies: Implementations, Findings and Frameworks. Information Science Reference. Information Science Reference - IGI Global, London, igi global edition.

Noy and McGuinness, 2003) Noy, N. F. and McGuinness, D. L. (2003). Ontology development 101: A guide to creating your first ontology. Technical report, Stanford University.

Nogueira, B. M., Santos, T. R. A., and ZÃ¡rate, L. E. (2007). Comparison of classifiers efficiency on missing values recovering: Application in a marketing database with massive missing data. In Proceedings of the 2007 IEEE Symposium on Computational Intelligence and Data Mining (CIDM 2007).

Ozimek, J. (2004). Case studies: The 2003 information management project awards. Journal of Database Marketing & Customer Strategy Management, 12(1):55.

Pearce, J. E., Webb, G. I., Shaw, R. N., and Garner, B. (2002). A systemic approach to the database marketing process. ANZMAC Conference Proceedings, 1:2941-2948.

Perez-Rey, D., Anguita, A., and Crespo, J. (2006). Biological and Medical Data Analysis, volume 4345/2006 of Lecture Notes in Computer Science, chapter OntoDataClean: Ontology-Based Integration and Preprocessing of Distributed Data, pages 262-272. Springer Berlin / Heidelberg.

Phillips, J. and Buchanan, B. G. (2001). Ontology-guided knowledge discovery in databases. In ACM, editor, International Conference On Knowledge Capture 1st international conference on Knowledge capture, pages 123-130. International Conference On Knowledge Capture

Pinto, F. (2006). A descoberta de conhecimento em bases de dados como suporte a actividades de business intelligence - aplicaÃ§Ã£o na Ã rea do database marketing. Master's thesis, Universidade do Minho.

Pinto, F., Santos, M. F., and Marques, A. (2009). WSEAS Transactions on Business and Economics, volume 6, chapter Database marketing intelligence supported by ontologies, pages 135-146. World Scientific and Engineering Academy and Society.

Quine, W. V. (1992). Theories and Things (Revised ed.). Harvard University Press.

Quinlan, R. (1986). Induction of decision trees. Machine Learning, 1(1):81-106.

Rebelo, C., Brito, P. Q., Soares, C., and Jorge, A. (2006). Factor analysis to support the visualization and interpretation of clusters of portal users. In WI 2006: Proceedings of the 2006 IEEE/WIC/ACM International Conference on Web Intelligence, pages 987–990, Washington, DC, USA. IEEE Computer Society.

Rothenfluh, T. E., Gennari, J. H., Eriksson, H., Puerta, A. R., Tu, S. W., and Musen, M. A. (1996). Reusable ontologies, knowledge-acquisition tools, and performance systems: Protege-ii solutionsto sisyphus-2. International Journal of Human-Computer Studies 44: 303-332., 44:303–332.

Santos, M. F., Cortez, P., Quintela, H., and Pinto, F. (2005). A clustering approach for knowledge discovery in database marketing. Data Mining VI: Data Mining, Text Mining and their Business Applications, 35:399–407.

Seller, M. and Gray, P. (1999). A survey database marketing. Technical report, Center for Research on information Technology and Organizations.

Sen, S. and Tuzhiln, A. (1998). Making sense of marketing data: Some mis perspectives on the analysis of large data sets. Journal of Market Focused Management, 3:91–111.

Sharma, S. and Osei-Bryson, K.-M. (2008). Framework for formal implementation of the business understanding phase of data mining projects. Expert Systems with Applications, page in press.

Shepard, D. (1998). The New Direct Marketing: How to Implement A Profit-Driven Database Marketing Strategy. David Shepard Ass, 3rd edition.

Schoenbachler, D. D., Gordon, G. L., Foley, D., and Spellman, L. (1997). Understanding consumer database marketing. Journal of Consumer Marketing, 14(1):5–19.

Smith, R. G. and Farquhar, A. (2008). The road ahead for knowledge management: An ai perspective. American Association for Artificial Intelligence, 1:17–40.

Sowa, J. F. (2000). Knowledge Representation: Logical, Philosophical, and Computational Foundations. Brooks Cole Publishing Co.

Staab, S. and Studer, R. (2004). Handbook on ontologies. International handbooks on information systems. Springer-Verlag.

Swartout, B., Patil, R., Knight, K., and Russ, T. (1996). Ontosaurus: A tool for browsing and editing ontologies. Knowledge Acquisition Workshops, 1.

Tao, Y.-H. and Yeh, C.-C. R. (2003). Simple database marketing tools in customer analysis and retention. International Journal of Information Management, 23:291–301.

Tudorache, T. (2006). Employing Ontologies for an Improved Development Process in Collaborative Engineering. PhD thesis, University of Berlim, Germany.

van Heijst, G., Schreiber, A. T., and Wielinga, B. J. (1997). Using explicit ontologies in kbs development. International Journal of Human-Computer Studies, 46(2):183–292.

Verhoef, P. and Hoekstra, J. (1999). Status of database marketing in the dutch fast moving consumer goods industry. Journal of Market Focused Management, 3:313â€"331.

Wehmeyer, K. (2005). Aligning it and marketing - the impact of database marketing and crm. Journal of Database Marketing & Customer Strategy Management, 12(2):243.

Welty, C. and Murdock, J. W. (2006). Towards knowledge acquisition from information extraction. In Springer, editor, In Proceedings of ISWC-2006., Athens.

Weng, S.-S. and Chang, H.-L. (2008). Using ontologies network analysis for research document recommendation. Expert Systems with Applications, 34:1857–1869.

Witten, I. H. and Frank, E. (2000). Data Mining: Practical Machine Learning Tools and Technique. The Morgan Kaufmann Series in Data Management Systems, 2nd edition.

Zairate, L. E., Nogueira, B. M., Santos, T. R. A., and Song, M. A. J. (2006). Techniques for missing value recovering in imbalanced databases: Application in a marketing database with massive missing data. In IEEE International Conference on Systems, Man, and Cybernetics, pages 2658–2664, Taiwan. IEEE.

Zhou, X., Geller, J., and Halper, Y. P. M. (2006). An Application Intersection Marketing Ontology, chapter Theoretical Computer Science, pages 143–163. Lecture Notes in Computer Science. Springer Berlin / Heidelberg.

Zineldin, M. and Vasicheva, V. (2008). Cybernization management in the cyber world: a new management perspective. Problems and Perspectives in Management, Volume 6, Issue 1, 2008, 1:113–126.

Zwick, D. and Dholakia, N. (2004). Whose identity is it anyway? consumer representation in the age of database marketing. Journal of Macromarketing, 24(1):31–43.

3

Parallel and Distributed Data Mining

Dr (Mrs). Sujni Paul
Karunya University
Coimbatore,
India

1. Introduction

Data mining is a process of nontrivial extraction of implicit, previously unknown, and potentially useful information (such as knowledge rules, constraints, and regularities) from data in databases. In fact, the term "knowledge discovery" is more general than the term "data mining." Data mining is usually viewed as a step towards the process of knowledge discovery, although these two terms are considered as synonyms in the computer literature. The entire life cycle of knowledge discovery includes steps such as data cleaning, data integration, data selections, data transformation, data mining, pattern evaluation, and knowledge presentation.

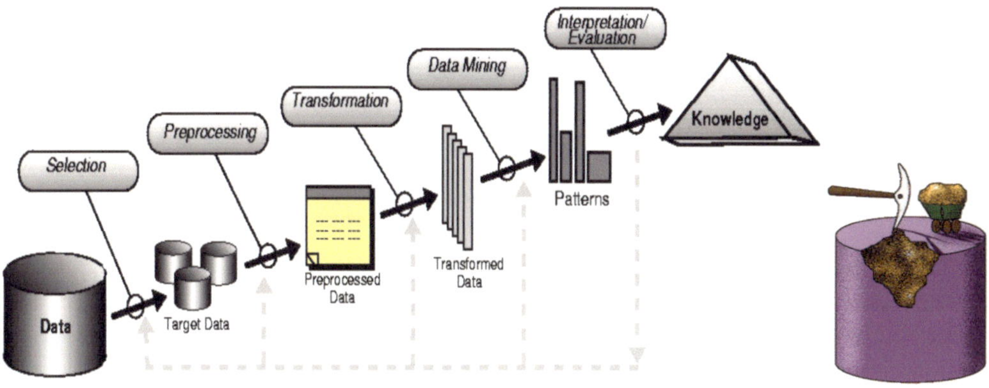

Fig. 1. Life Cycle of knowledge presentation

Data cleaning is to remove noise and inconsistent data. Data integration is to combine data from multiple data sources, such as a database and data warehouse. Data selection is to retrieve data relevant to the task. Data transformation is to transform data into appropriate forms. Data mining is to apply intelligent methods to extract data patterns. Pattern evaluation is to identify the truly interesting patterns based on some interestingness measures. Knowledge evaluation is to visualize and present the mined knowledge to the user. There are many data mining techniques, such as association rule mining, classification, clustering, sequential pattern mining, etc.
Since this chapter focuses on parallel and distributed data mining, let us turn our attention to those concepts.

2. Distributed data mining

Data mining algorithms deal predominantly with simple data formats (typically flat files); there is an increasing amount of focus on mining complex and advanced data types such as object-oriented, spatial and temporal data. Another aspect of this growth and evolution of data mining systems is the move from stand-alone systems using centralized and local computational resources towards supporting increasing levels of distribution. As data mining technology matures and moves from a theoretical domain to the practitioner's arena there is an emerging realization that distribution is very much a factor that needs to be accounted for.

Databases in today's information age are inherently distributed. Organizations that operate in global markets need to perform data mining on distributed data sources (homogeneous / heterogeneous) and require cohesive and integrated knowledge from this data. Such organizational environments are characterized by a geographical separation of users from the data sources. This inherent distribution of data sources and large volumes of data involved inevitably leads to exorbitant communications costs. Therefore, it is evident that traditional data mining model involving the co-location of users, data and computational resources is inadequate when dealing with distributed environments. The development of data mining along this dimension has lead to the emergence of distributed data mining. The need to address specific issues associated with the application of data mining in distributed computing environments is the primary objective of distributed data mining. Broadly, data mining environments consist of users, data, hardware and the mining software (this includes both the mining algorithms and any other associated programs). Distributed data mining addresses the impact of distribution of users, software and computational resources on the data mining process. There is general consensus that distributed data mining is the process of mining data that has been partitioned into one or more physically/geographically distributed subsets.

The significant factors, which have led to the emergence of distributed data mining from centralized mining, are as follows:

- The need to mine distributed subsets of data, the integration of which is non- trivial and expensive.
- The performance and scalability bottle necks of data mining.
- Distributed data mining provides a framework for scalability, which allows the splitting up of larger datasets with high dimensionality into smaller subsets that require computational resources individually.

Distributed Data Mining (DDM) is a branch of the field of data mining that offers a framework to mine distributed data paying careful attention to the distributed data and computing resources. In the DDM literature, one of two assumptions is commonly adopted as to how data is distributed across sites: homogeneously and heterogeneously. Both viewpoints adopt the conceptual viewpoint that the data tables at each site are partitions of a single global table. In the homogeneous case, the global table is horizontally partitioned. The tables at each site are subsets of the global table; they have exactly the same attributes. In the heterogeneous case the table is vertically partitioned, each site contains a collection of columns (sites do not have the same attributes). However, each tuple at each site is assumed to contain a unique identifier to facilitate matching. It is important to stress that the global table viewpoint is strictly conceptual. It is not necessarily assumed that such a table was physically realized and partitioned to form the tables at each site.

3. Parallel and distributed data mining

The enormity and high dimensionality of datasets typically available as input to the problem of association rule discovery, makes it an ideal problem for solving multiple processors in parallel. The primary reasons are the memory and CPU speed limitations faced by single processors. Thus it is critical to design efficient parallel algorithms to do the task. Another reason for parallel algorithm comes from the fact that many transaction databases are already available in parallel databases or they are distributed at multiple sites to begin with. The cost of bringing them all to one site or one computer for serial discovery of association rules can be prohibitively expensive.

For compute-intensive applications, parallelisation is an obvious means for improving performance and achieving scalability. A variety of techniques may be used to distribute the workload involved in data mining over multiple processors. Four major classes of parallel implementations are distinguished. The classification tree in Figure 1 demonstrates this distinction. The first distinction made in this tree is between *task parallel* and *data-parallel* approaches.

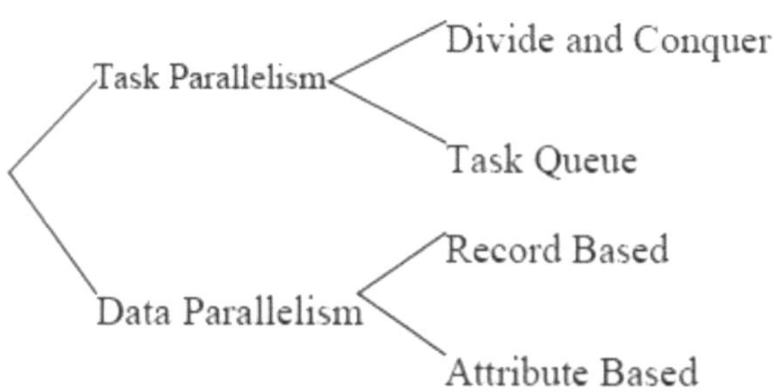

Fig. 2. Methods of Parallelism

Task-parallel algorithms assign portions of the search space to separate processors. The task parallel approaches can again be divided into two groups. The first group is based on a *Divide and Conquer* strategy that divides the search space and assigns each partition to a specific processor. The second group is based on a task queue that dynamically assigns small portions of the search space to a processor whenever it becomes available. A task parallel implementation of decision tree induction will form tasks associated with branches of the tree. A Divide and Conquer approach seems a natural reflection of the recursive nature of decision trees.

However the task of parallel implementation suffers from load balancing problems caused by uneven distributions of records between branches. The success of a task parallel implementation of decision trees seems to be highly dependent on the structure of the data set. The second class of approaches, called data parallel, distributes the data set over the available processors. Data-parallel approaches come in two flavors. A partitioning based on records will assign non-overlapping sets of records to each of the processors. Alternatively a partitioning of attributes will assign sets of attributes to each of the processors. Attribute-based approaches are based on the observation that many algorithms can be expressed in terms of primitives that consider every attribute in turn. If attributes are distributed over multiple processors, these primitives may be executed in parallel. For example, when constructing decision trees, at each node in the tree, all independent attributes are considered, in order to determine the best split at that point.

There are two basic parallel approaches that have come to be used in recent times - *work partitioning* and *data partitioning*.

Work Partitioning - These methods assign different view computations to different processors. Consider, for example, the lattice for a four dimensional data cube. If a name is assigned to the dimensions as "ABCD", 15 views need to be computed. Given a parallel computer with p processors, work partitioning schemes partition the set of views into p groups and assign the computation of the views in each group to a different processor. The main challenges for these methods are load balancing and scalability.

Data Partitioning - These methods work by partitioning the raw data set into p subsets and store each subset locally on one processor. All views are computed on every processor but only with respect to the subset of data available at each processor. A subsequent *merge* procedure is required to agglomerate the data across processors. The advantage of data partitioning methods is that they do not require all processors to have access to the entire raw data set. Each processor only requires a local copy of a portion of the raw data which can, e.g., be stored on its local disk. This makes such methods feasible for shared-nothing parallel machines.

4. Why parallelize data mining?

Data-mining applications fall into two groups based on their intent. In some applications, the goal is to find explanations for the most variable elements of the data set that is, to find and explain the *outliers*. In other applications, the goal is to understand the variations of the majority of the data set elements, with little interest in the outliers. Scientific data mining seems to be mostly of the first kind, whereas commercial applications seem to be of the second kind ("understand the buying habits of most of our customers"). In applications of the first kind, parallel computing seems to be essential. In applications of the second kind, the question is still open because it is not known how effective sampling from a large data set might be at answering broader questions. Parallel computing thus has considerable potential as a tool for data mining, but it is not yet completely clear whether it represents the future of data mining.

5. Technologies

- **Parallel computing**
  Single systems with many processors work on same problem.
- **Distributed computing**
  Many systems loosely coupled by a scheduler to work on related problems.
- **Grid Computing (Meta Computing)**
  Many systems tightly coupled by software, perhaps geographically distributed, are made to work together on single problems or on related problems.

5.1 Properties of algorithms for association discovery

Most algorithms for association discovery follow the same general procedure, based on the sequential *Apriori* algorithm. The basic idea is to make multiple passes over the database, building larger and larger groups of associations on each pass. Thus, the first pass determines the "items" that occur most frequently in all the transactions in the database; each subsequent pass builds a list of possible frequent item tuples based on the results of the previous pass, and then scans the database, discarding those tuples that do not occur frequently in the database. The intuition is that for any set of items that occurs frequently, all subsets of that set must also occur frequently.

Notice that, for large association sets, this algorithm and its derivatives must make many passes over a potentially enormous database. It is also typically implemented using a hash tree, a complex data structure that exhibits very poor locality (and thus poor cache behavior).

Although there exist workable sequential algorithms for data mining (such as Apriori, above), there is a desperate need for a parallel solution for most realistic-sized problems. The most obvious (and most compelling) argument for parallelism revolves around database size. The databases used for data mining are typically extremely large, often containing the details of the entire history of a company's standard transactional databases. As these databases grow past hundreds of gigabytes towards a terabyte or more, it becomes nearly impossible to process them on a single sequential machine, for both time and space reasons: no more than a fraction of the database can be kept in main memory at any given time, and the amount of local disk storage and bandwidth needed to keep the sequential CPU supplied with data is enormous. Additionally, with an algorithm such as Apriori that requires many complete passes over the database, the actual running time required to complete the algorithm becomes excessive.

The basic approach to parallelizing association-discovery data mining is via database partitioning. Each available node in the networking environment is assigned a subset of the database records, and computes independently on that subset, usually using a variation on the sequential *Apriori* algorithm. All of the parallel data mining algorithms require some amount of global all-all or all-one communication to coordinate the independent nodes.

5.2 Problems in developing parallel algorithms for distributed environment

There are several problems in developing parallel algorithms for a distributed environment with association discovery data mining which is being considered in this research work. These are:

- **Data distribution:** One of the benefits of parallel and distributed data mining is that each node can potentially work with a reduced-size subset of the total database. A parallel algorithm in distributed environment must effectively distribute data to allow each node to make independent progress with its incomplete view of the entire database.
- **I/O minimization:** Even with good data distribution, parallel data mining algorithms must strive to minimize the amount of I/O they perform to the database.
- **Load balancing:** To maximize the effect/efficiency of parallelism, each workstation must have approximately the same amount of work to do. Although a good initial data distribution can help provide load-balancing, with some algorithms, periodic data redistribution is required to obtain good overall load-balancing.
- **Avoiding duplication:** Ideally, no workstation should do redundant work (work already performed by another node).
- **Minimizing communication:** An ideal parallel data mining algorithm allows all workstations to operate asynchronously, without having to stall frequently for global barriers or for communication delays.
- **Maximizing locality:** As in all performance programming, high-performance parallel data mining algorithms must be designed to reap the full performance potential of

hardware. This involves maximizing locality for good cache behavior, utilizing as much of the machine's memory bandwidth as possible, etc.

Achieving all of the above goals in one algorithm is nearly impossible, as there are tradeoffs between several of the above points. Existing algorithms for parallel data mining attempt to achieve an optimal balance between these factors.

5.3 Algorithms in parallel and distributed data mining

The major algorithms used for parallel and distributed data mining are:

- **Count Distribution:** this algorithm achieves parallelism by partitioning data. Each of N workstations gets $1/N^{th}$ of the database, and performs an *Apriori*-like algorithm on the subset. At the end of each iteration however, is a communication phase, in which the frequency of item occurrence in the various data partitions is exchanged between all workstations. Thus, this algorithm trades off I/O and duplication for minimal communication and good load-balance: each workstation must scan its database partition multiple times (causing a huge I/O load) and maintains a full copy of the (poor-locality) data structures used (causing duplicated data structure maintenance), but only requires a small amount of per-iteration communication (an asynchronous broadcast of frequency counts) and has a good distribution of work.
- **Data Distribution:** This algorithm is designed to minimize computational redundancy and maximize use of the memory bandwidth of each workstation. It works by partitioning the current maximal-frequency itemset candidates (like those generated by *Apriori*) amongst work stations. Thus, each workstation examines a disjoint set of possibilities; however, each workstation must scan the entire database to examine its candidates. Thus this algorithm trades off a huge amount of communication (to fetch the database partitions stored on other workstations) for better use of machine resources and to avoid duplicated work.
- **Candidate Distribution:** This algorithm is similar to data distribution in that it partitions the candidates across workstations, but it attempts to minimize communication by selectively partitioning the database such that each workstation has locally the data needed to process its candidate set. It does this after a fixed (small) number of passes of the standard data distribution algorithm. This trades off duplication (the same data may need to be replicated on more than one node) and poor load-balancing (after redistributing the data, the workload of each workstation may not be balanced) in order to minimize communication and synchronization. The effects of poor load balancing are mitigated somewhat, since global barriers at the end of each pass are not required.
- **Eclat:** This sophisticated algorithm avoids most of the tradeoffs above by using an initial clustering step to pre-process the data before partitioning it between workstations. It thus achieves many of the benefits of candidate distribution without the costs. Little synchronization or communication is needed, since each node can process its partitioned dataset independently. A transformation of the data during partitioning allows the use of simple database intersections (rather than hash trees), maximizing cache locality and memory bandwidth usage. The transformation also drastically cuts down the I/O bandwidth requirements by only necessitating three database scans.

6. Role of intelligent agents in distributed data mining

Agents are defined as software or hardware entities that perform some set of tasks on behalf of users with some degree of autonomy. In order to work for somebody as an assistant, an agent has to include a certain amount of *intelligence*, which is the ability to choose among various courses of action, plan, communicate, adapt to changes in the environment, and learn from experience. In general, an intelligent agent can be described as consisting of a *sensing* element that can receive events, a *recognizer* or *classifier* that determines which event occurred, a *set of logic* ranging from hard-coded programs to rule-based inferencing, and a *mechanism* for taking action.

Data mining agents seek data and information based on the profile of the user and the instructions she gives. A group of flexible data-mining agents can co-operate to discover knowledge from distributed sources. They are responsible for accessing data and extracting higher-level useful information from the data. A data mining agent specializes in performing some activity in the domain of interest. Agents can work in parallel and share the information they have gathered so far.

Pericles A. Mitkas et al's work on Software agent technology has matured enough to produce intelligent agents, which can be used for controlling a large number of concurrent engineering tasks. Multi-agent systems are communities of agents that exchange information and data in the form of messages. The agents' intelligence can range from rudimentary sensor monitoring and data reporting, to more advanced forms of decision making and autonomous behavior. The behavior and intelligence of each agent in the community can be obtained by performing data mining on available application data and the respected knowledge domain. An Agent Academy a software platform is designed for the creation, and deployment of multiagent systems, which combines the power of knowledge discovery algorithms with the versatility of agents. Using this platform, agents are equipped with a data-driven inference engine, can be dynamically and continuously trained. Three prototype multi-agent systems are developed with Agent Academy.

Agent-based systems belong to the most vibrant and important areas of research and development to have emerged in information technology. Because of the lively extensive spreading of directions in research no publicly accepted solid definitions of agent-based systems and their elements - agents is provided. Hence, in context of this paper some general definitions are used: Software agent is software that acts as an agent for another as in a relationship of agency. When several agents act they may form a multi-agent system. Intelligent Agent (IA) refers to a software agent that exhibits some form of artificial intelligence. According to Wooldridge intelligent agents are defined as agents, capable of flexible autonomous action to meet their design objectives. They must involve:

- Reactivity: to perceive and respond in a timely fashion to changes occurring in their environment in order to satisfy their design objectives. The agent's goals and/or assumptions that form the basis for a procedure that is currently executed may be affected by a changed environment and a different set of actions may have to be performed.
- Pro-activeness: ability to exhibit goal-directed behavior by taking the initiative, responding to changes in their environment in order to satisfy their design objectives.
- Sociability: capability of interacting with other agents (software and humans) through negotiation and/or cooperation to satisfy their design objectives.

During the mining process the mobile intelligent agents can be used as it keeps monitoring the different workstations in the geographically distributed areas.

7. Architectures

Agent-based distributed data mining systems employ one or more agents to analyze and model local datasets, which generate local models. These local models generated by individual agents can then be composed into one or more new 'global models' based on different learning algorithms, for instance, JAM and BODHI. JAM Java Agents for Meta-learning is a Java-based distributed data mining system that uses a meta-learning technique. The architecture consists of local databases of several financial institutes, learning agents and meta-learning agents. Agents operate on a local database and generate local classifiers. These local classifiers then are imported to a data location where they can be aggregated into a global model using meta-learning.

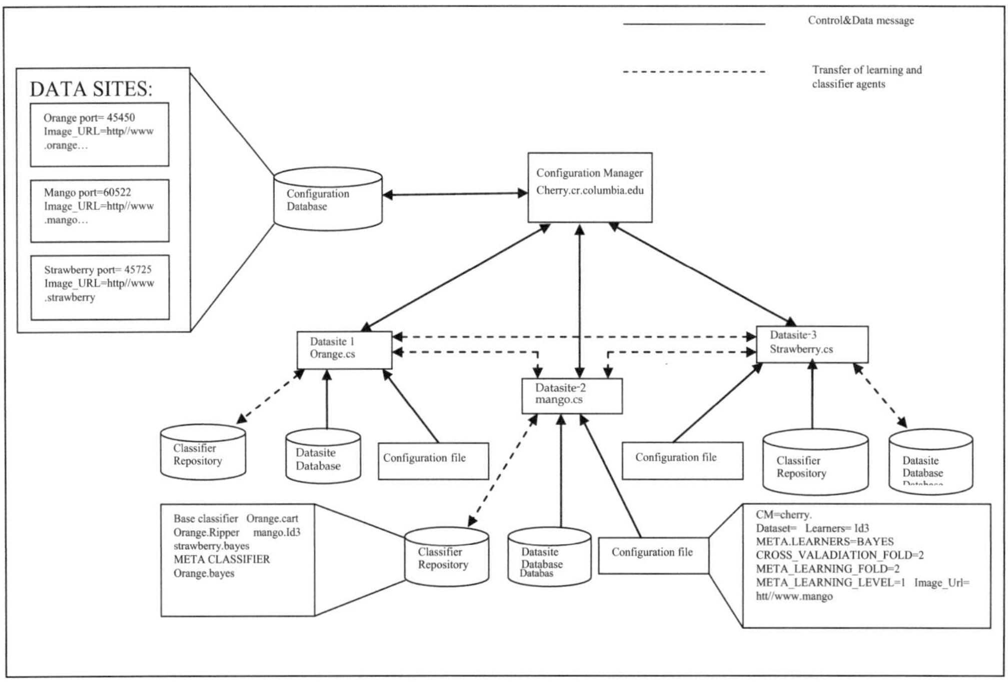

Fig. 3. JAM architecture with 3 datasites

BODHI is a Java and agent based distributed data mining system. BODHI also notes the importance of mobile agent technology. As all of agents are extensions of a basic agent object, BODHI can easily transfer an agent from one site to another site, along with the agent's environment, configuration, current state and learned knowledge. Figure 2.1 shows the BODHI architecture.

PADMA Architecture

The PADMA is an agent based architecture for parallel / distributed data mining. The goal of this effort is to develop a flexible system that will exploit data mining agents in parallel. Its initial implementation used agents specializing in unstructured text document classification.

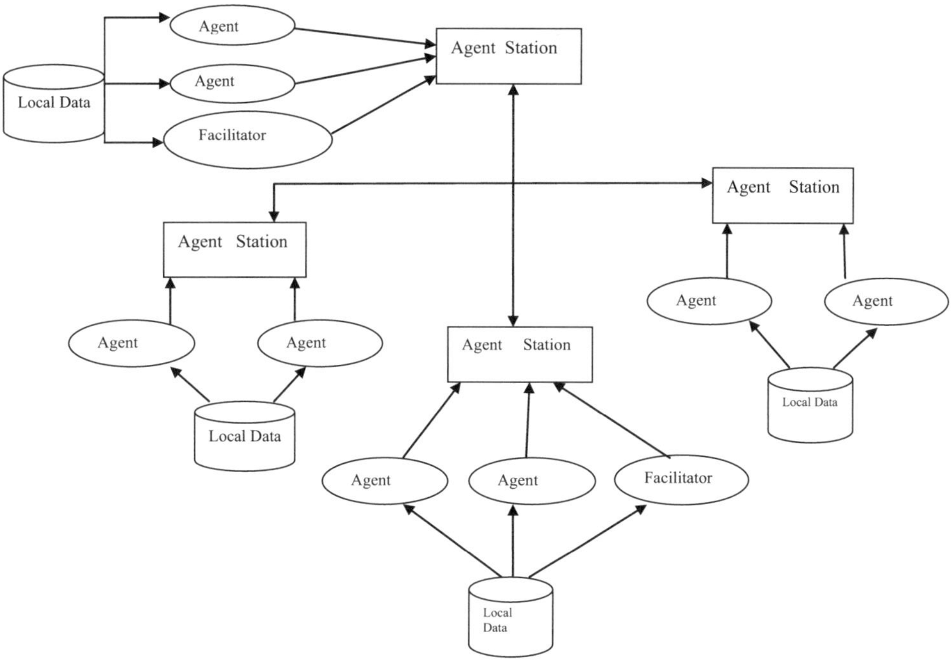

Fig. 4. BODHI: Agent-based distributed data mining system

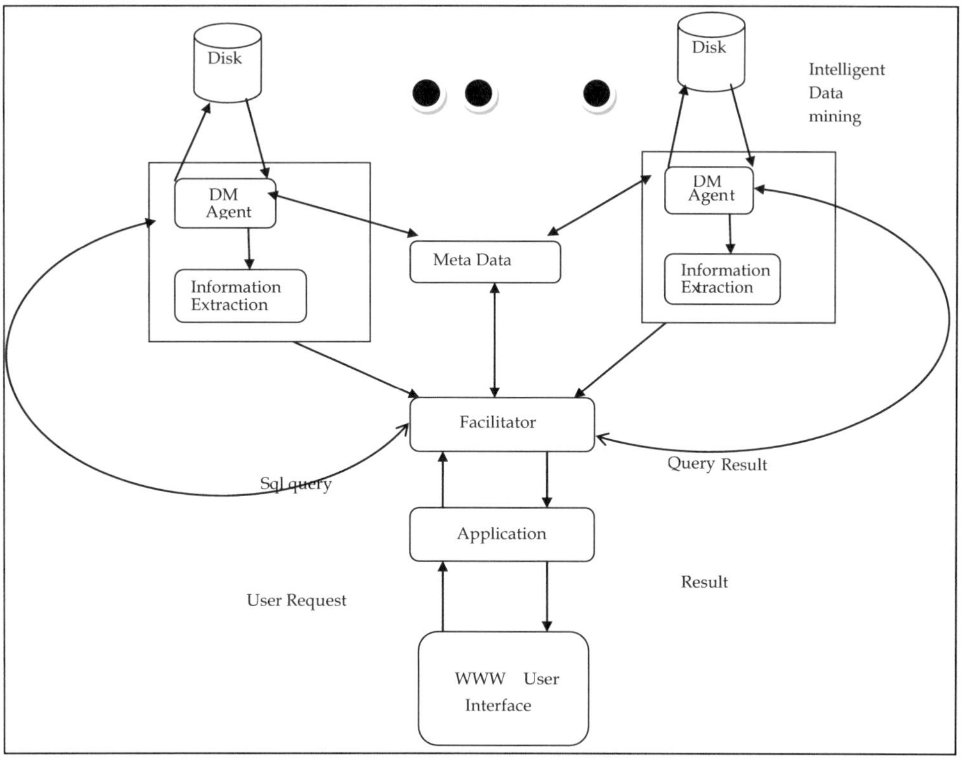

Fig. 5. PADMA architecture

PADMA agents for dealing with numeric data are currently under development. The main structural components of PADMA are 1. Data mining agents 2. Facilitator for coordinating the agents and 3. User interface. Agents work in parallel and share their information through facilitator.

8. Mathematical modeling

Distributed Data Mining (DDM) aims at extraction of useful pattern from distributed heterogeneous databases in order, for example, to compose them within a distributed knowledge base and use for the purposes of decision making. From practical point of view, DDM is of great concern and ultimate urgency.

Rough set theory is a new mathematical approach to imperfect knowledge. The problem of imperfect knowledge has been tackled for a long time by philosophers, logicians and mathematicians. Recently it became also a crucial issue for computer scientists, particularly in the area of artificial intelligence. There are many approaches to the problem of how to understand and manipulate imperfect knowledge. Rough set theory was developed by Zdzislaw Pawlak in the early 1980's. Rough set deals with classification of discrete data table in a supervised learning environment. Although in theory rough set deals with discreet data, rough set is commonly used in conjunction with other technique to do discrimination on the dataset. The main feature of rough set data analysis is non-invasive, and the ability to handle qualitative data. This fits into most real life application nicely. Rough set have seen light in many researches but seldom found its way into real world application.

Knowledge discovery with rough set is a multi-phase process consisted of mainly:

- Discretization
- Reducts and rules generation on training set

The advantage of using mathematical models is beyond increasing performance of the system. It helps knowledge workers in deeper analysis of the business and underlying product/domain. This will increase awareness in the company, knowledge transfer within the company, and higher desire to learn better things. There are many techniques like regression and classification, which are some of the popular mathematical models; however predictive analytics are not limited to these methods.

Regression: Linear Regression, kNN, CART, Neural Net

Classification: Logistic Regression, Bayesian Methods, Discriminant Analysis, Neural Net, kNN, CART.

9. Applications in parallel and distributed data mining

The technology of parallel and distributed data mining can be applied on different real time applications. The major applications are

- Credit card fraudulent detection
- Intrusion detection
- Business analysis - prediction etc.
- Financial applications
- Astrological events
- Anomaly Detection

10. Softwares for result analysis

The RapidMiner (formerly YALE) Distributed Data Mining Plugin allows performing distributed data mining experiments in a simple and flexible way. The experiments are not actually executed on distributed network nodes. The plugins only simulate this. Simulation makes it easy to experiment with diverse network structures and communication patterns. Optimal methods and parameters can be identified efficiently before putting the system into use. The network structure can for example be optimized as part of the general parameter optimization. While this cannot replace testing the system in an actual network, it makes the development stage much more efficient.

The service oriented architecture (SOA) paradigm can be exploited for the implementation of data and knowledge-based applications in distributed environments. The Web Services Resource Framework (WSRF) has recently emerged as the standard for the implementation of Grid services and applications. WSRF can be exploited for developing high-level services for distributed data mining applications. Weka4WS adopts the WSRF technology for running remote data mining algorithms and managing distributed computations. The Weka4WS user interface supports the execution of both local and remote data mining tasks. Other options like Inhambu, Weka Parallel and Grid Weka could also be used.

11. Future research directions

Parallel and Distributed data mining with Neural networks and Fuzzy approach
New Algorithms for performing Association,Clustering and Classification.
Privacy preserving parallel and distributed data mining.
Incremental Mining Algorithms.
Mining heterogeneous dataset in a parallel and distributed environment.
Knowledge Integration in a parallel and distributed environment.
Ant Colony Optimization with parallel and distributed data mining.
Mathematical modeling for a parallel and distributed mining process.

12. References

[Agr, 96] R. Agrawal, J. Shafer: "Parallel mining of association rules". IEEE Transactions on Knowledge and Data Engineering, 8(6) 962-969, 1996.

[AIS, 93] R. Agrawal, T. Imielinski, and A. Swami, "Mining Associations between Sets of Items in Massive Databases," Proceedings of the ACM SIGMOD, Washington, DC, pp. 207-216, May 1993.

[AR, 04] Andrei L. Turinsky, Robert L. Grossman y "A Framework for Finding Distributed Data Mining Strategies That are Intermediate Between Centralized Strategies and In-Place Strategies", 2004.

[ARD, 03] Assaf Schuster, Ran Wolff, and Dan Trock, "A High-Performance Distributed Algorithm for Mining Association Rules". In Third IEEE International Conference on Data Mining, Florida , USA, November 2003.

[AS, 96] R. Agrawal and J. C. Shafer, "Parallel Mining of Association Rules". IEEE Transactions On Knowledge And Data Engineering, 8:962-969, 1996.

[ATO, 99] Albert Y. Zomaya, Tarek El-Ghazawi, Ophir Frieder, "Parallel and Distributed Computing for Data Mining", IEEE Concurrency, 1999.

[ATS, 02] M. Z. Ashra_, D. Taniar, and K. A. Smith, "A Data Mining Architecture for Distributed Environments". IICS 2002, pages 27-38, 2002.

[Ays, 99] Ayse Yasemin SEYDIM "Intelligent Agents: A Data Mining Perspective" Southern Methodist University, Dallas, 1999.

[BH, 02] Byung Hoon Park and Hilloi Karagupta, "Distributed Data Mining: Algorithms, Systems and Applications", University of MaryLand, 2002.

[CF, 04] Cristian Aflori, Florin Leon, "Efficient Distributed Data Mining using Intelligent Agents", in Proceedings of the 8th International Symposium on Automatic Control and Computer Science, 2004.

[FA, 01] Felicity George, Arno Knobbe, "A Parallel Data Mining Architecture for Massive Data Sets", High Performance Research Center, 2001.

[KKC, 99] Kargupta, H., Kamath, C., and Chan, P., "Distributed and Parallel Data Mining: Emergence, Growth and Future Directions, Advances in Distributed Data Mining, (eds) Hillol Kargupta and Philip Chan, AAAI Press, pp. 407-416, 1999.

[SS, 08] Dr. Sujni Paul, Dr.V.Saravanan, "Knowledge integration in a Parallel and distributed environment with association rule mining using XML data", IJCSNS International Journal of Computer Science and Network Security, VOL.8 No.5, May 2008.

4

Modeling Information Quality Risk for Data Mining and Case Studies

Ying Su
Information Quality Lab Resource Sharing Promotion Centre, Institute of Scientific and Technical Information of China, Beijing, China

1. Introduction

Today, information is a vital business asset. For institutional and individual processes that depend on information, the quality of information (IQ) is one of the key determinants of the quality of their decisions and actions (Hand, et al., 2001; W. Kim et al., 2003; Mucksch, et al., 1996). Data mining (DM) technology can discover hidden relationships, patterns and interdependencies and generate rules to predict the correlations in data warehouses (Y. Su, et al., 2009c).

However, only a few companies have implemented these technologies because of their inability to clearly measure the quality of data and consequently the quality risk of information derived from the data warehouse(Fisher, et al., 2003). Without this ability it becomes difficult for companies to estimate the cost of poor information to the organization (D. Ballou, Madnick, & Wang, 2003). For the above reasons, the risk management of the IQ for DM is been identified as a critical issue for companies. Therefore, we develop a methodology to model the quality risk of information based on the quality of the source databases and associated DM processes.

The rest of this chapter is organized as follows. After a review of the relevant in Section 2, we introduce a forma1 model proposed for data warehousing and DM that attempts to support quality risks of different levels in Section 3. In section 4, we discuss the different quality risks that need to be considered for the output of Restriction operator, Projection and Cubic product operators. Section 5 describes an information quality assurance exercise undertaken for a finance company as part of a larger project in auto finance marketing. A methodology to estimate the effects of data accuracy, completeness and consistency on the data aggregate functions Count, Sum and Average is presented(Y. Su, et al., 2009a). The methodology should be of specific interest to quality assurance practitioners for projects that harvest warehouse data for decision support to the management. The assessment comprised ten checks in three broad categories, to ensure the quality of information collected over 1103 attributes. The assessment discovered four critical gaps in the data that had to be corrected before the data could be transitioned to the analysis phase. Section 6 applies above methodology to evaluate two information quality characteristics - accuracy and completeness - for the HIS database. Four quantitative measures are introduced to assess the risk of medical information quality. The methodology is illustrated through a medical domain: infection control. The results show the methodology was effective to detection and aversion of risk factors(Y. Su, et al., 2009b).

2. Literature review

2.1 IQ dimensions

Huang et al. (1999, p. 33) state that information quality has been conventionally described as how accurate information is. In the last couple of years, however, it has become clear that information quality encompasses multiple dimensions beyond accuracy. These dimensions can be gathered in various ways (Huang, et al., 1999). Huang et al. (1999) distinguish between three different approaches: the intuitive, systematic, and empirical one. The intuitive approach is one where IQ-criteria are based on the intuitive understanding or experience of one or several individuals. The main disadvantage of this approach is that it does not yield representative results. The systematic approach, according to Huang et al., focuses on how information may become deficient during the information production process. Few research strategies have followed this deductive-analytic or ontological approach (where real-life states are compared to the represented data states). One reason may be the fact that it is difficult to convey the results to information consumers. The third approach is an empirical one. Here, the criteria are gathered by asking large sets of information consumers about their understanding of information quality in specific contexts (as we have done with the online focus groups described earlier). The disadvantage of this approach, according to Huang et al. (1999, p. 34) is that the correctness or completeness of the results cannot be proven based on fundamental principles (as in the deductive systematic approach). There is also a risk, in Eppler's view, that the empirical results will not always be consistent or free of redundancies. It is also unclear, whether information consumers are always capable of articulating the information quality attributes which are important to them. Besides distinguishing the ways in which the criteria can be gathered, one can also distinguish the types of criteria that exist (Eppler, 2006).
The coexistence of these different criteria to IQ in business processes may result in conflicting views of IQ among information providers and consumers. These differences can cause serous breakdowns in communications both among information suppliers and between information suppliers and consumers. But even with improved communication among them, each of the principal approaches to IQ shares a common problem: each offers only a partial and sometimes vague view of the basic elements of IQ.
In order to fully exploit favourable conditions of these criteria and avoid unfavourable ones, we present a definition approach of IQ that is based on characteristics of enterprise activities precedence relationship between them (Table 1.). Enterprise activities are processing steps within a process transforming objects and requiring resources for their execution. An activity can be classified as a structured activity if it is computable and controllable. Otherwise, it is categorized as a non-structured activity. Accounting, planning, inventory control, and scheduling activities are examples of structured activities. Typical examples of non-structured activities are human-based activities such as design, reasoning, or thinking activities.Table 1. gives the reference dimensions of upstream activity regarding the context in the business processes (Su & Jin, 2006).
Su and Jin summarized academic research on the multiple dimensions of IQ, and assigned the four cases based on types of relationship of enterprise activities, as the second and third columns of Table 1. The fifth column of Table 1. summarizes academic research on the multiple dimensions of IQ. The first row is Ballou and Pazer's (1985) study, which takes an empirical, market research approach of collecting data from information consumers to determine the dimensions of importance to them. Table 1. lists the dimensions uncovered in Zmud's (1978) pioneering IQ research study, which considers the dimensions of information

important to users of hard-copy reports. Because of the focus on reports, information accessibility dimensions, which are critical with on-line information, were not relevant.

Activity Taxonomy	Upstream Activity	Downstream Activity	Definition Approach	Reference Dimensions of IQ for Upstream Activity
CASE Ⅰ	Non-Structured	Non-Structured	User-based	Consistent representation, Interpretability, Case of understanding, Concise representation, Timeliness, Completeness (Ballou & Pazer, 1985), Value-added, relevance, appropriate, Meaningfulness, Lack of confusion (Goodhue, 1995). Arrangement, Readable, Reasonable (Zmud, 1978).
CASE Ⅱ	Non-Structured	Structured	Intuitive	Precision, Reliability, freedom from bias (DeLone & McLean, 2003).
CASE Ⅲ	Structured	Non-Structured	User-based	See also CASE Ⅰ
CASE Ⅳ	Structured	Structured	System	Data Deficiency, Design Deficiencies, Operation Deficiencies (Huang et al., 1999).
Inherent IQ	Accuracy, Cost, Objectivity, Believability, Reputation, Accessibility, Correctness (Wang & Strong, 1996), Unambiguous (Wand & Wang, 1996). Consistency (English, 1999).			

Table 1. Activity-based defining to the IQ dimensions

In our analysis, we consider risks associated with two well-documented information quality attributes: accuracy and completeness. Accuracy is defined as conformity with the real world. Completeness is defined as availability of all relevant data to satisfy the user requirement. Although many other information quality attributes have been introduced and discussed in the existing literature, these two are the most widely cited. Furthermore, accuracy and completeness can be measured in an objective manner, something that is usually not possible for other quality attributes.

2.2 Overview of BDM and data warehousing

Business data mining (BDM), also known as "knowledge discovery in databases"(Bose & Mahapatra, 2001), is the process of discovering interesting patterns in databases that are useful in decision making. Business data mining is a discipline of growing interest and importance, and an application area that can provide significant competitive advantage to an organization by exploiting the potential of large data warehouses.

In the past decade, BDM has changed the discipline of information science, which investigates the properties of information and the methods and techniques used in the acquisition, analysis, organization, dissemination and use of information (Chen & Liu, 2004).

BDM can be used to carry out many types of task. Based on the types of knowledge to be discovered, it can be broadly divided into supervised discovery and unsupervised discovery. The former requires the data to be pre-classified. Each item is associated with a unique label, signifying the class in which the item belongs. In contrast, the latter does not require pre-classification of the data and can form groups that share common characteristics. To carry out these two main task types, four business data mining approaches are commonly used: clustering(Shao & Krishnamurty, 2008), classification(Mohamadi, et al., 2008), association rules(Mitra & Chaudhuri, 2006) and visualization (Compieta et. al., 2007).
As mentioned above, BDM can be used to carry out various types of tasks, using approaches such as classification, clustering, association rules, and visualization. These tasks have been implemented in many application domains. The main application domains that BDM can support in the field of information science include personalized environments, electronic commerce, and search engines. Table 2. summarizes the main contributions of BDM in each application.
A data warehouse can be defined as a repository of historical data used to support decision making (Sen & Sinha, 2007). BDM refers to the technology that allows the user to efficiently retrieve information from the data warehouse (Sen, et al., 2006).
The multidimensional data model or data cube is a popular model used to conceptualize the data in a data warehouse (Jin, et al., 2005). We emphasize that the data cube that we are referring to here is a data model, and is not to be confused with the well-known CUBE operator, which performs extended grouping and aggregation.

Application	Approaches	Contributions
Personalized Environments	Usage mining	To adapt content presentation and navigation support based on each individual's characteristics.
	Usage mining with collaborative filtering	To understand users' access patterns by mining the data collected from log files.
	Usage mining with content mining	To tailor to the users' perceived preferences by matching usage and content profiles.
Electronic Commerce	Customer management	To divide the customers into several segments based on their similar purchasing behavior.
	Retail business	To explore the association structure between the sales of different products.
	Time series analysis	To discover patterns and predict future values by analyzing time series data.
Search Engine	Ranking of pages	To identify the ranking of the pages by analyzing the interconnections of a series of related pages.
	Improvement of precision	To improve the precision by examining textual content and user's logs.
	Citation analyses	To recognize the intellectual structure of works by analyzing how authors are cited together.

Table 2. Business data mining contributions

2.3 Research contributions

The main contribution of this research is the development of a rigorous methodology to confirm the information quality risks of data warehouses. Although little formal analysis of this nature has been addressed in previous research, two approaches proposed earlier have influenced our work. Michalski, G. (2008) provides a methodology to determine the level of accounts receivable using the portfolio management theory in a firm. He presents the consequences that can result from operating risk that is related to purchasers using payment postponement for goods and/or services, however, he don't provide a methodology for deriving quality risks for the BDM (Michalski, 2008). Cowell, R. G., Verrall, R. J., & Yoon, Y. K. (2007) construct a Bayesian network that models various risk factors and their combination into an overall loss distribution. Using this model, they show how established Bayesian network methodology can be applied to: (1) form posterior marginal distributions of variables based on evidence, (2) simulate scenarios, (3) update the parameters of the model using data, and (4) quantify in real-time how well the model predictions compare to actual data (Cowell, et al., 2007).

3. The cube model and risks

3.1 Basic definitions

A data cube is the fundamental underlying construct of the multidimensional database and serves as the basic unit of input and output for all operators defined on a multidimensional database. It is defined as a 6-tuple, $\langle C,A,f,d,O,L\rangle$ where the six components indicate the characteristics of the cube. These characteristics are:

- C is a set of m characteristics $C=\{c_1,c_2,\cdots c_m\}$ where each c_i is a characteristic having domain (dom) C.;
- A is a set of t attributes $A=\{a_1,a_2,\cdots a_t\}$ where each a_i is an attribute name having domain Dom A. We assume that there exists an arbitrary total order on A, $\leq A$. Thus, the attributes in A (and any subset of A) can be listed according to $\leq A$. Moreover we say that each $a_i \in A$ is recognizable to the cube C;
- f is a one-to-one mapping, $f: C \rightarrow 2^A$, which maps a set of attributes to each characteristic. a set of attributes to each characteristic. The mapping is such that attribute sets corresponding to characteristics are pairwise disjoint, i.e., $\forall i,j,i \neq j, f(c_i) \cap f(c_j)=\varnothing$. Also, all attributes are mapped to characteristics (i.e., $\forall x, x \in A, \exists c, c \in C, x \in f(c)$). Hence, f partitions the set of attributes among the characteristics. We refer to f(c) as the schema of c;
- d is a Boolean-valued function that partitions C into a set of dimensions D and a set of dimensions D and a set of measures M. Thus, $C=D \cup M$ where $D \cap M=\varnothing$. The function d is *defined is follows:*; $\forall x \in C, d(x)=\begin{cases}1 & if \ \ x \in D \\ 0 & otherwise\end{cases}$
- O is a set of partial orders such that each $o_i \in O$ is a partial order defined on $f(c_i)$ and $|O|=|C|$.
- L is a set of cube cells. A cube cell is represented as an $\langle address, content\rangle$ pair. The address in this pair is an n-tuple, $\langle \alpha_1,\alpha_2,\cdots \alpha_n\rangle$, where n is the number of dimensional attributes in the cube, i.e., $n=|A_d|$. The content of a cube cell is defined similarly. It is a k-tuple, $\langle \chi_1,\chi_2,\cdots \chi_n\rangle$, where k is the number of metric attributes in the cube; i.e.,

$k=|A_m|$, where A_m, represents the set of all metric attributes; For notational convenience, we denote the structural address component of L as *L.AC* and the structural content component as *L.CC*. We denote the ith address value component of cube cell *1* as *1.AC[i]* and the *i*th content value component as *l.CC[i]*.

We now provide an example to clarify this definition. Subsequently, this will be used as a running example for the rest of the chapter. Consider a cube Sales which represents a multidimensional database of sales figures of certain products. The Sales cube has the following features (note the correspondence of the example to the definition above).

- The data are described by the characteristics time, product, location, and sales. Hence, the cube has a characteristics set C = $\{$product,time, address,sales$\}$ (m=4).
- The time characteristic is described by the attributes day, week, month, and year; the product characteristic is described by the product_id, weight and name attributes; the location characteristic is described by the store_name, store_address, state, and region attributes. The sales characteristic is described by the store_sales and store_cost attributes. Thus, for the Sales cube, A={ day, week, month, year, product_id, weight, name, store_name, store_address, state, region, store_sales, store_cost} (t = 13).
- Each of the characteristics, as explained in the previous item, are described by specific attributes. In other words, for the Sales cube, the mapping f is as follows:

$$f(\text{time}) = \{\text{ day, week, month, year}\}$$
$$\text{f(product)} = \{\text{ product\_id, weight, name}\}$$
$$f(\text{location}) = \{\text{ store\_name, store\_address, state, region}\}$$
$$f(\text{sales}) = \{\text{ store\_sales, store\_cost}\}$$

Also note that the attribute sets shown above re mutually disjoint.

· An example of a partial order in *O* on the Sales given by the following:

$$O_{\text{time}} = \{ \langle \text{day, week} \rangle, \langle \text{day, month} \rangle, \langle \text{day, year} \rangle, \langle \text{month, year} \rangle \}$$
$$O_{\text{product}} = \{ \langle \text{product\_id, name} \rangle, \langle \text{product\_id, weight} \rangle \}$$
$$O_{\text{location}} = \{\text{ store\_name, store\_address, state, region}\}$$
$$O_{\text{sales}} = \{ \ \}$$

· To present a simple example of L, we assume the following attributes and corresponding domains for the Sales cube data:

$$\text{A} = \{\text{ year, product\_id, store\_address, store\_sales, store\_cost}\}$$
$$\text{Dom year} = \{2001,2002,2003,2004\}$$
$$\text{Dom product\_id} = \{\text{P1, P2, P3, P4}\}$$
$$\text{Dom store\_address} = \{\text{"Valley View","Valley Ave",Coit Rd.", "Indigo Ct"}\}$$
$$\text{Dom store\_sales} \in R$$
$$\text{Dom store\_cost} \in R$$

· Then an element $l \in L$ may be expressed as follows:

$$l = \langle l.AC, l.CC \rangle \text{ where:}$$

$$l.AC = \langle 2001, P1, \text{"4 Valley View"} \rangle \text{, corresponding to the structural components:}$$

$$l.AC = \langle \text{year, product\_id, store\_address} \rangle$$

$$l.CC = \langle 30,120 \rangle \text{, corresponding to the structural components:}$$

$$l.CC = \langle \text{store\_sales, store\_cost} \rangle$$

A possible cube using the data from above is shown below pictorially in Fig 1. Henceforth, we will work with cubes in the development of theory in this chapter.

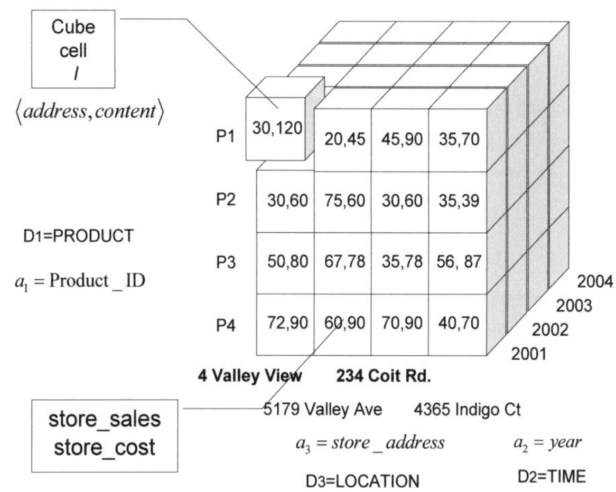

Fig. 1. Data Cube Example with Notation

Consider a cube C that contains tuples captured for a predefined real world entity type. Each tuple in C is either accurate, inaccurate, nonmember, or an incomplete. These terms are formally defined below:

- A tuple is accurate if all of its attribute values are accurate.
- A tuple is inaccurate if it has one or more inaccurate (or null) values for its nonidentifier attributes, and no inaccurate values for its identifier attribute(s).
- A tuple is a nonmember if it should not have been captured into C but it is. A nonmembership tuple might have inaccurate values either in its identifier attributes or nonidentifier ones which is mistakenly included in the cube.
- A tuple belongs to the incomplete set if it should have been captured into C but it is not.

We denote the set of accurate, inaccurate, nonmember and incomplete tuples by C_A, C_I, C_N, and C_C respectively. Then, we use the notion of a conceptual cube T in order to understand the relationship between tuples in C and the underlying entity instances in the real world. Cube T consists of tuples as they should have been captured in C if there were no errors in an ideal world. Tuples in T belong to three categories as follows:

- T_A, the set of instances in T that are correctly captured into C and thus remain accurate;
- T_I, the set of instances in T that are captured into C, and one or more of their nonidentifying attribute values are inaccurate or null;

- T_C, the set of instances in T that have not been captured into C and therefore form the incomplete dataset for C.

3.2 Cube-level risks

Based on the above definitions, we define the following quality risks for a cube C. $|L|$, $|L_A|$, $|L_I|$ $|L_N|$, and $|L_C|$ denote the cardinalities of the sets L, L_A, L_I, L_N, and L_C, respectively.

- Accuracy of C, measured as $\Pr_A(C) = |L_A|/|L|$, is the probability that a tuple in L accurately represents an entity in the real world.
- Inaccuracy of C, measured as $\Pr_I(C) = |L_I|/|L|$, is the probability that a tuple in L is inaccurate.
- Nonmembership of C, measured as $\Pr_N(C) = |L_N|/|L|$, is the probability that a tuple in C is a nonmember.
- Incompleteness of C, measured as $\Pr_C(C) = |L_C|/(|L| - |L_N| + |L_C|)$, is the probability that an information resource in the real world is not captured in C.

The data cube is a data model for representing business information using multidimensional database (MDDB) technology. The following example about a cube Sale illustrates these risks. Table 3. hows the data stored in the feature class C, and Table 4. shows the incomplete information for C. The attribute set $\{Time\_ID, Customer\_ID, Store\_Address\}$

Product_ID	Time_ID	Customer_ID	Store_Address	Store_Cost	Store_Sales	Tuple Status
1	2001	334-1626-003	5203 Catanzaro Way	10,031	100	A
2	2003	334-1626-001	1501 Ramsey Circle	7,342	200	A
3	2002	334-1626-004	433 St George Dr	**9,254**	300	I
4	2004	334-1626-005	1250 Coggins Drive	8,856	250	A
5	2000	334-1626-006	**4 Valley View**	8,277	120	I
6	1999	334-1626-007	5179 Valley Ave	9,975	360	A
7	**2002**	**334-1626-012**	**234 Coit Rd.**	**8,230**	**640**	**N**
8	**2004**	334-1626-002	4365 Indigo Ct	1,450	210	I
9	2005	**334-1626-019**	5006 Highland Drive	8,645	780	I

Table 3. Feature Class Cube C

ID	**Time_ID**	**Customer_ID**	**Store_Address**	**Store_Cost**	**Store_Sales**	**Tuple Status**
10	2004	334-1626-008	321 herry Ct.	11,412	365	C

Table 4. Incomplete Cube L_C

ID	**Rows Status**	**Error Description**
3	Inaccurate	Store_Cost should be "9,031"
5	Inaccurate	Store_Address should be "6 Valley View"
7	Nonmember	Should not belong to cube C
8	Inaccurate	Store_Sales should be "790"
9	Inaccurate	Customer_ID should be "334-1626-009"

Table 5. Errors Cube in L

Cube	Size	$\Pr_A(C)$	$\Pr_I(C)$	$\Pr_N(C)$	$\Pr_C(C)$
C	9	0.44	0.44	0.11	0.11

Table 6. Quality Profile for Cube C

forms the address for C. The Tuple Status column in Table 3. indicates whether a tuple is accurate (A), inaccurate (I), or a nonmember (N). Cells in C that are set in bold type contain inaccurate values, and the row set in bold type is a nonmember. Table 5. describes errors in C, and Table 6. provides the quality measures.

3.3 Risk measures for attribute-level

To assess the quality metrics of derived cubes based on the quality profile for the input cube, we need to estimate quality metrics at the attribute level for some of the relational operations. Let K_C and Q_C be the set of identifier and nonidentifier attributes of C. Furthermore, let k_C and q_C be the number of identifier and nonidentifier attributes, respectively. We make the following assumptions regarding the quality metrics for attributes of C.

Assumption 1. Error probabilities for identifier (nonidentifier) attributes are identically distributed. Error probabilities for all attributes are independent of each other.

Assumption 2. The probability of an error occurring in a nonidentifier attribute of a nonmember tuple is the same as the probability of such an error in any other tuple.

Let $\Pr_A(K_C)$ denote accuracy for the set of attributes K_C, and $\Pr_{Aa}(K_C)$ denote accuracy of each attribute in K_S. Thus $\Pr_A(K_C) = (|L_A| + |L_I|)/|L| = \Pr_A + \Pr_I$. From Assumption 1, we have $\Pr_A(K_C) = \Pr_A(k)^{k_C}$, and, therefore

$$\Pr_{Aa}(K_C) = (\Pr_A(C) + \Pr_I(C))^{1/k_S} \tag{1}$$

Let α_{Q_S} denote accuracy for the set of attributes Q_C and $\Pr_{Aa}(Q_C)$ denote accuracy of each attribute in Q_C. From assumption 2, we have $\Pr_A(Q_C) = \frac{|L_A|}{|L_A| + |L_I|} = \frac{\Pr_A(C)}{\Pr_A(C) + \Pr_I(C)}$. Because there are q_C nonidentifier attributes, we have $\Pr_A(Q_C) = \Pr_{Aa}(Q_C)^{q_C}$ and therefore

$$\Pr_{Aa}(Q_C) = \left(\frac{\Pr_A(C)}{\Pr_A(C) + \Pr_I(C)}\right)^{1/q_C} \tag{2}$$

4. Cube-level risks for proposed operations

4.1 Selection operation

The selection operator restricts the values on one or more attributes based on specified conditions, where a given condition is in the form of a predicate. Thus, a set of predicates is evaluated on selected attributes, and cube cells are retrieved only if they satisfy a given predicate. If there are no cube cells that satisfy P, the result is an empty cube. The algebra of the selection operator is then defined as follows:

Input: A cube $C_I = \langle C, A, f, d, O, L \rangle$ and a compound predicate P.

Output: A cube $C_O = \langle C, A, f, d, O, L_O \rangle$ where $L_0 \subseteq L$ and $L_0 = \{l | (l \in L) \wedge (l \text{ satisfies P})\}$
Mathematical Notation:

$$\sigma_P C_I = C_O \tag{3}$$

We define a conceptual cube (denoted by *U*) that is obtained by applying the predicate condition to the conceptual cube *T*. U_j denotes instances in T_j that satisfy the predicate condition for j = A, I, and C. Fig 1. shows the mapping between the subsets of the conceptual and stored and cubes. We make two assumptions that are widely applicable.

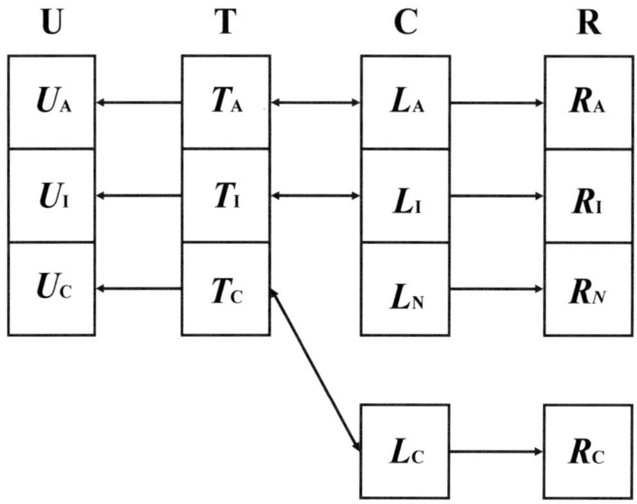

Fig. 2. Mapping Relations between the Concept and Physical

Assumption 3. Each true attribute value of an entity instance is a random (not necessarily uniformly distributed) realization from an appropriate underlying domain.
We then have

$$\frac{|U|}{|T|} = \frac{|U_A|}{|T_A|} = \frac{|U_I|}{|T_I|} = \frac{|U_C|}{|T_C|} \tag{4}$$

Assumption 4. The occurrences of errors in C are not systematic, or, if they are systematic, the cause of the errors is unknown.
This implies that the inaccurate attribute values stored in C are also random realizations of the underlying domains. It follows that

$$\frac{|U|}{|T|} = \frac{|R|}{|L|} = \frac{|R_{L_A}|}{|L_A|} = \frac{|R_{L_A}|}{|L_A|} = \frac{|R_{L_I}|}{|L_I|} = \frac{|R_{L_N}|}{|L_N|} = \frac{|R_{L_C}|}{|L_C|} \tag{5}$$

First, we consider the inequality condition. To illustrate this scenario, we use the cubes C and L_C as shown in Table 3. and Table 4. Consider a query to retrieve tuples on feature class whose Customer_ID end with letters that evaluates to greater than "005". R and R_C are shown in Table 7. and 2, respectively. R_A, R_I, and R_N refer to accurate, inaccurate, and nonmember subsets of R.

After query execution, all accurate tuples satisfying the predicate condition remain accurate in R. Similarly, all selected inaccurate and nonmember tuples continue to be inaccurate and nonmember in R, respectively. Tuples belonging to the incomplete dataset L_C that would have satisfied the predicate condition now become part of R_C, the incomplete set for R. Therefore, there is no change in the tuple status for the selected tuples. The expected value of $|R_{L_A}|$ is $|L_A|\cdot|R|/|L|$. Similarly, we have $|R_{L_I}| = |L_I|\cdot|R|/|L|$, $|R_{L_N}| = |L_N|\cdot|R|/|L|$, and $|R_{L_C}| = |L_C|\cdot|R|/|L|$. Using these identities in the definitions of $\Pr_A(R), \Pr_I(R), \Pr_N(R)$ and $\Pr_C(R)$, it is easily seen that $\Pr_A(R) = \Pr_A(C)$, $\Pr_I(R) = \Pr_I(C)$ $\Pr_N(R) = \Pr_N(C)$ and $\Pr_C(R) = \Pr_C(C)$. We show the algebra for $\Pr_C(R)$ here:

Product_ID	Customer_ID	Store_Address.	Store_Cost	Store_Sales	Tuple Status
4	334-1626-005	1250 Coggins Drive	8,856	250	A
5	334-1626-006	**4 Valley View**	8,277	120	I
6	334-1626-007	5179 Valley Ave	9,975	360	A
7	**334-1626-012**	**234 Coit Rd.**	**8,230**	**640**	**N**
8	334-1626-002	4365 Indigo Ct	1,450	210	I
9	**334-1626-019**	5006 Highland Drive	8,645	780	I

Table 7. Query Result R for Selection Operation

$$\Pr_C(R) = \frac{|R_C|}{(|R| - |R_N| + |R_C|)} = \frac{|R|\cdot|L_C|/|L|}{|R|\left[1 - (|L_N|/|L|) + (|L_C|/|L|)\right]} = \frac{|L_C|}{(|L| - |L_N| + |L_C|)} \tag{6}$$

4.2 Projection operation

The risky projection operator restricts the output of a cube to include only a subset of the original set of measures. Let S be a set of projection attributes such that $S \subseteq A_m$. Then the output of the resulting cube includes only those measures in C. The algebra of risky projection is defined as follows:

Input: A cube $C_I = \langle C, A, f, d, O, L\rangle$ and a set of projection attributes C.

Output: A cube $C_O = \langle C, A_O, f_O, d, O, L_O\rangle$ where $A_O = S \cup A_d$, $f_O: C \to 2^{A_O}$, such that $f_O(c) = f(c) \cup A_O$, and $L_O = \{l_O \mid \exists l \in L, l_O.AC = l.AC, l_O.CC = \langle l.CC[s_1], l.CC[s_2], \cdots, l.CC[s_n]\rangle\}$, where $\{s_1, s_2, \cdots, s_n\} = S$.

Mathematical Notation:

$$\Pi_S C_I = C_O \tag{7}$$

Fig. 3 illustrates the mapping between tuples in C and R. The notation $L_{I\to A}$, $L_{I\to I}$, and $L_{I\to N}$ refer to those inaccurate tuples in C that become accurate, remain inaccurate, and become nonmembers, respectively, in R. Each tuple in $L_{I\to N}$ contributes a corresponding tuple to the incomplete dataset R_C; we denote this contribution by $L_{I\to C}$. We denote by k_p and q_p the number of address and content attributes of C that are projected into R.

We estimate the sizes of the various subsets of R and of the set R_C using the attribute-level quality metrics derived in Equality (1) and (2). These sizes depend on the cardinality of the identifier for the resulting cube, and whether or not these attributes were part of the identifier of the original cube. Let k_R and q_R denote the number of identifier and nonidentifier attributes of R. We further define the following:

- $k_{p\to k}$: Number of projected identifier attributes of C that are part of the identifier for R.
- $q_{p\to k}$: Number of projected nonidentifier attributes of C that become part of the identifier for R.

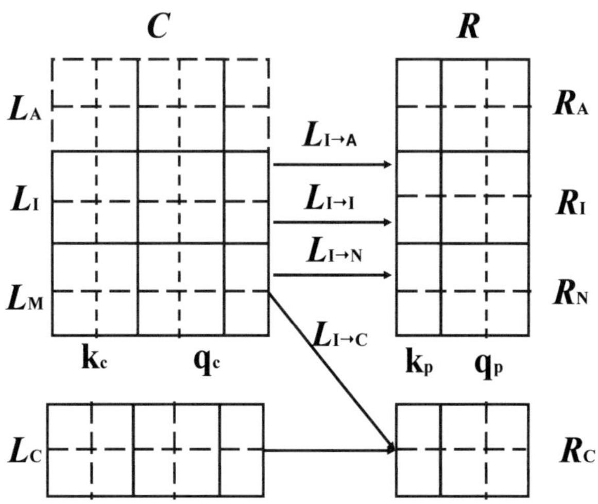

Fig. 3. Tuple Transformations for the Projection Operation

- $k_{p\to Q}$: Number of projected identifier attributes of C that become part of nonidentifiers of R.
- $q_{p\to Q}$: Number of projected nonidentifier attributes of C that are nonidentifier attributes of R.

The following equalities follow from our definitions:

$$k_p = k_{p\to k} + k_{p\to Q},\ q_p = q_{p\to k} + q_{p\to Q},$$

$$k_R = k_{p\to k} + q_{p\to K},\ and\ q_R = k_{p\to Q} + q_{p\to Q}.$$

A tuple in R is accurate only if all values of the projected attributes are accurate. From Equality (1), we know that each projected identifier attribute of C has accuracy $\Pr_{Aa}(K_C)$, whereas each projected nonidentifier attribute of C has an accuracy of $\Pr_{Aa}(Q_C)$ (2). The probability that a tuple is accurate in R is therefore given by

$$\begin{aligned}\Pr_A(R) &= \left[(\Pr_A(C)+\Pr_I(C))^{1/k_C}\right]^{k_{p\to K}} \bullet \Pr_{Aa}(Q_C)^{q_{p\to K}} \bullet \left[(\Pr_A(C)+\Pr_I(C))^{1/k_C}\right]^{k_{p\to Q}} \bullet \Pr_{Aa}(Q_C)^{q_{p\to Q}} \\ &= (\Pr_A(C)+\Pr_I(C))^{(k_{p\to K}+k_{p\to Q})/k_C} \bullet \Pr_{Aa}(Q_C)^{q_{p\to K}+q_{p\to Q}}\end{aligned} \quad (8)$$

Tuples in R are inaccurate if all the identifying attributes in R have accurate values, and at least one of the nonidentifying attributes of R is inaccurate. The size of the inaccurate set of

R can therefore be viewed as the difference between the set of tuples with accurate identifying attribute values and the set of accurate tuples. The former, which corresponds to $|R|(\Pr_A(R)+\Pr_I(R))$, is equal to $|R|(\Pr_A(C)+\Pr_I(C))^{k_{p\to K}/k_S} \bullet \Pr_{Aa}(Q_C)^{q_{p\to K}}$. It then follows that

$$\begin{aligned}\Pr_I(R)=&\left[(\Pr_A(C)+\Pr_I(C))^{k_{p\to K}/k_C}\bullet\Pr_{Aa}(Q_C)^{q_{p\to K}}\right]\\ &\bullet\left[1-(\Pr_A(C)+\Pr_I(C))^{k_{p\to Q}/k_C}\bullet\Pr_{Aa}(Q_C)^{q_{p\to Q}}\right]\end{aligned}. \quad (9)$$

Using the equality $\Pr_N(R)=1-\Pr_A(R)-\Pr_I(R)$, the nonmembership for R is obtained as $\Pr_N(R)=1-(\Pr_A(C)+\Pr_I(C))^{k_{p\to K}/k_C}\bullet\Pr_{Aa}(Q_C)^{q_{p\to K}}$.

The incomplete dataset R_C consists of the two parts: (i) tuples resulting from L_C and (ii) the inaccurate tuples in C that become nonmembers in R and contribute to R_C. Because $|L_{I\to C}|=|L_{I\to N}|$, we determine $|L_{I\to C}|$ as $|R_N|-|L_N|$.Nothing that $|R|=|L|$, it follows that

$$\begin{aligned}|R_C|&=|L_C|+|R_N|-|L_N|=|L|\bullet\frac{\Pr_C(L)\bullet(1-\Pr_N(L))}{1-\Pr_C(L)}+(\Pr_N(R)\bullet|R|)-(\Pr_N(C)\bullet|L|)\\ &=|R|[\Pr_C(L)-\Pr_N(L)+\Pr_N(R)(1-\Pr_C(L))]/(1-\Pr_C(L))\end{aligned} \quad (10)$$

Substituting $|R_C|$ in the definition of (6), after some algebraic simplification, this yields $\Pr_C(R)=[\Pr_C(C)-\Pr_N(C)+\Pr_N(R)(1-\Pr_C(C))]/(1-\Pr_N(C))$.

Because $\Pr_N(R)=1-\Pr_A(R)-\Pr_I(R)$, we have

$$\begin{aligned}\Pr_C(R)&=[\Pr_C(C)-\Pr_N(C)+(1-\Pr_A(R)-\Pr_I(R))(1-\Pr_C(C))]/(1-\Pr_N(C))\\ &=1-\frac{1-\Pr_C(C)}{1-\mu_C}(\Pr_A(R)-\Pr_I(R))\\ &=1-\frac{1-\Pr_C(S)}{1-\Pr_N(C)}\bullet\left[(\Pr_A(C)+\Pr_I(C))^{k_{p\to K}/k_C}\bullet\Pr_{Aa}(Q_C)^{q_{p\to K}}\right]\end{aligned} \quad (11)$$

4.3 Cubic product operation

The Cubic Product operator is a binary operator that can be used to relate any two cubes. Often it is useful to combine the information in two cubes to answer certain queries (which we will illustrate with an example). The algebra of the Cubic Product operator is defined as follows:

Input: A cube $C_1=\langle C_1,A_1,f_1,d_1,O_1,L_1\rangle$ and a cube $C_2=\langle C_2,A_2,f_2,d_2,O_2,L_2\rangle$

Output: A cube $C_O=\langle C_0,A_0,f_0,d_0,O_0,L_0\rangle$, where $C_0=\Lambda_{C1}(C_1)\cup\Lambda_{C2}(C_2)$;
$A_0=\Lambda_{C1}(A_1)\cup\Lambda_{C2}(A_2)$;
$L_0=\{l_0|\exists l_1,\exists l_2,l_1\in L_1,l_2\in L_2,l_0.AC=l_1.AC\bullet l_2.AC,l_0.CC=l_1.CC\bullet l_2.CC\}$ where $l_1.AC\bullet l_2.AC$ denotes the concatenation of $l_1.AC$ and $l_2.AC$. In addition:
$\forall c_i\in(C_1\cup C_2)$

$$f_O = \begin{cases} f_1 & \text{when applied to } c_i \in C_1 \bullet c_i \\ f_2 & \text{when applied to } c_j \in C_2 \bullet c_i \end{cases} \qquad \forall c_i \in (C_1 \cup C_2)$$

$$d_O = \begin{cases} d_1 & \text{when applied to } c_i \in C_1 \bullet c_i \\ d_2 & \text{when applied to } c_j \in C_2 \bullet c_i \end{cases}$$

$$\forall a_i \in (f(C_1) \cup f(C_2))$$

$$O_O = \begin{cases} O_1 & \text{when applied to } a_i \in f(C_1) \\ O_2 & \text{when applied to } a_j \in f(C_2) \end{cases}$$

Mathematical Notation:

$$C_1 \otimes C_2 = C_O \tag{12}$$

To evaluate the quality profile for the Cartesian product R of two specified cubes (say C_1 and C_2), we first need a basis to categorize tuples in R as accurate, inaccurate, and nonmember, and to identify tuples that belong to the incomplete dataset of R. To illustrate this, Let Feature and Employee Table are the two realized cubes with tuples as shown in Table 8. and Table 9.

Product_ID	**Time_ID**	**Customer_ID**	**Store_Address**	**Store_Cost**	**Store_Sales**	**Status**
P1	2001	334-1626-003	5203 Catanzaro Way	10,031	100	A
P2	2000	334-1626-006	**4 Valley View**	8,277	120	I
P3	**2002**	**334-1626-012**	**234 Coit Rd.**	**8,230**	**640**	N
P5	2004	334-1626-008	321 herry Ct.	11,412	365	C
P4	2004	334-1626-005	1250 Coggins Drive	8,856	250	A

Table 8. Actual Data Captured on Feature Table

Employee_ID	**Employee_Name**	**Position_Title**	**Tuple Status**
E1	**Sheri Nowmer**	**President**	Inaccuracy
E2	Derrick Whelply	Store Manager	Accuracy
E3	Michael Spence	VP Country Manager	Incompleteness
E4	**Kim Brunner**	**HQ Information Systems**	**Nonmember**

Table 9. Actual Data Captured on Employee Table

The Cartesian product for Features and Employees (denoted by R) is shown in Table 10.
The incomplete set is denoted by R_C and is shown in Table 11. Tuples in R_C are of two types: (a) tuples that are products of a tuple from $Feature_C$ and a tuple from $Employee_C$, and (b) tuples that are products of an accurate or inaccurate tuple from Features (Employees) and a tuple from $Employees_C$ ($Features_C$).
Formally, let C_1 and C_2 be two cubes on which the Cubic product operation is performed, and let R be the result of the operation. Furthermore, let t_1 be a tuple in C_1 (or C_{1C}), t_2 be a tuple in C_2 (or C_{2C}), and t be a tuple in R (or R_C). Table 12. summarizes how tuples should be categorized in R. Note that the concatenation of $t_1 \in C_{1N}$ and $t_2 \in C_{2C}$, and $t_1 \in C_{1C}$ and $t_2 \in C_{2N}$, are not meaningful to our analysis because they appear neither in the true world of R nor in the observed version of R.

Product_ID	Customer_ID	Store_Address	Store_Cost	Employee_ID	Employee_Name	Status
P1	334-1626-003	5203 Catanzaro Way	10,031	E1	**Sheri Nowmer**	I
P1	334-1626-003	5203 Catanzaro Way	10,031	E2	Derrick Whelply	A
P1	334-1626-003	5203 Catanzaro Way	10,031	**E4**	**Kim Brunner**	N
P2	334-1626-006	**4 Valley View**	8,277	E1	**Sheri Nowmer**	I
P2	334-1626-006	**4 Valley View**	8,277	E2	Derrick Whelply	I
P2	334-1626-006	**4 Valley View**	8,277	**E4**	**Kim Brunner**	N
P5	334-1626-008	321 herry Ct.	11,412	E1	**Sheri Nowmer**	N
P5	334-1626-008	321 herry Ct.	11,412	E2	Derrick Whelply	N
P5	334-1626-008	321 herry Ct.	11,412	**E4**	**Kim Brunner**	N

Table 10. The Cartesian Product Cube R

Product_ID	Customer_ID	Store_Address	Store_Cost	Employee_ID	Employee_Name
P1	334-1626-003	5203 Catanzaro Way	10,031	E3	Michael Spence
P2	334-1626-006	**4 Valley View**	8,277	E3	Michael Spence
P3	**334-1626-012**	**234 Coit Rd.**	**8,230**	E1	**Sheri Nowmer**
P3	**334-1626-012**	**234 Coit Rd.**	**8,230**	E2	Derrick Whelply
P3	**334-1626-012**	**234 Coit Rd.**	**8,230**	E3	Michael Spence
P4	334-1626-005	1250 Coggins Drive	8,856	E1	**Sheri Nowmer**
P4	334-1626-005	1250 Coggins Drive	8,856	E2	Derrick Whelply
P4	334-1626-005	1250 Coggins Drive	8,856	E3	Michael Spence

Table 11. Feature Class Cube C

$C_1 \times C_2$	$t_2 \in C_{2A}$	$t_2 \in C_{2I}$	$t_2 \in C_{2N}$	$t_2 \in C_{2C}$
$t_1 \in C_{1A}$	$t \in R_A$	$t \in R_I$	$t \in R_N$	$t \in R_C$
$t_1 \in C_{1I}$	$t \in R_I$	$t \in R_I$	$t \in R_N$	$t \in R_C$
$t_1 \in C_{1N}$	$t \in R_N$	$t \in R_N$	$t \in R_N$	–
$t_1 \in C_{1C}$	$t \in R_C$	$t \in R_C$	–	$t \in R_C$

Table 12. Tuple for the Cubic product Operation

The cardinality of the accurate, inaccurate, and nonmember tuples in R, and the incomplete tuples in R_C, are as shown below.
The cardinality of the accurate, inaccurate, and nonmember tuples in R, and the incomplete tuples in R_C, are as shown below.

$$|R_A| = |L_{1A}| \bullet |L_{2A}| \tag{13}$$

$$|R_I| = |L_{1A}| \cdot |L_{2I}| + |L_{1I}| \cdot |L_{2A}| + |L_{1I}| \cdot |L_{2I}| \quad (14)$$

$$|R_N| = |L_{1A}| \cdot |L_{2N}| + |L_{1I}| \cdot |L_{2N}| + |L_{1N}| \cdot |L_{2A}| + |L_{1N}| \cdot |L_{2I}| + |L_{1N}| \cdot |L_{2N}| \quad (15)$$

$$|R_C| = |L_{1A}| \cdot |L_{2C}| + |L_{1I}| \cdot |L_{2C}| + |L_{1C}| \cdot |L_{2A}| + |L_{1C}| \cdot |L_{2I}| + |L_{1C}| \cdot |L_{2C}| \quad (16)$$

Let $\Pr_A(i), \Pr_I(i), \Pr_N(i)$ and $\Pr_C(i)$ indicate the quality risks of S_i i =1, 2. $\Pr_A(R), \Pr_I(R), \Pr_N(R)$ and $\Pr_C(R)$ indicate the quality risks of the Cubic product R. Using $|R| = |R_1| \cdot |R_2|$ and the definitions in Section Cube-Level Risks, we have

$$|\Pr_A(R)| = \frac{|L_{1A}|}{|L_1|} \cdot \frac{|L_{2A}|}{|L_2|} = \Pr_A(C_1) \cdot \Pr_A(C_2) \quad (17)$$

$$\begin{aligned} |\Pr_I(R)| &= \frac{|L_{1A}| \cdot |L_{2I}| + |L_{1I}| \cdot |L_{2A}| + |L_{1I}| \cdot |L_{2I}|}{|L_1| \cdot |L_2|} \\ &= \Pr_A(C_1) \cdot \Pr_I(C_2) + \Pr_A(C_1) \cdot \Pr_I(C_1) + \Pr_I(C_1) \cdot \Pr_I(C_2) \end{aligned} \quad (18)$$

$$\begin{aligned} |\Pr_N(R)| &= \frac{|L_{1A}| \cdot |L_{2N}| + |L_{1I}| \cdot |L_{2N}| + |L_{1N}| \cdot |L_{2A}|}{|L_1| \cdot |L_2|} + \frac{|L_{1N}| \cdot |L_{2I}| + |L_{1N}| \cdot |L_{2N}|}{|L_1| \cdot |L_2|} \\ &= \Pr_N(C_1) \cdot (1 - \Pr_N(C_2)) + \Pr_N(C_2) \cdot (1 - \Pr_N(C_1)) + \Pr_N(C_1) \cdot \Pr_N(C_2) \\ &= \Pr_N(C_1) + \Pr_N(C_2) - \Pr_N(C_1) \cdot \Pr_N(C_2) \end{aligned} \quad (19)$$

From equality (17), we have

$$\frac{|R_C|}{|R|} = (1 - \Pr_N(C_1)) \cdot (1 - \Pr_N(C_2)) \cdot \frac{\Pr_C(C_1) + \Pr_C(C_2) - \Pr_C(C_1) \cdot \Pr_C(C_2)}{(1 - \Pr_C(C_1)) \cdot (1 - \Pr_C(C_2))}$$

Therefore, we have

$$\begin{aligned} \Pr_C(R) &= \frac{|R_C| / |R|}{1 - \Pr_M(R) + |R_C| / |R|} \\ &= \left[(1 - \Pr_N(C_1)) \cdot (1 - \Pr_N(C_2)) \cdot \frac{\Pr_C(C_1) + \Pr_C(C_2) - \Pr_C(C_1) \cdot \Pr_C(C_2)}{(1 - \Pr_C(C_1)) \cdot (1 - \Pr_C(C_2))} \right] \cdot \\ & \Bigg\{ 1 - (\Pr_N(C_1) + \Pr_N(C_2) - \Pr_N(C_1) \cdot \Pr_N(C_2)) \\ & + \left[(1 - \Pr_N(C_1)) \cdot (1 - \Pr_N(C_2)) \cdot \frac{\Pr_C(C_1) + \Pr_C(C_2) - \Pr_C(C_1) \cdot \Pr_C(C_2)}{(1 - \Pr_C(C_1)) \cdot (1 - \Pr_C(C_2))} \right] \Bigg\}^{-1} \\ &= \Pr_C(C_1) + \Pr_C(C_2) - \Pr_C(C_1) \cdot \Pr_C(C_2) \end{aligned} \quad (20)$$

From Equality (17), we can see that the accuracy of the output of the Cubic product operator is less than the accuracy of either of the input cubes, and that the accuracy can become very low if the participating tables are not of high quality. Nonmembership and incompleteness also increase for the output.

5. Reducing the information quality risk for a finance company

5.1 Introduction

This case was part of a project undertaken for an auto financing company (AFC) to predict the propensities of its customers to buy its profitable offerings. According to the framework proposed by Su et al (Su, et al., 2008; Su et al., 2009c), the work presented in this chapter would be classified as a 'Pragmatics' information quality risk assessment.
The quality risk was restricted to assessments of the data along the following three criteria.

- Accuracy risk: The extracted data had to be verified against the respective origins in the warehouse. The data in the warehouse were not assessed for accuracy.
- Completeness risk: It is a critical data quality attribute, in particular for data warehousing applications that draw upon multiple internal and external data sources.
- Consistency risk: The extracted data had to be consistent with the minimal information requirements for the project -as stipulated by the Project Regulation and as listed in the Information Requirements Document.

Aberrations in the data discovered in the course of the assessment were documented and submitted to the warehouse administrators. However, an evaluation of the warehouse data was beyond the immediate scope(D. J. Kim, et al., 2008).
The main contribution of this case is the development of quantitative models to confirm the information quality risks in decision support for this finance company.

5.2 Key components of risk

We will use the framework in knowledge intensive business services(Su & Jin, 2007) to briefly review the key components of company risk.

1. Internal environment is the organization's philosophy for managing risk (risk appetite and tolerance, values, etc.);
2. Objective setting identifies specific goals that may be influenced by risk events;
3. Event identification recognizes internal or external events that affect the goals;
4. Risk assessment considers the probability of an event and its impact on organizational goals;
5. Risk response determines the organization's responses to risk events such as avoiding, accepting, reducing, or sharing;
6. Control activities focus on operational aspects to ensure effective execution of the risk response
7. Information and communication informs stakeholders of relevant information;
8. Monitoring continuously evaluates the risk management processes;

For compliance-driven risk programs, information requirements play a central role in dictating the risk architecture. We provide a set of guidelines to this financial institution to perform risk-based capital calculations. To comply with these guidelines, AFC must show they have the data (and up to seven years of history) required to calculate risk metrics such as probability of accuracy, loss completeness and consistency, etc.

5.3 The quality risks

Upon examination of the Information requirements, and the associated extraction process, the focal points for the extraction process were identified as the following.

- Mappings: The data extraction required linking data from the business definitions, as identified by the Project Regulation, to their encoding for the warehouse. Quality risk required an examination of these mappings.
- Parallel extraction: The extraction process for certain data was identical across the twelve product categories. Information quality could be assessed through examination of such data for a single product category for a single month.
- Peculiar extraction: Certain data were peculiar to specific product categories. These data had to be examined individually for assurance of quality.

Risk assessment comprised comparison of the extracted data with the parent data in the warehouse, and risks on the code used in the extraction.

The risks on the 'mappings' were performed on the items in Table 13.

QR1	Product identifiers	It was checked that the roll-ups from the granular product levels to the product categories were accurate.
QR2	Transaction identifiers	It was checked that the transactions used to measure the relationships among the finance company and its customers were restricted to customer-initiated transactions.
QR3	Time identifiers	It was checked that the usage of the time identifiers to collate data from the fact tables was consistent with the encoding.
QR4	Monthly balances per product category	It was checked that the monthly balance for a certain customer in a certain product category was the sum of the balances for all the customer's accounts in that product category for the same month.
QR5	Valid accounts per product category	It was checked that the number of accounts held by a given customer in a given product category for a given month was calculated correctly.

Table 13. Mappings' assessed for quality

QR6	Loan limits.
QR7	Days to maturity.
QR8	Overdraft limits.
QR9	Promotional pricing information.
QR10	Life/Disability insurance indicators.

Table 14. Peculiarly extracted' data assessed for quality

Once it was verified that the mappings, as identified by Table 13, and had been accurately interpreted, the quality risks on the 'common extraction' items corresponded to verifying their extraction for a single month in any given product category. The quality risks for the 'parallel extraction' items were performed on the following.

The quality risks for the 'peculiar extraction' items were shown in Table 14. The quality risks comprised the verification of the respective data as the cumulative over all the accounts held by the customer in the particular product category.

5.4 Quality risk assessment

The data mining analysis did not directly use all the variables listed in the information requirements. However, it is easily seen that the existence of inaccurate, null, inconsistency, and incomplete attribute values have a direct impact on the aggregate values. For instance, consider the following query on the Loans table shown in Table 15.

Cust_ID	Prod_ID	Loans Date	Quantity	Loan Amount	Status
C1	P1	10-Mar-06	1000	100,031	A
C1	P1	22-apr-05	2000	76,342	A
C2	P2	06-may-06	**3000**	95,254	I
C3	P1	12-jun-07			C
C3	P2	10-sep-08	**1200**	**83,277**	I
C4	P1	14-aug-08	3600	90,975	A
C5	**P2**	15-apr-07	6400	82,230	M
C6	**P1**	18-jul-07	**2100**	**19,450**	I
C6	P3	23-nov-08	7800	**38,645**	I

Table 15. Customer Loans Table

SELECT SUM (Loans Amt) FROM Loans WHERE Prod ID = 'P1'

The query returns 286798 for the aggregate sum value. This, however, is not the true value because a) the inaccurate value 19,450 deviates from the actual value of 19,206; b) the inconsistency value 6400 contributes to this aggregate while it should not; c) the existential null value does not contribute to the sum while its true value of 3500 should; d) the values of 5200 and 7800 in the incomplete data set do not contribute to the sum while they should. Accounting for all the errors, the true aggregate sum value for this query is 65,500 which deviates about 23% from the query result.

It is, therefore, essential that the number of inaccurate, existential null, inconsistency, and incomplete values for each attribute be obtained in order to adjust the query result for the errors caused by these values. Auditing every single value in a database or data warehouse table that typically contains very large numbers of rows and attributes is expensive and impractical. Instead, sampling strategies can be used to estimate these errors as described next.

5.4.1 Strategies for reducing risk

In order to estimate the number of inconsistency, we draw a random sample without replacement from the set of identifier attributes of L and verify the number of accurate and inaccurate values; denoted by $n_{k:A}$ and $n_{k:I}$, respectively; in the sample as shown in Fig. 3.

Let $|L|$ denote the cardinality of L; let n_k be the sample size; and let $l_{k:A}$ be the total number of accurate identifiers in L that must be estimated. The maximum likelihood estimator (MLE) of $l_{k:C}$, denoted by $\hat{l}_{k:C}$, is an integer that maximizes the probability distribution of the accurate identifiers in *L*. This probability follows a hypergeometric distribution given by:

n_k	$K(k_1,\ldots,k_m)$	
$n_{k:C}$	$\forall v_{ki} \leftarrow C; i \in \{1,\ldots,m\}$	
$n_{k:I}$	$\exists\ \forall v_{ki} \leftarrow I; i \in \{1,\ldots,m\}$	Inconsistency

Fig. 3. Identifier sampling

$$p(n_{k:A}=x)=\frac{\binom{L_{k:A}}{x}\binom{|L|-l_{k:A}}{n_k-x}}{\binom{|L|}{n_k}} \tag{21}$$

Using the closed form expression we have:

$$\hat{l}_{k:A}=\left\lceil \frac{n_{k:A}(|L|+1)}{n_k} \right\rceil \tag{22}$$

where $\lceil \cdot \rceil$ is the ceiling for any given number. The MLE for the inaccurate identifiers in L (i.e., inconsistencys), denoted by $\hat{l}_{k:M}$ is then given by:

$$\hat{l}_{k:M}=|L|-\hat{l}_{k:A}=|L|-\left\lceil \frac{n_{k:A}(|L|+1)}{n_k} \right\rceil \tag{23}$$

In non-identifier attribute sampling, as shown in Fig. 4.

$K(k_1,\ldots,k_m)$	$q_i\ i \in \{1,\ldots,n\}$	n_q
$\forall v_{ki} \leftarrow A; i \in \{1,\ldots,m\}$	$v_{qi} \leftarrow A$	$n_{q:A}$
	$v_{qi} \leftarrow I$	$n_{q:I}$
	$v_{qi} \leftarrow N$	$n_{q:N}$
$\forall v_{ki} \leftarrow I; i \in \{1,\ldots,m\}$	$v_{qi} \leftarrow A$	
	$v_{qi} \leftarrow I$	Incompleteness
	$v_{qi} \leftarrow N$	

Fig. 4. Non-identifier sampling.

The corresponding identifier values are also retrieved since the non-identifier attribute values find their meaning only in conjunction with their corresponding identifiers.

Let $l_{q:A}$, $l_{q:I}$, and $l_{q:N}$ be the total numbers of accurate, inaccurate, and existential null values in q_i with an accurate identifier that need to be estimated. Their MLEs, denoted by $\hat{l}_{q:A}$, $\hat{l}_{q:I}$, and $\hat{l}_{q:N}$, are integers that maximize the probability distribution of these attribute value types in q_i. This probability function follows a multivariate hyper geometric distribution given by

$$p(n_{q:A}=x, n_{q:I}=y, n_{q:N}=z)=\frac{\binom{L_{q:A}}{x}\binom{L_{q:I}}{y}\binom{L_{q:N}}{z}}{\binom{\hat{l}_{k:A}}{n_q}} \tag{24}$$

A good approximation of MLEs can be obtained by assuming that $l_{q:A}$, $l_{q:I}$, and $l_{q:N}$ are integral multiples of n_q. Their estimates are then given by

$$\hat{l}_{q:A}=\left\lceil\frac{n_{q:A}(\hat{l}_{k:A}+1)}{n_q}\right\rceil; \hat{l}_{q:I}=\left\lceil\frac{n_{q:I}(\hat{l}_{k:A}+1)}{n_q}\right\rceil; \hat{l}_{q:N}=\left\lceil\frac{n_{q:N}(\hat{l}_{k:A}+1)}{n_q}\right\rceil \tag{25}$$

We propose using the Simple-Recapture sampling method to obtain an assessment for the size of the incomplete data set L_C. For this purpose, we assume that $|L|$ tuples have been sampled from T and $\hat{l}_{k:A}$ is obtained and this sampling has been done twice. The MLE estimates for $|L|$ and $|L_C|$ are then given by:

$$|\hat{T}|=\frac{|L|^2}{\hat{l}_{k:A}}; \; |L_C|=|\hat{T}|-|L|-\hat{l}_{k:M}=\frac{|L|^2}{\hat{l}_{k:A}}-\hat{l}_{k:A} \tag{26}$$

5.4.2 COUNT

COUNT is used to retrieve the cardinality of L or it functions on one of the identifier attributes, the true COUNT, denoted by $COUNT^T$, is the number of tuples with accurate identifiers plus the cardinality of the incomplete set:

$$COUNT^T(k_i)=\hat{l}_{k:A}+|\hat{L}_C| \tag{27}$$

When COUNT operates on one of the non-identifier attributes, the true count is the sum of accurate, inaccurate, and incomplete values:

$$COUNT^T(q_i)=\hat{l}_{q:A}+\hat{l}_{q:I}+\hat{l}_{q:N}+|\hat{L}_C| \tag{28}$$

5.4.3 SUM

The distributions of attribute value types within their underlying domains affect the assessment of the true SUM value. Therefore, we assume that the attribute value types could have a uniform distribution depending on the error generating processes. We use $\bar{\lambda}_{k:A}$ for each value in the incomplete data set and the estimated true sum will be given by

$$SUM^T(k_i)=\bar{\lambda}_{k:A}(\hat{l}_{k:A}+|\hat{L}_C|) \tag{29}$$

When SUM operates on a non-identifier attribute, the estimate for the true SUM value can be obtained by substituting the inaccurate, existential nulls and incomplete values with $\bar{\lambda}_{q:A}$ which is given by

$$SUM^T(q_i)=\bar{\lambda}_{k:A}(\hat{l}_{q:A}+\hat{l}_{q:I}+\hat{l}_{q:N}+|\hat{L}_C|) \tag{30}$$

5.4.4 AVERAGE

The estimated true value returned by the AVERAGE function on an identifier (non-identifier) attribute is given by the ratio of the estimated true SUM and true COUNT:

$$\text{AVERAGE}^{\text{T}}(\text{k}_{\text{i}}) = \frac{SUM^T(k_i)}{COUNT^T(k_i)} = \bar{\lambda}_{k:A} \tag{31}$$

$$\text{AVERAGE}^{\text{T}}(\text{q}_{\text{i}}) = \frac{SUM^T(q_i)}{COUNT^T(q_i)} = \bar{\lambda}_{q:A} \tag{32}$$

5.5 Quality risk initiatives

We present the nine key steps to successful deployment of an information quality program for a risk management initiative.

1. Identify the information elements necessary to manage credit risk. Identifying all the information elements and sources necessary to calculate company risk is no mean feat. Risk data such as QR1, QR2... QR10, for example, can each require the identification of several different product identifiers.
2. Define a information quality measurement framework.

The key dimensions that data quality traditionally measures include consistency (21), completeness (24), conformity, accuracy(26), duplication(28), and integrity(30). In addition, for risk calculations, dimensions such as continuity, timeliness, redundancy, and uniqueness can be important.

3. Institute an audit to measure the current quality of information.

Perform an information quality audit to identify, categorize, and quantify the quality of information based upon the decisions made in the previous step.

4. Define a target set of information quality metrics against each attribute, system, application, and company.

Based on the audit results and the impact that each attribute, application, database, or system will have on the ability of your organization to manage risk, the organization should define a set of information quality targets for each attribute, system, application, or company.

5. Set up a company wide information quality monitoring program, and use data to drive process change.
6. Identify gaps against targets.

The quality risks on the data discovered the following critical gaps.

QR1	**QR2**	QR3	QR4	QR5	QR6	**QR7**	QR8	**QR9**
0.6	**0.4**	0.8	0.5	0.8	0.6	**0.4**	0.8	**0.2**

Table 16. Critical Gaps

The issues listed in Table 16 after verification with the finance company analysts and the warehouse administrators.

Other quality issues were unpopulated data fields and unary data. In each case, these gaps were communicated to the warehouse, but were considered non-critical and did not require immediate address.

5.6 Remarks

The main contribution of this work is the illustration of a quantitative method that condensed the task of verifying the credit data to ten quality checks. The quality checks listed here can be transferred to other prediction analyses with a few modifications. However, their categorization as 'mappings', 'parallel extraction' and 'peculiar extraction' is a general, transferable framework. This proposition is elucidated in a methodology below.
We have provided a formal definitions of attribute value types (i.e., accurate, inaccurate, consistency, and incomplete) within the data cube model. Then, we presented sampling strategies to determine the maximum likelihood estimates of these value types in the entire data population residing in data warehouses. The maximum likelihoods estimates were used in our metrics to estimate the true values of scalars returned by the aggregate functions. This study can further be extended to estimate the IQ by the widely used Group By clause, partial sum, and the OLAP functions.

6. Case study for medical risk management

This section describes blood stream infection; we analyzed the effects of lactobacillus therapy and the background risk factors of bacteria detection on blood cultures. For the purpose of our study, we used the clinical data collected from the patients, such as laboratory results, isolated bacterium, anti-biotic agents, lactobacillus therapy, various catheters, departments, and underlying diseases.

6.1 Mathematical model

We propose entropy of clinical data to quantify the information quality. The entropy of clinical data is derived through modeling the clinical data as Joint Gaussian Random Variables (JGRVs) and applying the exponential correlation models that are verified by experimental data. We prove that a simple yet Effective Asynchronous Sampling Strategy (EASS) is able to improve the information quality of clinical data by evenly shifting the sampling moments of nodes from each other. At the end of this section, we derive the lower bound on the performance of EASS to evaluate its effectiveness on improving the information quality.

6.1.1 Entropy of clinical data

Without loss of generality, we assume clinical data from n different locations in the monitored area are JGRVs with covariance matrix C, whose element, ci,j , is given in the following:

$$c_{ij} = \begin{cases} \sigma_i^2 & i = j, for\ i \le n, j \le n, \\ \sigma_i \sigma_j \Pr_{i,j} & i \ne j, for\ i \le n, j \le n, \end{cases}$$

where σ_i and σ_j are the standard deviation of the clinical data S_i and S_j , respectively. Normalizing the covariance matrix leads to the correlation matrix A, which consists of the correlation coefficients of clinical data. The entry of A, $a_{i,j}$, is given as follows:

$$a_{ij} = \begin{cases} 1 & i = j, for\ i \le n, j \le n, \\ \Pr_{i,j} & i \ne j, for\ i \le n, j \le n, \end{cases} \tag{33}$$

Then, according to the definition of entropy of JGRVs, the entropy of the clinical data, H, is

$$H = \frac{1}{2}\log(2\pi e)^n \det C - \log\Delta \quad (34)$$

Where $\log\Delta$ is a constant due to quantization. detC is the determinant of the covariance matrix, which is:

$$\det C = \prod_{i=1}^{n} \sigma_i^2 \det A \quad (35)$$

For the sake of simplicity, we do not elaborate on the closed-form expression of the entropy. However, we will show, in the following, how to improve the information quality through increasing the entropy of clinical data.

6.1.2 Quality improvement

In the discussion on correlation model, we show that asynchronous sampling is able to produce less correlated data compared with synchronous sampling. With the entropy model based on correlation coefficients, the following discussion further explains that the information quality of clinical data improves through asynchronous sampling. Here, we quantify the information quality using entropy of the clinical data. Then, we need to prove $H \le \hat{H}$, where $\hat{H}$ is the entropy with respect to asynchronous sampling and H is that of synchronous sampling. Therefore, we have the following theorem and its proof:

$$H \le \hat{H} \quad (36)$$

$$H = \frac{1}{2}\log(2\pi e)^n \prod_{i=1}^{n} \sigma_i^2 \det A - \log\Delta \quad (37)$$

$$\hat{H} = \frac{1}{2}\log(2\pi e)^n \prod_{i=1}^{n} \sigma_i^2 \det \hat{A} - \log\Delta \quad (38)$$

As the entropy of sensory data increases after applying asynchronous sampling, we conclude that asynchronous sampling is able to improve the information quality of sensory data if the sensory data are temporal-spatial correlated.

6.1.3 Asynchronous sampling strategy

Through quantifying the information quality of sensory data, we show that asynchronous sampling can improve information quality by introducing non-zero sampling shifts. Instead of maximizing entropy through asynchronous sampling, we propose EASS that assigns equal sampling shifts to different locations. Given a set of sensors taking samples periodically, the sampling moments of the ith sensor is ti, ti + T, ti + 2T, … , where T is the sampling interval of the sensor nodes. Accordingly, we define the time shifts for sensor nodes, _i, as follows:

$$T_i = \begin{cases} t_{i+1} - t_i & i = 1,\dots,n-1, \\ T + t_1 - t_i & i = n \end{cases}$$

Thus we have

$$\sum_{k=1}^{n} \tau_k = T \tag{39}$$

For the proposed EASS, $\tau_i = \frac{T}{n}$, for $i \le n$.

Table 17 shows all the components of this dataset. The following decision tree shown in Fig. 5.was obtained as the relationship between the bacteria detection and the various factors, such as diarrhea, lactobacillus therapy, antibiotics, surgery, tracheotomy, CVP/IVH catheter, urethral catheter, drainage, other catheter. Fig. 5. shows the sub-tree of the decision tree on lactobacillus therapy = Y (Y means its presence.)

Item	Attributes
Patient' s Profile	ID, Gender, Age
Department	Department, Ward, Diagnosis
Order	Background Diseases, Sampling Date, Sample, No.
Symptom	Fever, Cathether(5), Traheotomy, Endotracheal intubation, Drainage(5)
Examination Data	CRP, WBC, Urin data, Liver/Kidney Function, Immunology
Therapy	Antibiotic agents(3), Steroid, Anti-cancer drug, Radiation Therapy, Lactobacillus Therapy
Culture	Colony count, Bacteria, Vitek biocode, β−lactamase
Susceptibility	Cephems, Penicillins, Aminoglycoside, Macrolides, Carbapenums, Chloramphenicol,Rifanpic, VCM, etc.

Table 17. Attributes in a Dataset on Infection Control

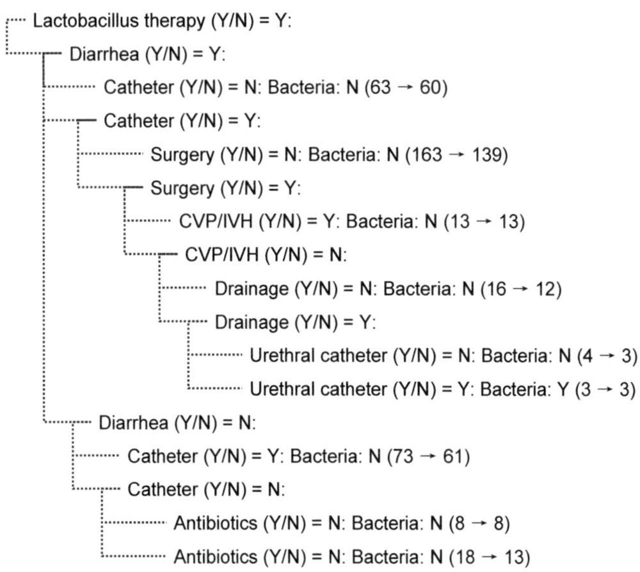

Fig. 5. Sub-tree on lactobacillus therapy(Y/N) = Y

6.2 Discussion and conclusion

Our methods can be used in hospital information system (HIS) analysis environments to determine how source data of different quality could impact medical databases derived using selection, projection, and Cartesian product operations. There was a lack of insight in which element of medical information quality (MIQ) was most relevant and a lack of insight into how implications of MIQ could be quantified. Our method would be useful in identifying which data sets will have acceptable quality, and which one will not. Based on this chapter four conclusions can be drawn:

- The formulation of the conceptual and mathematical model is general and therefore widely applicable.
- The model provides risk detection discovers patterns or information unexpected to domain experts
- The model can be used to a new cycle of risk mining process
- Three important process: risk detection, risk clarification and risk utilization are proposed.

The case study illustrated that the model could be parameterized with data collected from contractors through a database. Once parameterized with acceptable preciseness, applications valuable for society may be expected.

7. Conclusions

Our analysis can be used in business data mining environments to determine how source data of different quality could impact those DM derived using Restriction, Projection, and Cubic product operations. Because business data mining could support multiple such applications, our analysis would be useful in identifying which data sets will have acceptable quality, and which ones will not. Finally, our results can be implemented on top of data warehouses engine that can assist end users to obtain quality risks of the information they receive. The quality information will allow users to account for the reliability of the information received thereby leading to decisions with better outcomes.

8. Acknowledgment

We would like to thank NNSFC (National Natural Science Foundation of China) for supporting Ying Su with a project (70772021, 70831003).

9. References

Ballou, D.P., & Pazer, H.L. (1985). Modeling Data and Process Quality in Multi-Input, Multi-Output Information Systems. Management Science, 31(2), 150.

Bose, I., & Mahapatra, R.K. (2001). Business Data Mining - A Machine Learning Perspective. Information & Management, 39(3), 211-225.

Chen, S.Y., & Liu, X.H. (2004). The contribution of data mining to information science. Journal of Information Science, 30(6), 550-558.

Compieta, P., Di Martino, S., Bertolotto, M., Ferrucci, F., & Kechadi, T. (2007). Exploratory spatio-temporal data mining and visualization. Journal of Visual Languages and Computing, 18(3), 255-279.

Cowell, R.G., Verrall, R.J., & Yoon, Y.K. (2007). Modeling Operational Risk with Bayesian Networks. Journal of Risk and Insurance, 74(4), 795-827.

DeLone, W.H., & McLean, E.R. (2003). The DeLone and McLean model of information systems success: a ten-year update. Journal of Management Information Systems, 19(4), 9-30.

English, L.P. (1999). Improving data warehouse and business information quality methods for reducing costs and increasing profits New York: Wiley.

Eppler, M.J. (2006). Managing information quality increasing the value of information in knowledge-intensive products and processes (2nd ed.). New York: Springer.

Fisher, C.W., Chengalur-Smith, I., & Ballou, D.P. (2003). The impact of experience and time on the use of Data Quality Information in decision making. Information Systems Research, 14(2), 170-188.

Goodhue, D.L. (1995). Understanding user evaluations of information systems. Management Science, 41(12), 1827.

Hand, D.J., Mannila, H., & P. Smyth. (2001). Principles of Data Mining: MIT Press.

Huang, K.-T., Lee, Y.W., & Wang, R.Y. (1999). Quality information and knowledge. Upper Saddle River, N.J. : Prentice Hall PTR.

Jin, R., Vaidyanathan, K., Ge, Y., & Agrawal, G. (2005). Communication and Memory Optimal Parallel Data Cube Construction. IEEE Transactions on Parallel & Distributed Systems, 16(12), 1105-1119.

Kim, D.J., Ferrin, D.L., & Rao, H.R. (2008). A trust-based consumer decision-making model in electronic commerce: The role of trust, perceived risk, and their antecedents. Decision Support Systems, 44(2), 544-564.

Kim, W., Choi, B.J., Hong, E.K., Kim, S.K., & Lee, D. (2003). A Taxonomy of Dirty Data. Data Mining and Knowledge Discovery, 7(1), 81-99.

Michalski, G. (2008). Operational Risk in Current Assets Investment Decisions: Portfolio Management Approach in Accounts Receivable. Agricultural Economics-Zemedelska Ekonomika, 54(1), 12-19.

Mitra, P., & Chaudhuri, C. (2006). Efficient algorithm for the extraction of association rules in data mining. Computational Science and Its Applications - Iccsa 2006, Pt 2, 3981, 1-10.

Mohamadi, H., Habibi, J., Abadeh, M.S., & Saadi, H. (2008). Data mining with a simulated annealing based fuzzy classification system. Pattern Recognition, 41(5), 1824-1833.

Mucksch, H., Holthuis, J., & Reiser, M. (1996). The Data Warehouse Concept - An Overview. Wirtschaftsinformatik, 38(4), 421-&.

Sen, A., & Sinha, A.P. (2007). Toward Developing Data Warehousing Process Standards: An Ontology-Based Review of Existing Methodologies. IEEE Transactions on Systems, Man & Cybernetics: Part C - Applications & Reviews, 37(1), 17-31.

Sen, A., Sinha, A.P., & Ramamurthy, K. (2006). Data Warehousing Process Maturity: An Exploratory Study of Factors Influencing User Perceptions. IEEE Transactions on Engineering Management, 53(3), 440-455.

Shao, T., & Krishnamurty, S. (2008). A clustering-based surrogate model updating approach to simulation-based engineering design. Journal of Mechanical Design, 130(4), -.

Su, Y., & Jin, Z. (2006). A Methodology for Information Quality Assessment in the Designing and Manufacturing Process of Mechanical Products. In L. Al-Hakim (Ed.), Information Quality Management: Theory and Applications (pp. 190-220). USA: Idea Group Publishing.

Su, Y., & Jin, Z. (2007, September 21-23). In Assuring Information Quality in Knowledge intensive business services (Vol. 1, pp. 3243-3246). Paper presented at the 3rd International Conference on Wireless Communications, Networking, and Mobile Computing (WiCOM '07), Shanghai, China. IEEE Xplore.

Su, Y., Jin, Z., & Peng, J. (2008). Modeling Data Quality for Risk Assessment of GIS. Journal of Southeast University (English Edition), 24(Sup), 37-42.

Su, Y., Peng, G., & Jin, Z. (2009a, September 20 to 22). In Reducing the Information Quality Risk in Decision Support for a Finance Company. Paper presented at the International Conference on Management and Service Science (MASS'09), Beijing, China. IEEE Xplore.

Su, Y., Peng, J., & Jin, Z. (2009b, December 18-20). In Modeling Information Quality for Data Mining to Medical Risk Management (pp. 2336-2340). Paper presented at the The 1st International Conference on Information Science and Engineering (ICISE2009), Nanjing,China. IEEE.

Su, Y., Peng, J., & Jin, Z. (2009c). Modeling Information Quality Risk for Data Mining in Data Warehouses. Journal of Human and Ecological Risk Assessment, 15(2), 332 - 350.

Wand, Y., & Wang, R.Y. (1996). Anchoring data quality dimensions in ontological foundations. Association for Computing Machinery. Communications of the ACM, 39(11), 86-95.

Wang, R.Y., & Strong, D.M. (1996). Beyond accuracy: What data quality means to data consumers. Journal of Management Information Systems, 12(4), 5.

Zmud, R.W. (1978). AN EMPIRICAL INVESTIGATION OF THE DIMENSIONALITY OF THE CONCEPT OF INFORMATION. Decision Sciences, 9(2), 187-195.

5

Enabling Real-Time Business Intelligence by Stream Mining

Simon Fong and Yang Hang
University of Macau,
Macao SAR

1. Introduction

Traditionally Business Intelligence (BI) is defined as "a set of mathematical models and analysis methodologies that exploit the available data to generate information and knowledge useful for complex decision making processes" (Vercellis, 2009). The real-time aspect of BI seems to be missing from the classical studies. BI systems technically combine data collection, data storage, and knowledge management with analytical tools to present complex and competitive information to business strategic planner and decision makers (Negash, 2003). This type of BI systems or architectures has served for business usage for past decades (Rao, 2000).

Nowadays businesses evolved to be more competitive and dynamic than the past, which demand for real-time BI and capability of making very quick decisions. With this new business market demand, recently published works (Yang & Fong, 2010; Sandu, 2008) advocated that BI should be specified in four dimensions: strategic, tactical, operational and real-time. Most of the existing decision-support systems however are strategic and tactical; BI is produced by data mining either in forms of regular reports or some actionable information in digital format within a certain frame time. Although the access to the BI database (sometimes called Knowledge base) and the decision generated from data-mining rules are instant; the underlying historical data used for analysis may not be most up-to-the-latest-minute or seconds.

Compared with the operational BI, real-time BI (rt-BI) shall analyze the data as soon it enters the organization. The latency (data latency, analysis latency, decision latency) shall be zero ideally. In order to establish such real-time BI systems, relevant technologies to guarantee low/zero latency are necessary. For example, operational / real-time BI data warehouse techniques are able to provide fresh data access and update. Thus operational BI can be viewed as rt-BI as long as it can provide analytics within a very short time for decision making. The main approach is: system response time shall stay under a threshold that is less than the action taking time; and the rate of data processing shall be faster than the rate of data producing. However, there are many real-time data mining algorithms in theoretical fields, but their applicability and suitability towards various real-time applications are still vague; so far no one has conducted an in-depth study for rt-BI with consideration of stream-mining. We take this as the research motivation and hence the contribution of this chapter.

The chapter is structured in the following way: Section 2 is an overview of rt-BI system; the high-level framework, system architecture and process are described. Section 3 is a discussion of how rt-BI could be applied in several typical application scenarios. Section 4 details a set of experiments by simulating the different impacts of traditional data-mining and stream-mining in rt-BI architecture. A conclusion is drawn in the last section

2. rt-BI architecture

2.1 Overview of the rt-BI framework

rt-BI system relates to many technologies and tools evolved from strategic BI and tactical BI. Following previous research, a four-layer framework is proposed for rt-BI system in Figure 1. The main improvement is a real-time processing of whole knowledge discovery process.

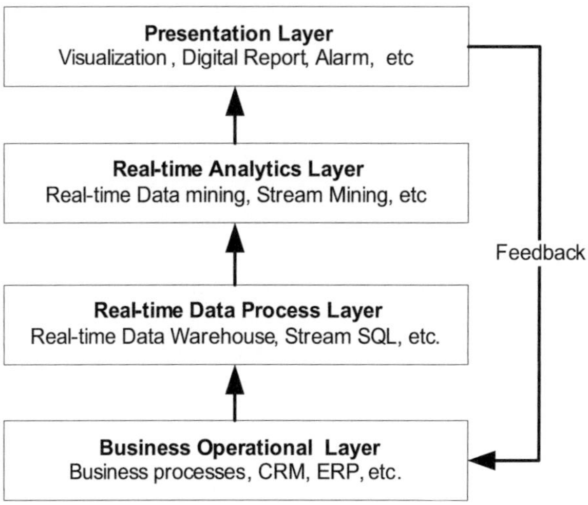

Fig. 1. Four-layer Framework

A. Business operational layer

This layer composes of two primary functions: business activity monitoring (BAM) and real-time process tuning (McCoy, 2002). Azvine (Azvine et al., 2006) presents the shortcoming of current BAM and process tuning technology for rt-BI: 1) current BAM can't make intelligent conclusion about the overall business process behavior; 2) and real business processes changes are carried throughout initiatives manually, that is expensive and time consuming. On the other hand, the level of automation is divided into two stages: semi- and fully-automatic. Our proposed framework tackles these problems with a fully-automated process. The system is built right on the top of business operations. It shall facilitate automated mapping of existing business operations within an organization, capture the knowledge to automate process tuning, optimization and re-engineering, and monitor people and systems for process conformance.

B. Real-time data process layer

This layer is responsible for providing qualified data to its upper layer - analytics layer. Data come from various resources in different formats. If the data contain too much noise, it will impair the business intelligence discovery. In this layer, the system is required to obtain the quality data within a time constraint. For this reason, preparation process should not take too long. Modern digital source is a kind of large volume and rapidly changing data.

Data stream technology (Botan, 2009) provides a good solution to build real-time data warehouse, with which increased refresh cycles to frequently update the data. This kind of data warehouse systems can achieve nearly real-time data updating, where the data latency typically is in the range from seconds to minutes.

C. Real-time analytic layer

Traditionally, data analyzing follows "analyst-in-the-middle" approach where human expert analysts are required to drive or configure the information with BI software and tools. But such manual task will incur analysis latency. To this end, the analysis tools should provide a high degree of automation, which is relating to artificial intelligence technology. Data miners serve as the kernel to build models or extract patterns from large amounts of information (Hand & Mannila, 2001; Hand, 1999, Hoffmann et al., 2001). Analytics layer uses fast data mining method to interpret data to information. So far there are many real-time data mining algorithms and methodologies. The four popular types are: clustering, classification, frequency counting, and time series analysis. Stream processing engines are also used based on sliding windows technology (Dong, 2003).

D. Presentation layer

This layer presents the BI to end-user in a highly interactive way in order to shorten action latency. The presentations vary in formats and designs. For examples, sophisticated time-series charts show a trend, and a KPI dashboard alarms off anomalies etc. Many companies provide these techniques as third party solutions, iNetSoft, SPSS, IBM, etc.

2.2 System architecture

Traditionally, the classic method to build model with data mining algorithm is training-then-testing approach. But the weakness is they may not suit large volume and high speed data.

A Mining Model Definition Language (MMDL) is used for stream mining system (Thakkar, 2008), but it has not illustrated how to design a stream mining system in a technical sense. A research (Stonebraker, 2005) proposed three real-time data stream processing architectures which can potentially be applied to solve high-volume low latency streaming problems but its both Rule Engine and Stream Process Engine architectures only rely on stream data querying (SQL). Mining data streams has been studied by many researchers. Gaber (Gaber, 2005) summarized the most cited data stream mining techniques with respect to different mining tasks, approaches and implementations. They proposed an adaptive resource-aware approach called Algorithm Output Granularity (AOG) (Gaber, 2004; Gaber, 2008).

The rt-BI system architecture described in this section is derived from the previous research in data mining and business intelligence. Different from the previous ones, the proposed architecture concentrates on constructing a system which is able to extract potential BI and return result to end-user in real-time.

Figure 2 shows a static view of rt-BI system architecture. *Firstly*, the rt-BI system collects a large amount of historical data from existing information system. *Secondly*, the system collects and monitors the new input data in real-time data process layer. If necessary it will transform the data into adequate forms. *Thirdly*, the system determines whether it relates to an established model in the real-time analytics layer. If so, the system matches it with the rules and returns BI result. Otherwise, the system runs on data-mining process in order to find new rules and BI. A newly found model is updated to the rule-based database. *Fourthly*, the discovered information is summarized as rt-BI result and presented in appropriate formats. During this process, any mis-prediction or incorrect-pattern will be updated to

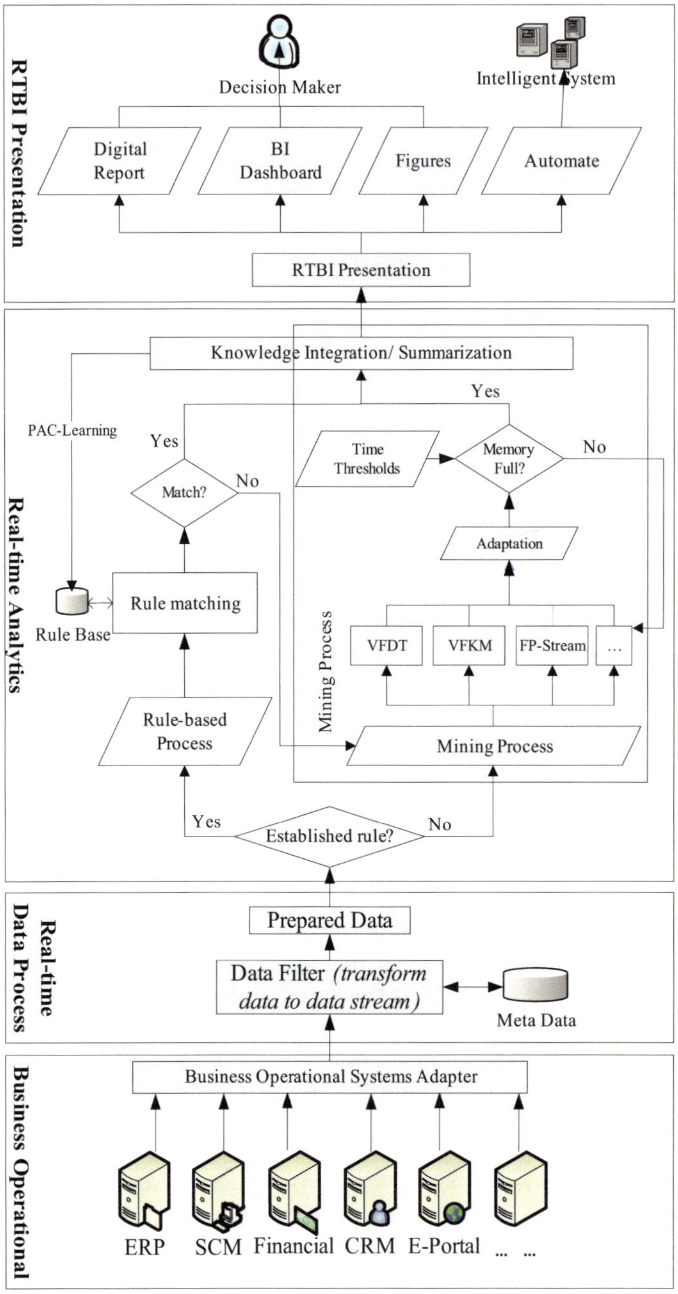

Fig. 2. rt-BI System Architecture

database in the case of next data mining happens. This process should be within a certain time threshold that the BI output is useful for decision making (to ensure no analytics latency). By this architecture, the system collects data and generates some prediction models in real-time. The data used to discover BI is not only dependent on historical but also the new incoming data.

2.3 rt-BI analyzing process

The analyzing kernel of an rt-BI system is the mining process. In this section, we show a dynamic diagram in Figure 3 to show how to implement the data mining process in RT-BI system.

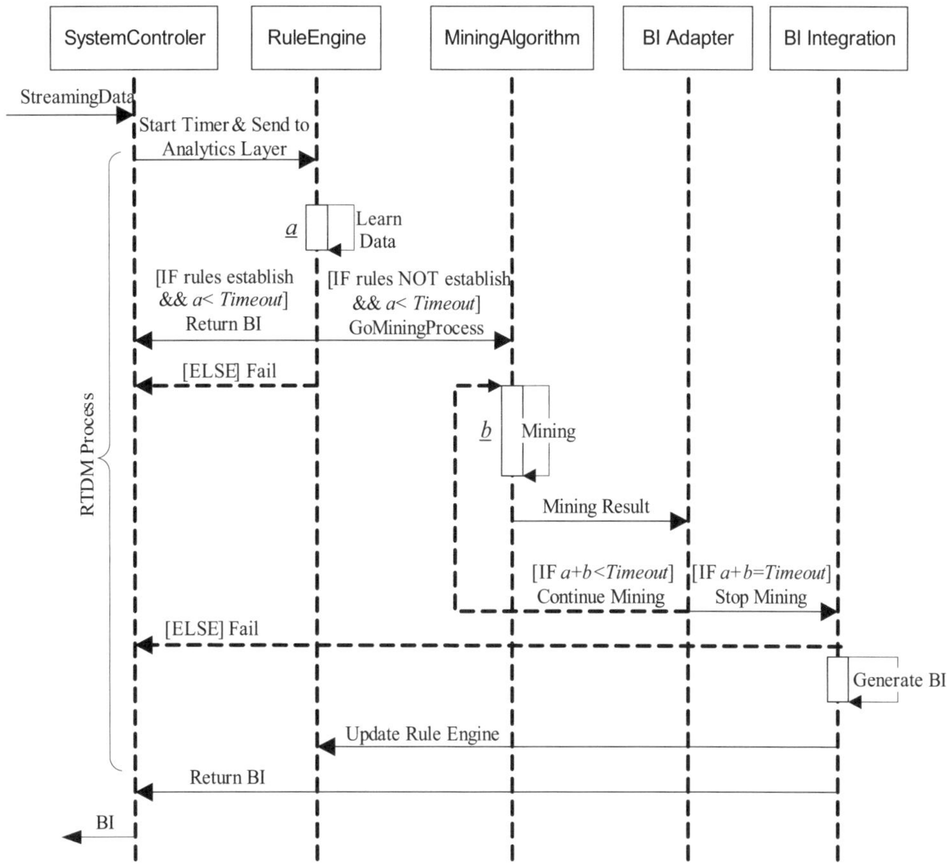

Fig. 3. rT-BI Generating Workflow

The process contains two segments: rule-based matching, and new BI mining. When new data comes, a timer is started to control the rt-BI running time so as to restrict analytics latency within an acceptable level. A timeout threshold is determined by the time required to make a decision, which restricts the rule-based matching time as well as the BI mining time. If new arrival data are correlating to the already established rules, the rule-based matching process activates and returns the BI within the time threshold. Otherwise, the new BI mining process will trigger. The determination should be within the time threshold. If it timeouts, the rt-BI system is deemed failed to discover new BI and returns the most recently updated information instead.

3. Applications of RT-BI system

The proposed system architecture can be applied in different applications. We illustrate four typical application domains. A more comprehensive comparison is presented in Table 1.

A. Anomaly detection and automated alerts

Anomaly Detection refers to detecting patterns in a given data set that do not conform to an established normal behavior (Hodge, 2004). The detected patterns are called anomalies, which are also referred to as outliers, surprise, aberrant, deviation, peculiarity, etc. and often translated to critical and actionable information in several application domains. Many anomaly detection techniques have been specifically developed for certain application domains, while others are more generic. Its application domains mainly include: insurance fraud detection (Phua et al, 2004), network attack detection (Zhengbing et al., 2008), and credit card fraud detection (Quah & Sriganesh, 2008; Whitrow et al., 2009), etc. A survey (Chandola et al., 2009) tries to provide a structured and comprehensive overview of the research on anomaly detection, but it doesn't give a generic design for such kind of rt-BI system. This type of applications is not only required to find the anomaly pattern from a large amount of data in real-time, but to present the result to end-user reliably and take action efficiently.

B. Prediction and suggestions recommender

Customer Relationship Management (CRM) systems apply data mining to analyze and predict the potential customer values. Although the analysis of available information for those customers who in the past have purchased product or services based on the historical data, and the comparisons with the characteristics of those who have not taken up the offer of the enterprise, it is possible to identify the segments with the highest potential. Commercial recommender systems use various data mining techniques to provide appropriate recommendations to users during real-time online sessions. E-business transactions usually take place over online networks. For analyzing e-Portal information, rT-BI system is recommends suitable suggestions to customers. A context-similarity based hotlinks assignment (Antoniou et al., 2009) analyzes the similarity of context between pages in order to suggest the placement of suitable hotlinks. Another real-time recommendation system based on experts' experiences is proposed in (Sun et al., 2008). It simplifies content-based filtering through computing similarity of the keywords and recommends common users the Web pages based on experts' search histories but not the whole Web pages.
Online recommender systems often use the suggested purchase items, or the items in which costumer may be also interested, as the presentation of rT-BI. These techniques widely used in call centers to make investigation service in terms of the telephone call data stream.

C. Forecast and markets analysis

Pricing network resources is a crucial component for proper resource management and the provision of quality of service guarantees in different markets. A model used data mining to forecast the stock market with time series (Dietmar et al., 2009). A competitive market intelligence system (Weiss & Verma, 2002) proposes to detect critical differences in the text written about a company versus the text for its competitor. However, the intelligence system is compelled to depend on empirical performance, which has to require human interaction to analyze the discovered patterns. As aforementioned, the latency is the primary constraint of operational BI and real-time BI. A business cannot respond to events as they happen if it cannot find out about these events for hours, days, or weeks. It also cannot immediately respond to events if the system that supplies the analyses of these events is down. If the problems of data latency and data availability are solved, then businesses react proactively to new information and knowledge rather than reactively.

Real-time business intelligence dashboards are used to bridge the gap between operational business intelligence and real-time business intelligence. It shall display not only historical information but also show the current status to support decision making.

D. Optimization and supply chain management

Supply Chain Management (SCM) is one of the hottest topics in e-Commerce. Online business transaction builds a dynamic pricing model that is integrated into a real-time supply chain management agent (Ku et al., 2008). Besides the pricing strategy, real-time supply chain management in a rapidly changing environment requires reactive and dynamic collaboration among participating entities. Radio Frequency Identification (RFID) is widely used in high-tech arena. It is described as a major enabling technology for automated contactless wireless data collection, and as an enabler for the real-time enterprise. Goods are supervised while they are embedded with RFID tags. The tags can send out electronic signal through its inside antenna. After capturing the data stream by sensors, RFID system is aware of the information of the goods, such as location and status. The real-time supervising and gaining visibility can achieve quick responsiveness and high efficiency in business flows, if RFID technology can be applied efficiently (Gonzalez et al., 2006).
The proposed architecture may address the challenge of processing high-volume, real-time data with requiring the use of custom code. rt-BI systems provide pattern discovery, trend detection, and visualization, controlling and improving the flow of materials and information, originating from the suppliers and reaching the end customers.

4. Experiments

4.1 Simulation setup

In our experiment, a simulation is programmed to verify the proposed framework. Simulated "real-time" environment runs through Massive Online Analysis (MOA), a framework for data stream mining. (Source: University of Waikato, www.cs.waikota.ac.nz). MOA consists of a library of open source JAVA API extending from WEKA data mining. The experiment platform is a PC with 2.99 GHz CPU and 1 GB RAM. The main procedure flow is shown in Figure 4.
Experiments are performed on both synthetic data and real data. Synthetic data are generated by Random Tree Generator provided by MOA. Real data are collected from PKDD'99 conference. (Source: http://lisp.vse.cz/pkdd99/Challenge/chall.htm). We chose them because they came from real-world financial and banking applications. This procedure is simulating *Business Operational Layer* process.
The collected data are in different formats. Thus, a data filter simulates *Real-time Data Process Layer*, emerging different tables, eliminating noisy data, and converting different types of files to MOA readable ARFF format. The sensor is accountable in implementing the following tasks: partition datasets from data source with a pre-configured size; and transfer partitioned data to a mining engine in an interval time, simulating a continuous stream flow.
Real-time Analytics Layer uses Hoeffding Tree (Hoeffding, 1963) as the core fast mining algorithms. As a pre-configured threshold of maximum memory size (window size), remaining available time (time out threshold), a decision tree is generated for each window in real-time. With the time passing by, the tree structure changes simultaneously. After a decision tree is built, a set of test stream data are used to test the accuracy. With the tree structure changing, a simple chart is reported in *Presentation Layer*.

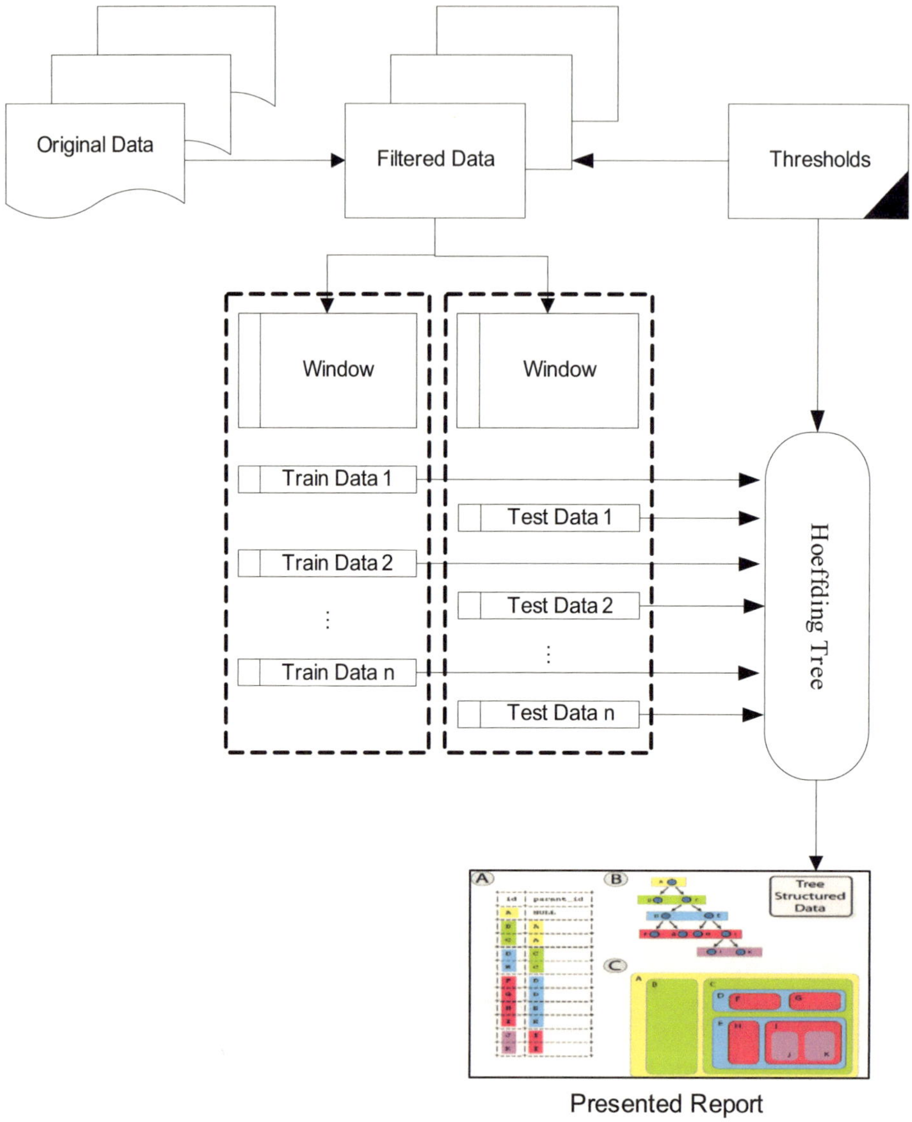

Fig. 4. Procedure Workflow

4.2 Results and discussions

Discussion of how rt-BI could be applied in several typical application scenarios.

In the simulation, Hoeffding Tree algorithm is the main algorithm of very fast decision tree classification for real-time data mining. It is used with VFML10 (Bernhard et al., 2008) numeric estimator. The accuracy percentage is calculated by the Basic Classification Performance Evaluator provided in MOA, which refers to following formula:

$$Accuracy = \frac{CorrectObervationNumber}{TotalObervationNumber} \times 100\%$$

A. Accuracy and window size

We extracted data segments of various sizes of windows from the same resource, respectively 1K, 5K, 10K, 100K, 250K, 500K, 750K and 1000K bytes. A streaming environment is simulated that data comes into rt-BI system continuously

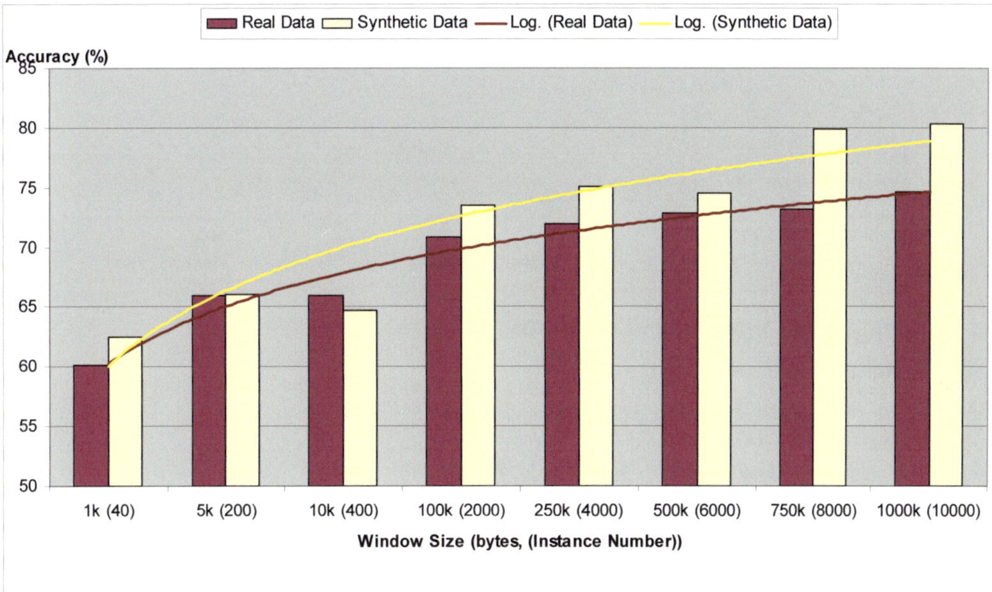

Fig. 5. Average Predication Accuracy Comparison

Generally, the synthetic data have a better performance than the real data result due to the controlled sparsity, but both the trends are correspondingly rising up. The accuracy increases with the window size growing (Figure 5). This experiment shows that: the larger the window size is, the higher accuracy. Thus, when it comes to designing a rt-BI system we have to consider what the optimal window size it should take. However, a large window size also yields certain delay.

B. Window size and complexity

Data mining algorithm has different efficiency in terms of its complexity. There are some factors influencing the complexity. For instance in our experiment, Hoeffding Tree's complexity is effected by the serialized size. The bigger this size is, the higher the complexity. This size also influences the need of computing resource. In our simulation, when the size of window gets large, the Java virtual machine was allocated a generous amount of memory. It strongly indicates that the serialized size was the cause. We tested different windows with increasing size from 1 Kb to 1M bytes, and observed this trend.

Figure 6 shows that: (1) a significant growth of serialized size appears from 1Kb to 500 Kb; (2) and a relatively slowly growing appears from 500 K to 1 M bytes. In other words, the relatively high complexity is found in the bigger data size region; the complexity becomes steady when a threshold arrives, so the increasing trend slows down. When we design a system, we shall consider this threshold and required response time together. If the required response time (timeout) is less than this threshold, we will achieve zero analysis latency as a result.

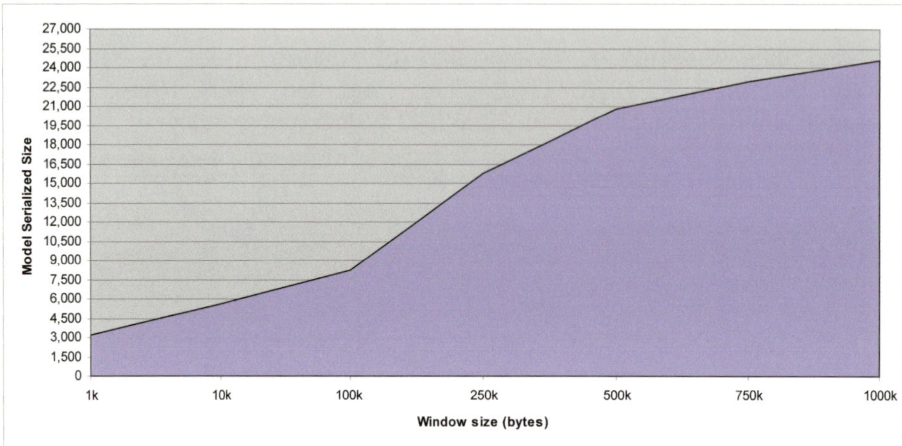

Fig. 6. Average Tree Complexity Comparison

C. Traditional and real-time learning methods

The biggest difference between traditional BI and rt-BI discovery is the data analyzing method. Due to the differences of the learning methods, rt-BI uses windowing technique, instead of training and testing the whole structured dataset as in traditional BI. The experimental data is the same as that in the previous experiments. From Figures 7 and 8, a classic classification method - Naïve Bayesian - is used in the traditional learning method. The ratio of training data size and testing data size is 1:1, 1:2, 2:1 respectively. rt-BI method based on Hoeffding Tree applies windowing technique. We can observe a significant trend that: traditional BI has a much better accuracy than rt-BI when the data size is relatively small; however, this advantage is not observed any more while the data size (window size) increases to a certain extent.

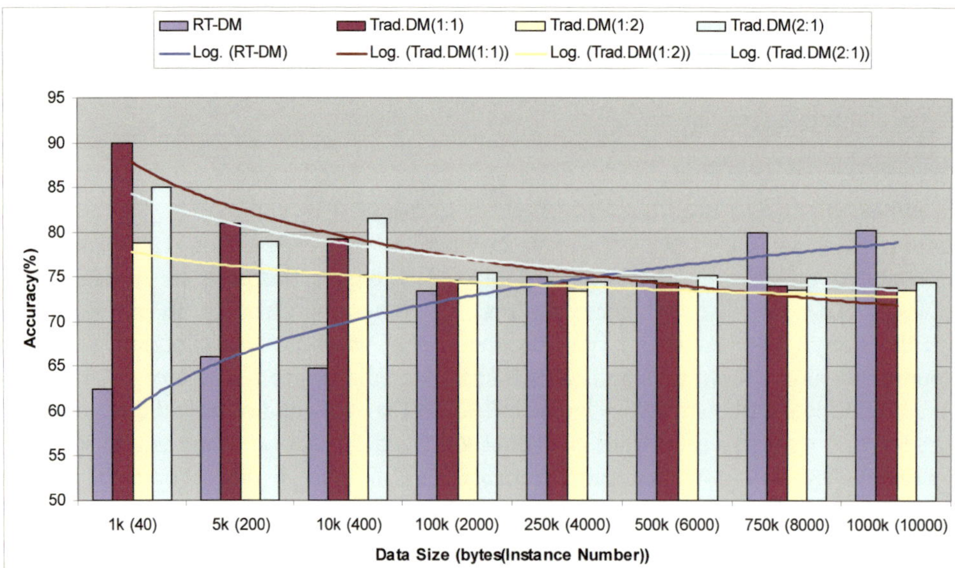

Fig. 7. Predication Accuracy Comparison between Bayesian and HTA

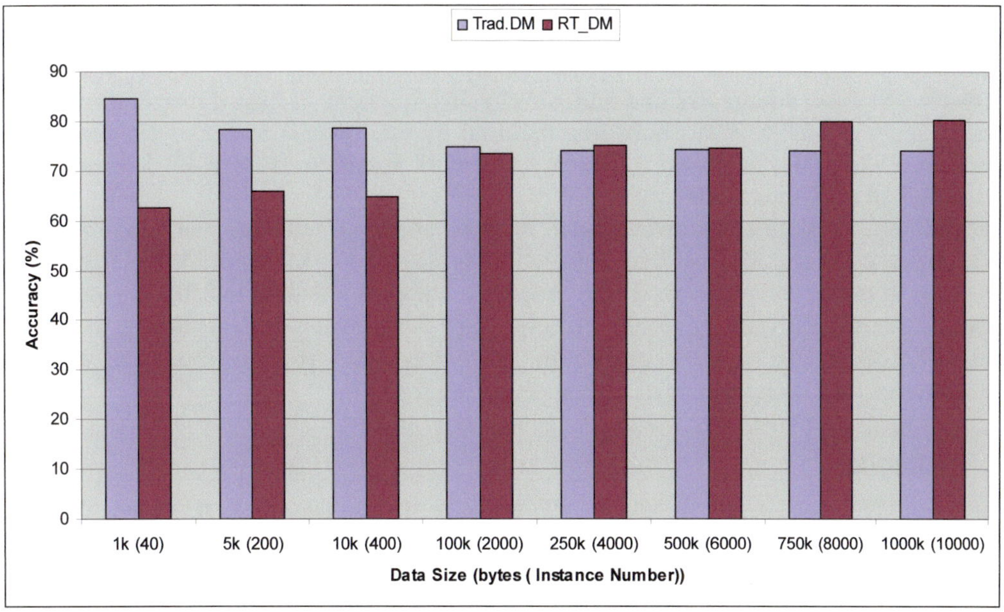

Fig. 8. Average Predication Accuracy Comparison between Bayesian and HTA

Figure 9 gives a comparison between a classic traditional decision tree J48 C4.5 and Hoeddfing Tree in our experiment. Synthetic data are used as input. We can see that both of them display an increasing accuracy while the data size is growing, C4.5 has a better performance than Hoeddfing tree but the former tree takes much more time than the latter one. For this reason, it may be unsuitable for rt-BI. Thus, we may make a short conclusion that: compared with traditional BI method (that is comprised of complete data training and testing), rt-BI equipped with stream data mining method obtains a better performance, and therefore it does suit environments characterized by huge and streaming data

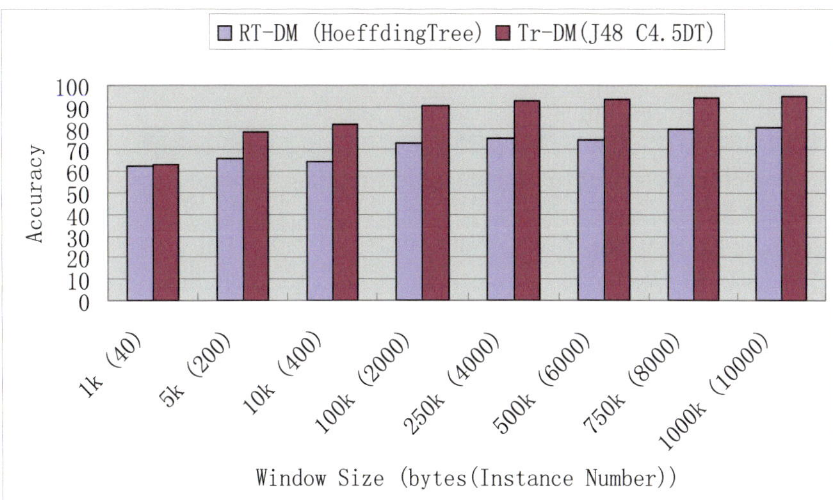

Fig. 9. Average Predication Accuracy Comparison by Window Sizes

5. Conclusion

Real-time business intelligence is a new concept in knowledge discovery. rt-BI requires exploring BI from a large volume and rapidly arriving data in business operations. rt-BI system aims to achieve very short time required in data process and analysis process for decision making. We proposed a generic framework architecture for rt-BI, followed by a discussion of rt-BI applications.

In addition, a simulation experiment is developed to validate the stream-mining performance. The results show that: 1) the window size is a key to determine the algorithm's accuracy in rt-BI system design; 2) the proposed framework is able to achieve nearly zero analysis latency within a threshold timeout. This shows using stream mining in rt-BI is desirable; 3) compared with traditional BI method, the rt-BI method has a better performance for a large volume of high speed streaming data.

6. References

Antoniou, D.; Garofalakis, J.; Makris, C.; Panagis, Y.; Sakkopoulos, E. (2009). Context-similarity based hotlinks assignment: Model, metrics and algorithm, Data & Knowledge Engineering, *In Press, Corrected Proof, Available online*, 4 May 2009.

Azvine, B.; Cui, Z.; Nauck, D. & Majeed, B. (2006). Real Time Business Intelligence for the Adaptive Enterprise. *Proceedings of the the 8th IEEE international Conference on E-Commerce Technology and the 3rd IEEE international Conference on Enterprise Computing, E-Commerce, and E-Services (CEC-EEE)*, pp. 29, San Francisco, CA, June 2006, IEEE Computer Society, Washington, DC

Bernhard, P.; Geoffrey, H. & Richard, K. (2008). Handling Numeric Attributes in Hoeffding Trees, *Lecture Notes in Computer Science*, Springer Berlin/Heidelberg Volume 5012, 2008, pp. 296-307.

Botan, I.; Cho, Y.; Derakhshan, R.; Dindar, N.; Haas, L., Kim, K. & Tatbul, N. (2009). Federated Stream Processing Support for Real-Time Business Intelligence Applications, *VLDB International Workshop on Enabling Real-Time for Business Intelligence (BIRTE'09)*, Lyon, France, August 2009

Chandola, V.; Banerjee, A. & Kumar, V. (2009). Anomaly Detection: A Survey, *ACM Computing Surveys*, Vol. 41(3), Article 15, July 2009

Dietmar, H.; Dorr, A. & Denton, M. (2009). Establishing relationships among patterns in stock market data, *Data & Knowledge Engineering*, Volume 68, Issue 3, March 2009, pp. 318-337

Dong, G.; Han, J.; Lakshmanan, L.V.S.; Pei, J.; Wang, H. & Yu, P.S. (2003). Online mining of changes from data streams: Research problems and preliminary results, *Proceedings of the 2003 ACM SIGMOD Workshop on Management and Processing of Data Streams. In cooperation with the 2003 ACM-SIGMOD International Conference on Management of Data*, San Diego, CA, June 2003

Gaber, M.; Zaslavsky, A. & Krishnaswamy, S. (2004). Towards an Adaptive Approach for Mining Data Streams in Resource Constrained Environments, *Proceedings of Sixth International Conference on Data Warehousing and Knowledge Discovery - Industry Track*, 2004

Gaber, M.; Zaslavsky, A. & Krishnaswamy, S. (2005). Mining data streams: a review. *SIGMOD*, Rec. 34, 2, 2005, pp. 18-26

Gaber, M. (2009). Data Stream Mining Using Granularity-Based Approach, *Studies in Computational Intelligence, Foundations of Computational*, Volume 6, 2009, pp. 47-66

Gonzalez, H.; Han, J. & Li, X. (2006). Mining compressed commodity workflows from massive RFID data sets. *Proceedings of the 15th ACM international Conference on information and Knowledge Management. CIKM '06*. ACM, New York, NY, 2006, pp. 162-171.

Hand, D. (1999). Statistics and Data Mining: Intersecting Disciplines, *ACM SIGKDD Explorations*, Vol.1, No.1, June 1999, pp. 16-19.

Hand, D.; Mannila, H. & Smyth, P. (2001). Principles of data mining, *MIT Press*, 2001

Hodge, V.J. & Austin, J. (2004). A Survey of Outlier Detection Methodologies. *Artificial Intelligence Review*, Kluwer Academic Publishers, 2004, pp. 85–126.

Hoeffding, W. (1963). Probability inequalities for sums of bounded random variables. *Journal of American Statistic Association*, Volume 58, 1963, pp. 13–30

Hoffmann, F.; Hand, D.J.; Adams, N.; Fisher, D. & Guimaraes, G. (2001). Advances in Intelligent Data Analysis. *Springer*, 2001

Ku, T.; Zhu, Y. & Hu, K. (2008). A Novel Complex Event Mining Network for RFID-Enable Supply Chain Information Security. *Proceedings of the 2008 international Conference on Computational intelligence and Security.* Volume 1, CIS. IEEE Computer Society, Washington, DC, 2008, pp. 516-521.

McCoy, D.W. (2002). Business Activity Monitoring: Calm Before the Storm, *Gartner Research*, ID: LE-15-9727

Phua, C.; Alahakoon, D. & Lee, V. (2004). Minority report in fraud detection: classification of skewed data. *SIGKDD Explore News*. Vol. 6, No. 1, June 2004, pp. 50-59.

Quah, J.T. & Sriganesh, M. (2008). Real-time credit card fraud detection using computational intelligence. *Expert Syst. Applications*. 35, 4, pp. 1721-1732.

Sandu, D. (2008). Operational and real-time Business Intelligence, *Revista Informatica Economică*, Vol. 3, No. 47, pp. 33-36

Stonebraker, M.; Çetintemel, U.; and Zdonik, S. (2005). The 8 requirements of real-time stream processing. *SIGMOD* Rec. 34, 4, 2005, pp. 42-47

Sun, J.; Yu, X.; Wu, Z. & Li, X. (2008). Real Time Recommendation Utilizing Experts' Experiences. *Proceedings of the 2008 Fifth international Conference on Fuzzy Systems and Knowledge Discovery (FSKD)*. Volume 5, IEEE Computer Society, Washington, DC, 2008, pp. 379-383

Whitrow, C.; Hand, D.J.; Juszczak, P.; Weston, D. & Adams, N. M. (2009). Transaction aggregation as a strategy for credit card fraud detection. *Data Mining and Knowledge. Discovery*. Vol. 18, No. 1, 2009, pp. 30-55.

Weiss, S. M. & Verma, N. K. (2002). A system for real-time competitive market intelligence.. *Proceedings of the Eighth ACM SIGKDD international Conference on Knowledge Discovery and Data Mining. KDD '02*. ACM, New York, NY, 2002, pp. 360-365.

Yang, H. & Fong, S. (2010). Real-time Business Intelligence System Architecture with Stream Mining, *Proceedings of the 5th International Conference on Digital Information Management (ICDIM 2010)*, July 2010, Thunder Bay, Canada, IEEE.

Zhengbing, H.; Zhitang, L. & Junqi, W. (2008). A novel Network Intrusion Detection System (NIDS) based on signatures search of data mining. *Proceedings of the 1st international Conference on Forensic Applications and Techniques in Telecommunications, information, and Multimedia and Workshop,* Adelaide, Australia, January 21 - 23, 2008, ICST, Brussels, Belgium, pp. 1-7.

6

From the Business Decision Modeling to the Use Case Modeling in Data Mining Projects

Oscar Marban[1], José Gallardo[2], Gonzalo Mariscal[3] and Javier Segovia[1]
[1]Universidad Politécnica de Madrid
[2]Universidad Católica del Norte
[3]Universidad Europea de Madrid
[1,3]Spain
[2]Chile

1. Introduction

In the current arena where companies face extreme competiveness and continuous changes, a rapid and flexible capability to respond to market dynamism is a key factor for the success or failure of any organization. In this context, the development of efficient strategic and operational decision-making support systems is essential for guaranteeing business success and survival. Nowadays, data mining systems are an effective technology for supporting organizational decision-making processes.

From the viewpoint of data mining development, the year 2000 marked the most important milestone: CRISP-DM (CRoss-Industry Standard Process for Data Mining) was published (Chatam, et al., 2002), (Piatetsky-Shaphiro, 2000). CRISP-DM is the most used model for developing data mining projects (Kdnuggets, 2007). Data mining had been successfully applied to many real problems. As a result, data mining has been popularized as the business intelligence tool with the greatest growth projection. In recent years, data mining technology has moved out of the research labs and into companies on the 'Fortune 500' list (Kantardzic & Zurada, 2005).

Even so, the scientific literature is dotted with many examples of failed projects, project planning delays, unfinished projects, or budget overruns (Eisenfeld et al., 2003), (Meta Group Research, 2003), (Maciaszek, 2005). There are two main reasons for this. On the one hand, there are no standard development processes to implement an engineering approach in data mining project development (Marbán, 2008). On the other hand, requirements are not properly specified. One of the critical success factors of data mining projects is the need for a clear definition of the business problem to be solved, where data mining is considered to be best technological solution (Hemiz, 1999). This indicates the need for a proper definition of project requirements that takes into account organizational needs based on a business model.

Historically, research in data mining has focused on the development of algorithms and tools, without any detailed consideration of the search for methodological approaches that ensure the success of a data mining project.

In this paper, we propose a methodological approach to guide the development of a business model of the decision-making process within an organization. The business decision-making model (represented in i* notation) is translated into use cases based on heuristics. In this way, the functional requirements of a data mining project can be associated with organizational requirements and the organization's strategic objectives.

This chapter is structured as follows. Section 2 summarizes the key dimensions to be considered in a requirements specification process and previous work related to requirements engineering. Section 3 presents a review of and concludes with a comparison of notations used in business modeling. Section 4 presents a business modeling process that takes into account the understanding of the business domain and the generation of a business decision-making model. Section 5 describes the process for creating the requirements model from the business decision-making model. In Section 6, the proposed methodology is applied to a case study. Finally, in Section 7 we summarize the conclusions of the presented research.

2. Requirements engineering and business modeling

Requirements engineering is a process covering all the activities involved in discovering, documenting and maintaining all the system requirements (Kotonya & Sommerville, 1998) (Sommerville, 2002), (Medina, 2004). Not only must a good requirements discovery process elicit what the customer wants, but it must also consider the analysis and understanding of the application and business domain in which the system will be used. The main dimensions that a requirements specification process should cover (Kotonya & Sommerville, 1998) are:

- Understanding of the application domain: This determines the minimum knowledge required about the domain in which the system is to be implemented.
- Problem understanding: This involves understanding the details of the business problem that the system is to solve.
- Business understanding: This means understanding how project development affects business components and what contribution it makes to achieving organizational goals.
- Understanding of stakeholder needs: This accounts for stakeholder needs, particularly regarding the work processes that the system is to support.

Taking into account the obvious need to apply requirements engineering in product development life cycles, many requirements engineering process models have been proposed in different areas of engineering. In software engineering, research has focused on requirements elicitation and monitoring for the design and implementation of software systems ((Cysneiros & Sampaio, 2004), (Gacitúa, 2001), (Gorschek & Claes, 2006)), since there is a broad consensus on the essentiality of the requirements elicitation phase in software development. There are several proposals ((Kotonya & Sommerville, 1998) (Davyt, 2001) (Sommerville, 2002)) that vary as to form and the emphasis they place on specific activities.

Rilston (Rilston et al. 2003) proposed the DWARF model (Data WArehouse Requirements deFinition) for OLAP and data warehouse development projects. DWARF supports management planning, specification, validation and requirements management. Bruckner et al. (Bruckner et al., 2001) define and discuss three abstraction levels for data warehouse requirements (business, user and system requirements), and show the requirements definition of a data warehouse system. Dale (Dale, 2004) presents a case study where the requirements definition process for developing a data warehouse is based on a modified Six Sigma Quality methodology.

In the e-commerce area, the E3-Value methodology (Gordijn et al., 2000) (Gordijn, 2003) has been proposed. It helps to systematically discover, analyze and evaluate e-business ideas. Requirements engineering is also used in the automotive industry. Weber and Weisbrod claim that the costs, sophistication and complexity involved in electrical and electronic automotive system development (telematics, interior and passenger comfort, driving assistance and safety-critical systems) are growing (Weber & Weisbrod, 2003).

Lately, the telecommunications field has expanded significantly. These advances have led to complex communications systems with different technologies. Therefore, the development of new high-quality services is a challenge for telecom operators. Gerhard presents the RATS (Requirements Assistant for Telecommunications Services) methodology (Gerhard, 1997).

There are many other areas where requirements engineering methodologies, techniques or activities are proposed and applied: control systems for nuclear power plants, avionics systems, lighting control, real-time embedded systems, complex systems (SCR method, Software Cost Reduction), intrusion detection systems, (Heitmeyer & Bharadwaj, 2000) (Heninger at al., 1978) (Heninger, 1980) (Slagell, 2002). There is also abundant research on security requirements engineering (Knorr, K. & Rohrig, 2005) (Leiwo et al., 2004). Firesmith defines different types of security requirements and gives some examples and guidelines associated with engineer training for specifying security requirements without unduly limiting security versus architecture (Firesmith, 2003).

In the case of data mining projects, there is not much research about applying requirements engineering techniques to requirements discovery and specification, as such projects are exploratory and return different types of results.

There is widespread agreement about the importance of business understanding in the requirements elicitation process (Kotonya & Sommerville, 1998). There are many references in the scientific literature to business process modeling for different purposes, such as a better organizational understanding, analysis and innovation, management or re-engineering (Martyn, 1995), (Koubarakis & Plexousakis, 1999), (Vérosle et al., 2003), (Gordijn & Akkermans 2007). However, there is little research on integrating the organizational model with definite requirements engineering activities (Mylopoulos et al., 2002), (Santander & Castro, 2002). Additionally, data mining projects are mainly developed to turn up knowledge or information to support decision-making at the strategic levels of an organization. This is an important issue because high-level decision-making processes are not structured, and hence are very difficult to model.

In this sense, business model development is essential for the requirements discovery and specification process in data mining projects, as the business model takes into account the main dimensions described above and relates project development to organizational strategic goals and objectives. To sum up, a better understanding of the business philosophy will help managers to make better decisions (Hayes & Finnegan, 2005).

3. Business modeling notations

There are different system specification techniques or methodology notations, where the term 'specification' is construed as the process of describing a system and its properties. A system specification can be described by a written document, a formal mathematic model, or a graphical representation. Each technique has advantages and disadvantages. Text descriptions are simpler and more flexible, but they are usually ambiguous, unclear or include many hard-to-process documents. Formal languages do not have these drawbacks, but they are complex, less flexible than written text; also their use requires additional effort (training) (Sommerville, 2002). On the other hand, group of stakeholders can easily and quickly understand the system described by graphical models, as they represent visual scenarios (Berenbach, 2004) (Sommerville, 2005). On the downside, the model becomes more and more complex as the amount of information it has to represent grows. In complex systems, a combination of natural language and graphical models can be a good choice.

Some standard graphical notations used for business modeling are UML, BPMN (Russell et al., 2006), (Wilcox & Gurau, 2003), (Agulilar-Saven, 2004), (Berenbach, 2004), (Vérosle et al., 2003), (Wohed et al., 2006), (White, 2004), and i* (Yu, 1995), (Yu, 1996), (Yu & Mylopoulos, 1997), (Alencar et al., 2000), (Castro, et al., 2001), (Santander & Castro, 2002). i* is described below. Taking into account the advantages of graphical system specification notations over other text (natural language) or formal notations (mathematical language), we opted to use a graphical notation in the research described in this chapter. After analyzing the described notations (UML, BPMN, framework i*), we selected the i* framework. The main reasons for this decision are:

1. The i* framework is more than just a modeling language (like UML and BPMN); it is also a modeling technique, as it defines a process for developing an organizational model.
2. The model is easy and intuitive to understand, as it is possible to build a multilevel view of the process to be modeled.
3. Not only are organizational requirements linked to the system functionalities under development, but data mining projects, real-time systems, or process control systems are also strongly related to global requirements such as reliability, security, etc. Requirements play a key role in these kinds of systems. UML or BPMN do not explicitly take into account these types of requirements. In contrast, the i* framework provides primitives related to non-functional requirements.
4. The i* framework explicitly states organizational goals, tasks and resources, and the network of SD relationships among various actors needed to achieve strategic goals and understand the reasons behind the decision-making processes.
5. The i* framework brings the requirements specification gradually closer to organizational requirements in a straightforward manner.

3.1 I* framework

The i* framework technique was proposed by Eric Yu (Yu, 1995) and has the following features:

- It helps organizations to represent the actors involved in the process.
- It helps to represent dependencies explicitly among different organizational actors.
- It helps to build a simplified view of the business to be represented, showing the actors, dependencies, resources and operations to achieve the defined business goals.
- It employs graphics with a small number of primitives.

The i* framework consists of two models: the **strategic dependency model (SD)** and the **strategic rationale model (SR)**. Both models are complementary and they are composed of a set of primitive actors, related by a dependency.

An *SD* model describes a network of dependency relationships among various actors in an organizational context. The actor is usually identified within the context of the model. This

model shows who an actor is and who depends on the work of an actor. An SD model consists of a set of nodes and links connecting the actors. Nodes represent actors and each link represents a dependency between two actors. Nodes represent actors and each link represents a dependency between two actors. In the context of the i* framework, actors refer to generic entities that have intentionality. To reflect different degrees of concreteness of agency, the concepts of roles, positions and agents are defined as specializations of actors.
An *SR* model (Yu, 1996) is useful for modeling the motivations of each actor and their dependencies, and provides information about how actors achieve their goals and soft goals. This model only includes elements considered important enough as to have an impact on the results of a goal. The *SR* model (Yu, 1996) shows the dependencies of the actors by including the SD model. According to these dependencies, the SR model specifies achievement goals, soft goals, tasks and resources. Compared with the SD model, SR models provide a more detailed level of modeling. Intentional elements (achievement goals, soft goals, tasks, resources) appear in the SR model not only as external dependencies, but also as internal elements linked by *means-ends* relationships and *task-decompositions*. The *means-end* links provide understanding about why an actor would engage in some tasks, pursue a goal, need a resource, or want a soft goal; the *task-decomposition* links provide a hierarchical description of intentional elements that make up a routine.
There are three different types of actors (Alencar et al., 2000):

1. The depending actor is called *depender*
2. The actor who is depended upon is called the *dependee.*
3. The *depender* depends on the *dependee* for something to be achieved: the *dependum.*

There are four types of dependency (Alencar et al., 2000), classed according to the type of freedom allowed in the relationship:

1. *Resource Dependency*: In a resource dependency, an actor depends on another for the availability of some entity. Resources can be physical or informational.
2. *Task Dependency*: In a task dependency, an actor depends on another to carry out an activity. The task specification prescribes how the task is to be performed.
3. *Goal Dependency*: In a goal dependency, an actor depends on another actor to bring about a certain state or condition in the world. The *dependee* is given the freedom to choose how to do this.
4. *Soft-Goal Dependency*: A soft-goal dependency is similar to a goal dependency except that there are no a priori, sharply defined success criteria. The meaning of the soft goal is elaborated on and clarified between the *depender* and the *dependee* in terms of the methods that might be used to address it.

4. Business modeling

The process of building a business model that could result in the requirements of a data mining project is divided into two phases. The first step of the process is to elicit information to gain a proper understanding of the business domain. In the second phase, the business decision-making model is then developed based on the collected information.

4.1 Business domain understanding

The business domain of an organization is usually fairly complex and should be fully understood before initiating the development of any project. The success of a data mining project will largely depend on the correct understanding of the project goals and requirements from a business or institutional viewpoint. So the objective here is to define a process to develop the task of understanding the business domain and establish a common vision with future users about the key project goals.

For the first phase of the data mining project life cycle (*Business Understanding*), the CRISP-DM development guide (Chapman, et al., 2000) proposes, among other things, two key tasks:

1. *Determine business objectives*: The first objective of the data analyst is to thoroughly understand, from a business perspective, what the client really wants to accomplish and which are the important factors that can influence the outcome of the project in the first instance.
2. *Assess situation*: This task involves more detailed fact-finding about all of the resources, constraints, assumptions and other factors that should be considered in determining the data analysis goal and project plan.

The above tasks are not easy to perform, and CRISP-DM does not suggest any methodological process for this purpose. Considering how important these tasks are for developing the business model, we present a methodological process that is designed to give project participants a better understanding of the organizational structure, strategic objectives, processes, business logic and other elements of the organization for which the future data mining system is to be developed.

The development of the proposal presented below involves identifying the relevant information to be elicited (based on the description of the essential components of a business model (Osterwalde et al., 2005), (Lagha et al, 2004)). This will give an overview of the business, identify the sources of such information and apply techniques and tools for requirements elicitation. The process of discovering and later specifying information related to the business domain is divided into two steps:

1. First, information is gathered to gain a view of the current company scenario (static vision of the business), that is, understand the components (tasks, organizational goals or requirements, organizational structure, products / services, market) that defines the organization and its environment at the start of the project.
2. Second, we have to elicit some information (see Figure 1) related to factors that influence or affect the achievement of objectives such as resources, capabilities, restrictions, SWOT analysis, etc. The achievement of organizational goals is in itself a definition of the future scenario of the organization.

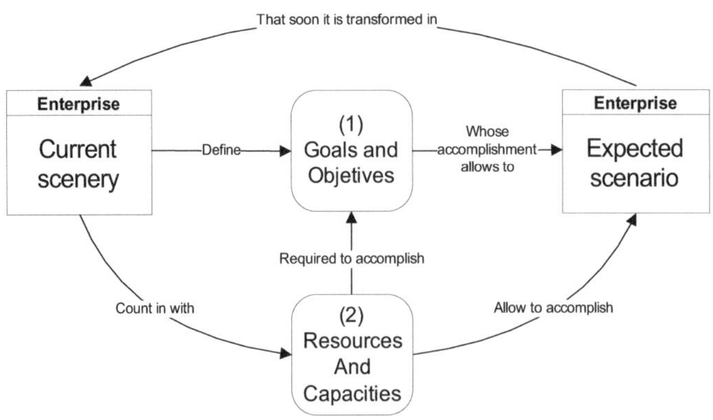

Fig. 1. Information about the business domain

Figure 2 shows a summary concept map. It includes a definition of the information that must be elicited in the above steps.
The aim of this concept map is to show, at a high level of abstraction, the key information (and its relevance) to be elicited to understand the business domain in the first instance.

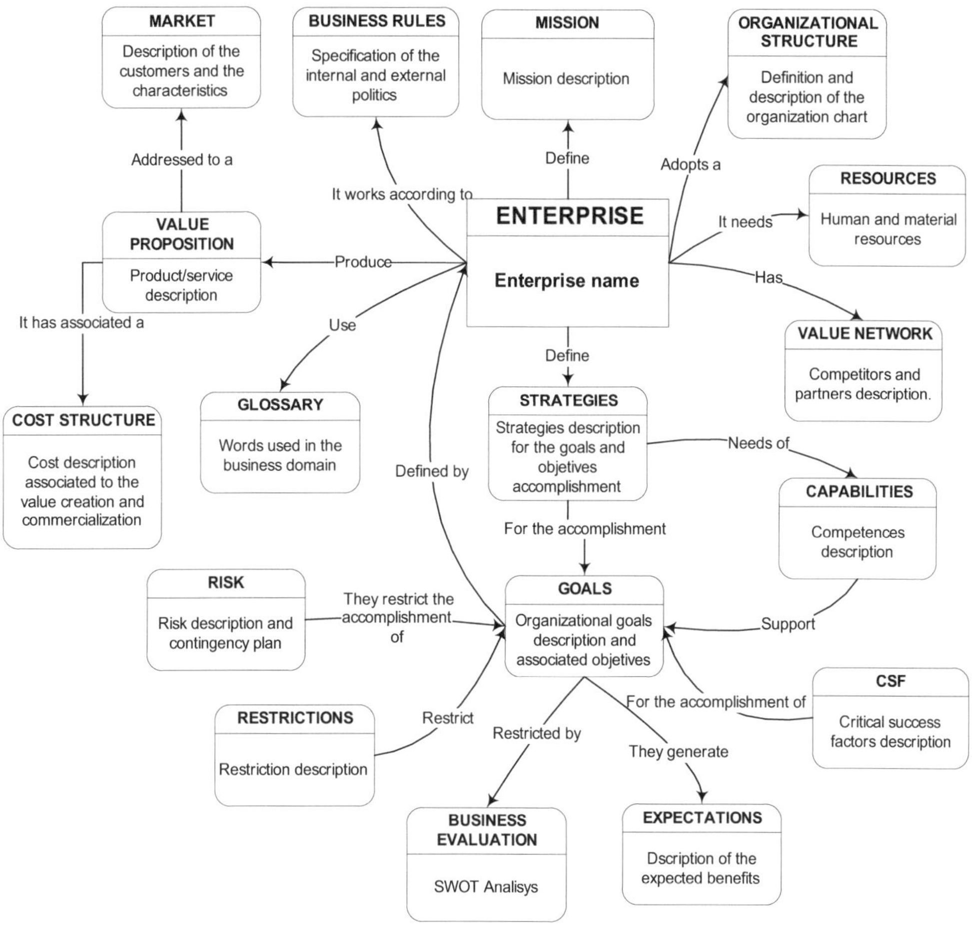

Fig. 2. Concept map that describes the business domain (based on (Ochoa, 2006))

4.2 Business decision-making model

After completing the business domain understanding phase and having identified the organizational goals, it is time to model the decision-making process. We propose a sequence of steps or stages for enacting this process (Figure 3).
The information required for each step can be elicited by requirements engineering and knowledge engineering techniques, such as interviews and questionnaires, JAD techniques, protocol analysis or laddering. A description by steps is given below.

4.2.1 Defining the initial goal of the decision-making process

This first step should identify the strategic goal underlying the decision-making process to be modeled from the organizational goals discovered in the business domain understanding

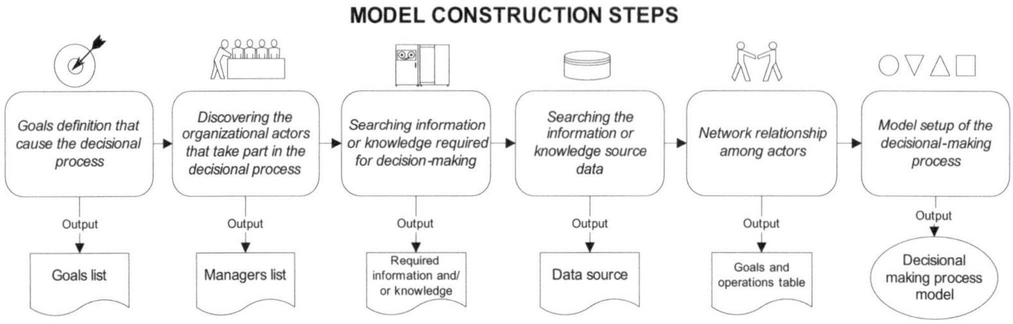

Fig. 3. Modeling process

step. Later, this goal will be the main objective to be achieved. It will be divided into a series of lower-level goals. These goals could then be further divided into a series of tasks developed by the organizational actors.

4.2.2 Discovering the organizational actors that take part in the decision-making process

Note, firstly, that there are different organizational actors inside an organization. These actors take part in the decision-making process at different levels of the organizational pyramid (Laudon & Laudon, 2004). The decisions made at the operational and knowledge levels are structured, that is, they are decisions based on procedures in place inside the organization. These decisions are not innovative and tend to recur. However, as the process progresses towards the strategic levels, decision-making becomes non-structured with less certain outcomes that affect the whole organization. Once all these considerations have been taken into account, the actors that make strategic decisions ('primary actors') must be identified at the respective level (Laudon & Laudon, 2004). Additionally, some actors that do not make decisions but do take part in the decision-making process also have to be identified ('secondary actors').

4.2.3 Eliciting the information or knowledge needed to make decisions

This third step should discover the information or knowledge to be gathered or assimilated for decision making by the primary organizational actors. This discovered information or knowledge will constitute potential goals to be achieved at the lowest level of the model on the way towards achieving the general goal underlying the decision-making process. In this step, there is an additional challenge for the knowledge modelers or engineers. This is to discover, as far as possible, all the factors that are not explicitly defined and could be unconsciously considered by the decision maker.

4.2.4 Determining useful data to be used as information or knowledge sources

The objective of this step is to determine all necessary data sources from which the decision makers can gather information or knowledge. At this point, it is important to consider that data are not necessarily available inside the organization. That is, data could be merged from diverse, both internal and external, organizational sources. Finally, it is important to discover and consider all necessary resources since data are the raw material of a data mining project.

4.2.5 Defining the dependency network among the different organizational actors

The purpose of this step is to determine how to establish the dependency network between the different actors involved in the decision-making process underlying the project. That is, the objective is to define how the actors are related to each other, and how responsible they are for the tasks required to achieve the established goals.

A refined goal tree can be built from the information elicited in the above steps (Glinz, 2000) (Martinez et al., 2002). In this goal tree, the highest-level goal is divided into achievement goals, operations and actors. All the recorded information will ultimately constitute the basic information for building a graphical representation of the decision-making process. Table 1 describes the notation used to define the refined goal tree.

SYMBOL	DEFINITION	SYMBOL	DEFINITION
GG	General Goals	AO	Associated Operations
AG	Achievement Goals	RA	Responsible Actors

Table 1. Acronyms to be used

4.2.6 Building the decision process model

Our proposal is to model the decision-making process in a five-step sequence (Figure 4).

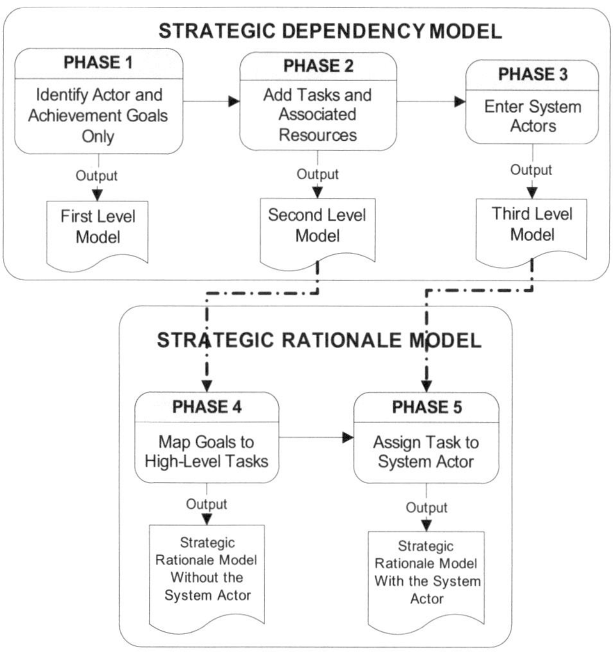

Fig. 4. Modeling Process

This is the last modeling process step and consists of applying the i* framework in order to graphically represent the information that was captured in the previous steps. To do this, we use the two complementary models defined by the technique: the *SD model* and the *SR model.*

a. *SD model*

This is the highest-level model, and its objective is to represent the actors who take part in the decision-making process and their dependency links. These links can be achievement goals, soft goals, tasks, or required and/or generated resources, necessary to achieve the general goals, previously identified in the first step of the process. A three-step incremental development is proposed:

Step 1. Develop a very basic preliminary model (first-level model) with a high level of abstraction. The objective of this model is for all the stakeholders to be able to understand what the model represents in the simplest way at an achievement goal level. This preliminary model only identifies actors that take part in the process or in the dependency network. The dependencies are defined in the refinement goal tree.

Step 2. Develop a second model (second-level model) with a higher level of detail. This second model represents the tasks originated by each achievement goal, the resources to achieve these goals and resources produced while developing process tasks or operations.

Step 3. Define a third model (third-level model) to complete the construction of the SD model), adding the "system" actors. The highest-level achievement goals initially defined in the first-level model are now divided into simpler tasks or operations. Subsequently, we analyze which tasks could be automated or which activities require the support of a software system. This information should be previously entered in the refinement goal tree. The tasks identified for automation are used by the system and converted at this point into new achievement goals that are linked to the system actor. These new goals will are potential use cases in the future system requirements model.

b. *SR model*

The second model's aim is to more explicitly represent the resources and the granular events (scenario) that originate the required activities to accomplish the achievement goals. The model can also be developed incrementally to give a better process understanding. The number of steps depends on many factors, such as the organizational complexity, modelers' experience, experts' business domain knowledge, and stakeholders' knowledge of the i* framework.

Step 4. For simplicity's sake, modeling is initially based on the second-level SD model that was output in Step 2. This does not include the system actor. In this step, the achievement goals from the SD model (which were part of the dependency model network) are mapped to high-level tasks. These tasks can be divided by the *task-decomposition* constructor into less complex tasks or into elementary operations that can, depending on their complexity level, be developed by some particular actor. The '*means-end*' constructor is used to represent more than one alternative to achieve a goal or task. Note also that every resource involved in the process involves the specification of the resource's sending and receiving operations in the '*dependee*' actor and in the '*depender*', respectively.

Step 5. To finish the modeling process, we have to take into account that some of the tasks that have to be developed by some organizational actors need software system support in order to process data and information. For that reason, we add the *system* actor, and consequently, this model has to be built depending on the third-level SD model (Step 3). All the tasks to be automated that were represented as achievement goals in the SD model are assigned to the *system* actor. Then, the achievement goals of the third-level SD model, which are mapped into high level tasks, are divided into more specific tasks depending on what resources there are and the specific problem's specialization level. Later, this decomposition of high-level tasks (achievement goals in the SD model) into simpler tasks and associated resources is destined to represent the use case scenario in the requirements model.

5. Deriving requirements

In this section, we describe how to build the use case model from the previously built business decision-making model (figure 5).

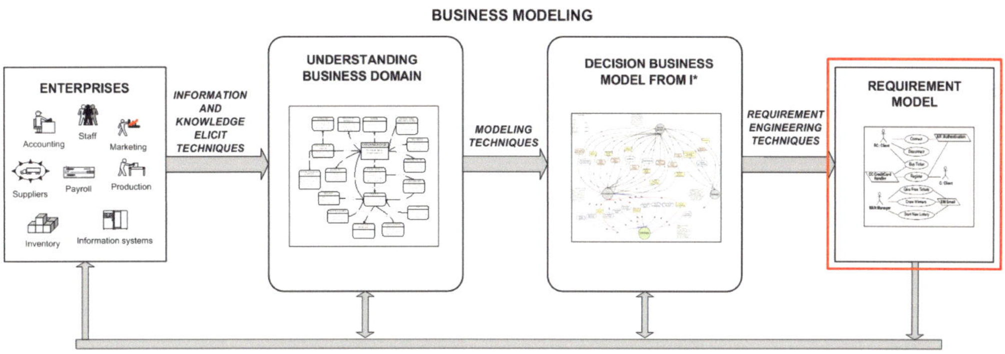

Fig. 5. Requirements modeling process

There are several approaches for extracting software requirements from a business model, like (Ortín et al., 2000), (Alencar et al., 2000) or (Santander & Castro, 2002). The transition guide used in this work is based on Santander and Castro's approach (Santander & Castro, 2002). In (Santander & Castro, 2002), transition from an organizational model to the requirements model is divided into three consecutive steps (see Figure 6). Unlike the approach presented in (Santander & Castro, 2002), use case definition in this research is restricted to the use cases that are derived from the achievement goal dependencies. This restriction is derived from the fact that, in a data mining system, a use case must basically represent the achievement goal that the user intends to achieve using the information or knowledge that the data mining system provides and never a task or goal as in a development-related process. In (Santander & Castro, 2002), use cases can be mapped from a goal dependency, a task dependency or a resource dependency.

Taking into account that we built an organizational model using the i* framework, identifying the actors that participate in the decision-making process, and the main achievement goals are part of a more general strategic goal, the main inputs for building the use case model will be the SD and SR models.

Step 1. ***Identifying system actors.*** There are several actors that participate in a business decision-making process (i* SD model). They are identified and placed in the refined goal tree; however use case actors are (directly or indirectly) linked to system actors by some kind of achievement goal dependency. Actors that are independent of the system actors cannot be considered use case actors. Additionally, if there are two or more actors that share any dependency linked by an is-a relationship in the i* model, they must be mapped as individual actors in the use case model, linked by a new generalization relationship.

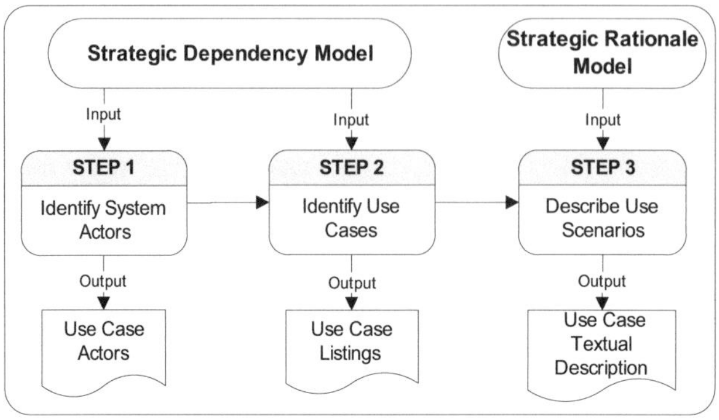

Fig. 6. Requirements modelling activities (based on (Santander & Castro, 2002))

Step 2. ***Identifying Use Cases.*** Taking the SD model as input, every goal dependency (dependum) must be identified. Actors identified in Step 1 play the dependee role or the depender role in the dependency relationship.

- An actor that plays the *dependee* role in a goal relationship must provide an informational resource and the dependency object (*dependum*) and the system will generate a use case as output.
- An actor that plays the depender role in a dependency with the system must provide knowledge and information in order to achieve the goals related to the identified use case. In this case, the dependency object (dependum) is again turned into a use case.

Step 3. ***Describing use case scenarios.*** The description of the use case scenario related to a specific actor is the third requirements modeling step. Therefore, it includes a description of the event sequence for carrying out tasks and getting resources related to goal achievement. The SR model graphically represents this event sequence. The description of the scenarios associated with use cases is no more than the textual description of a use case, including the field of action of every actor that participates in the achievement of a goal, task or resource represented in the SR model.

6. Case study

In this section, we describe a case study to illustrate the proposed methodology. This case study addresses the creation of a new program of studies at a technical-vocational training institute. The purpose of the case study is to assess the proposed procedure in a real situation in order to illustrate its use and get conclusions for refining the proposed methodology. The scope of developing a case study is limited to modeling the business decision-making process related to the creation of a new program of studies at a technical-vocational training institute (TVTI). This model will then be used to output a requirements model for a data mining system that supports the decision-making process. The assessment method consists of comparing the case study results with other project results in which the methodology was not used.

6.1 Understanding the business domain

This is the first step for modeling business decision-making. It consists of eliciting as much information as possible about the organization. This information will help stakeholders to assimilate all elements that they need to know to understand the organizational problems to be solved. For example, the elicited information is as follows:

The institution helps to provide people with technical-vocational training that is certified, whenever possible, by accredited bodies. To do this, it teaches the outcomes and values required by the region's industrial and service sectors. The organizational structure and decision-making levels at the institution are set out in the articles of the institution and in TVTI Council meeting minutes. The Council and Executive Committee are in charge of defining the organizational structure and decision-making levels.

In this case study, the head teacher is in charge of proposing the opening of new programs of study to the Council. The Council is responsible for studying and validating the information given by the Executive Director to support the proposal of opening a new degree. Finally, the Executive Director is assisted by a group of collaborators that advise and support the Executive Director, and they must collect and process the information related to the proposal.

On top of this, the institution has the mechanisms and structure required to identify and select the facilities and equipment needed to implement the program. Taking into account the knowledge and outcomes to be learned by the students, the Curricular Committee has to estimate the costs and investment needs for each program to decide whether existing equipment is to be used or it has to be renewed.

6.2 Modeling the decision-making process

In this section we describe the application of the guide proposed in Section 4.2 in order to obtain the decision-making process model of the case study.

6.2.1 Identifying the underlying goal of the decision-making process

From the information elicited in the understanding of the business domain step, we deduce that the underlying goal of the decision-making process is to materialize one of the strategic goals set by the organization: 'provide ongoing technical-vocational training programs that continuously meet the demands of the region's industrial and service sectors'.

6.2.2 Identifying organizational actors that participates in the decision-making process

In this step, we have to identify the actors that participate in the decision-making process. Table 2 shows the identified actors involved in opening the new degree process.

ROLE	ACTOR TYPE	ROLE	ACTOR TYPE
Executive Director	Primary	Consultants	Secondary
Council	Primary		

Table 2. Stakeholders

6.2.3 Eliciting information or knowledge needed to make decisions

According to the elicited information, the decision about whether or not to open a new degree depends on the following information or knowledge:

1. There is a market as companies are demandinmg technical professionals with the profile that the new degree offers, and there are future students interested in taking the new degree

2. Feasibility study
3. Support throughout time

6.2.4 Identifying data sources

Table 3 shows the data sources that are available at the beginning of the study. However, Table 3 also shows unavailable data sources that will be required later.

INFORMATION	DATA SOURCES	STATE	DESCRIPTION
Market	Sale management (training)	Available	Data about taught training courses
	Innovation	Available	Data derived from the use of new technologies or new procedures introduced by companies.
	...	...	...
Feasibility study	Utilities	Not Available	Data about utilities that the new degree offers.
	Cost structure	Not Available	Involved cost.
	...	...	...
Support	Student behaviour	Available	Useful data to predict drop-out and graduation rates.
	...	...	...

Table 3. Data sources (partial)

6.2.5 Defining the dependency network between different organizational actors

This step consists of refining the goals included in the goal tree (see Table 4) that defines the general goals, including derived operations, participant actors, and dependency level among actors. Column 1 in Table 4 shows a hierarchy of the identified goals. The general goal is located at the top. The next level contains the existing achievement goals. Finally, the derived operations are entered. Column 2 shows the type of the goal, operation, or available resource. Column 3 shows the actors involved in the process of achieving established goals and executing operations.

6.2.6 Decision process modeling

SD model

Step 1. This step builds the first-level model. The input is the refined goal tree (Table 4). The model includes the organizational actors that participate in the process and in the goal dependency network only. Figure 7 illustrates this first model for this case study. In the refined goal tree, the first actor in the actor column represents the *depender* and the second actor represents the *dependee* for each goal. The model shows, for instance, that the Executive Director actor (*depender*) depends on whether or not the Council actor (*dependee*) has validated the Reports (*dependum*) submitted by the Executive Director in the development of achievement goal 4.

GOAL NAME	TYPE	ACTORS
New program establishment	GG	Executive Director, Consultants, Executive Council
1. Market knowledge	AG	Executive Director - Consultants
1.1. Data supply	AO	Consultants - Executive Director
…	…	…
2. Feasibility	AG	Executive Director - Consultants
2.1. Data supply	AO	Consultants - Executive Director
…	…	…
3. Support	AG	Executive Director - Consultants
3.1. Data supply	AO	Consultores - Executive Director
…	…	…
4. Report validation	AG	Executive Director - Executive Council
4.1. Send report	AO	Executive Council - Executive Director
…	…	…

Table 4. Goal and operation table for the case under study (partial)

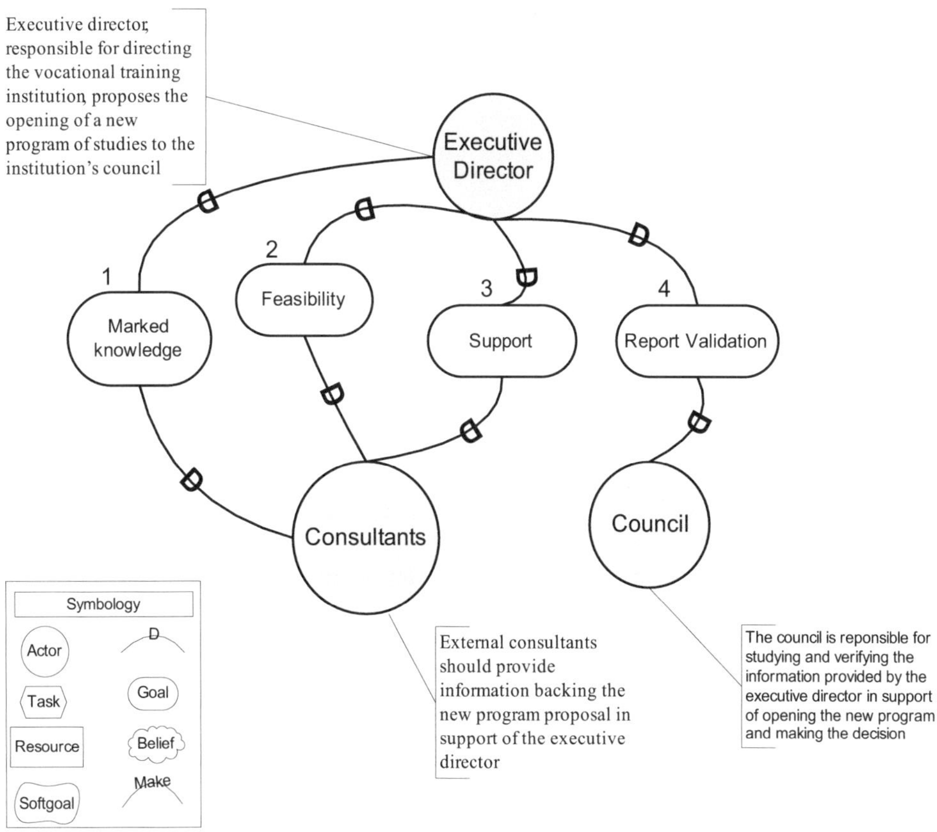

Fig. 7. First-level SD model

Step 2. This second model includes the tasks and resources needed by each achievement goal. Figure 8 shows the model output after completing this second step. For instance, this model specifies the tasks to be performed in order to achieve achievement goal 1 (market knowledge):

1. Executive Director actor (dependee in the task dependency relationship) must send required data to Consultants actor (depender)
2. Consultants actor (dependee) must develop the market analysis.
3. Consultants actor (dependee) must send analysis results to Director actor (depender).

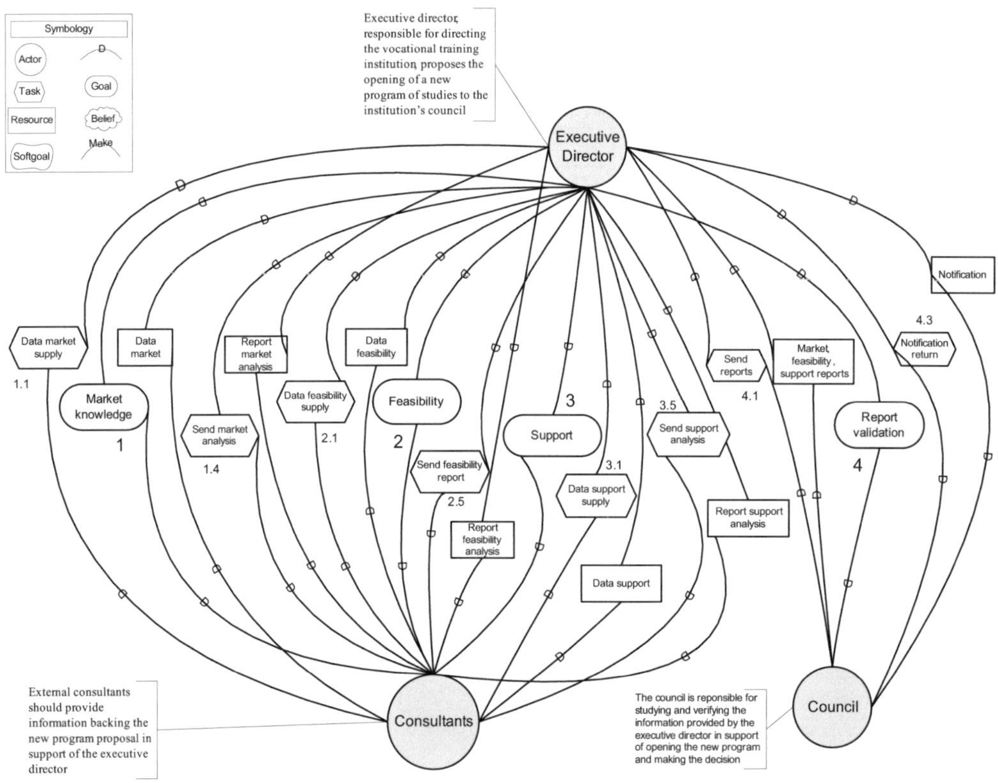

Fig. 8. Second-level SD model

Step 3. The final SD model (Figure 9) includes the system actor that is the responsible for the tasks and activities for which a software system is needed. In this third model, the Consultants actor delegates the data analysis involved in market, feasibility and support analysis to the system actor. Then, these tasks become achievement goals linked to the system actor, and the system actor becomes a *dependee* actor in the dependency relationship with the Consultants actor. It is important to include the system actor in this model since it will be easier to identify the main use cases later on.

SR Model

Following the modeling process, it is now time to build the SR model that justifies the dependencies between the different organizational actors in more detail.

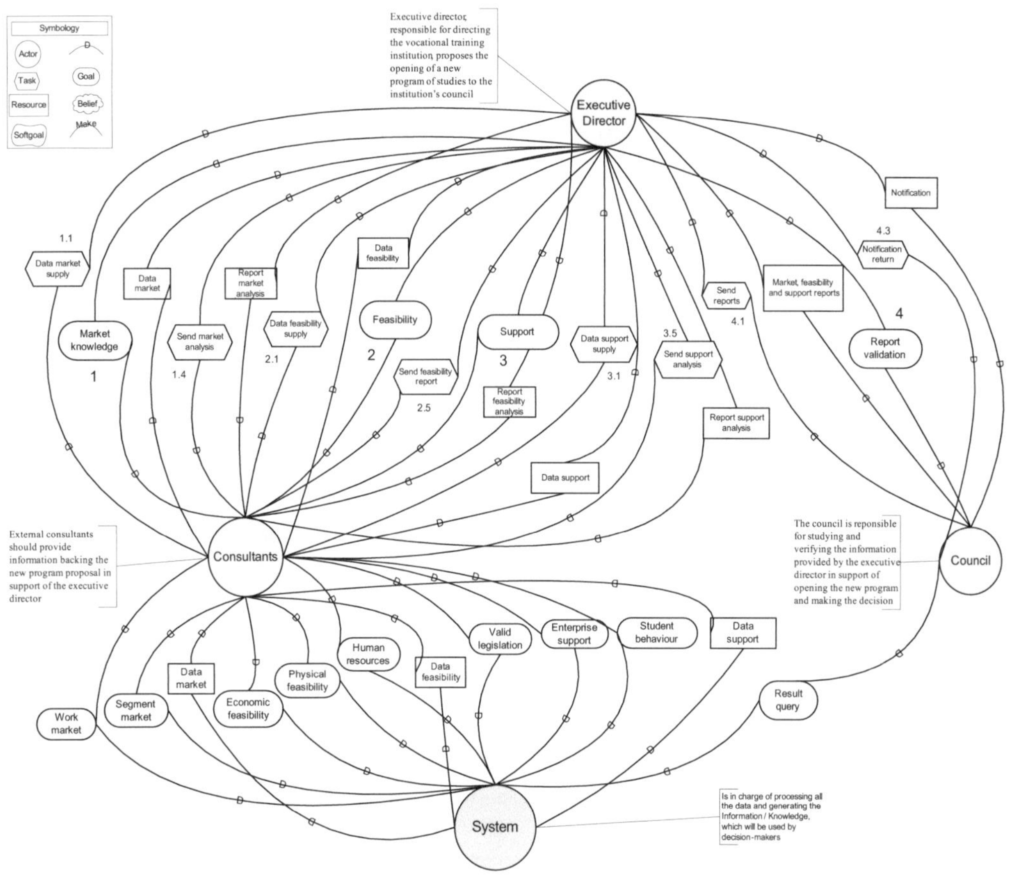

Fig. 9. Third-level SD model

Step 4. The second-level SD model will be used for modeling to gain a higher level vision. The general goal in this case study is *open a new program of study*. This general goal triggers a sequence of goals, such as *market, feasibility and support studies*. These studies are achievement goals (*dependum*) in the SD model, and they are linked to the *Executive Director* (*depender*) and *Consultants* (*dependee*) actors (Figure 10). These studies involve three high level tasks: *market study query, feasibility study query* and *support study query*. Consequently, the *Executive Director* delegates these studies to the *External Consultants* actor. Resource dependency networks are developed when the *Consultants* actor starts these tasks, and these tasks can be divided into smaller tasks such as writing and sending reports.

Step 5. The modeling process ends with the development of the SR Model (Figure 11), including the System actor. Achievement goals in the third-level SR model are converted into third-level tasks (business domain analysis, market analysis, economic feasibility analysis, etc.). At the same time, each task is divided into more specific tasks depending on the type of available resources and how specialized each problem is. For instance, the *surveys* subtask that uses survey and questionnaires data applied to several companies.

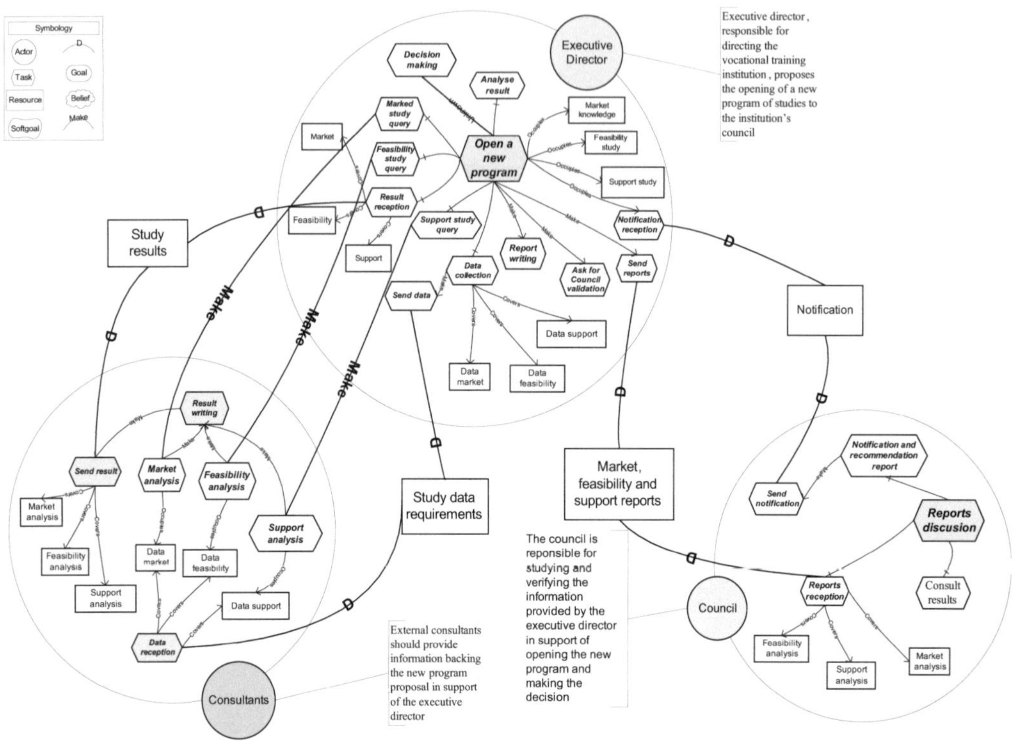

Fig. 10. SR Model

Another feature to be taken into account is the possibility of detailing the different alternatives to be weighed up to achieve a goal or perform a task. In this case study, for instance, tasks involved in the domain analysis can be achieved by validation, discovery and modeling.

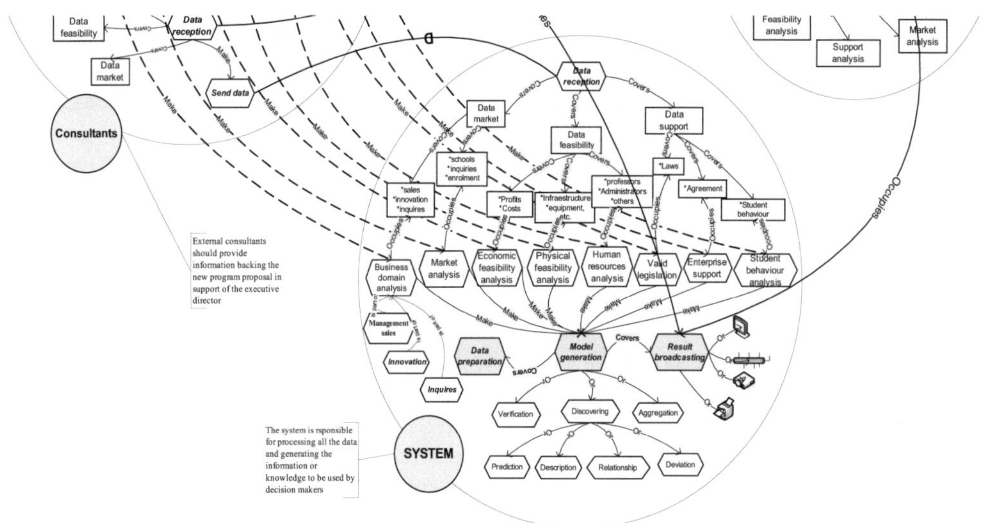

Fig. 11. SR Model with System actor (partial)

6.3 Modeling requirements

In the case under study, after applying the guidelines proposed in Section 4, they are as follows.

Step 1. Defining Use Case Studies:

Starting with the SD model output in the case under study (Figure 9) and applying the first step of the guidelines proposed in Section 4, three potential use case actors are identified: *Executive Director*, *External Consultants* and *Council*.

Looking at the model, we find that the *Council* actor has a dependency network with *System* actor by *'result query'* goal. The *'result query'* goal is a consequence of the *'report study'* achievement goal between *Council* and *Executive Director* actors. Therefore, *Council* actor is a potential actor.

The *External Consultants* actor is also a potential actor since there are dependency networks between *External Consultants* actor and *System* actor through several achievement goals.

There is no dependency network between *Executive Director* actor and *System* actor, therefore *Executive Director* is not considered an actor in the use case model.

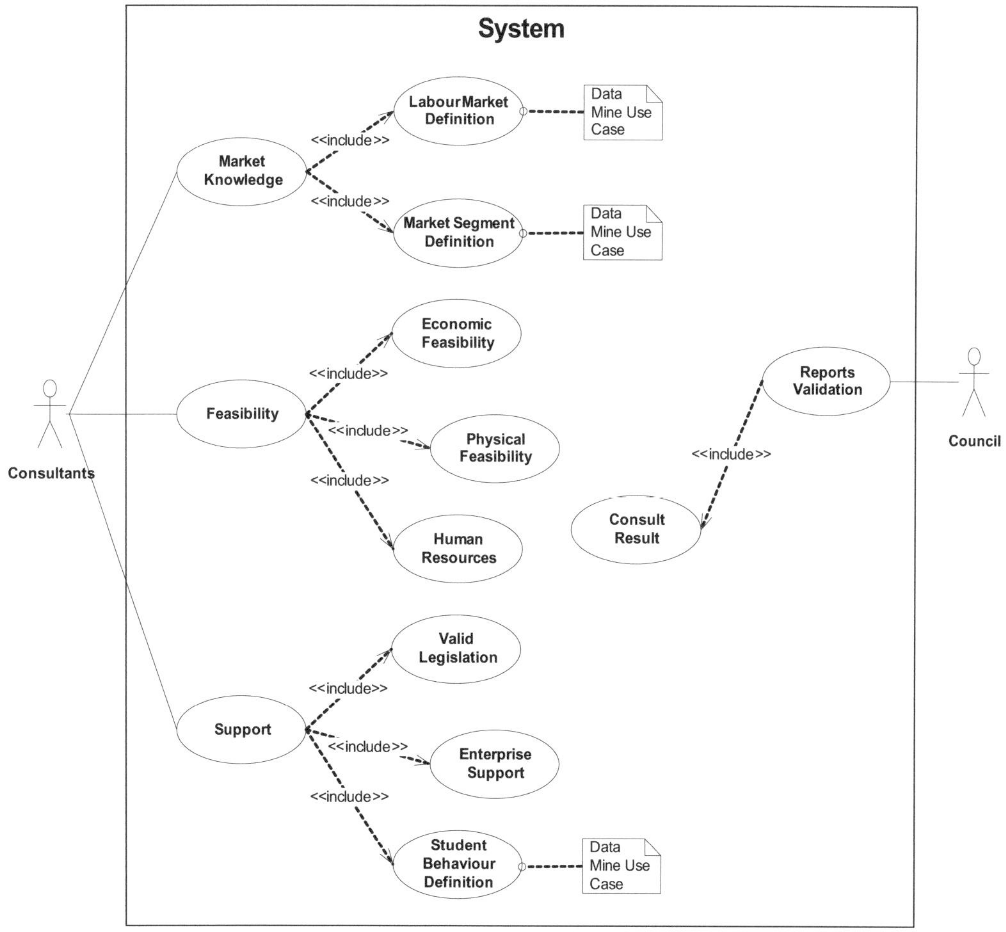

Fig. 12. Use case diagram for the system under study

***Step 2. Defining Use Cases*:**
Taking the SD model (Figure 9) as input, we can identify, according to Step 2 of the guidelines, the following use cases

1. Taking into account the identification of goal dependency networks in which previously identified actors play *a dependee* role in the dependency network, the following elements are identified:
   Actor: *Council* / Dependency objects: *Report Validation* / Actor: *Consultants* / Dependency objects: *Market knowledge, Feasibility, Support.*
2. Taking into account the identification of goal dependency networks, in which actors play a *depender* role in the dependency network with the System Actor, the following elements are identified:
   Actor: *Council* / Dependency objects: *Result query* / Actor: *Consultants* / Dependency objects: *Business domain, Market segment, Economic Feasibility, Physical Feasibility, Human Resources, Current Law, and Student Behavior.*

In the case under study, the use case diagram (Figure 12) obtained from i* models is based on standard UML notation. The graphical representation of the model shows the existing relationship between organizational actors and the system. The subsequent model description shows the event sequence that is triggered after an actor runs a use case.

Step 3. Describing the use case scenario

A description model is written for every identified use case to complete use case modeling. To do this, one of the templates proposed in the scientific literature (Robertson & Robertson, 1999) (Larman, 2003) can be used. The description must include actor intentions, and the responsibilities associated with the system.

Use Case	**Market Segment Definition** **ID: RQ_006** **Type: DM** **Creation Date: 22/11/07**
Description	This use case involves the data analysis of a specific market segment. It can predict potential students for a new program of studies.
Primary Actor	External Consultants
Assumptions	All the data required to run the study are available.
Resources	1. Regional school data 2. Results of surveys and questionnaires 3. Statistics related to Enrolment in Institutes and Universities
Steps	1. Provision of all the market data received by the head teacher by consultants 2. Definition of the data required for the study. 3. Data preparation 4. Definition of the models for developing the study 5. Results presentation

Table 5. Textual description of 'Market Segment Definition' use case

In this way, we will detail when actors ask for services or provide resources to the system and when the system gives information to the system actor. The information required to describe the use cases can be obtained from the SR Model (Figure 12). Table 5 shows an example of the description process for the 'Market Segment Definition' use case. After finishing the descriptions of all data mining use cases, the data mining requirements specification is developed.

7. Evaluation of the proposed methodology

In order to establish an evaluation baseline and estimate the benefit of the proposed methodology, we compare two instances in which a data mining project was developed. In both cases, the problem domain is the same and the objectives are similar; however, the users and the data analysts are different in both cases because the two project instances were developed at different times. The results are compared in Table 6.

CRITERIA	PROJECT A: NOT APPLYING THE METHODOLOGY	PROJECT B: APPLYING THE METHODOLOGY
Goal achievement	The objectives were established informally and therefore when the project ended it was difficult to establish if the business objectives were fulfilled.	The project's objectives were well-established and were clearly aligned with the business objectives.
User participation	User participation dropped significantly during the project development time.	Users participated actively in all stages of the project.
Development time	The development time was greater than initially planned (the project took over 30% longer)	The development time was as initially scheduled.
Effort	Workload was greater than initially planned (over 40% more than the initially estimated person/hours).	The development effort was as initially planned.

Table 6. Comparing two projects to report benefits of the methodology

Project A (developed without the implementation of the proposed methodology) tried to identify relevant factors, to discriminate between higher education students that failed and students who successfully completed their undergraduate programs. The search was based on information about the university students' income. Descriptive models were used to build predictive models to forecast the likelihood of a new student enrolling for an undergraduate program successfully completing the program.

Project B (developed using the proposed methodology) tried to support a specific and strategic goal of the organization, which is "to improve the academic work assessment and academic support systems, and the management control of financial resources and organizational materials".

In general, from the development of the data mining project applying the methodology, we found that the methodology actually brings together a number of relevant aspects that should be considered at the beginning of the development of a data mining project, such as the requirements to be met by the project, the necessary resources, the project risks and constraints and, generally, all important aspects to be taken into account and that emerge from the business domain understanding phase outlined by the CRISP-DM standard.

8. Conclusions

In the presented work, we proposed a new methodology that consists of a sequence of steps for developing a business model of a decision-making process in a company or organization. The methodology uses the business model is as input to get organizational requirements and use cases applied to data mining projects. A decision-making process model is useful for defining what tasks of the strategic decision-making process can be supported by a data mining project and, also, outputs the initial project requirements.

A requirements model ensures that data mining project results will meet users' needs and expectations, effectively supporting the decision-making process involved in achieving the organizational goals. The construction of the organizational model, which will be used to model the requirements, is based on an incremental and iterative process that provides a better understanding of the business. Additionally, it is useful for reaching agreement, negotiating and validating that the model faithfully represents the organization's decision-making process and checking that the business problem really requires the support of a data mining system.

Note that not only can the requirements model, output based on the organization's business model, identify data mining use cases; it can also pinpoint other functionalities that can be implemented by other conventional software systems that work together with the data mining systems in order to achieve organizational goals.

As regards the modeling technique used in this research, we have shown that the i* framework has valuable features that make a decision-making process model easier to develop. Another important idea is the fact that the i* framework is useful for explicitly representing non-functional requirements associated with functional requirements in the organizational business model. This can be done using the soft goal dependency objects.

9. References

Aguilar Savén R.S. (2004), "Business process modelling: Review and framework", International Journal of Production Economics. Vol. 90, No. 2, p. 129 - 149.

Alencar F., et al. (2000), "From Early Requirements Modeled by the i* Technique to Later Requirements Modeled in Precise UML", III Workshop de Engenharia de Requisitos.

Berenbach B. (2004), "Comparison of UML and Text based Requirements Engineering", 19th annual ACM SIGPLAN Conf. on Object-oriented programming systems, languages, and applications (OOPSLA'04).

BPMI. (2004), Business Process Management Initiative: Business Process Modeling Notation (BPMN), Specification Version 1.0, May 3.

BPMN_OMG. (2006), "Business Process Modeling Notation Specification", OMG Final Adopted Specification, OMG.

Bruckner R., et al. (2001), "Developing Requirements for Data Warehouse Systems with Use Cases", Seventh Americas Conference on Information Systems, pp. 329-335.

Castro, J., et al. (2001), "Integrating Organizal Requirements and Object Oriented Modeling", Proceedings of the 5th IEEE International Symposium on Requirements Engineering

Chapman P., et al. (2000), "CRISP-DM 1.0 step-by-step data mining guide", Technical report, 2000.

Chatam B., et al.(2002), "CMR's future: Humble growth through 2007".
Cysneiros L. & Sampaio, J. C. (2004), Nonfuncional Requirements: from elicitation to conceptual models, IEEE TRANSACTIONS ON SOFTWARE ENGINEERING, VOL. 30, NO. 5.
Dale M. (2004), "Defining user requirements for a large corporate data warehouse: an experiential case study", 9th Australian Workshop on Requirements Engineering, pp. 5.1-5.11.
Davyt N. (2001), "Ingeniería de requerimientos: una guía para extraer, analizar, especificar y validar los requerimientos de un proyecto", Facultad de Ingeniería, Universidad ORT del Uruguay.
DiLauro L. (2000), "What's next in monitoring technology? Data Mining Finds a Calling in Call Centers".
Eisenfeld B. (2003), et al., "42 percent of CMR software goes unused", http://www.gartner.com, February 2003.
Firesmith D. (2003), "Engineering Security Requirements", in *Journal of Object Technology*, vol. 2, no. 1, January-February, pp. 53-68
Gacitúa R. (2001), Identification of requirements: a focus based on a verb taxonomy, Theoria, Vol. 10: 67-78, ISSN 0717-196X.
Gerhard Armin P. (1997), "Requirements Acquisition and Specification for Telecommunication Services", tesis doctoral, University of Wales, Swansea, UK.
Glinz M. (2000), "Problems and Deficiencies of UML as a Requirements Specification Language", Proc. of the 10th Int. Workshop on Software Specification and Design (IWSSD'00).
Gordijn, J., et al. (2000), "Value Based Requirements Creation for Electronic Comerce Applications", Proceedings of the Hawaii Internacional Conf. On System Sciences, January 4-7, Hawaii.
Gordijn, J. (2003), "Value-based Requirements Engineering Exploring Innovative e-Commerce Ideas", VRIJE UNIVERSITEIT.
Gordijn J., & Akkermans. H. (2007), Business Models for Distributed Energy Resources In a Liberalized Market Environment. In *The Electric Power Systems Research Journal*, Vol. 77(9):1178–1188, Elsevier.
Gorschek T. & Claes W. (2006), "Requirements Abstraction Model", Requirements Eng, 11: 79–101, DOI 10.1007/s00766-005-0020-7.
Han J., & Kamber M. (2001), "Data Mining: Concepts and Techniques", Academic Press.
Hayes J. & Finnegan P. (2005), "Assessing the of potential of e-business models: towards a framework for assisting decision-makers", European Journal of Operational Research 160(2): 365-379.
Heitmeyer, C. & Bharadwaj, R. (2000), "Applying the SCR Requirements Method to the Light Control Case Study." *Journal of Universal Computer Science 6*, 7: 650-678.
Heninger, K., et al. (1978), "Software Requirements for the A-7E Aircraft." *Technical Report 3876*. Washington, D.C.: Naval Research Laboratory.
Heninger, K. L. (1980) "Specifying Software Requirements for Complex Systems: New Techniques and their Application." *IEEE Trans. on Software Engineering SE-6,* 1 (January): 2-13.
Hermiz, K. (1999), "Critical Success Factors for Data Mining Projects", DM Review Magazine, February, 1999,

http://www.dmreview.com/issues/19990201/164-1.html.

Johnston, S. (2004), "Rational UML Profile for Business Modeling", Julio, 2004, Disponible en línea http://www-128.ibm.com/developerworks/rational/library/5167.html#author1

Kantardzic M., & Zurada J. (2005), "Trends in Data Mining Applications:From Research Labs to Fortune 500 Companies", Next Generation of Data Mining Applications", IEEE, Wiley

Kelley Ch., & Adelman, S. (2003), "¿Where can I find sources about failed data mining projects and the reason for their failure?", DM Review Online Published in April 2003. DMReview.com.

Kdnuggets. (2007), http://www.kdnuggets.com/polls/2007/data_mining_methodology.htm.

Knorr, K. & Rohrig, S. (2001), "Security Requirements of E-Business Processes," 73-86. Towards the E-Society: E-Commerce, E-Business, and E-Government. First IFIP Conference on E-Commerce, E-Business, E-Government, Zurich, Switzerland, Oct. 4-5, 2001. Norwell, MA: Kluwer Academic Publishers, (ISBN 0792375297).

Kotonya G., & Sommerville I. (1998), *"Requirements Engineering. Processes and techniques"*, USA. J. Wiley.

Koubarakis M., & Plexousakis D., Business process, modelling and design: a formal model and methodology, BT Technol J Vol 17 No 4 October 1999.

Lagha B., et al. (2004), "An ontology for e-business models" In Value Creation from E-Business Models. W. Currie, Butterworth- Heinemann.

Larman C. (2003), "UML y Patrones, una introducción al análisis y diseño orientado a objetos y al proceso unificado", 2ª. Edición, Ed. Prentice Hall.

Laudon K., & Laudon J. (2004), *"Sistemas de Información Gerencial"*, Ed. Prentice Hall.

Leiwo, J. Et al. (1999), "Organizational Modeling for Efficient Specification of Information Security Requirements," 247-260. *Advances in Databases and Information Systems: Third East European Conference, ADBIS'99*. Maribor, Slovenia, Sept. 13-16, 1999.

Maciaszek L. (2005), *"Requirements Analysis and System Design"*, 2a Edition, Ed. Addison Wesley.

Marbán Ó., et al. (2008), "Towards Data Mining Engineering: a Software Engineering Approach", preprint submitted to Elsevier Science.

Martinez A., et al. (2002), "From Early Requirements to User Interface Prototyping: A methodological approach", 17th IEEE International Conference on Automated Software Engineering 2002, September 23-27, Edinburgh, UK

McDonald P.P., et al. (2006), "Growing its contribution: The 2006 CIO Agenda", Gartner group, http://www.gartner.com.

Medina, J. C. (2004), "Análisis comparativo de técnicas, metodologías y herramientas de Ingeniería de Requerimientos", Tesis Doctoral, CINVESTAV, Junio de 2004, México, D.F. México.

Meta Group Research. (2003), The Top 5 Global 3000 Data Mining Trends for 2003/04 Enterprise Analytics Strategies, Application Delivery Strategies, META Group Research-Delta Summary, 2061.

Mylopoulos J. et al. (2002), "Towards Requirements-Driven Information Systems Engineering: The Tropos Project.To appear in Information Systems", Elsevier, Amsterdam, The Netherlands.

Ochoa, A. (2006), "Uso de Técnicas de Educción para el Entendimiento del Negocio", Tesis de Magister en Ingeniería del Software. Escuela de Postgrado. Instituto Tecn. de Buenos Aires.

Ortín M. J. et al. (2000), "De los procesos de negocio a los casos de uso" , JISBD 2000, Valladolid, España Fecha: Noviembre 2000.

Osterwalder A. et al. (2005), "Clarifying business models: origins, present, and future of the concept", Communications of AIS, Volume 15, Article, May.

Martyn A. (1995), Business Processes - Modelling and Analysis for Re-engineering and Improvement. John Wiley & Sons, Chichester, England.

Pérez C. & Santín D. (2007), "Minería de Datos Técnicas y Herramientas", Ed. Thomson.

Piatetsky-Shaphiro G. & Frawley W. (1991), "Knowledge Discovery in Databases", AAAI/MIT Press, MA.

G. Piatetsky-Shaphiro. (2000), "Knowledge Discovery in Databases: 10 Years After", SIGKDD Explor. Newsl., 1(2):59-61.

Rilston F., Paim S., & Castro J. (2003), "DWARF: An approach for requirements definition and management of data warehouse systems", 11th IEEE International Requirements Engineering Conference (RE'03), p 75.

Robertson S. & Robertson J. (1999), "Mastering the Requirement Process", Ed. Addison - Wesley.

Russell, N., et al. (2006), "On the Suitability of UML 2.0 Activity Diagrams for Business Process Modelling", Third Asia-Pacific Conference on Conceptual Modelling (APCCM2006), Australia. Conferences in Research and Practice in Information Technology, Vol. 53.

Sánchez M. A. (2006), "Una recomendación para el desarrollo de software en un contexto de negocio bajo demanda de acuerdo a la especificación MDA y la arquitectura SOA", tesis doctoral, Universidad Pontificia de Salamanca.

Santander V. & Castro J. (2002), "Deriving Use Cases from Organizational Modeling", Proceedings of the IEEE Joint International Conference on Requirements Engineering (RE'02), IEEE.

Schewe K.D. (2000), "UML: A modern dinosaur? - A critical analysis of the Unified Modelling Language", 10th European - Japanese Conference on Information Modelling and Knowledge Bases, Saariselk, Finlandia.

Slagell, M., et al. (2002), "A Software Fault Tree Approach to Requirements Analysis of an Intrusion Detection System." Requirements Engineering 7, 4 (December): 207-220.

Sommerville I. (2002), "Ingeniería de Software", 6ta. Edición, Ed. Addison Wesley.

Sommerville I. (2005), "Ingeniería de Software", 7ma. Edición, Ed. Addison Wesley.

Sparx Systems (2008) (portal), "UML 2.1 Tutorial", [en línea], disponible en: http://www.sparxsystems.com.au, [Consulta: 13 de febrero de 2008].

Vérosle J., et al. (2003) A generic model for WLAN, hostpots- A roaming, business case in The Netherlands, WMASH'03, Septembre 19, San Diego, California, USA.

Weber M. & Weisbrod J. (2003), "Requirements engineering in automotive development: Experiences and challenges". IEEE Software, pages 16 -24, Enero/Febrero.

White S., IBM Corporation, "Introduction to BPMN", Stephen A. White. All Rights Reserved,
www.bptrends.com, BPTrends July, 2004.

Wilcox, P. & Gurau C. (2003), "Business modelling with UML: the implementation of CRM systems for online Retailing", Journal of Retailing and Consumer Services 10, 2003, available online at www.sciencedirect.com.

Wohed, Petia, et al. (2006), "On the Suitability of BPMN for Business Process Modelling", In proceedings, 4th International Conference on Business Process Management 4102/2006, pages pp. 161-176, Vienna, Austria.

Yu E. (1995), *Modelling Strategic Relationships for Process Reengineering*, Ph.D. thesis, Department of Computer Science, University of Toronto.

Yu Eric S.K. & Mylopoulos J. (1996). "AI Models for Business Process Reengineering.", in IEEE Expert Intelligent Systems and Their Applications. IEEE Computer Society. Volume 11, Number 4. pp. 16-23.

Yu, E. & Mylopoulos J. (1997), "Enterprise Modelling for Business Redesign: the i* Framework", Special Issue: Enterprise Modelling Papers, SIGGROUO, Vol.18, No. 1, April.

7

A Novel Configuration-Driven Data Mining Framework for Health and Usage Monitoring Systems

David He[1], Eric Bechhoefer[2], Mohammed Al-Kateb[2], Jinghua Ma[1], Pradnya Joshi[1] and Mahindra Imadabathuni[1]
[1]*The University of Illinois at Chicago*
[2]*Goodrich Sensors and Integrated Systems*
USA

1. Introduction

Health and Usage Monitoring Systems (HUMS) and Condition Based Maintenance (CBM) systems are closely related systems since the data collected by HUMS can be effectively used by CBM systems to generate condition and health indicators of air-crafts in order to find out the components on which maintenance is required. Efficient and comprehensive automation of such CBM systems is, therefore, of utmost importance to take an advantage of the massive amount of data continuously collected by HUMS.

In this chapter, we present a novel framework for automating the CBM systems, based on supervised learning practices established in UH-60 Condition Based Maintenance (CBM) manual [3]. The proposed framework is based upon a concept of building a configuration-driven data mining tool in which the maintenance decisions of aircrafts' components are driven by configuration metadata. We seek to address a key design goal of building a generic framework that can be easily instantiated for various CBM applications. This design goal, in turn, raises the challenges of building a system that features modularity (i.e., the software structure is based on a composition of separate modules, which jointly incorporate with each other.), extendibility (i.e., the software should be easy to extend.), and maintainability (i.e., the software should be easy to maintain and update.).

To meet this design goal, we adopted a layered architecture for the proposed framework. The framework consists of three layers; 1) Storage layer, which concerns the storage of source data and configuration metadata used by the system; 2) Extraction layer, in which the source data and configuration metadata are extracted and passed to the upper (processing) layer; and 3) Processing layer, which is responsible for executing mining algorithms and reporting necessary maintenance actions.

This layered architecture uses two prominent techniques, namely XML-based metadata storage, and dynamic code generation and execution. The XML-based metadata storage provides a generic platform for storing configuration meta-data, whereas dynamic code generation and execution allows applications to be extended with non-compiled source code, which is stored within configuration metadata. Both the generic storage platform and the on-the-fly code generation features help significantly reduce the cost of the software development life cycle (including software validation, verification, and maintenance), by allowing system engineers to supplement new functions, modify existing algorithms, consider new data sets, and conduct advanced analysis operations, without having to issue a new software release.

We have developed a functional software prototype of the proposed framework and examined the utility of the prototype to retrieve configuration metadata and, consequently, generate various maintenance reports. We will present examples of the reports generated by the software prototype, and an estimate of the time saved over the manual system. We will also demonstrate the exceedances report that shall list all simple exceedances, the associated count, and duration of those exceedances, as well as fault BIT report that shall list all BIT failures and their total instances. The software prototype provides the user with advanced and simplified modes for generating reports. The advanced mode gives the user a control on the report generation to specify, for instance, the type of aircrafts and analysis, the source of data and configuration files, the information to be displayed and hidden in the report, etc. The simplified, on the other hand, generates, in one single execution, all reports defined in the configuration files and using the default system settings.

We present two examples of the reports generated by the software prototype for the S-92A; the first example is for the fault BIT report that lists all BIT failures and their total instances, and the second example is for the exceedances [4, 5] report that lists all simple exceedances and their associated count. (See [6] for comprehensive list and details of the set of reports generated by the system).

In the research work presented in this chapter, we make the following contributions: 1) We address the motivation and demand for an automation of the HUMS CBM systems. 2) We present a novel framework for building Automated Condition Based Maintenance Checking Systems (ACBMCS). 3) We demonstrate the software prototype and explore the steps of generating various maintenance reports, in light of fault BIT and exceedances reports.

The remainder of this chapter is organized as follows. First, we outline the system and software requirement specifications. Second, we present the framework architecture. Third, we discuss in details the design of XML-based configuration. Fourth, we demonstrate an example of using the software prototype to generate maintainable reports. Finally, we conclude this chapter.

2. Requirement specifications

In this section we outline the system and software requirement specifications, which identify the end-users needs and expectations from the software application.

2.1 System requirements

The proposed framework has been designed to accommodate the following system requirements:

- The system should be configurable across various types of aircrafts.
- The system should perform different types of analysis to determine the health conditions.
- The system should process all the parameters required by analysis type and aircraft type.
- The system should configure the application algorithms based on the type of aircraft and the type of analysis being performed.

- The system should process all types of data used to monitor the various aircraft state parameters.
- The system should display the report to the user based on the algorithm executed.

2.2 Software requirements
The primary requirement for the software is to be generic. This generality has been address by building the software with the following features: 1) Modularity: The software structure is based on a composition of separate modules, which incorporate with each other through interfaces. 2) Integrity: Data, information, and knowledge stored and manipulated by the software must be correct and the relationship between them is consistent. 3) Extendibility and maintainability: The software should be easy to extend and maintain.

3. Framework architecture

The framework architecture is illustrated in Figure 1, which demonstrates that the software is composed of three connected layers; 1) Storage layer, 2) Extraction layer, and 3) Processing layer.
The storage layer concerns the storage of configuration metadata that drives the processing of the systems, as well as source data on which analysis is being done.
The extraction layer is the layer in which the source data and configuration metadata are extracted and passed to the upper (processing) layer.
The processing layer is responsible for executing the mining algorithms, based on the configuration metadata, against the corresponding data retrieved from source data files.

3.1 Storage layer
The storage layer is the lower lever layer which stores configuration metadata that drives the processing of the systems, as well as source data on which analysis is being done.
The configuration metadata (i.e., information representing aircrafts, analysis, parameters, algorithms, and actions report) is stored as a collection of XML documents. These XML documents are designed in a normalized way in order to reduce, or possibly remove, any information redundancy. To assure the integrity of XML documents content, these XML document are built according to an XML schema that expresses constraints on the structure and content of the XML documents. In addition, the XML schema employs the concept of archetypes which provides means of defining user-defined data types in the XML schema in a way that reduces nested definitions, as well as the concept of restrictions which defines acceptable values for XML elements or attributes. The design details of XML-based configuration are further discussed in the following section.
The source data, on the other hand, comes in the form of Raw Data Files (RDF) and Activity Data Files (ADF). An RDF is a collection of aircraft health data for a single aircraft operation, whereas an ADF is a set of indexes, to an RDF file, that provides a performance-optimized approach of retrieving source data of a single aircraft operation.

3.2 Extraction layer
This layer carries out the extraction of data from the source files. This data extraction is derived by the content of configuration metadata.

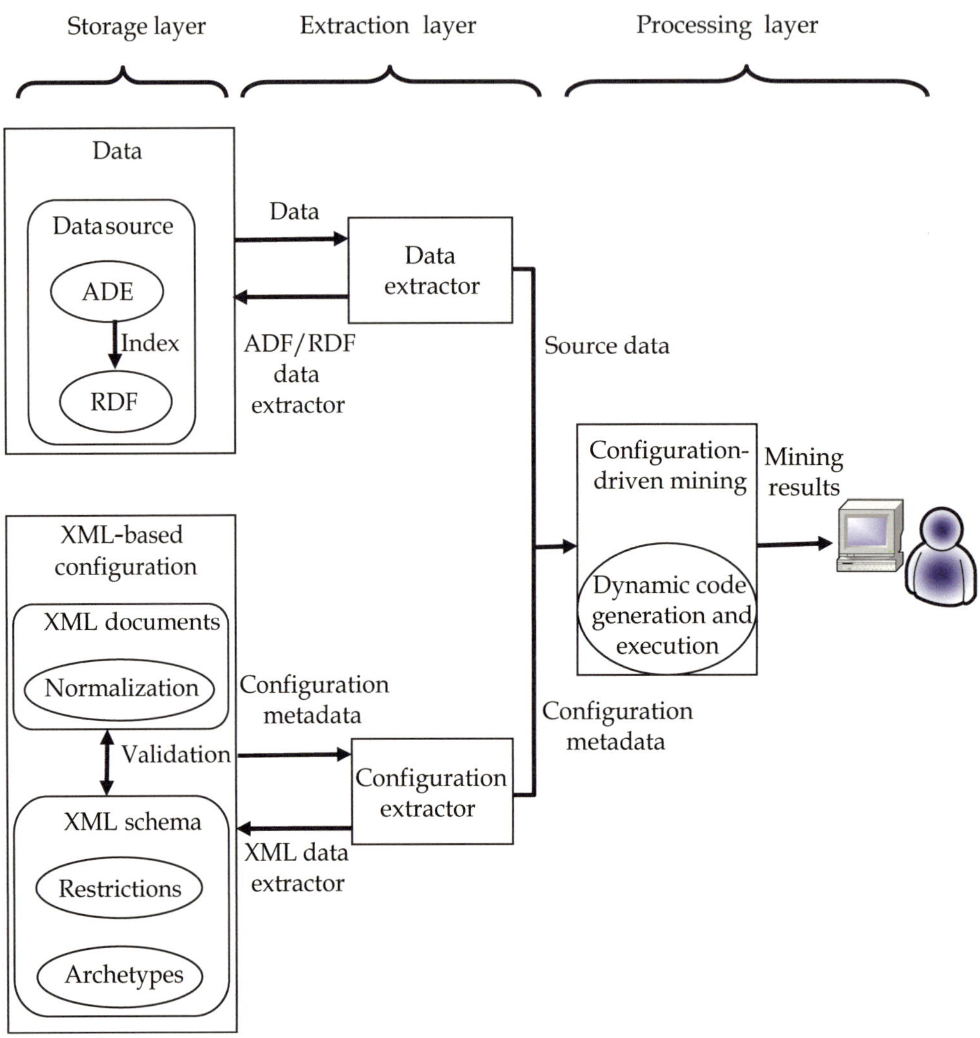

Fig. 1. Framework architecture

3.3 Processing layer

The processing layer is responsible for executing the mining algorithms, based on the configuration metadata, against the corresponding data retrieved from source data files. This layer uses dynamic code generation and execution technique to load algorithms, which should be executed, on the run-time from configuration metadata. The dynamic code generation and execution technique is a key building block of the proposed framework that allows the software to dynamically; 1) Wrap the code into fully-functional assembly source code (with all the required dependencies); 2) Compile the source code into an assembly; and 3) Use the assembly reference to create an instance of the application object.

4. XML-based configuration

The XML elements in the XML-based configuration and their interaction are shown in Figure 2.

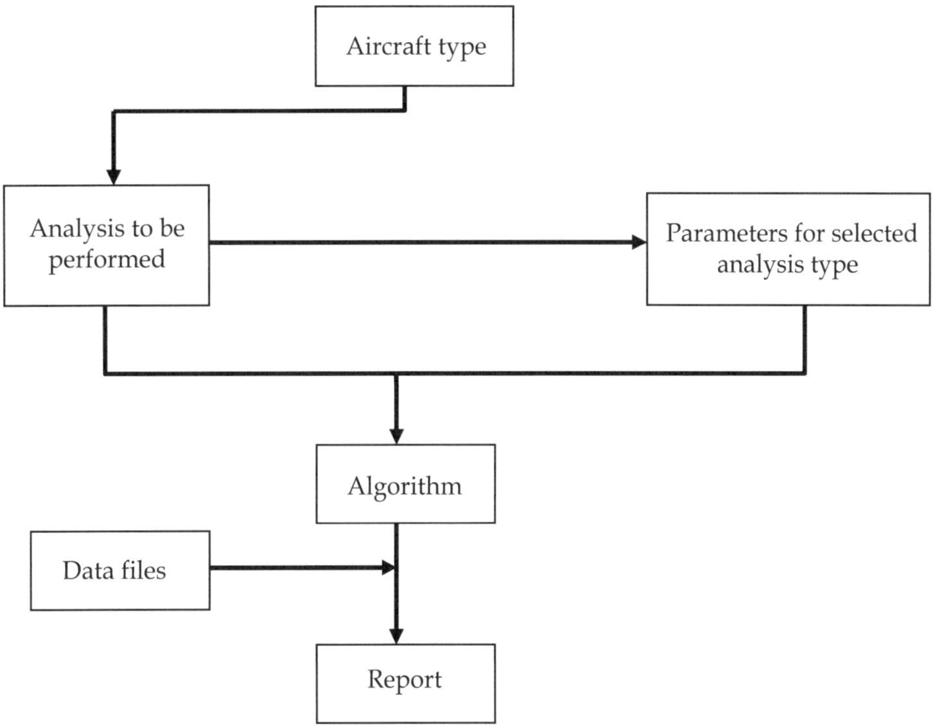

Fig. 2. XML elements in XML schema

The XML-based configuration design involves design of the XML schema and the XML documents holding the configuration information. The XML schema includes information regarding the organization of the elements, sub-elements and attributes which is in accordance with the structure of the system. The different restrictions are assigned on each of the elements, sub-elements and attributes to ensure data integrity. The XML documents, which contain the actual configuration information, are then validated against the schema to check for discrepancies and insure data integrity.

4.1 XML schema elements

XML schema of configuration files models five key elements illustrated in Figure 2:

- AIRCRAFT: The aircraft element consists of the main element Aircrafts in which all possible aircraft types can be defined. The sub-element Aircraft, of the main element Aircrafts, gives the details of one type of aircraft. Each aircraft is given a specific ID, defined as an attribute called airID, to distinguish it from other aircrafts and help in referencing. The sub-element airname of Aircraft contains the information of the name of the aircraft. Figure 3 shows the structure of this element.

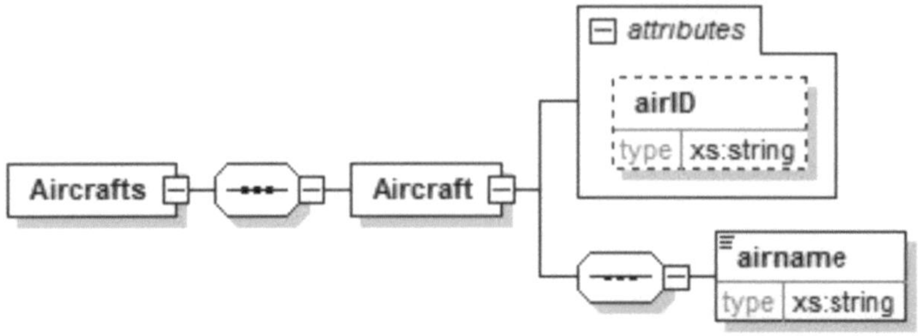

Fig. 3. Structure of the AIRCRAFT element

- ANALYSIS: The analysis element, as illustrated in Figure 4, consists of the main element AnalysisSets, which defines the set of all possible types of analysis that can be performed in CBM. The element AnalysisSets contains a sub-element Analysis, which carries the information regarding the analysis type. The sub-element name of Analysis gives the name of the analysis, and the attribute anaID assigns a specific ID to each analysis type.

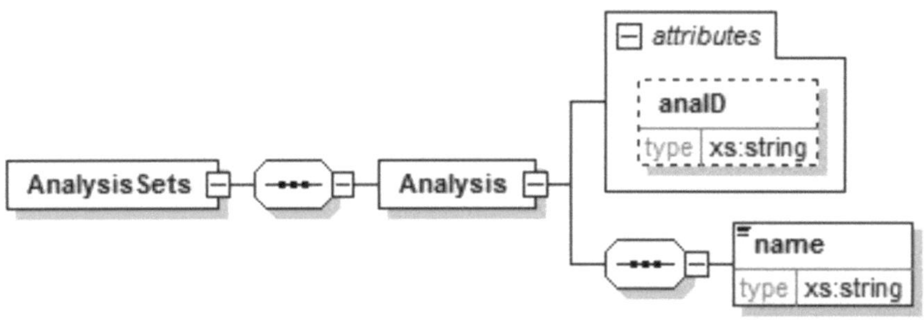

Fig. 4. Structure of the ANALYSIS element

- PARAMETER: The parameter element consists of the main element Parameters. As shown in Figure 5, it has a sub-element Parameter which holds the information of every parameter type. The attribute paramID assigns a unique ID to each parameter type which is used to call it by reference later. The sub-element paramname gives the name of the parameter and usedAt assigns the parameter to analyses and aircraft types at which the parameter is used. The sub-element assignment of usedAt holds this information in the attributes analysisID and aircraftID.
- ALGORITHM: Figure 6 demonstrates that the algorithm element consists of the main element algorithms, which has a sub-element algorithm in which every type of possible algorithm is defined. The attribute algoID assigns a unique ID to each algorithm type that is defined. The algorithm type is distinguished by the analysis and aircraft that uses it as well as the way it is executed. The sub-element used assigns the algorithm to analyses and aircraft types that use the algorithm. The sub-element assignement used holds this information in the attributes IDanalysis and IDaircraft. The sub-element algoinfo holds the information regarding the types of conditions to be executed in

condition and the types of possible actions on executing the algorithm condition in action. The element algoinfo is modeled as IF condition THEN action. The types of conditions and actions are defined as archetypes called conditiontype and actiontype, respectively.

- REPORT: The report element, illustrated in Firgure 7, consists of the main element reports". It has a sub-element report in which every type of report to be generated is defined. The attribute repID assigns a unique ID to each type of report that is defined. The type of report is distinguished by the algorithm that uses it and by the way it is executed. The sub-element for assigns the report to a type of algorithm. The sub-element result of for holds this information in the attribute algoID. The sub-element reportinfo holds the information regarding the types of conditions to be executed in condition and the types of possible actions on executing the algorithm condition in action. The element reportinfo is modeled as IF condition THEN action. Similar to the algoinfo element, the types of conditions and actions are defined as archetypes called conditiontype and actiontype, respectively.

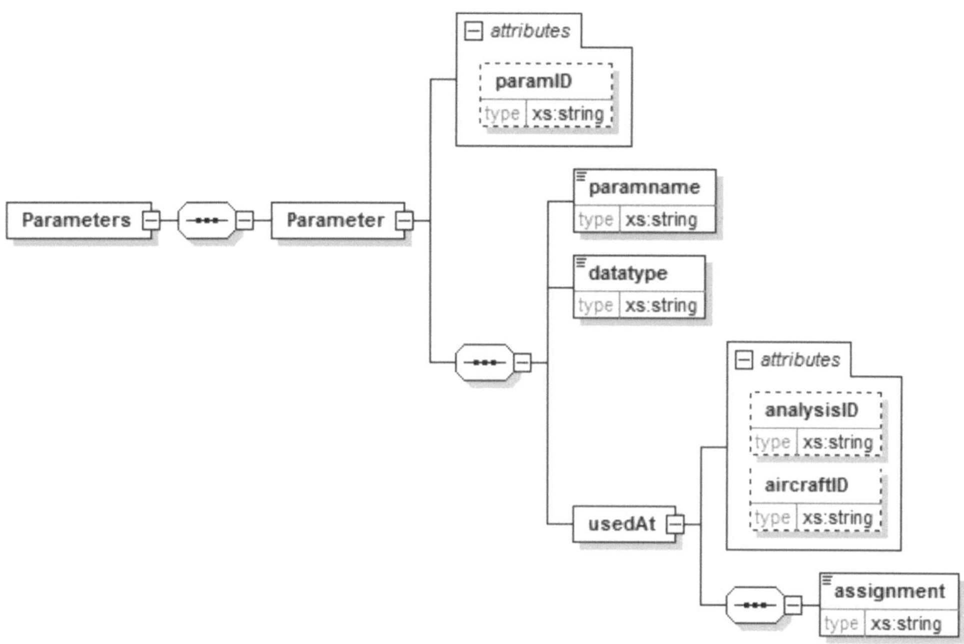

Fig. 5. Structure of the PARAMETER element

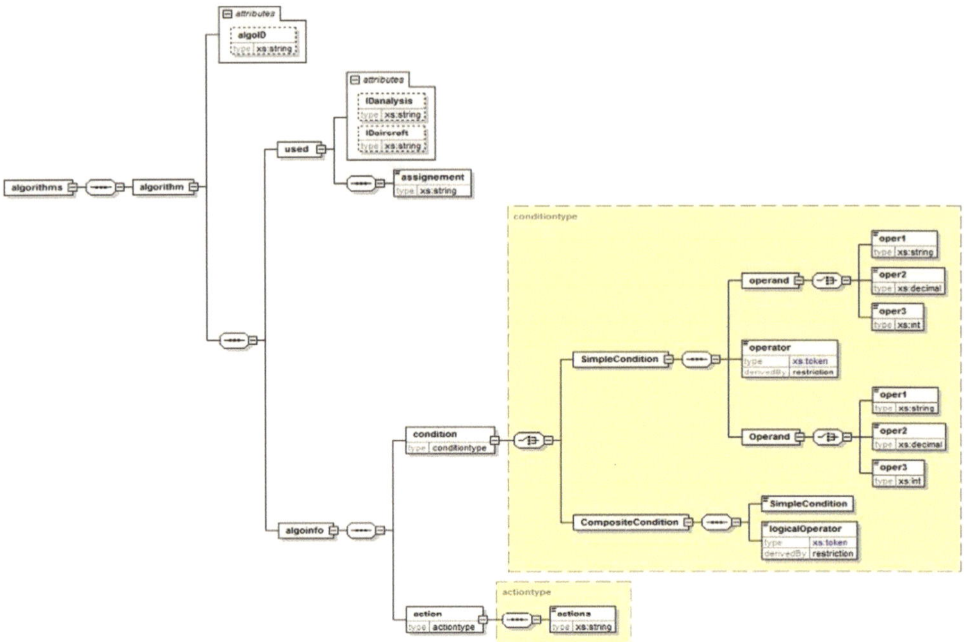

Fig. 6. Structure of the ALGORITHM element

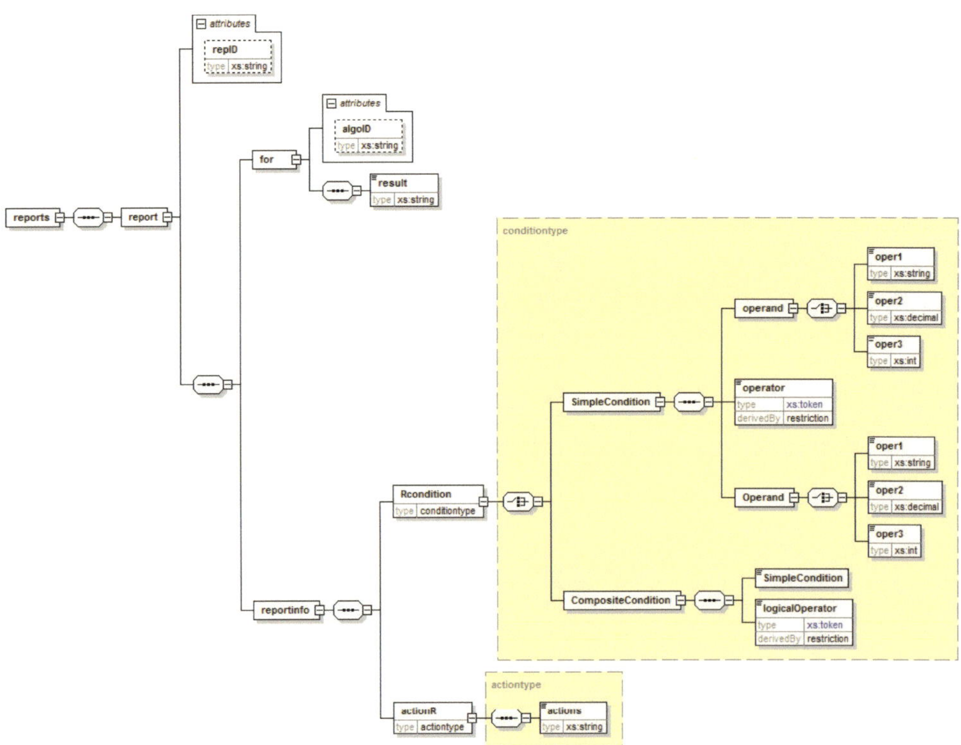

Fig. 7. Structure of the REPORT element

4.2 XML schema restrictions

In the design of XML schema, we employ the concept of archetypes which provides means of defining userdefined data types in the XML schema in a way that reduces nested definitions. The following archetypes are defined in the schema:

- CONDITIONTYPE: As shown in Figure 8, the conditiontype element is modeled as a choice element where the choices are simpleCondition and compositeCondition. The sub-element simpleCondition is a sequence element of operand, operator and operand. compositeCondition is a sequence element of simpleCondition, logicalOperator and compositeCondition.

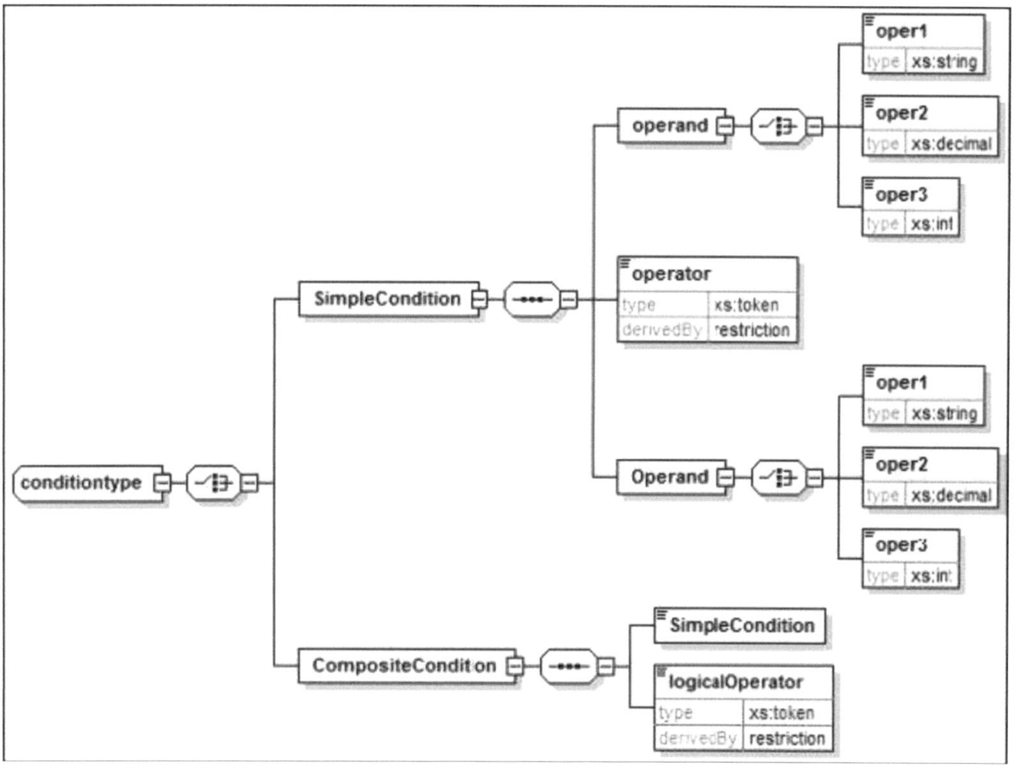

Fig. 8. Structure of the CONDITIONTYPE archetype

- ACTIONTYPE: The element actiontype, illustrated in Figure 9, consists of the sub-element actions where the corresponding action to a condition is listed.

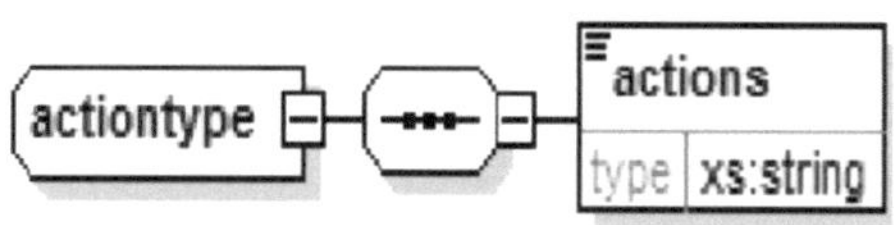

Fig. 9. Structure of the ACTIONTYPE archetype

5. Software prototype

To examine the utility of the proposed framework, we have developed a functional software prototype of the framework. The prototype has been developed under .Net Framework 3.5, in C# using Microsoft Visual Studio 2008 Professional. In this section, we present a step-by-step example of using the software prototype to generation fault BIT and exceedances reports.

5.1 Software installation

The software release comes in the form of a single MSI (Windows Installer) file. Running this installation file guides the user in the installation process of the software application. Figure 10, Figure 11, and Figure 12, respectively show the initial installation screen, the installation options, and the installation confirmation screen which indicates that all software components have been actually and successfully installed.

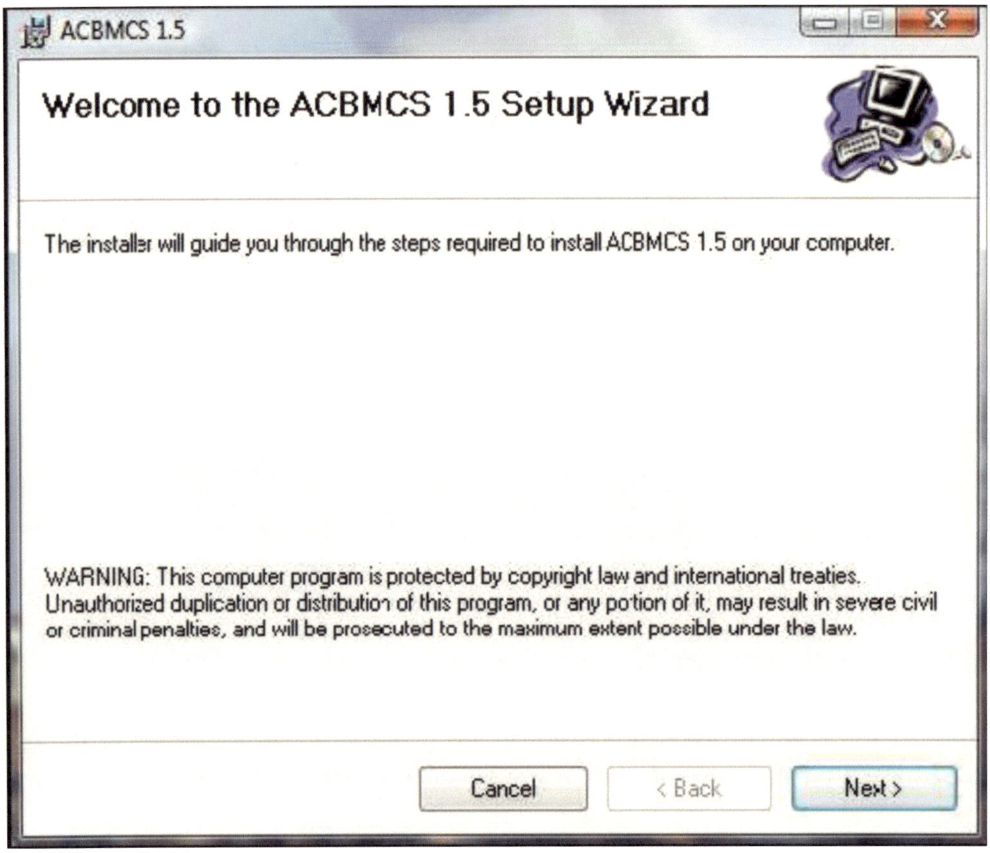

Fig. 10. Initial screen of installation wizard

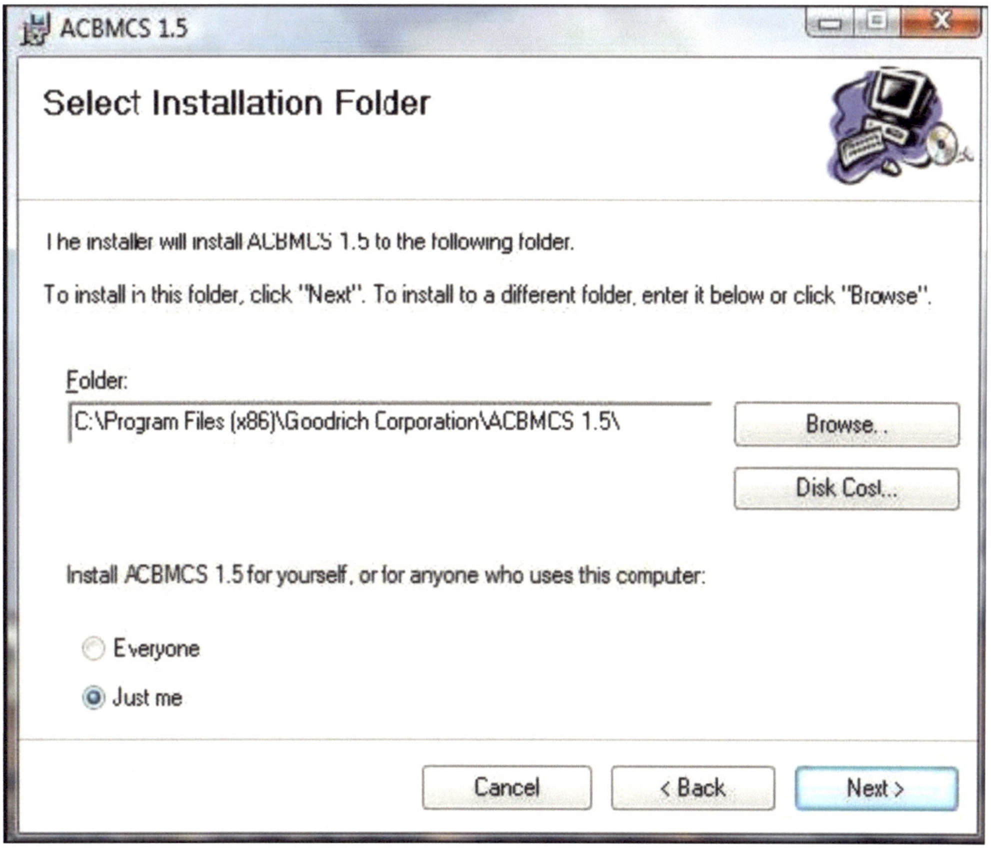

Fig. 11. User can select installation folder and security level

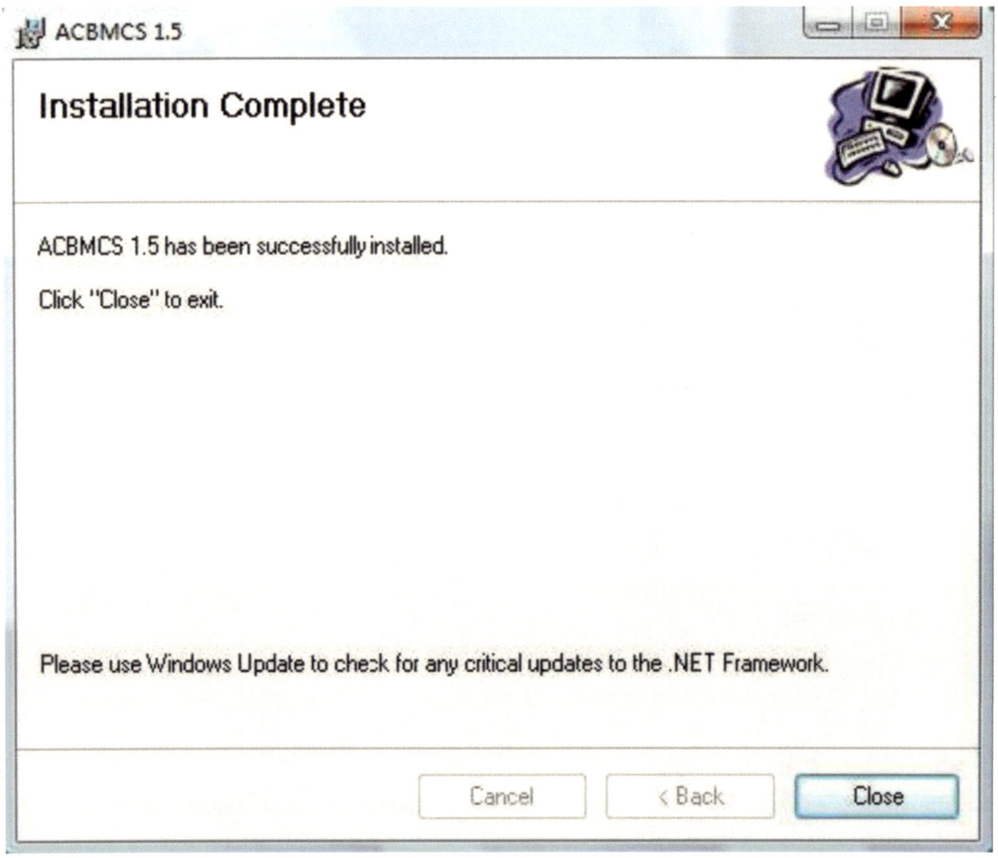

Fig. 12. Software installation confirmation

5.2 Application modes

As illustrated in Figure 13, the software features two modes available for the user; an advanced mode and a simplified mode.

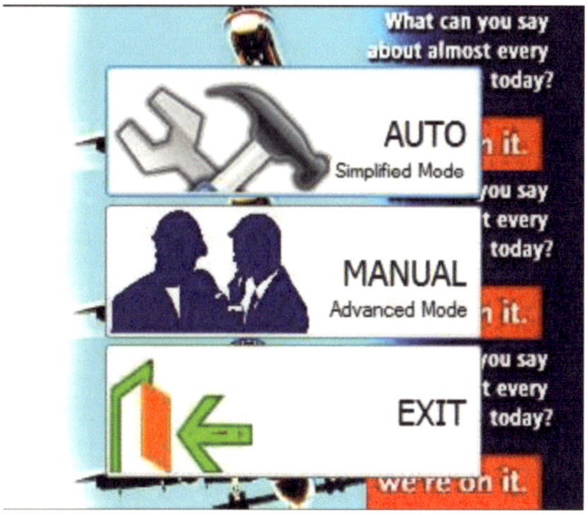

Fig. 13. Advanced and simplified modes

5.3 Advanced mode

The advanced mode gives the user a control on the report generation to specify:

- The source of configuration files: The application initially loads configuration files located in the default path (Figure 14). However, the software provides the user with the option of changing the path configuration files (Figure 15 and Figure 16).

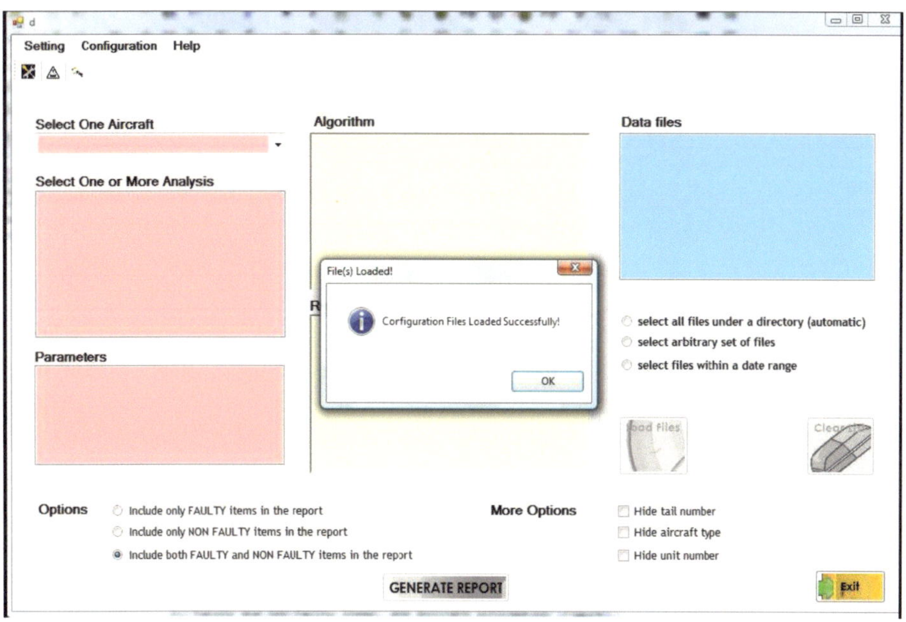

Fig. 14. Configuration files loaded from the default path

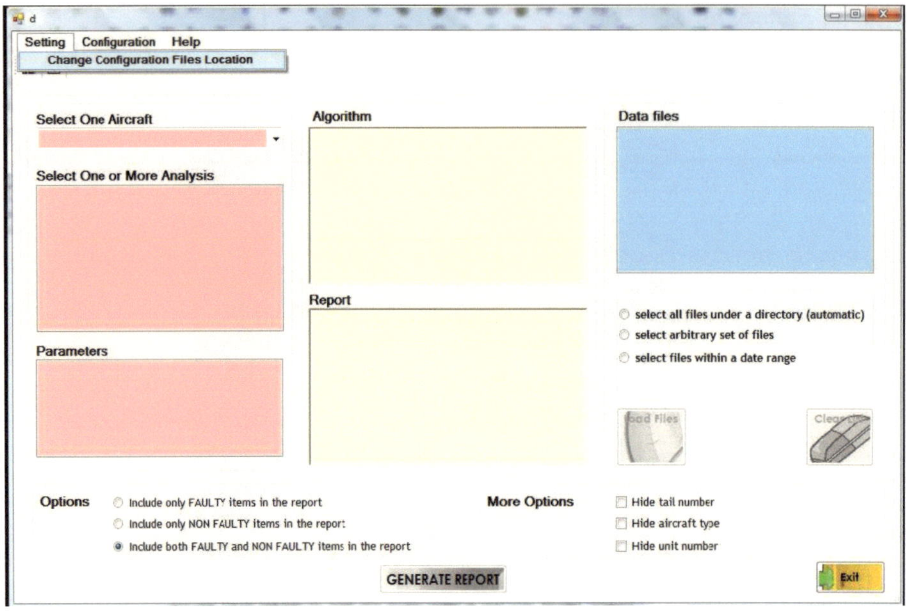

Fig. 15. Change the path of configuration files

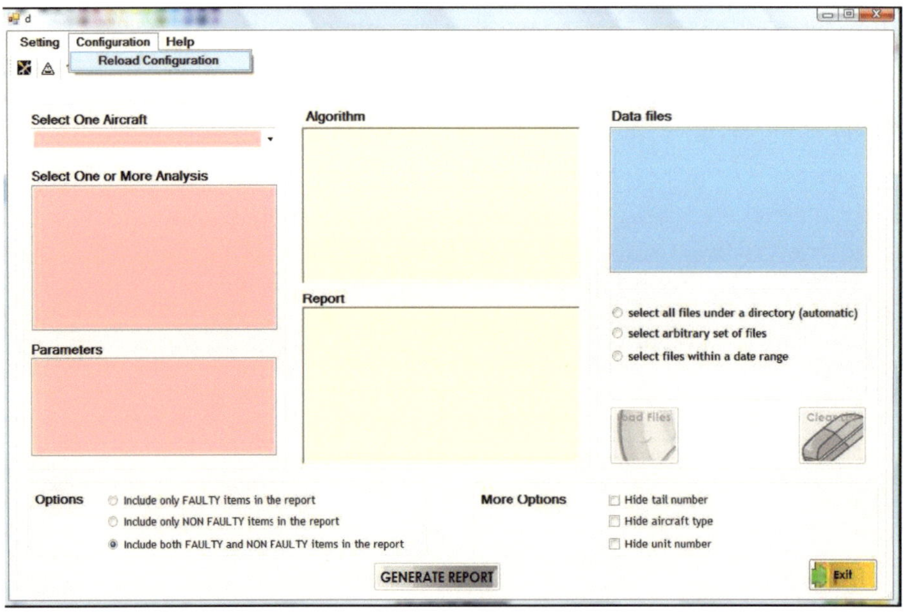

Fig. 16. Reload the configuration files

- The type of aircrafts and analysis (Figure 17): The user first selects the type of aircraft, and based on the selection, the related analysis are displayed. Upon the selection of the analysis (which can be multi-selection), a list of the related parameters and the corresponding algorithm(s) and report(s) are displayed.

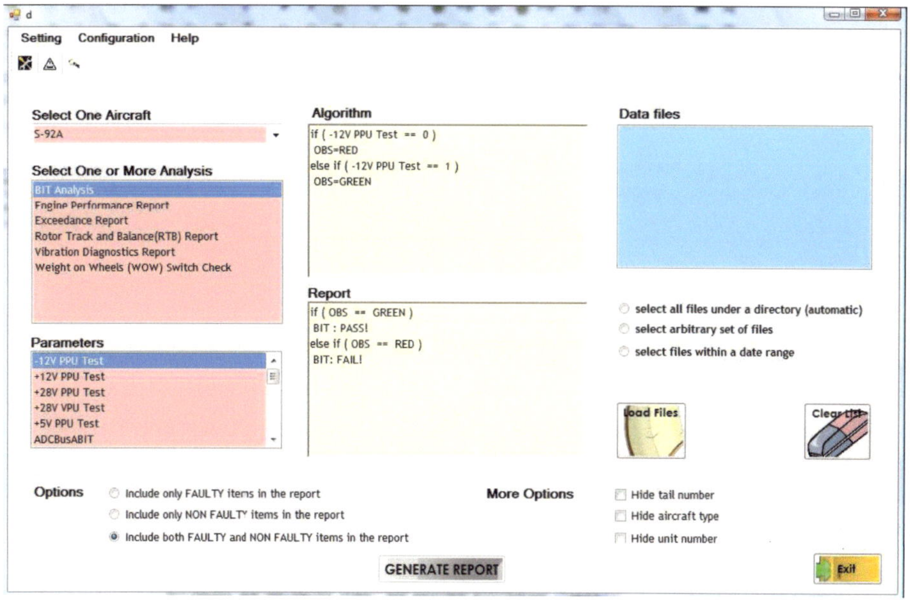

Fig. 17. Select aircraft and analysis

- The source of data files: The user has three options to load source data files. The first option is to load all files under a specific folder (Figure 18). The second option is to load a set of arbitrary files (Figure 19). The third option is to load files within a certain range of dates (Figure 20).

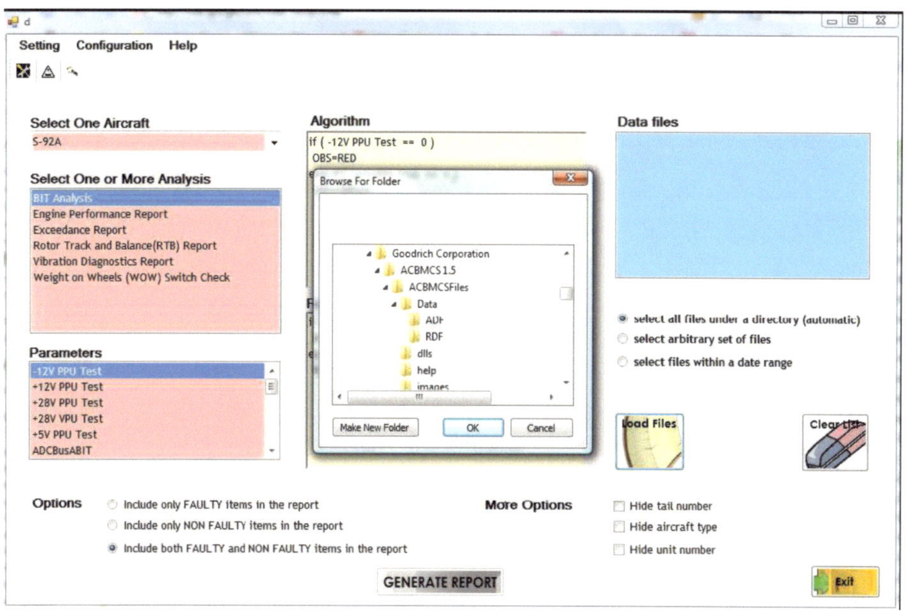

Fig. 18. Load all files under a specific folder

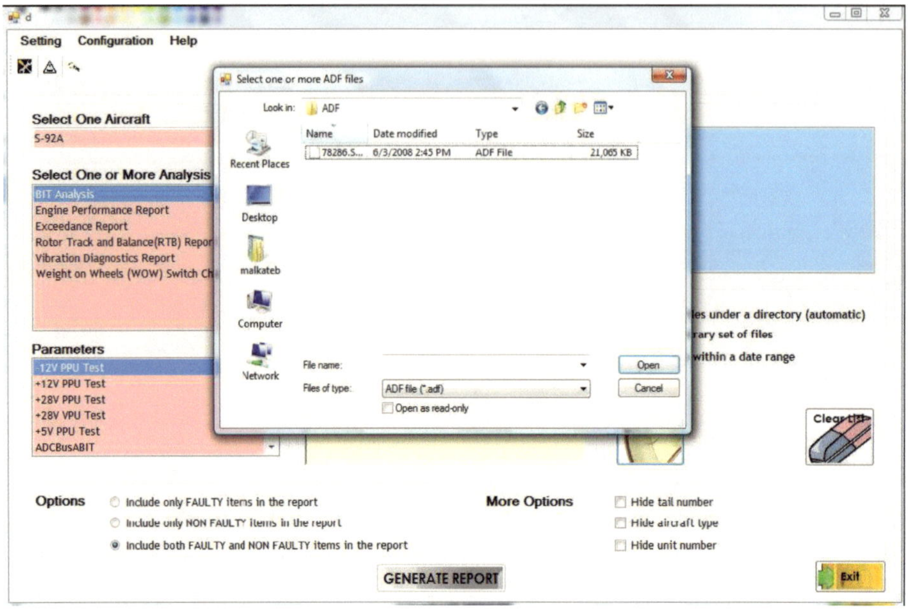

Fig. 19. Load a set of arbitrary files

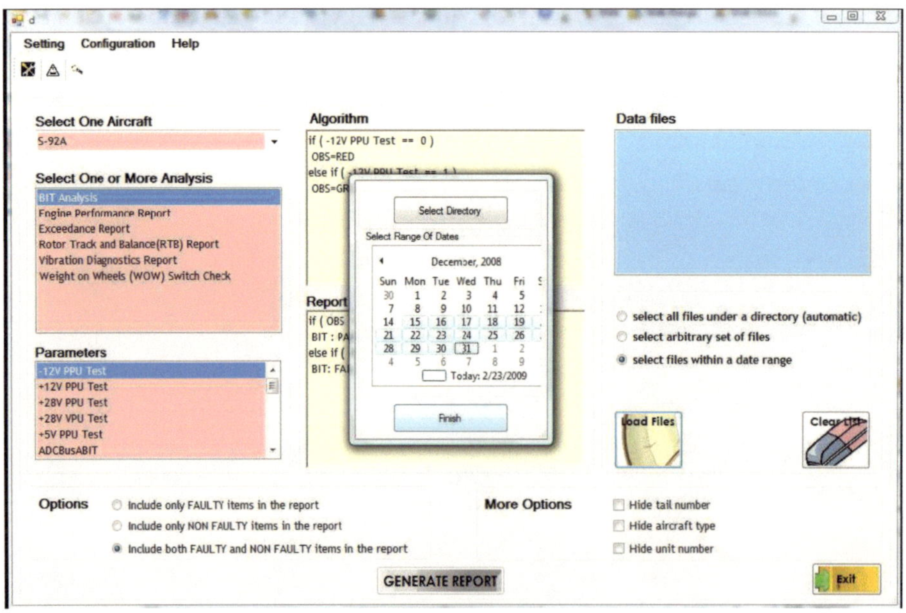

Fig. 20. Load files within a certain range of dates

- The information to be displayed and hidden in the report; faulty and non-faulty items (Figure 21), and aircraft information (Figure 22).

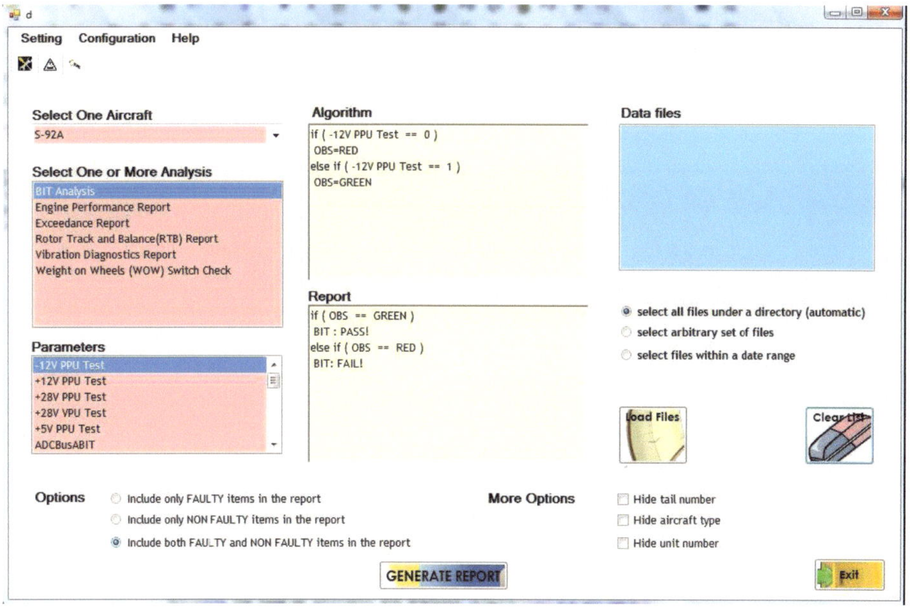

Fig. 21. Display faulty items, non-faulty items, or both

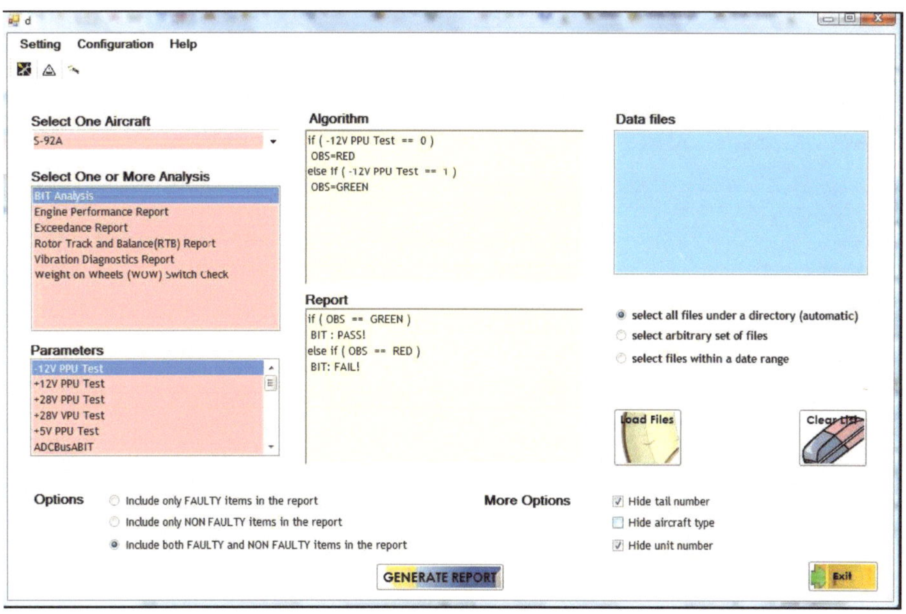

Fig. 22. Show or hide aircraft information

The last step is to generate the maintenance reports, which is achieved by clicking on the GENERATE REPORT button. Figures 23 and 24 and Figures 25 and 26 show the output maintenance reports for the fault BIT and exceedances analysis, respectively.

HUMS-ACBMCS GOODRICH

MAINTENANCE REPORT

DATE:

2/23/2009 3:52:18 PM

DESCRIPTION:

This report is generated by the Automated Condition Based Maintenance Checking System (ACBMCS) to demonstrate the recommended maintenance action.

ANALYSIS TYPE:

BIT Analysis

Fig. 23. Report header of the fault BIT analysis

RECOMMENDED MAINTENANCE ACTION:

Parameter Name	Parameter Value	Report Result
-12V PPU Test	1	BIT : PASS!
+12V PPU Test	1	BIT : PASS!
+28V PPU Test	1	BIT : PASS!
+28V VPU Test	1	BIT : PASS!
+5V PPU Test	1	BIT : PASS!
ADCBusABIT	Missing value	
ADCBusBBIT	Missing value	
AFCSBusBBIT	Missing value	
AHRSBusABIT	Missing value	
AHRSBusBBIT	Missing value	
BMUBusBIT	Missing value	
DTU BIT STATUS	Missing value	
MDCBusBIT	Missing value	
MPS SBIT	1	BIT : PASS!
PPU Arinc 429 Test	1	BIT : PASS!
PPU DRAM Test	1	BIT : PASS!
PPU Frequency Test	1	BIT : PASS!
PPU PBIT	1	BIT : PASS!
Tracker Power Test	1	BIT : PASS!
VPU SBIT	1	BIT : PASS!

Failure Count = 0

Fig. 24. Report body of the fault BIT analysis

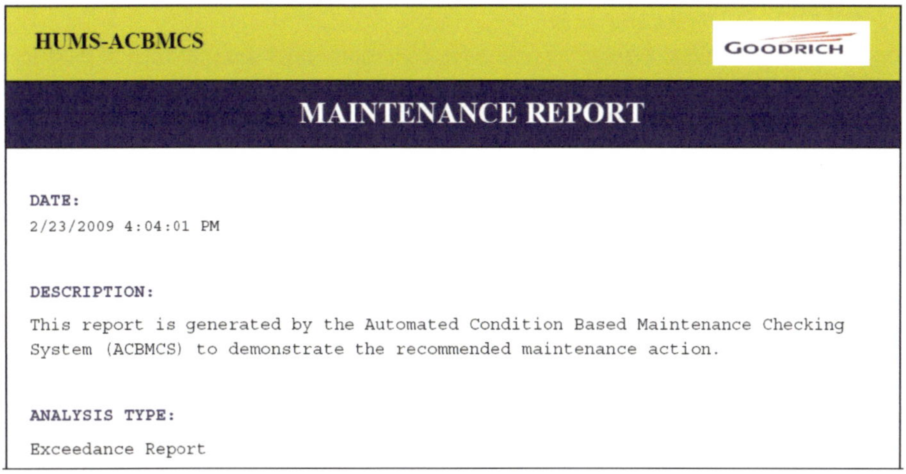
HUMS-ACBMCS

GOODRICH

MAINTENANCE REPORT

DATE:
2/23/2009 4:04:01 PM

DESCRIPTION:
This report is generated by the Automated Condition Based Maintenance Checking System (ACBMCS) to demonstrate the recommended maintenance action.

ANALYSIS TYPE:
Exceedance Report

Fig. 25. Report header of the exceedances analysis

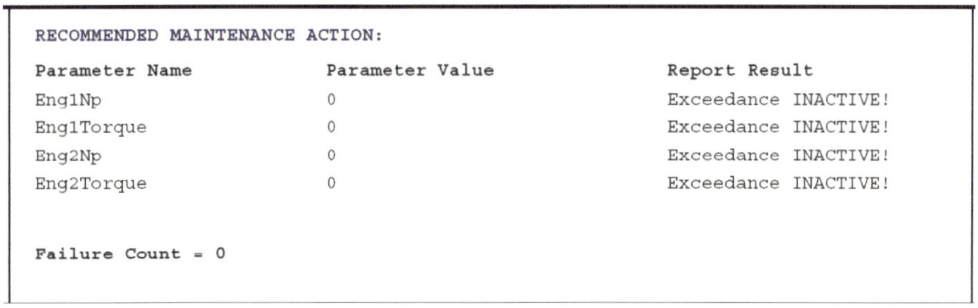
RECOMMENDED MAINTENANCE ACTION:

Parameter Name	Parameter Value	Report Result
Eng1Np	0	Exceedance INACTIVE!
Eng1Torque	0	Exceedance INACTIVE!
Eng2Np	0	Exceedance INACTIVE!
Eng2Torque	0	Exceedance INACTIVE!

Failure Count = 0

Fig. 26. Report body of the exceedances analysis

5.4 Simplified mode

The simplified mode generates, in one single execution, all reports defined in the configuration files by using the default system settings. Default settings reflect the default path of both the configuration files and source data files.

6. Conclusion

In this chapter, we present new framework for automating CBM systems. The utility of the proposed framework has been verified through a software prototype that demonstrates various functionality provided by the framework.

This work opens an avenue for several future works including, for instance, extending the data extraction module to manipulate the Health Indicators (HI) data from source data files, as well as conducting further complicated and advanced data mining and analysis operations using the proposed framework.

7. References

[1] Robert Hess, Alan Duke, and David Kogut (1999). Helicopter track and balance theory. Aircraft Maintenance Technology,

http://www.amtonline.com
[2] Goodrich Corporation. *Design standard for condition based maintenance system for army aircraft.* ADS-79-SP CBM
[3] US Army Aviation and Missile Command. *Uh-60 condition based maintenance (cbm) manual.*
[4] Goodrich Corporation. *Configuration requirements specifications for the s-92 hums exceedance processing and monitoring.* DOC.NO.: 3019554-CRS-0104
[5] Goodrich Corporation. *S-92 imd hums system specification.* DOC.NO.: SES-920273
[6] Mahindra Imadabathuni, Pradnya Joshi, David He, Mohammed Al-Kateb, and Eric Bechhoefer (2009). Application of the automated condition based maintenance checking system for aircrafts. Processings of The International Conference on Industrial Engineering and Systems Management (IESM 2009). MONTREAL - CANADA

8

Data Mining in Hospital Information System

Jing-song Li, Hai-yan Yu and Xiao-guang Zhang
Zhejiang University,
China

1. Introduction

Data mining aims at discovering novel, interesting and useful knowledge from databases. Conventionally, the data is analyzed manually. Many hidden and potentially useful relationships may not be recognized by the analyst. Nowadays, many organizations including modern hospitals are capable of generating and collecting a huge amount of data. This explosive growth of data requires an automated way to extract useful knowledge. Thus, medical domain is a major area for applying data mining. Through data mining, we can extract interesting knowledge and regularities. The discovered knowledge can then be applied in the corresponding field to increase the working efficiency and improve the quality of decision making.

This chapter introduces the applications of data mining in HIS (Hospital Information System). It will be presented in three aspects: data mining fundamentals (part 1 and part 2), tools for knowledge discovery (part 3 and part 4), and advanced data mining techniques (part 5 and part 6). In order to help readers understand more intuitively and intensively, some case studies will be given in advanced data mining techniques.

2. Part 1 Overview of data mining process

Nowadays, data stored in medical databases are growing in an increasingly rapid way. Analyzing that data is crucial for medical decision making and management. It has been widely recognized that medical data analysis can lead to an enhancement of health care by improving the performance of patient management tasks. There are two main aspects that define the need for medical data analysis.

1. Support of specific knowledge-based problem solving activities through the analysis of patients' raw data collected in monitoring.
2. Discovery of new knowledge that can be extracted through the analysis of representative collections of example cases, described by symbolic or numeric descriptors.

For these purposes, the increase in database size makes traditional manual data analysis to be insufficient. To fill this gap, new research fields such as knowledge discovery in databases (KDD) have rapidly grown in recent years. KDD is concerned with the efficient computer-aided acquisition of useful knowledge from large sets of data. The main step in the knowledge discovery process, called data mining, deals with the problem of finding interesting regularities and patterns in data.

A simple data mining process model mainly includes 6 steps:

1. Assembling the data

Data mining requires access to data. The data may be represented as volumes of records in several database files or the data may contain only a few hundred records in a single file. A common misconception is that in order to build an effective model a data mining algorithm must be presented with thousands or millions of instances. In fact, most data mining tools work best with a few hundred or a few thousand pertinent records. Therefore once a problem has been defined, a first step in the data mining process is to extract or assemble a relevant subset of data for processing. Many times this first step requires a great amount of human time and effort. As in healthcare industry, we need domain experts such as doctors, nurses, hospital managers and so on to work closely with the data mining expert to develop analyses that are relevant to clinical decision making. There are three common ways to access data for data mining:

1. Data can be accessed from a data warehouse.
2. Data can be accessed from a database.
3. Data can be accessed from a flat file or spreadsheet.

Because medical data are collected on human subjects, there is an enormous ethical and legal tradition designed to prevent the abuse of patients' information and misuse of their data. In data assembling process, we should pay more attention to the five major points:

- Data ownership
- Fear of lawsuits
- Privacy and security of human data
- Expected benefits
- Administrative issues

2. The data warehouse

A common scenario for data assembly shows data originating in one or more operational database. Operational databases are transaction-based and frequently designed using the relational database model. An operational database fixed on the relational model will contain several normalized tables. The tables have been normalized to reduce redundancy and promote quick access to individual records. For example, a specific customer might have data appearing in several relational tables where each table views the customer from a different perspective. But medical data is almost the most heterogeneous data which contains images like SPECT, signals like ECG, clinical information like temperature, cholesterol levels, urinalysis data, etc. as well as the physician's interpretation written in unstructured texts. Sometimes the relational database model can't describe the heterogeneous data with tables and we can use post-relational database model.

The data warehouse is a historical database designed for decision support rather than transaction processing. Thus only data useful for decision support is extracted from the operational environment and entered into the warehouse database. Data transfer from the operational database to the warehouse is an ongoing process usually accomplished on a daily basis after the close of the regular business day. Before each data item enters the warehouse, the item is time-stamped, transformed as necessary, and checked for errors. The transfer process can be complex, especially when several operational databases are involved. Once entered, the records in the data warehouse become read-only and are subject to change only under special conditions.

A data warehouse stores all data relating to the same subject (such as a customer) in the same table. This distinguishes the data warehouse from an operational database, which stores information so as to optimize transaction processing. Because the data warehouse is subject-oriented rather than transaction-oriented, the data will contain redundancies. It is the redundancy stored in a data warehouse that is used by data mining algorithms to develop patterns representing discovered knowledge.

3. Relational database and flat files

If a data warehouse does not exist, you can make use of a database query language to write one or more queries to create a table suitable for data mining. Whether data is being extracted for mining from the data warehouse or the data extraction is via a query language, you will probably need a utility program to convert extracted data to the format required by the chosen data mining tool. Finally, if a database structure to store the data has not been designed, and the amount of collected data is minimal, the data will likely be stored in a flat file or spreadsheet.

4. Mining the data

Prior to giving the data to a data mining tool, preprocessing of the data is necessary. Preprocessing the data includes multiple steps to assure the highest possible data quality, thus efforts are made to detect and remove errors, resolve data redundancies, and taking into account of the patient privacy, to remove patient identifiers. Data are analyzed using both statistical and data mining methods to produce information; output formats will vary depending upon the method used. Predictive modeling efforts are iterative, thus statistical and data mining results are repeated with different permutations until the best results (metrics) are obtained.

Patients and health care consumers are increasingly concerned about the privacy of their personal health information. All data mining should carefully attempt to create completely anonymous data before analyses are begun.

Anticipating that data will be 100% complete and error free is unrealistic when working with patient data which collected in complex health care systems. Cleaning the data is proved a nontrivial and tedious task. Data error identification is both an automated and a manual process, and required an iterative procedure that drew upon expertise from the clinical experts as well as statistical experts and the data warehouse engineer. Errors that detected out-of-range values (for example, a systolic blood pressure of 700) are identified by the clinical experts and eliminated from the research data sets. Errors where a variable included inconsistently recorded text require an iterative extraction and programming solution; clinical experts reviewe the text extraction and provide guidelines for converting data for consistency, coding, or deleting the variable if data conversion is not possible.

Medical data is often very high dimensional. Depending upon the use, some data dimensions might be more relevant than others. In processing medical data, choosing the optimal subset of features is such important, not only to reduce the processing cost but also to improve the usefulness of the model built from the selected data. So before the step of mining, we have several choices to make.

1. Should learning be supervised or unsupervised?
2. Which instances in the assembled data will be used for building the model and which instances will test the model?
3. Which attributes will be selected from the list of available attributes?
4. Data mining tools require the user to specify one or more learning parameters. What parameter settings should be used to build a model to best represent the data?

5. Interpreting the results

Result interpretation requires us to examine the output of our data mining tool to determine if what has been discovered is both useful and interesting. If the results are less than optimal we can repeat the data mining step using new attributes and/or instances. Alternatively, we may decide to return to the data warehouse and repeat the data extraction process.

As most medical datasets are large and complex, only those models that are validated by experts are retained in the knowledge base for system testing and verification. There are several techniques to help us make decisions about whether a specific model is useful (Evaluating Performance):

- Evaluating supervised learner models
- Two-class error analysis
- Evaluating numeric output
- Comparing models by measuring lift
- Unsupervised model evaluation

For example, if we use several fuzzy modeling methods to process medical data. When interpreting the results, concerning only the accuracy values might be misleading and not revealing other important information, as demonstrated by Cios and Moore. To double check seven other performance measures including sensitivity (a.k.a. recall in information retrieval community), specificity, precision, class weighted accuracy, F-measure, geometric mean of accuracies, and area under the receiver operating characteristics (ROC) curve were also needed to be computed for the top rank result obtained for each dataset.

Medical data mining using some fuzzy modeling methods without or with the use of some feature selection method. Belacel and Boulassel developed a supervised fuzzy classification procedure, called PROAFTN, and applied it to assist diagnosis of three clinical entities namely acute leukaemia, astrocytic, and bladder tumors. By dividing the Wisconsin breast cancer data (the version with 10 features) into 2/3 for training and 1/3 for testing, test accuracy of 97.9% was reported. Seker et al. used the fuzzy KNN classifier to provide a certainty degree for prognostic decision and assessment of the markers, and they reported that the fuzzy KNN classifier produced a more reliable prognostic marker model than the logistic regression and multilayer feedforward backpropagation models. Ruiz-Gomez et al. showed the capabilities of two fuzzy modeling approaches, ANFIS and another one that performs least squares identification and automatic rule generation by minimizing an error index, for the prediction of future cases of acquired immune deficiency syndrome.

6. Result application

Our ultimate goal is to apply what has been discovered to new situations. Data mining methods offer solutions to help manage data and information overload and build knowledge for information systems and decision support in nursing and health care. For instance, we can build nursing knowledge by discovering important linkages between clinical data, nursing interventions, and patient outcomes.

Applying data mining techniques enhances the creation of untapped useful knowledge from large medical datasets. The increasing use of these techniques can be observed in healthcare applications that support decision making, e.g., in patient and treatment outcomes; in healthcare delivery quality; in the development of clinical guidelines and the allocation of medical resources; and in the identification of drug therapeutic or adverse effect associations. Recent studies using data mining techniques to investigate cancer have focused on feature extraction from diagnostic images to detect and classify, for example, breast cancers.

3. Part 2 Techniques of data mining

Health care now collects data in gigabytes per hour volume. Data mining can help with data reduction, exploration, and hypothesis formulation to find new patterns and information in data that surpass human information processing limitations. There is a proliferation of reports and articles that apply data mining and KDD to a wide variety of health care problems and clinical domains and includes diverse projects related to cardiology, cancer, diabetes, finding medication errors, and many others.

Over the past two decades, it is clear that we have been able to develop systems that collect massive amounts of data in health care, but now what do we do with it? Data mining methods use powerful computer software tools and large clinical databases, sometimes in the form of data repositories and data warehouses, to detect patterns in data. Within data mining methodologies, one may select from an extensive array of techniques that include, among many others, classification, clustering, and association rules.

3.1 Classification

Classification maps data into predefined groups or classes. It is often referred to as supervised learning because the classes are determined before examining the data. Classification algorithms require that the classes be defined based on data attribute values. They often describe these classes by looking at the characteristics of data already known to belong to the classes. Pattern recognition is a type of classification where an input pattern is classified into one of several classes based on its similarity to these predefined classes.

One of the applications of classification in health care is the automatic categorization of medical images. Categorization of medical images means selecting the appropriate class for a given image out of a set of pre-defined categories. This is an important step for data mining and content-based image retrieval (CBIR).

There are several areas of application for CBIR systems. For instance, biomedical informatics compiles large image databases. In particular, medical imagery is increasingly acquired, transferred, and stored digitally. In large hospitals, several terabytes of data need to be managed each year. However, picture archiving and communication systems (PACS) still provide access to the image data by alphanumerical description and textual meta information. This also holds for digital systems compliant with the Digital Imaging and Communications in Medicine (DICOM) protocol. Therefore, integrating CBIR into medicine is expected to significantly improve the quality of patient care.

Another application is constructing predictive model from severe trauma patient's data. In management of severe trauma patients, trauma surgeons need to decide which patients are eligible for damage control. Such decision may be supported by utilizing models that predict the patient's outcome. To induce the predictive models, classification trees derived from a commonly-known ID3 recursive partitioning algorithm can be used. The basic idea of ID3 is to partition the patients into ever smaller groups until creating the groups with all patients corresponding to the same class (e.g. survives, does not survive). To avoid overfitting, a simple pruning criterion is used to stop the induction when the sample size for a node falls under the prescribed number of examples or when a sufficient proportion of a subgroup has the same output.

From the expert's perspective, classification tree is a reasonable model for outcome prediction. It is based on the important representatives from two of the most important groups of factors, which affect the outcome, coagulopathy and acidosis. The two mentioned features, together with body temperature, are the three that best determine the patient's outcome.

3.2 Clustering

Clustering is similar to classification except that the groups are not predefined, but rather defined by the data alone. Clustering is alternatively referred to as unsupervised learning or segmentation. It can be thought of as partitioning or segmenting the data into groups that might or might not be disjointed. The clustering is usually accomplished by determining the similarity among the data on predefined attributes. The most similar data are grouped into clusters.

Cluster analysis is a clustering method for gathering observation points into clusters or groups to make (1) each observation point in the group similar, that is, cluster elements are of the same nature or close to certain characteristics; (2) observation points in clusters differ; that is, clusters are different from one another. Cluster analysis can be divided into hierarchical clustering and partitioning clustering. Anderberg (1973) believed that it would be objective and economical to take hierarchical clustering's result as the initial cluster and then adjust the clusters with partitioning clustering. The first step of cluster analysis is to measure the similarity, followed by deciding upon cluster methods, deciding cluster manner of cluster method, deciding number of clusters and explanations for the cluster. Ward's method of hierarchical clustering is the initial result. K-means in partitioning clustering adjusts the clusters.

A special type of clustering is called segmentation. With segmentation a database is partitioned into disjointed groupings of similar tuples called segments. Segmentation is often viewed as being identical to clustering. In other circles segmentation is viewed as a specific type of clustering applied to a database itself.

Clustering can be used in designing a triage system. Triage helps to classify patients at emergency departments to make the most effective use of resources distributed. What is more important is that accuracy in carrying out triage matters greatly in terms of medical quality, patient satisfaction and life security. The study is made on medical management and nursing, with the knowledge of the administrative head at the Emergency Department, in the hope to effectively improve consistency of triage with the combination of data mining theories and practice. The purposes are as follows:

1. Based on information management, the information system is applied in triage of the Emergency Department to generate patients' data.
2. Exploration of correlation between triage and abnormal diagnosis; cluster analysis conducted on variables with clinical meanings.
3. Establishing triage abnormal diagnosis clusters with hierarchical clustering (Ward's method) and partitioning clustering (K-means algorithm); obtaining correlation law of abnormal diagnosis with decision trees.
4. Improving consistency of triage with data mining; offering quantified and scientific rules for triage decision-making in the hope of serving as a foundation for future researchers and clinical examination.

3.3 Association rules

Link analysis, alternatively referred to as affinity analysis or association, refers to the data mining task of uncovering relationships among data. The best example of this type of application is to determine association rules. An association rule is a model that identifies specific types of data associations. These associations are often used in the retail sales community to identify items that are frequently purchased together. Associations are also used in many other applications such as predicting the failure of telecommunication switches.

Users of association rules must be cautioned that these are not causal relationships. They do not represent any relationship inherent in the actual data (as is true with functional dependencies) or in the real world. There probably is no relationship between bread and pretzels that causes them to be purchased together. And there is no guarantee that this association will apply in the future. However, association rules can be used to assist retail store management in effective advertising, marketing, and inventory control.

The discovery of new knowledge by mining medical databases is crucial in order to make an effective use of stored data, enhancing patient management tasks. One of the main objectives of data mining methods is to provide a clear and understandable description of patterns held in data. One of the best studied models for pattern discovery in the field of data mining is that of association rules. Association rules in relational databases relate the presence of values of some attributes with values of some other attributes in the same tuple. The rule [A = a]) ⇨ [B = b] tells us that whenever the attribute A takes value a in a tuple, the attribute B takes value b in the same tuple. The accuracy and importance of association rules are usually estimated by means of two probability measures called confidence and support respectively. Discovery of association rules is one of the main techniques that can be used both by physicians and managers to obtain knowledge from large medical databases.

Medical databases are used to store a big amount of quantitative attributes. But in common conversation and reasoning, humans employ rules relating imprecise terms rather than precise values. For instance, a physician will find more appropriate to describe his/her knowledge by means of rules like "if fever is high and cough is moderate then disease is X" than by using rules like "if fever is 38.78C and cough is 5 over 10 then disease is X". It seems clear that rules relating precise values are less informative and most of the time they seem strange to humans. So nowadays, some people apply semantics to improve the association rules mining from a database containing precise values. We can reach that goal by

1. Finding a suitable representation for the imprecise terms that the users consider to be appropriate, in the domain of each quantitative attribute,
2. Generalizing the probabilistic measures of confidence and support of association rules in the presence of imprecision,
3. Improving the semantics of the measures. The confidence/support framework has been shown not to be appropriate in general, though it is a good basis for the definition of new measures,
4. Designing an algorithm to perform the mining task.

4. Part 3 A KDD Process Model

The terms knowledge discovery in database (KDD) and data mining are distinct.

KDD refers to overall process of discovering useful knowledge from data. It involves the evaluation and possibly interpretation of the patterns to make the decision of what qualifies as knowledge. It also includes the choice of encoding schemes, preprocessing, sampling, and projections of the data prior to the data mining step.

Data mining refers to the application of algorithms for extracting patterns from data without the additional steps of the KDD process.

The KDD process is often to be nontrivial; however, we take the larger view that KDD is an all-encompassing concept. KDD is a process that involves many different steps. The input to this process is the data, and the output is the useful information desired by the users. However, the objective may be unclear or inexact. The process itself is interactive and may require much elapsed time. To ensure the usefulness and accuracy of the results of the process, interaction throughout the process with both domain experts and technical experts might be needed.

Data mining is the step in the process of knowledge discovery in databases, that inputs predominantly cleaned, transformed data, searches the data using algorithms, and outputs patterns and relationships to the interpretation/evaluation step of the KDD process. The definition clearly implies that what data mining (in this view) discovers is hypotheses about patterns and relationships. Those patterns and relationships are then subject to interpretation and evaluation before they can be called knowledge. Fig. 3.1 illustrates the overall KDD process.

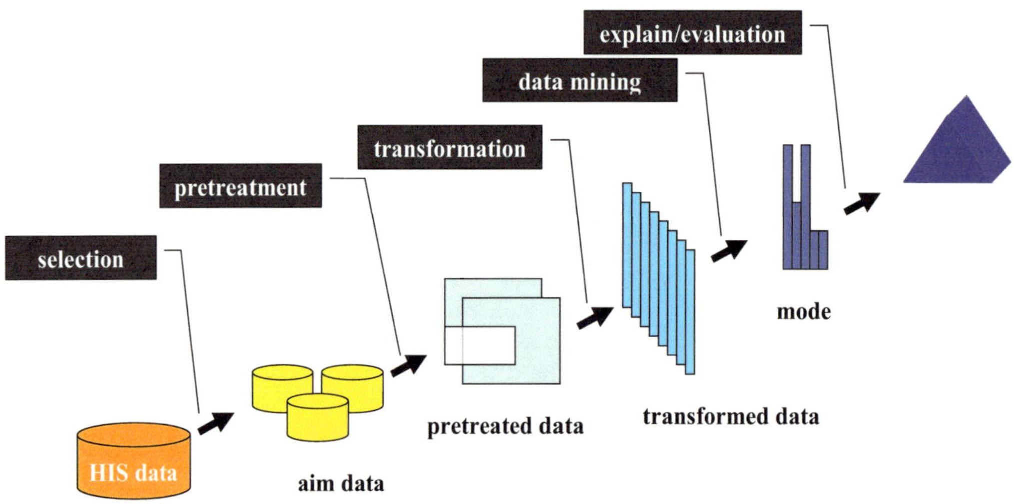

Fig. 3.1 KDD process

The KDD process consists of the following five steps:

1. Select a target data set: The data needed for the data mining process may be obtained from many different and heterogeneous data sources. This first step obtains the data from various databases, files, and nonelectronic sources. With the help of one or more human experts and knowledge discovery tools, we choose an initial set of data to be analyzed.
2. Data preprocessing: The data to be used by the process may have incorrect or missing data. There may be anomalous data from multiple sources involving different data types and metrics. There may be many different activities performed at this time. We use available resources to deal with noisy data. We decide what to do about missing data values and how to account for time-sequence information.
3. Data transformation: Attributes and instances are added and/or eliminated from the target data. Data from different sources must be converted into a common format for processing. Some data may be encoded or transformed into more usable formats. Data reduction may be used to reduce the number of possible data values being considered.

4. Data mining: A best model for representing the data is created by applying one or more data mining algorithms. Based on the data mining task being performed, this step applies algorithms to the transformed data to generate the desired results.
5. Interpretation/evaluation: We examine the output from step 4 to determine if what has been discovered is both useful and interesting. Decisions are made about whether to repeat previous steps using new attributes and/or instances. How the data mining results are presented to the users is extremely important because the usefulness of the results is dependent on it. Various visualization and GUI strategies are used at this last step.

Another important step not contained in the KDD process is goal identification. The focus of this step is on understanding the domain being considered for knowledge discovery. We write a clear statement about what is to be accomplished. Hypotheses offering likely or desired likely or desired outcomes can be stated. A main objective of goal identification is to clearly define what is to be accomplished. This step is in many ways the most difficult, as decisions about resource allocations as well as measures of success need to be determined. Whenever possible, broad goals should be stated in the form of specific objectives. Here is a partial list of things to consider at this stage:

- A clear problem statement is provided as well as a list of criteria to measure success and failure. One or more hypotheses offering likely or desired outcomes may be established.
- The choice of a data mining tool or set of tools is made. The choice of a tool depends on several factors, including the level of explanation required and whether learning is supervised, unsupervised, or a combination of both techniques.
- An estimated project cost is determined. A plan for human resource management is offered.
- A project completion/product delivery data is given.
- Legal issues that may arise from applying the results of the discovery process are taken into account.
- A plan for maintenance of a working system is provided as appropriate. As new data becomes available, a main consideration is a methodology for updating a working model.

Our list is by no means exhaustive. As with any software project, more complex problems require additional planning. Of major importance is the location, availability, and condition of resource data.

The data mining process itself is complex. As we will see in later chapters, there are many different data mining applications and algorithms. These algorithms must be carefully applied to be effective. Discovered patterns must be correctly interpreted and properly evaluated to ensure that the resulting information is meaningful and accurate.

5. Part 4. Warehouse and OLAP

5.1 Data warehousing

The term data warehouse was first used by William Inmon in the early 1980s. He defined data warehouse to be a set of data that supports DSS and is "subject-oriented, integrated, time-variant, and nonvolatile." With data warehousing, corporate-wide data (current and historical) are merged into a single repository. Traditional databases contain operational data that represent the day-to-day needs of a company. Traditional business data processing (such as billing, inventory control, payroll, and manufacturing support) support online transaction processing and batch reporting applications. A data warehouse, however, contains informational data, which are used to support other functions such as planning and forecasting. Although much of the content is similar between the operational and informational data, much is different. As a matter of fact, the operational data are transformed into the informational data.

The basic components of a data warehousing system include data migration, the warehouse, and access tools. The data are extracted from operational systems, but must be reformatted, cleansed, integrated, and summarized before being placed in the warehouse. Much of the operational data are not needed in the warehouse and are removed during this conversion process. This migration process is similar to that needed for data mining applications except that data mining applications need not necessarily be performed on summarized or business-wide data. The applications to access a warehouse include traditional querying, OLAP, and data mining. Since the warehouse is stored as a database, it can be accessed by traditional query language.

The data transformation process required to convert operational data to informational involves many functions including:

- Unwanted data must be removed.
- Converting heterogeneous sources into one common schema. This problem is the same as that found when accessing data from multiple heterogeneous sources. Each operational database may contain the same data with different attribute names. In addition, there may be multiple data types for the same attribute.
- As the operational data is probably a snapshot of the data, multiple snapshots may need to be merged to create the historical view.
- Summarizing data is performed to provide a higher level view of the data. This summarization may be done at multiple granularities and for different dimensions.
- New derived data may be added to better facilitate decision support functions.
- Handling missing and erroneous data must be performed. This could entail replacing them with predicted or simply removing these entries.
- When designing a data warehouse, we must think of the uniqueness of medical data carefully. Below we comment on some unique features of medical data.
- Because of the sheer volume and heterogeneity of medical databases, it is unlikely that any current data mining tool can succeed with raw data. The tools may require extracting a sample from the database, in the hope that results obtained in this manner are representative for the entire database. Dimensionality reduction can be achieved in two ways. By sampling in the patient-record space, where some records are selected, often randomly, and used afterwards for data mining; or sampling in the feature space, where only some features of each data record are selected.
- Medical databases are constantly updated by, say, adding new SPECT images (for an existing or new patient), or by replacement of the existing images (say, a SPECT had to be repeated because of technical problems). This requires methods that are able to incrementally update the knowledge learned so far.
- The medical information collected in a database is often incomplete, e.g. some tests were not performed at a given visit, or imprecise, e.g. "the patient is weak or diaphoretic."

- It is very difficult for a medical data collection technique to entirely eliminate noise. Thus, data mining methods should be made less sensitive to noise, or care must be taken that the amount of noise in future data is approximately the same as that in the current data.
- In any large database, we encounter a problem of missing values. A missing value may have been accidentally not entered, or purposely not obtained for technical, economic, or ethical reasons. One approach to address this problem is to substitute missing values with most likely values; another approach is to replace the missing value with all possible values for that attribute. Still another approach is intermediate: specify a likely range of values, instead of only one most likely. The difficulty is how to specify the range in an unbiased manner.

The missing value problem is widely encountered in medical databases, since most medical data are collected as a byproduct of patient-care activities, rather than for organized research protocols, where exhaustive data collection can be enforced. In the emerging federal paradigm of minimal risk investigations, there is preference for data mining solely from byproduct data. Thus, in a large medical database, almost every patient-record is lacking values for some feature, and almost every feature is lacking values for some patient-record.

- The medical data set may contain redundant, insignificant, or inconsistent data objects and/or attributes. We speak about inconsistent data when the same data item is categorized as belonging to more than one mutually exclusive category. For example, a serum potassium value incompatible with life obtained from a patient who seemed reasonably healthy at the time the serum was drawn. A common explanation is that the specimen was excessively shaken during transport to the laboratory, but one cannot assume this explanation without additional investigation and data, which may be impractical in a data mining investigation.
- Often we want to find natural groupings (clusters) in large dimensional medical data. Objects are clustered together if they are similar to one another (according to some measures), and at the same time are dissimilar from objects in other clusters. A major concern is how to incorporate medical domain knowledge into the mechanisms of clustering. Without that focus and at least partial human supervision, one can easily end up with clustering problems that are computationally infeasible, or results that do not make sense.
- In medicine, we are interested in creating understandable to human descriptions of medical concepts, or models. Machine learning, conceptual clustering, genetic algorithms, and fuzzy sets are the principal methods used for achieving this goal, since they can create a model in terms of intuitively transparent if . . . then . . . rules. On the other hand, unintuitive black box methods, like artificial neural networks, may be of less interest.

5.2 OLAP

Online analytic processing (OLAP) systems are targeted to provide more complex query results than traditional OLTP or database systems. Unlike database queries, however, OLAP applications usually involve analysis of the actual data. They can be thought of as an extension of some of the basic aggregation functions available in SQL. This extra analysis of the data as well as the more imprecise nature of the OLAP queries is what really differentiate OLAP applications from traditional database and OLTP applications. OLAP tools may also be used in DSS systems.

OLAP is performed on data warehouse or data marts. The primary goal of OLAP is to support ad hoc querying needed to support DSS. The multidimensional view of data is fundamental to OLAP applications. OLAP is an application view, not a data structure or schema. The complex nature of OLAP applications requires a multidimensional review of the data. The type of data accessed is often (although not a requirement) a data warehouse.

OLAP tools can be classified as ROLAP or MOLAP. With MOLAP (multidimensional OLAP), data are modeled, viewed, and physically stored in a multidimensional database (MDD). MOLAP tools are implemented by specialized DBMS and software systems capable of supporting the multidimensional data directly. With MOLAP, data are stored as an n-dimensional array (assuming there are n dimensions), so the cube view is stored directly. Although MOLAP has extremely high storage requirements, indices are used to speed up processing. With ROLAP (relational OLAP), however, data are stored in a relational database, and a ROLAP server (middleware) creates the multidimensional view for the user. As one would think, the ROLAP tools tend to be less complex, but also less efficient. MDD systems may presummarize along all dimensions. A third approach, hybrid OLAP (HOLAP), combines the best features of ROLAP and MOLAP. Queries are stated in multidimensional terms. Data that are not updated frequently will be stored as MDD, whereas data that are updated frequently will be stored as RDB.

There are several types of OLAP operations supported by OLAP tools:

- A simple query may look at a single cell within the cube.
- Slice: Look at a subcube to get more specific information. This is performed by selecting on one dimension. This is looking at a portion of the cube.
- Dice: Look at a subcube by selecting on two or more dimensions. This can be performed by a slice on one dimension and the rotating the cube to select on a second dimension. A dice is made because the view in slice in rotated from all cells for one product to all cells for one location.
- Roll up (dimension reduction, aggregation): Roll up allows the user to ask questions that move up an aggregation hierarchy. Instead of looking at one single fact, we look at all the facts. Thus, we could, for example, look at the overall total sales for the company.
- Drill down: These functions allow a user to get more detailed fact information by navigating lower in the aggregation hierarchy. We could perhaps look at quantities sold within a specific area of each of the cities.
- Visualization: Visualization allows the OLAP users to actually "see" the results of an operation.

To assist with roll up and drill down operations, frequently used aggregations can be precomputed and stored in the warehouse. There have been several different definitions for a dice. In fact, the term slice and dice is sometimes viewed together as indicating that the cube is subdivided by selecting on multiple dimensions.

6. Part 5 Embedded real-time KDD process

6.1 A modified KDD process

As referred in Part 3, traditional knowledge discovery process includes five steps: selection, pretreatment, transformation, data mining, and interpretation and evaluation. It is not a

simple linear course, but an iterative one including recurrence between every two steps. Refine and deepen the knowledge continuously, and finally make it easier to understand.
Medical data is huge and disorganized generally because of residing in different information systems. This makes data mining of medical data different from others. Data mining in the HIS database is an important work for hospital management. Hospital managers can utilize the knowledge mined sufficiently into decision-making for the hospital with the final purpose to provide the hospital better development. A modified KDD process was proposed for medical data mining using Intersystems BI tool DeepSee (Fig. 5.1).

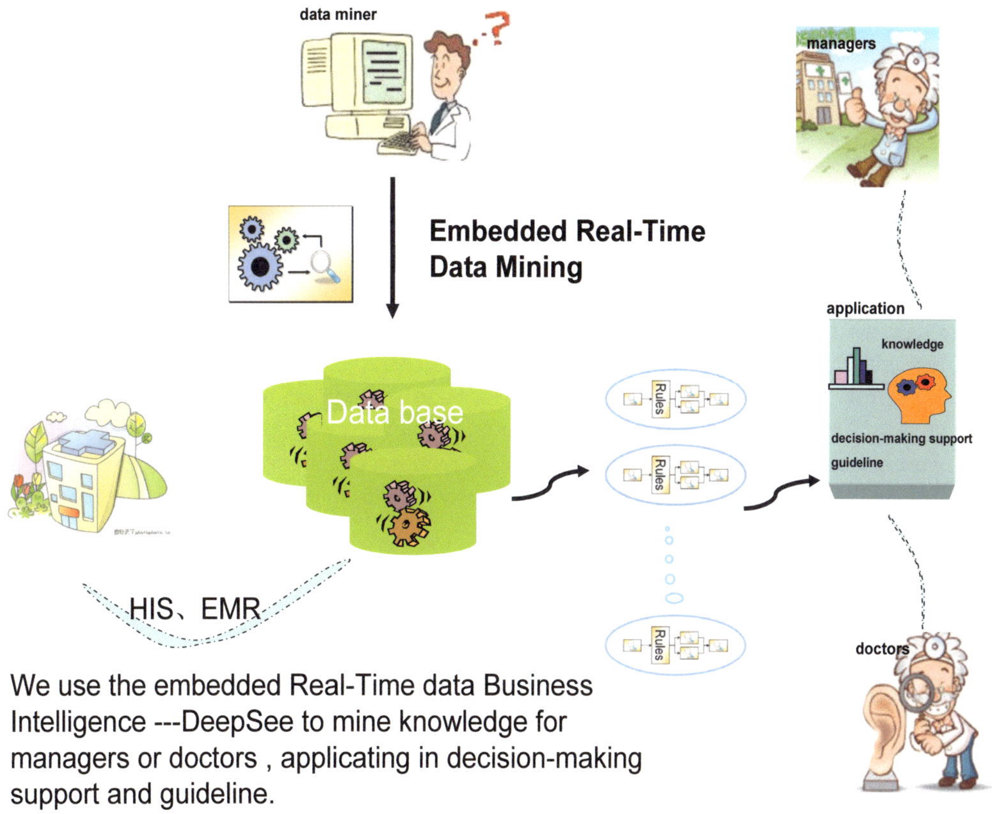

Fig. 5.1 Embedded real-time process mining

6.2 Embedded real-time process mining

DeepSee is innovative software that enables data miners to embedded real-time business intelligence capabilities into the existing and future transactional applications. Embedded real-time business intelligence is different from the traditional data mining process. That's because it's focused on providing every user with useful, timely information related to making operational decision. InterSystems DeepSee is used for supporting the decision-making process in hospital management. With DeepSee, hospital managers can look at what's happening in the hospital while it's actually taking place and they can make the changes needed to improve the medical process.

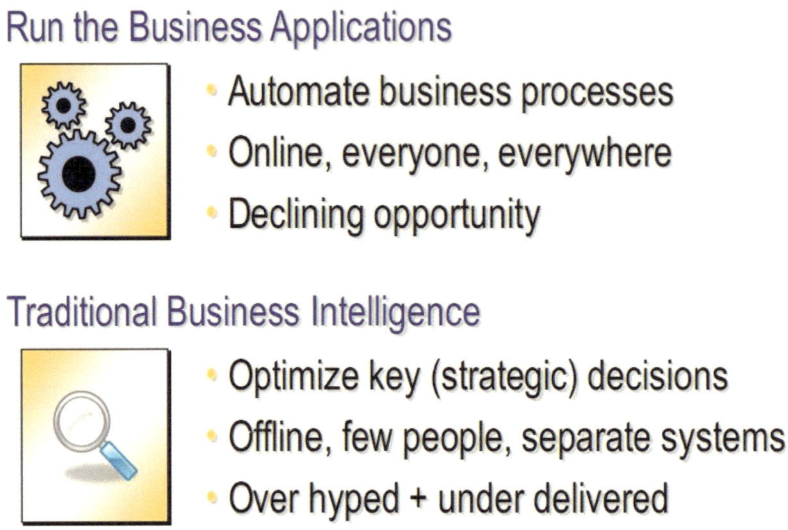

Fig. 5.2 Market Evolution of DeepSee

1. **Business Intelligence** is the art of putting the data collected by applications to good use-analyzing it to provide information that helps managers make better business decisions. Traditionally, such analysis has been performed by small groups of "data experts" working with specialized tools, looking at data gathered into a data warehouse. Because loading data into a warehouse often takes considerable time, the information gleaned from traditional business intelligence is usually historical in nature.
2. **Real-time Business Intelligence** takes the data warehouse out of the picture. It allows timely analysis of data stored within transactional applications. Because the data is "fresh", real-time business intelligence helps users make better operational decisions.
3. **Embedded Real-time Business Intelligence** means that the capability to turn operational data into immediately useful in formation is included as a feature of the transactional application. Users don't have to be data analysis experts or use separate tools to gain insight from their data.

With DeepSee, business intelligence is:

- Fast- Utilizing InterSystems' breakthrough transitional bit indexing map technology that provides excellent retrieval performance for complex queries plus top-tier update performance for high-volume transaction processing, information is accessible in real time.
- Easy- Using DeepSee, application developers rapidly build interactive dashboards containing graphs, charts, filters, images, links, etc.
- Cost-effective- DeepSee removes the costly requirement to create and maintain a data warehouse because, unlike traditional BI, it accesses your current transactional data.

Managers can monitor every branch department to compare the results of local hospital activities at any point during the medical process. Depending on the information delivered by operational BI, decisions can be made in real time to implement activities that are proving successful in other locations- a promotion for high interest bearing account, for example- and to immediately cut off promotions that aren't working effectively in certain locations. The emphasis of data mining is on an implementation of a general approach to rule based decision-making.

Four steps to embedded BI with DeepSee

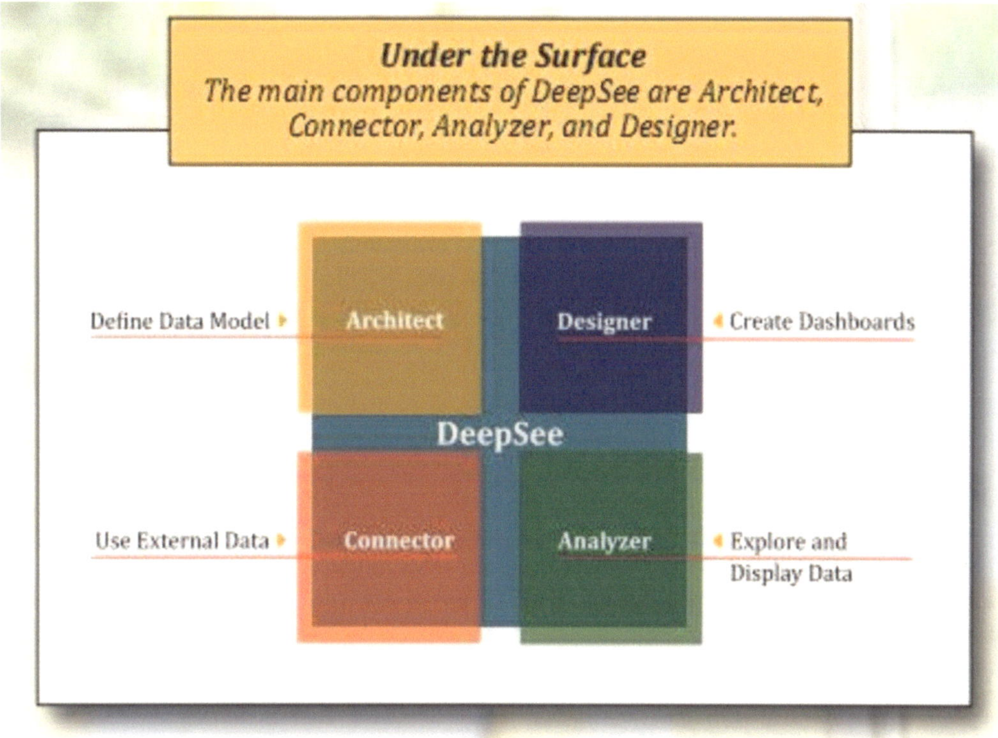

Fig. 5.3 The main four components of DeepSee

Step 1. Determine Key Performance Indicators

Better than anyone, your users know how to do their jobs. And they can tell you what knowledge they need to be able to do their jobs better. Through discussions with end users, you can figure out what key performance indicators they want to be able to analyze in real time. A key performance indicator might be a particular bit of raw data that is collected by your application, or it might be a measurement that is calculated from disparate solutions. The best way to determine meaningful, useful performance indicators is to talk to your users.

Step 2. Define a data model

Your data model is a definition of how to organize the raw data that aggregates into various key performance indicators. If a performance indicator must be calculated from raw data, the data model will define how that is done. The data model is also where you can give data, dimensions, and key performance indicators names that will be intuitive and meaningful for end users.

The dimensions of a data model determine how many ways a performance can be analyzed, and thus what raw data needs to be included in your model. In order to speed analysis time, some of those dimensions may have indices defined within your model. DeepSee works with transactional data, so information will be organized and indexed by your data model in real time.

The task of defining a data model is accomplished using the DeepSee Architect.

Step 2a. (if necessary): Incorporate "foreign" data

If any of the raw data needed in your data model comes from applications or repositories that are not powered InterSystems' technology, that data must be incorporated using Ensemble and the DeepSee Connector. The Connector provides a "snapshot" of the external data, which may be transformed (through the use of configurable business rules) to fit into your data model. The snapshot can be a one-time import, or occur on a scheduled basis. Incremental updates are supported.

Step 3. Build components

The DeepSee Analyzer enables point-and-click or drag-and-drop creation of pivot tables, graphs, and charts that use data models defined by the DeepSee Architect. These components are dynamic, allowing users to drill all the way down to the underlying detail data.

Step 4. Design a dashboard

With the DeepSee Designer, you will create dashboards that include the graphs, charts, and pivot tables you built with the DeepSee Analyzer, as well as links, combo-boxes, lists, and other user interface components. Dashboards can be tailored to specific topics, functions, or individuals. You can control how much flexibility users have when exploring data for example, pre-defined filters can exclude sensitive data from users who have no need to see it.

The dashboards you create with the Designer are Web pages that can easily be embedded within the user interface of your application. Users do not have to be data analysis experts to reap the benefits of real-time business intelligence. They merely need a working knowledge of your application.

7. Part 6 Two case studies of data mining in HIS

7.1 KDD based on DeepSee

DeepSee contains four main components:

A: Connector

- For non-Caché data, the Connector can extract data from external sources so that it can be modeled using the Architect.
- The connector is not used if the data is already in Caché (or Ensemble).

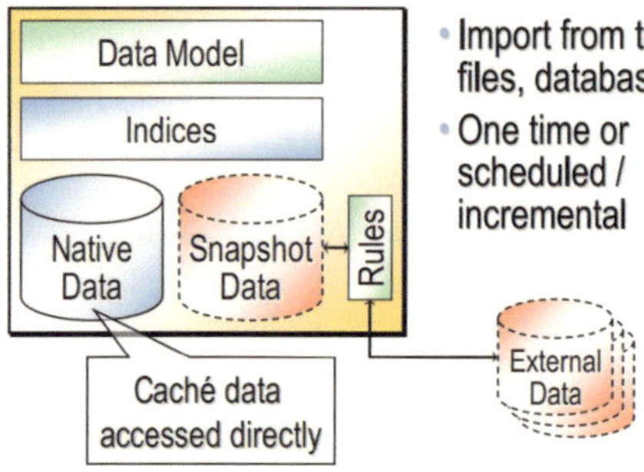

Fig. 6.1 DeepSee Connector

B: Architect

- Defines the data models to be used by the Analyzer.
- A data model defines the dimensions and measures by which data can be analyzed.
- High-performance bitmap indices are created for optimal performance.
- Models are based on current transactional data-no data warehouse is required.

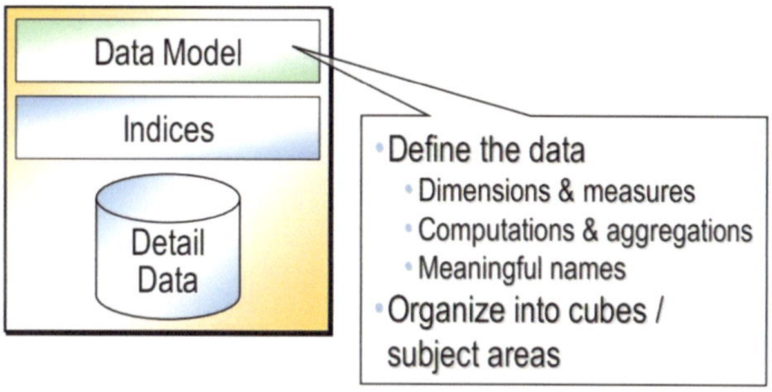

Fig. 6.2 DeepSee Architect

C: Analyzer

- Point-and-click/ drag-and-drop creation of pivot tables and graphs.
- Uses data models defined by the Architect.
- Dynamic drill down all the way to the underlying detail data.

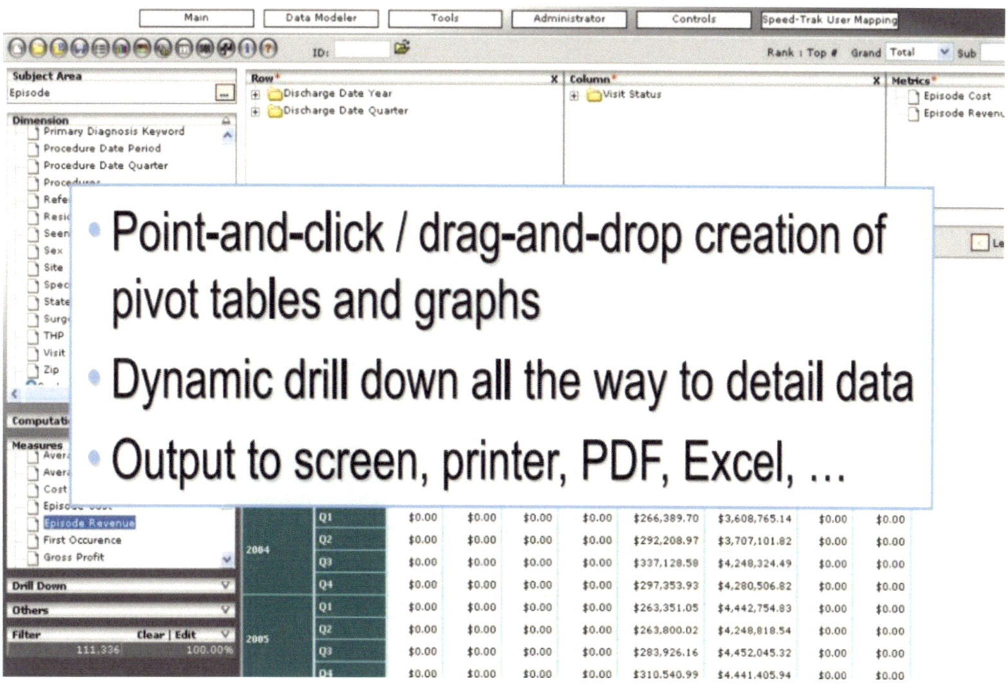

Fig. 6.3 DeepSee Analyzer

D: Designer

- Create dashboards that use the pivot tables and graphs built with the Analyzer.
- Dashboards are Web pages that can be embedded into applications.
- Dashboards can also include interactive UI controls like combo-boxes, lists, radio buttons, links, etc.

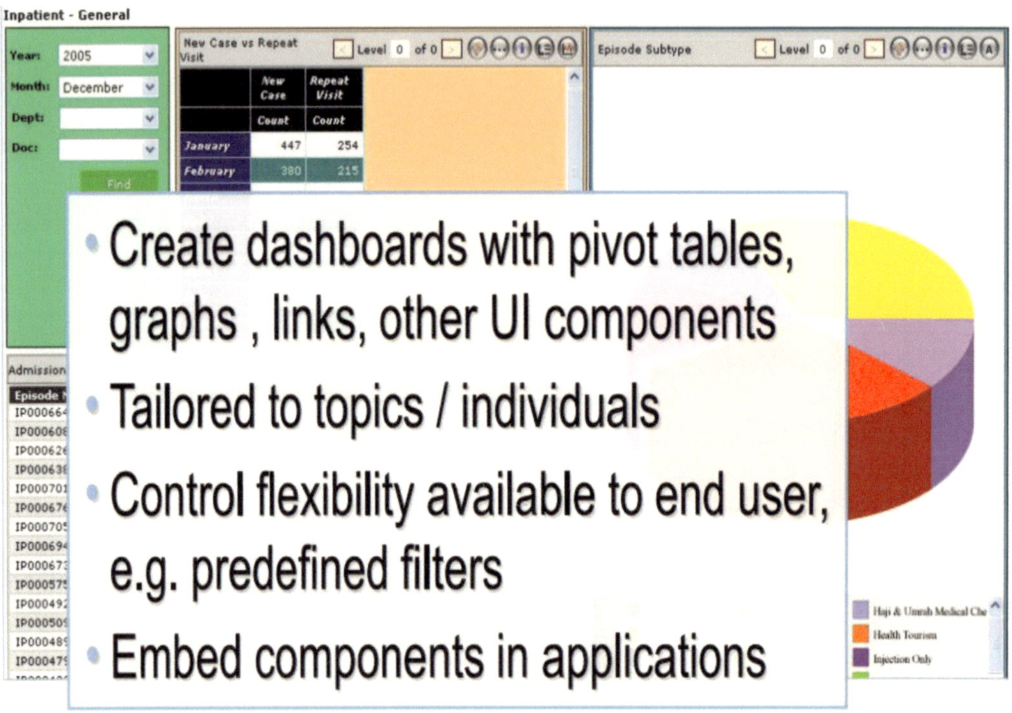

Fig. 6.4 DeepSee Designer

In the following part, we will introduce two KDD examples using DeepSee.

7.2 KDD of Inpatient Fees

Health care organizations are increasing expenditures on information technology as a means to improve safety, quality, and access. Decision-making is the core of hospital management, and goes widely throughout the whole hospital behavior. It is pivotal for hospitals to make appropriate decision, which is closely related to hospital development. Managers suffer pressure to make decision, when the knowledge from Hospital Information System is not so high-quality, comprehensive or reliable. Therefore it is important to integrate data from different Hospital Information Systems, carry out data mining and subsequently discover the knowledge in the mining result to promote the hospitals' competition.

HIS database involves fee information related to the whole medical behavior, such as examinations, tests, treatments, prescriptions, nursing and supplies et al. We can relevantly construct models based on various themes for data mining. The database contains information as follow: 1. patient information, 2. diagnostic information (diseases category and diagnose information), 3. medical information (surgeries, radio chemotherapies, nursing, prescriptions, examinations, and treatment orders, treatment departments and corresponding managers) 4. fee information (treatment fee details, beds and medical consumables), 5. insurance patient data, 6. time information (starting time and duration of the whole medical behavior). All the information can be discovered to provide knowledge for decision-making support.

7.2.1 Modeling of inpatient fee

For every theme, the dimensions, relevant indexes and data source each instance should be defined. A model is built based on inpatient fee to analyze HIS data (in the duration from 2001 to 2007) of a hospital in Zhejiang Province in China. The dimensions and data source defined, accordingly, are in Table 1 as follow:

Theme	**Inpatient fees**
Dimensionalities	Date dimensionalities (duration, day, week, month, quarter, year)
Related indexes	Fee category, medical insurance category, department, net payment
Dataset and the sources (summary)	Inpatient master records: PAT_VISIT Inpatient master index: PAT_MASTER_INDEX Inpatient settle master: INP_SETTLE_MASTER Inpatient settle details: INP_SETTLE_DETAIL
Data details	Charge class: FEECLASSNAME.FEECLASSNAME Discharge time: RCPTNO.visitfk.DISCHARGEDATETIME Admission time: RCPTNO.visitfk.ADMISSIONDATETIME Admission department: RCPTNO.visitfk.DEPTADMISSIONTO.DEPTNAME Discharge department: RCPTNO.visitfk.DEPTDISCHARGEFROM.DEPTNAME Admission form: RCPTNO.visitfk.PATIENTCLASS Discharge form: RCPTNO.visitfk.DISCHARGEDISPOSITION Insurance type: RCPTNO.visitfk.INSURANCETYPE Payment: PAYMENTS

Table 6.1 Theme and dimensions

Then a data model is built in the HIS database according to the data source. It is object model below (Fig. 6.5) to explain the relationship between the data:

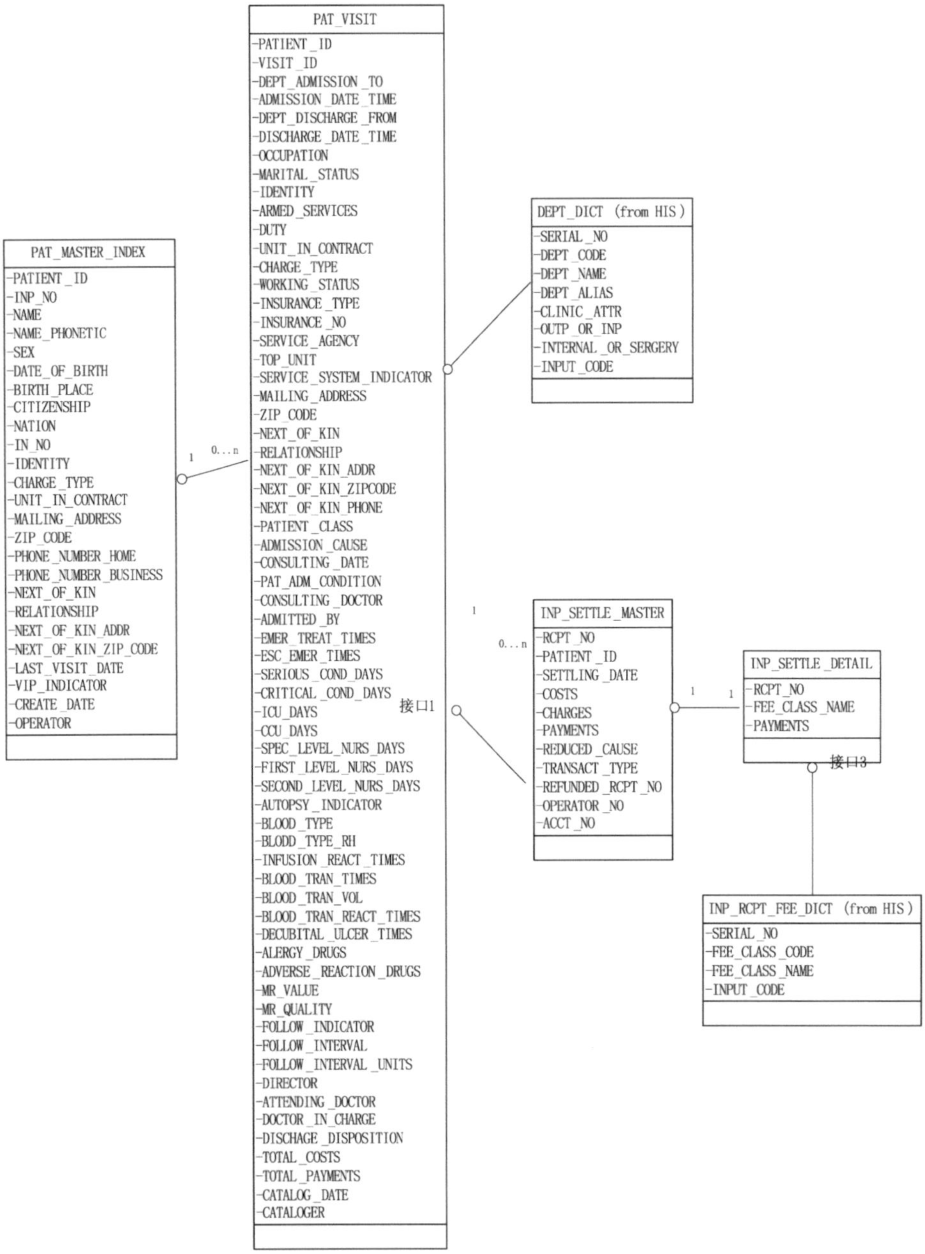

Fig. 6.5 Object model of inpatient fees

This model will be analyzed in three aspects: medical insurance fee, department annual fee and fee compositions.

7.2.2 Related work and results

Based on the model built above, the embedded real-time DeepSee is used to carry out data mining for the model of inpatient fee theme. It will be analyzed from three aspects.

7.2.2.1 *Analysis of medical insurance fee*

The data mining result of medical insurance fee from 2001 to 2007 is illustrated in Fig. 6.6. It can be seen that public retire staff occupies the maximum proportion of 22.35%, and the unemployed people least, 0.72%. It is important for the hospital to receive public retire staffs due to the high proportion. Hospital managers should adjust guidelines accordingly to provide higher quality treatment for these patients in advance.

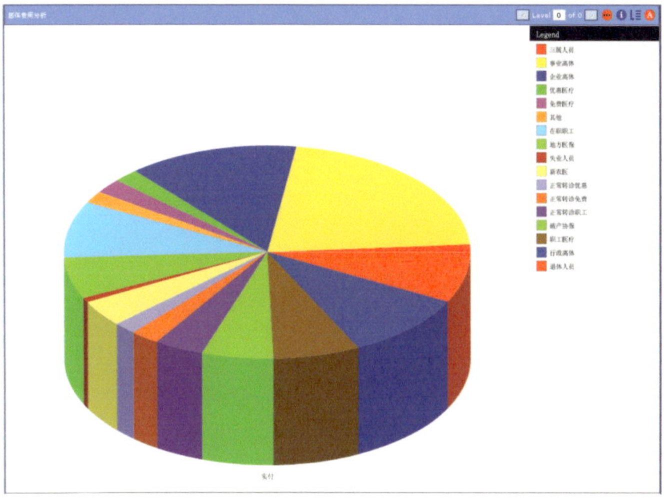

Fig. 6.6 Medical insurance fees from 2001 to 2007

7.2.2.2 *Analysis of the annual fee*

From Fig. 6.7, the conclusion can be reached that the department annual fee rose continuously from the year 2001 to 2007, with the amount rising from 9,346.86 million to 19,788.85 million and the growth rate is about 1.17.

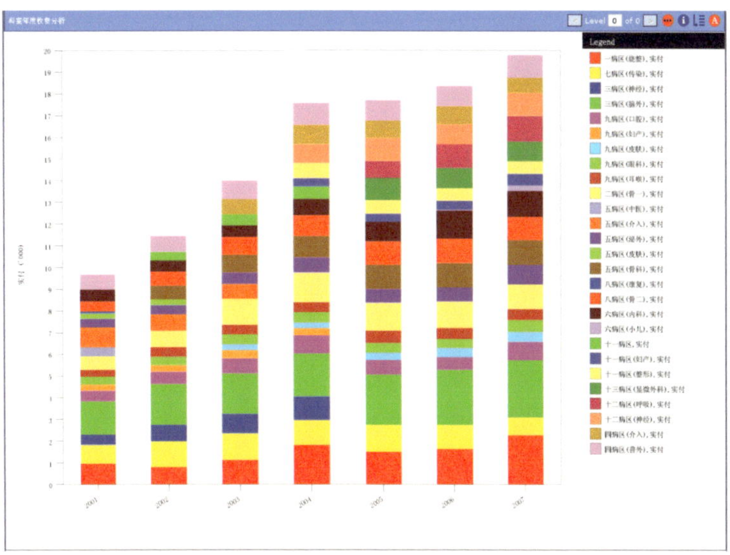

Fig. 6.7 Department annual fee from 2001 to 2007

Conclusion could be got from Fig. 6.8 that the third endemic area (cerebral surgery) had the most proportion, followed by the first endemic area (burn and plastic) and second endemic area (orthopaedics).

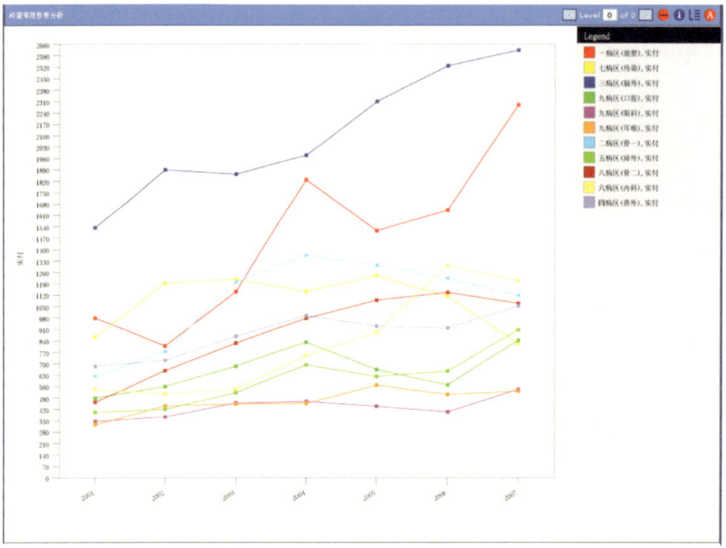

Fig. 6.8 Trend of each department annual fee from 2001 to 2007

7.2.2.3 *Analysis of fee compositions*

Inpatient fees include drugs, examinations, treatments, test and operations et al. We can reach the conclusion that the fees of western medicine, treatment and operation occupied a fairly large proportion, according to Fig. 6.9.

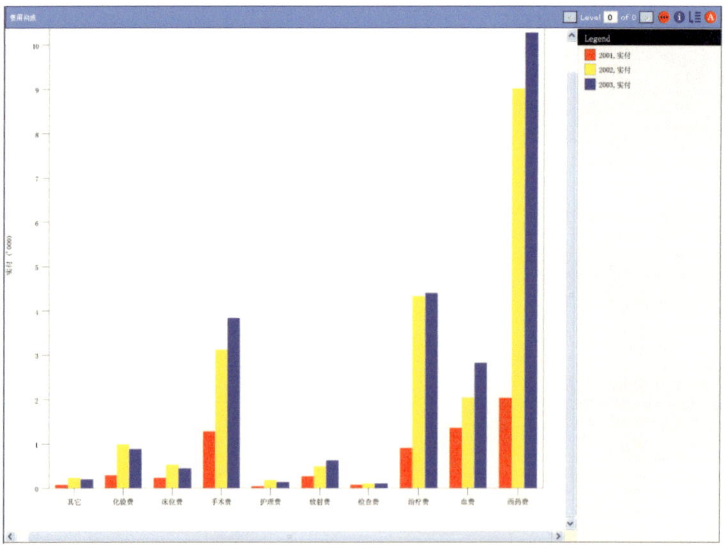

Fig. 6.9 Fee proportion from 2001-2003

When the fee proportion of drugs, examination or test is too high, managers can analyze the compositions of every inpatient fee according to data mining results, and finally control over treatment pertinently.

7.3 KDD of Pharmacy

Pharmacy is the main place of drug storage and supply base in hospital. Pharmacy managers have a responsibility to guarantee the medicinal safety, effect and abundance. Correctness of pharmaceutical expenditure accounts influences hospital operating results directly, so it has financial significance to enhance management during drug circulation. Hospital Information System (HIS) database contains all data related to pharmacy.

7.3.1 Modeling of pharmacy theme

A model is built based on the pharmacy data (in the duration from 2001 to 2005) of a hospital in Zhejiang Province in China. The dimensions and data source defined, accordingly, are in Table 6.2 as follow:

Theme	**Pharmacy**
Dimensionalities	Date dimensionalities
Related indexes	Drug name, Stock name, Annual inventory, Inventory profit, Stock amount, Supplier
Dataset and the sources (summary)	Drug dictionary: Drug_Dict Drug supplier catalog:DRUG_SUPPLIER_CATALOG Drug stock balance: DRUG_STOCK_BALANCE Drug storage dept dictionary: DRUG_STORAGE_DEPT
Data details	Drug name: drugfk.DRUGNAME Drug code: drugfk.DRUGCODE Export money: EXPORTMONEY Annual inventory: INVENTORY Profit: PROFIT Storage name: STORAGE.STORAGENAME Supplier: FIRMID.SUPPLIER Time: YEARMONTH （ps: drugfk is the foreign key of DRUG_CODE and DRUG_SPEC）

Table 6.2 Theme and dimensions

Then pharmacy model is established according to the data source in the HIS database. It's an object model in Fig. 6.10 to explain the relationship between the tables. The model includes four tables: Drug stock balance, Drug storage dept dictionary, Drug dictionary and Drug supplier catalog. Drug stock balance is the main table for analysis, and it includes 246,016 records data involving 11,655 kinds of drugs. The relationship between these tables is one to one correspondence. Subsequent data mining is all based on this pharmacy model, analyzing in four aspects: delivery trend, stocks, stock department profitability and profitability from different supplier.

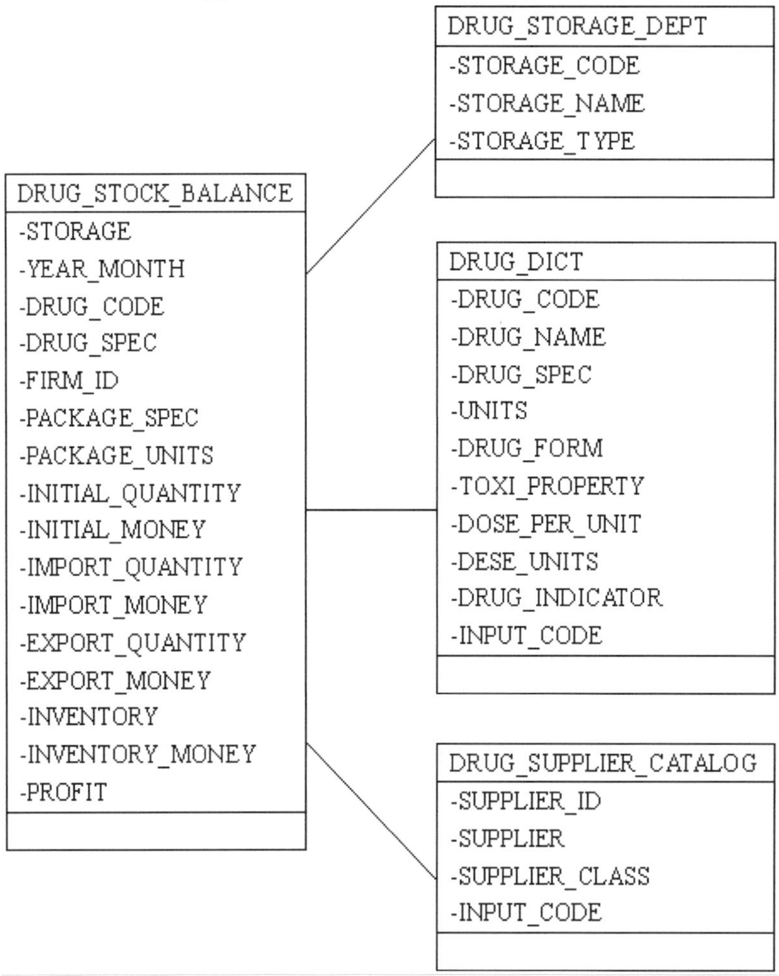

Fig. 6.10 Object model based on pharmacy theme

7.3.2 Related work and results

Data mining analysis is established based on the object model above. Main data mining dashboard (Fig. 6.11) contains three parts: project selection, main panel and filter. Analysis will be expatiated from four aspects: delivery trend, stocks, stock department profitability and profitability from different supplier. The main panel can be chosen to display the topic in statistical data or graphics. Data will be filtered by time, drug name and stock units.

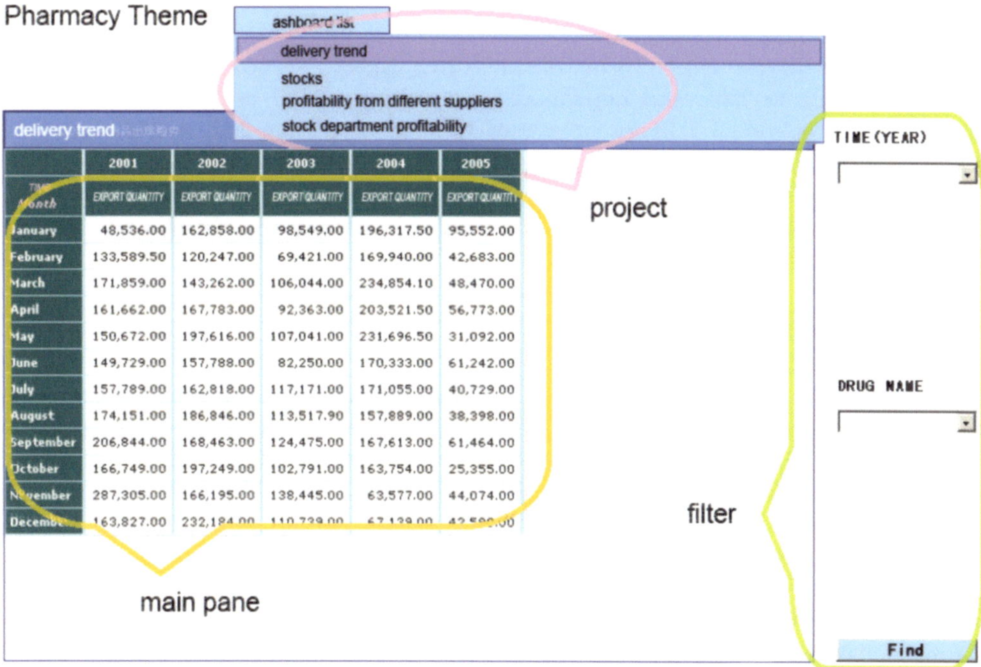

Fig. 6.11 Main data mining dashboard

7.3.2.1 *Analysis of Delivery Trend*

By observing delivery trend graphical, managers can adjust the drug inventory and warehousing in the next year. On the other hand, managers can speculate epidemics while there are fluctuation or peak valley in the trend graphics.

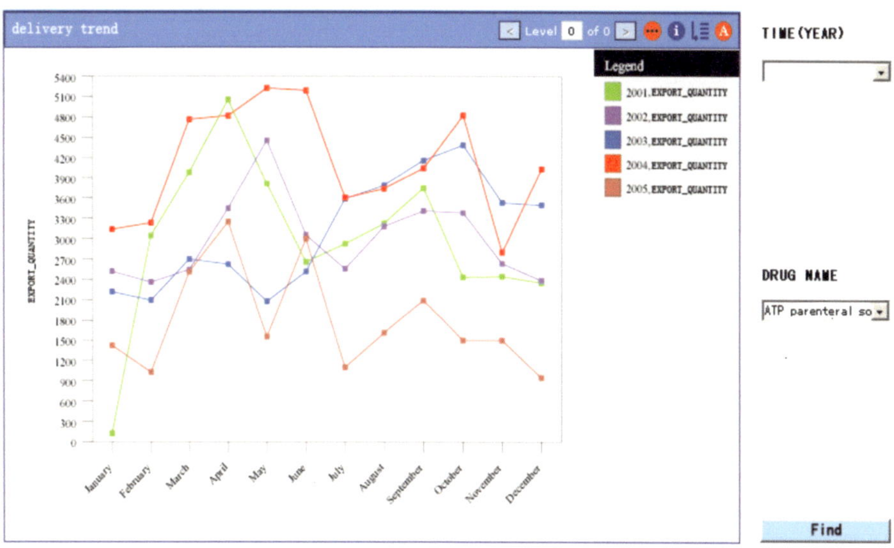

Fig. 6.12 Delivery trend of ATP Injection

The delivery trend of ATP Injection from 2001 to 2005 is illustrated in Fig. 6.12, horizontal axis as the time month, vertical axis as delivery volume, different colors corresponding to different year. Analysis will be carried through two aspects: vertically the global delivery trends from 2001 to 2005, and horizontally the delivery trend of ATP Injection in the assigned year. The global delivery volume of ATP Injection from 2001 to 2005 keeps in a relatively stable state. In most years, there is a delivery peak around April, and then the trend line declines slowly, and reaches a new peak around October. Pharmacy managers can investigate the actual situation according to these fluctuations and peaks, and adjust the pharmacy more reasonably.

7.3.2.2 *Analysis of Stock*

Stock analysis will be carried out in table and graphics tow forms. In table, red data indicates warning signal. Maximum stock and minimum stock were presupposed. There will be a warning signal any time when stock is higher than maximum stock or lower than minimum stock. Warning signal reminds pharmacy mangers to stop stocking in or stock in time. In graphics, horizontal axis is the time month and vertical axis is stock volume, different colors representing different stock department.

Fig. 6.13 is the table form stock of Leucogen in 2002. It has been below the minimum stock from March in the whole year. According to the delivery trend of Leucogen in the main data mining dashboard, it is the large amount of delivery which causes the warning signal. Pharmacy managers should stock in Leucogen in time to avoid emergency storage. Fig. 6.14 is the graphics form of Leucogen in 2002, which is much more visual than table form.

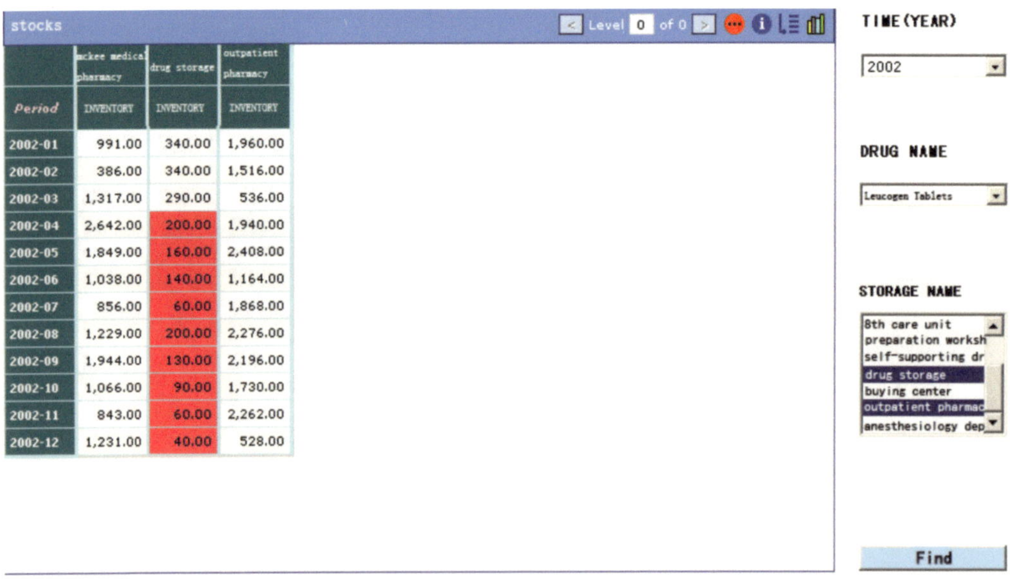

	mckee medical pharmacy	drug storage	outpatient pharmacy
Period	INVENTORY	INVENTORY	INVENTORY
2002-01	991.00	340.00	1,960.00
2002-02	386.00	340.00	1,516.00
2002-03	1,317.00	290.00	536.00
2002-04	2,642.00	200.00	1,940.00
2002-05	1,849.00	160.00	2,408.00
2002-06	1,038.00	140.00	1,164.00
2002-07	856.00	60.00	1,868.00
2002-08	1,229.00	200.00	2,276.00
2002-09	1,944.00	130.00	2,196.00
2002-10	1,066.00	90.00	1,730.00
2002-11	843.00	60.00	2,262.00
2002-12	1,231.00	40.00	528.00

Fig. 6.13 Stock table of Leucogen

7.3.2.3 *Analysis of Stock Department profitability*

Profitability of department has been paid lots of attention. Departments contain the center pharmacy, pharmaceutical workshop, self-supporting pharmacy, drug storage, procurement center and out-patient pharmacy. Fig. 6.15 exhibits the profitability of each department referred above from 2001 to 2005, horizontal axis as the year, vertical axis as profitability, different colors corresponding to different departments. As can be seen, drug storage profits stably and accounts for 77.79% to 99.98% from 2001 to 2005. The center pharmacy profits secondly, and pharmaceutical workshop the least.

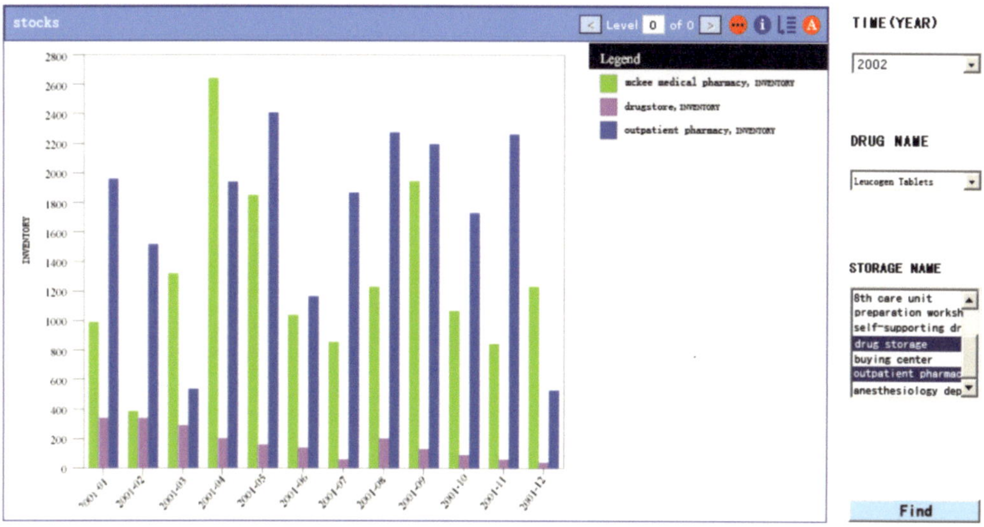

Fig. 6.14 Stock graphics of Leucogen

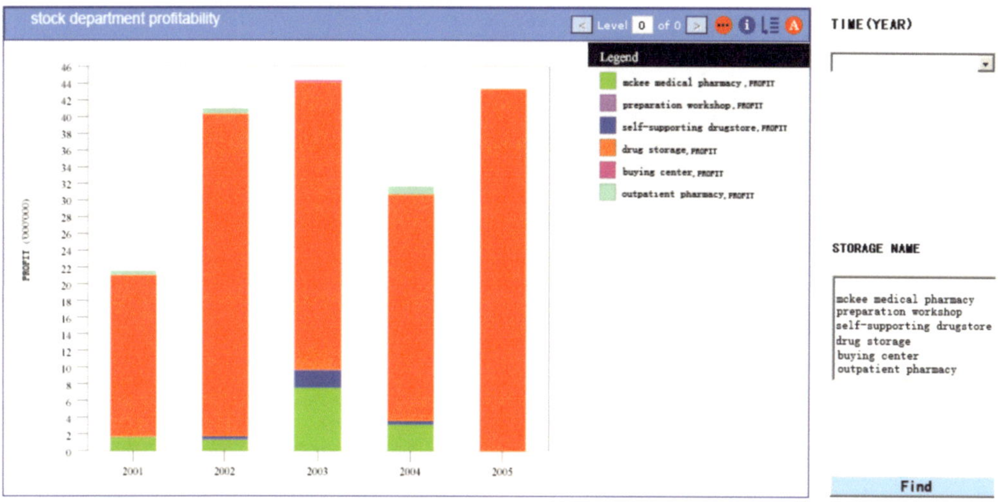

Fig. 6.15 Profitability of each stock department

7.3.2.4 *Analysis of profitability from different suppliers*

Different suppliers make different profitability, which is fairly important to hospital finance. Both the drug price and delivery volume would affect total profitability. Fig. 6.16 is profitability of Mannitol Injection from different suppliers, horizontal axis as suppliers' name, vertical axis as profitability, different colors corresponding to different years.

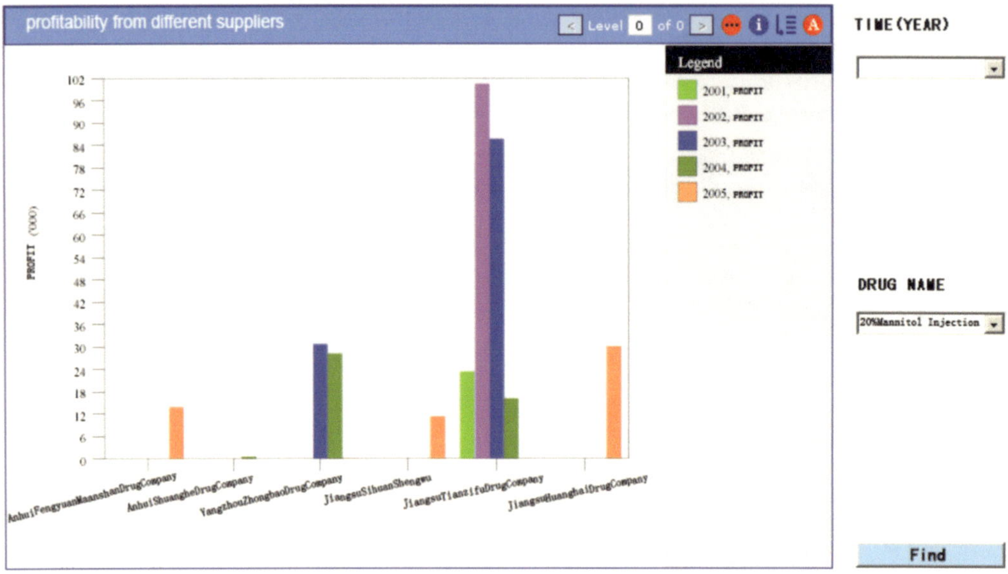

Fig. 6.16 Profitability from different suppliers

It can be seen in Fig. 6.16 that profitabilitys steadily increase from 2001 but gradually decrease from 2004. Jiangsu Tianzifu Drug Company accounts for the largest proportion which means the pharmacy buy large volume of Mannitol Injection from the supplier.

Decision-making throughout hospital activities is the core of hospital management. How to access high-quality decision-makers in time makes key deciders feel tremendous pressure. Pharmacy is the source of medication in hospital. Data mining of pharmacy in HIS database and monitoring on it is an important way to ensure safe medication and adequate stocks. In this part, we use Deepee as a data mining tool. Managers can utilize the knowledge mined sufficiently into decision-making for the hospital with the final purpose to provide the hospital better development.

8. References

[1] Krzysztof J. Cios, G. William Moore. Uniqueness of medical data mining. Artificial Intelligence in Medicine 26: 1-24, 2002.

[2] Linda Goodwin, Michele VanDyne, Simon Lin. Data mining issues and opportunities for building nursing knowledge. Journal of Biomedical Informatics 36: 379-388, 2003.

[3] Thomas M. Lehmanna, Mark O. Gu¨ld, Thomas Deselaers. Automatic categorization of medical images for content-based retrieval and data mining. Computerized Medical Imaging and Graphics 29: 143-155, 2005.

[4] Sean N. Ghazavi, Thunshun W. Liao. Medical data mining by fuzzy modeling with selected features. Artificial Intelligence in Medicine: 43, 195—206, 2008.

[5] Belacel N, Boulassel MR. Multicriteria fuzzy assignment method: a useful tool to assist medical diagnosis. Artificial Intelligence in Medicine 21: 201—207, 2001.

[6] M.R. Smith, X. Wang, R.M. Rangayyan. Evaluation of the sensitivity of a medical data-mining application to the number of elements in small databases. Biomedical Signal Processing and Control 4: 262–268, 2009.
[7] Wen-Tsann Lin, Shen-Tsu Wang, Ta-Cheng Chiang. Abnormal diagnosis of Emergency Department triage explored with data mining technology: An Emergency Department at a Medical Center in Taiwan taken as an example. Expert Systems with Applications 37: 2733–2741, 2010.
[8] Janez Demsˇar, Blazˇ Zupan, Noriaki Aoki. Feature mining and predictive model construction from severe trauma patient's data. International Journal of Medical Informatics 63: 41–50, 2001.
[9] AndrewKusiak, Bradley Dixon, Shital Shah. Predicting survival time for kidney dialysis patients: a data mining approach. Computers in Biology and Medicine 35: 311–327, 2005.
[10] Gloria Phillips-Wren, Phoebe Sharkey, Sydney Morss Dy. Mining lung cancer patient data to assess healthcare resource utilization. Expert Systems with Applications 35: 1611–1619, 2008.
[11] Miguel Delgado, Daniel SaÂnchez, MarõÂa J. MartõÂn-Bautista. Mining association rules with improved semantics in medical databases. Artificial Intelligence in Medicine 21: 241 – 245, 2001.
[12] Po Shun Ngan, Man Leung Wong, Wai Lam. Medical data mining using evolutionary computation. Artificial Intelligence in Medicine 16: 73–96, 1999.
[13] Richard J. Roiger, Michael W. Geatz.DATA MINING A TUTORIAL-BASED PRIMER. Pearson Education.2003.
[14] Margaret H. Dunham. DATA MINING Introductory and Advanced Topics. Pearson Education.2003.
[15] Soukup, T., & Dabifdon, I. Visual data mining: Techniques and tools for data visualization and mining. New York: Wiley.2002. http://www.intersystems.com/
[16] Yu Hai-Yan, Li Jing-Song. Data mining analysis of inpatient fees in hospital information system. ITME2009, August 14.
[17] Chae, Y.M., Kim, H.S. Analysis of healthcare quality indicator using data mining and decision support system. Expert Systems with Applications, 2003, 24-, 167-172.J. Clerk Maxwell, A Treatise on Electricity and Magnetism, 3rd ed., vol. 2. Oxford: Clarendon, 1892, pp.68–73.
[18] Chae, Y.M., Kim, H.S. et al. Analysis of healthcare quality indicator using data mining and decision support system. Expert Systems with Applications, 2003, 24-, 167-172.
[19] Se-Chul Chun, Jin Kim, Ki-Baik Hahm, Yoon-Joo Park and Se-Hak Chun, Data mining technique for medical informatics: detecting gastric cancer using case-based reasoning and single nucleotide polymorphisms. Expert Systems, May 2008, Vol.25, No.2
[20] Delen, D., Walker, G. Predicting breast cancer survivability: A comparison of three data mining methods. Artificial Intelligence in Medicine, 2005, 34(2), 113-127.
[21] Koh H, Tan G. Data mining applications in healthcare. J Healthc Inf Manag, 2005, 19(2).
[22] Milley A. Healthcare and data mining. Health Manag Technol, 2000, 21(8).

[23] Ozcan YA.Forecasting. In: Quantitative methods in health care management, California: Josey-Bass; 2005.p.10-44 [Chapter 2].

9

Data Warehouse and the Deployment of Data Mining Process to Make Decision for Leishmaniasis in Marrakech City

Habiba Mejhed, Samia Boussaa and Nour el houda Mejhed
[1]*Université Cadi Ayyad, Marrakech Département Génie Informatique, Laboratoire Micro Informatique Systèmes Embarques Systèmes sur Puce. Ecole Nationale des sciences appliquees,*
[2]*Université CadiAyyad, Marrakech Laboratoire d'Ecologie et Environnement, Faculté des Sciences Semlalia,*
[3]*&Université Louis Pasteur-Strasbourg I, Laboratoire de Parasitologie, Faculté de Pharmacie,*
[4]*Universite Sidi Mohammed Ben Abdallah, Fes Département Génie Informatique, Ecole Nationale des sciences appliquées de Fes.*
[1,2,4]*Morocco*
[3]*France*

1. Introduction

In the last decade, the epidemiology applied more and more tools to help to make decision. The aim is to translate epidemic data using the modelling concepts of health information systems for the decision-making. The information is a value-increasing necessary to plan and control the activities of an organism with effectively. It is the raw material that will be transformed by information systems. Often, the availability of data makes it very difficult, if not impossible, to extrapolate the information that really matter. It is essential to have rapid and complete information needed for the decision-making process: the strategic indicators are extrapolated mainly operational data in a database, through a selection process or synthetic gradually. The widespread use of data analysis techniques has made the information system a strategic element and policy framework for achieving the business.

Therefore, the decision-making systems have emerged in the 80s (decision support system) and offer techniques and means to extract information from a set of memorized data. As a result, the volume of information collected during an epidemiological case study enables the development of new observing systems to analyze and extract some indicators as appropriate clinical decision and public health.

The clinical decision support provided epidemiologist technologies necessary to facilitate this difficult task (Degoulet & Fieschi, 1998), (Gilbert, 2004), (Teh, 2009).

The data warehouse remains a valuable tool for storage and data accessibility, it is defined as a collection of information that integrates and reorganize the data from a variety of sources and make them available for analysis and assessment to scheduling and decision making.

If the data warehouse used to store historical data, with the finality analysis, the data mining is defined as a process of exploration and modelling data in order to discover new correlations, to find trends and stable patterns in the data. It proposes a number of tools from different disciplines, in particular, to decision making in epidemiology [Daniel, 2005), [René & Gilles, 2001), (Pascal et all, 2007), (Stéphane, 2007), (Egmont et all, 2002), (Hang & Xiubin, 2008). Data mining combines between various sciences domains (Databases, Statistics, Artificial Intelligence) to construct models from the data, and under the criteria fixed in advance and make a maximum of knowledge useful to make decision.
In Morocco, leishmaniasis remains a severe public health problem. Many foci were described in rural areas of Ouarzazate (Rioux et all 1986), Essaouira (Pratlong et all, 1991), Azilal (Rhajaoui et all, 2004), Chichaoua (Guernaoui et all 2005) and Al Haouz (Boussaa et all, 2009), (Rioux et all, 1986) but also in suburban areas, in Taza (Guessous et all, 1997) and Fez (Rhajaoui et all, 2004) Marrakesh is an interesting study site because it lies close to the focus of cutaneous leishmaniasis in the south of Morocco (Ouarzazate, Chichaoua and Al Haouz), and current studies have classified the area of Marrakesh as being at risk of cutaneous leishmaniasis (Boussaa et all, 2005), (Boussaa et all, 2007).
As the best choice of a vector-control strategy is dictated by sandfly ecology, we try to simplify this complex of diseases and quantify the climatic factors which can determine the distribution and activity of sandflies vectors in Marrakesh city. According to the WHO (2005), the activity of sandfly fauna is affected by many climatic factors as temperature, humidity and wind, besides seasons and according to sandfly species.
In this chapter we present a simple contribution to the fight against leishmaniasis in Morocco. The idea is to propose to epidemiologists an application based on tools of data warehouse and data mining to help them to make decision. In the first time, we conceived and modelled our information system to establish the pattern of the database on which we are going to work. Then, we develop a data warehouse to store and extrapolate data collected in Marrakech city, and we used a data mining tools for Leishmaniasis data analysis to get a better decision-making.
We studied three forms of leishmaniasis according to sandfly vectors collected in Marrakech city by (Boussaa et all, 2005), (Boussaa et all, 2007): Phlebotomus papatasi proven vector of zoonotic cutaneous leishmaniasis with Rodents as a reservoir; P. sergenti proven vector of anthroponotic cutaneous leishmaniasis and P. longicusis potential vector of visceral leishmaniasis with canine as reservoir hosts.

2. Material and methods

A. Sandfly collections

Specimens were collected in Marrakech city (31°36′N, 8°02′W, 471m a.s.l.) between October 2002 and September 2003 as described by (Boussaa et all, 2005). The specimens caught were preserved in 70% ethanol. They were cleared in potash 20% and Marc-Andre solution, then dehydrated and mounted in Canada balsam (Abonnenc, 1972). The identification was made by examining the morphology of male genitalia, female spermathecae and pharynges. For Larroussius species, we revised our specimens according to results of [Boussaa et all, 2008).

B. Data analysis

We have a data file.xls containing all the information on the activity of sandflies P.Papatasi, P. Sergenti and P. Longicuspis based on climate change (date, temperature and density). We can present data from Excel files in the following diagrams:

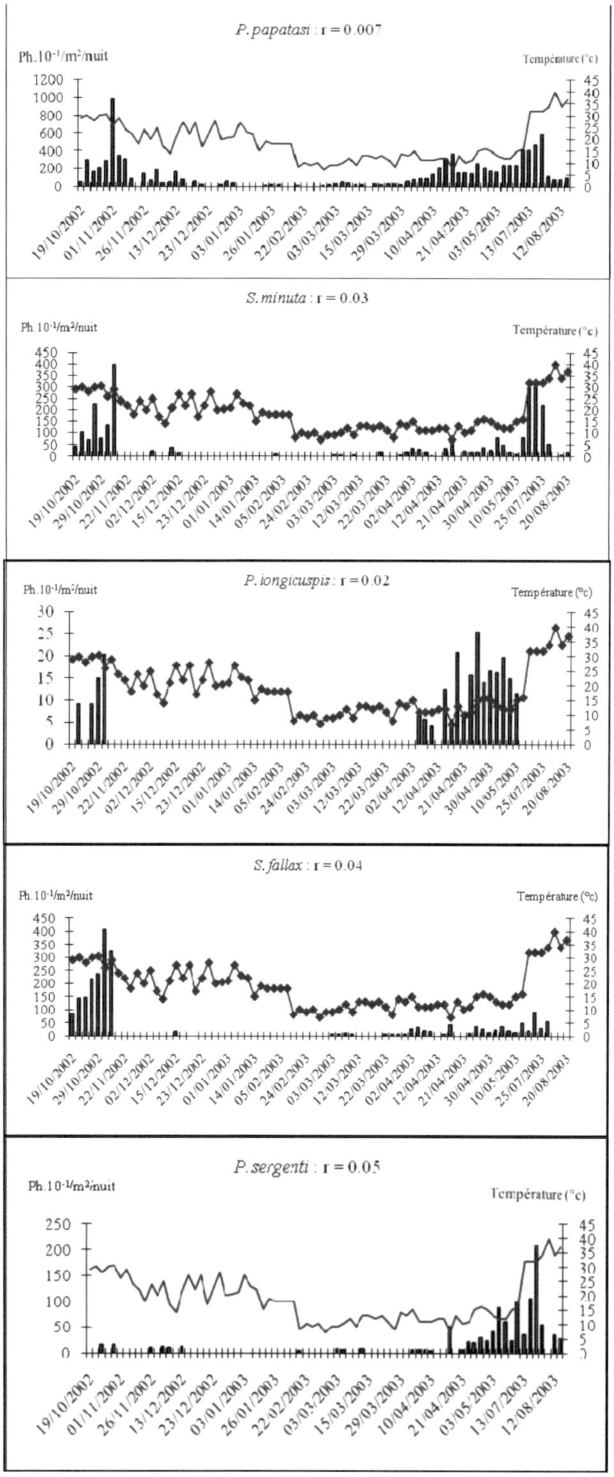

Fig. 1. The activity of sandfly population in Marrakech area

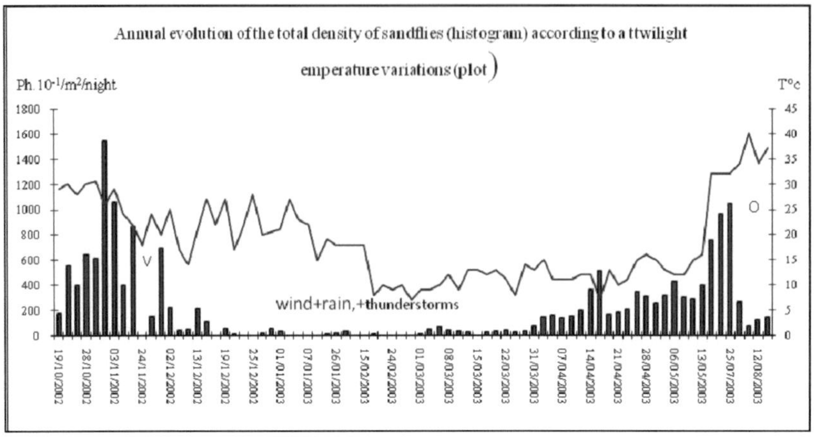

Fig. 2. Annuel evolution of the global density of the sandflies vector according to the time and the climatic change

3. Development of a data warehouse Leishmaniasis

In this section we proceed to the conception of our data scheme. Our investigations on the sandflies collections were carried out in Marrakech city. The goal is to design a database, to develop DW and to load this database, and then the relationships in the cube are built automatically to give the answer to question posed in this case.

3.1 Background

The creation of a data warehouse involves several steps:

The conception: the implementation of a data warehouse usually begins by framing the project, define the needs and goals expressed by policymakers, modeling and designing a data structure. There are two data models, the star pattern, in this model, we must define one (or more) table (s) made with one or several measures (values of indicators). Both must have multiple dimension tables whose primary keys form the primary key tables done. Warning: The dimension tables are not linked.

Then the model snowflake which is derived from the star schema where the tables are standard size (of the table remains unchanged). With this scheme, each dimension is divided according to his (or her) hierarchy (s).

The acquisition of data: The data will be extracted from the sources.

a. The static extraction will be performed when the DW must be loaded for the first time and is conceptually a copy of operational data.
b. The incremental extraction, is used for the periodic updating of the DW, and captures just the changes in data sources at the last extraction.

The choice of extracting data is based mainly on their quality, selection of data from the database is not a simple task to do.

Data cleaning: This phase will improve the quality of duplicate data, inconsistencies between the values logically related, missing data, unexpected use of a field, impossible value or wrong ...

Loading DW: The loading of data in the DW is the process is to load the data cleaned and prepared in the DW.

3.2 Needs specification

We have developed the analysis tools concerning, the population of sandflies, according to the various species listed in Marrakech city and their density, we considered the human population which may become affected after bites of infected sandflies.
These tools allow knowing the following information: (a) The density of each species of sandflies listed, (b) The period at risk for the spread of the disease, (c) The rate of infection of humans by infected sandflies, (d) The rate per unit time, which a man loses her immunity and becomes susceptible, (e) The rate of infected and susceptible in humans.
To meet the needs of decision makers, we implemented the DW with respect to the architecture described in the following section.

3.3 Data warehouse architecture

Schematic below shows the architecture of the data warehouse applied to Leishmaniasis data.

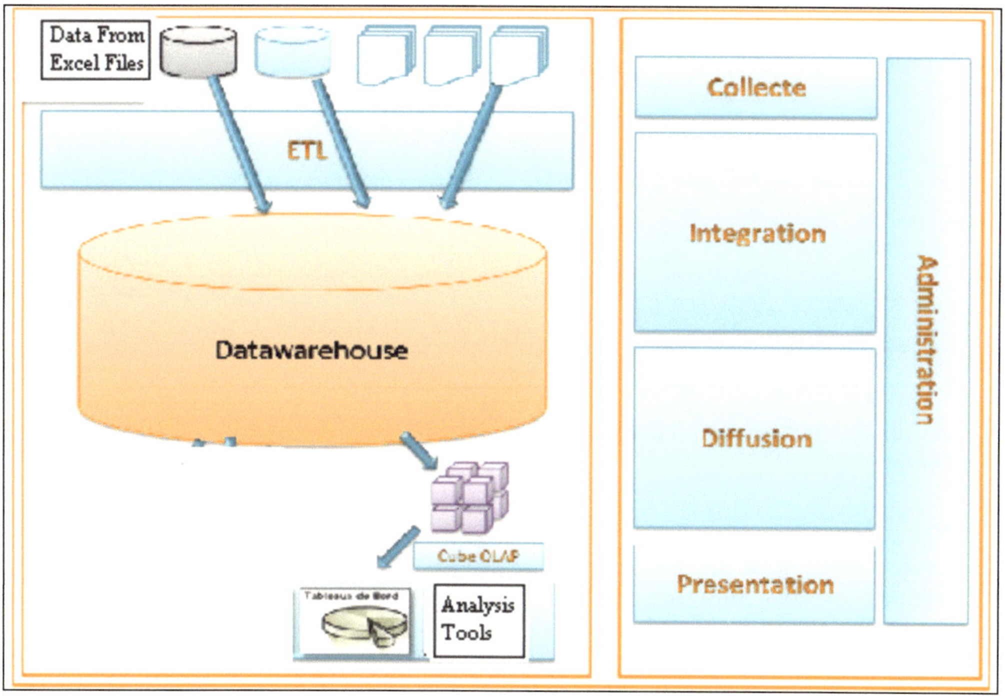

Fig. 3. Data warehouse Architecture

To ensure a robust, flexible and portable solution, we adopted a software architecture divided into several parts:
Collection of raw data files: the job of this module is periodically connected to all servers, to check the generation of new data files
Conversion of the Files: The application of this module is written in Java. This module convert the data files collected by the module above, and filter the information contained therein. It permits to leave only the information that will be used in the future treatments.
Loading data into the data warehouse: ETL process allows Extraction, Transformation and Loading of data from various sources (databases, files) into DW. ETL process is the most

important module to design a Data warehouse with respecting two constraints: data sources and data types (data quality).
Building of multidimensionnel cubes :

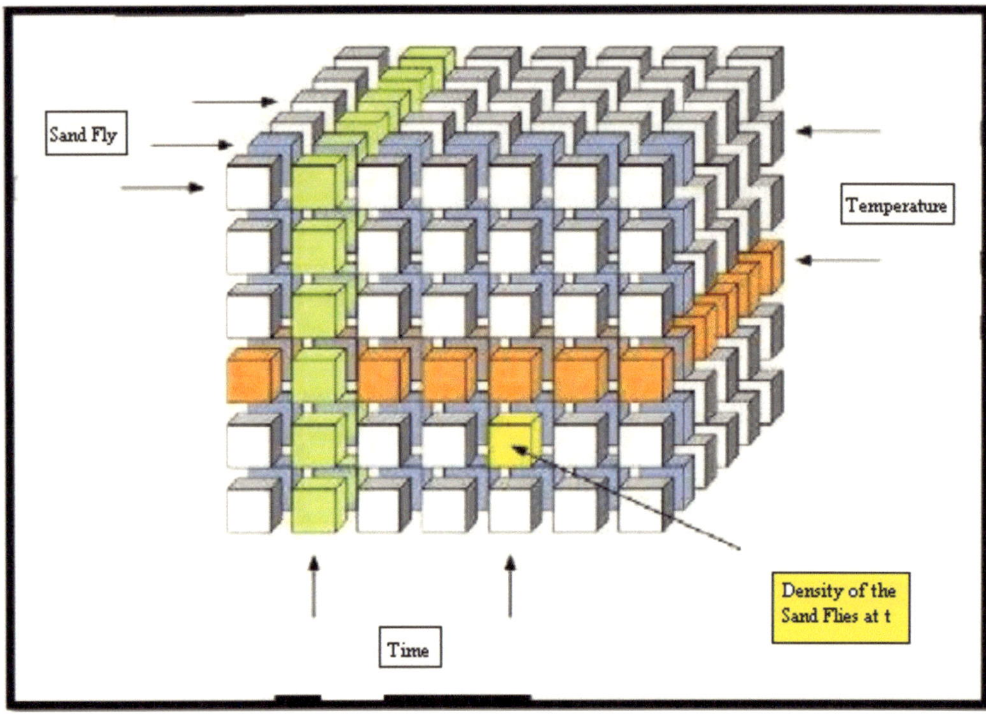

Fig. 4. Example of multidimensional view (Cube) of the Leishmaniasis data.

Creation of the graphical interfaces, graph and report: used for operation, querying cubes and creating reports.

3.4 Data model

This section deals with the transmission of the Leishmaniasis disease from the sandflies vector to human. There are four actors in this case, sandflies species, climatic change and Time and Human. The data dictionary given in the following table:

data	Description of data
Human	Sexe Age statut
sandflies	specie Name
Temperature	Degree
time	wear Month Day

The data layer architecture of Leishmaniasis is illustrated schematically by:

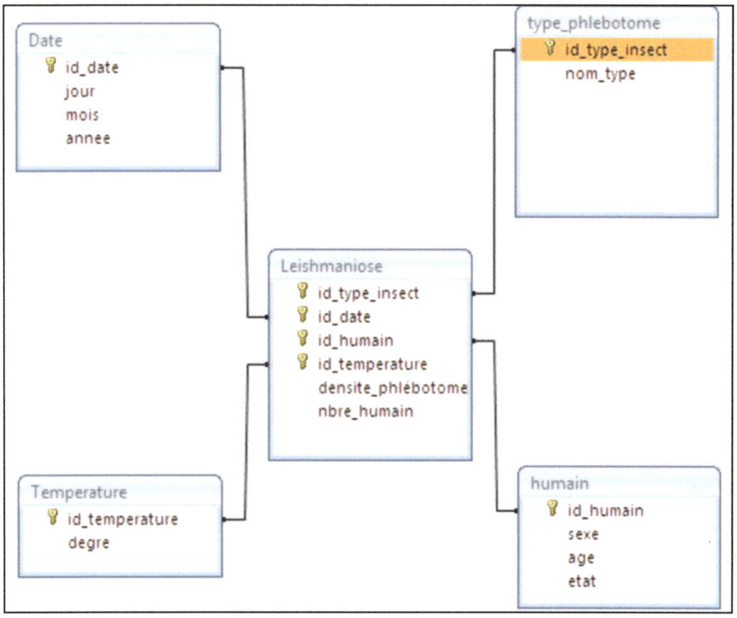

Fig. 5. The model data warehouse diagram

The model chosen must comply with the requirements and needs of use, in our case, we opted for a star pattern respecting the nature of the information we have.
Dimension Tables: Date, Temperature, Sandflies (P. Sergenti, S. Minuta, S. Fallax, P. Logicuspis, P. Papatasi), Human.
Fact Table: Leishmaniose.
Data is extracted from Excel files using java code. The program consists of two classes, one for extraction and one for export useful data to the database.

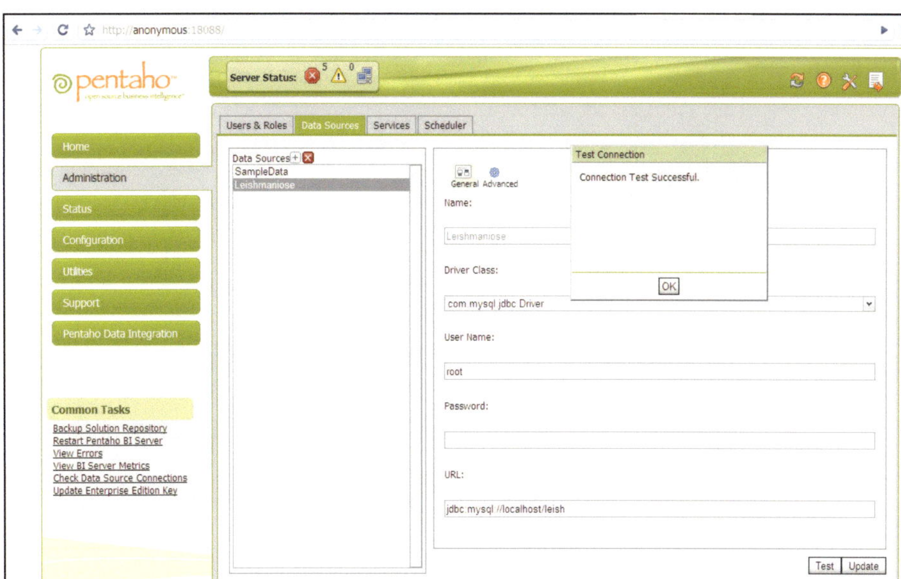

3.5 Dimensional cube

Pentaho integr a CubeDesign tool, it allows to have the cube in XML format and to publish it in the User Pentaho Console. Cube creation through 5 steps as shown in the below:

Step 1. With the CubeDesigner we establish the connection to database Leishmaniose.

Step 2. Select tables and views useful to visualise the Cube. For example, to calculate the density of the P. Sergenti and the infected human in a fixed interval time.

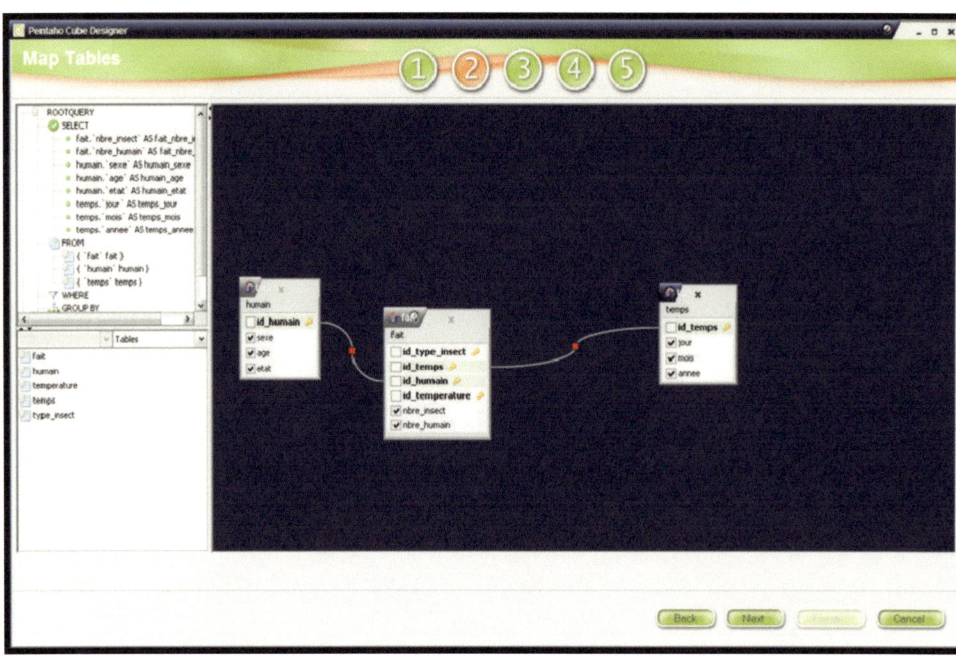

Step 3. Choose of the measures: Infected human

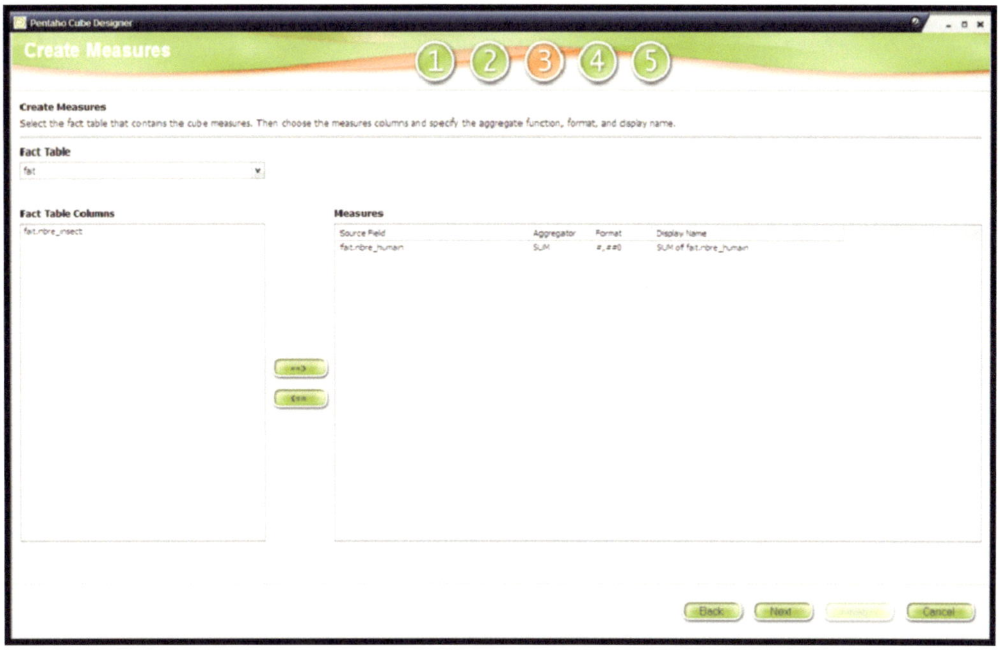

Step 4. All the dimensions and their aggregation will be specified via the interface below.

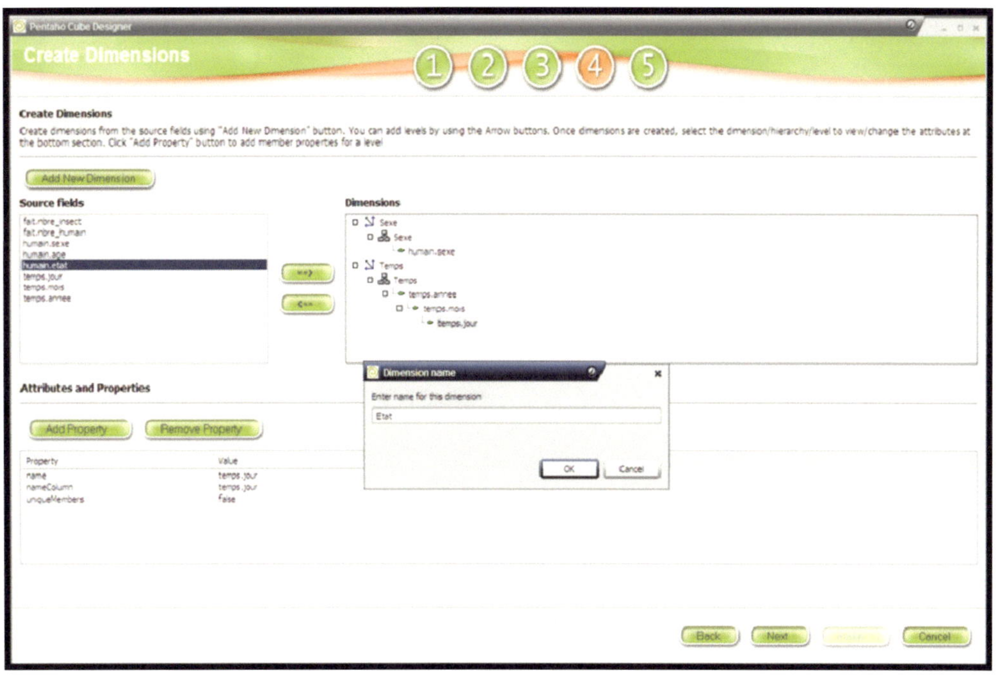

Step 5. The interface below allows us to view the file for the model; it's possible to update it as needed.

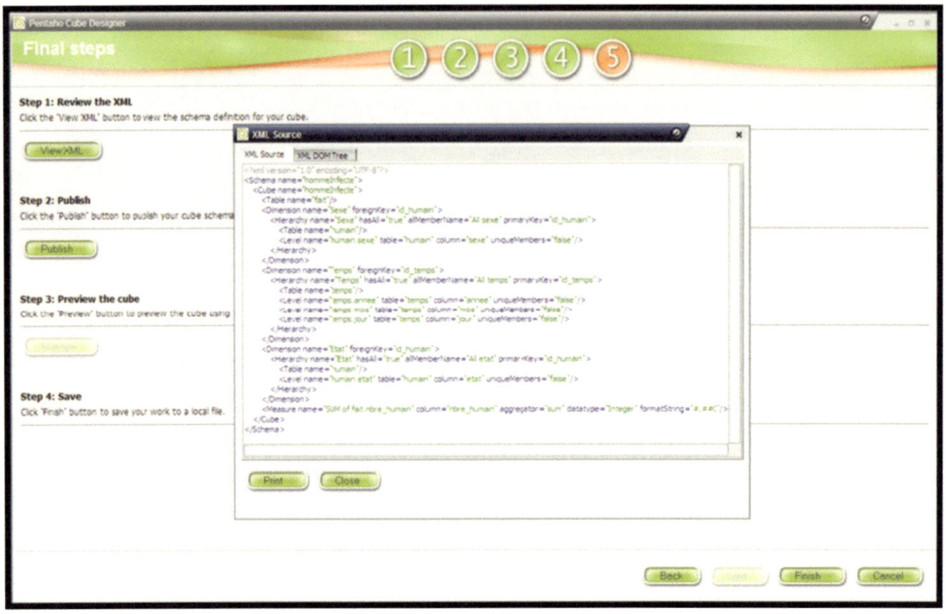

Finally, the pattern is saved

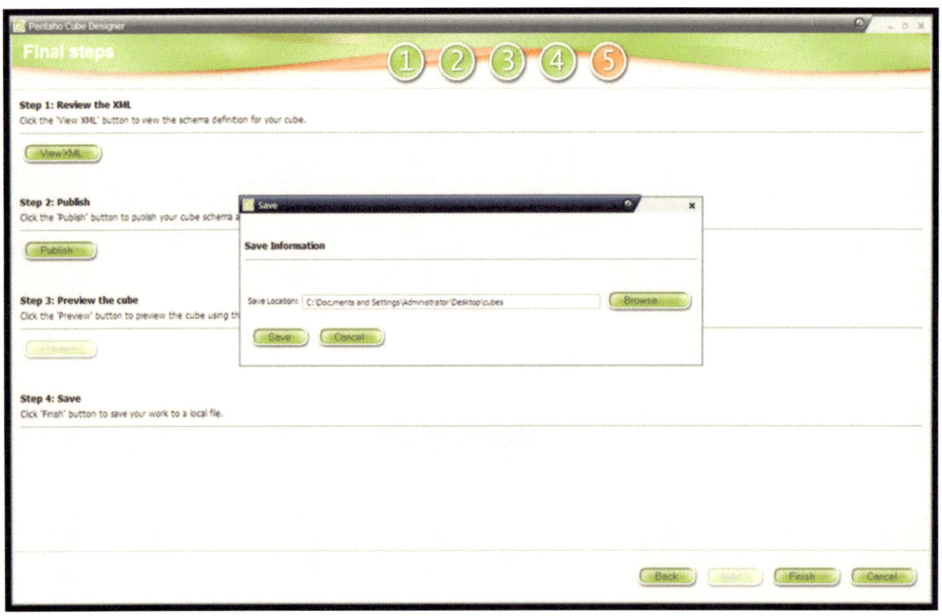

Tree files are generated : (a) Xml file to save the pattern produced by CubeDesigner. (b) Properties file : for the allocation of the database. (c) Xaction file : presents a set of all protocols to data access.

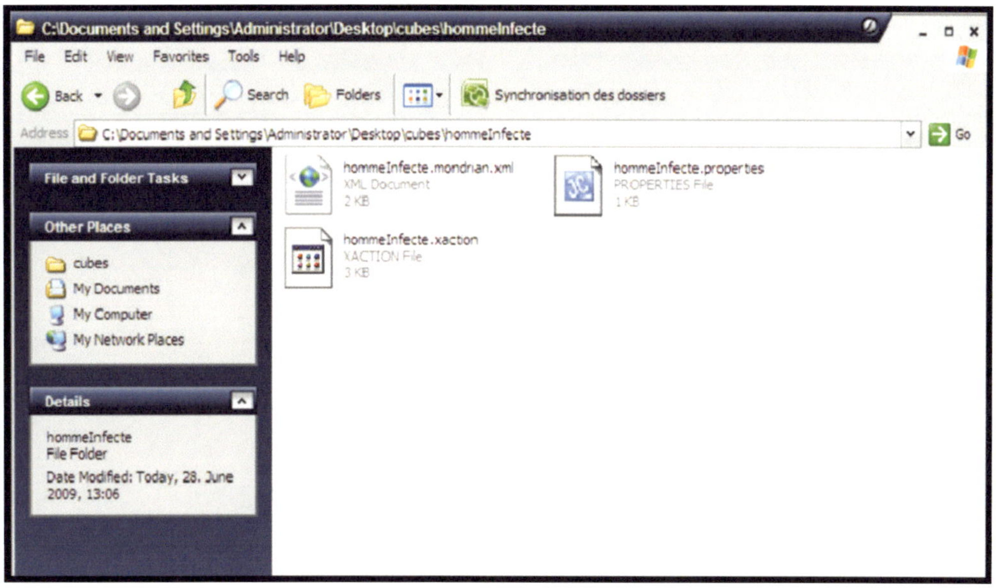

3.6 Pattern publication with workbench

Workben is a tool to create diagrams, for our case it is just used to refine and publish the pattern designed by CubeDesigner.

Step 1. Configuration of the Workbench references to establish connection to database.

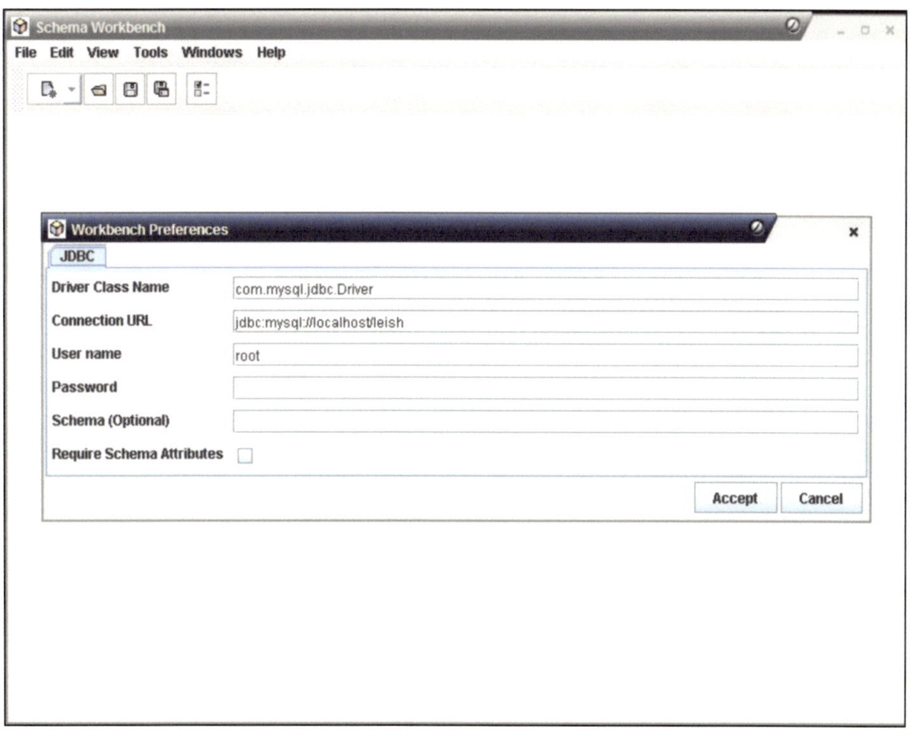

Step 2. Pattern raffinement.

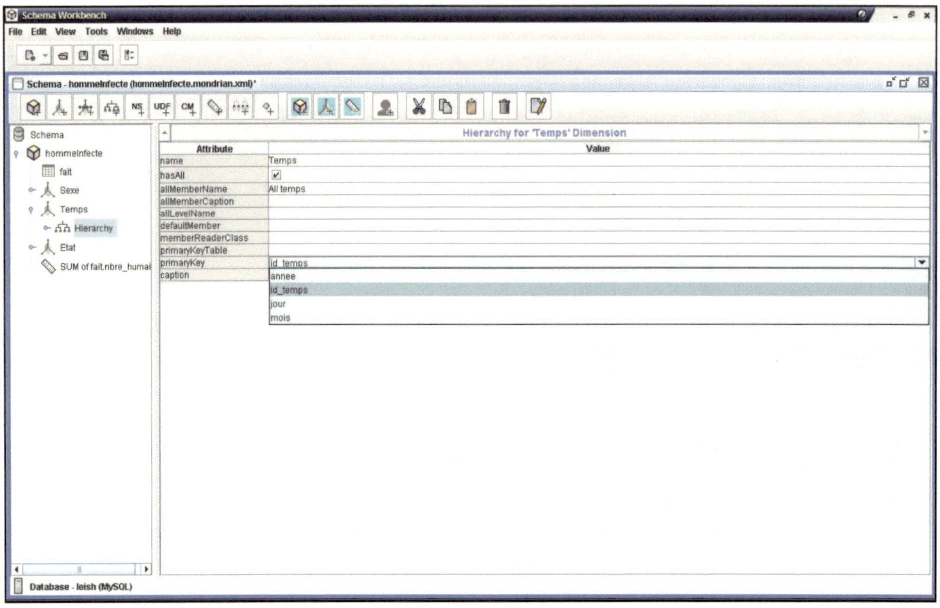

Step 3. Now, it is important to have URL for the host user, The password for the publisher and The login and password of the user server.

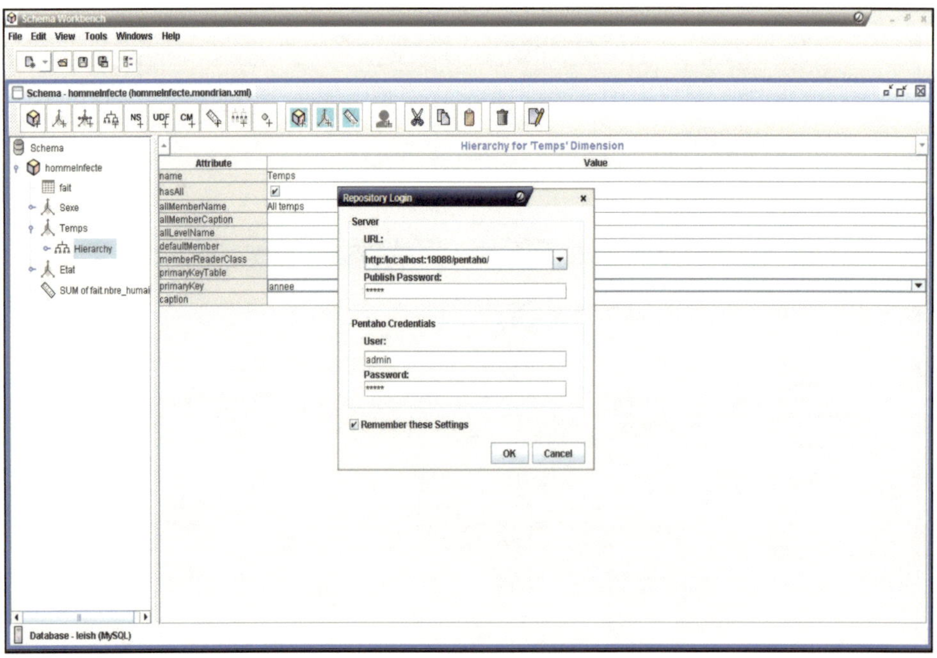

3.7 Visualization phase

'User Console' tool gives different views of the pattern previously published.

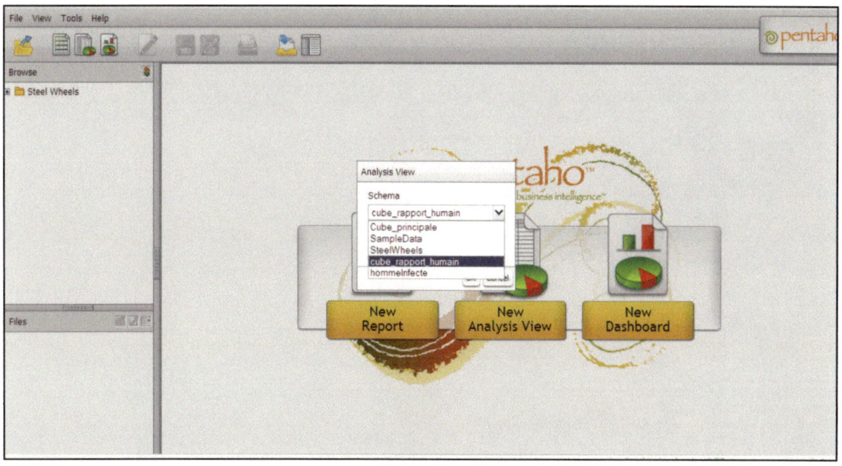

It's possible to have several modes to visualize data from database. As illustrated in the following figures.

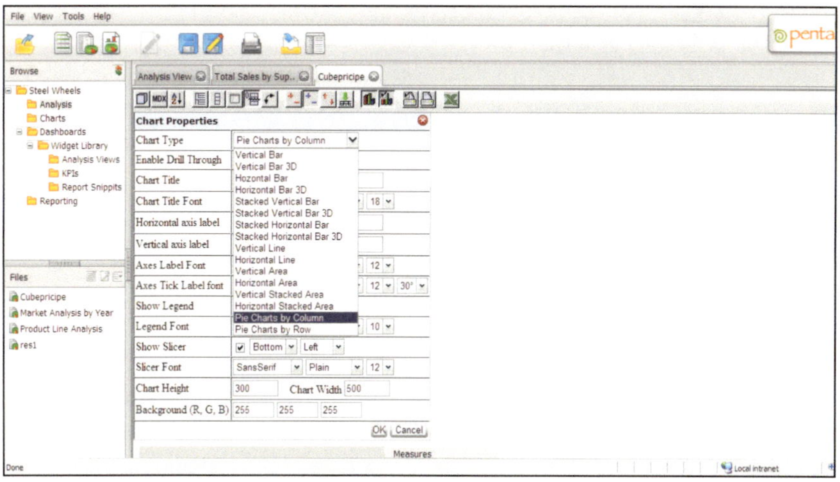

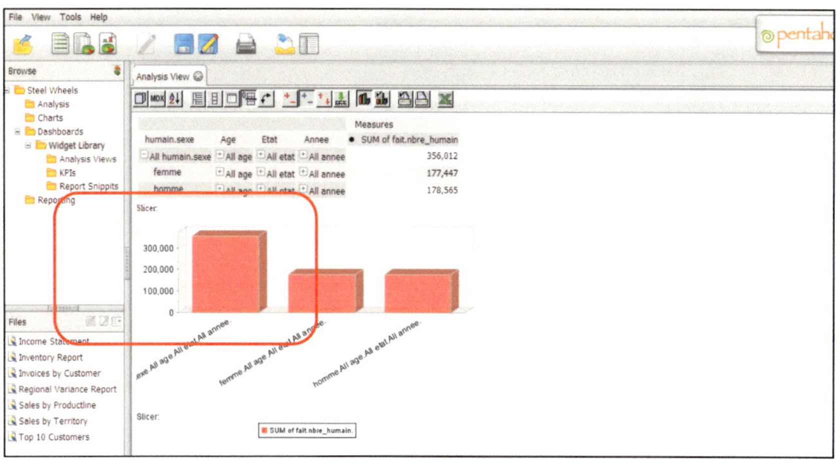

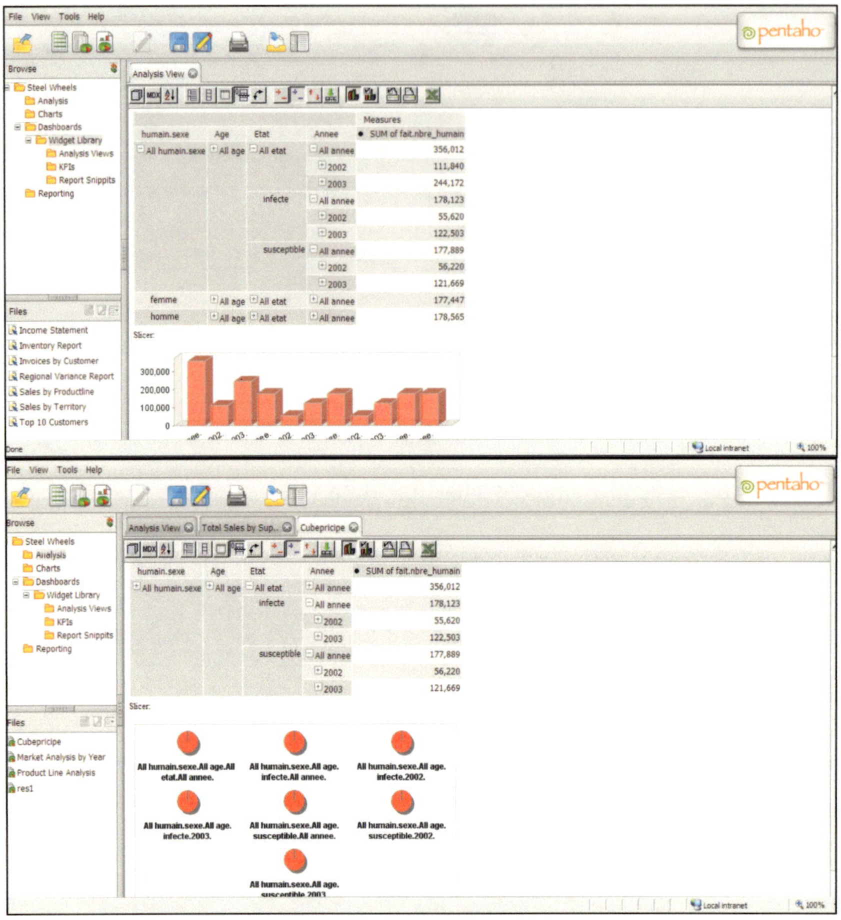

The hearlth professional may use OLAP concept to fialter and visualize other type of information.

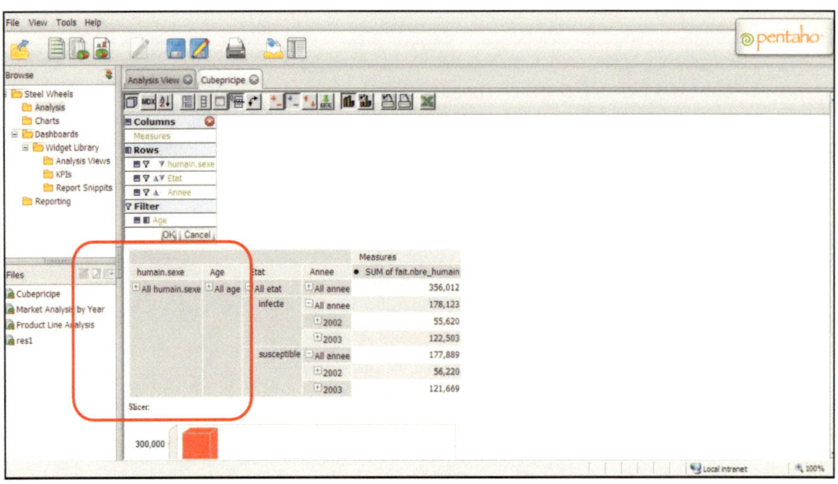

4. Data mining: application to the Leishmaniasis

Given the seriousness of leishmaniasis in Morocco, it was essential to deploy easy methods to reduce its exploitable spread if not eradicate it completely. Our proposal aims to exploit tools of data mining process on this infectiou disease. By definition, the data mining attempts to extract knowledge from vast volumes of data.
The wealth of information transmitted on vectors of disease allows us to apply these tools to identify methods and anticipate behaviour, therefore, make a good decision.

4.1 K-means and deployment

The technologies that are on the market, offers comprehensive platforms and integrated data analysis to meet all requests of indicators developed in the industry. We are able to accede to any type of data stored in our data base, to implement operations to analyze the data and present results in a need predefined by the user.
The software that we have developed our application offers a wide range of approaches ranging from methods of descriptive statistical analysis to predictive modeling methods.
The first step is to create a new diagram and import the data as shown in the screenshot below.

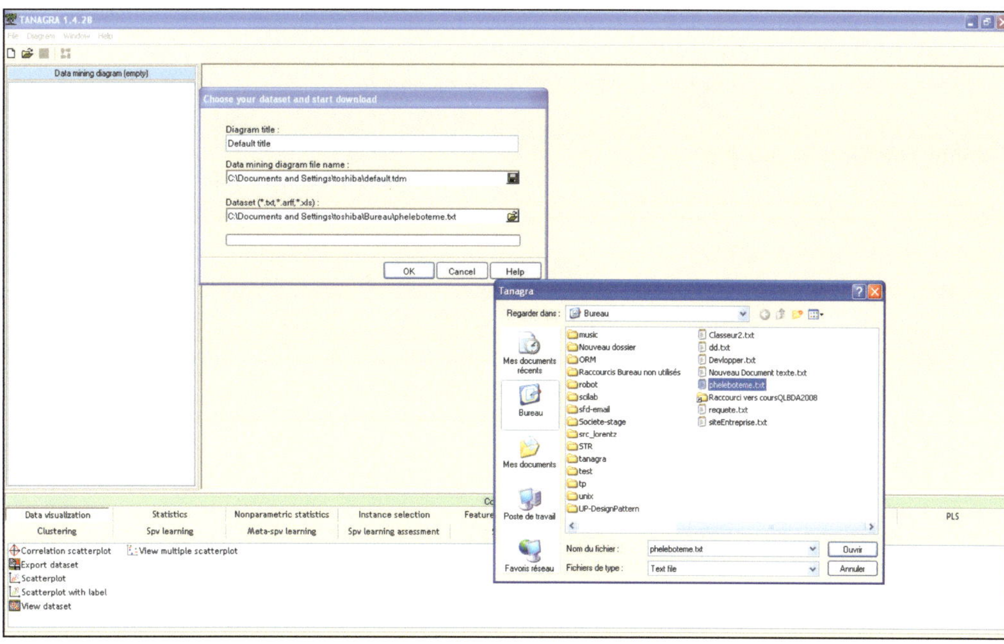

4.2 Descriptive statistics

We can do descriptive statistics to variables. We calculate the frequency histograms on all columns to count the number of active and additional comments.

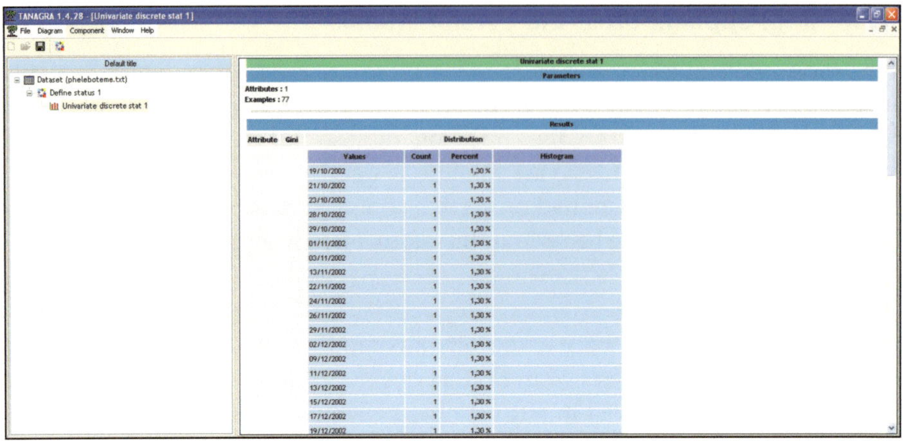

4.3 Method principal component analysis (ACP)

They are three categories of data mining algorithms: supervised methods, unsupervised methods and methods of data reduction. Each category is based on a number of techniques. In this section, we chose the third type using the method of principal component analysis (ACP).

Given a set of observations described by variables exclusively digital (x1, x2, ..., xp), the APC aims to describe the same data set with new variables in reduced numbers. These new variables will be linear combinations of original variables. Principal component analysis can therefore be seen as a technique to reduce dimensionality.

4.4 Visualization of our data

To implement the ACP method, we can see, for example, date and temperature data concerning P. longicuspis. After we define an analysis of the variables studied. The result is given in the following figure:

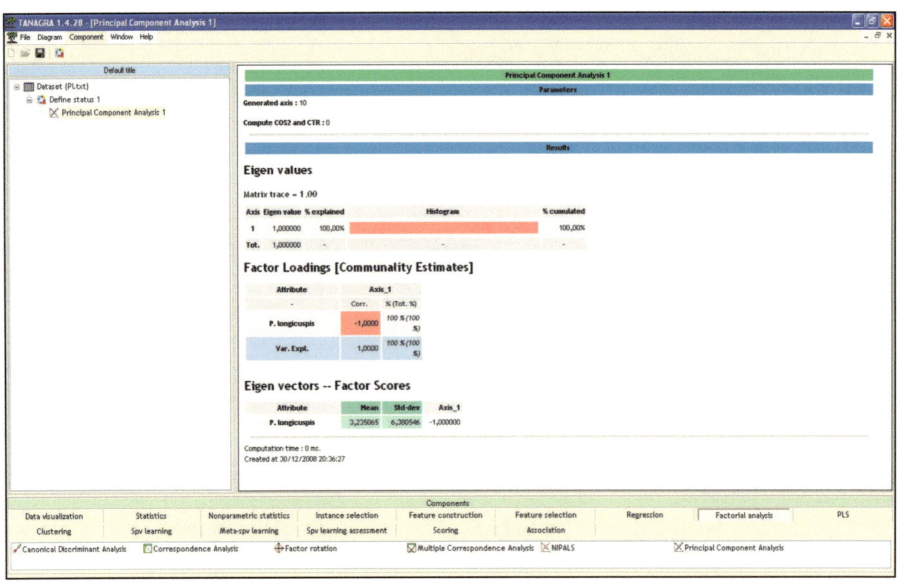

To better assess the relative positions to sandflies in the first factorial design, we add the component display. We put abscissa variable representing the first axis, calculated using the ACP, and ordered the second axis. We get the point cloud :

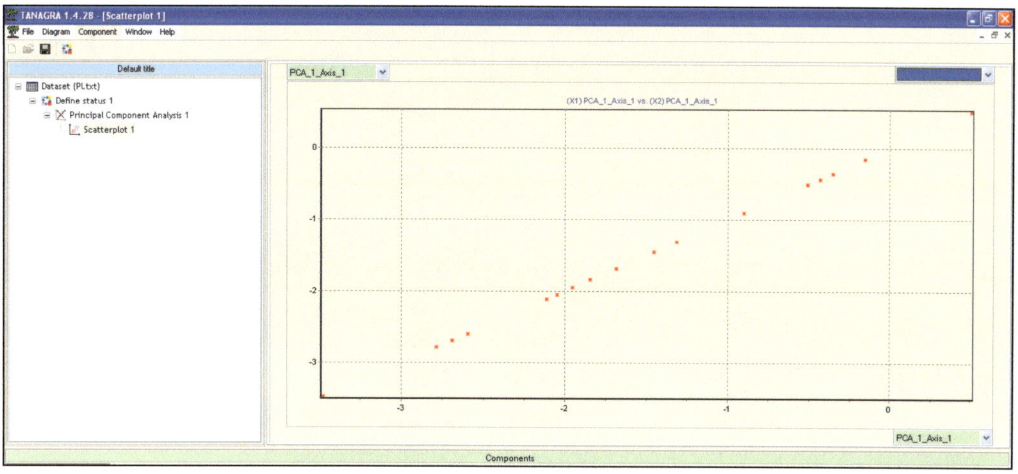

Fig. 6. Point cloud data on (date, temperature, for P. longicuspis)

Among the variables are, we want to check the effect of the variable date that can distort our results. We will color the points according to this variable, we select as a variable component as is shown in this illustrative visualization.

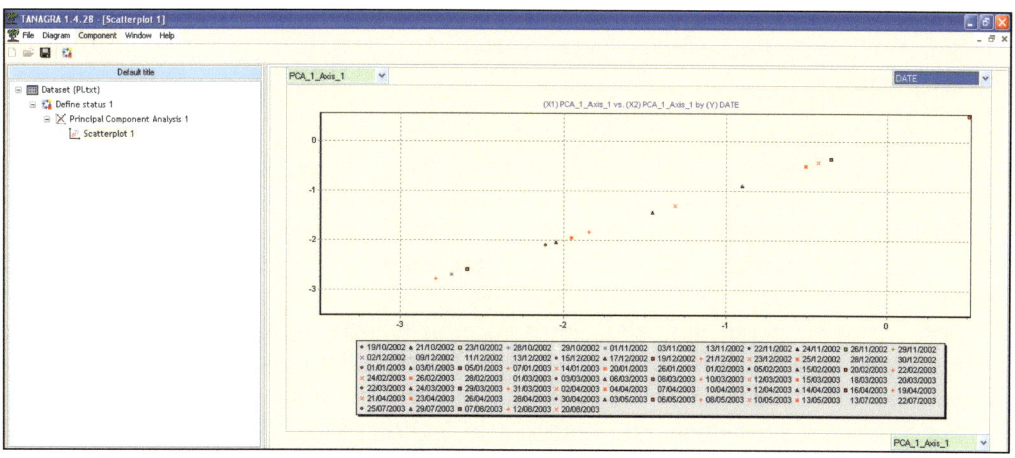

Fig. 7. Using the date_format as illustrative variable

Now we apply the ACP method on all data:

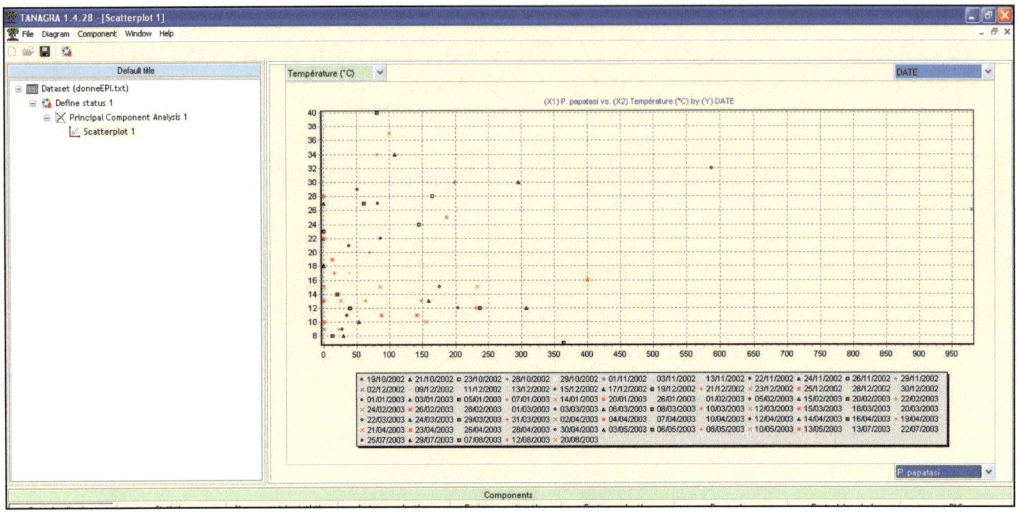

Fig. 8. Implementation of the ACP method on sandflies data

The most difficult decision in any project is to determine what method should be implemented. In our case, we prefer use the open source tools:

a. ETL « Talend Open Studio » Talend Open Studio offer: A complete range of components, Traces and statistics of treatment in real time, the addition of specific code and the integration on the decisional open source.
b. MySQL to create the database and data warehouse for the persistent storage area.
c. Pentaho BI Suite: cover many areas of Business intelligence through various software (owned by Pentaho or integrated into).
d. Pentaho Analysis (Mondrian + JPivot), Cube Designe, schema Workbench. For analysis OLAP
e. Open source data mining software Tanagra.

5. Discussion

Our investigations were conducted in Akioud, an urban district in Marrakech city, during one-year-study. This site was selected, considering the presence, of all the sandfly species inventoried in the urban area of Marrakech (Boussaa et all, 2007).

According to the correlation between the weekly density of the three vectors (P. papatasi, P. sergenti and P. longicuspis) and the factor R0, we can prevent the risk of leishmaniasis in this area.

a. For P. papatasi population, R0 factor is superior to 1 during two periods of the year: November and May-June-July, which correspond to the periods of risk of zoonotic cutanous leishmaniais caused by L. major in this area.
b. For P. sergenti population, R0 is superior to 1 during the period of July–August and inferior to 1 in the rest of the year. So, this period corresponds to the phase of risk of anthroponotic cutanous leishmaniais caused by L. tropica in this area. We observe that R0 reaches its peak during the period of August when the temperature is very high.
c. For P. longicuspis, the results have shown two periods of risk of visceral leishmaniasis in this area: October and May-June.

(Boussaa et all, 2005) classified Marrakech area as being at risk of cutaneous leishmaniasis because of the high density of P. papatasi throughout the year, its position close to the cutaneous leishmaniasis foci in the arid region (Rioux et all, 1986) and the omnipresence of Meriones shawi, main L. major reservoir host in Morocco. In this work, we approve the conclusion of [Boussaa et all, 2005) and we exploit these data to assist in the decision on the issue of the fight against leishmaniasis in Morocco.
Indeed, these are spatio-temporal models which permit to follow and control the evolution of leishmaniasis in terms of time and region, and to find the appropriate threshold of the population of sandflies for stopping the multiplication of the disease. In Chichaoua (70 Km from Marrakech city), focus of anthroponotic cutanous leishmaniais, (Bacaër and Guernaoui, 2006) suggest that the epidemic could be stopped if the vector population were reduced by a factor (R0)2 = 3.76.

6. Conclusion

To fight against the spread of the cutaneous and visceral leishmaniasis and to address the need of the responsible for population health to set the policies that determine the nature of health care provided, and most importantly, for fast evaluation of the severity of the multiplication of the disease, we proposed to develop a model of data warehouse to storage appropriate data of the sandflies seasonality and the information about the susceptible human (patient with suspected Leishmania infection). Then, structural key and functional parameters will be measured to ensure the advanced treatment. By employing data mining process we have the ability to extract knowledge and to generate summaries for better health decision-making. Through this complete and operational platform, it will be easy to control the sandflies seasonality and the rate of the transmission disease.

7. References

P. Degoulet et M. Fieschi (1998). *Informatique et santé Collection, Paris, Springer-Verlag,* Volume 10,

Gilbert Saporta (2004). Data mining ou fouille de données, RST « Epidémiologie » *Data Mining.*

Daniel T. Larose (adaptation française T. Vallaud) (2005). Des données à la connaissance : Une introduction au data-mining (1Cédérom), *Vuibert.*

René Lefébure et Gilles Venturi (2001). Data Mining : Gestion de la relation client, personnalisations de site web, *Eyrolles,* mars 2001.

Pascal Poncelet, Florent Masseglia and Maguelonne Teisseire (Editors) (2007). Data Mining Patterns: New Methods and Applications, Information Science Reference, ISBN: 978-1599041629, October 2007.

Stéphane Tufféry (2007). Data Mining et Statistique Décisionnelle, Technip, nouvelle édition revue et enrichie, juin 2007.

Egmont-Petersen, M., de Ridder, D., Handels, H. (2002). Image processing with neural networks -a review. *Pattern Recognition 35*: pp. 2279–2301. doi: 10.1016/S0031-3203(01)00178-9. 2002.

Boussaa, S., Guernaoui, S., Pesson, B., Boumezzough, A. (2005). Seasonal fluctuations of phlebotomine sand fly populations (Diptera: Psychodidae) in the urban area of Marrakech, Morocco. pp. 86–91, *Acta Trop.* 95.

Boussaa, S., Pesson, B., Boumezzough, A. (2007). Phlebotomine sandflies (Diptera: Psychodidae) of Marrakech city, Morocco. pp. 715-724, *Ann. Trop. Med. Parasitol.* 101.

WHO (2005). Lutte contre les leishmanioses. *Série de Rapports Techniques.*

Rhajaoui, M., Fellah, H., Pratlong, F., Dedet, J.P., Lyagoubi, M. (2004). Leishmaniasis due to Leishmania tropica MON-102 in a new Moroccan focus. *Trans. R. Soc. Trop. Med. Hyg.* 98, pp. 299–301.

Teh and All (2009). Development of a Data warehouse for Lymphoma Cancer Diagnosis and Treatment Decision Support. *Proceedings of the 10th WSEAS International Conference on MATHEMATICS and COMPUTERS in BIOLOGY and CHEMISTRY,* Pp. 15 _24. ISSN: 1790-5125, ISBN: 978-960-474-062-8.

Abonnenc E. (1972). Les phlébotomes de la région éthiopienne (Diptera: Phlebotomidae). *Mémoire de l'ORSTOM.* 55, pp. 1–289.

Bacaër, N., Guernaoui, S. (2006). The epidemic threshold of a simple seasonal model of cutaneous leishmaniasis. *J. Math. Biol.* 53, pp. 421–436.

Boussaa, S., Boumezzough, A., Remy, P. E., Glasser, N., Pesson, B. (2008). Morphological and isoenzymatic differentiation of Phlebotomus perniciosus and Phlebotomus longicuspis (Diptera: Psychodidae) in Southern Morocco. *Acta Trop.* 106, pp. 184–189.

Boussaa, S., Pesson, B., Boumezzough, A. (2009). Faunistic study of the sandflies (Diptera: Psychodidae) in an emerging focus of cutaneous leishmaniasis in Al Haouz province, Morocco. *Ann. Trop. Med. Parasitol.* 103, pp. 73-83.

Guernaoui, S., Boumezzough, A., Pesson, B., Pichon, G. (2005). Entomological investigations in Chichaoua: an emerging epidemic focus of cutaneous leishmaniasis in Morocco. J. *Med. Entomol.* 42, pp. 697–701.

Guessous-Idrissi, N., Chiheb, S., Hamdani, A., Riyad, M., Bichichi, M., Hamdani, S., Krimech, A. (1997). Cutaneous leishmaniasis: an emerging epidemic focus of Leishmania tropica in north Morocco. *Trans. R. Soc. Trop. Med. Hyg.* 91, pp. 660–663.

Pratlong, F., Rioux, J.A., Dereure, J., Mahjour, J., Gallego, M., Guilvard, E., Lanotte, G., Périères, J., Martini, A., Saddiki, A. (1991). Leishmania tropica au Maroc. IV. *Diversité isozymique intrafocale. Ann. Parasitol. Hum. Comp. 66,* pp. 100–104.

Ramaoui, K., Guernaoui, S., Boumezzough, A. (2008). Entomological and epidemiological study of a new focus of cutaneous leishmaniasis in Morocco. *Parasitol.* Res. 103, pp. 859-863.

Rioux, J.A., et all (1986). Les leishmanioses cutanées du bassin méditerranéen occidental: de l'identification enzymatique à l'analyse éco-épidemiologique, l'exemple de trois 'foyers', tunisien, marocain et français. Montpellier, France: *Institut Méditerranéen d'Etudes Épidémiologiques et Ecologiques.* pp. pp.365–395.

Hang Xaio, Xiubin Zhang (2008). Comparison Studies on Classification for Remote Sensing Image Based on Data Mining Method, *WSEAS TRANSACTIONS on COMPUTERS.* Volume 7, ISSN: 1109-2750, pp. 552 558.

10

Data Mining in Ubiquitous Healthcare

Viswanathan, Whangbo and Yang
Carnegie Mellon University, Adelaide, Australia

1. Introduction

Ubiquitous healthcare is the next step in the integration of information technology with healthcare services and refers to the access to healthcare services at any time and any place for individual consumers through mobile computing technology. Further, ubiquitous healthcare is able to provide enhanced services for patient management such as services that collect patients' data real-time and provide health information by analyzing the data using biomedical signal measurement instruments, which can be carried anytime, anywhere and by everyone online as well as offline.

The emergence of these tremendous data sets creates a growing need for analyzing them across geographical lines using distributed and parallel systems. Implementations of data mining techniques on high-performance distributed computing platforms are moving away from centralized computing models for both technical and organizational reasons (Kumar & Kantardzic, 2006).

In this paper, we present and discuss the designed prototype for a ubiquitous healthcare system that will provide advanced patient monitoring and health services. Subsequently we introduce and present empirical analysis of a preliminary distributed data mining system. The integration of such a distributed mining system is studied in the context of the decision support framework for our ubiquitous healthcare system.

2. Ubiquitous healthcare initiatives

A growing number of ubiquitous healthcare projects are being pursued by large enterprises owning healthcare related companies and government bodies. MobiHealth project (MobiHealth, 2004) is a mobile healthcare project supported by the EC with countries such as Netherlands, Germany, Spain and Sweden participating in it, and companies such as Philips and HP are providing technical support. EliteCare, is an elderly care system developed in the USA that monitors patients using various sensors and provides emergency and health information services. Tele-monitoring service is being developed by the Philips Medical system, where centers analyze data that is collected from homes and transmitted by biomedical signal collection devices, and provide health management and related information. CodeBlue is a sensor network based healthcare system being developed to treat and deal with emergencies, rehabilitation of stroke patients, and in general, to use health signal data in addition to hospital records in real time treatment decisions. The UbiMon (Kristof Van Laerhoven et al., 2004) project which stands for Ubiquitous Monitoring Environment for Wearable and Implantable Sensors is studying mobile monitoring using sensors and real-time biomedical data collection for long time trend analyses. The Smart Medical Home project developed at the University of Rochester in New York aims to develop a fully integrated personal health system with ubiquitous technology based on infrared and bio sensors, computers, video cameras and other devices. Sensor data is collected and transmitted to a center for further analysis and preventive care.

There are several ubiquitous challenges in the development of such healthcare frameworks and systems. These include:

- issues of security and privacy related to information transfer through unsecured infrastructure, potentially lost or stolen devices, legal enforcement and other scenarios;
- determining current context and user activity in real-time and locating context dependent information such as automatic discovery of services based on user health needs;
- development of low-power sensors to monitor user context and health condition;
- information management through development of techniques to collect, filter, analyze and store the potentially vast quantities of data from widespread patient monitoring and applying privacy preserving data mining at several levels;
- simple patient interaction systems to provide guidance, feedback and access to medical advice in acute situations;
- Adaptable network infrastructures to support large-scale monitoring, as well as real-time response from medical personnel or intelligent agents.;
- integration of specialized local u-Health architectures for unified data access and connection to National grids;

3. U-healthcare system framework

The components of the ubiquitous system prototype are summarized in this section. A system user in this paper refers to a patient who has a contract with a provider to use the ubiquitous healthcare services and regularly receives medical treatment at a hospital. Fig. 1 shows an overview of the ubiquitous healthcare service framework as suggested in this paper.

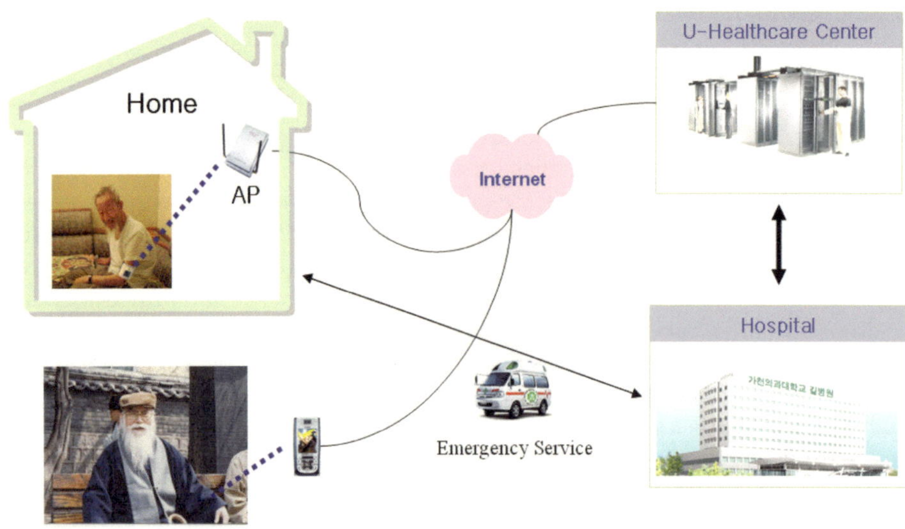

Fig. 1. Ubiquitous Healthcare Framework

The user wears a sensory device, provided by the hospital, on his wrist. The sensor regularly transmits collected data to a healthcare center through networking or mobile devices, and the transmitted data is stored at the u-healthcare center. In the center, monitoring staff are stationed to answer the user' queries, monitor his biomedical signals, and call an emergency service or visit the patient to check his status when an abnormal pattern is detected. The hospital monitors the collected data and judges the patient's status using the collected biomedical signals in his periodic check-up.

3.1 Biomedical signal collection and transmission

A wrist sensor is used to collect biomedical signals. The wrist sensor, attached to a user's wrist throughout the day, collects data such as the user's blood pressure, pulse, and orientation and transmits the collected data to the user's mobile phone or access point (AP) at home using a wireless ZigBee device. ZigBee is established by the ZigBee Alliance and adds network, security and application software to the IEEE 802.15.4 standard. Owing to its low power consumption and simple networking configuration, ZigBee is considered the most promising for wireless sensors.

Biomedical signals can be collected while moving in and out of the user's residence. The data collected inside of the house is sent to the AP in the house using Zigbee module. The AP stores the collected data and sends it regularly to the data storage at the healthcare center. When the user is outside of the house, the sensor sends the collected data to the user's mobile phone and then using CDMA module of the mobile phone, transmits the data to the center.

A light-weight data mining component is being developed for the mobiles and APs which briefly analyzes the data collected. This component has the responsibility of judging if an emergency occurs by analyzing the biomedical signals collected by the sensor. It also includes a function to call an emergency service using a motion detector attached to the sensor if it detects a fall-down, that is, when the user collapses.

3.2 Healthcare center

The healthcare center has two primary roles. First, it provides storage and management for the biomedical data collected from the users, and second, it monitors the users' health status and takes appropriate emergency or preventive action when required. A database server in the healthcare center stores and manages data including the medical, personal, family and other information for all registered users as well as biomedical signals collected from them. This data is used for real-time monitoring of users in case of emergencies and is also useful in periodic checkups.

The healthcare center also includes personnel who are stationed to keep monitoring users' health status and provide health information as well. Some of their responsibilities include regular phone checks, personal visits to users and emergency assistance if any abnormal signals are detected from a user.

3.3 CDSS (Clinical Decision Support System)

The CDSS supports long-term and short-term decision making processes by using models from distributed data mining, developing alternative plans and performing comparison analysis. In the short-term it assists in optimal planning to solve various decision making problems confronted in emergencies by utilizing the biomedical sig-nals. The goal of this system is to provide an information system environment where a decision maker can solve problems easily, accurately and promptly such that users are benefited. The CDSS needs to be integrated with a distributed data mining system that can provide global models.

3.4 Emergency response

Emergencies in a U-health framework require robust and quick recognition followed by an efficient emergency response. In this framework we employ a three pronged emergency recognition drive. Firstly, personnel monitoring the streaming biomedical data may detect abnormal signs and check user through phones or visits. Secondly, abnormal signs are also detected while mining the biomedical data collected over a period by the CDSS. Lastly, motion detectors mounted on sensors detect occurrence of falls and erratic movement.
The emergency management system uses a variety of hardware and software components that aim to improve emergency counteractions at the appropriate time and lower preventable deaths. This includes portable personal terminals comprising of RFID tags, portable RFID readers, an ambulance information system, a hospital in-formation system and a healthcare information system. The efficiency of the treatment in emergency rooms is increased by using RFID tags and readers. Since the system is well integrated it also transfers patient information in real-time to hospitals, and therefore medical teams who will provide treatment during emergencies can be well-prepared.

3.5 Short range wireless communication module

Biomedical signals collected from sensors are sent to mobile phones or APs using Zigbee, a short range wireless communication module. Zigbee is easy to control by complementing Bluetooth's weaknesses, provides multi hopping, and has low power consumption, which allows users to control the network size freely inside and outside of their houses (Hill et al., 2004). As Zigbee is a competitive short range wireless communication technology in vertical applications' area like a senor network, a large scale sensor network can be configured by combining a low power Zigbee transceiver and a sensor (Smithers & Hill, 1999).

3.6 Remote monitoring system

With increasing urbanization, shrinking of living space and shifting concepts of the family, elderly people often tend to live alone without any assistance at home. In such cases prompt responses are most important when a medical emergency occurs. The remote monitoring system is used to detect falls and erratic movement occurring at homes remotely using cameras or by checking current situations when an abnormal sign is detected. There may be signals that cannot be detected even with motion detectors mounted on sensors, or false alarms may occur. In these cases, the situations can be checked using in-house video cameras. The remote monitoring system is not only a management system for patient monitoring but aims for general health improvement of consumers through prevention of diseases, early detection, and prognosis management. Thus a customized personal healthcare service is established, maintained and controlled continuously (Jardine & Clough, 1999).

4. Clinical decision support with data mining

Data mining research is continually coming up with improved tools and methods to deal with distributed data. There are mainly two scenarios in distributed data mining (DDM): A database is naturally distributed geographically and data from all sites must be used to optimize results of data mining. A non-distributed database is too large to process on one machine due to processing and memory limits and must be broken up into smaller chunks that are sent to individual machines to be processed. In this paper we consider the latter scenario (Park & Kargupta, 2003). In this section we discuss how distributed data mining plays an important role within the CDSS component of the ubiquitous health-care system.

4.1 CDSS and DDM

In a ubiquitous healthcare framework DDM systems are required due to the large number of streams of data that have a very high data rate and are typically distributed. These need to be analyzed/mined in real-time to extract relevant information. Often such data come from wirelessly connected sources which have neither the computational resources to analyze them completely, nor enough bandwidth to transfer all the data to a central site for analysis. There is also another scenario where the data collected and stored at a center needs to be analyzed as a whole for creating the dynamic profiles. The preliminary empirical analysis with the prototype distributed data mining system discussed in this paper is suited towards this latter situation. The integration of the CDSS component of the ubiquitous healthcare framework with such a DDM is important.

As mentioned earlier the CDSS utilizes source data such as a user's blood pressure, pulse and temperature collected from the sensor, medical treatment history and other clinical data and integrates them for guidance on medical decision making. This involves both centralized and decentralized decision making processes and thus needs to employ distributed data modelling techniques. There are several levels of data mining involved in this process. Local mining of individual user data based on personalized medical history as well as global mining with respect to groups is required.

Data mining techniques used in the decision making system divide patients into groups. As a collection of patients have their own characteristics, they should be divided properly, and group properties are found through applying cluster analysis modelling techniques and searching created groups in the group analysis step. Secondly, finding causes and developing a model using mining techniques. Important causes of each subdivided group can be understood by the created cause and effect model, and through this, proper management for each patient can be achieved. Finally, a dynamic profile of the patient can be created using past history and domain knowledge in con-junction with sensory data. Each patient's risk rate is calculated by a system reflecting mining results, and administrators can see patients' risk rankings from the risk rates and give priority to patients with higher rates.

4.2 Distributed data mining architecture

This section describes a prototype system for DDM. For a detailed exposition of this system see (Viswanathan et al., 2000). The DDM system is build from various components as seen in figure 2. The DDM system takes source data and using SNOB (Wallace & Dowe, 2000), a mixture modeling tool, partitions it to clusters. The clusters get distributed over the LAN using MPI (developed by the Message Passing Interface Forum). Data models are developed for each cluster dataset using the classification algorithm C4.5 (Quinlan, 1993).

Finally the system uses a voting scheme to aggregate all the data models. The final global classification data model comprises of the top three rules for each class (where available). Note that MPI is used in conjunction with the known maximum number of hosts to classify the clusters in parallel using the C4.5 classification algorithm. If the number of clusters exceeds the available number of hosts then some hosts will classify multiple clusters (using MPI). Also the aggregation model scans all Rule files from all clusters and picks the best rules out of the union of all cluster rule sets. During the classification phase we have also classified the original dataset and produced rules modeling this data. To finally ascertain if our DDM system is efficient we compare our global model to this data model from the un-partitioned database. We compare the top three rules for each class from this model with our rules from the global model. If our global model is over 90% accurate in comparison to the data model from the original database we consider this as a useful result.

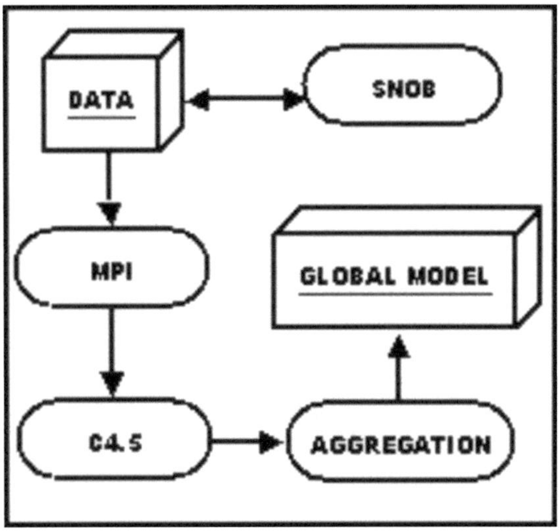

Fig. 2. DDM System Components

4.3 Preliminary results

The DDM system was tested on a number of real world datasets in order to test the effectiveness of data mining and the predictive accuracy. Detailed empirical analysis can be studied from (Viswanathan et al., 2005). In this section we present the DDM system performance results on the 'Pima-Indians-Diabetes' dataset from the UCI KDD Archive (Merz & Murphy, 1998). The diagnostic is whether the patient shows signs of diabetes according to World Health Organization criteria.

In order to study the usefulness of the system we compare the top three rules (where available) for each class from the partition-derived classification rules and rules from the original dataset. The aim of this testing is to find out the effect of our clustering process in partitioning, to the efficiency of our classification model and its predictive accuracy. We will consider 10% to be our threshold, average error rates of rules from partitions greater then 10% of that of the corresponding original rules is an undesirable result.

We can observe in figure 3 that the graphs comparing rules from partitions and original rules approximately follow the same gradient with the average error rate of partition rules staying above the original rules throughout with this gap closing as we approach higher classes. In general the distributed data mining system offers useful performance in the presence of a number of factors influencing the predictive accuracy. However many improvements and further research is needed in order to optimize the DDM system.

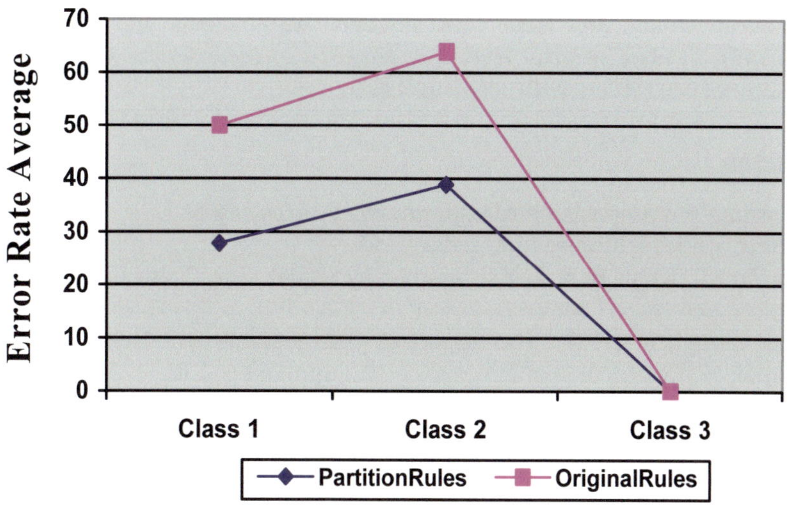

Fig. 3. Results from Partitioning

5. Conclusions and future challenges

As the elderly population constitutes a larger proportion of the aging society, providing quality long term care becomes an increasingly critical issue over the world. Our research aims to enable a patient-centric ubiquitous healthcare environment instead of the existing hospital-centric approach. The use of traditional verification-based approaches to analysis is difficult when the data is massive, highly dimensional, distributed, and uncertain. Innovative discovery-based approaches to health care data analysis with the integration of distributed data mining techniques warrant further attention.

This paper commences by describing a ubiquitous healthcare framework designed to provide consumers with freedom from temporal and spatial restrictions in their access to professional and personalized healthcare services anytime and anywhere - even outside of the hospital. Components of the system framework are discussed in brief. A prototype distributed data mining system is introduced with results from preliminary experiments on data. The plausibility of integrating such a DDM system with the clinical decision support component (CDSS) of the ubiquitous healthcare frameworks is highlighted.

However, there are several problems to solve, and the first one is accuracy. If sensors collect incorrect data, doctors can misjudge or misunderstand patients' emergency situations. Further analysis from the data mining mechanism is of great importance. The second is that there are controversial factors such as permissible ranges, certifications of doctors, and responsibility in case of the remote treatment. The existing law puts a limitation on the qualification of remote medical technicians, which impedes the spread of the system. Therefore, to activate the remote medical service, permissible ranges should be widened, and various remote medical technologies should be imported. The third is privacy protection. All user information employed such as bio-medical data collected from the remote monitoring systems or sensors should be handled with care to protect patients' privacy, and careful study is required to decide how much personal information should be open to the public. The fourth is security of biomedical signals. In this ubiquitous healthcare environment, sensors transmit collected biomedical signals to centers through wired or wireless communication, and these collected data are analyzed and used by the CDSS monitoring staff. Various security levels are required to control access to biomedical data stored in intermediate centers with access authorization.

6. References

CodeBlue. http://www.eecs.harvard.edu/~mdw/proj/codeblue.

EliteCare. http://www.elitecare.com/index.html.

Hill, J.; Horton M.; Kling R. & L. Krishnamurthy (2004). The Platforms enabling Wireless Sensor Networks. *Communications of the ACM*, Vol. 47 pp. 41-46.

Jardine, I. & Clough K. (1999). The Impact of Telemedicine and Telecare on Healthcare. *Journal of Telemedicine and Telecare*, Vol. 5, Supplement 1 127-128.

Kumar A. & Kantardzic M. (2006). Distributed Data Mining: Framework and Implementations, *IEEE Internet Computing*, vol. 10, no. 4, 2006, pp. 15-17.

Kristof Van Laerhoven et. al. (2004). Medical Healthcare Monitoring with Wearable and Implantable Sensors, *Proceedings of 2nd International Workshop on Ubiquitous Computing for Pervasive Healthcare Applications*.

MobileHealth. http://www.mobihealth.org/.

Message Passing Interface Forum (1994). "MPI: A message-passing interface standard". *International Journal of Supercomputer Applications*, 8(3/4):165-414.

Merz, C. & Murphy, P. (1998). *UCI repository of machine learning databases*. Irvine, CA: University of California Irvine, Department of Information and Computer Science. Internet: http://www.ics.uci.edu/~mlearn/MLRepository.html.

Park B. H., Kargupta H. (2003). "Distributed data mining: Algorithms, systems, and applications". *The Handbook of Data Mining*.Nong Ye (ed) Lawrence Erlbaum, New Jersey.

Quinlan, J. (1993). *C4.5: Programs for machine learning*. San Mateo, CA: Morgan Kaufmann.

Smithers C. R. and Hill N. Options for Wireless Technology in Telemedicine and Telecare Applications. *Journal of Telemedicine and Telecare*, Vol. 5, Supplement 1 138-139.

Smart Medical Home. University of Rochester, Center for Future Health, Rochester, NY U.S.A. http://www.futurehealth.rochester.edu/smart_home/Smart_home.html.

Tele-Monitoring: http://www.medical.philips.com.

United Nations Population Division Publications (2002). UN World Population Ageing 1950~2050. http://www.un.org/esa/population/publications/worldageing19502050/.

Viswanathan M.; Yang Y. K. & Whangbo T. K (2005). Distributed Data Mining on Clusters with Bayesian Mixture Modeling, *Lecture Notes in Computer Science*, Volume 3613, Jul, Pages 1207 - 1216.

Wallace C. & Dowe D. (2000). "MML clustering of multi-state, Poisson, von Mises circular and Gaussian distributions". *Statistics and Computing*, 10(1), pp. 73-83, January.

11

Data Mining in Higher Education

Roberto Llorente and Maria Morant
Universidad Politécnica de Valencia,
Spain

1. Introduction

Higher Education targets to develop complex theoretical, abstract and analytical reasoning capabilities in the alumni. This objective can be accomplished addressing four major steps: Theoretical foundation, practice, communication and assessment (Petry, 2002). Theoretical background and practical exercise comprise the basic knowledge building process at initial stages. Assessment guides the alumni through higher complexity studies permitting the student to identify the weak points in the knowledge building where further theory study and/or practice is required.

Theoretical foundation and problem-solving practice are well known aspects in Higher Education. High-quality materials in printed and electronic format, sometimes including multimedia -audio, video or computer graphics–, sometimes delivered through the Internet are readily available today. Teaching-aids as computer-feed overhead projectors or electronic blackboards in the classroom are common place and facilitate the knowledge-building process. Moreover, computers in the classroom are a powerful tool linking theory and problem-solving practice in engineering studies (Beyerlein et al., 1993).

On the other hand, the assessment process has been evolving slowly in the last decades. Pen-and-paper examination techniques have been translated to the computer-enabled classroom as software applications that present an exam in the screen and record the student answers. This process can be seen as an external assessment targeting to evaluate the skills of the student in order to give a pass/fail on a given subject. The external evaluation can be useful for the student in order to know the skill level, but usually fails short when the student wants to now "what's wrong", i.e. to know not only what question was missed but also what knowledge areas the student is finding difficulties. Weak areas identification cannot be done from a single question or set of questions. It requires the assessment process, examination or similar, to be considered as a whole. Student attention time or time spent thinking on a specific question -relative to the other question, as some students think faster than others- clearly indicates the areas where difficulties hide, by example. The pattern followed when answering the exam questions, by example, is another useful indicator. The student will try to answer first the questions he feels more comfortable with. Dubitation on the answer -change the answer several times- is another useful parameter. All these parameters and many others can be compiled and processed by the unprecedented analytic processing capabilities of modern data mining techniques.

Collaborative assessment appears as a the natural evolution from the individual learning to the collaborative learning, which was proposed as a suitable technique to speed-up development of analytical reasoning as different approaches are continuously suggested

(Sharan & Sharan, 1992). Working in group provides opportunities for developing the student generic skills such as organization, team work, delegation and cooperation. Group work can be used in science career studies for introducing the students in real world work as it provides the opportunity to work in multidisciplinary teams. The aim of group work is to produce better results in presentations and reports. This is achieved combining the individual talent of each member of the group, contributing knowledge and ideas. Nevertheless, cooperative learning is usually disregarded because groupal work assessment cannot provide individual marks. This can be seen as an unfair evaluation method becoming an important issue when the student faces competition in his initial career stages.

Data mining can remove the assessment roadblocks in the collaborative learning scenario altogether providing an unprecedented level of information pinpointing the learning process bottlenecks. This breakthrough approach permits accurate per-student marks when using cooperative learning. In this way, collaborative work and groupal assessment could be regarded as fair, efficient knowledge-building technique.

In this chapter, a generic data mining based assessment technique applied to Higher Education is proposed and analysed. An ad-hoc online evaluation software for deep data-gathering is described in Section 2. Parameters, learning patterns and bottleneck identification techniques are discussed considering a case study. Next in Section 3, an overview of groupal activities methodologies and the associated data mining assessment technique is presented. Finally Section 4 summarizes the main conclusions.

1.1 Educational data mining principle

Data mining addresses data analysis by software in order to find patterns, regularities or the opposite -irregularities- in very large information sets. A lot of companies use data mining to comb through databases and adapt their business plans. Readily examples can be found in supermarkets where data mining is used in order to figure out which of their products sells best and where. Data mining processing can be successfully extended to the education environment, specifically at Higher Education levels.

A data mining process can be defined and applied for exploring and analysing data to identify useful patterns in the evaluation results. In this section, the state-of-the-art of data mining definitions applied to education is summarized highlighting the main steps, phases and factors to be considered. Educational Data Mining (EDM) is defined as the process used for transforming raw data compiled by education systems in useful information that could be used by the lecturers to take corrective actions and answer research questions (Heiner et al., 2006). EDM is the application of data mining in the educational field, with the main objective of better understanding the student learning process in order to improve the quality of the education system.

Fig.1 shows the process of applying educational data mining on the results obtained from educational methodologies. The lecturers are the responsible of designing and planning the classes using different methodologies. The students use and participate in these activities working individually or in groups. The data obtained are processed by data mining in order to classify, identify patterns or associate different terms.

The main objective is to identify the learning pattern of each student according to its student profile. As it is already known, we can find different student profiles in the same class, from which we can classify in two big groups: those who are able to self-regulate their own learning processes and do prefer a free approach of exploring the subject, and those who prefer close teacher control and need more guidance. It is necessary to identify these profiles in order to evaluate the learning pattern of each student.

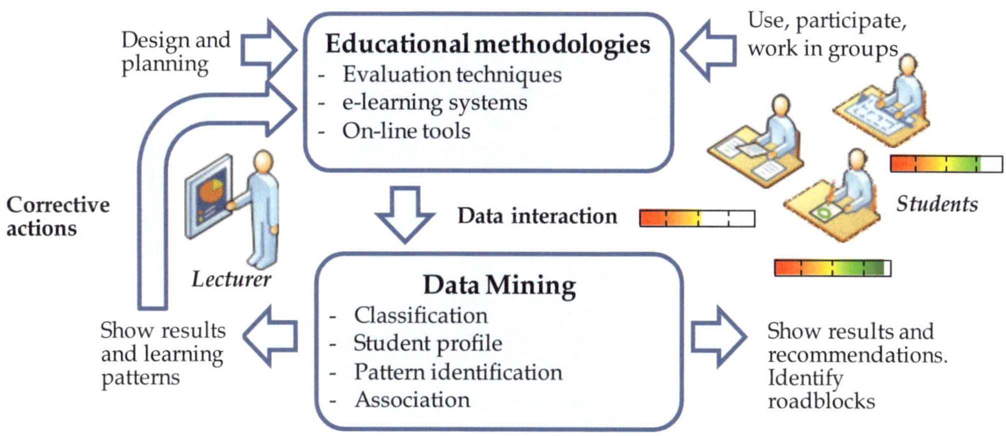

Fig. 1. Data mining for identification of the student' learning pattern

As a conventional data mining processes, several steps should be performed for EDM analysis. The different steps can be summarized in:

1. **Data pre-processing:** In this phase the data to be studied are processed before being analysed. Usually it consists of calculating descriptive data summarizations and measures of central tendency (such as mean and mode) and data dispersion (like quantiles, variances and standard deviation). Data cleaning methods can be applied too in order to handle missing values or inconsistent data. Integration and transformation of the data may be applied before starting the data mining study.
2. **Data mining:** The data are processed performing correlations to identifying associations in the information gathered. Frequency pattern mining analysis should be applied at this stage.
3. **Classification:** In this stage the metric is evaluated using decision tree and decision rule induction. They can be used linear or non-lineal models for classification. Cluster analysis and sequence or trend analysis can be applied over the classified information.
4. **Visualization:** The data mining results are presented in a readable form. Two main outputs are presented: One for the students and the other one for the lecturer. It is important to give feedback to the students on their learning patterns pointing out the roadblocks identified so they can take action to solve them. Further tracking on the bottlenecks identified for a given student, can also identify the problem. In that way, they can use that knowledge to address learning tasks with more intention, thereby achieving positive results in terms of assessments of performance and interaction with other students. On the other hand, the analysis of the information provided by data mining can be used by the lecturers for introducing corrective actions, instructional changes and other improvements, which were derived from the learning pattern results.

1.2 Assessment state-of-the-art

Usually, qualitative methods are used for evaluation with different criteria. General criteria for judging qualitative studies are different depending on the purpose. In order to achieve collaborative learning it is required that the lecturers develop an effective plan. This plan is in reality like a route-map that the students should follow. In order to prepare a suitable plan the lecturers must know the actual situation (where you are in the map) and define the goals (where you want to go). In learning, like in other situations, the development of successes is uncertain and the plan must be adaptive in order to add corrective actions. To do this, appropriate evaluation tools are needed.

The evaluation tools typically employed in Higher Education can be classified in written and oral techniques. Written examination so far tries to bring the students to their maximum potential after several years of studies. The examination procedure can be oral, but chances of successful computer-processing are reduced as human voice - to machine translation techniques are not sufficiently advanced.

Written assessment techniques can summarised in:

- **Questionnaires:** A questionnaire consists of a number of questions of given concepts that the student has to answer. A distinction is made between open-answer and closed-answer questions as it will be explained later.
- **Problem solving:** A mathematical problem is given to the student to be solved in every step till reaching the final answer. The student should explain how each step is achieved and the reasons. In this case, not only that the final correct answer is achieved is considered, the steps to reach it are taken into account too.
- **The portfolio:** One of the last evaluation methods which includes an assessment technique of the portfolio as a collection of materials of the students' abilities and achievements that can be used as a method for testing and examinations (Lupton, 2005). These are individual techniques which require time-consuming stand-alone work.
- **Rubrics:** A rubric is a scoring tool used for linking the students' criteria to the learning objectives. One of the key advantages of the rubrics for the lecturers is that they establish clear benchmarks for achieving success and make grading more efficient.
- **Concept maps:** Diagrams showing the relationships among different concepts. When establishing the key concepts and their relationships the student demonstrates the knowledge about the subject.
- **Notebook revision:** The teachers review the student's notebooks where they take notes and develop the concepts given in class.
- **Academic work:** Written documents prepared by the student developing a given task. This can be applied to summarize ideas for a given concept, describe processes, compiling information or state-of-the-art between others.
- **Essays:** The student writes a short document giving its opinion of a concept or develops an idea from a topic.
- **Study case:** A real-life example is given to the student who should understand it, study the problem to propose solutions and develop it.
- **Project:** The students develop a technical project document. This is used to integrate concepts and apply them to a project case.
- **One minute paper:** This technique consists in a writing activity of very short duration (it should take one minute or less to complete it) developing a proposed subject or specific question. This technique has been commonly introduced in Higher Education to prompt the students to summarize the day's lesson.

Typical oral assessment techniques:

- **Oral exam:** The students should present the answer of a question or a summary of a concrete subject orally to the teacher. In this case other aspects more than the knowledge of the question can be evaluated (speech techniques, body language, etc.)
- **Presentation:** Activities done in the classroom where the student gives a short presentation of a work that he has prepared and explains it to the rest of the class.

- **Open discussions and debate:** Dialogue between the members of the class guided by the lecturer.

The questionnaires are probably the most used evaluation technique as it provides objective assessment and it is well suited to computerized or online assessment format. Many questionnaires formats are used in Higher Education that can be classified in two main groups: Closed-questions (multiple choice, yes/no questions, ordering, etc.) and open-questions (short questions, extended-response questions, problems to develop, filling the gaps, essays…). The difference between the two groups relies on if there is only one correct answer (closed question), or if the answer should be explained by the student and interpreted by the lecturer (open question). Inside each group there are different methodologies that can be summarized in:

Closed-question types

a. **Multiple-choice question:** This kind of question comprises a statement followed by different answer options that are given to the student (from which only one is the correct answer). These questions are commonly used not only for evaluating theoretical concepts but for short mathematical problem resolution on which achieving the right number results is what matters.
b. **Yes/No or True/False question:** It is a multiple-choice question but with only two options. In this case the student should answer if the statement presented in the question is true or false. This can be used to identify basic concepts.
c. **Ordering question:** In these questions the student must put a list of concepts in the correct order. This can be used for example for describing the phase order of a given process or for chronological ordering.
d. **Matching question:** In these questions there are two or three columns of information and the student should relate each item from one column with one item from another column. This has multiple applications such as selecting the opposite meaning or the similar one, pair combination, etc.

Open-question types

a. **Filling the gaps:** These questions appear as a statement with missing words in the sentence (called gaps) that the students should fill in with the proper words.
b. **Short questions:** In this case, the student should answer the given question in a few lines. This type of questions develop the skills of summarizing and synthetizing the main concepts.
c. **Extended-response questions:** In this case, the student should develop in detail about a given concept or idea given in the statement.
d. **Problem solving:** A technical problem is presented to the student which must use calculations to produce the answers. Analytical description of the steps taken is usually required.

Multiple-choice questions are the most interesting strategy to be employed in data mining applications as different variables can be defined addressing pre-defined "information bits" useful to assess the learning pattern. Of course, the information bits must be defined by the lecturer in advance. Some examples of information bits can, by example, the "answer toggling", i.e. if the student changes his answer several times. Other example of a useful information bit is the time thinking spent before answering a given question. This indicates that the student doubts and a roadblock in the learning process is pinpointed. Moreover, considering the specific two answers on which the student is in doubt, the roadblock in the learning process can be identified with high precision.

1.3 Higher education framework

The European Higher Education Area, intended to be established by end of 2010 according to the Bologna Process (The Bologna Declaration of June 1999), established deep reforms targeting a more European Higher Education more compatible and attractive for the students (European Commission, 1999). In the new European Higher Education Area the students will be able to choose from a wide range of high quality courses in a transparent way with the benefit from smooth recognition procedures. Three main objectives of the Bologna process can be summarized in: introduction of the three cycle system (defined as bachelor, master and doctorate), quality assurance and recognition of qualifications and periods of study.

Moreover, in the European Higher Education Area based on the Bologna principles, laboratory lessons have been incorporated in all the subjects of the internal curricular units. According to this, almost all science graduate students will use a laboratory at some point in their graduate careers. Laboratory work in engineering studies involves not only practise on-the-field work but team-work. In fact, what enterprises are looking for are mature graduates with a good understanding of the principles of engineering as well as excellent team-working and management skills. To achieve this, the curriculum must incorporate active, engaging and relevant learning, teaching and assessment strategies to develop self-aware, well-motivated, enterprising and independent learners. In addition, assessment and feedback must be used to promote, as well as to measure, the student learning and progress. In order to introduce successfully cooperative learning in Higher Education it is required to assess the precise and accurate tracking of the learning process and to be able to identify and separate the individual outcomes from the outcome of each member of the group. This tracking can be performed by data mining on the collection of several variables during the learning process both individually and also in the cooperative work. All this information can be processed by deep data mining. For this, some variables can be considered in order to obtain two key outcomes: First, an accurate estimation of the effectiveness of the learning process. And second, a precise identification of the bottlenecks of areas where the student is facing problems in the knowledge acquisition process. This is of great importance in order to take corrective actions by the lecturer if necessary.

Laboratory lessons can be used as discovery process for the students as they uncover the mechanisms behind important scientific principles described in theory. In the laboratory, the student learns how to use the related instrumentation and techniques to obtain useful data. The practical work is thoroughly guided in the first parts but, eventually, the student must become autonomous in the measurements. The laboratory time is intended to practice the theoretical concepts previously introduced in the theoretical lessons. The student qualification includes the practice marks obtained in the laboratory sessions. In this chapter we study different strategies to evaluate the laboratory lessons and group-work in engineering studies.

To evaluate this kind of activities in group-work, ordinary exams in the laboratory sessions are time-consuming and most of the times produce lack of interest in alumni due to the large number of sessions. In fact, according to the 2009 "Eurobarometer" survey on Higher Education reform among students (Gallup Organization, 2009), this lack of interest is affecting the engineering students who were the least likely to intend to go on to further study with a 32% vs. 71% of medical students who had plans to continuing their studies doing a Doctorate or another Masters course. Also the number of students per session (around 35) prevents the possibility of oral or individual exams. For this reason, on-line

evaluation techniques based in test using multiple-choice, filling the gaps or short questions have been commonly introduced and accepted at the university in the last years.
The tests are powerful educational tools that if are carefully designed can be used for evaluating accurately the student learning. These tests can reinforce learning by providing students with indicators of what topics they should revise.
But this type of evaluation and e-learning activities needs a control of the evolution of the learning skills in order to validate the results. This can be solved applying data mining to the examination results and advising the lecturer with the student success rate statistics broke down by the concepts introduced in the session. E-learning techniques are used too for distance education where web-based technology was very quickly adopted and used for course delivery and knowledge sharing (Zaïne, 2001). In Section 2 of this chapter, an overview of data mining techniques that can be used for enhance on-line education not only for the students but for the lecturers is included. These techniques offer researchers unique opportunities to study how students learn and what approaches to learning lead to success (Minaei-Bidgoli et al., 2003). This allows classifying students in order to predict their final grade based on features extracted from the collected data during the web-based on-line evaluation tool. Some example cases applied to real could dataset results are commented in this chapter according to (Minaei-Bidgoli et al., 2003), (Llorente & Morant, 2009), (Merceron & Yacef, 2005).
However, this becomes more difficult when we add group-centric work as it is more complicated to identify the work done and skills developed by each member of the group individually. When we talk of cooperative work we mean collaboration between all the partners. As we know, good collaboration is not achieved only having students sit side-by-side called collaborative work, a group must have clear positive interdependence: members must promote each other's learning and face-to-face interaction. But the evaluation and qualification of this kind of problem-based results it is also a much deeper issue, as it is very difficult to identify the level of each member of the group in the whole result. In Section 3 of this chapter, a groupal evaluation technique is proposed taken into account for data mining calculations for obtaining a fair evaluation result. In order to obtain an accurate learning pattern of each student it is necessary to identify small bits of information that can be analysed by data mining.

2. Data mining and e-Learning

With the insertion of the new technologies in education, novel evaluation techniques appeared in order to make the evaluation process simpler and different for the students. Moreover, using evaluation tools for monitoring the students learning evolution can be extended to study deeply the learning pattern of the students. This can be achieved if more information is taken into account apart from only the answer in the exams. There are a lot of bits of information that, despite if you look at them separately they have no obvious meaning, when analysed with data mining can give us exact relation with learning concepts and predict roadblocks in the learning process. In this Section we will describe how data mining techniques can be applied in Higher Education studies.

2.1 Data gathering

The main goal of a lecturer should be to make the most effective use of the lecturing time in order to give students a beneficial experience of doing science. In order to achieve this, lecturers can use different methods to include technical and practical aspects to the concepts they want to explain, for example laboratory and seminar sessions. About engineering studies, different aspects have to be considered that are, most of the times, interrelated and complementary: a pedagogy factor to determining the best teaching methods for the desired outcomes, and a logistic factor to ensuring that the evaluation process is correct and that the students understand the tasks they need to accomplish.

Several tools can be used by the lecturers and lecturers in order to evaluate the learning pattern of the students. We can classify some as:

- Native applications that run in a computer or mobile devices to compile information presenting several questions to the user. This type of applications has been extended for work in the field using PDA without the necessity of having a computer. Applications running in the PDA can be used for updating the stock of a company, user surveys in the street, etc.
- Pure online applications that run in a website navigator such as Microsoft Explorer, Mozilla Firefox, Opera, Safari, etc. Nowadays they use commonly HTML4 or HTML5 and usually require connectivity to Internet. This kind of applications has main the advantage that the data compilation can be done remotely from several users at different locations. The data can be stored in the same database and it is transparent to the final user.
- Middleware software based on XML, SOAP and Web services. This is an extension of the only application where not only the website navigator is needed but a custom-made application must be installed to run the program. These service-oriented architectures provide a more functional set of application programming interfaces that can be applied for online testing. An example could be Adobe Air applications.

2.2 Data analysis

In (Llorente & Morant, 2009) the data mining technique in Higher Education is proposed for monitoring the learning tracking at the end of the lesson using a web-based exam. The exam comprises a questionnaire showing the questions in increasing difficulty order. The developed application stores the results and other information that can be analysed by data mining to identify roadblocks. This technique consists of five phases which can be summarized as:

- Data collection: This phase starts with the initial data collection using the on-line test application described before. In this phase we get familiar with the data, to identify data quality problems, or to detect interesting subsets to form hypotheses for hidden information. This could be very useful for lecturers that need to update the contents of their lessons depending on the results obtained in the previous ones.
- Data preparation phase: This phase covers the activities needed to construct the final database. This phase is included in the on-line test programming to record the data that is needed for data mining directly in a database. However, data preparation tasks are likely to be performed multiple times, as after using this technique some variations could be needed to add parameters that could be interesting to study or to remove data that is not significant to the study.
- Modelling phase: In this phase, various data mining techniques can be selected and applied. Typically, there are several techniques for the same data mining problem type. Some techniques have specific requirements on the form of data. Therefore, stepping back to the data preparation phase is often needed.

- Evaluation stage: This phase comprises the knowledge building assessment. The lecturer monitoring the obtained data. In this phase, the lecturer takes decisions about the concepts that need to be clarified and includes the corresponding changes in the deployment phase.

The information gathered during the process is stored and following data mining processes will benefit from the information of the previous ones. The phase sequence shown in Fig. 2 is not strict. The arrows indicate the most important and frequent dependencies between the phases. Moving back and forth between different phases can be done if it is required. It depends on the outcome of each phase or which particular task has to be performed next.

The life cycle of a data mining process is based on a modification of the CRoss-Industry Standard Process for Data Mining (named CRISP-DM). The outer circle in Fig. 2 represents the cyclic nature of data mining itself.

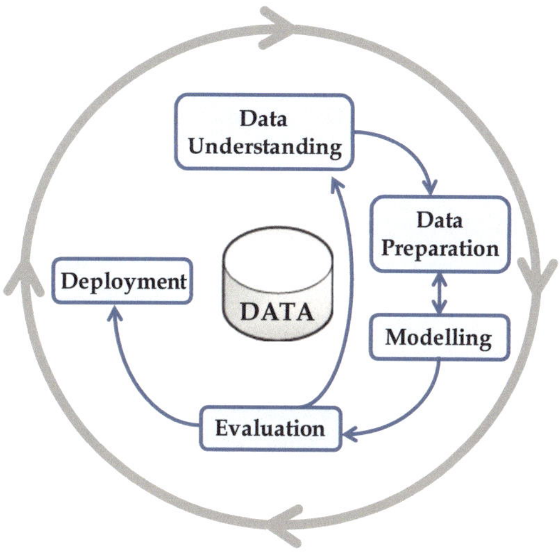

Fig. 2. Educational data mining structure (Llorente & Morant, 2009)

2.3 Information bits and pattern identification

The special importance of the proposed technique is that data mining is done at class-level and also at student-level, which permits the proper guide of the knowledge building process at personal level capturing and analysing individual bits of information.

We could say that the technique is based on relationship mining, which main goal is to discover if there are relationships between variables in the data set saved containing a large number of bits of information. In this may we try to find out which variables are most strongly associated with a single variable of particular interest or discover which relationships between any two variables are strongest.

Sequential pattern mining is interesting too. In this case, the objective is to find temporal associations between events, for example to determine which kind of student behaviours lead to an eventual event or result.

The procedure for correcting the assessment on-line tests is, naturally, the individuation of right and wrong answers. The control panel system applies tailored deep data mining (Witten & Frank, 2005) to track the knowledge construction process of the alumni. This aims to monitor the results and the quality of the learning in the laboratory.

Usually the computer is the responsible for finding the patterns by identifying the underlying rules and features in the data. In this case, data mining is applied over a large set of variables which are tracked during a simple on-line exercise done at the end of the laboratory lesson. As we said before, in data mining, the process of using a model to derive predictions or descriptions of behaviour that is yet to occur is called "scoring". Following a traditional analysis, a new model of database has to be built to score new data, or the data has to be moved from relational tables. But the on-line application for laboratory test used in this case records directly in a data base the obtained score of the alumni. This application has been modified to include other parameters that are useful for data mining evaluation of the results performance of the students. The bits of information considered for deep data mining in this case can be classified in three levels depending on the complexity of the relation that analyses:

First level: Answer

- *Answer*: Selected answer. This value is the first one to be taken into account in order to know if the answer provided by the student is correct or not. Afterwards other information will be evaluated in order to find out the procedure the student followed to reach that answer and elaborate the learning pattern.

Second level: Timing

- *Ts*: Time spent by the student observing the question on-screen. This value can give the lecturer an idea about if the group has discussed about the answer selection a lot of less time. This parameter can have several meanings. For example, if the theoretical concept that the question is addressing is well understood or should be recalled in the next lesson to be clarified. Another meaning could be if the question is in a wrong format. This monitoring can give the lecturer the opportunity of giving the students another question in the same topic to observe the results and explain the concept again if necessary.

Third level: Sequence

- *Tr*: Number of times the student has recalled the question to be presented in the screen. This parameter includes at the background the internal relationships between the questions presented to the students. If a question is recalled after answering it, the reason could be because the students has understood the concept after solving a question that was presented afterwards, and they want to change the previous selection.
- *Ai*: Number of times the studies has changed the answer. This parameter is related with the two previous ones. The students can spend some time observing the question and if the selected answer is changed many times it indicates that there is no agreement of all the members of the group. This variable is related with *Tr* if the question is recalled after answering.
- *Seq_a*: Sequence of answers selected by the student when changing the answer of a given question. This is a very important parameter to be considered. Data mining studies can point out if any question was wrong-answered but if the previous selected answers contained the correct one. Moreover, it is interesting to consult this parameter if a question has been recalled after answering it, because most of the times when an test answer is changed the previously selected was the correct one.
- *Seq_q*: Sequence of questions requested by the student after the first presentation. This parameter contains the questions the students wanted to recall after answering the complete test.
- *Lq*: Last question answered by the student.

Additional data gathered:

- *S1… SN*: Individual scores per question.
- *S*: Final score.

The correlation of the different variables above is analysed in order to identify the bottlenecks or roadblocks in the student learning process. This is taken into account in the web application developed for the case study example explained in next point for laboratory evaluation purposes dealing with Fourier and Laplace domains in Telecommunication engineering. This on-line application includes a "control panel" of the subject which is presented in real-time to the lecturer during the realisation of the on-line exercise. This control panel is a translation of the business control panel that can be found in advanced business administration techniques. See by example (Romero et al., 2008).

2.4 Examination tool example

An e-learning tool has been developed targeting to solve the low assistance and relatively poor results obtained in laboratory sessions. The implemented tool combines adaptive examination with on-the-fly data mining techniques in the e-learning examination phase (Monk, 2005). The examination consists in an on-line exam for groups of two or three students to be done in the last 15 minutes of every laboratory session. The exam is composed on-the-fly by an examination server that chooses the questions from a question database, and saves the student results in a result database (answers and spent time are recorded). The results database is analysed by data mining and continually monitored in order to track the success rate of the different concepts addressed in the exam. If a particular concept is detected to be too difficult (a local minima during the data mining is identified), then the exam generator is instructed to go further, presenting questions with fine details to other students in order to identify the concept that has not been properly understood (Cheng et al., 2005).

The examination tool has been implemented as a web application employing HTML and JavaScript. Data storing, retrieval and analyse has been implemented employing ActiveX Data Objects (ADO) modules for database access.

This technique was introduced for the first time in the academic year 2006/2007 in the subject *Análisis de Sistemas Contínuos* (ASC), in Telecommunication Engineering studies at the *Escuela Politécnica Superior de Gandia* (Universidad Politécnica de Valencia, Spain) (www.epsg.upv.es). This subject (ASC) is a single term subject that became a keystone in Telecommunication studies, as it includes basic circuit analysis in continuous time and the Fourier and Laplace transforms tools.

ASC subject comprises 75 lecturing hours and provides the theoretical basis (80 % time) and laboratory sessions (20 % time) deep into time invariant systems characterisation using the impulse response, convolution operation, continuous time Fourier Transform, and signal and system analysis in the Laplace domain. Interactive seminars are included as a part of the theoretical classes to apply the explained concepts to solve a proposed problem. Using this method students resolve proposed problems first as a team in the seminars, then with a partner in the laboratory sessions, and finally during the lecturing via examples and in-class resolved problems. This makes easier to the student to prepare this very problem-solving oriented subject. The application was developed using Oracle Data Mining (ODM) software. This software contains several data mining and data analysis algorithms for classify, predict, clustering, and for making regression, associations and anomaly detection. This platform provides means for the creation and management of data mining models inside a given

database. ODM simplifies model deployment by offering Oracle SQL functions to score data stored right in the database. ODM is employed for extract the important information in the control panel application developed for ASC laboratory evaluation.
A first study identifies alumni who have the same doubts about the same topic, and generates the relation with the questions that have been answered correctly and wrong. Several functions and algorithms can be selected in ODM depending on the usage and the features of the data.
Table 1 shows an example of the stored data for data mining evaluation. In this case five questions are presented and the different parameters described before are recorded in the database. In this case the control panel obtains the overall difficulty level of each question.
Based on this results the cross correlation factor between the presented questions is obtained, as is shown for the same example in Table 2. The obtained cross correlation factor points out that the question Q3 is estimated of similar difficulty as Q5.

Question	Q1	Q2	Q3	Q4	Q5
Ts (s)	154	132	214	202	197
Tr	3	1	5	3	2
Ai	0	0	1	0	1
Seq_a	"1"	"2-1"	"1"	"1"	"3-2"
Seq_q	"1"	"2"	"3"	"4"	"3-5"
Lq		"1"	"2"	"3"	"3"
S	1	1	1	1	0
Difficulty Level	18.00	18.43	23.29	21.43	25.07

Table 1. Capture example of the stored data for data mining

	Q1	Q2	Q3	Q4	Q5
Q1	1				
Q2		1			
Q3			1		1
Q4				1	
Q5					1

Table 2. Cross correlation factor of the difficulty of the presented questions

This is particularly true in the case presented, as both question address Fourier Transform particular aspects. In particular, the questions were:

Q3: “Giving the coefficients of Fourier Series decomposition given below, indicate which of the signals presented in the figure corresponds with the original continuous-time signal.”

Q5:”Observe carefully the spectrum shown in the Figure below. This spectrum corresponds to a continuous signal. Indicate the number of sinusoidal signals present, their frequency, amplitude and phase.”

After the development of the data mining tool and the introduction of this panel, several bottlenecks in the subject taught were identified. Corrective lecturing actions like allocating more time for the Fourier Analysis lecturing, where introduced and the pass-rate of the laboratory work in the subject increased by in 37% the compared with the first year the laboratory work was introduced (academic year 2003/2004). This improvement has been sustained over time, as can be observed in the final marks historic series for the last four academic years shown in Fig. 3.

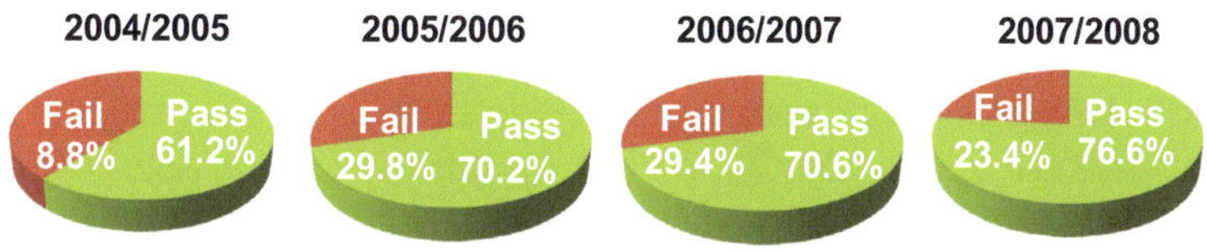

Fig. 3. Evaluation results, before and after introducing the data mining tool

It should be pointed out that the introduction of the on-line evaluation tool in the laboratory in 2005/2006 made a 32% increase in attendance to the laboratory sessions, and 9% increase in alumni passing the subject. In 2007/2008 with the data mining tool a 6% increase was observed.

3. Data mining for collaborative learning

Cooperative learning is based in small teams conformed by students of different levels of ability that interact to improve their understanding of a subject. Each member of the group is responsible not only for learning what is taught but also for helping their team mates to learn. If cooperative learning is correctly structured, it engages people working in teams to accomplish a common goal, under conditions that involve both positive interdependence (all members must cooperate to complete the task) and both individual and group accountability (each member is accountable for the complete final outcome).

But cooperative work is not achieved only having students sit side-by-side at the same desk. To be cooperative a group must have clear positive interdependence: members must promote each other's learning and face-to-face interaction. Interaction between teacher and students and between students plays a fundamental role in the whole learning process. In many cases also the practical application in the laboratory or in seminar activities of the notions acquired by the students constitutes a very important step.

3.1 Collaborative work

As previously discussed, it is important that the students develop working-in-group skills. This leads to incorporate practise lessons and discussion activities in Higher Education in order to introduce cooperative learning.

In cooperative learning, the team members work together in the classroom for the success of their team and not only for individual success. Students have to get rid of its self-interest for the larger interest of the team. In order to achieve the goals, students have to assist and help each other to solve the problems. The members of the group have a positive interdependence on each other. By communicating with each other, they get to learn from their partners.

Cooperative learning in the classroom has many advantages over the conventional or traditional ways of learning. The traditional ways of learning involves working individually without much interaction with other students. Using this technique probably the students will remain unaware of the new methods of problem solving. The quality of work reported delivered by students working in a group will better as compared to the students working individually. This is because in a group, every suggestion is cross-checked by the other members of the team which minimize the chances of errors.

Cooperative learning can also speed up the completion of the task as those working in a group will complete their work faster than those working individually. Moreover, working in group provides opportunities for developing the student generic and social skills such as organisation, team work, delegation, cooperation, gender and creativity (Gokhale, 1995).
Group work can be used in engineering studies for introducing the students in real world work as it provides the opportunity to work in multidisciplinary teams. The aim of group work is to produce better results in presentations and reports. This is achieved combining the individual talent of each group member, contributing knowledge and ideas.
Obviously, from the teacher point of view, it is mandatory to evaluate if the success of the work comes from the entire team and not to only from any particular member of the team, which is studied in this section.

3.2 Groupal assessment

In (Llorente & Morant, 2009) interactive groupal seminars were proposed for encouraging collaborative work. Based on this we can propose evaluation techniques in order to obtain a deeper knowledge of the skills acquired by the individual students, decorrelating the group evaluation scores from the actual individual score by different approaches.
The groupal seminar technique proposed is shown in Fig. 4. and it is developed in four phases as:

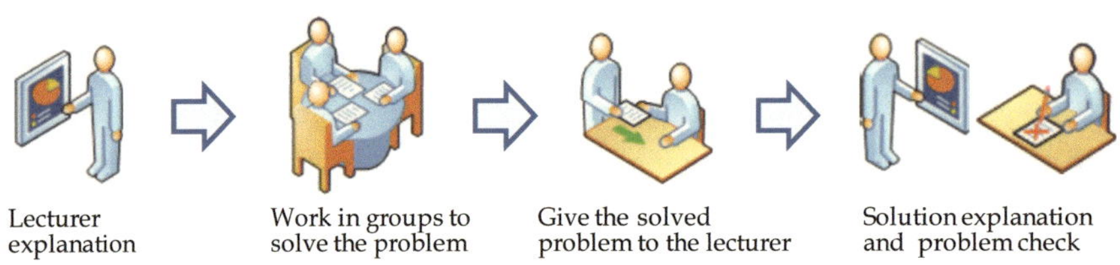

Fig. 4. Proposed seminar technique

1. In the first part of the seminar the alumni listen to the lecturer explanation of theoretical concepts related with the problem that will be proposed afterwards. This focuses student attention on the material to be learned. In this phase the lecturer clearly defines the assignment, teaches the required concepts and strategies. It is needed to specify the positive interdependence and individual accountability and give the criteria for success.
2. In the second phase, the students work in group trying to solve the proposed problem. The group size is a factor to take into account. Smaller groups (of three students) contain less diversity of thinking styles and make more difficult the management (as it means that there will be a larger number of groups in the same class). Conversely, in larger groups it is difficult to ensure that all members participate (Gokhale, 1995). In this study the group were set up to five students.

This phase needs the organisation of the class to be changed. Effective classroom organisation maximises time spent on teaching and learning experiences by eliminating or minimising the distractions caused by behaviour problems. For this reason, during this phase the classroom organisation is changed as shown in Fig. 5. During the first phase of the seminar the classroom organisation remains as in a usual lesson, in order to make easier to the students attending the lecturer explanation. After the explanation, the placement of furniture is changed grouping 5 students in small clusters of desks to form different groups of work. This provides a separated area of work for each group of students (that facilitates small group cooperative learning) and ease of movement around the room for the teacher.

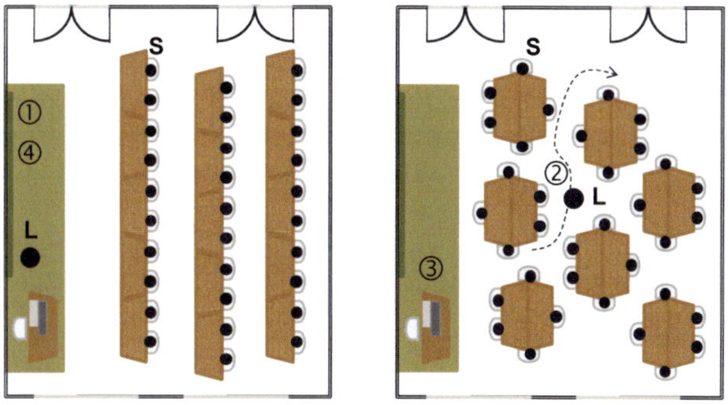

Fig. 5. Plan view of the organisation of the class for the different phases of the seminar, L: Lecturer, S: Students. The numbers represents the different phases

3. In the third step of the seminar, the students give the solution of the proposed problem to the lecturer that will return it solved back in the next session.
4. The fourth and last phase consist in the exposition of the problem solution by the lecturer.

This technique can be used by the lecturers to monitor the quality of the results. In the last phase of the seminar the lecturer can go deeper in the concepts that were not clear during the development of the problem inside the group.

In most of the cases, a group is comprised by students with different levels of ability and it is a challenge for the lecturer to evaluate individually each member. This can be solved using decorrelation techniques in the evaluation process. The herein proposed technique targets to obtain a deeper knowledge of the skills acquired by decorrelating the group evaluation scores evaluation from the individual scores by different approaches:

Group score

The first decorrelation technique evaluates the results obtained by the group during the groupal seminar. In this score all group members are pooled together, taking into account the quality the intermediate steps used by the student to solve the problem (Si) and if the correct solution of the problem is achieved (Ss). Including this score in the evaluation process aims to promote a positive interdependence inside the group, as the team members perceive that they need each other in order to complete the group's task. This is important as it and avoids the effect of pseudo-learning group. The called pseudo-learning group effect occurs when students are assigned to work together but they have no interest in doing so. Sometimes students think that they will be evaluated by being ranked from the highest performer to the lowest performer, so they start competing between them. They see each other as a rival who must be defeated, and in this case, students would achieve better results if they were working alone.

However, it would be not fair using only this score to evaluate the students, as remains the commented possibility of the work was left to one or a few students of the whole group. Cooperation is not assigning a task to a group of students where one or a few students do all the work and the others only put their names on the report as well. This is the reason why decorrelation techniques are needed to evaluate the individual members of the group.

Individual participation

A second technique is based on evaluating the participation of each student inside the group. This promotes face-to-face interaction, assessing the quality and quantity of each member's contributions to the group.

During the second phase of the seminar, the lecturer observes each group and records the frequency with which each member contributes to the group's work. Based on this information, the lectures assigns an individual score (Sp) to each student depending on its participation inside the group. The final score is given by the score obtained by the group presented solution weighted by the individual score Sf=Sp*(Si+Ss).

Peer-to-peer student evaluation

The third technique takes into account on peer-to-peer student evaluation at group level. Lecturers need to ensure that all the members of the cooperative learning group are involved in the task. Groups need to describe what member actions are helpful and unhelpful.

This technique is based on each student gives a score to each student inside the same group. The lecturer provides time and a structure for the students of each learning group to process how effectively they have been working together. When a given score is recorded for the student in different groups, this correction factor is accurate.

Percentile evaluation

The last technique is based on a percentile evaluation for the group and session. In order to avoid conflicts in the group where some students can be too domineering or do not do their share of the work, the student groups must be different in each groupal seminar session. It is important to change student groupings frequently. This ensures each student interacts with different students throughout the semester.

Small groups can be formed in different ways: randomly (i.e. by seat proximity), teacher-selected or student-selected.

The individual scores are extracted from the percentile of the group scores over all sessions on different group environment. If a large number of scores are recorded, the final score of each student is precisely the percentile above the mean of the class.

3.3 Case study example

The case study was evaluated in the same subject in the Universidad Politécnica de Valencia UPV over three years involved with the interactive seminar technique: a preliminary period of a year without using this technique, and engagement with interactive seminars for two academic years comprising 406 students.

	2004/2005	2006/2007
Pass	61.2%	70.6%
Fail	38.8%	29.4%

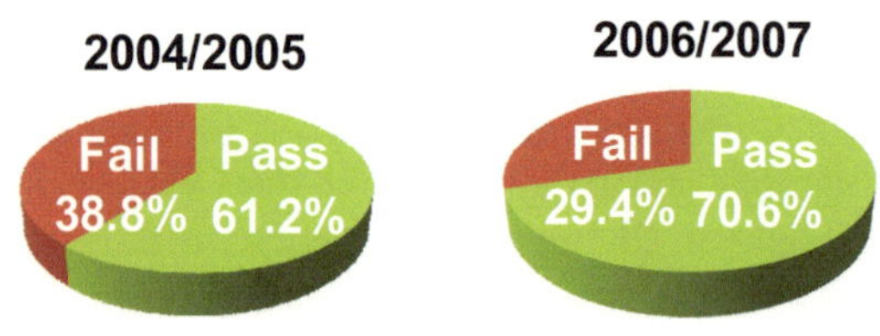

Fig. 6. Evaluation results of the subject ASC in the academic year 2004/2005 and 2006/2007

The introduction of the groupal seminar was reflected in an increase of 9.4% of the passing alumni (from 61.2 % to 70.6 % of the presented alumni) in the analysed year (2006/2007) over the first year of the curricula of the ASC subject was set (2004/2005).

The feasibility of the groupal seminal method presented in this paper is demonstrated in a case study of 16 alumni in 3 seminar sessions in the academic year 2006/2007. In Table 3 are shown the alumni score of the proposed problem without employing these evaluation techniques, for shake of comparison the variance is obtained comparing with the practical online exam results.

The seminar score of the problem is based on if the correct solution was achieved and, in this case, the score is recorded using a gradual scale of B (equivalent to 9 points), R+ (corresponding to 8 points), and R (to 6 points). In Table 3 can be observed that the variance compared with the results obtained in the practical online exam achieves values of even 0.88. For this reason the different decorrelation techniques should be used to improve the evaluation method of the seminar lessons.

Student	Sp score Seminar 1	Sp score Seminar 2	Sp score Seminar 3	Seminar Mean	Online Exam	Variance
#1	8 (R+)	8 (R+)	6 (R)	7.33	7.9	0.16
#2	6 (R)	8 (R+)	6 (R)	6.66	7.6	0.43
#3	9 (B)	8 (R+)	9 (B)	8.66	8.3	0.067
#4	8 (R+)	9 (B)	9 (B)	8.66	8	0.22
#5	9 (B)	8 (R+)	9 (B)	8.66	8.6	0.002
#6	8 (R+)	9 (B)	9 (B)	8.66	9.3	0.2
#7	6 (R)	9 (B)	6 (R)	7	5.8	0.72
#8	9 (B)	8 (R+)	9 (B)	8.66	8.6	0.002
#9	8 (R+)	8 (R+)	6 (R)	7.33	6.5	0.34
#10	9 (B)	9 (B)	9 (B)	9	9.3	0.045
#11	6 (R)	8 (R+)	9 (B)	7.66	8.6	0.43
#12	8 (R+)	8 (R+)	9 (B)	8.33	7.6	0.26
#13	8 (R+)	8 (R+)	9 (B)	8.33	9.6	0.8
#14	8 (R+)	8 (R+)	9 (B)	8.33	9.2	0.37
#15	8 (R+)	6 (R)	9 (B)	7.66	7.6	0.0022
#16	6 (R)	8 (R+)	9 (B)	7.66	9	0.88

Table 3. Case study: Seminar Session 1

In Table 4 are shown the results of the case study for two seminar sessions where the described decorrelation techniques have been implemented. These tables contain several data:

- **Group (G):** Four groups were formed in each seminar session and labelled 1, 2, 3 and 4 respectively in order to obtain the mean score of the group and the percentile study. It can be observed that each student is in a different group in each session to ensure the percentile evaluation described before.
- **Si:** Quality of the intermediate steps used by the student to solve the problem
- **Ss:** Score of the problem considering if the correct solution was achieved.
- **Sp:** Individual participation inside the group. This value is recorded by the lecturer during the seminar session. This parameter has a maximum value of 0.5.
- **Sf:** Score obtained by the group presented solution weighted by the individual score Sf=Sp*(Si+Ss).
- **Peer-to-peer (P2P):** Score given by each student to the other student inside the same group. The lecturer asks the student to record each score with an integer number.
- **Final (F):** Final score of the seminar session. This score is weighted in this way: Final=0.6*Sf+0.4*P2P.

It can be observed in Table 4 that the peer-to-peer score has a high value in the first session. This is normal due to the general impression that this score could mask the final mark. For this reason the final score of the seminar is not obtained as the mean of the lecturer evaluation and the students' evaluation. The final score is weighted to avoid that most popular students could achieve better scores for friendship.

Student	Seminar Session 1							Seminar Session 2						
	G	Si	Ss	Sp	Sf	P2P	F S1	G	Si	Ss	Sp	Sf	P2P	F S2
#1	1	10	8	0.4	7.2	9	7.92	4	9	8	0.4	6.8	7	6.88
#2	2	6.5	6	0.5	6.25	9	7.35	4	9	8	0.4	6.8	9	7.68
#3	3	9.5	9	0.4	7.4	8	7.64	4	9	8	0.4	6.8	9	7.68
#4	1	8.5	8	0.4	6.6	7	6.76	1	9.5	9	0.3	5.55	8	6.53
#5	3	9.5	9	0.4	7.4	8	7.64	3	9	8	0.4	6.8	8	7.28
#6	1	8.5	8	0.5	8.25	9	8.55	1	9.5	9	0.5	9.25	9	9.15
#7	2	6.5	6	0.3	3.75	7	5.05	1	9.5	9	0.3	5.55	7	6.13
#8	3	9.5	9	0.5	9.25	9	9.15	2	8.5	8	0.4	6.6	9	7.56
#9	1	8.5	8	0.3	4.95	7	5.77	2	8.5	8	0.3	4.95	8	6.17
#10	3	9.5	9	0.5	9.25	9	9.15	1	9.5	9	0.4	7.4	9	8.04
#11	2	6.5	6	0.5	6.25	9	7.35	2	8.5	8	0.5	8.25	9	8.55
#12	4	10	8	0.4	7.2	7	7.12	4	9	8	0.3	5.1	8	6.26
#13	4	10	8	0.5	9	9	9	3	9	8	0.5	8.5	9	8.7
#14	4	10	8	0.5	9	9	9	3	9	8	0.5	8.5	8	8.3
#15	4	10	8	0.4	7.2	7	7.12	2	6.5	6	0.4	5	7	5.8
#16	2	6.5	6	0.5	6.25	9	7.35	3	9	8	0.5	8.5	9	8.7

Table 4. Case study: Seminar Session 1 and 2

However, it can be observed in next tables that this impression changes and the students gives more realistic score to their partners.

Student	Seminar 1	Seminar 2	Seminar 3	Seminar Mean	Online Exam	Variance
#1	7.92	6.88	6.96	7.25	7.9	0.20
#2	7.35	7.68	5.72	6.93	7.6	0.22
#3	7.64	7.68	7.64	7.65	8.3	0.20
#4	6.76	6.53	8.75	7.34	8	0.21
#5	7.64	7.28	9.15	8.02	8.6	0.16
#6	8.55	9.15	8.75	8.81	9.3	0.11
#7	5.05	6.13	5.32	5.5	5.8	0.045
#8	9.15	7.56	7.24	7.98	8.6	0.19
#9	5.77	6.17	5.72	5.88	6.5	0.18
#10	9.15	8.04	9.15	8.78	9.3	0.13
#11	7.35	8.55	8.04	7.98	8.6	0.19
#12	7.12	6.26	8.75	7.37	7.6	0.024
#13	9	8.7	9.15	8.95	9.6	0.21
#14	9	8.3	9.15	8.81	9.2	0.073
#15	7.12	5.8	8.04	6.98	7.6	0.18
#16	7.35	8.7	9.15	8.4	9	0.18
Mean				7.66	8.21	0.16

Table 5. Evaluation results and variance comparing with the practical online exam score

Table 5 summarizes the obtained results for the case study of 16 students in 3 seminar sessions. Comparing scores obtained from the groupal work including the correction by the four decorrelation techniques with the individual score obtained in the practical work score.

This is a comparable measurement as the practical work score is obtained via an on-line exam almost at the same dates during the course progress. A maximum variance of 0.22 is obtained comparing the result of the decorrelating technique proposed with the practical on-line exam. The low variance obtained indicates the suitability of the approach proposed, compared with the results obtained without using the proposed decorrelation techniques shown in Table 3.

The overall satisfaction of the alumni regarding groupal interaction has been as measured by the "Instituto de Ciencias de la Educación" (ICE), an internal education-quality control organism of the Universidad Politécnica de Valencia. The obtained results of satisfaction of the alumni rose from 6.86 (over 10) to 8.24 points (over 10) in the academic year 2006/2007. This means a 20.12% increase compared with the previous year.

4. Conclusion

In this chapter, deep data mining analysis applied to evaluation techniques in Higher Education was proposed as an assessment technique permitting to identify the learning pattern of each student according to the student profile. Data mining takes advantage of computer assisted evaluation techniques used in e-Learning. Data mining is applied to decorrelate the incomes in groupal activities such as laboratory lessons or seminars.

Data mining for e-learning

It has been presented that data mining can be applied over bits of information taken during the online evaluation. These small pieces of information can be classified in three levels depending on the complexity of the relation that analyses, mainly: answer, timing and sequence. The correlation of these bits of information can be analysed in order to identify the bottlenecks or roadblocks in the student learning process.

Data mining for groupal assessment

Data mining applied to groupal activities was also presented in order to decorrelate the inputs of each member of the group. Interactive groupal seminars were proposed as a problem-based evaluation method suitable for engineering studies.

A case study over a real subject comprising laboratory lessons and seminar was presented confirming the validity of the proposed techniques to identify the learning pattern of the students. Further improvements can be introduced in the proposed techniques by using deeper data mining analysis and corrective techniques in the following years.

5. References

Beyerlein, S., Ford, M., & Apple, D. (1993) Using a Learning Process Model to Enhance Learning with Technology. *Proceedings of Frontiers in Education Conference 1993*, pp. 456-460, ISBN: 0-7803-1482-4, Washington, USA, Nov. 2003.

Cheng, S-C., Yueh-Min Huang, Y-M., Chen, J-N., & Lin., Y-T. (2005). Automatic Leveling System for E-Learning Examination Pool Using Entropy-Based Decision Tree. Advances in Web-Based Learning ICWL 2005, pp. 273-278, Springer.

European Commission (1999). The European Higher Education Area. The Bologna Declaration of 19 June 1999. Joint declaration of the European Ministers of Education. Available at http://ec.europa.eu/

Gallup Organization (2009). 2009 Eurobarometer survey on Higher Education reform among students. In: Eurobarometer surveys on Higher Education in Europe, March 2009, available at the website: http://ec.europa.eu/education/higher-education/doc/studies/barometersum_en.pdf

Gokhale, A. A. (1995). Collaborative Learning Enhances Critical Thinking. *Journal of Technology Education*, Vol. 7, No. 1, ISSN 1045-1064, 1995.

Heiner, C., Baker, R. & Yacef, K. (2006). Preface in *Proceedings of the Workshop on Educational Data Mining at ITS 2006*, Jhongli (Taiwan), 2006.

Llorente, R. & Morant, M. (2009). Accurate knowledge evaluation by deep data-mining in telecommunication engineering studies. *Proceedings of EAEEIE Annual Conference Innovation in Education for EIE*, ISBN 978-84-8363-428-8, Valencia (Spain), June 2009, IEEE.

Llorente, R. & Morant, M. (2009). The control panel: a deep data-mining technique for the lecturing of engineering-related studies. *Proceedings of INTED 2009*, ISBN 978-84-612-7578-6, Valencia (Spain), March 2009, Ed. IATED.

Lupton, K. (2005). Portfolio versus syllabus methods in experiential education. *Innovative Higher Education*. Vol. 4, Number 2, pp. 114-126, DOI: 10.1007/BF01080440.

Merceron, A. & Yacef, K. (2005). Educational Data Mining: a Case Study. In: *Artificial Intelligence in Education*, IOS Press, ISBN 1-58603-530-4, Amsterdam (Netherlands).

Minaei-Bidgoli, B. ; Kashy, D.A.; Kortemeyer, G. & Punch, W.F. (2003). Predicting student performance: an application of data mining methods with the educational web-based system LON-CAPA. *Proceedings of SEE/IEEE Conference 2003* ISBN 0-7803-7444-4, Boulder, CO, November 2003, IEEE.

Monk, D. (2005). Using Data Mining for e-Learning Decision Making. *Electronic Journal of e-Learning*, Vol. 3, Issue 1, pp. pp 41-54.

Petry, E. (2002). Architectural education: evaluation and assessment *Proceeding of Frontiers in Education 2002*, Vol. 2, ISBN: 0-7803-7444-4.

Rau W. & Heyl B. S. (1990). Humanizing the college classroom: Collaborative learning and social organization among students. *Teaching Sociology*, Vol. 18, pp. 141-155, American Sociological Association, April 1990.

Romero, C.; Ventura, S.; Espejo, P. & Hervas, C. (2008). Data mining algorithms to classify students. *Proceedings of EDM 2008*. pp. 182-185, ISBN 0-6153-0629-2, Montreal (Canada), June 2008.

Sharan, Y. & and Sharan, S. (1992). *Expanding Cooperative Learning through Group Investigation*, Ed. Teachers College Press, ISBN 0-8077-3190-0.

Smith, K. A. (1995). Cooperative Learning: Effective Teamwork for Engineering Classrooms. *Proceedings of IEEE Frontiers in Education Conference*, pp. 13-18, ISBN 0-7803-3022-6, Atlanta (USA), November 1995, IEEE.

Witten, I. H. & Frank, E. (2005). *Data Mining: Practical Machine Learning Tools and Techniques*, Ed. Morgan Kaufman, ISBN 0-12-088407-0, San Francisco, CA.

Zaïane, O. R. (2001). Web usage mining for a better web-based learning environment. *Proceedings of Conference on Advanced Technology for Education 2001*, pp. 60–64, Banff, AB, June 2001

12

EverMiner – Towards Fully Automated KDD Process

M. Šimůnek and J. Rauch
Faculty of Informatics and Statistics, University of Economics, Prague, Czech Republic

1. Introduction

A man-controlled data-mining process has its limits - there is a limited number of data mining tasks an user is capable to create, a limited number of results he or she is able to digest, a limited number of task parameters changes he or she is able to try to get better results and so on. Significantly improved results from data mining could be in contrast obtained from huge amount of data-mining tasks run automatically in iteration steps with changing task parameters. These changes are based on results from previous runs combined with background knowledge about given domain. Not only task parameters but also types of patterns the automated process is looking for could be influenced by previous results and changed during iterations.

This text specifies further and in more details the thoughts published in previous works of [Rauch & Šimůnek, 2005a], [Rauch & Šimůnek, 2007], [Rauch & Šimůnek, 2009a] and mainly in the paper [Rauch, 2010] where a formal architecture of the automated data-mining process was firstly proposed.

The text is organized as follows. There are main research-goals presented in the next section together with references to the work that has been already done, mainly in form of the academic KDD system LISp-Miner (see [Šimůnek, 2003], [LISp-Miner]) and tightly related project SEWEBAR for dealing with background knowledge that is necessary for every successful data mining process (see [Kliegr et. al., 2009], [SEWEBAR]). The third section introduces the EverMiner system and its global concept of two loops and its phases. These particular phases are described then in details in the fourth section of this chapter. Conclusions and plans of future work are outlined in the fifth section. The text ends with acknowledgements and references of cited works.

2. Prerequisites

The KDD research on the UEP started in the year 1995 and we are developing since the LISp-Miner system - an academic system for KDD, see [LISp-Miner]. It consists now of eight data mining procedures mining for syntactically rich patterns with much higher possibilities to express relations in analysed data than the simple *association rules* proposed by [Agrawal et. al., 1993]. Instead, those procedures are based on an original Czech data-mining method called GUHA (see [Hájek & Havránek, 1978]) with a deep theoretical background and history of development since 1966. Thus, the LISp-Miner system incorporates a core data-mining algorithm with greater capabilities than the *a-priori* algorithm proposed by [Agrawal et. al., 1996]. For details about alternative approach to mine for patterns with a rich syntax see [Rauch & Šimůnek, 2005b] and [Hájek et. al., 2010]. A new feature to run also data-mining tasks remotely on a computer grid was implemented recently into all the procedures of the LISp-Miner system.

We concentrate now in our research on the significant problems of today's KDD, mainly to offer solutions for:

- to present results of data mining to data owners in a readable form, especially in the form of analytical reports;
- to incorporate background/domain knowledge to (a) formulate reasonable *Local Analytical Questions* (LAQ, see section 4.2 later in this chapter) to be answered by data mining tasks and (b) to prune results of trivial or of already-known facts;
- to automate the whole process of KDD, mainly its three phases - *Data Preprocessing*, *Data Analysis* and *Results Interpretation*. The EverMiner project (see the next section) has been started to deal with this problem especially.

For the whole automation to be feasible there are some necessary prerequisites that had to be accomplished first:

1. Long-time experiences with solving different types of data-mining tasks and a large set of heuristics and hints how to pre-process data and how to fine-tune task parameters to obtain suitable amount of valuable results.
2. Theoretical background of mathematical logic with a language to describe properties of mined syntactically rich patterns and with logically valid rules for deduction and induction of new knowledge based on already known facts and newly mined patterns.
3. Implemented portfolio of data-mining procedures mining for different kinds of patterns. The most suitable one of these procedures will be chosen in each step of iteration to answer given *Local Analytical Question*.
4. Implemented computer grid feature to solve many tasks simultaneously (and possibly very fast) on a computer grid (dedicated one or an one consisting of ordinary PCs linked together).
5. A *Knowledgebase* where all the above-mentioned heuristics, rules etc. are stored together with the already known domain background knowledge collected previously from domain specialists.
6. Good approach to present the mined results in a human readable form to domain specialists (and in a way suitable for them).

Eight data mining procedures were implemented already in the LISp-Miner system and they are proved through many years of using in data-mining analysis, both the real world and academic ones in teaching courses (see e.g. [Lín et. al., 2004], [Rauch et. all., 2005], [Rauch & Šimůnek, 2005b], [Rauch & Šimůnek, 2005c]). Sets of heuristics and rules for data-mining process automation were proposed and a theoretical logical backgrounds were established (see e.g. [Rauch, 2005], [Rauch, 2009]). Distributed solving of data mining tasks using the computer grid was implemented (see [Šimůnek & Tammisto, 2010]). The first version of the *Knowledgebase* for storing domain knowledge has been built within the LISp-Miner *LM DataSource* module (see [Rauch & Šimůnek, 2008]) and is now refined further in cooperation with the SEWEBAR project (see e.g. [Kliegr et. al., 2009]). Functions were implemented for an automated export of mined results into the SEWEBAR to be published in form of analytical reports. So the logical step now is to combine all the already existing parts together and to start truly automated KDD process.

The above mentioned complex patterns and rich syntax offered by those already implemented data-mining procedures of the LISp-Miner system have a good potential for fine-tuning of the task parameters and for types of mined patterns to be chosen from in each step. We see a great benefit of allowing these DM procedures to crawl automatically through the analysed data and to digest true nuggets by several iterations of answering analytical questions and provide newly found knowledge to domain specialists.
But we admit also that fulfilling this goal is not an easy task to do and there are several related problems that had to be solved. Among others, it is to provide results to the domain specialist in an understandable form. A tightly related SEWEBAR project (see section 3.5 later in this text) is aiming at this problem and is already delivering the first results in improving communication with domain experts in both directions (i.e. gathering already known facts from specialists and delivering results using analytical reports in the opposite direction).

3. EverMiner

The EverMiner project aims at developing such a system that would automatically run many data-mining tasks in several iterations and will possibly find interesting results without any user interaction. The main goals of the EverMiner project are:

1. To mine automatically in the data for all the hidden patterns which were not discovered yet and for which it is a great potential that they will be of some interests for domain specialists (i.e. not to mine obvious or already-known facts nor their consequences).
2. To free data-miners from majority of the necessary work and time spent during the KDD process. And to allow even the domain specialists themselves to do successful data-mining analysis without any need to have the analytical know-how that is necessary to discover some really useful new knowledge but which an ordinary domain specialist is not willing to learn (or has no time to learn to work with a data-mining tool).

Let us remind that a similar project has been proposed already under the name of GUHA80 and mentioned in [Hájek & Havránek, 1982] and [Hájek & Ivánek, 1982] but has been never realized. The project presented here differs completely from the GUHA80, albeit it is based on the GUHA method too.
The global concept of the EverMiner is in Fig. 1. Analysed data provide input for the data-mining process although they need to be pre-processed first. The most important property of the proposed automated data mining is its cyclic nature. Immediately after the *Data Preprocessing* phase, a main cycle of data-mining process begins (the *Outer Loop*) with an inner loop inside for a fine-tuning of the currently processed task parameters to obtain a reasonable amount of patterns (at least some, but not too many).
A brief description follows of all the phases presented in Fig 1. A detailed explanation is in the section 4.

3.1 Analysed data

Generally, any empirical data obtained through experiments, observations or transactional databases that we want to analyse and to uncover interesting relationships in them. In this text we suppose that they represent a finite many properties of finite many objects and that they are store in a table of a relational database. We expect also that the data concern some given domain where a set of typically involved properties could be identified and formally

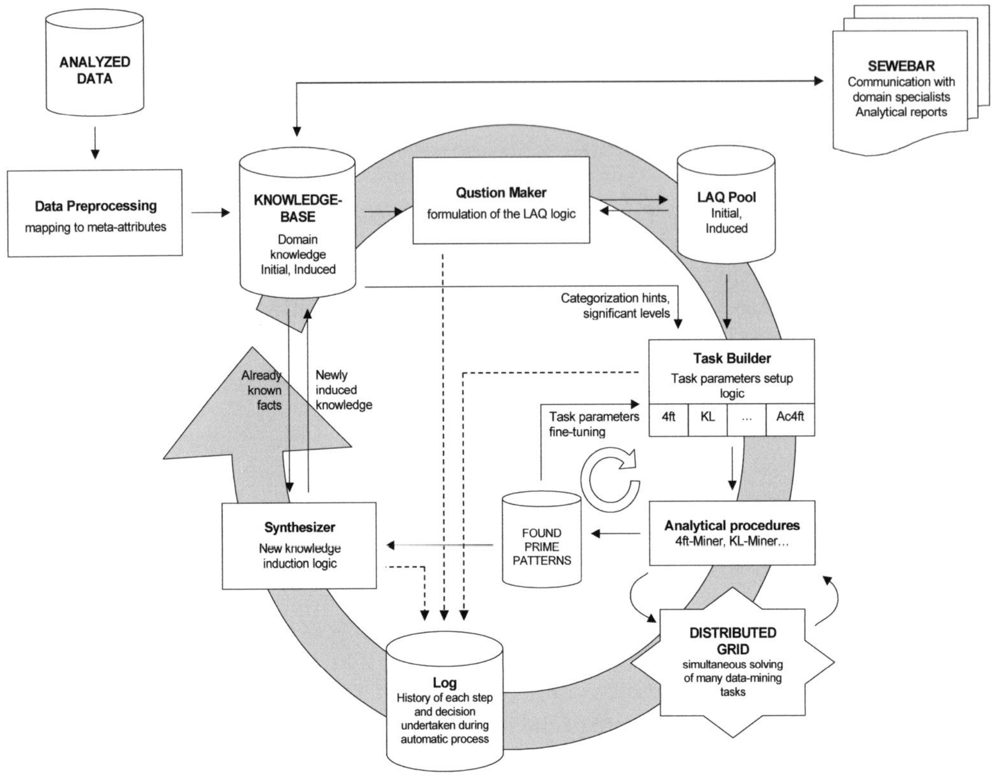

Fig. 1. Global concept of the EverMiner

described. Examples of analysed data are transactions on bank accounts, polling results, standardized records of patients etc.

3.2 Data preprocessing

Data Preprocessing phase is equally important for an automated process as it is for a manually done data-mining analysis. Understanding of analysed data structures and suitable transformations of data have significant influence on quality of the data-mining analysis results. The most important parts are mapping of analysed data columns to meta-attributes defined in the *Knowledgebase* and categorization of values based on the hints - for details see section 4.1 further in this text.

This phase is not part of the main cycle so user-feedback could be requested in case of an ambiguity - e.g. a column good be mapped to more than one meta-attribute or two possible categorization hints could be applied.

3.3 Outer loop

The *Outer Loop* is inspired by the main phases of the KDD process as described e.g. in the CRISP-DM methodology [CRISP-DM] - i.e. the *Domain Understanding, Data Transformation, Analytical Procedures* and *Results Interpretation* - and its cyclical nature.

Each of iterations of this cycle takes into account current state of the domain knowledge (stored in the *Knowledgebase*) and tries to mine new knowledge mimicking steps of the man-controlled data-mining analysis done by a user:

The *Question Maker* module formulates set of *Local Analytical Questions* (LAQ) based on the current level of knowledge. *LAQs* are stored into the *LAQ Pool* where they wait to be processed. (There could be also an initial set of *LAQs* provided manually.) The *Task Builder* module takes the *LAQs* one by one from the *LAQ Pool* and creates a data-mining task(s) to answer them in the same way as would be case in a man-controlled data-mining. Results in form of found prime patterns are handed to the *Synthetizer* module. Here, they are examined if they do not follow from some already known facts. Only those really novel patterns are added into the *Knowledgebase* and eventually reported to domain specialist in form of *Analytical Reports* via the SEWEBAR. Changes to the *Knowledgebase* make possible another set of *LAQs* to be formulated by the *Question Maker* module (e.g. "*Are they any exceptions to newly found patterns?*") and these new *LAQs* are again stored into the *LAQ Pool*. The *Task Builder* module periodically checks the *LAQ Pool* for not-yet-answered *LAQs* and the whole process is repeated. The *Outer Loop* ends if there are no further *LAQs* in the *LAQ Pool*.

There could be more than one data-mining task necessary to answer a single *LAQ*. Actual number of tasks and types of patterns it is looking for will depend on structure and complexity of the processed *LAQ*. Generally, the automated data mining proposed here will lead to a very large number of data-mining tasks to be solved by different GUHA-procedures for each step of the *Outer Loop*, in contrast to much lower number of data-mining tasks ever created by users during some data-mining analysis done manually.

3.4 Inner loop

Initial task parameters setting could be done only roughly, as is the case even for a man-controlled data-mining analysis. The precise settings could be chosen only after task is solved for many times and the data-miner could see number and quality of found patterns. It has therefore an iterative nature.

The *Inner Loop* takes care of this iterative nature while looking for the right task parameters. Results of every single task run are checked and task parameters could be tweaked if there are no patterns found (parameters are too strict) or too many of them are found (parameters are too loose). It is important to say that the background logic of implemented GUHA-procedures already filters found patterns to be prime only - not easily deducted from other already found patters (for details see e.g. [Rauch, 2005]).

3.5 SEWEBAR

The aim of the SEWEBAR project is to develop a framework of the same name that acts as a platform to illicit the background knowledge from domain specialists and - in an opposite direction - to present mined results in an understandable way (in form of structured analytical reports). There has been developed a specialised BKEF XML schema for storing background knowledge and an open-source content management system (CMS) called *Joomla* is used for preparation of structured analytical reports using created authoring tools.

The SEWEBAR project is tightly related to the KDD research at Department of Knowledge Engineering of the University of Economics Prague, but is independent of the LISp-Miner and the EverMiner projects. For more details about the SEWEBAR project see [SEWEBAR], [Kliegr et. al., 2009] and [Balhar et. al., 2010].

There is a two-way communication established between the EverMiner and the SEWEBAR framework. All the necessary knowledge will be provided automatically by the SEWEBAR to the EverMiner at request. Simultaneously, the EverMiner will send all the results and all the updates of the *Knowledgebase* (newly found knowledge about given domain) to the

SEWEBAR to be presented to domain specialists in easily understandable form of analytical reports and of graphical visualisations of the *Knowledgebase*.

4. Detailed description of the proposed phases

Each of the above-mentioned proposed phases is described in the following sub-sections.

4.1 Domain knowledge and data preprocessing

The *Knowledgebase* (i.e. the *knowledge repository*) contains all the available knowledge about given domain that was either provided by domain specialists (as a results of the domain specialists communication with the SEWEBAR before the beginning of the analysis) or induced from the results of automated iterations of the EverMiner's *Outer Loop*.
There are several levels of knowledge present in the *Knowledgebase* and described in the following paragraphs (see also [Rauch and Šimůnek, 2009], [Rauch, 2010]).

4.1.1 Meta-attributes

The basic level of knowledge consists of meta-attributes. The meta-attributes are typical properties (characteristics) of objects for a given domain. They are identified in advance by domain specialists and contain the following knowledge:

- Name (of list of possible typical names) of the concerned attribute in future analysed data.
- Cardinality type of values stored (*nominal, ordinal, cardinal*) and expected *Data type* of values (*integer, float, text, date, Boolean*).
- Categorization hints - describing either enumeration of typical values (e.g. *Sun, Mon, Tue, ..., Sat*) or allowed range for numerical values and proposed lengths of intervals to categorize them. There could be several categorization hints provided for a single meta-attribute to differentiate among different goals of analysis.
- Important values (i.e. significant levels) that have some special meaning (e.g. 100 °C as a threshold for boiling water). They could be used for categorization or setting-up data-mining tasks (e.g. *"Are there any exceptions for X when Temperature is below 100)?"*) because domain specialists are used to them and interpretation of results with such thresholds is easily understandable for them.

All this information about meta-attributes is used then to map (automatically) database columns from the analysed data to meta-attributes. It is necessary to find an appropriate meta-attribute for each database column to do a proper pre-processing of database column values - i.e. to categorize them accordingly to the categorization hints provided.
Mapping columns to meta-attributes is difficult given availability of typical names and data-types of concerned meta-attributes only. There will be lots of ambiguities and missing definitions, especially for a newly created *Knowledgebase*. Fortunately, the *Data Preprocessing* phase is not part of the *Outer Loop* so it is possible to ask user for feedback to resolve such an ambiguity or to update definition of meta-attributes if there is no appropriate meta-attribute to map a database column to.

4.1.2 Hierarchy of meta-attributes

Defined meta-attributes are associates with meta-attribute *groups*. Each meta-attribute must have its *Basic group* associated. A meta-attribute could moreover belong to an unlimited number of other meta-attribute *groups* too. Therefore it is possible to group meta-attributes

according to several criterions at once. Attributes created from database columns of the analysed data inherit associations to *groups* from its master meta-attribute on behalf of which they were created.
Groups are organized in a hierarchy with the *Root-Group* at the top of it and each subsequent *group* having its *Parent group* defined to be either the *Root-Group* or any other *group* already present in the hierarchy. This hierarchical structure allows for a clever using of *groups* in further processing (e.g. while formulating the *LAQs* – see the next section). So every mention of a *group* covers simultaneously all the attributes belonging directly to the *group* plus others in any *Child-group* having the given *group* as its *Parent group*.

4.1.3 Mutual dependency

Mutual dependency aims at visualizing relationships among meta-attributes in an easily and understandable way for domain experts. Not only known dependencies among meta-attributes are recorded but also clues for what are users interested in to be answered (and for what not). For any pair of meta-attributes (or sometimes for the whole *groups* of attributes) we could specify:

- *Type of dependency* … describes (based on the best-available knowledge of domain experts) possible dependency between values of the first meta-attribute and values of the second meta-attribute. Examples are:
  - ↑↑ … a positive influence ⇒ the higher values of the first meta-attribute the higher values of the second meta-attribute; applicable for cardinal or ordinal meta-attributes only.
  - ↑↓ … a negative influence ⇒ the higher values of the first meta-attribute the lower values of the second meta-attribute; applicable for cardinal or ordinal meta-attributes only.
  - $\mathcal{F}$ … a function-like dependency, e.g. "*velocity*" is defined as ½ $a\ t^2$ where "*a*" is acceleration and "*t*" is time. So "velocity" is dependent on "*acceleration*" and "*time*" in a function-like manner; applicable for cardinal attributes only.
  - ↑+ … a positive increase of relative frequencies ⇒ the higher values of the first meta-attribute (cardinal or ordinal) the higher probability of occurrence of some property described by the second meta-attribute (Boolean).
  - ? … an unknown influence, need to be specified by future analysis.
  - \- … no influence at all.
  - ≈ … there is some influence but is not specified further (yet).
  - ⊗ … we are not interested in determining type of influence between this pair of *meta-attributes*.
- *Scope* … whether such dependency has a global scope (has been observed in the whole domain) or is supposed to be specific only to the current sample of analysed data. Options are:
  - Data specific
  - Domain specific
- *Validity* … whether the knowledge is supported by the results of the data-mining analysis. This allows to track progress in changes of the domain knowledge. Options are:
  - Proven
  - Rejected

- Unknown

Several two-dimensional grids containing selected subsets of attributes could be constructed where graphical symbols do express possible options of mutual dependencies among them - see example in Fig. 2.

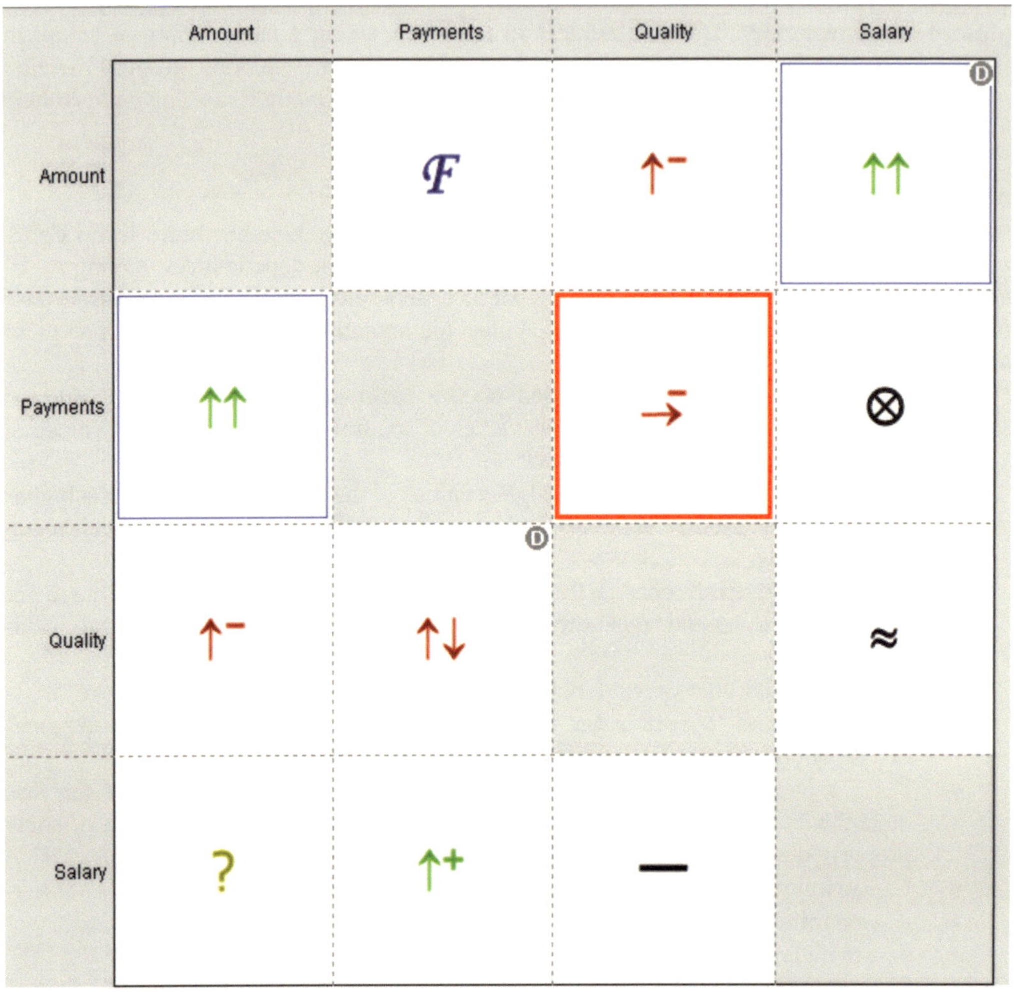

Fig. 2. Grid of mutual dependencies among subset of meta-attributes (from the *LM DataSource* module)

Proven dependencies are framed in blue, rejected dependencies in red. Dependencies with a limited scope of validity for the analysed data only are marked with the (D) sign - i.e. dependencies that do not hold globally but only for given sample of the analysed data (e.g. due to conditions how data were collected or pre-processed).

This visual presentation helps to gather as much information about given domain as possible because it seems that domain experts are keen with expressing their knowledge this way and they are happy even to input data themselves in a suitable (internet) application. It is especially important while presenting a newly found knowledge when experts are expected to approve it and to give a necessary feedback.

Although the above-mentioned *Knowledgebase* was implement first in the *LM DataSource* and the *LM KnowledgeSource* modules of the LISp-Miner system (see [Rauch & Šimůnek, 2008] and [LISp-Miner]) its future development was moved now into the SEWEBAR project.

4.1.4 Meta-attribute distribution

Another type of knowledge - about every single meta-attribute - could be included in the *Knowledgebase* too. This kind of knowledge represents conditional distributions of frequencies of values or big differences of types of distributions between two subsets of analysed data. For example, the *Education level* could be of a *Gaussian* distribution among the whole population but could be expected to be skewed towards higher levels of education in the capital/university city where highly educated people are of high demand. This type of knowledge could be used again both for the formulation of the *LAQs* and for the pruning results of well-known facts.

This type of knowledge is related to the *CF-Miner* and *SDCF-Miners* data-mining procedures of the LISp-Miner system and needs to be investigated further.

4.2 Question maker and local analytical questions

The *Question Maker* module formulates new *Local Analytical Questions* (*LAQs*) based on the current level of domain knowledge and newly mined knowledge in previous cycles. Any *LAQ* describes a question user wants to answer in a formalized way but using plain language so the *LAQ* is understandable to domain experts. Examples of *LAQs* are:

- "Are there any relations between characteristics of *Body-Mass-Index* and *Success of therapy* in analysed data?"
- "Are there any exceptions to the patterns found for the previous question depending on level of *Physical activity* when these patterns do not hold?"

Not only single attributes could be used to formulate a *LAQ* - the whole groups of meta-attributes could be instead to formulate more general analytical questions:

- "Are there any relations between *Social characteristics* of patients and *Cardiovascular risk factors*?"
- "Are there any exceptions to the patterns found for the previous question depending on *Physical activities* when these patterns do not hold?"

4.2.1 LAQ templates

After several years of experiences with data mining analyses we have observed that there is only a limited number of *LAQ* types that are typically formulated. There is of course infinite number of particular groups or even attributes that could appear in *LAQs* but the skeleton of the *LAQ* remains still the same. Thus, it is possible to prepare reasonably small number of so called *LAQ Templates* with active positions prepared where a particular group of attributes could be inserted to formulate a proper *LAQ*. Examples of such *LAQ Templates* are:

- "Are there some strong relationships in sense of <*interest measure*> between patients characteristics given by <*group of attributes A*> and by <*group of attributes S*> in subsets of data given by Boolean conditions based on <*group of attributes C*>? We are however interested in already known and proven facts."
- "Are there any exceptions to the patterns found for the previous question depending on <*group of attributes C*> when these patterns do not hold?"

It is easy then to formulate new *LAQs* given the pre-defined *LAQ Templates*, list of possible *groups of attributes* (available from the background knowledge of concerned domain) and list of available *interest measures* to describe type of looked-for relationships in data.

List of available *LAQ Templates* is not strictly closed and a new template could be added if a new type of typical user's questions emerges. List of available *groups of attributes* is provided by the *Knowledgebase* and it contains additional information about each attribute (derived from its associated master meta-attribute) - e.g. its *cardinality type* (whether its values are *nominal*, *ordinal* or *cardinal*). This could restrict positions in *LAQ templates* where such attribute could be used.

A newly created *LAQ* should be checked against already accumulated domain knowledge (both the initial and induced). It is not necessary to proceed to data-mining phase if the *LAQ* could be answered (either directly or by a deduction) from the already known facts in the *Knowledgebase*. Otherwise, a new data-mining task will be created based on it and solved.

Initially, a pool of unanswered *LAQs* will consists of the *LAQs* prepared in advance by the user, if they are such. Next, the *Question Maker* will create as many further *LAQs* as possible given the actual content of the *Knowledgebase*. Together they will be sent to the *Task Builder* module (see the next sub-section) to find answers to them. Found answers to given *LAQs* will eventually lead to a new knowledge and these new facts will be added into the *Knowledgebase*. This might offer a new possibility for the *Question Maker* module to formulated another *LAQ(s)* - e.g. using the "*are there any exceptions to newly found patterns?*" *LAQ Template*. Therefore, the actual number of unanswered *LAQs* in the *Pool* fluctuates as a *LAQ* is removed when corresponding data-mining task(s) is/are created and simultaneously as new *LAQs* are formulated as a reaction to a fresh knowledge in the *Knowledgebase* being newly induced from the results of just solved data-mining tasks.

4.2.2 LAQ grid

Again, a grid could be constructed to keep track of already processed *LAQs* - grid of combinations of available group of attributes (or its subset) - see Fig. 3.

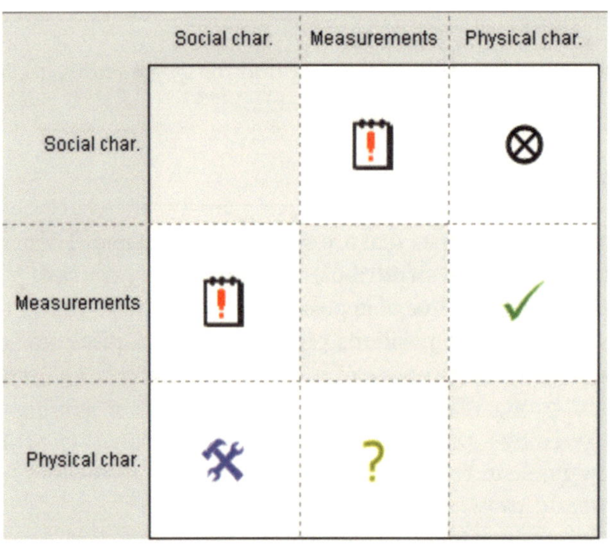

Fig. 3. *LAQ-template* Grid (from the *LM LAQManager* module)

So the user continually knows which *LAQs* are already solved (marked with ✓), which are just being processed now (marked with ⚒), which ones are waiting to be processed (marked with [!]) or we are not concerned in this *LAQ* (marked with ⊗).

4.3 Task builder

Once a *LAQ* is formulated it needs to be answered by results from solved data-mining task(s). One *LAQ* could be answered with a single task for a single analytical procedure or more tasks for different analytical procedures might be necessary to answer it.

Set-up of the task depends on structure of the *LAQ* it is supposed to answer and its structure is in turn influenced by the *LAQ Template* that was used to formulate the *LAQ* in the first place. There are prepared rules in advance how to set-up task(s) for given *LAQ Template*.

There are many task parameters available that influence significantly the size and the quality of mined results. These parameters include minimal and maximal lengths of Boolean attributes involved in constructing of patterns. Task parameteres include also criterions based on *interest measure(s)* to specify types and tightness of relationships inside to be found patterns.

First version of heuristics was prepared to guide the *Task Builder* module while setting of initial parameters for a new task. The heuristics are based on number of attributes and number of theirs categories and on experiences with expressing the most typical kinds of relationships inside patters - i.e. types of quantifiers used and suitable levels for theirs parameters - for details see the *Analytical procedures* section or [Rauch & Šimůnek, 2005b]. Once a task is created it is dispatched to a corresponding analytical procedure to be solved.

The *Task Builder* role is not limited to setting up tasks based on the given *LAQs*. It is also involved in the *Inner Cycle* of the EverMiner process - to fine-tune task parameters to get a reasonable number of results from the *Analytical procedures* phase to answer the given *LAQs*. It is very often that either too many patterns are found given the initial settings of task parameters or that no pattern is found at all. This is typical even for man-prepared task parameters because of an unknown character of the analysed data and because of complexity of possible parameters settings. Thus, the data mining process has to be done iteratively so long as the right values of task parameters are found. The *Task Builder* module is equipped with another set of heuristics to be able to restrict searched solution-space (i.e. to decrease number of found patterns) or to enlarge it (i.e. to increase number of found patterns). The *Inner Loop* could be described in detail as visible in Fig. 4.

When the number of found patterns is too small (or no patterns found at all), task parameters are changed to be looser (to allow for not so strong patterns) or to search through an enlarged search-space (to prove more possible combinations). When the number of found patterns is too big, task parameters are made stricter so a smaller number of strong patterns will be found in the next round. This *Inner Loop* is repeated as many times as needed. There are of course limits to fine-tuning of parameters, especially when no patterns had been found, because it makes no sense to make task parameters very loose. Therefore, it is possible that no patterns for a given *LAQ* are supported by the analysed data and this particular *LAQ* is rejected.

It depends on the underlying *LAQ*, used analytical procedure and found types of patterns what is assumed to be an "acceptable" number of found patterns. Some kinds of relationships in the analysed data (e.g. of the $\uparrow\uparrow$ or the $\mathcal{F}$ mutual dependency) could be expressed with large number of *4ft-associational rules* in the *4ft-Miner* procedure compared to a single *KL-pattern* as a result of the *KL-Miner procedure*. As a rule of thumb an "acceptable" number of patterns is more than none and less than two hundred.

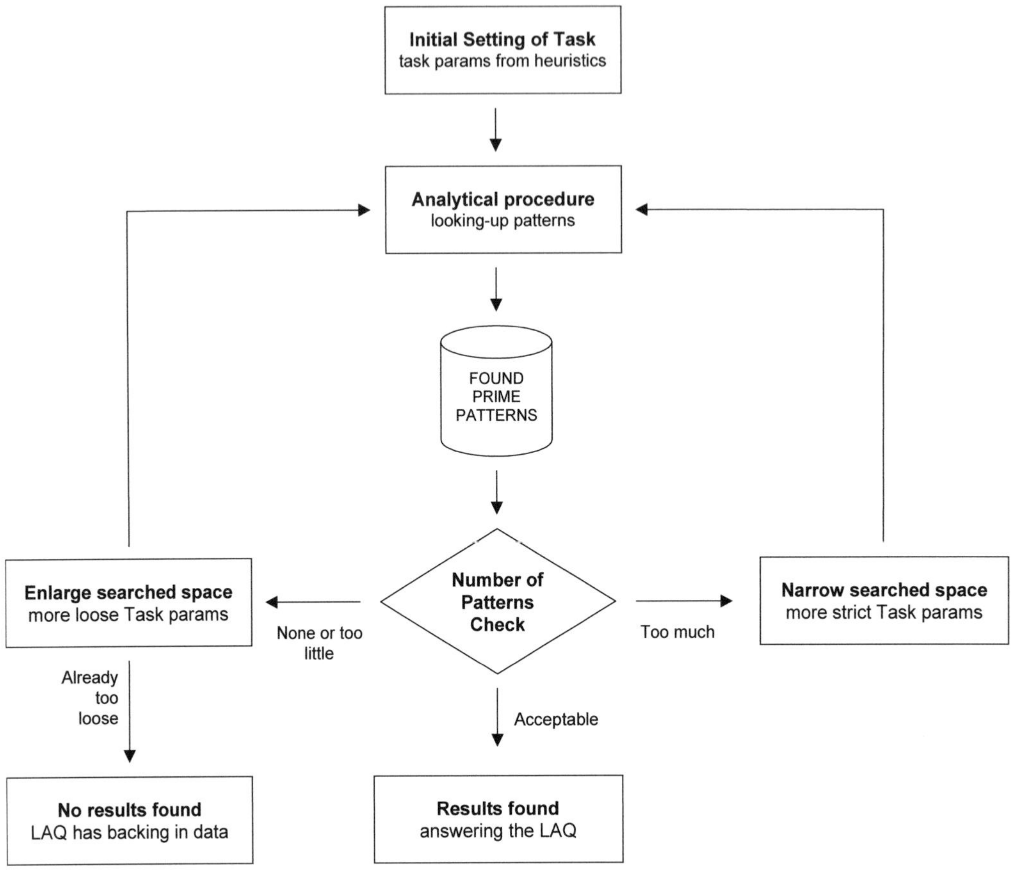

Fig. 4. Detail Description of the Inner Loop

4.4 Analytical procedures

There are seven analytical procedures implemented already in the LISp-Miner system:

- *4ft-Miner* procedure expressing found patterns as (conditional) *4ft-associational rules* with a rich syntax;
- *SD4ft-Miner* procedure looking for *SD4ft-patterns* - comparing two sub-sets in the analysed data in sense of two (conditional) *4ft-associational rules;*
- *Ac4ft-Miner* procedure looking for *4ft-action rules* describing some kind of action resulting in a change of characteristics in objects from the analysed data;
- *KL-Miner* procedure looking for KL-patterns in form of K×L contingency tables of two multi-categorical attributes and under some (richly defined) condition;
- *SDKL-Miner* procedure comparing two sub-sets in the analysed data in sense of two *KL-patterns;*
- *CF-Miner* procedure looking for *CF-patterns* in form of distribution of frequencies for a single multi-categorical attribute and under some (richly defined) condition;
- *SDCF-Miner* procedure comparing two sub-sets in the analysed data in sense of two *CF-patterns.*

All the implemented procedures are so called GUHA-procedures (in sense of [Hájek & Havránek, 1978]). Theirs input consists of the analysed data and a simple definition of a large space of potentially interesting patterns. And theirs output is set of all interesting patterns that are supported by the analysed data. For more detail see [Rauch & Šimůnek, 2005a], [Hájek et. al., 2010].

The most important feature is a really rich syntax of looked-up patterns that could be defined in relatively simple way. Each implemented data-mining procedure offers a rich syntax how to describe potentially interesting pattern we are looking for. They mine not for associational rules only but for an enhanced version called *4ft-asociational rules* (see [Rauch & Šimůnek, 2005a]) and for other types of patterns - e.g. conditional frequencies, K×L conditional frequency tables ([Lín et. al., 2004]), *Set-differs-from-set* (SD) rules or for *4ft-actional rules* (see [Ras & Wieczorkowska, 2000], [Rauch & Šimůnek, 2009b]). This rich syntax makes possible to involve semantically features of logical reasoning and deduction ([Rauch, 2009]).

4.4.1 Optimisation

Number of patterns in the search-space each analytical procedure has to walk-through is enormous, especially because of the rich syntax of mined-for patterns. Several optimisation techniques were incorporated therefore into analytical procedures implementations.

As an example of such an optimisation we could mention the *bit-string* structures for very fast computing of frequencies of derived *Boolean attributes* to construct contingency tables (for details see e.g. [Rauch & Šimůnek, 2005b]). For simplicity reasons we would discuss only *4ft-association rule* syntax that is used in the *4ft-Miner* procedure. A conditional *4ft-association rule* has form of:

$$\varphi \approx \psi / \chi$$

Where φ, ψ and χ are derived *Boolean attributes* automatically derived from basic *Boolean attributes* as theirs *conjunctions, disjunctions* and *negations*. The symbol $\approx$ is called *4ft-quantifier*. To compute frequencies from contingency table we need to know frequencies of each derived *Boolean attribute* and hence frequencies of concerned basic *Boolean attributes*. Values of each *Boolean attribute* in the analysed data are represented with binary arrays of zeros and ones, which allow an easy compounding with binary arrays of another *Boolean attribute* by bit-wise operations of AND, OR and NOT. Thus a bit-string representation of any derived *Boolean attribute* could be quickly prepared from involved basic *Boolean attributes*. Moreover bit-string representations of partial derived Boolean attributes are cached during walking-through the search-space, so a new derived *Boolean attribute* representation have not to be prepare from scratch.

Another technique of skips over the search-space is implemented that significantly reduces number of patterns that have to be constructed. The whole branches of the search-space are skipped when there is no chance of verified patterns could be present there based on logic of associational rules and actual data-mining task parameters.

4.4.2 Filtering of found patterns

There are usually many patterns found, so users could easily get overwhelmed and get lost without a chance to spot really interesting results. There were therefore implemented means to decrease number of patterns without losing any information.

Found true patterns are filtered according to theirs logical properties - only so called prime-patterns are included into results. Thus only the patterns that do not easily follow from (a more simple ones) already presented in results are included. For details see e.g. [Rauch, 2005]. This technique has also inspired the filtering of truly novel patterns in the *Synthesizer* module - see section 4.6 later.

4.5 Distributed solving of tasks using grid

For the whole automated data-mining process to be feasible, there must be a way to compute each step of the *Inner Loop* iteration very quickly. Although there are several optimisation techniques already incorporated (see the previous section), there are clear limits for shortening solution times on a single computer. One possible solution how to significantly increase the computing power and hence to decrease solution times is to use computer grid to divide solution of single task among many grid nodes.

4.5.1 Grid type chosen

There were two possible options regarding the type of grid used - the dedicated grid or the PC-Grid consisting of ordinary PCs linked together as clients of the grid server. The dedicated-grid main advantage is its huge processing power and constant availability of this power because it has nothing else to do than to wait for assigned task to be solved. Meanwhile, computers in the PC-Grid are obliged to serve their primary users first and only the remaining computing power is available for the grid. On the other hand the main advantage of the PC-Grid are low initial costs and its easy scalability - just another PCs are registered. Being an academic institution where money funds are often scarce we opt for the PC-Grid.

The Techila PC-Grid [Techila] was successfully installed on the University of Economics computer network and now we would like to increase number of participation grid nodes by registering more PCs from offices, computer labs and even dormitories.

4.5.2 Core data mining algorithm overhaul

The main problem that had to be addressed while incorporating grid features into the LISp-Miner system was how to divide data-mining task into sub-tasks that could be solved (in parallel) on particular grid nodes. The goal was to find a general solution that could be used in all the implemented GUHA procedures within the LISp-Miner system, although they mine for different patterns and theirs core data-mining algorithm is different. Different strategies of task partitioning could lead to different complexity of each atomic sub-task and therefore to very different total computing times on the grid.

4.5.3 Implementation

Two strategies were chosen and already implemented - for details see [Šimůnek & Tammisto, 2010]. The most important feature of this solution is that no changes to the original optimised core data-mining algorithms are needed and this solution is applicable for all the GUHA-procedures implemented in the LISp-Miner system so far.

All the necessary communication with the grid using provided API was implemented on the user side and new modules for solving sub-tasks on grid nodes were created (one module for each of the eight data-mining procedures). This new modules use the same program code as is used for local solving of tasks. There is no change from the point of view of user -

only a new dialog window appears to decide whether to solve the concerned task locally or by the grid. Communications links and the grid access-privileges were secured by certificates.

A real data analysis was undertaken using distributed grid verification and results were compared to solving-times of the same task on a single computer. Two procedures were selected for benchmark tests - the *4ft-Miner* procedure as the currently most used one and the *Acft-Miner* procedure (looking up the *4ft-action-rules*) where the grid potential is even higher due to a more complex pattern syntax. A significant improvement in solution times was observed right from the first tasks. The grid overhead (due to division of a task into sub-tasks, to uploading all the necessary data to the grid and then to downloading the results) is reasonably small and its relative importance decreases by growing complexity of tasks. There was observed a near linear dependency between number of grid nodes involved and reduction in task-solution times. For example a task running for more than 30 hours on a single PC was solved within 6 hours on grid consisting from just 5 grid nodes. And the same task was solved in just one hour using 24 grid nodes (albeit more powerful ones, in 1,2 factor approximately).

The undertaken experiments proved that the implemented grid feature brings significant improvements to solutions times and is easily up-scaled for even better times by simply registering more PCs as grid nodes.

4.6 Synthesizer and inducing new knowledge

After new results are mined they are handed to the *Synthesizer* module to be confronted with the existing knowledge already stored in the *Knowledgebase* and possibly to induce a new knowledge. Remember, please, that new results have been already pruned of logically dependent patterns and only so called prime-patterns are passed to this phase.

4.6.1 What to not report

Even the prime-patterns could describe many kinds of true but (from the point of view of domain experts) completely worthless facts. Examples of such "gems" are: "*There is at least a 99% probability that a person giving birth to a child will be a women*" or "*Body temperature of patients is in range from 34 to 40 °C in more than 90 % of cases*". There is many more such statements that are certainly true but will irritate domain experts and maybe they will even break they faith in results of analysis. Thus, it is very important to automatically filter out as many of such statements as possible.

There is no sense too in reporting the same patterns over and over if they were already presented to users in previous rounds of analysis. So every found pattern has to be checked against knowledge already present in the *Knowledgebase* and only really novel facts will be append there are reported in analytical reports.

4.6.2 Filtering of already-known knowledge

A technique similar to prime-rule testing is proposed for comparing newly found patterns with knowledge already in the *Knowledgebase*.

It is possible to translate any kind of *Mutual Dependency* knowledge stored in the *Knowledgebase* to one (or more) patterns looked-up by one of analytical procedures. For example, the dependency of *Education* ↑↓ *BMI* (stating that a higher level of education leads generally to a lower level of the *Body-Mass-Index*) could be translated into *4ft-asociational rules* in form of:

$$\text{Education}(\alpha_{right\_cut\_n}) \Rightarrow_{p,B} \text{BMI}(\beta_{left\_cut\_m})$$

where

- $\alpha_{right\_cut\_n}$ is so-called *right cut* of categories of the attribute *Education* with the length of *n* (i.e. *n* of highest categories of the concerned ordinal attribute)
- $\beta_{left\_cut\_m}$ is so-called *left cut* of categories of the attribute BMI with the length of *n* (i.e. *n* of lowest categories of the concerned ordinal attribute)
- $\Rightarrow_{p,B}$ is the *4ft-quantifier* of *Found implication* based on the confidence value of *a/(a+b)*.

Similar translations are available for remaining types of *Mutual Dependency* using possibly another types of quantifiers or whole analytical procedures and their patterns (*KL-patterns, CF-patterns* and even *SD4ft-*, *SDKL-* and *SDCF-patterns*) – for more details see [Rauch, 2010].

This translation of *Mutual dependencies* needs to be done only once (either before the EverMiner analysis begins or after each change of the *Knowledgebase*). When a new pattern is mined and sent to the *Synthesizer* module it will be checked against subsets of this translated patterns (only those for the same analytical procedure). What we want to resolve is whether it (logically) follows from some (simpler) pattern already present in the *Knowledgebase.* So the same approach could be used as for the prime-rule testing described above. But this time the set of patterns it is checked against the one translated from the *Knowledgebase.*

If deduction rules prove that the newly found pattern logically follows from a pattern representing a *Mutual dependency* already present in the *Knowledgebase,* it could be either filtered-out or this *Mutual dependency* could be flagged that it is supported by the analysed data.

4.6.3 Inducing new knowledge

If a newly found pattern meets test of novelty it need to be added into the *Knowledgebase* in form of the new *Mutual dependency* knowledge. Again, there are translations-rules available for each analytical procedure (and its type of patterns) how to construct a new *Mutual dependency* based on the found pattern.

When a new *Mutual dependency* is created and inserted into the *Knowledgebase,* it is compared to already existing *Mutual dependencies* for the same pair of (meta-) attributes. If they are two different types of *Mutual dependencies* now in the *Knowledgebase,* it should be investigated further whether they are complementary or contradictory. Complementary dependencies could coexist e.g. in case of:

$$\text{Education} \uparrow\downarrow \text{BMI and Education} \downarrow\uparrow \text{BMI}$$

In this special case, a tighter Mutual dependency of $\mathcal{F}$(Education, BMI) stating that there is a strict function-like dependency between the level of education and value of the BMI could be used to formulate a new LAQ (and eventually to prove it).

On the other hand, the contradictory *Mutual dependencies*, e.g. in case of:

$$\text{Education} \uparrow\uparrow \text{BMI and Education} \uparrow\downarrow \text{BMI}$$

leads to the "*rejected in the analysed data*" flag to be set for the first mutual dependency and the found contradiction need to be highlighted in the analytical report.

4.6.4 Groups of related patterns

The same dependency in the analysed data could be expressed in more than one way by different types patterns of different analytical procedures. For example, where a single *KL-pattern* could be sufficient to describe a function-like dependency between two attributes, tens of *4ft-associational rules* could be necessary to express the same. Too many found rules make results hard to understand and complicate reaching right conclusions. It is necessary therefore to identify groups of patterns that describe a single dependency in the analysed data and possibly to use another type of the *LAQ Template* and therefore another analytical procedure to answer it. This feature is not understood well and has to be addressed in future research.

4.7 Complete history of analysis

Every decision taken during both *Loops* and even the intermediate results need to be logged so the whole history of the automated KDD process could be checked afterwards. No information of any kind is ever deleted. This will not only help during development of the EverMiner but also will allow an analytical audit of the whole reasoning behind delivered results and to prove the validity of newly induced knowledge. Types of stored information are:

- used mapping of attributes from the analysed data to the meta-attributes in the *Knowledgebase*;
- formulated *LAQs* and its parameters (used *Template*, groups of meta-attributes)
- created tasks; each task is associated to the *LAQs* it is supposed to answer;
- information about task-parameters changes during fine-tuning in the *Inner Loop*;
- found prime patterns of each task-run;
- answers to the *LAQs* derived from the found prime patterns - together with information whether they support the already known facts in the *Knowledgebase*;
- changes made to the *Mutual Dependency* type of knowledge.

The necessary infrastructure for storing this kind of information is already in place for man-controlled data-mining and could be used for the EverMiner too:

- Every created attribute has already an optional link to its master *meta-attribute*.
- Formulated *LAQs* are stored in database and their status could be monitored.
- Each data-mining task must belong to a task-group. So a task-group will be created for every *LAQ* and all data-mining tasks designed to answer it will be included in this group (remember that there could be more than one task necessary to answer a single *LAQ*).
- Already implemented feature of task-cloning will be utilized for keeping track of task-parameters evolution during the *Inner Loop* - a new clone of the task with current version of task-parameters will be created in each iteration before task-parameters are changed. The name of the newly cloned task will be the same and task will be inserted into the same task-group. Only the "iteration" index will be increased to provide information about sequence of steps in the *Inner Loop*.
- Found results are routinely stored within data-mining task data to be visible to users in man-controlled data-mining analysis. This feature allows keeping results from all iterations because each task-parameters version is stored in corresponding cloned-task and identified with its "iteration" number.

- Every newly synthesized knowledge is added in form of the *Mutual Dependency* into the *Knowledgebase*. Three important properties accompany it - whether it is created by some user (domain specialist) or by the *Synthesizer* module; the time-stamp - when it was created; and finally links to data-mining results the new knowledge is based upon. Incorporation of the time-stamp allows storing multiple instances of mutual dependence to a single pair of meta-attributes while preserving the whole evolution of who and when made any change. Thus, a mutual dependency relationship could be marked as "*proven*" when results from a data-mining task will prove them, or could be marked as "*rejected*" otherwise. And a complete "evolution graph" of the *Knowledgebase* could be constructed afterwards to provide users with deep explanation why some new knowledge was induced and based on what patterns in the analysed data.

5. Conclusion and further work

All the phases necessary to build an automated data-mining system were proposed. Some parts were already implemented and the remaining pieces have a sufficient theoretical background to be implemented in a near future.
Our goal is to proceed in partial steps and gradually build the functioning EverMiner system. Currently, we are working on the communication with the SEWEBAR project repositories to be able to gather relevant information into the EverMiner *Knowledgebase* regarding processed attributes. A first version of the *QuestionMaker* for formulating some simple kinds of *LAQs* based on the knowledge already stored in the *Knowledgebase* will be implemented then. It will allow to launch first analytical procedures tasks and to solve them using the already implemented grid feature.
After obtaining the first results we will be able then to deploy appropriate rules for the fine-tuning of the task parameters, based on the number and quality of found prime patterns. Another kinds of knowledge could be possibly stored into the Knowledge to help either during the *Data Preprocessing* phase, during formulation of *LAQs* or during pruning results of already-known facts.

6. Acknowledgements

This text was prepared with the support of "Institutional funds for support of a long-term development of science and research at the Faculty of Informatics and Statistics of The University of Economics, Prague".

7. References

Agrawal, R.; Iimielinski, T.; Swami, A. (1993). Mining associations between sets of items in massive databases. *Proceedings of the ACM-SGMOD 1993 Int. Conference on Management of Data*, pp. 207-216, 1993, Wasghington D.C.

Agrawal, R.; Manilla, H.; Srikant, R.; Toivonen, H.; Verkamo, A. (1996) *Fast Discovery of Association Rules*. In: Advances in Knowledge Discovery and Data Mining, Fayyad, U. M. et al., (Eds.), pp. 307–328, AAAI Press/The MIT Press

Balhar, T.; Kliegr, T.; Šťastný, D.; Vojíř, S. (2010). Elicitation of Background Knowledge for Data Mining. *Proceedings of Znalosti 2010*, s. 167–170, ISBN 978-80-245-1636-3, Jindřichův Hradec, February 2010, Oeconomica, Praha

CRISP-DM: *Cross Industry Standard Process for Data Mining* [online]. [cit. 18. 12. 2009], available from WWW: http://www.crisp-dm.org

Hájek, P. & Havránek, T. (1978). *Mechanising Hypothesis Formation – Mathematical Foundations for a General Theory*. Springer-Verlag, Berlin - Heidelberg - New York, 1978, 396 pp.

Hájek, P. & Havránek, T. (1982). GUHA80: An Application of Artificial Intelligence to Data Analysis. *Computers and Artificial Intelligence*, Vol. 1, 1982, pp. 107-134

Hájek, P. & Ivánek, J. (1982). Artificial Intelligence and Data Analysis, *Proceedings of COMPSTAT'82*, Caussinus H., Ettinger P., Tomassone R. (Eds.), pp. 54-60, 1982, Wien, Physica Verlag

Hájek, P.; Holeňa, M.; Rauch, J. (2010). The GUHA method and its meaning for data mining. *Journal of Computer and System Sciences*, Vol. 76, 2010, pp. 34-48, ISSN: 0022-0000

Kliegr, T.; Ralbovský, M.; Svátek, V.; Šimůnek, M.; Jirkovský, V.; Nemrava, J.; Zemánek, J. (2009). Semantic Analytical Reports: A Framework for Post-processing data Mining Results, *Proceedings of Foundations of Intelligent Systems*, pp. 88–98, ISBN 978-3-642-04124-2, ISSN 1867-8211, Praha, September 2009, Springer Verlag, Berlin

Lín, V.; Dolejší, P.; Rauch, J.; Šimůnek, M. The KL-Miner Procedure for Datamining, *Neural Network World*, Vol. 5, 2004, pp. 411–420, ISSN 1210-0552.

LISp-Miner - academic KDD system [online], [cit 2010-07-15], available from WWW http://lispminer.vse.cz

Ras, Z. & Wieczorkowska, A. (2000). Action-Rules: How to Increase Profit of a Company. *Proceedings of PKDD 2000*, Zighed, D.A., Komorowski, J., Zytkow, J.M. (Eds.), pp. 587–592, LNCS (LNAI) Vol. 1910, Springer, Heidelberg

Rauch J. (2005): Logic of Association Rules. *Applied Intelligence*, Vol. 22, 2005, pp. 9 - 28, ISSN 0924-669X

Rauch J. (2009): Considerations on Logical Calculi for Dealing with Knowledge in Data Mining, In: *Advances in Data Management*, Ras Z. W., Dardzinska A. (Eds.), pp. 177 - 202, Springer, 2009

Rauch, J. (2010). EverMiner - Consideration on a Knowledge Driven Permanent Data Mining Process, EverMiner - Consideration on a Knowledge Driven Permanent Data Mining Process, *International Journal of Data Mining, Modelling and Management*, ISSN: 1759-1171 (Online), 1759-1163 (Print), accepted for publication

Rauch, J. & Šimůnek, M. (2005a). GUHA Method and Granular Computing, *Proceedings of IEEE 2005*, HU, Xiaohua, LIU, Qing, SKOWRON, Andrzej, LIN, Tsau Young, YAGER, Ronald R., ZANG, Bo (Eds.), pp. 630–635, ISBN 0-7803-9017-2, Beijing, July 2005, IEEE, Piscataway

Rauch, J. & Šimůnek, M. (2005b). An Alternative Approach to Mining Association Rules. In: *Foundations of Data Mining and Knowledge Discovery*, LIN, Tsau Young et. al. (Eds.), pp. 211–231, ISBN 3-540-26257-1, ISSN 1860-949X, Springer, Berlin

Rauch, J. & Šimůnek, M. (2005c). New GUHA procedures in LISp-Miner system, *Proceedings of COST 274: Theory and Applications of Relational Structures as Knowledge Instruments*. pp. 73–85, Universidad de Málaga, April 2005, Málaga

Rauch, J. & Šimůnek, M. (2007). Semantic Web Presentation of Analytical Reports from Data Mining - Preliminary Considerations, *Proceedings of the WEB INTELLIGENCE*, pp. 3–7, ISBN 0-7695-3026-5, San Francisco, November 2007, IEEE Computer Society, Los Alamitos

Rauch, J. & Šimůnek, M. (2008). LAREDAM - Considerations on System of Local Analytical Reports from Data Mining, *Proceedings of Foundations of Intelligent Systems*, pp. 143–149, ISBN 978-3-540-68122-9, ISSN 0302-9743, Toronto, May 2008, Springer-Verlag, Berlin

Rauch, J. & Šimůnek, M. (2009a). Dealing with Background Knowledge in the SEWEBAR Project. In: *Knowledge Discovery Enhanced with Semantic and Social Information*, BERENDT, Bettina, MLADENIČ, Dunja, GEMMIS, Marco de, SEMERARO, Giovanni, SPILIOPOULOU, Myra, STUMME, Gerd, SVÁTEK, Vojtěch, ŽELEZNÝ, Filip (Eds.), pp. 89–106, Springer-Verlag, ISBN 978-3-642-01890-9. ISSN 1860-949X, Berlin. URL: http://www.springer.com/engineering/book/978-3-642-01890-9.

Rauch, J. & Šimůnek, M. (2009b). Action Rules and the GUHA Method: Preliminary Considerations and Results, *Proceedings of Foundations of Intelligent Systems*, pp. 76–87, ISBN 978-3-642-04124-2. ISSN 1867-8211, Praha, September, 2009, Springer Verlag, Berlin

Rauch, J.; Šimůnek, M.; Lín, V. (2005). Mining for Patterns Based on Contingency Tables by KL-Miner - First Experience. In: *Foundations and Novel Approaches in Data Mining*, LIN, Tsau Young, OHSUGA, Setsuo, LIAU, C. J., HU, Xiaohua (Eds.), pp. 155–167, ISBN 3-540-28315-3. ISSN 1860-949X, Springer-Verlag, Berlin

SEWEBAR project [online], [cit 2010-17-14], available from WWW http://sewebar.vse.cz

Šimůnek, M. (2003). Academic KDD Project LISp-Miner. *Proceedings of Advances in Soft Computing – Intelligent Systems Desing and Applications*, ABRAHAM, A., FRANKE, K., KOPPEN, K. (Eds.), pp. 263–272, ISBN 3-540-40426-0, Tulsa, 2003, Springer-Verlag, Heidelberg

Šimůnek, M. & Tammisto, T. (2010). Distributed Data-Mining in the LISp-Miner System Using Techila Grid. *Proceedings of Networked Digital Technologies*, ZAVORAL, Filip, YAGHOB, Jakub, PICHAPPAN, Pit, El-QAWASMEH, Eyas (Eds.), pp. 15–21, ISSN 1865-0929, ISBN 978-3-642-14291-8, Praha, July 2010, Springer-Verlag, Berlin

Techila PC-Grid [online], [cit: 2010-07-10], see http://www.techila.fi

13

A Software Architecture for Data Mining Environment

Georges Edouard KOUAMOU
National Advanced School of Engineering, Cameroon

1. Introduction

Data Mining also called Knowledge Discovery consists in analyzing a large set of raw data in order to extract hidden predictive information. It is a discipline which is at the confluence of artificial intelligence, data bases, statistics, and machine learning. The questions related to the knowledge discovery present several facets whose principal ones are: classification, clustering and association. Several models of algorithms are used for each aspect: Neural Networks, Lattice, Statistics, Decision trees, Genetic Algorithms (Mephu, 2001).

Technically, data mining is the process of analyzing data from many different dimensions or angles, and summarizing the relationships identified. For example, analysis of retail point of sale transaction data can give information on which products are selling and when. The summary of this information on retail can be analyzed in the perspective of promotional efforts to provide knowledge of consumer buying behavior. Based on the acquired knowledge, a manufacturer or retailer could determine which items are most susceptible to promotional efforts. Although several tools were developed for this purpose, we note the lack of software environments which are able to support the user activities in a coherent way during the process of data mining.

A software environment can be seen as a set of components which are able to work in cooperation. Each component offers services to other components and it can require some services from them. The role of the environment consists in coordinating the execution of the components which it incorporates, in order to complete the tasks which are assigned to him. The required goal is to offer a support to the software process i.e. the scheduling of the various stages which describe the goal to reach. In software Engineering in general, this goal is related to the capacity of production and evolution of software. In this case we talk about Software Environment Engineering (SEE) also known as CASE tools. When an applicative software environment is concerned, it is specific to a given theme like data mining, thus it consists of a set of tools designed to analyze and produce information likely to improve the choice of the decision makers.

In general, software environments must evolve to take into account changes and new requirements. For instance, the addition of new tools which implies new functionalities, the removal or the replacement of an existing one in the system becomes essential. These modifications should not involve a consequent restructuring of the whole system. For that, it is interesting to reason on the structure of the environment in order to determine its possibilities of modularity and adaptation to its context. This capacity of evolution of the software environments is different to the monolithic vision which consists in statically binding all the elements together during compilation. Several mechanisms are available to implement this approach of construction of the extensible environments with the support of software reuse in particular Design Patterns, software architectures and component based development.

In this chapter, we are interested in the environments of data mining. The purpose of this study is to describe an open software architecture, which is able to be instantiated by the adding of components which implement the various algorithms, in the view to develop environments for knowledge discovery. This architecture must face many constraints:

- to take into account the various models of algorithms,
- to provide the mechanisms of interoperability among the models,
- to be integrated into the existing Information System since it makes up the main source of data.

Being given the interest that express the business community and the researchers for the acquisition and/or the development of these types of environment, it is necessary to find the means of reducing the efforts necessary to this effect in particular in a context where powerful human resources are missing. Through the content of this chapter, we will explore the design of such a generic architecture by detailing the possible solutions to resolve the associated constraints.

2. The problem

The activities in the domain of data mining were formerly carried out by the researchers. With the maturity of the algorithms and the relevance of the problem which are addressed, the industrial are interested from now on to this discipline. In this section, we explore what is done by other researchers and the industrialists.

2.1 Context

In the research domain, the interest relates to the development of algorithms and the improvement of their complexity. The tools which result from the implementation of these algorithms are used separately on sets of targeted and formatted data quite simply because, the researchers remain in the situations of test on academic cases.

There are efforts to gather these various tools in a common environment. In this regard, the experience of the University of WAIKATO gave place to a homogeneous environment in term of programming language called WEKA (Witten and Frank, 2005). However the algorithms must be written in java programming language to be integrated into this platform. Also the mechanisms of interoperability or exchange the models among tools are not provided.

Concerning the industrialists, they are trying to implement the data mining algorithms on top of DBMS (Hauke et al., 2003), or to integrate them with ERP (Enterprise Resource Planning) in order to increase the capabilities of their CRM (Customer Resources Management) (Abdullah et al., 2009). Indeed, the algorithms are mature and the tools which result from them are efficient and consistent so that they outperform the old statistical methods. In addition the ability to store large databases is critical to data mining.

The major problem with existing Data mining systems is that they are based on non-extensible frameworks. In fact tools are independent even in an integrated data mining framework; no models sharing, nor of interaction exchange between tools. Consequently the mining environments are non-uniform because the user interface is totally different across implementations of different data mining tools and techniques. Also a model obtained from one tool is not accessible to another tool.

Thus the needs of an overall framework that can support the entire data mining process is essential, in other words the framework must accommodate and integrate all data mining phases. Also the corresponding environment should provide a consistent, uniform and flexible interaction mechanism that supports the user by placing the user at the center of the entire data mining process. The key issue of this observation will be the construction of an open architecture, allowing extensions and integration of different algorithms implemented by third parties in possibly any language.

Conscious of this disappointment, some studies are undertaken on the subject, but while approaching the question more under the angle of presentation (Khimani, 2005; Poulet, 2001). The aim of their studies consists of developing an effective user-centered graphical environment dedicated to data mining; improving comprehensibility of both the data and the models resulting of data mining algorithms, improving interactivity and the use of various algorithms.

2.2 Contribution

It is a necessity to consider such environments in its globality. The plan consists in reconciling data mining discipline and software engineering with a view to improve the structure of these environments. It is a question of studying the structure of a modular and extensible environment whose design would profit from the current best practices from software engineering which let to implement the advanced techniques to manage the heterogeneity, the distribution and the interoperability of the various components, and especially the reuse and structuring approaches.

As being mentioned early, some reflections are carried out to provide a uniform view on data mining processes. In this way this study is trying to bring together the various approaches to integration (Wasserman, 1990; Ian and Nejmah, 1992) in data mining process. One approach deals with the presentation dimension to integration. The aim is to help users navigate through enormous search spaces, help them gain a better insight into multi-dimensional data, understand intermediate results, and interpret the discovered patterns (Han and Cercone, 2000; Khimani et al., 2004). Another approach is closed to the data dimension to integration. The goal of this approach is to avoid manual data manipulation, and manual procedures to exchange data and knowledge models between different data mining systems (Kurgan and Musilek, 2006).

3. Process of data mining

There is a confusion of terms, between Data Mining and Knowledge Discovery, which is recurrent despite Data Mining concerns application, under human control, which in turn are defined as algorithms designed to analyze data, or to extract patterns in specific categories from data; while Knowledge Discovery is a process that seeks new knowledge about an application domain (Klosgen and Zytkow, 1996). This process consists of many steps among with one of them being data mining.

The process is defined as a set of steps to follow to achieve a goal. In software development discipline, the process consists of a set of activities necessary to transform needs and

requirements expressed by the customer into a software product. The description of the process permits to identify the suitable tools and their sequence, since each tool will be associated to an activity to carry out a task. Software engineering adopted Waterfall model (Roy, 1970), Spiral model (Boehm, 1988) and Iterative models (Kroll and Kruchten, 2003; Highsmith, 2002) that became well-known standards in this area.
Concerning knowledge discovery several different process models have been developed both by research and industrial (Kurgan and Musilek, 2006). We notice that all process models are closed to iterative process model in software development because they often include loops and iterations. The major difference between them is the granularity of the processing steps. From these observations, we think that a data mining process model could emphasize main steps, each gathers the steps of different models as sub-steps or elementary task. Thus the data mining environment support a process including: Data Preparation or Pre-processing, Data Mining itself, Evaluation and knowledge Deployment.

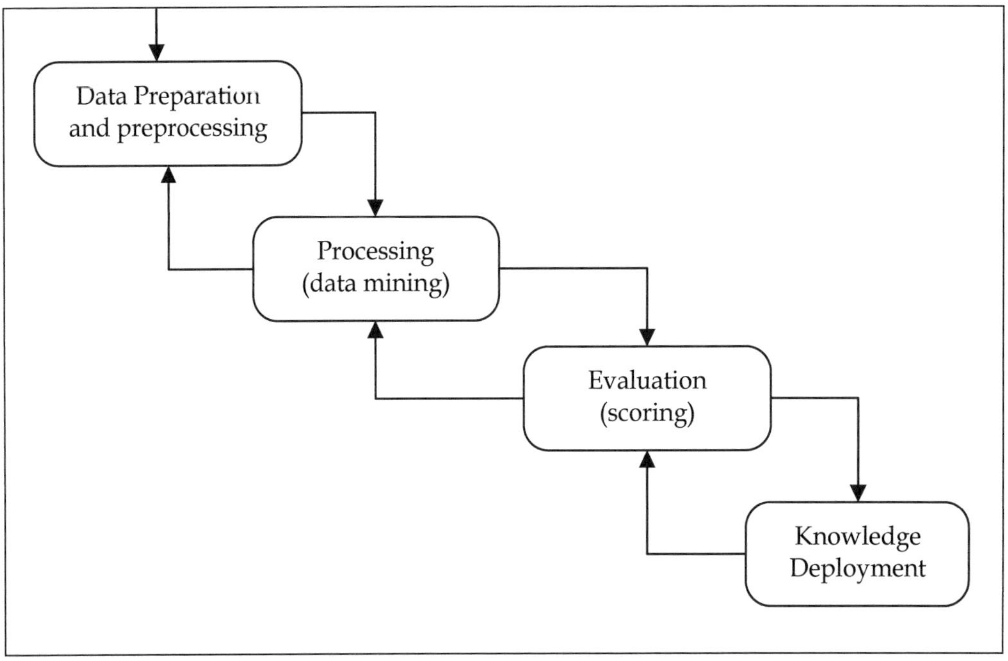

Fig. 1. Description of activities of the data mining process

Preparation and Preprocessing phase: from different sources of heterogeneous data (DB, structured text file, spreadsheet,...) to build a warehouse by combining the various data and removing inconsistency between them. This phase covers all the tasks involved in creating the case table from the data gathered in the warehouse. Data preparation tasks are likely to be performed multiple times, and not in any prescribed order. Tasks include table and attribute selection as well as data cleaning and transformation. For example, you might transform a nominal attribute into binary values or number; you might insert new columns or replace values for example the average in cases where the column is null.
Data mining phase is the phase which consists in processing data to build models. Different methods are applied to extract patterns. The tools used result from the algorithms of

classification, clustering and association rule. The persistent patterns are saved as models in the data warehouse for a later use.

Evaluation also known as scoring is the process of applying a model to new data. Data mining is accomplished by building models. A model uses an algorithm to act on a set of data. The notion of automatic discovery refers to the execution of data mining models. Data mining models can be used to mine the data on which they are built, but most types of models are generalizable to new data.

Knowledge Deployment is the use of data mining within a target environment. In the deployment phase, insight and actionable information can be derived from data. Deployment can involve scoring (the application of models to new data by using either the same tool that produces the given model or another tool), the extraction of model details (for example the rules of a decision tree), or the integration of data mining models within applications, data warehouse infrastructure, or query and reporting tools.

From this description follows the architecture of the environment structured in a layered style including a data warehouse, tools slots and presentation components.

4. Architectural structure

Software architecture is a concept which refers more to the design than with the implementation. It embodies the concepts necessary to describe the system structure and the principles guiding its evolution. Our reflection is based on the following definition: the software architecture of a program or computing system is the structure or structures of the system, which comprise software components, the externally visible properties of those components, and the relationship among them (Clemens et al., 2003).

From this point of view, we can gather the components according to three layers:

- the components of user interface which ensure the dialog with the user. The actions of the user cover the choice of the tool to be used, the method for the evaluation and the capture of the options (modification of its parameters),
- the business components which ensure the (pre) processing. They consist of four groups of tasks.
- The storage system and the data connectors which get into memory the data contained in the warehouse and arrange in the warehouse the persistent entities to be exploited later.

4.1 Data warehouse

The data warehouse makes it possible to store, organize and manage the persistent data and extracted knowledge. Data can be mined whether it is stored in various format either flat files, spreadsheets, database tables, or some other storage format. The important criterion for the data is not the storage format, but its applicability to the problem to be solved. Although many data mining tools currently operate outside of the warehouse, they are requiring extra steps for extracting, importing, and analyzing the data. Thus connectors must be provided to ensure the interactions between the tools and the warehouse. To guarantee its independence with respect to the processing tools and the management system of the warehouse, it is necessary to provide with the generic interfaces. Furthermore, when new insights require operational implementation, integration with the warehouse simplifies the application of results from data mining.

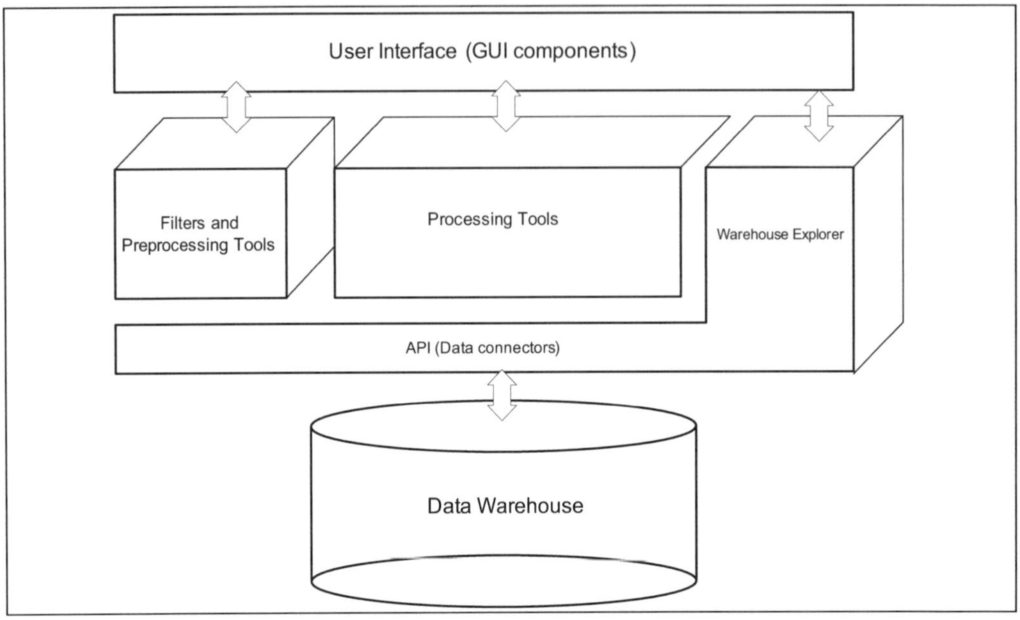

Fig. 2. A layered Architecture for Data Mining environments

4.2 Tools slots

The slots are designed to accommodate the new tools to plug in the environment. These tools are used for raw data preprocessing or data analysis. There are numerous algorithms for business tier, from attributes selection which is a part of data preprocessing to the analysis phase (Han and Kamber, 2006). The commonly used techniques are:

- **Artificial neural networks**: Non-linear predictive models that learn through training and resemble biological neural networks in structure.
- **Decision trees**: Tree-shaped structures that represent sets of decisions. These decisions generate rules for the classification of a dataset. Specific decision tree methods include Classification and Regression Trees (CART) and Chi Square Automatic Interaction Detection (CHAID).
- **Genetic algorithms**: Optimization techniques that use processes such as genetic combination, mutation, and natural selection in a design based on the concepts of evolution.
- **Nearest neighbour method**: A technique that classifies each record in a dataset based on a combination of the classes of the k record(s) most similar to it in a historical dataset (where $k \geq 1$). Sometimes called the k-nearest neighbour technique.
- **Rule induction**: The extraction of useful if-then rules from data based on statistical significance.
- **Lattices**: also known as Galois Lattices are mathematical structure allowing to represent the classes, described from a set of attributes, which are underlying to a set of objects.

The business components of this tier are related to data preparation and data mining itself. The phase of preparation consists of cleaning data in order to ensure that all values in a dataset are consistent and correctly recorded. The data mining analysis tools can be categorized into various methods (Klemettinen et al., 1999):

1. Classification: The process of dividing a dataset into mutually exclusive groups such that the members of each group are as "close" as possible to one another, and different groups are as "far" as possible from one another, where distance is measured with respect to specific variable(s) you are trying to predict.
2. Clustering: The process of dividing a dataset into mutually exclusive groups such that the members of each group are as "close" as possible to one another, and different groups are as "far" as possible from one another, where distance is measured with respect to all available variables.
3. Association rule: Data can be mined to identify associations. In this case data mining model is a set of rules describing which attribute implies another on what confidence and support.
   - **Support:** Support of a rule is a measure of how frequently the items involved in it occur together. Using probability notation, support (A=>B) = P(A, B).
   - **Confidence:** Confidence of a rule is the conditional probability of B given A; confidence (A => B) = P (B | A), which is equal to P(A, B) or P(A).

This categorization helps to define the interfaces independently to the nature of the algorithm and its implementation. That is while multiple implantations could be plugged with respect to the same interface.

4.3 User interface

The user interface ensures the presentation aspect. It permits to explore datawarehouse, to launch a tool and to visualize knowledge in various formats. Insofar as the expert must play a central role during the process, a particular accent must be put on interactive dimension with the user. Visualization must be graphic with possibilities of edition, this to increase interactive dimension with the user. Finally all new tool plugged in the environment will have to adapt to the user interface provided and to reach the warehouse to recover data or to store its results there.

4.4 Documenting the architecture of data mining environment

The architecture focuses on the low layers (business and data), with the hope that the user interface will profit from the results of the existing studies (Khimani and Al, 2004). Since extensibility and reuse are the main features of the environment, the description of architecture is based on the Design Pattern (Gamma and Al, 1996) and UML (Booch et al.,) will be used as language of expression.

The reasoning is based on the families of tools given that they define a common interface under which can be grafted several different implementations. The crucial question consists in finding the appropriate structure of these various interfaces (common attributes and operations).

4.4.2 Classification and clustering

Classification and clustering algorithms proceed in two phases:

- the training which consists in building the classifier who describes a predetermined sets of classes of data; during this phase, the classifier creates the internal model which carries knowledge necessary to classify any object.
- the classification which consists in using the classifier built to assign a class to a new object. At the end of this phase, an evaluation of the model is carried out to produce a confusion matrix.

The confusion matrix shows the dispersion of the examples. It is a matrix of which the columns are equal to the number of initial classes and the rows are equals to the classes determined by the classifier/cluster algorithm. The value of the cell (i,j) represents the examples of the initial class i which has been put in the class j by the classifier. To ensure this, one of the following evaluation methods is considered: holdout, leave-one-out, cross-validation, resubstitution:

- **Holdout**: data are partitioned in two subsets. One set is use for learning and the other set is used for testing the pertinence of hypothesis.
- **Leave-one-out**: each example is used once to test the hypothesis obtained from the others.
- **Cross validation:** the data are partitioned in several subsets of identical size; each one of them is used once to test the hypothesis obtained from the remainder of subsets.
- **Resubstitution:** the set of examples which are used for learning are also used for testing.

The design patterns "Classifieur" and "Cluster" respectively define the skeleton of the algorithms of classification and clustering. However each concrete classifier/Cluster has the responsibility to redefine certain aspects which are specific to the model that it uses. For this layer, we define a succession of abstract entities which make it possible to adapt the concrete components by implementing the appropriate interface.

4.4.2 Association rule

The algorithms of association rule present two facets: the research of the rules of association and the research of the sequences. In the case of the rules of associations, the model consists of all the rules found by the algorithm. The relevance of each rule is evaluated through the metric one used by the algorithm. In general it is confidence. Each rule consists of two whole of items characterized by their support. The first being the antecedent or premise and the second is the conclusion or consequence. One Item indicates an article or a pair attribute/value of the data source. In the case of sequential reasons, the model is rather made up of a set of sequences. A sequence being a continuation of Itemsets ordered in time. The design pattern « Association » is used to define the interface of the algorithms related to this family of data mining algorithms. As in the case of classification, this interface let the implementation to the concrete association algorithm.

4.4.3 Data manipulation and representation

All the algorithms input a context. Let O be a set of objects, and A a set of attributes. A *Context* is a relation $I=O\times A$ such as:

- $I(o_i,a_j) = v$ which represents the value of attribute a_j for the object o_i
- $I(o_i,a_j) =$ Null if the value a_j is unknown for the object o_i

Then an example represents a line of this relation. The Figura 3 is an illustration of a relation I using O={1,2,3,4,5} and A={a,b,c}

	a	b	c
1	v_{a1}	v_{b1}	v_{c1}
2	v_{a2}	v_{b2}	v_{c2}
3	v_{a3}	v_{b3}	v_{c3}
4	v_{a4}	v_{b4}	v_{c4}
5	v_{a5}	v_{b5}	v_{c5}

Fig. 3. An illustration of context

The Context is the representation in memory of the data stored on the disc (in the warehouse). The structure of table is adapted for its representation. In object perspective orientation, a context has composite entity formed by examples each being a line of the tabular structure.

4.4.4 Logical structure of the data mining environment

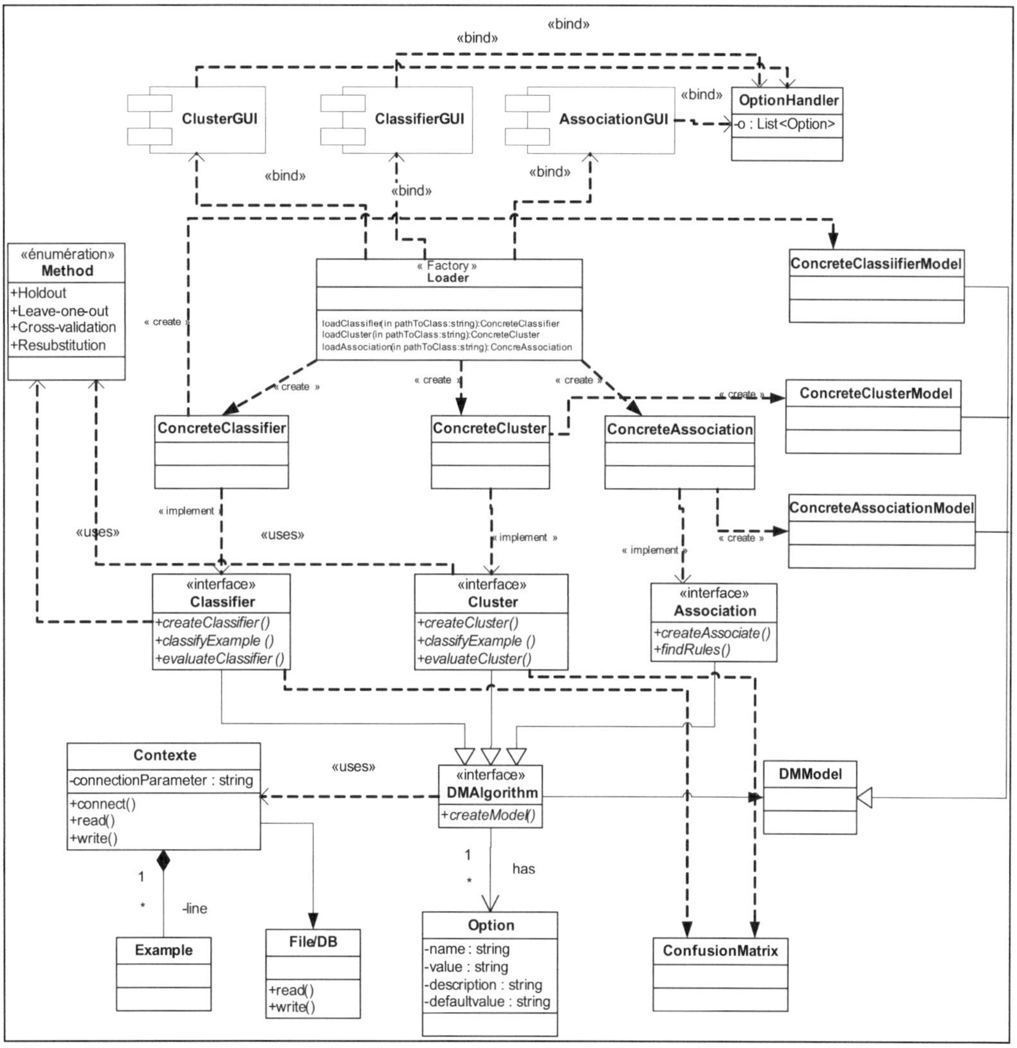

Fig. 4. A logical view of the environment

The environment shall be configured with different families of algorithms. For each family, just their interface is exposed. The loader is responsible for the instantiation of each algorithm in the sense that it implements the operations to create concrete algorithms. The information necessary to this task will be stored in a repository which could be a configuration file in this case. The data mining algorithms manipulate model (or knowledge). The models are created from contexts which can be seeing as proxy since it

provides an image in the memory for data in the warehouse. Classifier (resp. Cluster) algorithms encapsulate the knowledge of which confusion matrices are created. The concrete algorithms redefine the operations to return the appropriate model and the appropriate confusion matrix.
Because of the complexity of GUI components, there are designed as black box subsystems intending that the suitable GUI framework which is more adapted to the needs of the environment will be plug in this structure.

5. Discussion and future trends

As this study is going on, there are several issues we may decide to consider while bearing in mind the state of the technology. The technological capabilities, principally the use of standards, are an important factor that influences the openness and the acceptance of such environments. These issues include:

- Integration : adding new tools in the environment;
- Interoperability over multiple dimensions: vertical (interaction between adjacent layers), horizontal (interaction between components of the same layer) and the interaction with other framework.
- Compatibility between legacy tools while plugging in the environment and its accommodation with the interoperability mechanism which is implemented.

5.1 Integration and interoperability issues

Since this environment is developed to provide a framework for integrating the entire data mining process, the main issue to deal with consists in supporting interoperability between the data mining tools in the same environment or interoperability between the data mining environment and other external software (Cios and Kurgan, 2005). Interoperability refers to the ability of a computer system and/or data to work with other systems or data using common standards or processes (Wileden et al., 1991). From the data mining perspective, the management of interoperability can help to achieve multiple goals:

- to standardize communication between diverse data mining tools and storage systems;
- to provide standard mechanisms for sharing data between data mining tools that work on different software platforms.

Interoperability within the scope of the data mining supposes simply the exchange of the data and knowledge between different software tools. The stake of such an operation is to compare the relevance of results provided by two different algorithms. Conscious of this situation of the reuse of the models from one environment to another, the DMG (Data Mining Group) proposed the Predictive Modelling Markup Language (PMML) (PMML, 2001). The PMML is a specification of the XML (DTD, XML Schema) to represent efficiently the characteristics that allow reusing a model independently of the platform which has built this model. It is currently used by the most important industrials in the domain of data mining environments (IBM, Microsoft, Oracle, SAS, SPSS, etc). However the existing research platforms do not integrate easily this standard because the common work undertaken within this framework relies on the improvement of the complexity and the performance of the algorithms.
The PMML provides specifications (DTD or XML schema) to represent the characteristics of a model independently of the platforms. To reuse the models, the platform consuming the model needs the configuration of the data to use. In general they are the types of the

attributes and their role in the model. Accordingly, the management of interoperability consists in studying the possibility of extracting the generic characteristics which are common to models of the same nature. This abstraction permits to maintain the algorithms without rewriting them. By using PMML, different applications taking from different places can be used across the process in the same environment; one application can generate data models, another application analyzes them, another evaluates them, and finally yet another application is used to visualize the model. In this sense, any subsystem of the environment could be satisfied simply by choosing the suitable software components which have already incorporated the PMML language. For instance on the level of the presentation layer, VizWiz (Wettschereck et al., 2003) can be used for visualization of models, PEAR (Jorge et al., 2002) for exploration and visualization of association rules.
The use of XML language and the related standard to achieve the interoperability in such environment has many advantages unless the compatibility with the legacy systems is assured. XML permits the description and storage of structured or semi-structured data, and to exchange data in a tool-independent way.

5.2 Compatibility issue

Compatibility is a consequence of the integration perspective of the environment. If the new tools can be developed according to the principles of the environment, the integration of the legacy tools is a challenge. We notice that several environments were developed in the commercial world and the world of research for the retrieval of knowledge starting from the data. These environments are heterogeneous on several aspects such as the handled formats of data or the supported platforms, the types of algorithms and built models, the access mode to the data, etc (Goebel & Gruenwald, 1999). In spite of these differences, the objective of very model of dated mining is to store relevant information obtained by data analysis to facilitate decision making by carrying out predictions of the events for example. The problem of incompatibility relates to two aspects: data (to solve the heterogeneity of the data) and interfaces tools (incompatibility of the interfaces).
Since XML is the standard in fact to support interoperability, the solution to face the heterogeneity of the legacy tools, candidate with integration in the environment, consists in conforming them to this standard without however modifying their internal structure. The implementation of the wrappers (Kouamou & Tchuente, 2008) is a technique often used in such circumstances. The wrapper will be charged to transform the data to represent them in a format conforms to that awaited by the legacy tool.

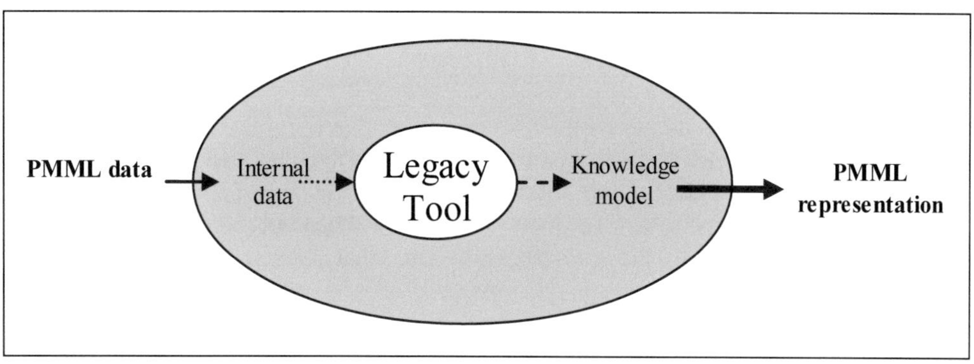

Fig. 5. Overview of the wrapper

The other function of the wrapper is to convert the interface of a legacy tool into one of the main interfaces the loader class expects. Thus the wrapper lets classes work together that couldn't otherwise because of incompatible interfaces.

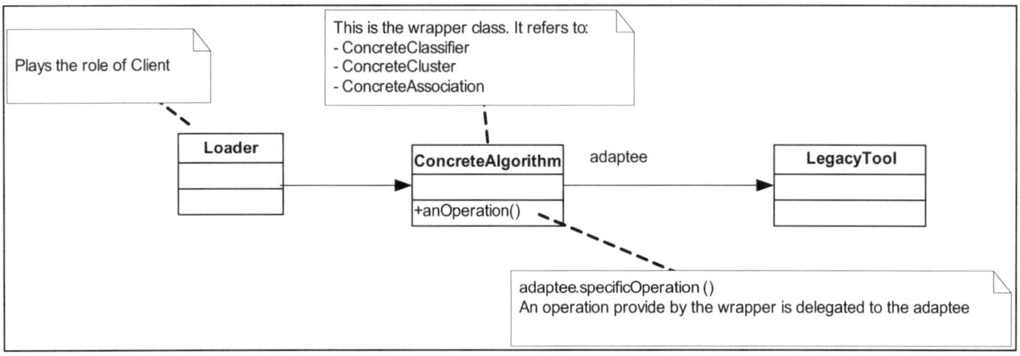

Fig. 6. The structure of the wrapper

The wrapper can be structured in two different ways (Gamma et al., 1995): (i) by interface inheritance or (ii) by delegation. Considering the fact that legacy tool may be heterogeneous in term of programming languages, the second approach is more appropriate in this circumstance.

5.3 Implementation issue

Since the implementation of a data mining environment as described here requires enormous human resources for its construction, to gain in productivity and time, it is important to gradually try out the various aspects developed within the framework of this study. Another issue concern the reuse of the available material principally the software components which are able to realize a part of it. That is while we choose WEKA (Witten & Frank, 2005) as the backbone of experiment because it is a freeware and it has gained considerable popularity in both academia and research communities.

WEKA was developed at the University of WAIKATO. Written in JAVA, it groups a diversity of data mining algorithms based on bayesian network, neural network, Decision Trees and Statistics. Briefly it is more diversified than the concurrent frameworks. However our intention is to evaluate the performance of this framework according to the principles which have been described previously. This evaluation consist to integrate some new types of algorithms, then to appreciate how PMML can be introduced in this framework to assure pattern exchange with other frameworks.

5.3.1 Extending WEKA

For this purpose, we proceeded to the reverse engineering to rebuild the architectural model of this environment in order to determine the extension points where new algorithms can be plugged in. However, we focused our attention mainly on the classifiers taking into account the implementations available for this stage of our study. Thus we could integrate four new tools without deteriorating the configuration of what exists. These tools are the implementation of the algorithms LEGAL, GALOIS, GRAND and RULEARNER which are based on the lattices as learning model (Mephu & Njiwoua, 2005).

This experiment shows that WEKA provides a set of abstract classes, one for each family of algorithms. A new algorithm must inherit the abstract class relevant to it family, then it must implement the available abstract methods. The class loader uses a configuration file as tool repository.

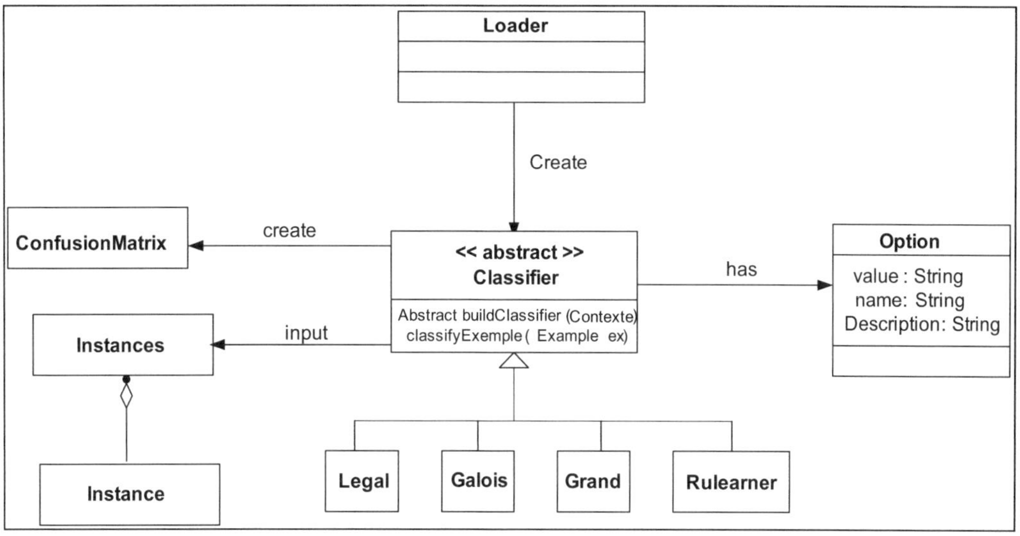

Fig. 7. A partial view of WEKA with the new classification algorithms

In WEKA the extension is done through inheritance. The choice of this approach supposes that algorithms are written in Java. The management of heterogeneity through the reuse of algorithms written in other programming languages relies on the competence of the developer. So the next step will consist to provide the mechanism which could easy the adaptation of heterogeneous algorithms.

5.3.2 Managing interoperability in WEKA platform

The algorithms implements into the WEKA environment (classifier, cluster and association rule) use as in parameter, the data under an owner format (ARFF, Attribute Relation File Format). They produce at output textual unstructured descriptions. The absence of an explicit description of the characteristics of the models thus built does not allow the reuse of extracted knowledge. From this flat structure could be extracted the main characteristics of each type of model. In the case of the association rules, the model consists of all the rules found by the algorithm. The importance of each rule is evaluated through the metric used by the algorithm. In general it is about confidence. Each rule consists of two sets of items (called Itemset) characterized by their support. The first is being the antecedent or premise and the second the conclusion or consequence. One Item indicates an article or a pair attribute/value of the data source. In the case of sequential motifs, the model is rather made up of a set of sequences (called Sequence). A sequence being a chronological series of Itemsets.

Three major concepts permit to characterize the rules independently of the platforms and the algorithms: items, ItemSets and rules. The same reasoning can be applied easily to the other types of model in order to extract their characteristics.

Figura 9 presents the process which has been used to export the models from the algorithm of the associate rule family in WEKA.

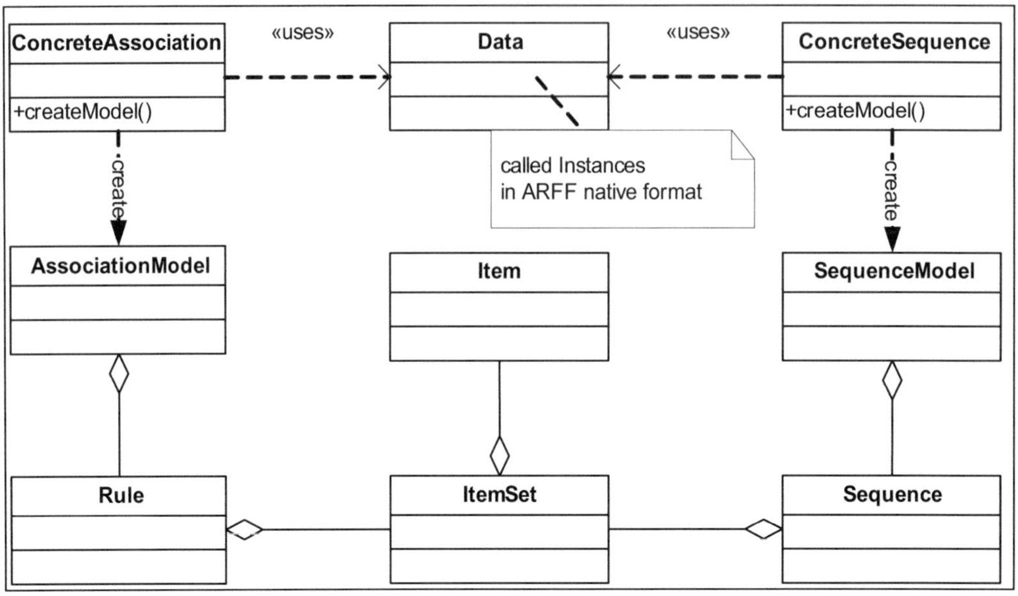

Fig. 8. A view of the association rules model

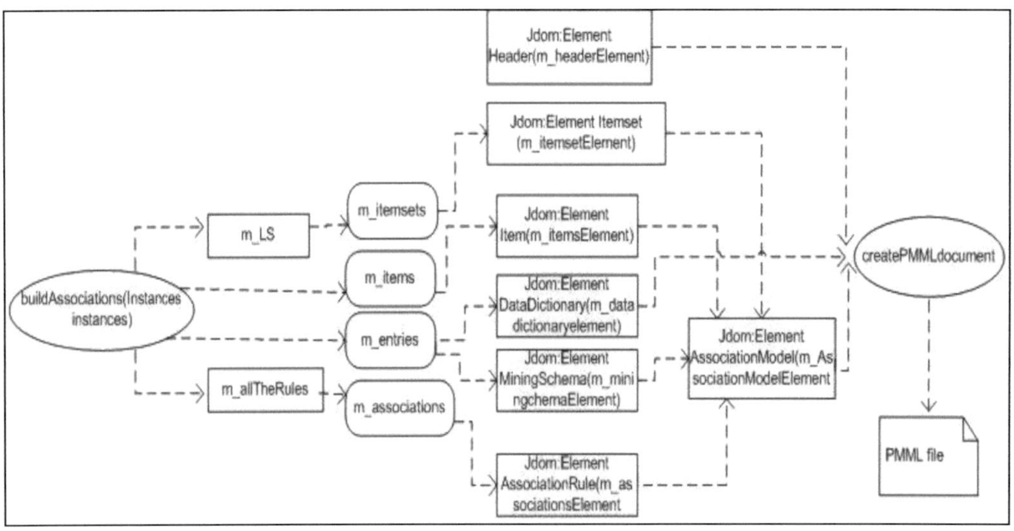

Fig. 9. Exportation of a associate model

From the execution of the association algorithm (buildAssociations operation is executed), the description of the entries of the model (items) is built starting from the instances of ARFF file provides as parameter. The sets of items are built using the structure m_LS which contains the whole frequent items resulting from the execution of the algorithm. The rules are obtained from the structure m_allTheRules. All these parameters make it possible to build the elements of JDOM tree which will be assembled to build the model according to the PMML standard using the method "createPMMLdocument" of the wrapper entity.

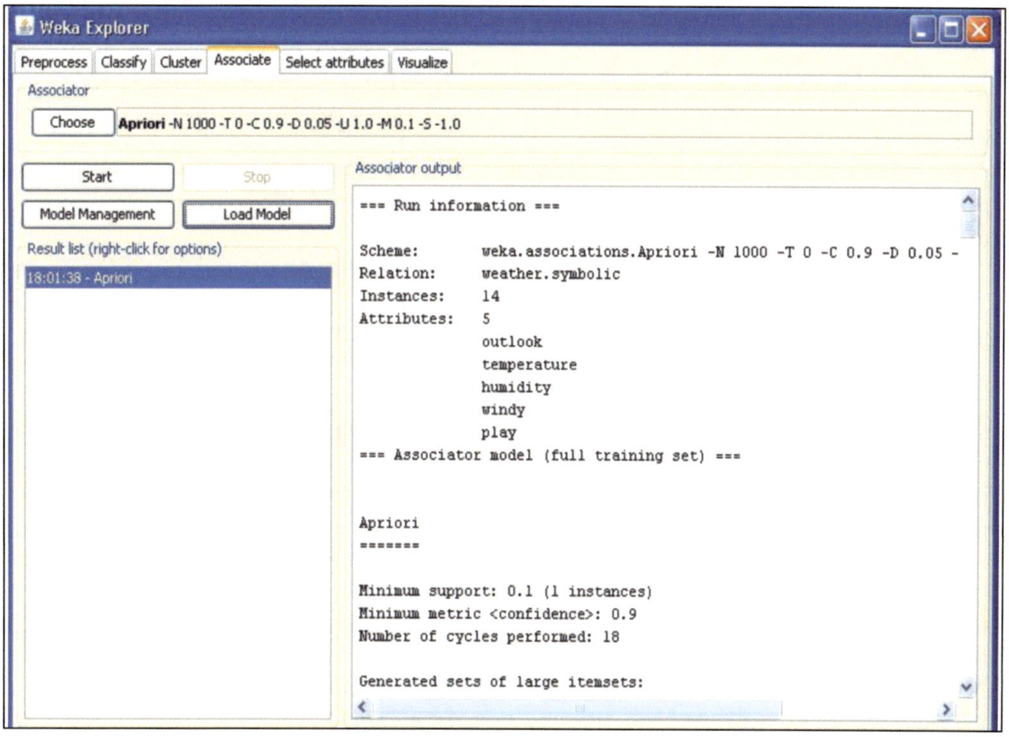

Fig. 10. User Interface with the introduction of the new functionalities

The generated rules and the performance of the algorithms, the number of cycles carried out remain the same. It is proposed the means of handling the model obtained and of being able to export it in PMML format (command button *ModelManagement*) or of importing an external model (button Load Model). A new panel is provided to manage the PMML structure of a model obtained from a WEKA tool or imported from a external framework.

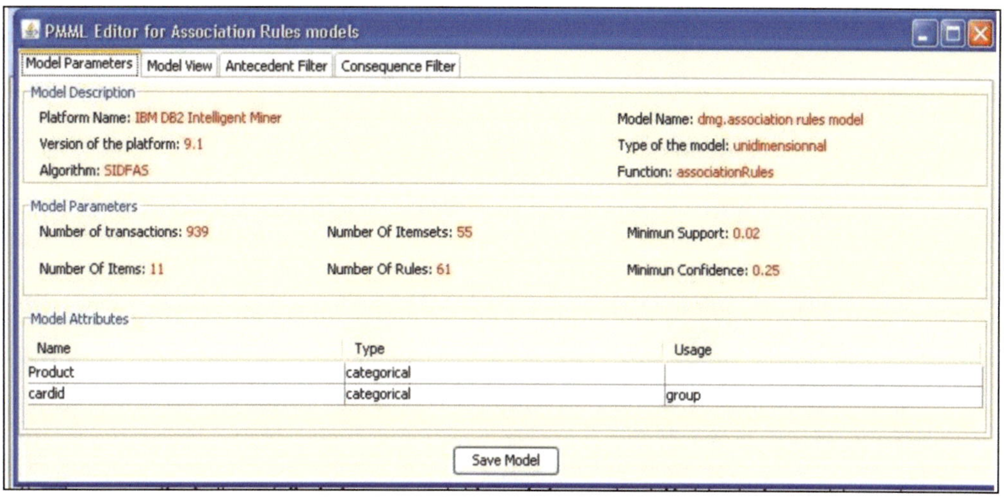

Fig. 11. The panel provided as PMML editor in the WEKA environment

6. Conclusion

Data mining becomes gradually an emergent technology beside the industrial. To favour its use by this target, it is good to be care with the major problems that are facing existing data mining systems: They are based on non-extensible frameworks, they provide a non-uniform mining environment - the user is presented with totally different interface(s) across implementations of different data mining techniques. That is why it is necessary to design a data mining environment which has the following features:

- Open with well defined extension points since new algorithms can be added to the environment,
- Modular because any compatible component is supposed to substitute another,
- Possible integration of different tasks/tools e.g allow to reuse the output of a task by another task
- User flexibility and enablement to process data and knowledge, to drive and to guide the entire data mining process.

This kind of environment is based on a process which is summarized in four steps. Because the components of the environment are made to support the tasks carried out within each step, the process let to the design of the important entities which could be found in such case. This study described the logical structure of data mining environment while insisting on its main issues. In short, integration and interoperability of modern data mining environments may be achieved by application of modern industrial standards, such as XML-base languages. Such synergic application of several well-known standards let the developer gather experiences from other team in the sense that the use of standard favours the reuse of legacy systems (Kurgan & Musilek, 2006).

The adoption of standards in this discipline already made it possible to develop procedures of data exchange between various platforms. At the same time there are reflections on the standardization of a data mining process model. From these efforts, the challenge for the future is to develop and popularize widely accepted standards in data mining environment that, if adopted, will stimulate major industry growth and interest. This standard will promote development and delivery of solutions that use business language, resulting in performing projects faster, cheaper, more manageably, and more reliably.

7. References

A. Abdullah; S. Al-Mudimigh, B. Farrukh Saleem, C. Zahid Ullah. (2009). Developing an integrated data mining environment in ERP-CRM model - a case study of MADAR. *International Journal Of Education and Information Technologies*, Volume 3, N° 2.

Bass, L.; Clements, P. & Kazman, R. (2003). *Software Architecture in Practice*, Second Edition, Addison-Wesley.

Boehm, B. (1998). A spiral model of software development and enhancement. *IEEE Computer*, Vol 21, N°5, pp 61-72.

Cios, K. and Kurgan, L. (2005). Trends in data mining and knowledge discovery. In Pal, N and Jain, L (eds). *Advanced Techniques in Knowledge Discovery and Data Mining*, Springer, pp. 1-26.

Gamma, E.; Helm, R.; Johnson, R. & Vlissides, J. (1995). *Design Patterns: Elements of Reusable Object-Oriented Software*; Addison Wesley.

Goebel, M. & Gruenwald, L. (1999). A survey of data mining and knowledge discovery software tools. *ACM SIGKDD.*

Han, J. & Cercone, N. (2000). RuleViz: a model for visualizing knowledge discovery process, In *Proceedings of the 6th ACM SIGKDD International Conference on Knowledge Discover and Data Mining*, pp. 244–253.

Han, J. & Kamber, M. (2006). *Classification and Prediction, in Data Mining: Concepts and Techniques*, 2nd Edition, Morgan Kaufmann Publishers.

Hauke, K.; Owoc, M. L.& Pondel, M. (2003). Building Data Mining Models in the Oracle 9i Environment, *Informing Science*, pp 1183-1191.

Highsmith, J. (2002). *Agile Software Development Ecosystems*, Addison Wesley, 448 pages.

Ian, T.& Nejmah B. (1992). Definitions of Tool Integration for Environments", *IEEE Software*, Vol. 9, N° 3 pp. 29–35.

Jorge, A.; Pocas, J. & Azevedo, P. (2002). Post-processing operators for browsing large sets of association rules. *In Proceedings of the ECML/PKDD'02 workshop on Integrating Aspects of Data Mining, Decision Support and Meta-Learning*, pp. 53–64.

Kimani, S.; Lodi, S.; Catarci, T.; Santucci, G. & Sartori, C. (2004). VidaMine: a visual data mining environment, *Journal of Visual Languages & Computing*, Volume 15, Issue 1, pp 37-67.

Klemettinen, M.; Mannila, H. & VERKAMO, A. I. (1999). Association rule selection in a data mining environment. *Lecture notes in computer science*, vol. 1704, pp. 372-377.

Klosgen, W and Zytkow, J. (1996). Knowledge discovery in databases terminology. In Fayyad, U, Piatetsky-Shapiro, G, Smyth, P and Uthurusamy, R (eds) *Advances in Knowledge Discovery and Data Mining*. AAAI Press, pp. 573–592.

Kouamou, G., E. & Tchuente, D. (2008). Experience with Model Sharing in Data Mining Environments. In Proceedings of the 4th ICSEA, Malta.

Kroll, P. & Kruchten, P. (2003). *Rational Unified Process Made Easy: A Practitioner's Guide to the RUP*, Addison Wesley, 464 pages

Kurgan, L., A. and Musilek, P. (2006). A survey of Knowledge Discovery and Data Mining process models. *The Knowledge Engineering Review*, Vol. 21:1, 1-24., Cambridge University Press.

Mephu, N., E. & Njiwoua, P. (2005). Treillis de Concepts et Classification supervisée. *Techniques et Sciences Informatiques*, Vol 24(2), Hermes, Paris.

Mephu, N., E. (2001). Extraction de Connaissances basée sur le Treillis de Galois: Méthodes et Applications, HDR thesis, Université d'Artois, 2001.

Perrin, O. & Boudjlida, N. (1993) Towards a Model for persistent data integration, In *Proceedings of CAISE'93, the 5th Conference on Advanced Information Systems Engineering*, Lecture Notes in Computer Science, pp 93-117, Paris, France.

PMML (2001). Second Annual Workshop on the Predictive Model Markup Language, San Francisco, CA.

Roy, W. (1970). Managing the development of large software system concepts and techniques. In *Proceedings of the WESCON. IEEE*, pp. 1–9.

Seifert, J. W. (2004). Data Mining: An Overview, Congressional Research Service, The Library of Congress.

Wasserman, A. I. (1990). Tool Integration in Software Engineering Environments. In Software Engineering Environments. *International Workshop on Environments, Lecture Notes in Computer Science* N° 467, pp.137-149. Berlin

Wettschereck, D.; Jorge, A. & Moyle, S. (2003). Visualization and evaluation support of knowledge discovery through the predictive model markup language. In *Proceedings of 7th International Conference on Knowledge-Based Intelligent Information and Engineering Systems*. Springer, pp. 493–501.

Wileden, J.C.; Wolf, A.L.; Rosenblatt, W.R. and Tan, P.L. (1991) Specification Level Interoperability, *Communications of the ACM* , Volume 34(5), pp. 73–87.

Witten, I. H. & Frank, E. (2005). *Data Mining: Practical Machine Learning Tools and Techniques* (Second Edition), Morgan Kaufmann, 525 pages, ISBN 0-12-088407-0

14

Supervised Learning Classifier System for Grid Data Mining

Henrique Santos, Manuel Filipe Santos and Wesley Mathew
University of Minho,
Portugal

1. Introduction

During the last decades, applications of data mining techniques have been receiving increasing attention from the researchers and computer professionals (J. Luo, et al, 2007). Data mining on localized computer environments no longer meets the demands of solving today's complex scientific and industrial problems because of the huge amount of data that is stored in geographically distributed worldwide databases (M. F, Santos et al, 2009 J. Luo et al, 2007).

The purpose of this work is to generate a global model from distributed data sets. We consider two platforms for distributed data mining: one is based on divers distributed sites and the other on a global site (central site). There are two main methods for solving the data mining challenge in the distributed data set. The first method is to collect all data from the different repositories and store it in one location and then apply data mining on the collected data in order to make the global model. The second method applies the data mining in each distributed location generating local models, then collects and merges those models as a way to make the global model. The first method is defined as Centralized Data Mining (CDM) and the second method as Distributed Data Mining (DDM). This paper compares the performance of these two methods on three different data sets: two synthetic data sets (Monk 3 and 11 multiplexer) and a real-world data set (Intensive Care Unit (ICU) data).

Classification is one of the most popular data mining technologies that can be defined as a process of assigning a class label to a given problem, given a set of problems previously defined (A. Orriols, et al 2005). Considering the actual level of data distribution, classification becomes a challenging problem. Current advances in Grid technology make it a very proactive in developing distributed data mining environment on grid platform.

In this work grid is designed in a parallel and distributed fashion. Supervised learning method is used for data mining in the distributed sites. Data mining is applied in every node in the grid environment. The main objective of this work is to induce a global model from the local learning models of the grid. Every node of the grid environment manages an independent supervised classifier system and such nodes transmit learning models to the central site for making global model. This global model can show complete knowledge of all nodes.

The construction of the global model is based on already induced models from distributed sites. This paper presents different strategies for merging induced models from each

distributed site. The different strategies tested are Weighted Classifier Method (WCM), Specific Classifier Method (SCM), Generalized Classifier Method (GCM), and Majority Voting Method (MVM) (M. F, Santos et al, 2009).
The remaining sections of this paper are organized as follows: Section 2 gives the background information about grid based supervised learning classifier systems. This section explains the grid data mining, distributed data mining, Supervised Classifier System (UCS), and GridClass learning classifier system. Section 3 explains the different methods for constructing and optimizing techniques for global model. Section 4 explains the experimental work and results. Experimental setup of Monk 3 problem and 11 multiplexer problem and ICU data are explained here. Section 5 discusses the results obtained so far based on the performance of different strategies used in the system and further illustrates some aspects of the DDM and CDM methods. The final section presents conclusion and the future work.

2. Background

The grid and agent technology assure to supply reliable and secure computing infrastructure facilitating the perfectly consistent use of distributed data, tools, and systems to solve complex problems in different areas such as health care, research centre and business management (J. Luo etal 2006). Distributed data mining, which executes data mining in distributed fashion, uses the technologies available for data mining in distributed environments like distributed computing, cluster computing, grid computing and cloud computing. Grid computing is applied in this work, because of the compatibility for data mining in grid platform. Supervised classifier system is a newly introduced, successive implementation of learning classifier system (K. Shafi, et al, 2007). The following subsections give detailed explanation of supervised classifier system, distributed data mining, grid data mining and details of Gridclass system.

2.1 Supervised Classifier System (UCS)

Supervised Classifier System (UCS) is a Learning Classifier System (LCS) derived from XCS and is designed for supervised learning scheme (A Orriols_Puig, et al, 2007). UCS adopts main components and patterns of the XCS which are accepted for supervised learning (A Orriols_Puig, et al, 2007). LCS gives accurate response for each environmental problem because it is an adaptive model. LCS was introduced by John H Holland in 1970. The XCS follows reinforcement learning scheme. In the supervised learning classifier, the environment shows the correct action only after the learner chooses (predict) the action (H. H. Dam, 2008).
Basic function of UCS is to generate the learning model and check the accuracy of that model. The population of a UCS is based on a kind of rules (containing a condition and an action), the Classifiers. A set of parameters should be defined in order to govern the UCS execution. The parameters include: *Accuracy, Number of Match, Number of Correct, Correct Set Size, Numerosity, Last Time this was in the GA* (Experience).
Fitness of the classifiers in the UCS is a measure of their performance and is calculated based on the accuracy of the classifier (H. H. Dam, 2008, A Orriols_Puig, et al, 2007). Classifiers are grouped in two categories, the correct and incorrect classifiers. Correct classifiers are those receiving the highest payoff contrasting with incorrect classifiers that receive the lowest payoff. Correct classifiers have more chance to sustain in the population because incorrect classifiers are receiving less fitness.

Training and testing are the two fundamental processes in the UCS system. During the training phase, the system receives inputs from the environment and develops the population related to the input data. When new input enters into the system, it matches the input data with current population of classifiers. If there is some classifiers in the population that matched with condition and action parts of the new input data, those matched classifiers are stored in the correct set (C) (H. H. Dam, 2008, A Orriols_Puig, et al, 2007, K. Shafi, et al, 2007). Otherwise, correct set would be empty. Genetic Algorithm (GA) and covering are the two different training processes in the classifier system. In UCS, if the correct set is empty, then covering method will be executed; otherwise, if the average experience of the classifiers in the correct set is greater than user defined constant *GA_Throshold*, then GA will be executed (H. H. Dam, 2008, A Orriols_Puig, et al, 2007).
The parameters associated to each classifier are updated only in the training period. When a classifier condition part matches with condition part of the training data, then the *number of match* of that classifier will be increased by one, similarly when a condition and action parts of a classifier match with condition and action part of the training data, then the *number of correct* will be increased by one (H. H. Dam, 2008). User can set the maximum size of the population. When population reaches the maximum size, then the system has to find space for the new classifier by removing one classifier from the population. After the training process, UCS will find the accuracy of generated population (training model) with testing data. User has to give two files to UCS, one file for training and another file for testing. Figure 1 show the life cycle of the UCS system. Table 1 displays the configuration parameters of the UCS system.

Parameters	**Default value**	**Meaning**
coveringProbability	0.33	Probability of covering
crossoverProb	0.8	The probability of choosing instead of mutation to perform on a rule condition
GaThreshold	25	Threshold value for genetic algorithm
inexperiencePenalty	0.01	The factor by which to discount when experience is too low
mutationProb	0.05	The probability of mutation a single point in a rule condition.
Noise	0.0	Probability of class noise being added to each example in the training data.
Onlinelearning	TRUE	Boolean value to decide online learning or offline learning
POPMAXSIZE	400	Maximum size of population
Probabilityofclasszero	0.5	Balance of class distribution in the training data
ThetaDel	20	Deletion vote experience threshold
ThetaDelFrac	0.10	Deletion vote fraction
ThetaSub	20	Subsumption experience threshold
V	20	Parameter controlling fitness evaluation for UCS

Table 1. Configuration parameters of the UCS system

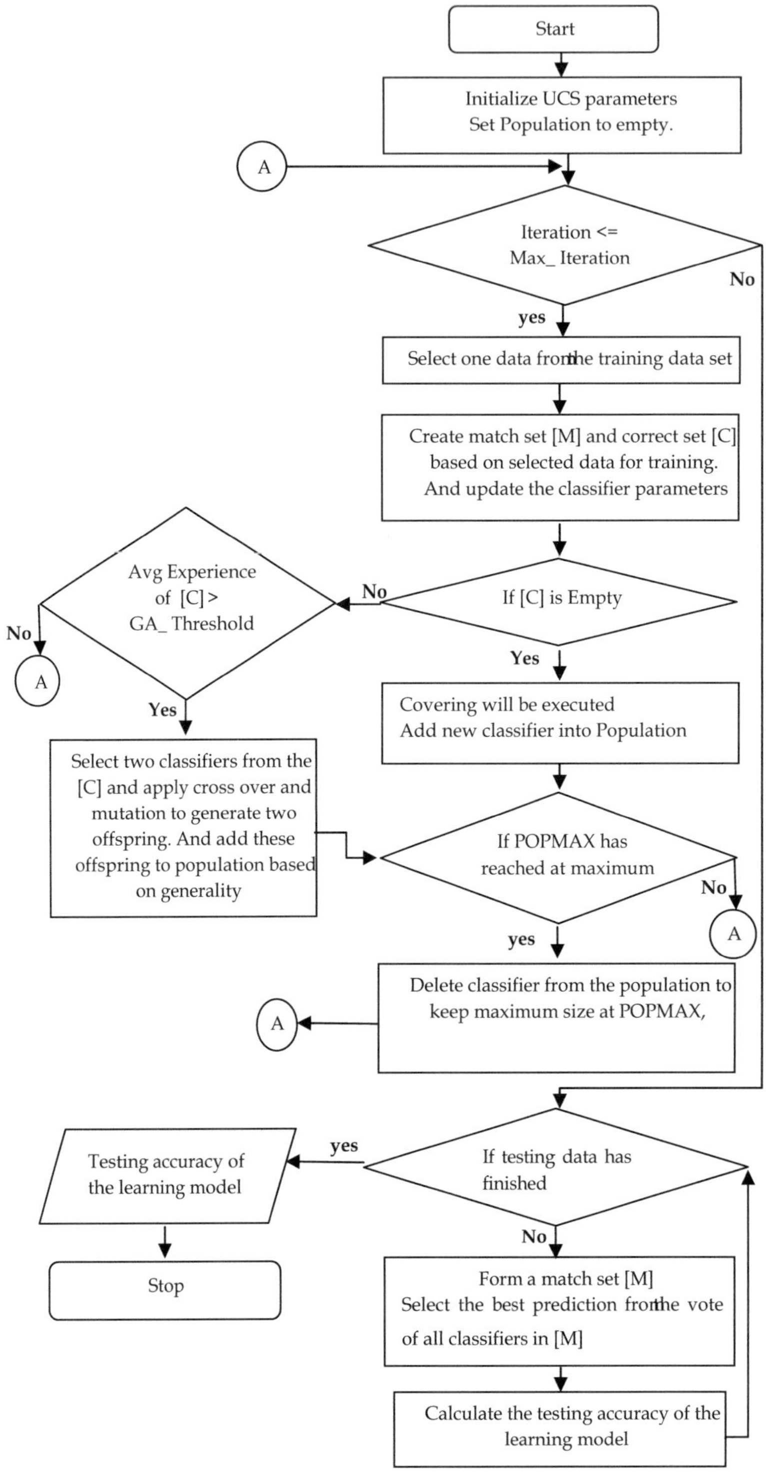

Fig. 1. Flow chart of the UCS system.

2.2 Grid Data Mining (GDM)

Grid computing is the next generation of distributed and parallel computing technologies. Grid integrates the technologies of both distributed and parallel computing, focused on large-scale and higher-level, so it can manage more complex distributed data mining tasks (I. Foster, 2001). Grid computing gives higher throughput computing by taking the benefits of other computers, which are connected by a network thus, grid computing is viewed as virtual computing (V. Stankovski et al, 2007). Under distributed computing, one or more resources is shared by other resources (computers) in the same network, hence every resource in the network is shared in grid computing (M. F. Santos, et al 2009). Grid computing is a distributed heterogeneous computer network with storage and network resources, which gives secure and feasible access to their combined capabilities. Grid environment makes it possible to share, transfer, explore, select and merge distributed heterogeneous resources. In grid, all computer resources in the network are connected together and share their computing capability to elaborate the computing power like a supercomputer so that users can access and leverage the collected power of all the computers in the system (M. F. Santos, et al, 2009). Grid computing can increase the efficiency, decrease the cost of computing by reducing the processing time, optimize resources, and distribute workloads. Therefore, users can achieve much faster results on massive operations at lower costs.

The grid platform has the facility to apply parallel computing and dynamic allocation of resources. Decentralized method for data mining is suitable for grid based DM. Grid platform can offer data management services and computations for distributed data mining process of parallel data analysis and decentralization. The objective of grid computing is to create distributed computing environment for organizations and provide application developers the ability to utilize computing resources on demand.

2.3 Distributed Vs centralized data mining.

The goal of distributed data mining is to get global knowledge from the local data at distributed sites (N. Zhang, et al, 2009). Recently, many companies, organizations and research centers have been generating and manipulating huge amounts of digital data and information. The digital data are stored in distributed repositories for more reliable and fast access of information. Basically two approaches can be used for mining data from the distributed database: one is Distributed Data Mining (DDM) and the other is Centralized Data Mining (CDM) (M. F. Santos, et al, 2010, C. Clifton et al, 2002).

Centralized Data Mining is also known as warehousing method (N. Zhang, et al, 2009). In CDM, data is stored in the different local databases, but for mining purpose, all data has to be transferred from local databases to the centralized data repository. There are many excising applications that are used this principle of collecting data at centralized site and running an algorithm on that data. Figure 2 depicts the centralized method when considering three geographically distributed databases. These three databases may be the parts of one organization, while the execution of distributed data mining, the data which is stored in the local database has to send to the central repository. The data mining algorithm is applied on that collected data, which is in the central repository and generate global model.

The size and security of data are two main concerns in the centralized mining method. The large size of the data will increase the communication and computational cost of mining process. The size of the local data may vary from one site to another and it is not controlled

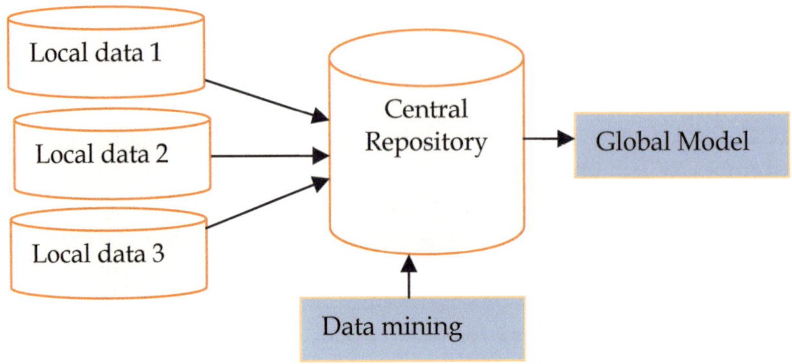

Fig. 2. Centralized data mining method.

by the user. Algorithm can retrieve local data depending on the requirement of the user, but the size is not predictable. High bandwidth communication channel is required for sending large sized data to a central site; otherwise, it will take longer to send data to central site. After receiving all data from different nodes, mining algorithm would be applied to the centralized data. Because of the large size of the data, generating the centralized model would be slower, resulting in higher computational cost. The privacy is another main issue of sending data to a central repository. For example, an insurance company with different branches may be unwilling to transmit large amounts of data across a network (C. Clifton et al, 2002).

Distributed data mining means data mining in the distributed data sets (N. Zhang, et al, 2009). In DDM, data sets are stored in different local data sets, and hosted by local computers that are connected through a computer network (N. Zhang, et al, 2009). First, data mining is executed in all local environments, and then all these local models (results) from local nodes are combined. The combined model (result) is called Global Model (GM). Figure 3 depicts the DDM method with three geographically distributed databases. The first process of the DDM is to make three local models by applying mining algorithm at each site in parallel fashion. Central node will receive all these three local models and merge them to develop the GM.

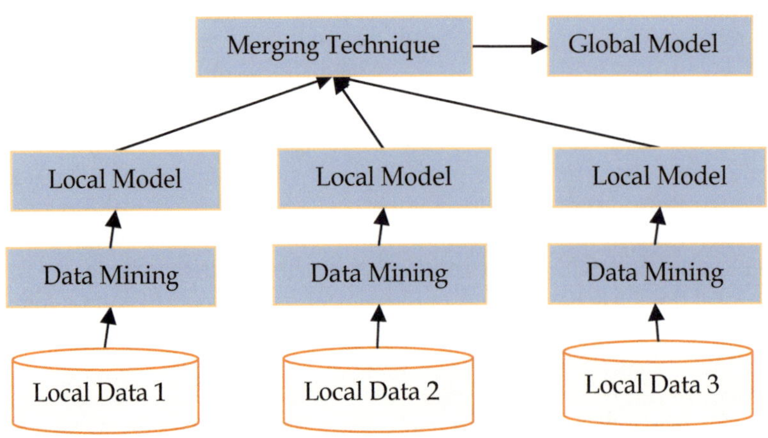

Fig. 3. Distributed data mining method

The DDM has several advantages compared to the CDM. First, the DDM system doesn't need to send original data to the central node; instead, system can send local trained models to the central site, making DDM more secure than CDM. Second, the local model has a fixed size, which is set by the user. Since the size of the local model would be less than the size of training data, DDM doesn't require high bandwidth for communicational channel thus reducing the communication cost. Third, the computational cost of the DDM is less because in DDM paradigm, data mining is executed in parallel fashion on small data sets from each node.

2.4 Gridclass system

Gridclass is a grid based UCS structured for grid data mining in a parallel and distributed fashion. Gridclass should be installed in every node in the distributed environment in order to use the training data to develop the local models (M. F. Santos et al, 2010). The execution of basic UCS system needs one training data set and one testing data set. The initial population can be empty, or a given population generated in previous runs of the Gridclass (incremental learning). Incremental learning mechanism uses previous experience to improve the learning model. This helps to improve the quality of the classifiers (M. F. Santos et al, 2010). If user does not give the predefined population, Gridclass starts the training process with an empty population. The Gridclass system writes its training model into an XML file, and the training and testing data sets are stored in CSV files.

When placing a predefined population in the current population, Gridclass makes some modification in the parameters of the classifiers. The parameters *Number of Match, Number of Correct, Accuracy and Numerosity* are the same as in the previous model, but the parameters *Last Time This Was In The GA* and *Correct Set Size* are set to zero. If the maximum size of population is less than the predefined population, then the number of classifiers copied would be equal to the maximum size. The training process is the process of generating and updating the classifiers in the population based on the training data.

Condition and action are the two parts of each row of the training data set and are matched with the classifier's condition and action parts respectively. The action part is defined in a binary language and has only two possible values in the Gridclass system: 0 or 1 (yes or no). Genetic Algorithm (GA) and covering are the two methods for the learning process. The classifiers, whose condition part is correctly matched with the condition value of the training data, compose the match set (M) (H. H. Dam, 2008, A Orriols_Puig, et al, 2007, K. Shafi, et al, 2007). Similarly the classifiers, which are correctly matched with condition and action part of the training data are considered as the correct set (C) (H. H. Dam, 2008, A Orriols_Puig, et al, 2007, K. Shafi, et al, 2007).

The covering is executed only when the correct set becomes empty; otherwise, if the average experience of classifier in the correct set is greater than the *GA_ Threshold,* then GA is executed (H. H. Dam, 2008, A Orriols_Puig, et al, 2007, K. Shafi, et al, 2007, M. F. Santos, et at, 2010). Covering is the process of generating new classifiers into the population. While covering, condition part of the training data is used as the condition part of the new classifier, and action part of the training data is used as the action part of the new classifier. Each position of the condition part of the new classifiers is checked against the covering probability. If any position is less than the covering probability, then that position is changed with don't care symbol (#). Don't care symbol is the substitution of all the possible values in that position (T. Kovacs, 2004). The "#" symbol can represents both 0 and 1 in binary data.

In the case of genetic algorithm, two classifiers are selected from the correct set; these two classifiers are known as parent classifiers. In crossover function, the parent classifiers are split to generate two new classifiers, which are known as child classifiers (offspring). If any position of the new classifier is less than the mutation probability, then the mutation process is applied to that position. After the mutation, classifier checks the generality of new classifier. If the child classifier is more general than the parent classifier, then new child classifier is added into the population.

Accuracy of the child classifier is the average of parent *Accuracy*, and *Correct Set Size* of the child classifier is the average of parent *Correct Set Size*. Other parameters such as *Number of Match, Number of Correct, Numerosity* and *Last Time This Was In The GA* are set to 1. If the parent classifier is more general than the child classifier, then the parent classifier is added again into the population (H. H. Dam, 2008).

The parameters of classifier are updated only during the training process. These parameters are *Number of Match, Number of Correct, Accuracy, Numerosity, Last Time This Was In The GA,* and *Correct Set Size*. When the classifier's condition part is correctly matched with the condition part of the training data, the *Number of Match* of that classifier is increased by one (H. H. Dam, 2008, A Orriols_Puig, et al, 2007, K. Shafi, et al, 2007). Likewise, when the condition and action of one classifier is correctly matched with condition and action of one training data, the *Number of Correct* is increased by one (H. H. Dam, 2008, A Orriols_Puig, et al, 2007). *Accuracy* of the classifier is the *Number of Correct* divided by *Number of Match* (H. H. Dam, 2008, A Orriols_Puig, et al, 2007, K. Shafi, et al, 2007). Fitness is based on the *accuracy* of the classifier, i.e. Accuracy ^v (H. H. Dam, 2008, A Orriols_Puig, et al, 2007, K. Shafi, et al, 2007). In UCS, *Numerosity* of the classifier is always one, and *Correct Set Size* of classifier is the average size of all correct sets when the classifier takes part in correct set.

The supervised classifier system has a maximum size for the population. During the training, if the number of classifier reaches the maximum population size the system removes one classifier from the population to make room for the new one.

Testing is used to check the *Accuracy* of the population. Each node in the distributed site has a separate testing data set. This data set has the same format as the training data set but the data may be different. Each row in the testing data set is matched with the classifiers in the population to create the match set. Classifiers in this match set are used to predict the action of the testing data. The system finds the sum of the *fitness* and *Numerosity* of classifiers in the match set based on the action. Then the ratio of *fitness* and *Numerosity* are found. The action that corresponds to the maximum ratio is selected as predicted action. During testing, the population of classifiers is not changed.

3. Methods for generating the global model

The most critical task of this work is to optimize the global model generated from all local models in the distributed sites. A challenge in optimizing the global model is combining local models without losing the benefits of any classifier (M. F. Santos, et al, 2010). Local models only represent their own training data (problem defined in the node) but the global model should represent all local models from the grid environment (M. F. Santos, et al, 2010).

Two main approaches have been considered while generating the global model from the local models in the grid environments: 1) managing the size of global model, 2) keeping the benefits of each classifier while modifying the parameters. The size of the local model is fixed; it will not change during execution (dynamically). But, in the optimized global model, system does not add all the classifiers from the distributed sites. So, the global model size depends on the strategies used for constructing the global model, and on the classifiers in the local models. While training, the local model parameters of the classifiers are updated, but the parameters of the classifiers in the global model are updated during the merging of different local models.

Basically, there are two situations when we need to update the parameters: first, if two classifiers are the same, then there is no need to add repeated classifier in the global model. In this case, keep one classifier in the global model and update the parameters of that classifier with the parameters of the other. Second, if one classifier is more general than the other one, then the more general classifier is kept in the global model and the less general classifier is removed from the global model. The parameters of the more general classifier are updated with the parameters of the less general classifier. Next we present four different strategies for constructing and optimizing the global model (Figure 4): Weighted Classifier Method (WCM), Majority Voting Method (MVM), Specific Classifier Method (SCM), and Generalized Classifier Method (GCM).

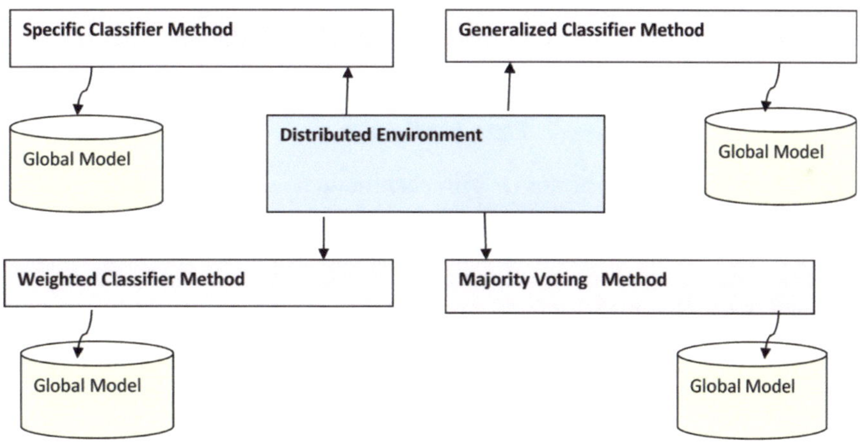

Fig. 4. Different methods for combining and optimizing local models

3.1 Weighted Classifier Method (WCM)

WCM is used to construct the global model considering the highest weighted classifier from the local models and keeping with the size of global model (M. F. Santos, et al, 2010). Global model size is set by the average size of local models. Weight of the classifier (Wgt) is derived from the parameters of *Number of Match (Nm), Number of Correct (Nc),* and *Accuracy (Acc)* as given by expression 1.

$$Wgt = Nm * Nc * Acc \tag{1}$$

When a new classifier comes to the global model, it is compared with all other classifiers that are already stored in the global model. If the weight of the new classifiers is higher than the weights of any classifier in the global model, then the new classifier is added to the population. If the population size reaches the maximum, then one classifier whose weight is less than those of all other classifiers in the population is removed from the population. The

populations of global model may repeat same classifier many times, but the global population size should not change dynamically.
Expression 2 defines the computing processing efficiency (Eff) of the classifiers.

$$Eff = Teval + Tupdate \tag{2}$$

In the above expression, *Teval* stands for the evaluation time and *Tupdate* is the Update time, where evaluation time represents the time needed to check whether the classifier needs to be kept in the global model, and update time is the time needed to update the parameters of the classifier in the global model.
The total time of evaluation is computed from expression 3.

$$Teval = T1eval * Pop \tag{3}$$

T1eval is the time needed for evaluating one classifier.
The total time of update is computed using expression 4.

$$Tupdate = T1update * Pop \tag{4}$$

T1update is the time need for updating the parameters of one classifier and pop is the total number of classifier given by expression 5.

$$Pop = N * Popmax\ . \tag{5}$$

In the above, *N* is the number of nodes with each node having fixed number of classifiers, and *Popmax* is the number of classifier in a single node.
In the case of weighted classifier method, each classifier only needs to be evaluated and not updated. So the processing efficiency of weighted classifier, *Effweighted* is: *Teval.*
In this method, each classifier needs to be compared to the global model only once, and there is no need to update the classifier parameters. So the processing efficiency is high.

3.2 Specific Classifier Method (SCM)

SCM is another strategy for constructing and optimizing a global model. In this method, the global model preserves discrete classifiers (M. F. Santos, et al, 2010). Here discrete classifiers mean that there are no two classifiers with the same condition and action parts. Two classifiers are considered to be similar if the condition and action parts of one classifier are the same as the condition and action parts of the other classifier. For example, consider three classifiers:

c1= 0,#,0 ->1
c2= 0,1,0 ->1
c3= 0,0,0 ->1

These three classifiers have the same action, that is "1", and a condition part represented with 3 bits of data. "#" symbol represents the wildcard. The classifier c1 is more general than classifier c2 and c3; even though in SCM, these three classifiers are considered as three different classifiers.
If a classifier is repeated, its parameters are updated with those of the repeating classifier. The size of the global model generated by SCM is dynamic. Expressions 6 and 7 defining how the parameters of SCM are updated are given below.

$$GNm = GNm + NNm \tag{6}$$

$$GNc = GNc + NNc \tag{7}$$

In the above expressions, *GNm* is the *Number of Match* of the current classifier in the global model, *NNm* represents the *Number of Match* for the new classifier, *GNc* stands for the *Number of Correct* of current classifier in the global model, *NNc* is the *Number of Correct* for the new classifier.
Accuracy of current classifier in the global model (*GAcc*) is computed in expression 8.

$$GAcc = \frac{(GNm * GNc * GAcc) + (NNm * NNc * NAcc)}{(GNm * GNc) + (NNm * NNc)} \tag{8}$$

The parameter, *Last Time This Was In The GA* of the classifier in the global model is updated with the maximum value of *Last Time This Was In The GA*. *Numerosity* and *Correct Set Size* are not updated.
The total processing efficiency, *Effspecific* of SCM is based on the evaluation time of the classifier and modification time of the parameters in the global mode as defined in expression 9.

$$Effspecific = Teval + Tupdate \tag{9}$$

Teval is the total evaluation time and *Tupdate* is the total update time.

3.3 Majority Voting Method (MVM)

MVM is a third method for constructing and optimizing the global model from the distributed local models. This approach finds one cut-off-threshold value to benchmark the classifiers in the global population from all discrete classifiers in the local model (M. F. Santos, et al, 2010). The global population size of the MVM is not previously fixed by the user. Here, the system first selects the discrete classifiers from the local models. If a new classifier is already in the global model, then parameters of the existing classifier are modified based on the parameters of the new classifier. After reading the entire local models from the distributed site, the system calculates the average value of *accuracy*, which is considered as cut-of-threshold value of Majority Voting. If the classifier accuracy is less than this threshold value, then that classifier is removed from the global model. This method helps to maintain the valid classifiers in the global model. Parameter updates of the classifiers in Majority Voting are the same as the SCM.
The processing efficiency of Majority Voting is calculated as the sum of the processing efficiency of discrete classifiers and the processing efficiency of applying the cutoff threshold to those discrete classifiers. The processing efficiency of discrete classifiers was derived in the above section (SCM). For the execution of cutoff threshold, the system evaluates all discrete classifiers. Total processing efficiency of majority voting, *Effmajority* is given by expression 10.

$$Effmajorityvoting = Effspecific + NS * T1eval \tag{10}$$

Where *NS* represents the size of a discrete classifier and *NS*T1eval* represents the processing efficiency for applying cutoff threshold to a classifier.

3.4 Generalized Classifier Method (GCM)

GCM is the last method for constructing and optimizing the global model from distributed local models. This strategy is used to keep only *more general* and discrete classifiers in the global model (M. F. Santos, et al, 2010). The phrases *less general* and *more general* refer to the degree of generality of classifiers. Each classifier in the local model would be compatible to any one of four different situations: 1) Global model may have the same classifier, 2) Global model may have more general classifier than the new classifier, 3) New classifier may be more general than the classifier in the global model, and 4) New classifier may be completely new (M. F. Santos, et al, 2010).

In the first case, a classifier just updates its value and does not allow a new classifier to enter the global model. In the second case, classifiers in the global model, which are more general, updates its parameter values with new classifier parameters and does not let a new classifier to enter into the global model. In the third case, classifiers which are less general are removed from the global model, and the parameters of the new classifier are updated with the parameters of the classifiers that are removed from the global model. The new classifier is then added into the global model. In the fourth case, new classifiers directly enter into the global model. For example, consider three classifiers:

c1 = 0,1,0 -> 1
c2 = 0,#,0 -> 1
c3 = 0,0,0 -> 1

These three classifiers have the same action that is set to 1 and a condition part represented by 3 bits of data. Assuming that they come in that order, with classifier c1 as the first classifier, the system only keeps classifier c2, because the other two are less general than classifier c2. The first classifier c1 will be saved in the global model, but when the classifier c2 arrives, classifier c1 is removed because classifier c1 is less general than classifier c2, and parameters of classifier c2 are updated with those of classifier c1. Classifier c3 will not be saved because it is less general than classifier c2 that is already in the global model. The parameters of classifier c2 are again updated with those of classifier c3. The size of the global model in this method is dynamic and it is smaller than the size of the global model generated by other methods. In this model, the classifiers are very general, but the testing accuracy is normally very low. Parameters that are updated by the GCM are the same as those updated by SCM as given by expressions 11 and 12.

$$GNm = GNm + LNm \tag{11}$$

$$GNc = GNc + LNc \tag{12}$$

The new accuracy, *Newacc*, is computed by expression 13.

$$Newacc = \frac{(GNm * GNc * GAcc) + (LNm * LNc * LAcc)}{(GNm * GNc) + (LNm * LNc)} \tag{13}$$

Where *GNm* is the *Number of Match* of more general classifier, *LNm* stands for the *Number of Match* of less general classifier, *GNc* represents the *Number of Correct* of more general classifier, *LNc* is the *Number of Correct* of less general classifier, *GAcc* is the *Accuracy* of more general classifier, and *LAcc* is the *Accuracy* of less general classifier.

The parameter, *Last Time This Was In The GA* of the classifier in the global model is updated with the maximum value of *Last Time This Was In The GA*. *Numerosity* and *Correct Set Size* are not updated. The processing efficiency of GCM is the sum of processing efficiency of SCM, processing efficiency of classifier modification, and processing efficiency of deleting less general classifier. The processing efficiency of SCM is the same as that for GCM. The processing efficiency of classifier modification is the efficiency of matching each classifier in the global model with every other classifier in the global model to update the more general classifier. The modification efficiency is calculated by the sum of the evaluation time and update time of the discrete classifier: *NS*T1eval+NS*T1update*.
The processing efficiency of removing the less general classifier is equal to the evaluation time of classifiers in the global model; so, the evaluation time of this process is *NS*T1eval*. The total efficiency of generalized classifier, *Effgeneral*, is given by expression 14.

$$Effgeneral = Effspecific + NS * T1eval * 2 + NS * T1update \tag{14}$$

4. Experimental work and results

Experiment was done with Monk3 problem and 11 multiplexer problems and Intensive Care Unit (ICU) data. Two sets of experiments were done in monks3 problem and 11 multiplexer problem and one experiment was done with ICU data. Each experiment differs by the way it generates training data and testing data. For training, all experiments were done with 5000 iterations. For the various experiments it was considered a grid environment with four nodes (sites) each one containing a local model.
In order to promote a benchmark among the strategies, all four strategies were applied in each problem.

4.1 Eleven multiplexer problem

Boolean multiplexer has an ordered list of 11 bits; therefore 11 multiplexer problems have 2048 different ordered lists. First 3 bits of the 11 multiplexer (a0 - a2) are considered as the address bits and next 8 bits (d0 - d7) are considered as answer bits. The data format of the 11 multiplexer problems is typically a string a0, a1, a2, d0, d1, d2, d3, d4, d5, d6, d7.
In learning classification, multiplexers are used as a class of addressing problem. The action class is merged with each problem data; the action has two possibilities, either zero or one. The following example elucidates the above description:

01101100110 =>class 1
01011100110 =>class 0
10011100110 =>class 0
11001100110 =>class 1
00101100110 =>class 0

4.1.1 Experimental setup for 11 multiplexer problem

The two experiments of the 11 multiplexer are differentiated by the way they choose training and testing data. The entire data was divided into two parts, 70% of the data was taken for training and 30% for testing. The training data was divided into four equal portions for four nodes. Similarly the testing data also was divided into four equal portions for four nodes. So the size of training data set is 340 examples and the size of testing data set is 172 examples.

In the first experiment, the training data in each node is completely different from the data in other nodes and the same was true for the testing data. In the second experiment, the training and testing data in the four nodes shared some common classifiers because the data for each node was selected randomly. The centralized training data sets were created by combining four training data sets in the distributed site, so the total size of the centralized training data set is 1360 (340*4) . Similarly, the centralized testing data was created by combining four testing data sets in the distributed sites, being the centralized testing data set size equal to 688(172*4).

4.1.2 Results from 11 multiplexer problem

Table 2 displays the different testing accuracies of global models, which are generated by using the four different strategies in both experiments. The global model size of the WCM is set to 400 and the sizes of the other three methods are not fixed.

First Experiment		
Strategy	**Accuracy**	**Global model Size**
GCM	0.7848	238
SCM	0.9534	772
MVM	0.8953	503
WCM	0.9127	400
Second Experiment		
GCM	0.7965	220
SCM	0.9302	775
MVM	0.9186	507
WCM	0.9476	400

Table 2. Testing accuracies of the global model for the 11 multiplexer problems.

Table 3 displays the testing accuracy of centralized learning models of both experiments. It shows testing accuracies for different sizes of learning model ranging from 100 to 800. The size of the centralized learning model is varied so that the results can be compared with those of the distributed method. Five thousand training iteration were done in each execution of the centralized method.

The testing accuracy of SCM is the highest in the first experiment when compared to the other strategies used in the Gridclass system. In the first experiment, testing accuracy is also good for WCM and MVM. The testing accuracy of SCM and WCM were the best in the second experiment. The performance of GCM is very low in both experiments.

Table 3 shows that the accuracy of the learning model is dependent on the size of the learning model, because the accuracy increases with the global model size. Here it is difficult to compare the results of distributed and centralized methods, because the differences in the sizes of learning models. In the case of distributed models, except for WCM, the size of the global model is not fixed because its size is based on the local model. But in the centralized model, global model size is defined by the user.

Comparison of WCM with the centralized model shows that in both experiments, WCM has better accuracy than the centralized method according to the related global model size.

Comparison of other strategies such as SCM, GCM, and MVM with the centralized model shows that both experiments of these three strategies resulted in almost similar accuracy based on global model size.

Centralized model of 11 multiplexer problem		
Experiment	**Testing Accuracy**	**learning model size**
1	0.53	100
2	0.64	100
1	0.72	200
2	0.81	200
1	0.92	300
2	0.85	300
1	0.90	400
2	0.87	400
1	0.90	500
2	0.95	500
1	0.94	600
2	0.96	600
1	0.96	700
2	**0.94**	**700**
1	**0.99**	**800**
2	**0.95**	**800**

Table 3. Testing accuracies of centralized model based on different sizes of learning model in the 11 multiplexer problems.

4.2 Monks3 problem

In the second experiment, environmental problems are defined by Monks3 problem that has 8 attributes and 432 instances. Table 4 shows the position and available values for each attribute in the Monks3 problem.

Attributes	**Allowed Values**
Class	0,1
a1	1,2,3
a2	1,2,3
a3	1,2
a4	1,2,3
a5	1,2,3,4,5
a6	1,2
a7	ID

Table 4. Attributes of monk3 problem.

The table 4 describes the allowed values for each position of the classifiers in the monks3 problem. The class has only two possible values: 1 and 0. The permitted values of the first, second and forth positions (a1, a2, a4) of monks 3 problem vary from 1 to 3, the third and sixth positions (a3, a6) can have values 1 and 2, and the fifth position can have values from 1 to 5. The seventh position is used to identify each instance of the data. In data mining applications class is used as action and a1 to a6 are used for representing condition of the training and testing data. The position a7 (Id) is not necessary for data mining problems. Examples of data patterns are shown below:

Class	a1,	a2,	a3,	a4,	a5,	a6,	Id
1	1	3	1	1	3	2	data_1
0	2	2	2	3	4	1	data_2
1	3	1	1	3	3	2	data_3

4.2.1 Experimental setup for Monks 3 problem

Two different experiments were done. First experiment toke 144 examples in each training data set and 72 examples in each testing data set; second experiment had 72 examples in each training data set and 36 examples data in each testing data set. The differences of training size in both experiments were introduced to find the importance of training size. In the centralized data mining, training data was made by combining all four training data in the distributed sites, so the first training data set size became 576 (144*4) and testing data set size became 288 (72*4). For the second experiment, training data set size was 288 (72*4) and testing data set size was 144 (36*4). The size of each local model was 400 classifiers.

4.2.2 Results from Monks3 problem

Table 5 displays the different testing accuracies of global models, which are generated by using the four different strategies. The results of the four strategies are given from two different experiments in two groups. The global model size of WCM is set to 400, and the sizes of the other three methods are not fixed.

First Experiment		
Strategy	**Accuracy**	**Global model Size**
GCM	0.7222	39
SCM	1	196
MVM	1	167
WCM	1	400
Second Experiment		
GCM	0.75	17
SCM	0.9583	276
MVM	0.8333	240
WCM	0.9583	400

Table 5. Testing accuracies of global models from Monk3 problem.

The size of the training and testing data are the basic differences in these two experiments. Here, accuracy of the first experiment is better than the accuracy of the second experiment. In the first experiment, WCM, MVM and SCM attained 100% of accuracy. In the second experiment, WCM and SCM have given better accuracy than other two strategies. The Accuracy of MVM is significantly better in the first experiment than in the second experiment. The accuracy of GCM in both experiments is poor.
Table 6 displays the testing accuracy of centralized learning model of both experiments. The training iteration of centralized model was 5000 and the size of the learning model was set to 400. These experiments help to compare the distributed data mining and centralized data mining.

Centralized Model		
Experiment	**Accuracy**	**Learning Size**
1	1	400
2	1	400

Table 6. Testing accuracies of Centralized model from Monk3 problem.

In centralized model, both experiments reached 100% of accuracy. In the first experiment, the testing accuracies of the centralized model and the distributed model are similar, but in the second experiment, the testing accuracy of the centralized model is better than the testing accuracy of the distributed model.

4.3 ICU data

The Intensive Care Unit data is about the prediction of organ failure about 6 different organic systems (M. Vilas-Boas, et al, 2010). The data have been collected from three distinct sources: the electronic health record, ten bed side monitors, and paper based nursing record. There is a total 31 fields of data in this problem. The data was collected from thirty two patients' information for first five days. The total number of records in this data set is 2107, but this data was not balanced (the number of resulting ones and zeros were not equal). Consequently, the data set was extracted for balancing the output. Hence the final data set has 3566 records.

4.3.1 Experimental setup for ICU data

The ICU data was divided into two parts: 70% of the data was selected as training data and the rest 30% was selected as testing data. Four different data sets with 624 records were selected from the training data to make the four different training data sets in the distributed sites. Similarly, four different data sets with 268 records were selected from the testing data for four different testing data sets in the distributed sites. In the centralized data mining, training data is made by combining all those four training data sets, so the training data set size became 2496 (624*4), similarly testing data set was made by combining all those four testing data sets, so the testing data set size became 1072 (268*4).

4.3.2 Results from ICU data

Table 7 shows the different testing accuracies of global model, which are generated by using the four different strategies used for constructing global model.

First Experiment		
Strategy	Accuracy	Global model Size
GCM	0.84	1382
SCM	0.85	1466
MVM	0.89	1416
WCM	0.73	400

Table 7. Testing accuracies of global models from Monk3 problem.

The results showed in table 7 correspond to an interesting result when the ICU data is used. The MVM has the best result but the GCM and SCM also are very close. Table 8 displays the testing accuracy of centralized learning model. The training iteration of centralized model was 5000 and the size of the learning model was set to 400.

Centralized Model		
Experiment	Accuracy	Learning Size
1	0.68	400

Table 8. Testing accuracies of centralized model from ICU data.

The testing accuracy of CDM from ICU data is 0.68 (68%). In this problem, testing accuracy of CDM has less accuracy than the testing accuracies of DDM. The global model sizes of WCM and CDM are the same even though the testing accuracy of CDM is less than the global model testing accuracy of WCM.

5. Discussion

Three axes will be considered to analyze the experimental results:

1. Significance of the training size;
2. Efficiency of different strategy for generating global model;
3. Comparison of DDM and CDM.

The training data size affects the quality of models in the distributed sites. In monks 3 problem, training size of each node in the first experiment corresponds to double the training size of each node in the second experiment; therefore, global model of the first experiment is more general than the global model of the second experiment. That is why the accuracy of the global model in the first experiment is better than the accuracy of the second experiment.

Now let's examine the operating efficiency of each strategy used for making global model. Here, less processing efficiency means that the processing time of the strategy is higher, and more processing efficiency means those strategies need less processing time. The best processing efficiency model is the WCM; because the WCM does not have any updates (parameter modification) instead of it has only evaluation process (comparison). The processing efficiency of SCM is lower than the WCM because SCM has not only the update process, but also the evaluation process. The first process of the GCM and MVM is to develop discrete classifier in the global model, up to SCM function. Hence the processing efficiency of these two methods is lower than WCM and SCM. The GCM has less processing efficiency than MVM because the GCM has two more processes after developing discrete classifier, but the MVM has only one more process after the generation of discrete classifiers. The global model of GCM and SCM represents all the local models. When the global model is generated by WCM or MVM, some classifiers are removed from the global models. The WCM keeps only the highest weighted classifiers in the global model therefore other classifiers have to be removed from the global model. The number of classifiers kept in the population is equal to the predefined size of the global model. In the MVM, the classifiers which are above the threshold value are kept in the global model, other classifiers which are less than the threshold value must be removed from the global model. The size of SCM is bigger than those of all other methods and the accuracy of the global model also comparatively better.

In the 11 multiplexer problems, centralized accuracy and distributed accuracy are almost similar in both experiments. In the first experiment monks 3 problem centralized testing accuracy and distributed testing accuracy are similar, but in the second experiment centralized testing accuracy is better than the distributed testing accuracy.

Four main disadvantages of the CDM are: i, ii) the communication and computation are higher; iii) less privacy of local data; and iv) the cost of implementation is higher. The communicational cost of CDM is always higher because CDM has to send huge amount of data from each distributed site to the central repository. Collected data in the central repository would be very large therefore the computational cost of the CDM would be higher (M. F. Santos, et al, 2010). There is some privacy issue to send private data of each branch of the organization to central repository. Another constraint is that the cost of implementation would be higher because the CDM requires high bandwidth communicational channel for sending huge sized data, also very large sized storage repository is required in the central repository because central repository has to store a large size of data for centralized data mining. On the other hand, the DDM only needs to send the local models from the distributed sites to the global site. The local model size would be very smaller than the size of the processed data therefore the communicational cost is less. Data mining is applied in every node in the distributed sites hence the computational cost of DDM would be less than the computational cost of the CDM. In DDM, there is no privacy issue because in DDM system doesn't need to send data to central repository also the cost of implementation is less because there is no need of high bandwidth communicational channel and large size of storage device in the central repository. The main advantage of CDM is that the global model of the centralized method represents the whole data set. So the global model generated by the centralized method is more general than the global model generated from the distributed method.

6. Conclusions and future work

The main objective of this work is to find the benefits of the DDM relative to the CDM. Above sections describe the benefits of the DDM, such as less implementation cost, less communication cost, less computation cost, and no privacy issue. In addition to these benefits, the accuracy of the global model in the DDM and the CDM are almost similar, which means that we can change from CDM to DDM without losing accuracy. Therefore, this work shows that DDM is the best method for implementing data mining in a distributed environment.

Constructing and optimizing the global model was the second objective of this work that describes and test four different strategies. The strategies of SCM and WCM achieved accuracies that are close to those of CDM. Among those four strategies, GCM performed worse.

The results also show that the size of the training data affect the quality of the models in the Gridclass system.

Future work will address testing of bigger size of real world data. The communication and computational cost of DDM and CDM would be included in the study for better understanding of the performance of those two methods. Likewise further work would also include more dynamic strategies to induced global model from the distributed local learning model.

7. Acknowledgment

The authors would like to express their gratitudes to FCT (Foundation of Science and Technology, Portugal), for the financial support through the contract GRID/GRI/81736/2006.

8. References

A. Orriols-Puig, A Further Look at UCS Classifier System. *GECCO'06, Seattle, Washington, USA*, 2006.

A. Orriols, EsterBernado-Mansilla, Class Imbalance Problem in UCS Classifier System: Fitness Adaptation..,*Evolutionary Computation, 2005. The 2005 IEEE congress on*, 604-611 Vol.1 2005.

A. Orriols, EsterBernado-Mansilla, Class Imbalance Problem in Learning Classifier System: A Preliminary study. *GECCO'05 Washington DC, USA, ACM* 1-59593-097-3/05 2006, 2006

A. Meligy, M. Al-Khatib, A Grid-Based Distributed SVM Data Mining Algorithm. *European Journal of Scientific Research* ISSN 1450-216X, Vol.27, No.3, pp313-321, 2009.

C. Clifton, M. Kantarcioglu, J. Vaidya, X. Lin, M. Y. Zhu, Tool for Privacy Preserving Distributed Data Mining. *Sigkdd Explorations* volume 4, 2002.

G. Brown., T. Kovacs., J. Marshall., UCSpv: Principled Voting in UCS Rule Populations. *GECCO 2007, Genetic and Evolutionary Computation Conference proceeding of the 9th annual conference on Genetic evolutionary computation*, 2007.

H. H. Dam, A scalable Evolutionary Learning Classifier System for Knowledge Discovery in Stream Data Mining, *M.Sci. University of Western Australia, Australia, B.Sci. (Hons) Curtin University of Technology, Australia. Thesis work* 2008.

H. Lu., E. Pi., Q. Peng., L. Wang., C. Zhang.,: A particle swarm optimization-aided fuzzy cloud classifier applied for plant numerical taxonomy based on attribute similarity. *Expert system with applications,* volume 36, pages 9388-9397 (2009).

I. Foster, The Anatomy of the Grid: Enabling Scalable Virtual Organizations, *1st International Symposium on Cluster Computing and the Grid* (CCGRID'01), Brisbane, Australia, IEEE.

J. H. Holmes., P. L.. Lanzi., S. W. Wilson., W. Stolzmunn., Learning Classification System: New Models Successful Applications., *Information Processing Letters,* 82 (23- 30), 2002.

J. Luo, M. Wang, J. Hu, Z. Shi, Distributed data mining on Agent Grid: Issues, Platform and development toolkit. *Future Generation computer system* 23, 61-68, 2007.

K. Shafi, T. Kovacs, H. A. Abbass, W. Zhu, Intrusion detection with evolutionary learning classifier system. *Springer Science+ Business Media B. V.* 2007.

M. F. Santos, W. Mathew, T. Kovacs, H. Santos, A grid data mining architecture for learning classifier system. *WSEAS TRANSACTIONS on COMPUTERS* Volume 8, ISSN: 1109-2750 2009.

M. F. Santos, W. Mathew, H. Santos, GridClass: Strategies for Global Vs Centralized Model Construction in Grid Data Mining. *Workshop on Ubiquitous Data Mining, Artificial Intelligence (ECAI2010), in Portugal,* 2010.

M. F. Santos, H. Quintela, J. Neves, Agent-Based learning Classifier System for Grid Data Mining. . *GECCO, Seattle, WA, USA* 2006.

M. F. Santos. Learning Classifier System in Distributed environments, *University of Minho School of Engineering Department of Information System. PhD Thesis work* 1999.

M.Cannataro, A. Congiusta, A. Pugliese, D.Talia, P. Trunfio, Distributed Data Mining on Grid: Services, Tools, and Applications. *IEEE TRANSACTIONS ON SYSTEM, MAN, AND CYBERNETICS- PART B: CYBETNETICS,* VOL. 34 NO6, DECEMBER 2004.

M. Plantie., M. Roche., G. Dray., P. Poncelet.,: Is voting Approach Accurate for Opinion Mining? Proceedings of the 10th international conference on Data Warehousing and Knowledge Discovery 2008.

M. Vilas-Bous, M. F. Santos, F. Portela, A. Silva, F. Rua, Hourly prediction of organ failure and outcome in intensive care based on data mining techniques. *ICEIS 2010 conference,* 2010.

M. Y. Santos., A. Moreira., Automatic Classification of Location Contexts with Decision Tree. *Proceeding of the Conference on Mobile and Ubiquitius System,* 2006.

N. Zhang, H. Bao, Researchon Distributed Data Technology Based on Grid. *First International Workshop on Database Technology and Applications* 2009.

T. Kovacs, Strength or Accuracy: Credit Assignment in Learning Classifier Systems. Distinguished Dissertation,. *Springer-Verlag London limited, page 26,* 2004.

V. Stankovski, M. Swain, V. Kravtsov, T. Niessen, D. Wegener, J. Kindermann, W. Dubitzky, Grid-enabling data mining applications with DataMiningGrid: An Architectural perspective. *Future Generation Computer System*24, 256- 279, 2008.

Part 2

New Data Analysis Techniques

15

A New Multi-Viewpoint and Multi-Level Clustering Paradigm for Efficient Data Mining Tasks

Jean-Charles LAMIREL,
LORIA, Campus Scientifique,
France

1. Introduction

Data mining or knowledge discovery in database (KDD) refers to the non-trivial process of discovering interesting, implicit, and previously unknown knowledge from databases. Such a task implies to be able to perform analyses both on high-dimensional input data and large dataset. The most popular models used in KDD are the symbolic models. Unfortunately, these models suffer of very serious limitations. Rule generation is a highly time-consuming process that generates a huge number of rules, including a large ratio of redundant rules. Hence, this prohibits any kind of rule computation and selection as soon as data are numerous and they are represented by very high-dimensional description space. This latter situation is very often encountered with documentary data. To cope with these problems, preliminary KDD trials using numerical models have been made. An algorithm for knowledge extraction from self-organizing network has been proposed in [8]. This approach is based on a supervised generalized relevance learning vector quantization (GRLVQ) which is used for extracting decision trees. The different paths of the generated trees are then used for denoting rules. Nevertheless, the main defect of this method is to necessitate training data. On our own side, we have proposed a hybrid classification method for mapping an explicative structure issued from a symbolic classification into an unsupervised numerical self-organizing map (SOM) [15]. SOM map and Galois lattice are generated on the same data. The cosine projection is then used for associating lattice concepts to the SOM classes. Concepts properties act as explanation for the SOM classes. Furthermore, lattice pruning combined with migration of the associated SOM classes towards the top of the pruned lattice is used to generate explanation of increasing scope on the SOM map. Association rules can also be produced in such a way. Although it establishes interesting links between numerical and symbolic worlds this approach necessitates the time-consuming computation of a whole Galois lattice. In a parallel way, in order to enhance both the quality and the granularity of the data analysis and to reduce the noise which is inevitably generated in an overall classification approach, we have introduced the multi-viewpoint analysis and multi-level clustering approach based on a significant extension of the SOM model, named MultiSOM [19][25]. The viewpoint building principle consists in separating the description of the data into several sub-descriptions corresponding different property subsets or even different data subsets. In MultiSOM each viewpoint is represented by a single SOM map.

The conservation of an overall view of the analysis is achieved through the use of a communication mechanism between the maps, which is itself based on Bayesian inference [1]. The advantage of the multi-viewpoint analysis provided by MultiSOM as compared to the global analysis provided by SOM [11][12] has been clearly demonstrated for precise mining tasks like patent analysis [19]. Another important mechanism provided by the MultiSOM model is its on-line generalization mechanism that can be used to tune the level of precision of the analysis. Furthermore, using free topology clustering methods like the method of the Neural Gas family [23] or those of the K-means family [22] as a new basis, we have proposed in [2] to extent the MultiSOM model into a more general multi-viewpoint and multi-level clustering paradigm, named Multi-Viewpoints Data Analysis (MVDA). The main advantage of the new MDVA paradigm it that it can imbed various clustering methods which might well prove more efficient than SOM model for classification tasks where explicit visualization of the clustering results is not required. Hence, thanks to the loss of topographic constraints as compared to SOM, the free topology clustering methods, like K-means, Neural Gas or its extensions, like Growing Neural Gas (GNG) [7], Incremental Growing Neural Gas (IGNG) [26], or Improved Incremental Growing Neural Gas (I_2GNG) [9], tends to better represent the structure of the data, yielding generally better clustering results [2].

In this chapter we will propose a new approach for knowledge extraction that consists in using the MVDA paradigm as a front-end for efficiently extracting association rules in the context large datasets constituted by high-dimensional data. In our approach we exploit both the generalization and the intercommunication mechanisms of our new paradigm. We also make use of our original recall and precision measures that derive from the Galois lattice theory and from Information Retrieval (IR) domains. The first introduces the notion of association rules. The second section presents the MVDA model. The third section gives an overview of the specific clustering quality criteria that are used in our approach. The fourth section presents the rule extraction principles based both on the MVDA model and on the formerly presented quality criteria. The experiment that is presented on the last section shows how our method can be used both to control the rules inflation that is inherent to symbolic methods and for extracting the most significant rules.

2. The symbolic model and association rules extraction

The symbolic approach to Database Contents Analysis is mostly based on the Galois lattice model [30]. A Galois lattice, *L(D,P)*, is a conceptual hierarchy built on a set of data *D* which are described by a set of properties *P* also called the intention (Intent) of the concept of the lattice. A class of the hierarchy, also called a "formal concept", is defined as a pair *C=(d,p)* where *d* denotes the extension (Extent) of the concept, i.e. a subset of *D*, and *p* denotes the intention of the concept, i.e. a subset of *P*. The lattice structure implies that it exists a partial order on a lattice such that:

$$\forall C_1, C_2 \in L, C_1 \Leftrightarrow \text{Extent}(C_1) \subseteq \text{Extent}(C_2) \Leftrightarrow \text{Intent}(C_1) \supseteq \text{Intent}(C_2)$$

Association rules are one of the basic types of knowledge that can be extracted from large databases. Given a database, the problem of mining association rules consists in generating all association rules that have some user-specified minimum support and confidence. An association rule is an expression $A \to B$ where A and B are conjunctions of properties. It means that if an individual data possesses all the properties of A then he necessarily possesses all the properties of B as regard to the studied dataset[1]. The support $supp(A \cup B)$ of the rule is equivalent to the number of individuals of the verifying both properties A and B, and the confidence $conf(A \cup B)$ is given by: $conf(A \cup B) = supp(A \cup B)/supp(A)$. An approach proposed by [28] shows that a subset of association rules can be obtained by following the direct links of heritage between the concepts in the Galois lattice. Even if no satisfactory solution regarding the rule computation time have been found, an attempt to solve the rule selection problem by combining rules evaluation measures is described in [3].

3. The MVDA model

In [13][14], Lamirel and al. firstly introduced the dynamic cooperation between clustering models in the context of information retrieval. This new approach has been originally used for analyzing the relevance of user's queries regarding the documentary database contents. It represents a major amelioration of the basic clustering approach. From a practical point of view, the *MultiView Data Analysis paradigm* (MVDA), introduces the use of viewpoints associated with the one of unsupervised Bayesian reasoning in the clustering process. Its main advantage is to be a generic paradigm that can be applied to any clustering method and that permits to enhance the quality and the granularity of data analysis while suppressing the noise that is inherent to a global approach.
The principle of the MVDA paradigm is thus to be constituted by several clustering models which have been generated from the same data or even from data that share the same overall description space. Each model is issued from a specific viewpoint and can be generated by any clustering method. The relation between the models is established through the use of an inter-models communication mechanism relying itself on unsupervised Bayesian reasoning.
The inter-models communication mechanism enables to highlight semantic relationships between different topics (i.e. clusters) belonging to different viewpoints related to the same data or even to the same data description space. In the MDVA context, this communication is based on the use of the information that can be shared by the different clustering models, like data associated to clusters or labels associated to their descriptions (see Fig. 1).
The inter-models communication is established by standard Bayesian inference network propagation algorithm which is used to compute the posterior probabilities of target model's nodes (i.e. clusters) T_k which inherited of the activity (evidence Q) transmitted by their associated data or descriptor nodes. This computation can be carried out efficiently because of the specific Bayesian inference network topology that is associated to the set of models by the MVDA paradigm [1]. Hence, it is possible to compute the probability $P(ac_m t \mid t_k, Q)$ for an activity of modality act_m on the model node t_k which is inherited from activities generated on the source model. This computation is achieved as follows:

$$P(act_m|t_k,Q) = \frac{\sum_{d \in act_m, t_k} Sim(d,s_d)}{\sum_{d \in t_k} Sim(d,s_d)} \quad (1)$$

such that s_d is the source node to which the data d has been associated, $Sim(d, s_d)$ is the cosine correlation measure between the description vector of the data d and the one of its source

[1] An association rule cannot be considered as a logical implication, because his validity directly depends on the dataset from which it is extracted.

node s_d and $d \in act_m, t_k$, if it has been activated with the positive or negative modality act_m from the source model.
The nodes of the target model getting the highest probabilities can be considered as the ones who include the topics sharing the strongest relationships with the topics belonging to the activated nodes of the source model.
One of the richness of this paradigm is that there are very various ways to define viewpoints. One possible way consists in separating the description space of the data into different subspaces corresponding to different criteria of analysis. As an example, an image can be simultaneously described using 3 different viewpoints represented by: (1) a keyword vector; (2) colour histogram vector; (3) a feature vector. A multi-view analysis that is performed on such data can thus highlight the most interesting correspondences between the domains of colours, shapes and image topics while letting the opportunity to figure out specific relationships existing inside each specific domain.

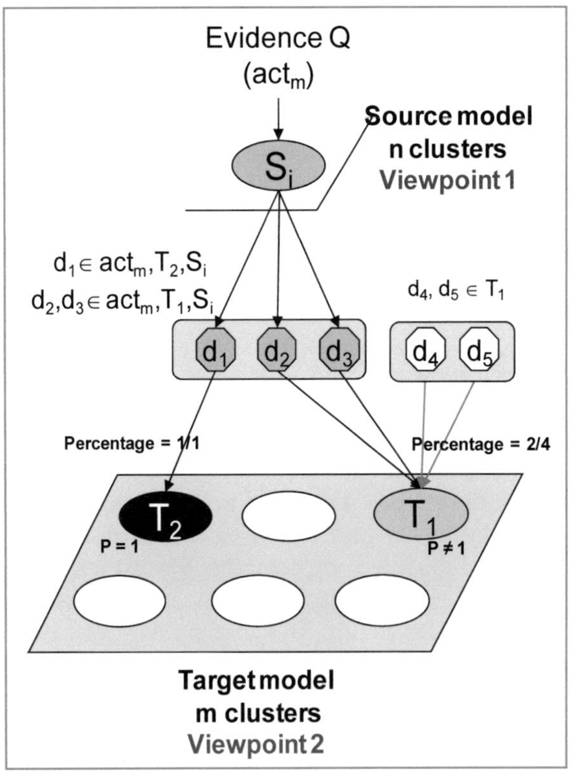

Fig. 1. The MVDA inter-models communication principle.

The relation between maps is established through the use of two main mechanisms: the inter-maps communication mechanism presented formerly and the generalization mechanism that we present hereafter.
The main roles of the MVDA generalization mechanism are both to evaluate the coherency of the topics that have been computed on an original clustering model and to summarize the contents of this later into more generic topics with the advantage of avoiding applying any further learning process. Our generalization mechanism [2] creates its specific link structure

in which each node of a given level is linked to its 2-nearest neighbours (see Fig. 2). For each new level node n the following description vector computation applies:

$$W_n^{M+1} = \frac{1}{3}\left(W_n^M + \sum_{n_k \in V_n^M} W_{n_k}^M \right) \tag{2}$$

where $V_n{}^M$ represents the 2-nearest neighbour nodes of the node n on the level M associated to the cluster n of the new generated level $M+1$.

After description vectors computation, the repeated nodes of the new level (i.e. the nodes of the new level that share the same description vector) are summarized into a single node. Our generalization mechanism can be considered as an implicit and distributed form of a hierarchical clustering method based on neighbourhood reciprocity [21]. Existing clustering algorithms, such as growing hierarchical self-organizing map (GHSOM) [24], represents a dynamically growing architecture which evolves into a descending hierarchical structure. Nevertheless, the weak point of such methods is to isolate lower level models without regards to their potential links with the other levels. As opposed, our generalization method has the advantage of preserving the original neighbourhood structure between nodes on the new generated levels. Moreover, we have shown in [2] that this method produces more homogeneous results than the classical training approach which should be repeated at each level, while significantly reducing time consumption. Lastly, the inter-model communication mechanism presented in the former section can be used on a given viewpoint between a clustering model and its generalizations as soon as they share the same projected data.

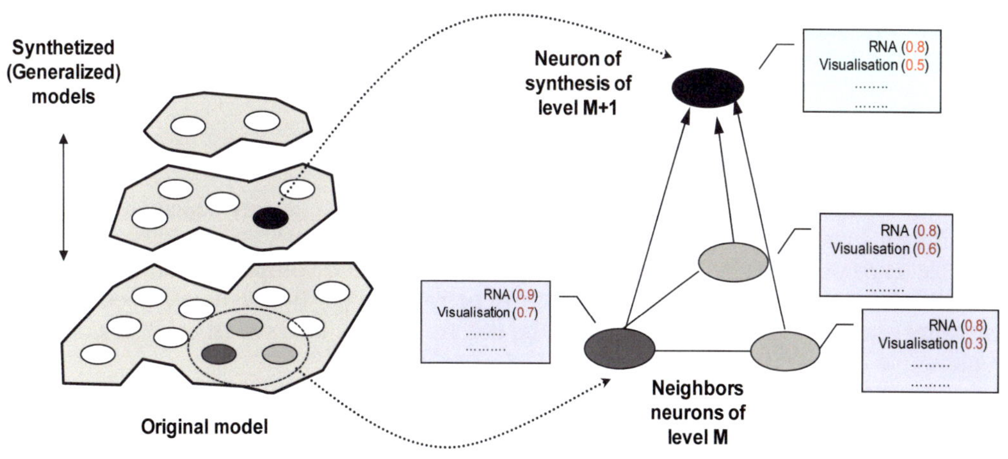

Fig. 2. MVDA generalization mechanism applied on a Neural Gas clustering model (2D representation of gas is used only for the sake of clarity of the figure)

The MVDA paradigm has been chosen as one of the two reference approaches of the IST-EISCTES European project [6]. Its most recent version has opened new perspectives for automatic link analysis in webometrics by allowing to automatically combining referencing and textual information [18]. In section 4, we show this model can be exploited for efficient rule extraction. Our association rule extraction approach makes use of this model in combination with specific clustering quality indexes that we present in the next section.

4. Quality of classification model

When anyone aims at comparing clustering methods, or even evaluating clustering results, he will be faced with the problem of choice of reliable clustering quality indexes. The classical evaluation indexes for the clustering quality are based on the intra-cluster inertia and the inter-cluster inertia [4] [5][21]. Thanks to these two indexes, a clustering result is considered as good if it possesses low intra-cluster inertia as compared to its inter-cluster inertia. However, as it has been shown in [17], the distance based indexes are often strongly biased[2] and highly dependent on the clustering method. They cannot thus be easily used for comparing different methods, or even different clustering results issued from data whose description spaces have different sizes. Moreover, as it has been also shown in [Ka], they are often properly unable to identify an optimal clustering model whenever the dataset is constituted by complex data that must be represented in a both highly multidimensional and sparse description space, as it is often the case with textual data. To cope with such problems, our own approach takes its inspiration both from the behavior of symbolic classifiers and from the evaluation principles used in Information Retrieval. Our Recall/Precision and F-measures indexes exploit the properties of the data associated to each cluster after the clustering process without prior consideration of clusters profiles [17]. Their main advantage is thus to be independent of the clustering methods and of their operating mode.

In IR, the **Recall *R*** represents the ratio between the number of relevant documents which have been returned by an IR system for a given query and the total number of relevant documents which should have been found in the documentary database [27]. The **Precision *P*** represents the ratio between the number of relevant documents which have been returned by an IR system for a given query and the total number of documents returned for the said query. **Recall** and **Precision** generally behave in an antagonist way: as **Recall** increases, **Precision** decreases, and conversely. The ***F*** function has thus been proposed in order to highlight the best compromise between these two values [29].

It is given by:

$$F = \frac{2(R * P)}{R + P} \tag{3}$$

Based on the same principles, the *Recall* and *Precision* quality indexes which we introduce hereafter evaluate the quality of a clustering method in an unsupervised way[3] by measuring the relevance of the clusters content in terms of shared properties. In our further descriptions, a cluster's content is supposed to be represented by the data associated with this latter after the clustering process and the descriptors (i.e. the properties) of the data are supposed to be weighted by values within the range [0,1].

Let us consider a set of clusters C resulting from a clustering method applied on a set of data *D*, the local *Recall* (Rec) and *Precision* (Prec) indexes for a given property *p* of the cluster *c* can be expressed as:

$$\underset{c}{\text{Rec}}(p) = \frac{|c_p^*|}{|D_p^*|}, \quad \underset{c}{\text{Prec}}(p) = \frac{|c_p^*|}{|c|} \tag{4}$$

---

[2] A bias can occur when the intrinsic dimensions of the obtained clusters (number of non-zero components in the reference vectors describing the clusters) are not of the same order of magnitude than the intrinsic dimensions of the data profiles (see [17] for more details).

[3] Conversely to classical **Recall** and **Precision** indexes that are supervised.

where the notation X^*_p represents the restriction of the set X to the set members having the property p.
Fig. 3 illustrates the basic principle of the new unsupervised **Recall** and **Precision** indexes that have been formerly presented.

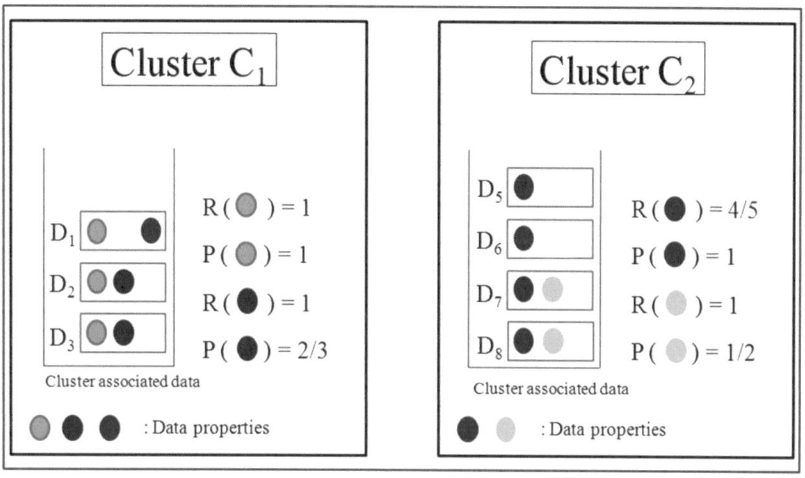

Fig. 3. Principle of Recall(R)-Precision(P) quality indexes
(in this example, for the sake of simplicity data are considered to have Boolean properties).

Then, for estimating the overall clustering quality, the averaged **Recall** (R) and **Precision** (P) indexes can be expressed as:

$$R = \frac{1}{|\bar{C}|}\sum_{c\in\bar{C}}\frac{1}{S_c}\sum_{p\in S_c}\underset{c}{\text{Rec}}(p)\,,\quad P = \frac{1}{|\bar{C}|}\sum_{c\in\bar{C}}\frac{1}{S_c}\sum_{p\in S_c}\underset{c}{\text{Prec}}(p) \tag{5}$$

where S_c is the set of properties which are peculiar to the cluster c that is described as:

$$S_c = \left\{ p \in d,\, d \in c \,\middle|\, \overline{W}^p_c = \underset{c' \in C}{Max}\left(\overline{W}^p_{c'}\right) \right\} \tag{6}$$

where $\bar{C}$ represents the peculiar set of clusters extracted from the clusters of C, which verifies:

$\bar{C}$ verifies
$$\bar{C} = \left\{ c \in C \,\middle|\, S_c \neq \varnothing \right\} \tag{7}$$

and:
$$\overline{W}^p_c = \frac{\sum_{d\in c} W^p_d}{\sum_{c'\in C}\sum_{d\in c'} W^p_d}$$

where W^p_x represents the weight of the property p for element x.

Similarly to IR, the **F-measure** (described by Eq. 3) could be used to combine averaged **Recall** and **Precision** results. Moreover, we demonstrate in Annex A that if both values of

averaged **Recall** and **Precision** reach the unity value, the peculiar set of clusters C represents a Galois lattice. Therefore, the combination of this two measures enables to evaluate to what extent a numerical clustering model can be assimilated to a Galois lattice natural classifier. The stability of our **Quality** criteria has also been demonstrated in [20].
Macro-Recall and *Macro-Precision* indexes defined by (Eq. 5) can be considered as cluster-oriented measures because they provide average values of *Recall* and *Precision* for each cluster. They have opposite behaviors according to the number of clusters. Thus, these indexes permit to estimate in a global way an optimal number of clusters for a given method and a given dataset. The best data partition, or clustering result, is in this case the one which minimizes the difference between their values (see Fig. 4).

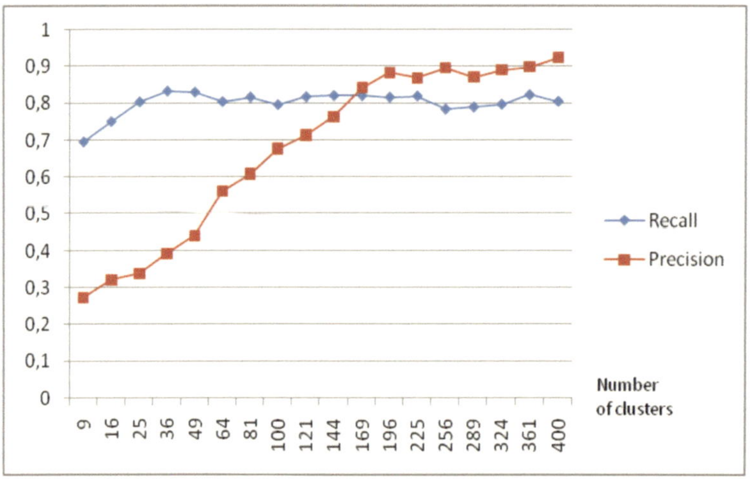

Fig. 4. Evolution of quality criteria for optimal clustering model detection. The optimal model is found at the break-even point between the Recall and Precision quality indexes, letting varying the number of clusters. Here the optimal clustering model is obtained at 169 clusters.

5. Rules extraction from a MultiGAS model

An elaborated unsupervised clustering model, like a MultiGAS model, which represents itself an extension of the Neural Gas model relying on the MDVA paradigm, is a natural candidate to cope with the related problems of rule inflation, rule selection and computation time that are inherent to symbolic methods. Hence, its synthesis capabilities that can be used both for reducing the number of rules and for extracting the most significant ones. In the knowledge extraction task, the generalization mechanism can be specifically used for controlling the number of extracted association rules. The intercommunication mechanism will be useful for highlighting association rules figuring out relationships between topics belonging to different viewpoints.

5.1 Rules extraction by the generalization mechanism

We will rely on our local cluster quality criteria (see Eq. 4) for extracting rules from the classes of the original gas and its generalizations. For a given class c, the general form of the extraction algorithm (**A1**) follows:

$\forall p_1, p_2 \in P_c^*$
1. ***If*** (Rec(p_1) = Rec(p_2) = Prec(p_1) = Prec(p_2) = 1) ***Then***: $p_1 \leftrightarrow p_2$ (equivalence rule)
2. ***ElseIf*** (Rec(p_1) = Rec(p_2) = Prec(p_2) = 1) ***Then***: $p_1 \rightarrow p_2$
3. ***ElseIf*** (Rec(p_1) = Rec(p_2) = 1) ***Then***
   If (Extent(p_1) $\subset$ Extent(p_2)) ***Then***: $p_1 \rightarrow p_2$
   If (Extent(p_2) $\subset$ Extent(p_1)) ***Then***: $p_2 \rightarrow p_1$
   If (Extent(p_1) $\equiv$ Extent(p_2)) ***Then***: $p_1 \leftrightarrow p_2$

$\forall p_1 \in P_c^*$, $\forall p_2 \in P_c - P_c^*$
4. ***If*** (Rec(p_1) = 1) ***If*** (Extent(p_1) $\subset$ Extent(p_2)) ***Then***: $p_1 \rightarrow p_2$ (*)

where Prec and Rec respectively represent the local *Precision* and *Recall* measures, Extent(p) represents the extension of the property p (i.e. the list of data to which the property p is associated), and P_c^* represent the set of peculiar properties of the class c.
The optional step 4) (*) can be used for extracting **extended rules**. For **extended rules**, the constraint of peculiarity is not applied to the most general property. Hence, the extension of this latter property can include data being outside of the scope of the current class c.

5.2 Rules extraction by the inter-gas communication mechanism

A complementary extraction strategy consists in making use of the extraction algorithm in combination with the principle of communication between viewpoints for extracting rules. The general form of the extraction algorithm (**A2**) between two viewpoints v_1 and v_2 will be:

$\forall p_1 \in P_c^*$, $\forall p_2 \in P_{c'}^*$ and $c \in v_1$, $c' \in v_2$
1. ***If*** (Rec(p_1) = Rec(p_2) = Prec(p_1) = Prec(p_2) = 1) ***Then*** *Test_Rule_Type;*
2. ***ElseIf*** (Rec(p_1) = Rec(p_2) = Prec(p_2) = 1) ***Then*** *Test_Rule_Type;*
3. ***ElseIf*** (Rec(p_1) = Rec(p_2) = Prec(p_1) = 1) ***Then*** *Test_Rule_Type;*
4. ***ElseIf*** (Rec(p_1) = Rec(p_2) = 1) ***Then*** *Test_Rule_Type;*

where *Test_Rule_Type* procedure is expressed as:

1. ***If*** (Extent$_{v1}$(p_1) $\subset$ Extent$_{v2}$(p_2)) ***Then***: $p_1 \rightarrow p_2$
2. ***If*** (Extent$_{v2}$(p_2) $\subset$ Extent$_{v1}$(p_1)) ***Then***: $p_2 \rightarrow p_1$
3. ***If*** (Extent$_{v1}$(p_1) $\equiv$ Extent$_{v2}$(p_2)) ***Then***: $p_1 \leftrightarrow p_2$

Extended rules will be obtained as:

a. $\forall p_1 \in P_c^*$, $\forall p_2 \in P_{c'}$: Substituting respectively Rec(p_2) and Prec(p_2) by the *viewpoint-based measures* Rec$_{v1}$(p_2) and Prec$_{v1}$(p_2), related to the source viewpoint, in the previous algorithm.
b. $\forall p_1 \in P_c$, $\forall p_2 \in P_{c'}^*$: Substituting respectively Rec(p_1) and Prec(p_1) by the *viewpoint-based measures* Rec$_{v2}$(p_1) and Prec$_{v2}$(p_1), related to the destination viewpoint, in the previous algorithm.

6. Experimental results

Our test database is a database of 1000 patents that has been used in some of our preceding experiments [19]. For the viewpoint-oriented approach the structure of the patents has been parsed in order to extract four different subfields corresponding to four different viewpoints: **Use, Advantages, Patentees** and **Titles**. As it is full text, the content of the textual fields of the patents associated with the different viewpoints is parsed by a standard lexicographic analyzer

in order to extract viewpoint specific indexes. The obtained indexes are then normalized by an expert of the patent domain. Table 1 summarizes the results of the indexing phase.
Each of our experiments is initiated with optimal gases generated by means of an optimization algorithm based on our quality criteria [17] (see also Fig. 4). In a first step, original optimal gases are generated for all the viewpoints. In a second step, generalized gases are generated for each viewpoint by applying successive steps of generalization on the original optimal gases. The results of these two steps are summarized in Table 2.
Our first experiment consists in extracting rules from each single viewpoint. Both the original gases and their generalizations are used for extracting the rules. The algorithm is first used without its optional step, and a second time including this step (for more details, see Algorithm A1). The overall results of rule extraction are presented in Table 3.
Some examples of extracted rules related to each viewpoint are given hereafter:

- *Refrigerator oil* → *Gear oil* (supp = 7, conf = 100%) (Use)
- *Wide viscosity range* → *Thermal and oxidative stability* (supp = 3, conf = 100%) (Advantages)
- *Surfactant system* → *Calcium* (supp = 7, conf = 100%) (Title)
- *Infineum* → *Hexxon* (supp = 10, conf = 100%) (Patentees)

	Use	Advantages	Patentees	Titles
Number of indexed documents	745	624	1000	1000
Number of rough indexes generated	252	231	73	605
Number of final indexes (after normalization)	234	207	32	589

Table 1. **Summary of the patent indexation process.** Some remarks must be made concerning the results shown in this table. (1). The index count of the **Titles** field is significantly higher than the other ones. Indeed, the information contained in the patent titles is both of higher sparseness and of higher diversity than in the **Use** and **Advantages** fields. (2) The number of final patentees has been significantly reduced by grouping the small companies in the same general index. (3) Only 62% of the patents have aN **Advantages** field, and 75% an **Use** field. Consequently, some of the patents will not be indexed for these viewpoints.

	Original level: Optimal	**Generalized levels**												
		1	**2**	**3**	**4**	**5**	**6**	**7**	**8**	**9**	**10**	**11**	**12**	**13**
Use	100	79	62	50	40	31	26	16	11	-	-	-	-	-
Advantages	121	100	83	75	64	53	44	34	28	23	18	13	-	-
Patentees	49	31	24	19	16	12								
Titles	144	114	111	105	95	83	71	59	46	35	27	22	18	14

Table 2. **Summary of the gas generation process.** For all viewpoints, the generalization limit has been fixed to levels that have more than 10 neurons. Hence, for a given viewpoint, the number of generalization levels depends both on the initial count of neurons of its associated optimal gas and on the homogeneity of the data distribution relatively to this viewpoint.

For evaluating the complexity of our algorithm based on a numerical approach, as compared to a symbolic approach, we use following efficiency factor (EF) computation:

$$EF = (RC * MLC) / (MRC * LC) \tag{9}$$

where RC=rules count, MRC=maximum rules count (symbolic), LC=loops count, MLC=maximum loop count (symbolic).
A global summary of the results is given in Table 3. Said table includes a comparison of our extraction algorithm with a standard symbolic rule extraction method as regards to the amount of extracted rules. In single viewpoint experiment, when our extraction algorithm is used with its optional step, it is able to extract a significant ratio of the rules that can be extracted by a classical symbolic model basically using a combinatory approach. In some case, such as the **Patentees** viewpoint, all the rules of 100% confidence can be extracted from a single level of the gas (see Fig. 9). Alternatively, as in the case of the **Use** viewpoint, the combination of gas levels of the same viewpoint can be used for extracting all the rules of 100% confidence (see Table 3 and Fig. 6). The worse extraction performance is obtained with the **Titles** viewpoint. This relatively low performance (58% of rules of 100% confidence extracted using all the gas levels) can be explained both by the higher sparseness and by the higher diversity of the data related to this viewpoint. Nevertheless, it is compensated by the much better extraction efficiency, as compared to the symbolic model. Moreover, in the case of this viewpoint, the extracted rules have an average support which is higher than the average support of the overall rule set (see Table 3 and Fig. 10).
Even if no rule selection is performed when the extraction algorithm is used with its optional step, the main advantage of this version of the algorithm, as compared to a classical symbolic method, is the computation time. As a matter of fact, the computation time is significantly reduced, since our algorithm is class-based. Moreover, generally speaking, the lower the generalization level, the more specialized will be the classes, and hence, the lower will be the combinatory effect during computation (see Fig. 6,7,8, 9 and 10). Another interesting result is the behaviour of our extraction algorithm when it is used without its optional step. Fig. 7 shows that, in this case, a rule selection process that depends on the generalization level is performed: the higher the generalization level, the more rules will be extracted. We have already done some extension of our algorithm in order to search for partial rules. Complementary results showed us that, even if this extension is used, no partial rules will be extracted in the low level of generalization when no optional step is used. This tends to prove that the standard version of our algorithm is able to naturally perform rule selection.
Our second experiment consists in extracting rules using the intercommunication mechanism between the Use and the Advantage viewpoints. The communication is achieved between the original gas of each viewpoint, and furthermore, between the same levels of generalization of each viewpoint (see Fig. 5). For each single communication step the extraction algorithm is applied is a bidirectional way.
Some examples of extracted rules are given hereafter:

- *Natural oil* (Advantages) $\rightarrow$ *Catapult oil* (Use) (supp = 8, conf = 100%)
- *Natural oil* (Advantages) $\rightarrow$ *Drilling fluid* (Use) (supp = 8, conf = 100%)

The results of our multi-viewpoint experiment are similar to the ones of our single viewpoint experiment (see Table 3). A rule selection process is performed when the standard version of our algorithm is used. The maximum extraction performance is obtained when *viewpoint-based Recall* and *viewpoint-based Precision* viewpoint are used (see Algorithm A2).

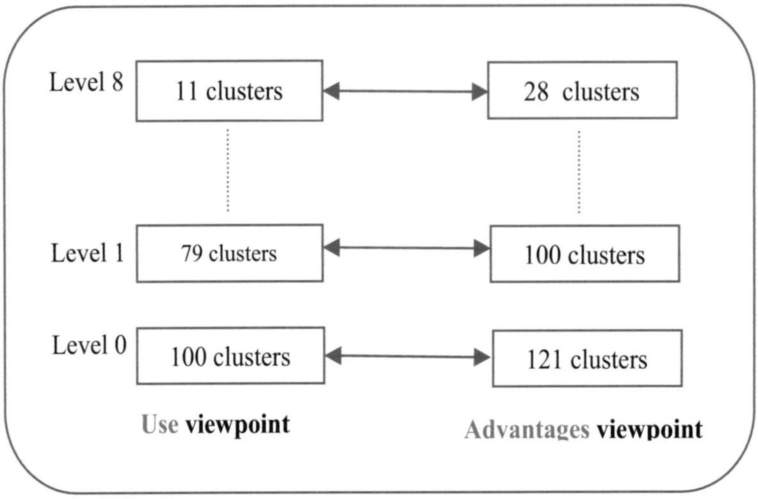

Fig. 5. **Overview of the communication process.** For the generalization process, only 9 levels have been used for both viewpoints, starting at level 0 from the optimal gases.

		Patentees	Titles	Use	Advantages	Use ↔ Advantages
Symbolic model	Total rule count	12	2326	536	404	649
	Average confidence	100%	100%	100%	100%	100%
	Average support	3.583	1.049	1.139	1.042	1.081
	Global rule count	26	4912	2238	1436	2822
	Average confidence	53%	59%	59%	44%	45%
MultiGAS model	Peculiar rule count	12	422	251	287	250
	Average confidence	100%	100%	100%	100%	100%
	Extended rule count	12	1358	536	319	642
	Average confidence	100%	100%	100%	100%	100%
	% of symbolic total	100%	58%	100%	79%	99%
	Average support	3.583	1.081	1.139	1.050	1.073

Table 3. **Summary of results.** The table presents a basic comparison between the standard symbolic rule extraction method and the MultiGAS-based rule extraction method. The global rule count defined for the symbolic model includes the count of partial rules (confidence<100%) and the count of total rules (confidence=100%). In our experiments, the rules generated by the MultiGAS model are only total rules. The peculiar rule count is the count of rules obtained with the standard versions of the extraction algorithms. The extended rule count is the count of rules obtained with the extended versions of the extraction algorithms including their optional steps.

7. Conclusion

In this paper we have proposed a new approach for knowledge extraction based on a MultiGAS model, which represents itself an extension of the Neural Gas model relying on the MDVA paradigm. Our approach makes use of original measures of unsupervised Recall and Precision for extracting rules from gases. Thanks to the MultiGAS model, our experiments have been conduced on single viewpoint classifications as well as between multiple viewpoints classifications on the same data. They take benefit of the generalization and the inter-gas communication mechanisms that are embedded in the MVDA paradigm. Even if complementary experiments must be done, our first results are very promising. They tend to prove that a clustering model, as soon as it is elaborated enough, represents a natural candidate to cope with the related problems of rule inflation, rule selection and computation time that are inherent to symbolic models. One of our perspectives is to more deeply develop our model in order to extract rules with larger context like the ones that can be obtained by the use of closed set in symbolic approaches. Another interesting perspective would be to adapt measures issued from information theory, like IDF or entropy, for ranking the rules. Furthermore, we plan to test our model on a reference dataset on genome. Indeed, these dataset has been already used for experiments of rule extraction and selection with symbolic methods. Lastly, our extraction approach can be applied in a straightforward way to a MultiSOM model, or even to a single SOM model, when overall visualization of the analysis results is required and less accuracy is needed.

8. References

[1] Al-Shehabi S., and Lamirel J.-C. (2004). Inference Bayesian Network for Multi-topographic neural network communication: a case study in documentary data. Proceedings of ICTTA, Damas, Syria, April 2004.

[2] Al Shehabi S., and Lamirel J.C. (2005). Multi-Topographic Neural Network Communication and Generalization for Multi-Viewpoint Analysis. International Joint Conference on Neural Networks - IJCNN'05, Montréal, Québec, Canada, August 2005.

[3] Bayardo Jr. R. J., and Agrawal R. (1999). Mining the most interesting rules. In Proc. of the 5th ACM SIGKDD Int'l Conf. on Knowledge Discovery and Data Mining, p.145-154, August 1999.

[4] Calinski T. and Harabasz J. (1974). A dendrite method for cluster analysis. Communications in Statistics, 3 (1974), 1–27.

[5] Davies D., and Bouldin W. (1979). A cluster separation measure. IEEE Trans. Pattern Anal. Machine Intell. 1 (1979) 224–227.

[6] François C., Hoffmann M., Lamirel J.-C., and Polanco X. (2003). Artificial Neural Network mapping experiments. EICSTES (IST-1999-20350) Final Report (WP 9.4), 86 p., September 2003.

[7] Frizke B. (1995). A growing neural gas network lerans topologies. Tesauro G., Touretzky D. S., leen T. K., Eds., Advances in neural Information processing Systems 7, pp 625-632, MIT Press, Cambridge MA.

[8] Hammer B., Rechtien A., Strickert M., and Villmann T. (2002). Rule extraction from self-organizing networks. ICANN, Springer, p. 877-882.

[9] Hamza H., Belaïd Y., Belaîd. A, and Chaudhuri B. B. (2008). Incremental classification of invoice documents. 19th International Conference on Pattern Recognition - ICPR 2008.

[10] Kassab R., and Lamirel J.-C., (2008). Feature Based Cluster Validation for High Dimensional Data. IASTED International Conference on Artificial Intelligence and Applications (AIA), Innsbruck, Austria, February 2008.

[11] Kaski S., Honkela T., Lagus K., and Kohonen, T. (1998). WEBSOM-self organizing maps of document collections, Neurocomputing, vol. 21, pp. 101-117.

[12] Kohonen T. (2001). Self-Organizing Maps. 3rd ed. Springer Verlag, Berlin.

[13] Lamirel J.-C., and Créhange M. (1994). Application of a symbolico-connectionist approach for the design of a highly interactive documentary database interrogation system with on-line learning capabilities. Proceedings ACM-CIKM 94, Gaitherburg, Maryland, USA, November 94.

[14] Lamirel J.C. (1995). Application d'une approche symbolico-connexionniste pour la conception d'un système documentaire hautement interactif. PhD Thesis, Université of Nancy 1, Henri Poincaré, Nancy, France.

[15] Lamirel J.C., Toussaint Y., and Al Shehabi S. (2003). A Hybrid Classification Method for Database Contents Analysis, FLAIRS 03 Conference, p. 286-292.

[16] Lamirel J.C., Al Shehabi S., Hoffmann M., and Francois C. (2003). Intelligent patent analysis through the use of a neural network : experiment of multi-viewpoint analysis with the MultiSOM model. Proceedings of ACL, Sapporo, Japan, p. 7-23.

[17] Lamirel J.C., Al Shehabi S., Francois C., and Hoffmann M. (2004). New classification quality estimators for analysis of documentary information: application to web mapping. Scientometrics, Vol. 60, No. 3, p. 445-462.

[18] Lamirel J.C., Al Shehabi S., François C., and Polanco X. (2004). Using a compound approach based on elaborated neural network for Webometrics: an example issued from the EICSTES Project. Scientometrics, Vol. 61, No. 3, p. 427-441.

[19] Lamirel J.-C., and Al Shehabi S. (2006). MultiSOM: a multiview neural model for accurately analyzing and mining complex data. Proceedings of the 4th International Conference on Coordinated & Multiple Views in Exploratory Visualization (CMV), London, UK, July 2006.

[20] Lamirel J.C., Ghribi M., and Cuxac P. (2010). Unsupervised Recall and Precision measures: a step towards new efficient clustering quality indexes. 19th International Conference on Computational Statistics (COMPSTAT'2010), Paris, France, August 2010.

[21] Lebart, L. , Morineau A., and Fénelon J. P. (1982). Traitement des données statistiques. Dunod, Paris, France.

[22] McQueen J.B. (1967). Some methods of classification and analysis of multivariate observations. L. Le Cam and J. Neyman (Eds.), Proc. 5th Berkeley Symposium in Mathematics, Statistics and Probability, Vol. 1: 281-297, Univ. of California, Berkeley, USA.

[23] Martinetz T., and Schulten K. (1991). A "neural-gas" network learns topologies. In T. Kohonen, K. Mäkisara, O. Simula, and J. Kangas, editors, Artificial neural networks, North-Holland, Amsterdam, p. 397-402.

[24] Ontrup J. and Ritter H. (2005). A hierarchically growing hyperbolic self-organizing map for rapid structuring of large data sets. In Proceedings of 5th Workshop On Self-Organizing Maps - WSOM 05, Paris 1 Panthéon-Sorbonne University.
[25] Polanco X., Lamirel, J.C., and François C. (2001). Using Artificial Neural Networks for Mapping of Science and technology: A Multi self-organizing maps Approach. Scientometrics, Vol. 51, N° 1, p. 267-292.
[26] Prudent Y., Ennaji A. (2005). An Incremental Growing Neural Gas learns Topology. ESANN2005, 13th European Symposium on Artificial Neural Networks, Bruges, Belgium, 27-29April 205, published in Neural Networks, 2005. IJCNN apos;05. Proceedings. 2005 IEEE International Joint Conference , vol. 2, no. 31 pp 1211 - 1216, July-4 Aug. 2005.
[27] Salton G. (1971). The SMART Retrieval System: Experiments in Automatic Document Processing, Prentice Hall Inc., Englewood Cliffs, New Jersey.
[28] Simon A., and Napoli A. (1999). Building Viewpoints in an Object-based Representation System for Knowledge Discovery in Databases. Proceedings of IRI'99, Atlanta, Geogia, S. Rubin editor, The International Society for Computers and Their Applications, ISCA, p. 104-108, 1999.
[29] Van Rijsbergen C. J. (1975). Information Retrieval. Butterworths, London, England, 1975.
[30] Wille R. (1982). Restructuring Lattice Theory: An Approach Based on Hierarchies of Concepts. In Ordered Sets, (I. Rival, ed.), D. Reidel: 1982, p. 445-470.

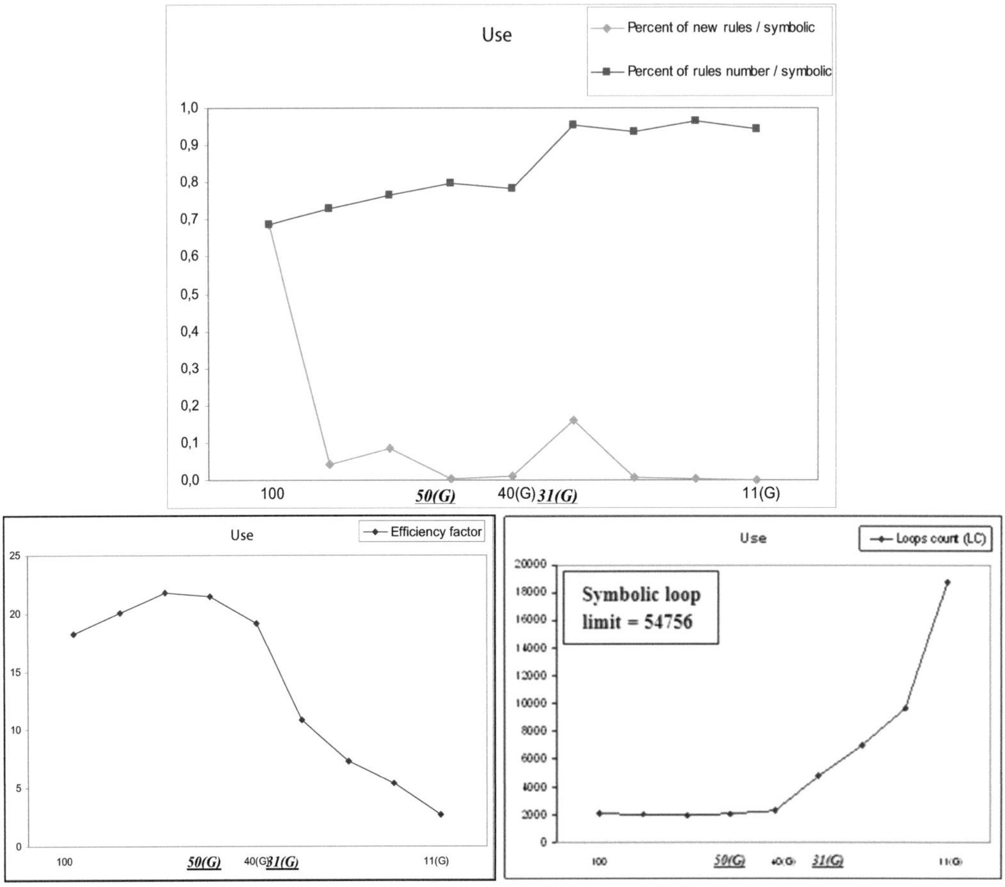

Fig. 6. **Rule extraction results for the Use viewpoint (extraction algorithm A1 with optional step).** The 50(G) level can be considered as an optimal level since it provides the best compromise between the percentage of extracted rules (80% of all the rules) and the computation complexity (2033 loops). However, if the percentage of extracted rules is considered as prior to the computation complexity, the 31(G) level (95% of all the rules, 4794 loops) should be considered as a more optimal level.

New rules: rules that are found at a given level but not in the preceding ones.
Symbolic loop limit: number of loops used by a symbolic approach for extracting the rules.
x(G): represents a level of generalization of x neurons).

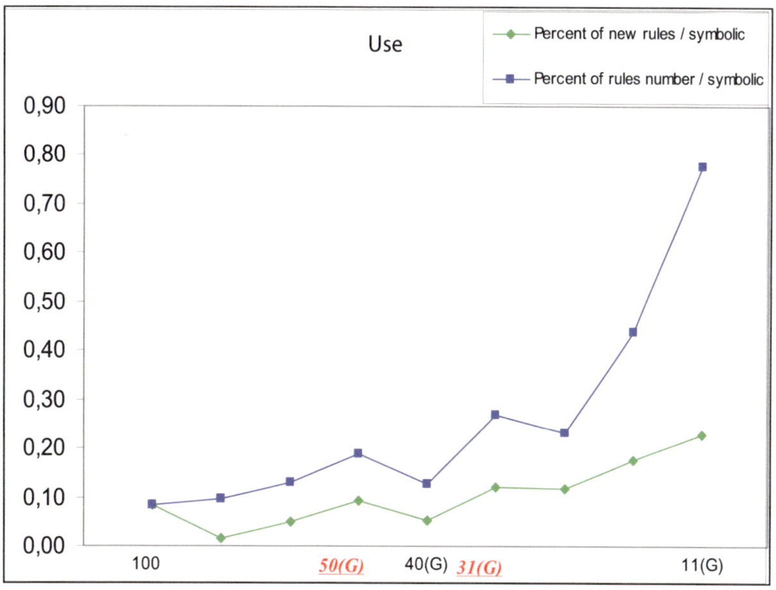

Fig. 7. **Rule extraction results for the Use viewpoint (extraction algorithm A1 without optional step).** Only peculiar rules are extracted with this version of the algorithm. In this case, a rule selection process that depends on the level of generalization is performed: the higher the level of generalization, the lower will be the selection. The good performances of the respective 50(G) and 31(G) levels are also highlighted with this version of the algorithm (see fig. 3 for a comparison with the other version of the algorithm).

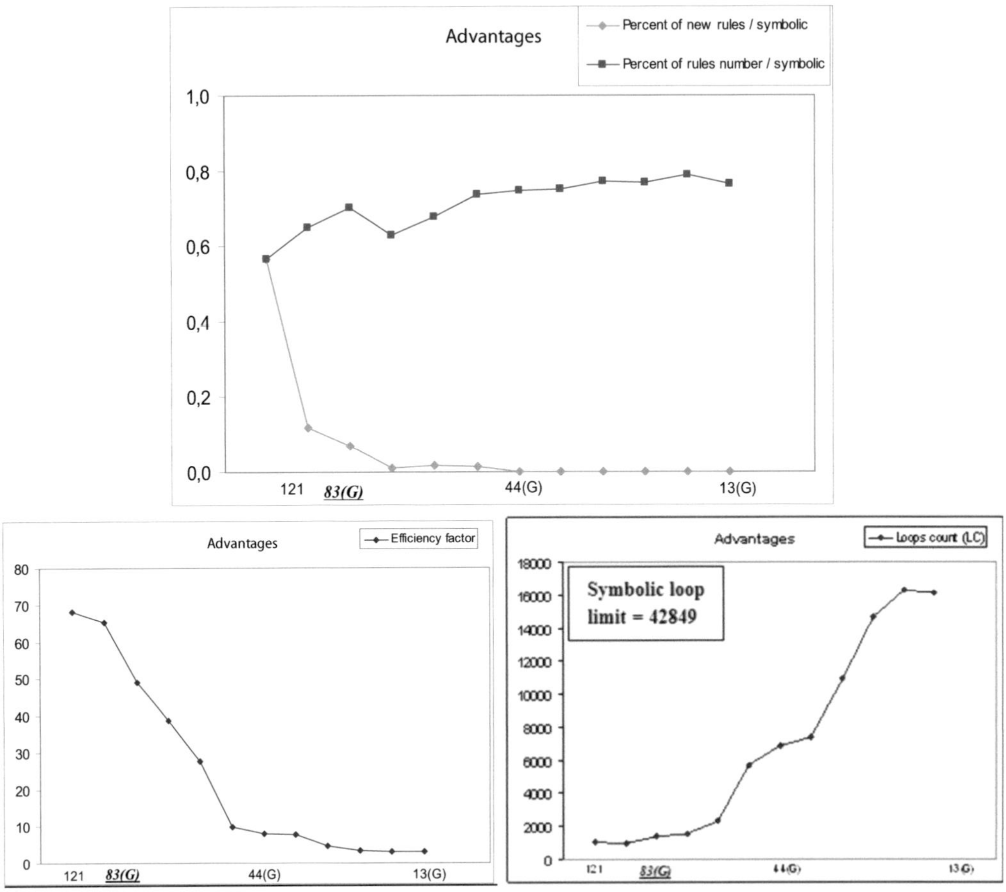

Fig. 8. **Rule extraction results for the Advantages viewpoint.** The 83(G) level can be considered as the level representing the optimal compromise: 70% of all the rules are extracted using 1402 loops.

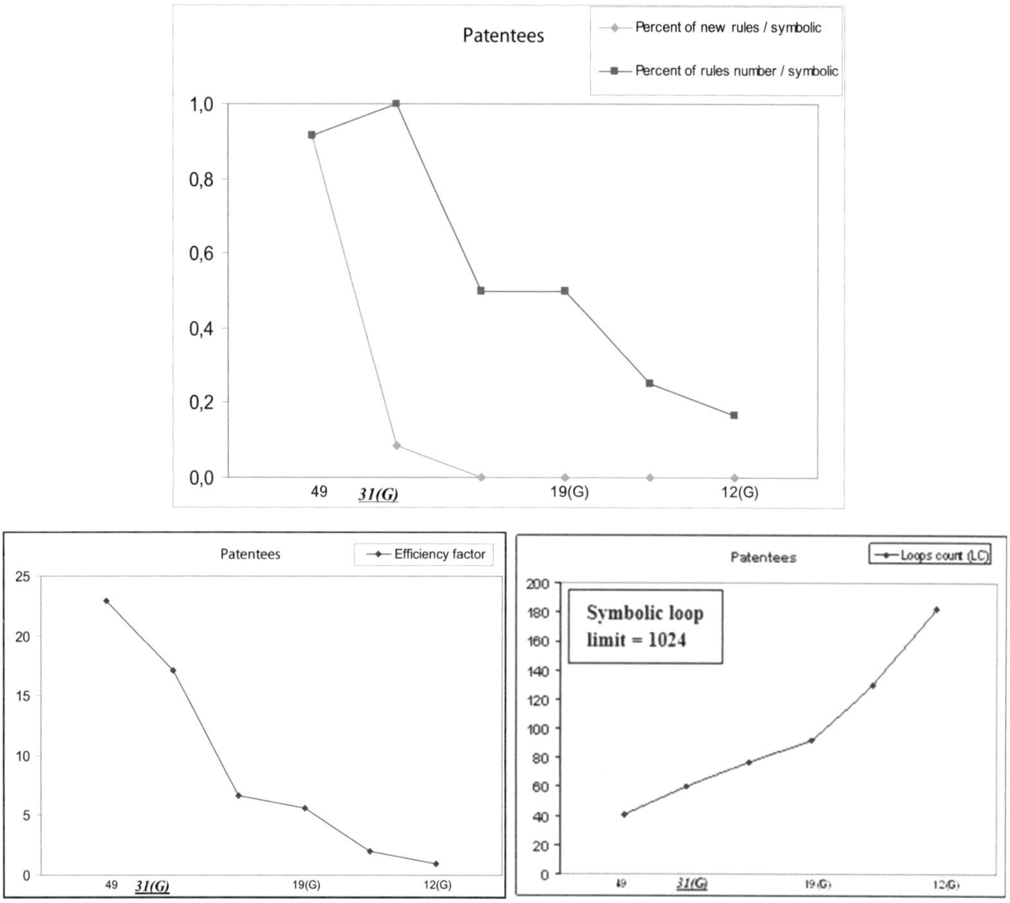

Fig. 9. **Rule extraction results for the Patentees viewpoint.** The 49(G) level can be considered as an optimal level since it provides the best compromise between the percentage of extracted rules (92% of all the rules) and the computation complexity (41 loops). Nevertheless, if the percentage of extracted rules is considered as prior to the computation complexity, the 31(G) should be considered as a more optimal level: all the rules are extracted using 61 loops. The decrease of the rules extraction performance for high generalization levels is due all together to the specific indexation characteristics of this viewpoint (the average number of indexes per document is near to 1), to the initial gathering effect of the winner-takes-most NG learning strategy, to the further effect of the generalization process and to the rule extraction strategy based on the distribution of single properties. Hence, when generalization is performed, the documents described by combination of indexes that have been initially gathered into the same classes by the initial learning strategy will be spread into specific classes. In such a way, the distribution of single properties into the classes will become more heterogeneous for intermediary generalization levels than for the initial level.

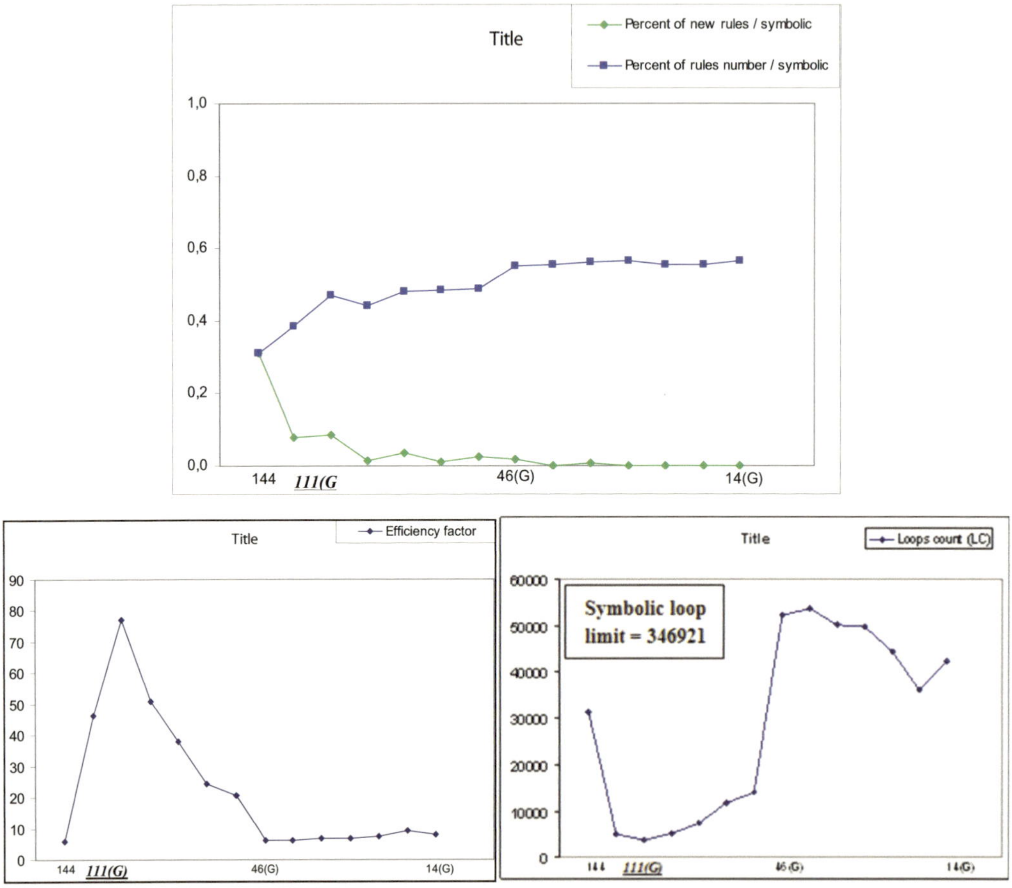

Fig. 10. **Rule extraction results for the Titles viewpoint.** The 111(G) level can be considered as an optimal level. Hence, even if the percentage of extracted rules is relatively low (48% of all the rules), this level provides a very good extraction efficiency (Efficiency factor=76 and 3619 loops) as compared to the symbolic model. The high rule computation complexity of the first gas level (optimal level), as compared to the next generalization levels, is due both to the sparseness of indexation of the **Titles** viewpoint and to the gathering effect of the winner-takes-most NG learning strategy (see also fig. 6 concerning that point). Hence, when data distribution is sparse, this learning strategy tends to gather the data into a few number of classes, letting some other classes empty. This effect will increase significantly the complexity of rule computation on the original level since non empty classes will have relatively heterogeneous descriptions. It should be noted that this complexity will be reduced at intermediary steps of generalization since unrelated data will be spread into different classes by the generalization process.

Annex 1: Galois lattice equivalence

Let D being a given dataset and P being the set of properties associated to the data of D,
Let $f : P \rightarrow D$ being a function associating to a set of properties p, the set of data which possess at least all the properties of p
Let $g : D \rightarrow P$ being a function associating to a set of data d, the set of properties which are at least common to all the data of d

Let $\bar{C}$ be a set of peculiar clusters issued from D with:
(see Section 3 for peculiar cluster definition)

$\forall c \in \bar{C}, D_c = \{d_1, d_2, \ldots, d_n\}$ being the set of data associated to the cluster c, $\forall d_i \in D_c, p_i$ being the set of peculiar properties of the data d_i and $P_C = p_1 \cup p_2 \cup \ldots p_n$ being the whole set of peculiar properties of the cluster c

$\bar{C}$ represents a Galois lattice if it verifies the condition:

$\forall c \in \bar{C}, h(P_c) = P_c$ *with* $h(P_c) = gOf(P_c)$
(Galois lattice definition given in [Lamirel and Toussaint, 2000])

Let c being a cluster of $\bar{C}$:

$$
\begin{aligned}
f(P_c) &= f(p_1 \cup p_2 \cup \ldots p_n) \\
&= f(p_1) \cap f(p_2) \cap \ldots f(p_n) \text{ by construction of } f \\
&= \{d_1, d_2, \ldots, d_n\} \\
&= D
\end{aligned}
$$

A value of **Precision** of **1** implies that all each peculiar property p_i of a cluster c is possessed at least by all the data of D_c, *thus:*

$$\forall p_i, f(p_i) \supseteq D_c \tag{1}$$

A value of **Recall** of **1** implies that all the data possessing a peculiar property p_i of a cluster c are included in this cluster, *thus:*

$$\forall p_i, D_c \supseteq f(p_i) \tag{2}$$

Hence, by (1) and (2),

$$f(p_1) = f(p_2) = \ldots f(p_n) = D_c$$

and subsequently:

$$D = D_c \tag{3}$$

$$
\begin{aligned}
g(D_c) &= g(d_1 \cup d_2 \cup \ldots d_n) \\
&= g(d_1) \cap g(d_2) \cap \ldots g(d_n) \text{ by construction of } g \\
&= \{p_1, p_2, \ldots, p_n\} \\
&= P
\end{aligned}
$$

A value of **Precision** of **1** implies that each data d_i of a cluster c possesses at least all the properties of P_c, *thus:*

$$\forall d_i, g(d_i) \supseteq P_c \tag{1}$$

A value of **Recall** of **1** implies that each property p_i of a cluster c is belonged exclusively by the data of this cluster, *thus:*

$$\forall d_i, P_c \supseteq g(d_i) \tag{2}$$

Hence, by (1) and (2),

$$g(d_1) = g(d_2) = \ldots g(d_n) = P_c$$

and subsequently:

$$P = P_c \tag{4}$$

Finally, $gOf(P_c) = g(f(P_c))$

$= g(D_c)$ from (3)

$= P_c$ from (4)

Conclusion: Joint unity values of **Recall** and **Precision** implies that the set of peculiar clusters of a numerical classification could be assimilated to a Galois lattice.

16

Spatial Clustering Technique for Data Mining

Yuichi Yaguchi, Takashi Wagatsuma and Ryuichi Oka
The University of Aizu
Japan

1. Introduction

For mining features from the social web, analysis of the shape, detection of network topology and corresponding special meanings and also clustering of data become tools, because the information obtained by these tools can create useful data behind the social web by revealing its relationships and the relative positions of data. For example, if we want to understand the effect of someone's statement on others, it is necessary to analyze the total interaction between all data elements and evaluate the focused data that results from the interactions. Otherwise, the precise effect of the data cannot be obtained. Thus, the effect becomes a special feature of the organized data, which is represented by a suitable form in which interaction works well. The feature, which is included by social web and it is effect someone's statement, may be the shape of a network or the particular location of data or a cluster.

So far, most conventional representations of the data structure of the social web use networks, because all objects are typically described by the relations of pairs of objects. The weak aspect of network representation is the scalability problem when we deal with huge numbers of objects on the Web. It is becoming standard to analyze or mine data from networks in the social web with hundreds of millions of items.

Complex network analysis mainly focuses on the shape or clustering coefficients of the whole network, and the aspects and attributes of the network are also studied using semistructured data-mining techniques. These methods use the whole network and data directly, but they have high computational costs for scanning all objects in the network.

For that reason, the network node relocation problem is important for solving these social-web data-mining problems. If we can relocate objects in the network into a new space in which it is easier to understand some aspects or attributes, we can more easily show or extract the features of shapes or clusters in that space, and network visualization becomes a space-relocation problem.

Nonmetric multidimensional scaling (MDS) is a well-known technique for solving new-space relocation problems of networks. Kruskal (1964) showed how to relocate an object into n-dimensional space using interobject similarity or dissimilarity. Komazawa & Hayashi (1982) solved Kruskal's MDS as an eigenvalue problem, which is called quantification method IV (Q-IV). However, these techniques have limitations for cluster objects because the stress, which is the attraction or repulsive force between two objects, is expressed by a linear formula. Thus, these methods can relocate exact positions of objects into a space but it is difficult to translate clusters into that space.

This chapter introduces a novel technique called Associated Keyword Space (ASKS) for the space-relocation problem, which can create clusters from object correlations. ASKS is based on

Q-IV but it uses a nonlinear distance measure, space uniformalization, to preserve average and variance in the new space, sparse matrix calculations to reduce calculation costs and memory usage, and iterative calculation to improve clustering ability. This method allows objects to be extracted into strict clusters and finds novel knowledge about the shape of the whole network, and also finds partial attributes. The method also allows construction of multimedia retrieval systems that combine all media types into one space.

Section 2 surveys social-web data-mining techniques, especially clustering of network-structured data. In Section 3, we review spatial clustering techniques such as Q-IV and ASKS. Section 4 shows the results of a comparison of Q-IV and ASKS, and also shows the clustering performance between ASKS and the K-nearest neighbor technique in a network. Section 5 explains an example application utilizing ASKS. Finally, we summarize this chapter in Section 6.

2. Related work

2.1 Shape of the network

Data-mining techniques for network-like relational data structures have been studied intensively recently. Examining the shape of a network or determining a clustering coefficient for each object is an important topic for complex networks (Boccaletti et al. (2006)), because these properties indicate clear features of whole or partially structured networks. Watts & Strogatz (1998) explained that human relationships exhibit a small-world phenomenon, and Albert & Barabási (2002) showed that the link structure of web documents has the scale-free property. These factors, the small-world phenomenon, which has $\log n$ of radius of n objects in the network, and the scale-free property, which has a power-law distribution of the rate number of degree, are found in many real network-like data such as protein networks (Jeong et al. (2001)), metabolic networks (Jeong et al. (2000)), routing networks (Chen et al. (2004)), costar networks (Yan & Assimakopoulos (2009)), and coauthor networks (Barabási & Crandall (2003)). The clustering coefficient (Soffer & Vázquez (2005)) is another measure of network shape and of the local density around an object in a network. Although the clustering of coefficients can extract "how much an object is included in a big cluster", it is not able to identify actual objects that are included in a cluster. Thus, to extract objects into a cluster, the nearest-neighbor technique can be applied to extract objects into the cluster (Wang et al. (2008)), but it is difficult to check the actual cluster size. Hierarchical clustering is another useful technique (Boccaletti et al. (2006)), but it is still difficult to find the density of a cluster.

2.2 Web mining categorization

Web mining applications can be categorized into the following three groups.

1. Web content mining retrieves useful information by performing text mining.
2. Web structure mining discovers communities and the relevance of pages based on hyperlink structures.
3. Web usage mining analyzes user access patterns from access logs and click histories.

An excellent review of Web mining can be found in Kosala & Blockeel (2000).

In terms of the above categorization, we have developed an algorithm for Web content mining Yaguchi et al. (2006); Ohnishi et al. (2006). This tool helps a user discover text information by displaying the hyperlink structure between related Web pages. The following subsection gives a summary of related work on Web content and structure mining methods.

2.3 Web data mining

Many schemes have used hyperlink structures to extract valuable information from the Web Carrière & Kazman (1997); Kleinberg (1999); Pirolli et al. (1996); Spertus (1997).
Dean et al. introduced two algorithms to identify related Web pages: one derived from the HITS algorithm Kleinberg (1999) and the other based on cocitation relationships. To increase accuracy, the HITS algorithm has been combined with content information Bharat & Henzinger (1998); Chakrabarti et al. (1999); Modha & Spangler (2000).
He et al. proposed a method to retrieve pages related to a query given by a user that grouped pages into distinct topics He et al. (2001). In the process, they introduced similarity metrics based on text information, hyperlink structure, and cocitation relationships.
Moise et al. treated the problem of how to find related pages effectively (Moise et al. (2003)). They proposed three approaches: hyperlink-based, content-based, and hybrid approaches. They developed an algorithm and showed that it outperformed conventional algorithms in the precision of its retrieved results.
In general, related Web pages are densely connected to each other by hyperlinks, and graph mining approaches can be used to discover such clusters of related Web pages, which are called "Web communities." Recent approaches to the discovery of Web communities are described in (Murata (2003)), and the requirements for graph mining algorithms suitable for the discovery of Web communities are also discussed.
Youssefi et al. applied data mining and information visualization techniques to Web domains, aiming to benefit from the combined power of human visual perception and computing ability (Youssefi et al. (2004)).
Liu et al. modeled a Web site's content structure in terms of its topic hierarchy by utilizing three types of information associated with a Web site: hyperlink structure, directory structure, and Web page content (Liu & Yang (2005)).

3. Spatial clustering

3.1 Nonmetric multidimensional scaling

The problem of creating a new N-dimensional space using the correspondence of pairs of objects is the same as the nonmetric multidimensional scaling (MDS) problem. The metric MDS was first proposed in Young and Householder's study (Young & Householder (1938)), where numerical affinity values were used, and the nonmetric MDS was also presented using only orders of affinities (Shepard (1972); Kruskal (1964)). We describe brief definition for nonmetric MDS of Kruskal's approach.
In the study of nonmetric MDS, let N denote the dimension of the space in which objects are allocated, and let each object be numbered i and its location be denoted by x_i. The similarity or dissimilarity (nonnegative value) between objects i and j is defined by δ_i and the Euclidean distance between them is defined as $d_{ij} = -(x_j - x_i)^2$. Now, object x_i is given a more suitable position $\hat{x}_i$ as a next state by utilizing δ_i, and the new distance between objects i and j is also set as $\hat{d}_{ij} = -(\hat{x}_j - \hat{x}_i)^2$. Then, the stress S can be defined as:

$$S = \sqrt{\frac{\sum\limits_{i<j} d_{ij}^2}{\sum\limits_{i<j} (d_{ij} - \hat{d}_{ij})^2}}. \qquad (1)$$

Finally, the goal of nonmetric MDS is able to express the following equation:

$$\min_{\text{all n-dimensional configurations}} \sqrt{\frac{\sum\limits_{i<j} d_{ij}^2}{\sum\limits_{i<j} (d_{ij} - \hat{d}_{ij})^2}}. \quad (2)$$

3.2 Quantification method IV

Komazawa & Hayashi (1982) solved the nonmetric MDS problem as an eigenvalue problem. Let M_{ij} denote the nonnegative value of the affinity measure between object i and j, and M_{ij} becomes bigger as the objects i and j become more similar. The location of object i is denoted by x_i in the N-dimensional space, and if two objects, i and j, are more similar, x_i and x_j are closer; if they are more dissimilar, the distance between them is larger. Practically, this problem is defined as the maximization of the following function ϕ:

$$\phi = \sum_{i=1}^{n}\sum_{j=1}^{n} -M_{ij}d_{ij} \rightarrow \max \quad (3)$$

$$d_{ij} = |x_i - x_j|^2. \quad (4)$$

Hence,

$$\begin{aligned} \phi &= -\sum_{i=1}^{n}\sum_{j=1}^{n} M_{ij}|x_i - x_j|^2 = -\sum_{i=1}^{n}\sum_{j=1}^{n} M_{ij}(|x_i|^2 - 2x_ix_j + |x_j|^2) && (5)\\ &= 2\sum_{i=1}^{n}\sum_{j=1}^{n} M_{ij}x_ix_j - \sum_{i=1}^{n}\sum_{j=1}^{n} M_{ij}|x_i|^2 - \sum_{i=1}^{n}\sum_{j=1}^{n} M_{ij}|x_j|^2 && (6)\\ &= \sum_{i=1}^{n}\sum_{j=1}^{n}(M_{ij} + M_{ji})x_ix_j - \sum_{i=1}^{n}|x_i|^2\sum_{j=1}^{n}(M_{ij} + M_{ji})x_{ij} = x_{ij} && (7) \end{aligned}$$

Let a_{ij} be:

$$a_{ij} = M_{ij} + M_{ji}. \quad (8)$$

Then:

$$\phi = 2\sum_{i=1}^{n}\sum_{j=1}^{n} a_{ij}x_ix_j - \sum_{i=1}^{n}|x_i|^2\sum_{j=1}^{n} a_{ij}. \quad (9)$$

If we eliminate $a_i i$ from this equation, then:

$$\phi = 2\sum_{i=1}^{n}\sum_{j=1,j\neq i}^{n} a_{ij}x_ix_j - \sum_{i=1}^{n}|x_i|^2\sum_{j=1,j\neq i}^{n} a_{ij} = \mathbf{x}'\mathbf{B}\mathbf{x} \quad (10)$$

$$B = \begin{pmatrix} -\sum\limits_{j=1,j\neq 1}^{n} a_{1j} & a_{12} & \cdots & a_{1n} \\ a_{21} & -\sum\limits_{j=1,j\neq 2}^{n} a_{2j} & \cdots & a_{2n} \\ \vdots & \vdots & \ddots & \vdots \\ a_{n1} & a_{n2} & \cdots & -\sum\limits_{j=1,j\neq n}^{n} a_{nj} \end{pmatrix}, x = \begin{pmatrix} x_1 \\ x_2 \\ \vdots \\ x_n \end{pmatrix}. \quad (11)$$

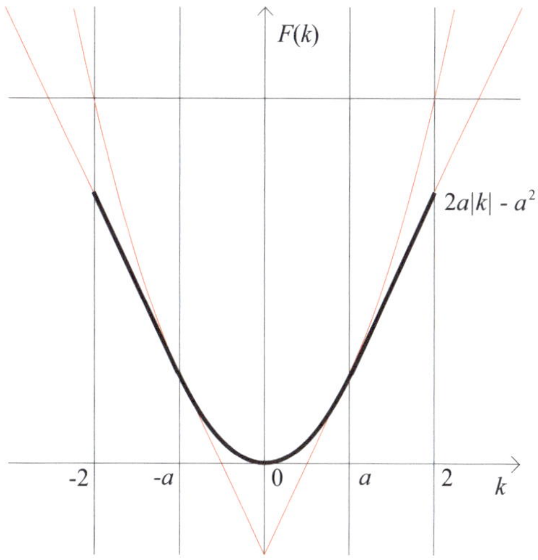

Fig. 1. Nonlinear function used in ASKS.

Maximizing $\mathbf{x}'\mathbf{B}\mathbf{x}$ under the condition $\mathbf{x}'\mathbf{x} = const$, requires solving equation (3):

$$\phi^* = \mathbf{x}'\mathbf{B}\mathbf{x} - \lambda\mathbf{x}'\mathbf{x} - \mathbf{c} \tag{12}$$

$$\frac{\partial\phi^*}{\partial x} = \mathbf{B}\mathbf{x} - \lambda\mathbf{I}\mathbf{x} = \mathbf{0} \tag{13}$$

. Finally, equation (3) becomes the following equation:

$$(\mathbf{B} - \lambda\mathbf{I})\mathbf{x} = \mathbf{0}. \tag{14}$$

This eigenvalue problem can be solved more quickly if matrix **B** is sparse. However, this method requires all N eigenvalues to be positive. Normally, to ensure eigenvalues are positive, a sufficiently large value must be subtracted from all elements of **B**. Thus, the calculation time and memory requirement becomes $O(N^2)$ in many cases.

3.3 Associated keyword space (ASKS)

ASKS is a nonlinear version of MDS and is effective for noisy data Takahashi & Oka (2001). This section explains ASKS and describes how to calculate it.
Let N denote the spatial dimension of an allocated object. Each object is indexed by i and its location is defined by x_i. The distance is measured by the formula F:

$$d_{ij} = -F(x_j - x_i). \tag{15}$$

F has a parameter a and is defined as:

$$F(k) = \begin{cases} |k|^2 & (|k| < a) \\ 2a|k| - a^2 & (|k| \geq a). \end{cases} \tag{16}$$

Figure 1 shows a plot of this function.
Three types of constraints on the distribution of objects are specified to decide the amount of space to be allocated to similar objects in distinguishable clusters:

1. make the original point the center of gravity for the objects;

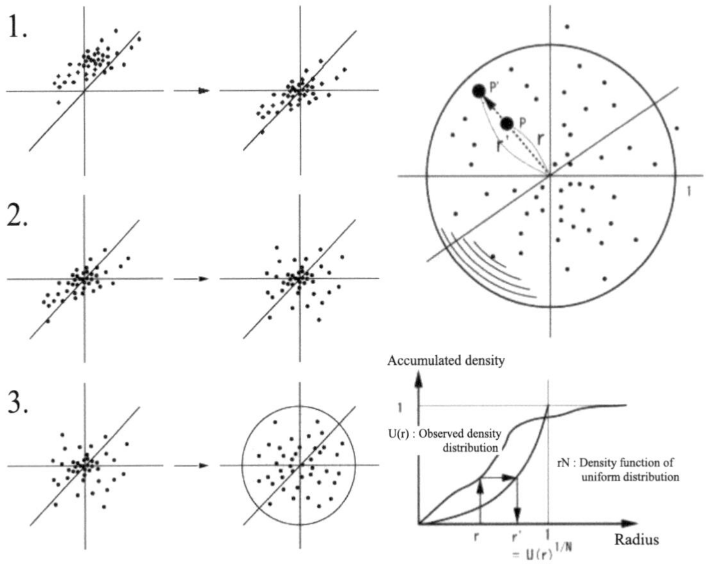

Fig. 2. Uniformalization types used in ASKS.

2. obtain covariance matrices such that dispersion in any direction creates the same value; and
3. uniformalize the objects in a radially from origin.

Figure 2 shows the method for uniformalization in the super-sphere. Uniformalization is useful for clustering noisy data that otherwise tend to distribute connections too evenly across the data.

3.4 Iterative solution of nonlinear optimization

The criterion function of ASKS is:

$$J(x_1, x_2, \ldots, x_n) = \sum_i \sum_j \{-M_{ij} F(x_j - x_i)\} \rightarrow \max \tag{17}$$

M_{ij} is an affinity (a nonnegative value) between objects i and j. It is calculated from the co-occurrence of objects i and j. The partial derivative of J with respect to x_i gives the formula for determining the values of x_i that maximize J:

$$\frac{\partial}{\partial x_i} \sum_i \sum_j \{-M_{ij} F(x_j - x_i)\} \equiv 0, \tag{18}$$

$$\sum_j M_{ij} F'(x_j - x_i) \equiv 0. \tag{19}$$

The derivative of F is:

$$F'(k) = \begin{cases} 2k & (|k| < a) \\ 2a\frac{k}{|k|} & (|k| \geq a), \end{cases} \tag{20}$$

and parameter a is junction of linear and non-linear distance measure for controlling density. Next, define D by:

$$D(k) = \begin{cases} 2 & (|k| < a) \\ \frac{2a}{|k|} & (|k| \geq a), \end{cases} \tag{21}$$

from which we derive the expression:

$$F'(x_j - x_i) = D(x_j - x_i)(x_j - x_i). \tag{22}$$

The following iterative computation converges to the solution x_i.

$$x_i^{t+1} = \frac{\sum_j M_{ij} D(x_j^{(t)} - x_i^{(t)}) x_j^{(t)}}{\sum_j M_{ij} D(x_j^{(t)} - x_i^{(t)})} \tag{23}$$

The three constraints must be enforced at each step of the iterative computation for all variables x_i $(i = 1, 2, \ldots, n)$.

4. Experiment

4.1 Comparison of Q-IV and ASKS

The effectiveness of ASKS is shown by comparing its performance with that of Q-IV.
Assume that 1,000,000 objects are to be clustered into C categories of 100, 1000, or 10,000 objects. We generated a set of affinity data between objects $M_{ij}(1 \leq i \leq C, 1 \leq j \leq C)$, where each M_{ij} took a value of 1 if objects i and j belonged to the same category, and 0 otherwise. We counted the numbers for the first case (N_i) and the second case (N_o), and then we defined R_i as the sum of the affinities in a class for the first case and R_o as the sum of the affinities between classes for the second case. If objects i and j belonged to the same category, then M_{ij} was set to $M_{ij} = 1$ with a probability of R_i / N_i, and the other values of M_{ij} were set to $M_{ij} = 0$. In the same way, if objects i and j belonged to different categories, the value of M_{ij} was set to $M_{ij} = 1$ according to R_o / N_o. The ratio of R_o / R_i expresses the level of noise, where a value of zero denoted no noise and larger values (which could be > 1.0) denoted a high level of noise. Both methods were applied to the case of 1000 categories. The Q-IV method is characterized by linear optimization and standard distributions of the various noise levels. The clustering results for the Q-IV approach are shown in Figure 3, where a subset of 20,000 objects belonging to 20 categories is plotted to aid visualization. The ASKS method is characterized by nonlinear optimization and a uniform distribution of the various noise levels. The results for the ASKS method under the same conditions are shown in Figure 4. These results show that the ASKS technique is superior to the Q-IV approach because ASKS can gather objects belonging to the same category into a more compact space and can distinguish categories at higher noise values.
To give a comparison numerically, we measured the ratio of the Standard Distribution (SD) in the associated spaces. The parameter S_i is the sum of the SD of objects i and j that belong to the same category, and S_o is the same sum when the objects are in different categories. An ideal MDS system would gather objects of the same category into a single point, causing the value $S_i = 0$. Therefore, we can compare the effectiveness of the above methods in terms of the ratio S_i / S_o.
Experiments were performed using a range of noise levels ($0.01 \leq R_i / R_o \leq 100.0$) and various numbers of categories. Figure 5(a) shows the results for 100,000 objects in 50 categories for the

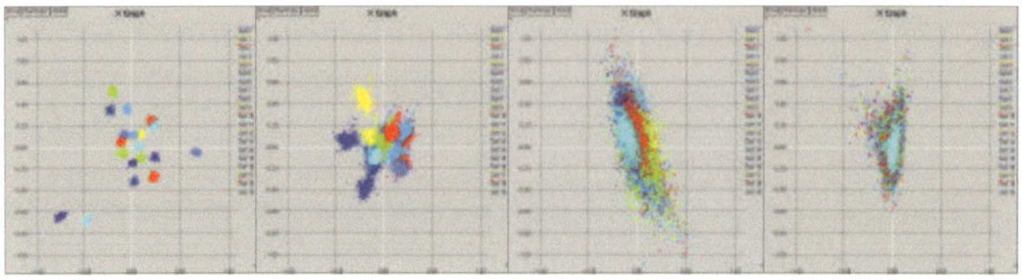

Fig. 3. Allocation of items by Q-IV. Noise level (Ro/Ri) [left = 0.01, 0.1, 1.0, right = 100.0].

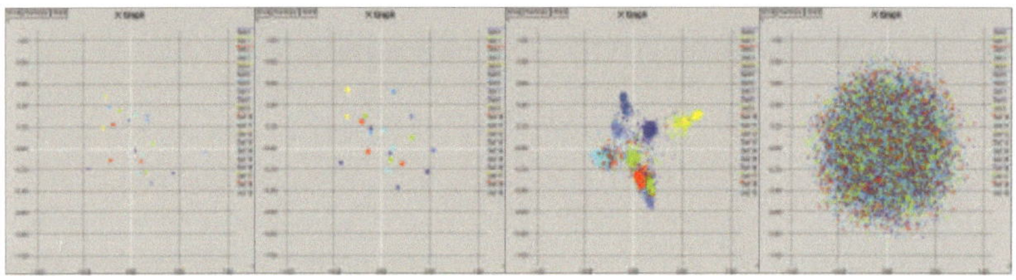

Fig. 4. Allocation of items by ASKS. Noise level (Ro/Ri) [left = 0.01, 0.1, 1.0, right = 100.0].

same conditions as those shown in Figures 3 and 4. Figure 5(b) shows the results for 100,000 objects with 500 categories, and Figure 5(c) shows the results for 5000 categories.

Another experiment was also performed to show the effect of parameter a in equation (20). If $a = 2$, then the function of ASKS is same as Q-IV without uniformalization. Thus, we can call this case as uniformalized Q-IV. Now, we set 100,000 samples, which belong to 1000 classes, into three-dimensional space. Figure 6 shows a comparison study on noise robustness between uniformalized Q-IV and ASKS with $a = 0.2$, and the number of iteration is set to 200. From this figure, Q-IV could not discriminate the classes when ratio $Ro/Ri = 0.1$ but ASKS still easily finds the clusters.

Figure 7 explains the effect of parameter a which is the junction of the group of linear and non-linear distance functions. In this figure, if parameter a is getting smaller, then each cluster becomes tighter but the speed of convergence is slower.

To check the dense of clustering, we separate the clustering space into $20 \times 20 \times 20$ boxes and we count the number of objects in each box. Figure 8 shows that the result, which is indicated by the red circled area, is perfectly clustered one or several groups, because each class in the dataset consists of 100 elements, and we can distinctively see in the graph where a box has more than 100 elements. Q-IV was unable to cluster these objects when $a = 0.01$ and $a = 0.1$, but ASKS was able to perform that clearly.

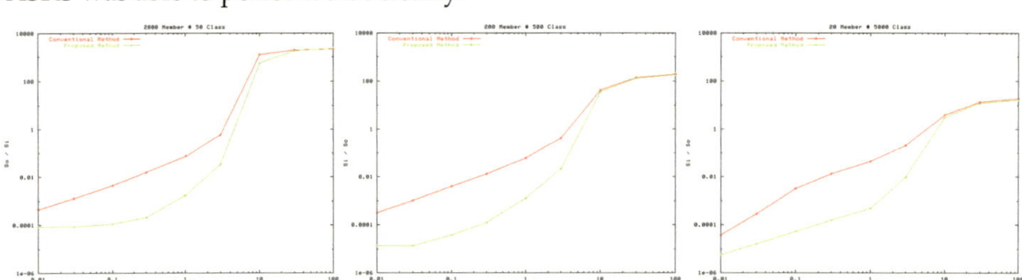

(a) 2000 Members * 50 Classes (b) 200 Members * 500 classes (c) 20 Members * 5000 classes

Fig. 5. Relationship between R_o/R_i and S_o/S_i using 100,000 samples: (a) 50, (b) 500, and (c) 5000 classes (for 2000, 200, and 20 samples/class, respectively.) For the larger noise levels ($R_o/R_i > 10$), there is little difference in efficiency between the conventional method (upper line) and the proposed method (lower line).

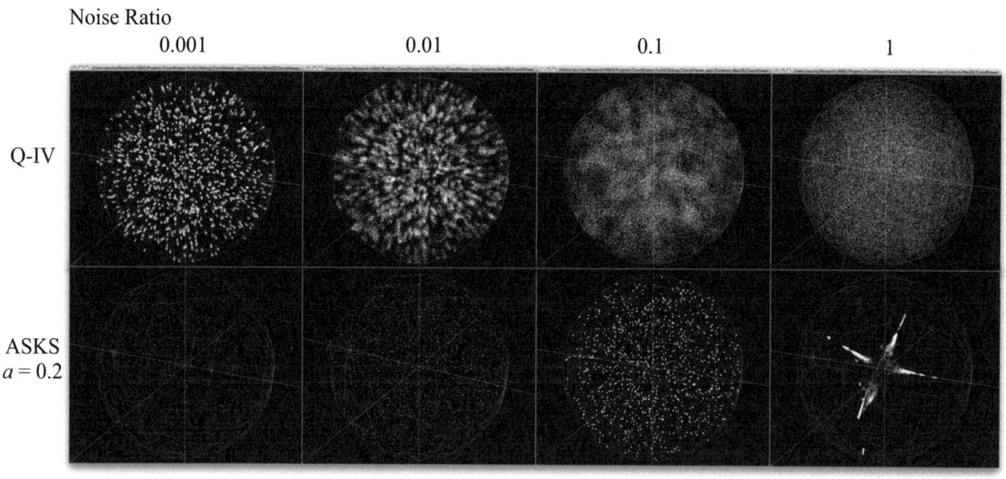

Fig. 6. Comparison study on noise robustness between uniformalized Q-IV and ASKS with $a = 0.2$.

5. Application examples

5.1 Text retrieval system

Takahashi & Oka (2001) constructed a text retrieval system using ASKS. From this study, they planned to search similar Japanese documents from fj news group which belongs to a news system on the Internet. It gathered 3.7 million articles from 1985 to 2000, and the number of words was approximately 520,000. The result of ASKS clustering shows that the study was able to find the associated word such as the word "Tabasco" and "Hot cod ovum" can be found around the word "Mustard" in the space which has same property "Hot", or "Rice", "Laver", "Soybean paste soup" and "Egg" also can be found around "Soybean paste", which are usually appeared in Japanese breakfast(figure 9).

5.2 Multimedia clustering

Wagatsuma et al. (2009) also constructed Web mining system using ASKS was performed as follows.

1. Create an affinity matrix for each of several media-content items and merge these matrices.
2. Create 3D coordinates and allocates each item (e.g., URL or text) by using ASKS.
3. Analyze the associated space.

In this experiment, Web pages were crawled from the page "Office of Prime Minister of Japan" [1] to a maximum hyperlink depth of four and with no restriction on URL domains. A total of 1371 pages were collected, with included words of 6948 types, and images of 579 types. Textual information was analyzed by MeCab [2], an open-source Japanese morphological analyzer. This study used three types of media, namely Web page hyperlinks, text, and image data.

---

[1] http://www.kantei.go.jp/

[2] http://mecab.sourceforge.net/

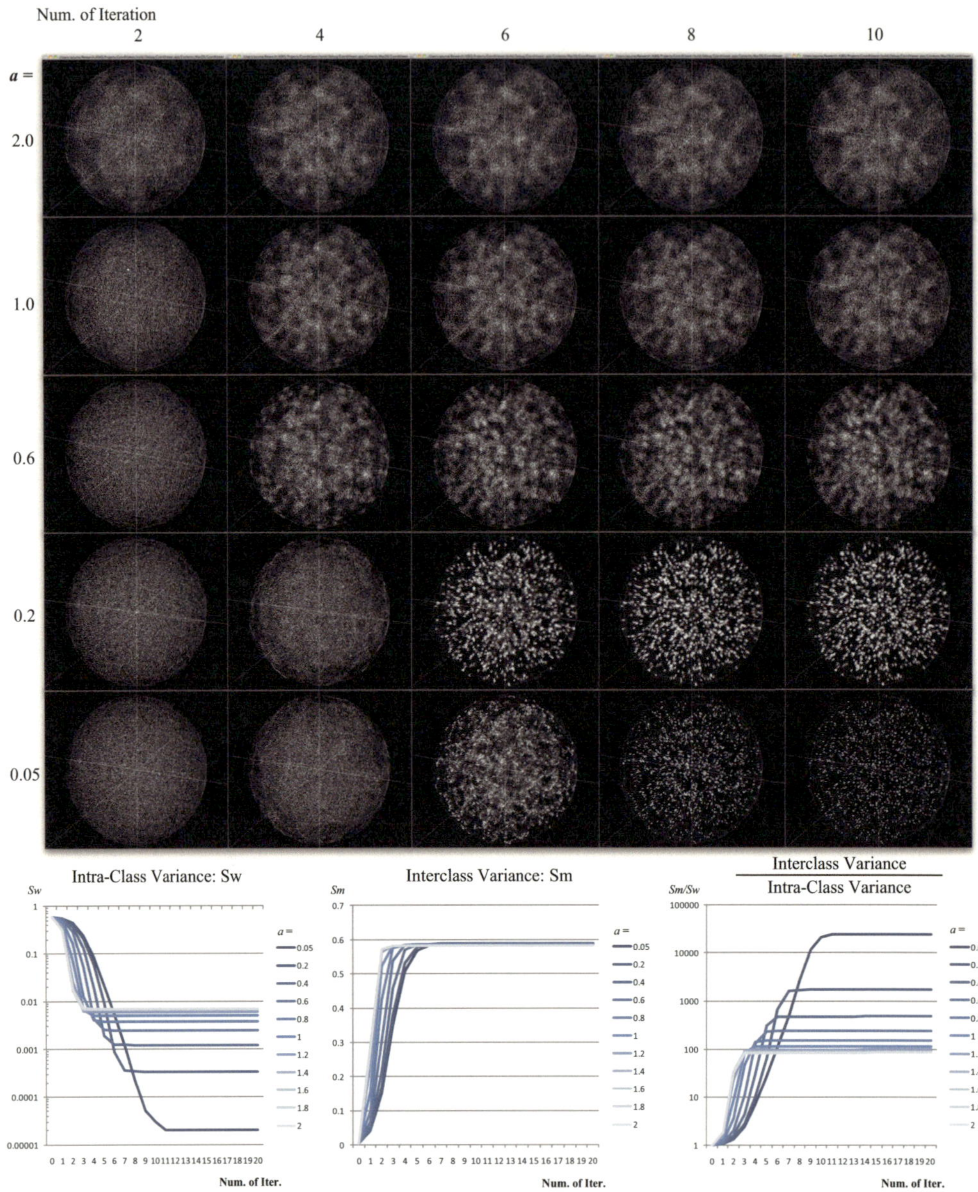

Fig. 7. Comparison study on the effect of parameter *a* to capability of clustering

5.2.1 Calculation of the affinity matrix

In this experiment, the affinity information could be specified in terms of six matrices (see Figure 10). This study defined the meaning of semantic similarity for each affinity matrix as follows.

1. *Web page hyperlink structure (page vs. page)*
   Increase affinity by 1 when there is a hyperlink from a page to the other page.

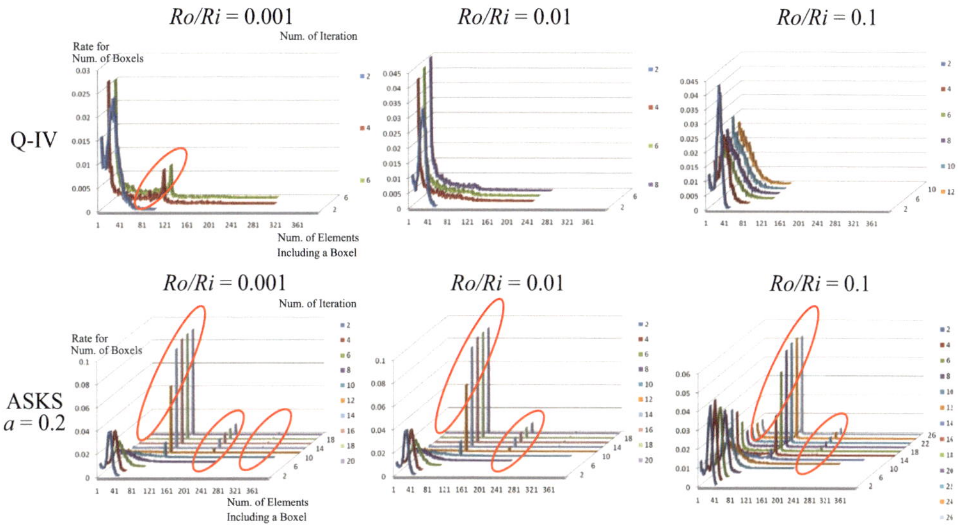

Fig. 8. Comparison study on clustering ability in 3D space: We set 20 × 20 × 20 small boxes into 3D affinity space, and count the number of boxes which have the same the number of objects inside.

2. *Word co-occurrence in a sentence (word vs. word)*
   If a word appears in a sentence with other words, then their affinity is calculated according to the interword distances. If word i and word j appear in a sentence, the distance d_{ij} is specified as 1 plus the number of words appearing between them. Then the affinity of the two words is defined as:

$$d_{ij} = 1 - \frac{d_{ij} - 1}{L},$$

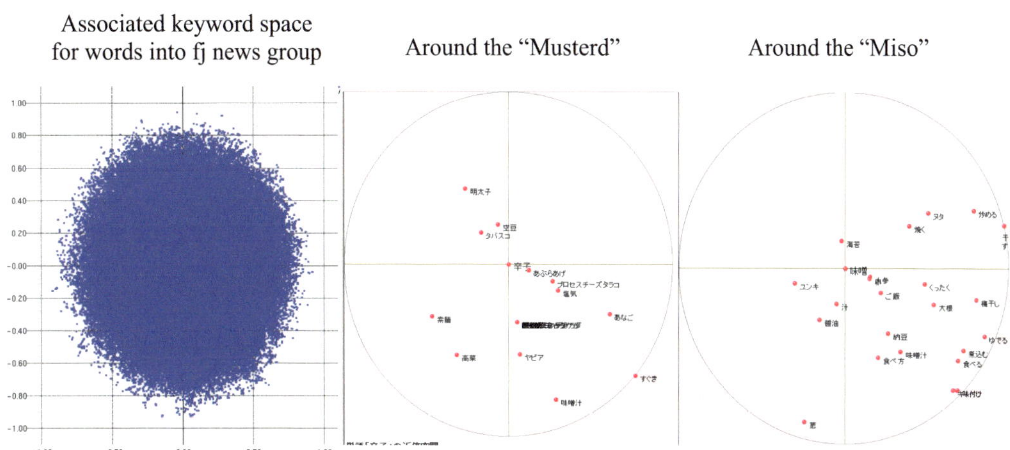

Fig. 9. ASKS in text retrieval system.

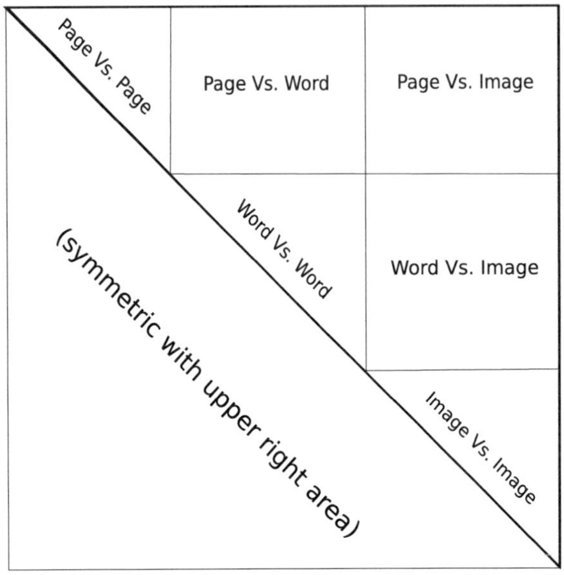

Fig. 10. The affinity matrix represents the presence of semantic similarity between types of media or content (Web page hyperlinks, text, and images.) This affinity matrix is created by merging six affinity matrices for the separate types.

where $L(=10)$ is the maximum allowed distance between two words. This definition was developed in Ohnishi et al. (2006).

3. *Similarity between images (image vs. image)*
All of the images used in a Web page have a mutual affinity. This affinity is most frequently calculated in terms of the distances of the correlation of their color histograms. To calculate the affinity between image i and image j, with histograms Hi and Hj, their distance d_{ij} is defined as:

$$d_{ij} = \frac{\langle H_i, H_j \rangle}{(\|H_i\| \cdot \|H_j\|)}$$

.

This study uses the binarized values:

$$d_{ij} = \begin{cases} 1 & if\ d_{ij} \geq 0.5, \\ 0 & otherwise. \end{cases}$$

4. *Word occurrence in a Web page (page vs. word)*
If a word appears in a certain page, then the affinity between them is calculated using the Term Frequency—Inverse Document Frequency (TF-IDF).

5. *Image occurrence in a Web page (page vs. image)*
If an image appears in a certain page, then the affinity between them is set to 1.

6. *Image occurrence with word (word vs. image)*
If an image has a word defined by an alt tag, then the affinity between the image and the alt word is available.

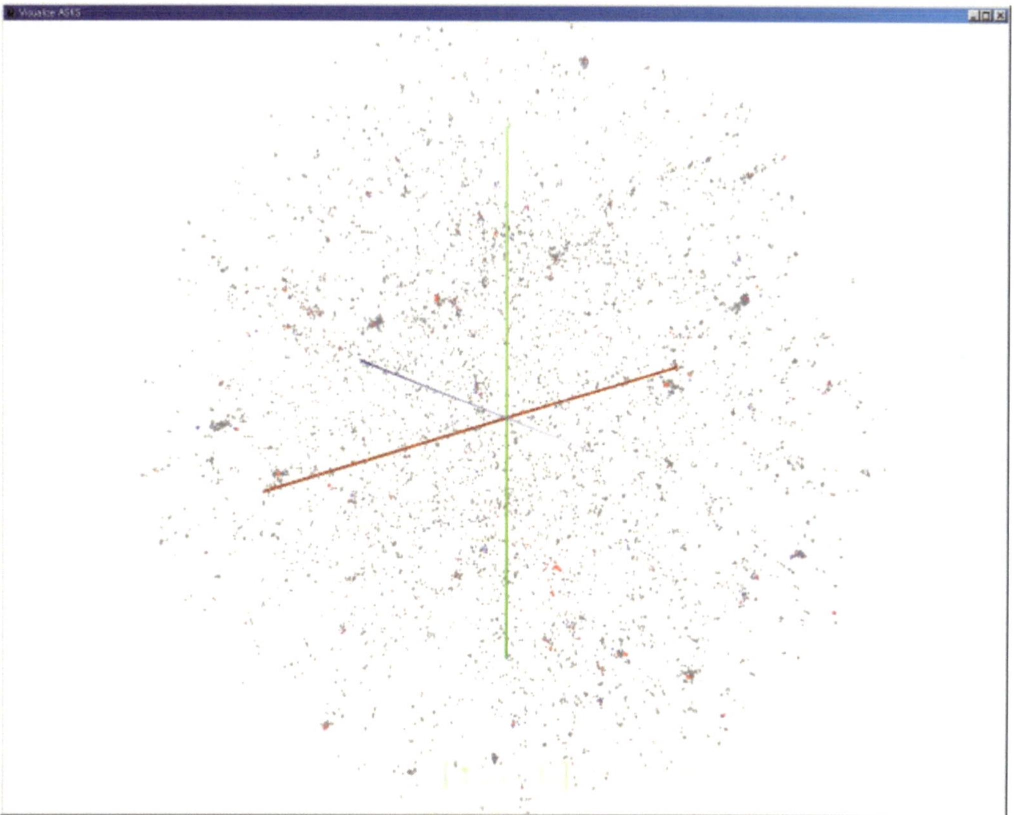

Fig. 11. Visualized associated space with merged affinity matrix. Each allocated node expresses a Web page, a word, or an image. This study can find several clusters in this associated space.

5.3 Merging the affinity matrices

After all six affinity matrices are created, they are simply concatenated into one matrix (see Figure 10). This merged affinity matrix represents the semantic similarities within the various types of media or content.

5.3.1 Visualization of the associated space

This study has developed software to visualize and analyze the 3D-associated space generated by the affinity matrix, called Visualize ASKS. It allows users to recognize the correlations between items more intuitively. The study also found several clusters in the associated space of our example (see Figure 11).

5.3.2 Cluster investigation

This study targeted one cluster constructed from neighboring items to analyze the features of the allocation in the association space generated by the affinity matrix involving several media. This study also selected one word within the cluster (the name of a previous Prime Minister of Japan "Junichiro Koizumi") as the source word, and analyzed the space within a 0.1 radius of this word. Note that the association space has a radius of 1.0.

The target area included the following three elements.

Fig. 12. Images gathered in the target area. There is little semantic similarity among them. These were all of the images in the Web pages reached by a few hyperlink steps from the seed page.

- *Pages:* A large number of Web page nodes existed in the target area, but semantically dissimilar pages were also mixed in with these pages.
- *Words:* Examples of several words in the target area (translated from Japanese into English) were

  cabinet official, prime minister, ministry, media person, interview, talk, cabinet secretariat, safety, and government.

  Many words linked to politics, the economy, and the names of the previous Prime Minister of Japan were gathered in the target area.
- *Images:* Three images were gathered in the target area, as shown in Figure 12. The first image appeared in a Web page referring to the Japanese governmental problem expressed the word "kidnapping" in Japanese [3]. The second image was used in the home page of the "Prime Minister of Japan and His Cabinet" [4]. The third image is a facial portrait image of the previous Prime Minister of Japan, "Junichiro Koizumi", found in the Web page "Introducing Previous Prime Ministers of Japan" [5].
  These images do not have high mutual semantic similarity scores, as calculated by our definition in Section refsubsec:definition. These were the only images in the Web pages reached by a few hyperlink steps from the seed page.

A noteworthy feature is that both of the items linked strongly to each other are found within the target area. However, many Web pages with semantically dissimilar information are also included. This Web page cluster was constructed from Web pages reached by a few hyperlink steps from the seed page.

5.3.3 Image allocation investigation

This study investigated the features of a collection of images having semantic similarity, being facial portraits of the previous Prime Minister of Japan (see Figure 13). These images were allocated to clusters in the associated space as shown in Figure 14.

[3]http://www.rachi.go.jp/
[4]http://www.kantei.go.jp/foreign/index-e.html
[5]http://www.kantei.go.jp/jp/koizumisouri/index.html

Fig. 13. Target images of the previous Prime Minister of Japan. These images have high mutual semantic similarity.

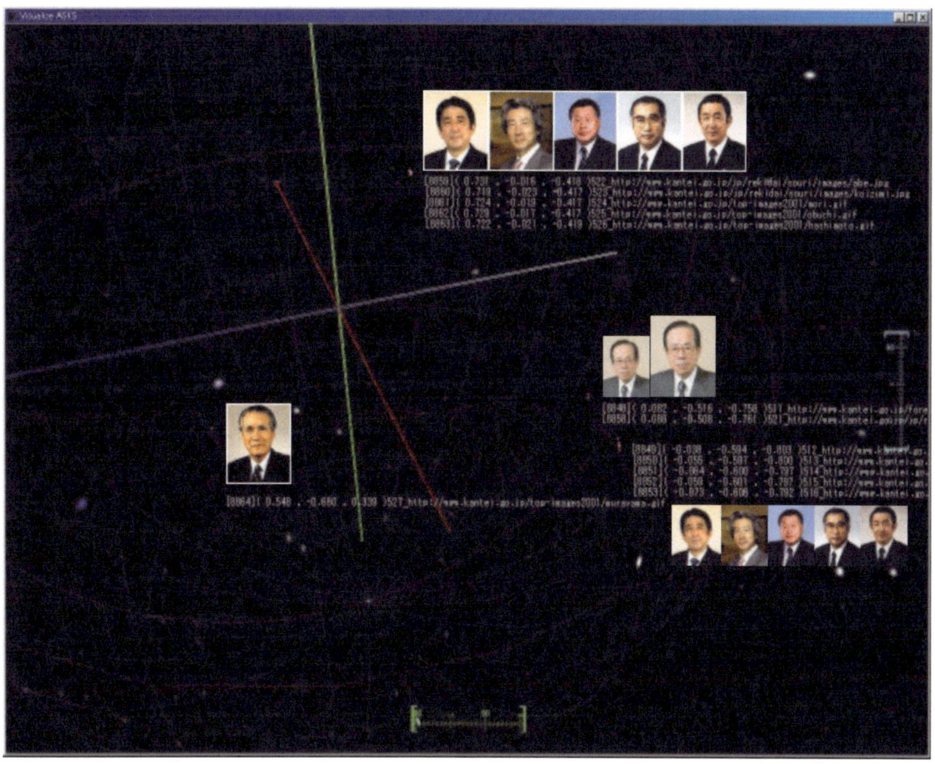

Fig. 14. Target images allocated to clusters. Images allocated to one cluster usually have similar domain names.

Images were allocated to several detached clusters, although they all had high mutual affinity values. From an analysis of the information about nodes around each image, we found that images allocated to the same cluster often have similar domain names. However, a few pairs of images in the same cluster have high affinities but different domain names. We therefore conclude that the allocation of image nodes is affected by other information.

6. Conclusion

We have introduced a novel spatial clustering technique that is called ASKS. ASKS can relocate objects into a new n-dimensional space from network structured data. Comparing ASKS with Q-IV, it improves the performance of clustering, and it can find actual clusters of objects and retrieve similar objects that are not related by an object of query, and it can be used in a multimedia retrieval system that combines words, Web pages and images.

We plan to pursue the following developments in future work. We expect that the visualized space used in this research will resemble existing relation graphs, which can be described by rubbery models or which may be easier to understand. Therefore, we should compare the visualization in this research with existing relationship graphs. Then there is the progression to categorization using clustering methods with visualized associated spaces to investigate the meaning of each category. In addition, if we apply categories, it may be possible to build a search system using the categorized information provided.

7. References

Albert, R. & Barabási, A. (2002). Statistical mechanics of complex networks, *Reviews of modern physics* 74(1): 47–97.

Barabási, A. & Crandall, R. (2003). Linked: The new science of networks, *American journal of Physics* 71: 409.

Bharat, K. & Henzinger, M. R. (1998). Improved algorithms for topic distillation in a hyperlinked environment, *Proceedings of the 21st annual international ACM SIGIR conference on Research and development in information retrieval*, ACM, pp. 104–111.

Boccaletti, S., Latora, V., Moreno, Y., Chavez, M. & Hwang, D. (2006). Complex networks: Structure and dynamics, *Physics Reports* 424(4-5): 175–308.

Carrière, S. & Kazman, R. (1997). WebQuery: Searching and visualizing the Web through connectivity, *Computer Networks and ISDN Systems* 29(8-13): 1257–1267.

Chakrabarti, S., Dom, B. E., Kumar, S. R., Raghavan, P., Rajagopalan, S., Tomkins, A., Gibson, D. & Kleinberg, J. (1999). Mining the Web's link structure, *Computer* 32(8): 60–67.

Chen, J., Gupta, D., Vishwanath, K., Snoeren, A. & Vahdat, A. (2004). Routing in an Internet-scale network emulator, *The IEEE Computer Society's 12th Annual International Symposium on Modeling, Analysis, and Simulation of Computer and Telecommunications Systems, 2004.(MASCOTS 2004). Proceedings*, pp. 275–283.

He, X., Ding, C., Zha, H. & Simon, H. (2001). Automatic topic identification using webpage clustering, *Proceedings of the 2001 IEEE international conference on data mining*, IEEE Computer Society, pp. 195–202.

Jeong, H., Mason, S., Barabási, A. & Oltvai, Z. (2001). Lethality and centrality in protein networks, *Nature* 411(6833): 41–42.

Jeong, H., Tombor, B., Albert, R., Oltvai, Z. & Barabási, A. (2000). The large-scale organization of metabolic networks, *Nature* 407(6804): 651–654.

Kleinberg, J. (1999). Authoritative sources in a hyperlinked environment, *Journal of the ACM*

(JACM) 46(5): 604–632.
Komazawa, T. & Hayashi, C. (1982). Quantification Theory and Data Processing, *Tokyo: Asakura-shoten* .
Kosala, R. & Blockeel, H. (2000). Web mining research: A survey, *ACM SIGKDD Explorations Newsletter* 2(1): 1–15.
Kruskal, J. (1964). Multidimensional scaling by optimizing goodness of fit to a nonmetric hypothesis, *Psychometrika* 29(1): 1–27.
Liu, N. & Yang, C. (2005). Mining web site's topic hierarchy, *Special interest tracks and posters of the 14th international conference on World Wide Web*, ACM, pp. 980–981.
Modha, D. S. & Spangler, W. S. (2000). Clustering hypertext with applications to web searching, *Proceedings of the eleventh ACM on Hypertext and hypermedia*, ACM, pp. 143–152.
Moise, G., Sander, J. & Rafiei, D. (2003). Focused co-citation: Improving the retrieval of related pages on the web, *Proceedings of the 12th International world wide web Conference (Budapest, Hungary, 2003)* .
Murata, T. (2003). Visualizing the structure of web communities based on data acquired from a search engine, *IEEE transactions on industrial electronics* 50(5): 860–866.
Ohnishi, H., Yaguchi, Y., Yamaki, K., Oka, R. & Naruse, K. (2006). Word space : A new approach to describe word meanings, *IEICE technical report. Data engineering* 106(149): 149–154.
Pirolli, P., Pitkow, J. & Rao, R. (1996). Silk from a sow's ear: extracting usable structures from the Web, *Proceedings of the SIGCHI conference on Human factors in computing systems: common ground*, ACM, p. 125.
Shepard, R. (1972). Multidimensional scaling: Theory and applications in the behavioral sciences, Seminar Press New York.
Soffer, S. & Vázquez, A. (2005). Network clustering coefficient without degree-correlation biases, *Physical Review E* 71(5): 57101.
Spertus, E. (1997). ParaSite: Mining structural information on the Web, *Computer Networks and ISDN Systems* 29(8-13): 1205–1215.
Takahashi, H. & Oka, R. (2001). Self-organization an associated keyword space for text retrieval, *WMSCI2010, World Multi-Conference on Systemics, Cybernetics and Informatics* pp. 302–307.
Wagatsuma, T., Yaguchi, Y. & Oka, R. (2009). Cross-media data mining using associated keyword space, *10th IEEE International Conference on Computer and Information Technology (CIT10)* 2: 289–294.
Wang, C., Au, K., Chan, C., Lau, H. & Szeto, K. (2008). Detecting Hierarchical Organization in Complex Networks by Nearest Neighbor Correlation, *Nature Inspired Cooperative Strategies for Optimization (NICSO 2007)* pp. 487–494.
Watts, D. & Strogatz, S. (1998). Collective dynamics of "small-world" networks, *Nature* 393(6684): 440–442.
Yaguchi, Y., Ohnishi, H., Mori, S., Naruse, K., Oka, R. & Takahashi, H. (2006). A mining method for linkedweb pages using associated keyword space, *IEEE/IPSJ International Symposium on Applications and the Internet (SAINT'06)* pp. 268–276.
Yan, J. & Assimakopoulos, D. (2009). The small-world and scale-free structure of an internet technological community, *International Journal of Information Technology and Management* 8(1): 33–49.
Young, G. & Householder, A. (1938). Discussion of a set of points in terms of their mutual

distances, *Psychometrika* 3(1): 19–22.
Youssefi, A., Duke, D. & Zaki, M. (2004). Visual web mining, *Proceedings of the 13th international World Wide Web conference on Alternate track papers & posters*, ACM, pp. 394–395.

17

The Search for Irregularly Shaped Clusters in Data Mining

Angel Kuri-Morales[1] and Edwyn Aldana-Bobadilla[2]
[1]*Instituto Tecnológico Autónomo de México*
[2]*Instituto de Investigaciones en Matemáticas Aplicadas y en Sistemas,UNAM México*

1. Introduction

One of the basic endeavours in Data Mining is the unsupervised process of determining which objects in the database do share interesting properties. The solution of this problem is usually denoted as "clustering", i.e. the identification of sets in the database which may be grouped in accordance with an appropriate measure of likelihood. Clustering can be considered the most important unsupervised learning problem. As every other problem of this kind, it deals with finding a structure in a collection of unlabeled data. A loose definition of clustering could be "the process of organizing objects into groups whose members are similar in some way". A cluster is therefore a collection of objects which are "similar" between them and are "dissimilar" to the objects belonging to other clusters. In clustering the more traditional algorithms are based on similarity criteria which depend on a metric. This fact imposes basic constraints on the shape of the clusters found. These shapes are hyperspherical in the metric's space due to the fact that each element in a cluster lies within a radial distance relative to a given center. Working with metric spaces works fine when the hyperspheres are well behaved. However, there are cases where there is an unavoidable degree of confusion because the hyperspheres do overlap to a certain extent. It has been shown (Haykin,1994) that iff the elements of the database exhibit a Gaussian behavior a Bayesian classifier will minimize the degree of confusion, even when classification errors are unavoidable. Several clustering methods have been proposed. Most exhibit the limitation discussed above. In this work, however, we discuss three alternatives of clustering algorithms which do not depend on simple distance metrics and, therefore, allow us to find clusters with more complex shapes in n-dimensional space.

a. Clustering based on optimization of validity indices.

b. Clustering based on optimization of entropy

c. Clustering based on optimization of membership.

This chapter begins with an account of the principles of the traditional clustering methods. From these it is evident that irregularly shaped clusters are difficult to deal with. With this limitation in mind we propose some non-traditional approaches which have shown to be effective in our search for possibly non-hyperspherical locus. The clustering process is a highly non-linear and usually non-convex optimization problem which disallows the use of traditional optimization techniques. For this reason we discuss some optimization techniques pointing to Genetic Algorithms as a good alternative for our purposes.

2. Clustering

Our problem will be focused under the assumption that the data under consideration correspond to numerical variables. This will not be always the case and several other methodologies have been devised to allow clustering with non-numerical (or categorical) variables.
Research on analyzing categorical data has received significant attention see (Agresti,2002), (Chandola et al.,2009),(Chang & Ding,2005) and (Gibson,2000). However, many traditional techniques associated to the exploration of data sets assume the attributes have continuous data (covariance, density functions, Principal Component's Analysis, etc.). In order to use these techniques, the categorical attributes have to be discarded, although they are loaded with valuable information. Investigation under way (Kuri & Garcia,2010) will allow us to apply the methods to be discussed in what follows even in the presence of categorical variables. Suffice it to say, however, that we shall not consider these special cases and, rather,focus on numerically expressible attributes of the data sets.

2.1 Definition

Clustering, as stated, is an unsupervised process that allows the partition of a data set X in k groups or clusters in accordance with a similarity criterion. Generally all elements of data set X belong to a *metric space D*, where there exist relationships between them that are expressible in terms of a distance. In the great majority of clustering methods, the similarity between two or more elements is defined as a measure of its proximity whose value is a consequence of such distance. The elements are rendered similar if its proximity is less than a certain threshold. This threshold represents the radius that defines the bound of a cluster as a n-dimensional spherical hull.

2.2 Metrics

Formally a metric is a function that defines the distance between elements of a set. The set with a metric is called a metric space.

Definition 1 *A metric on a set X is a function $d : X \times X \rightarrow R$ where R is the set of the real numbers. For all x, y, z in X this function must satisfy the following conditions*

1. $d(x,y) \geq 0$
2. $d(x,y) = 0 \quad if \quad and \quad only \quad if \quad x = y$
3. $d(x,y) = d(y,x)$
4. $d(x,z) \leq d(x,y) + d(y,z)$ (triangle inequality)

In a clustering process a popular set of metrics is one of the Minkowsky family (Cha,2008). Its value is defined by the following equation.

$$d_{mk}(P,Q) = \sqrt[\alpha]{\sum_{i=1}^{n} |P_i - Q_i|^{\alpha}} \tag{1}$$

where P and Q are two vectors in an n-dimensional space. The α value is an integer number that represents one particular metric ($\alpha = 2$ corresponds to the Euclidian Distance). However, this distance is sometimes not an appropriate measure for our purpose. For this reason sometimes the clustering methods use statistical metrics such as Mahalanobis'(Mahalanobis,1936), Bhattacharyya's (Bhattacharyya,1943) or Hellinger's (Pollard,2002), (Yang et al.,2000). These metrics statistically determine the similarity of the probability distribution between random variables P and Q.

2.3 Methods

Among the many approaches to clustering we wish to mention some of the better known ones. We are careful to mention at least one example of every considered approach, although this account is, by no means, exhaustive. In what follows we call "traditional" those methods which emphasize the use of a metric to determine a set of centroids. A centroid is, intuitively, the point around which all the elements of the cluster do group. This is the reason why metric-based methods yield hyperspherical clusters.

2.3.1 Traditional methods

As already mentioned, traditional methods typically yield well defined centroids. The algorithms supporting the method offer a wide variety. Some use concrete logic, others fuzzy logic; some approach the problem intuitively (even in a simplistic fashion) as is the case of hierarchical clustering. Others, on the other hand, approach the clustering problem as a (non-obvious) problem of competition (such as the ones stemming from Kohonen's approach).

2.3.1.1 K-means

The main idea is to define k centroids, one for each cluster. The next step is to take each point belonging to a given data set and associate it to the nearest centroid. When no point is pending, the first step is completed. At this point we need to re-calculate k new centroids as barycenters of the clusters resulting from the previous step. After we have these k new centroids, a new binding has to be done between the same data set points and the nearest new centroid. As a result of this loop we may notice that the k centroids change their location step by step until no more changes are done. This algorithm aims at minimizing an objective function, in this case a squared error function. The objective function is:

$$J = \sum_{i=1}^{n} \sum_{j=1}^{k} \left\| x_i - c_j \right\|^2 \tag{2}$$

where $\left\| x_i - c_j \right\|^2$ is s a chosen distance between a data point x_i and and the cluster center c_j. (For details see (MacQueen,1967))

2.3.1.2 Fuzzy C-means

This is a method which allows one object in the data set to belong to two or more clusters. It is based on minimization of the following objective function:

$$J = \sum_{i=1}^{n} \sum_{j=1}^{C} u_{ij}^{m} \left\| x_i - c_j \right\|^2 \qquad 1 \leq m < \infty \tag{3}$$

where m is any real number greater than 1, u_{ij} is the degree of membership of x_i in j, x_i is the $i-th$ of d-dimensional measured data, c_j is the d-dimension center of the cluster, and $\left\| x_i - c_j \right\|$ is any norm expressing the distance between any measured data and the center.

Fuzzy partitioning is carried out through an iterative optimization of the above equation by:

$$u_{ij} = \frac{1}{\sum_{k=1}^{C} \frac{\|x_i - c_j\|}{\|x_i - c_k\|}^{2/(m-1)}} \tag{4}$$

$$c_j = \frac{\sum_{i=1}^{n} u_{ij}^m x_i}{\sum_{i=1}^{n} u_{ij}^m} \tag{5}$$

the iterations will stop when

$$max_{ij} = \left\{ \left| u_{ij}^{k+1} - u_{ij}^{k} \right| \right\} < \epsilon \tag{6}$$

where $0 \le \epsilon \le 1$ and k is the iteration step. The reader can find more details in (Dunn,1973).

2.3.1.3 Hierarchical clustering

Given a set of N items to be clustered, and a distance matrix, the basic process is:

1. Start by assigning each item to a cluster, so that if you have N items, you now have N clusters, each containing just one item. Let the distances between the clusters be the same as the distances between the items they contain.
2. Find the closest pair of clusters and merge them into a single cluster, so that now you have one cluster less.
3. Compute distances between the new cluster and each of the old clusters.
4. Repeat steps 2 and 3 until all items are clustered into a single cluster of size N.

Of course there is no point in having all the N items grouped in a single cluster but, once you have gotten the complete hierarchical tree, for k clusters simply cut the $k-1$ longest links. Representative methods in this category are BIRCH (Zhang,1996), CURE and ROCK (Guha,1998).

2.3.1.4 Self organizing maps

These kind of neural networks basically allows the mapping of a set of vectors in n-dimensional space into a smaller set in (typically) 2-dimensional space. The idea is to assign every vector in the original n-space an XY coordinate in a way such that neighboring elements in XY plane (the so-called neurons) correspond to neighboring elements in the original n-dimensional space. This yields a map in XY where physically close sets of neurons define clusters in n dimensional space. The procedure for the training algorithm is:

1. Initialize
   - Define a grid on a Cartesian plane XY.
   - Every pair of coordinates in $\mathbb{N}$ is associated to a neuron.
   - The number of neurons is given by $N = max(X_i) \times max(Y_j)$
   - A weight vector $w_{ij} \in \mathbb{R}$ is associated to every neuron.
   - A set V, consisting of all elements of the data set, is defined. We denote the cardinality of V with J. That is $J = |V|$.
   - Define a maximum number of epochs E. An epoch consists of the (typically) random traversal of all J vectors.

- All elements of the weight vectors are assigned random numbers.
- A maximum number of epochs, T, is defined.
- A learning rate $\eta[e(t)]$ in $\mathbb{R}$ is defined, where $e(t)$ is the t-*th* epoch.
- A feedback function of neuron i to the winning neuron k in epoch t is defined, where $r_{ik}[e(t)] \in \mathbb{R}$

2. $i = 1$
3. An input vector V_j is randomly selected (without replacement).
4. A winning neuron k is determined as the neuron that has the minimum distance $d_k = min_i \|V - w_i\|$ to the input vector V_j.
5. The weight vectors are iteratively adapted according to the following function: $w_{ij}(t) = w_{ij}(t-1) + \eta[e(t)] * r_{ik}[e(t)] * (V_j - w_{ij}(t-1))$
6. If $i = J$

    $t \leftarrow t + 1$
    If $t > T$ end algorithm.
    Update $\eta[e(t)]$
    Update $r_{ik}[e(t)]$
    Go to step 2

   else

    $i = i + 1$
    Go to step 3.

   endif

Upon ending, the algorithm will have placed similar neurons in neighboring areas of the plane. That is, it will have organized (hence the name SOM) similar neurons to lie physically close to each other in XY. A cluster will, therefore, consist of those objects in the data set whose coordinates in the original space of attributes are pointed to by neighboring neurons in the Cartesian plane. A complete description of this method is found in (Kohonen,1997)

2.3.2 Limitations of traditional methods

In general a good clustering method must:

- Be able to handle multidimensional data sets.
- Be independent of the application domain.
- Have a reduced number of parameters.
- Be able to display computational efficiency.
- Be able to yield irregularly shaped clusters.

The last point is the most difficult to achieve for the following reason. If we assume that all elements of data set X belong to a *metric space D*, then there exist relationships between them that are expressible in terms of a distance. The elements are similar if its proximity is less than a certain threshold. This threshold represents the radius that defines the bound of a cluster as a n-dimensional spherical hull. This is illustrated in Fig. 1(a) (for $n = 2$) where the bound clusters are convex shapes. However an ideal case would allow us to obtain arbitrary shapes for the clusters that adequately encompass the data. Fig. 1(b) illustrates this fact.

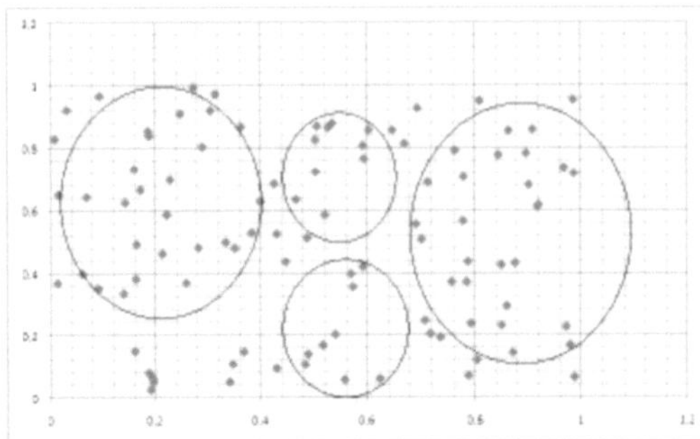

(a) Circular shapes

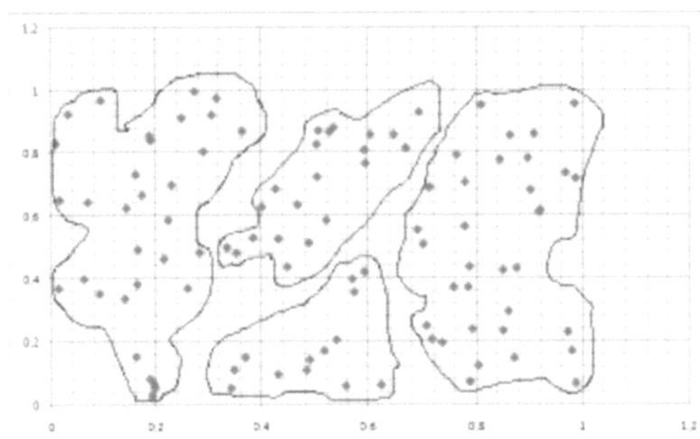

(b) Arbitrary shapes

Fig. 1. Differents ways of clustering for the same dataset

For example, assume we have a problem in 2-dimensional space (say $X - Y$) and that we define a metric which assigns greater merit to the coordinates in the Y axis than those in the X axis. To make this hypothesis definite, suppose that the values of the X-coordinates are k times as important as those of the Y-coordinates. We define a distance. Then a set of two hypothetical clusters would look like the ones illustrated in Fig. 2(a).
In this figure the coordinates (x_i, y_i) of point i are set in units of the same relative size. However, if we were to change the X axis so that every coordinate x_i is replaced by x_i' where $x_i' = kx_i$ then we would now see the same two clusters as shown in Fig. 2(b). Clearly, now the clusters exhibit a circular (hypersphere, for $n = 2$) shape. A similar experiment may be performed for any metric space. Working with metric spaces works fine when the hyperspheres are well behaved. This is illustrated in Fig. 3. Here (and in the following 2 figures) the elements of the database are assumed to lie on the surface of the sphere.
However, there are cases such as the one illustrated in Fig. 4(a) where there is an unavoidable degree of confusion.
In this case classification errors are unavoidable. An even more critical case is as the one shown in Fig. 4(b), where a metric algorithm will be unable to distinguish the clusters unless the width of the surface of the spheres is specified. A further example of the problems we may face is illustrated in Fig. 5, where highly irregular but, however, fairly "evident" clusters are shown. None of these would be found by a clustering algorithm based on a metric space.

2.4 Non-traditional methods

In this work we discuss three alternatives of clustering algorithms which do not depend on simple distance metrics and, therefore, allow us to find clusters with more complex shapes in n-dimensional space.

a. Clustering based on optimization of quality indices.

b. Clustering based on optimization of entropy

c. Clustering based on optimization of membership.

2.4.1 Clustering based on optimization of quality indices.

In this case, the clustering algorithm is based on the identification of those elements of the database which optimize some quality criterion. In the usual process, the clusters are found via some arbitrary clustering algorithm and then assigned a quality grade according to a certain quality index. An interesting alternative is to find the elements of the clusters from the indices directly. The problem with this approach is that the purported indices are usually expressed mathematically with some complex function which is not prone to optimization by any of the traditional methods. Hence, we analyze clusters resulting from the optimization of a given quality index with genetic algorithms (GA). In particular, we point out that any elitist GA has been proved to find a global optimum if given enough time (Rudolph,1994). Furthermore, we know that not all GAs are equally efficient and, further, that a variation called Vasconcelos GA (VGA) is best among a family of GAs (Kuri,2002). We point out that there have many attempts to prove that a specific quality index is relatively better than others (Kovacs,2006). We have selected some of the more interesting ones for our analysis. Applying VGA we have found clusters which depend on one of the following quality indices.

- Dunn and Dunn-like validity indices
- Davies-Bouldin validity index
- SD validity index
- Variance of the nearest neighbor (VNN)

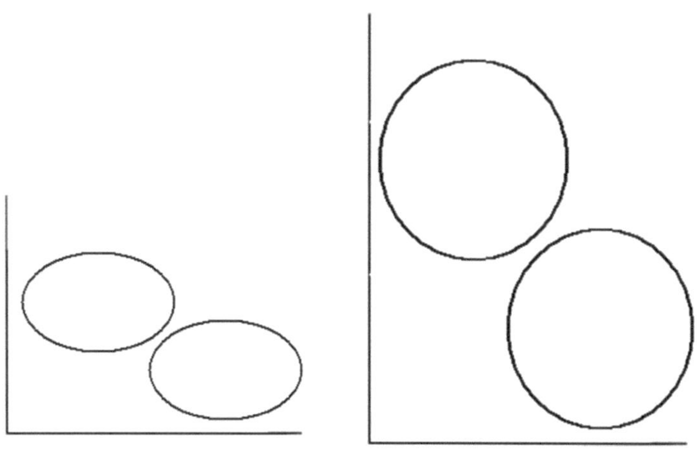

(a) Clusters in X-Y (b) Clusters in X-kY

Fig. 2. Hypothetical clustering

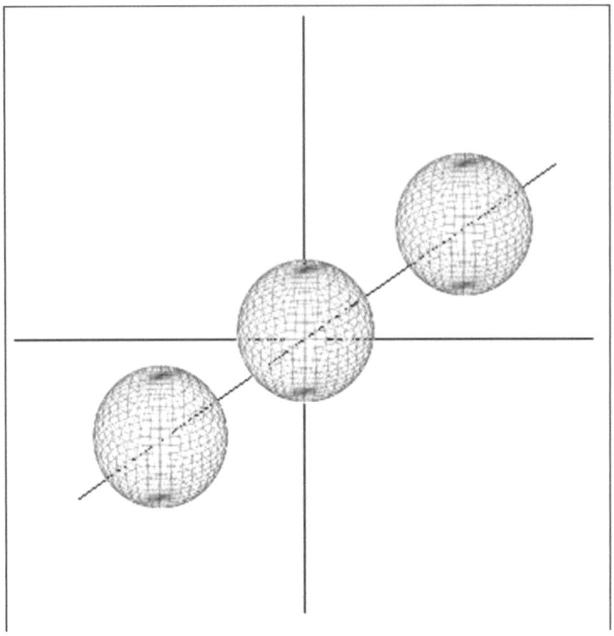

Fig. 3. Disjoint spherical clusters

None of the resulting clusters has an immediate spherical shape unless the coordinates of the space of solution are translated into the indices: a rather involved and sometimes downright impossible task.

2.4.2 Clustering based on optimization of entropy

In broad terms, the information of a data set may be expressed as the expected information for all the symbols in such set. From Shannon's information theory (Shannon,1949) we may write the entropy of a source S as:

$$H(S) = \sum_{i=1}^{n} p(s_i)I(s_i) = -\sum_{i=1}^{n} p(s_i)log_2(p(s_i)) \tag{7}$$

where $p(s_i)$ is the probability that symbol s_i is output by the source; $I(s_i)$ is the information present in symbol i in bits:$I(s_i) = -log_2 p(s_i)$. There are several possible approaches to clustering by considering the information in the data rather than a distance between their elements (COOLCAT). To solve these problems we apply a rugged genetic algorithm. In order to test the efficiency of our proposal we artificially created several sets of data with known properties in a tridimensional space. By applying this algorithm [called the Fixed Grid Evolutionary Entropic Algorithm (FGEEA) (Kuri & Aldana,2010)] we were able to find highly irregular clusters that traditional algorithms cannot. Some previous work is based on algorithms relying on similar approaches (such as ENCLUS'(Cheng,1999) and CLIQUE's (Agrawal et al.,1998)). The differences between such approaches and FGEEA will also be discussed.

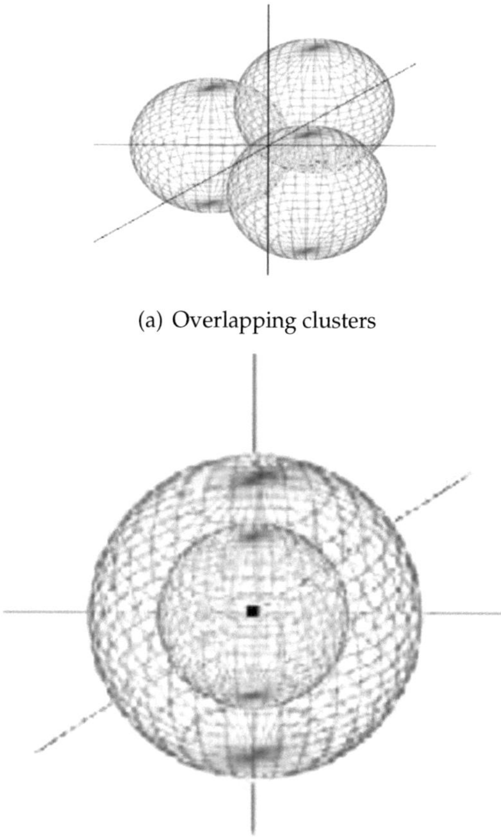

(a) Overlapping clusters

(b) Concentric clusters

Fig. 4. Clusters with different overlapping degree

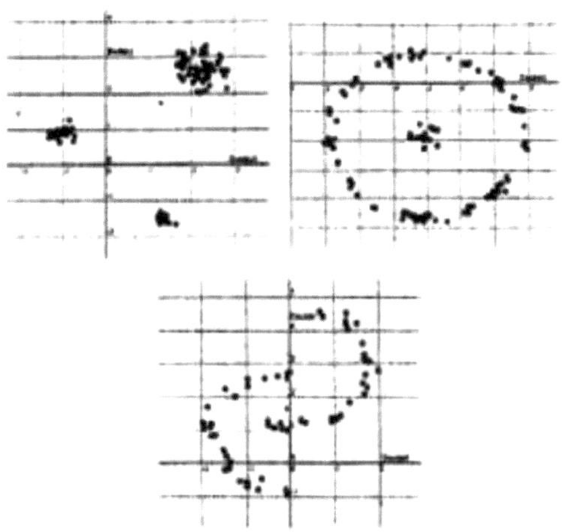

Fig. 5. Irregularly shaped clusters

2.5 Clustering based on optimization of membership

A final approach to be discussed is one in which the elements of a cluster are determined by finding a set of metric locus which encompass the elements of the database; one set per cluster. To make the idea definite a formula originally developed by Johan Gielis (Gielis,2003) (which has been called the "superformula") is examined. It allows the generation of n-dimensional bodies of arbitrary shape by modifying certain parameters. This approach allows us to represent a cluster as the set of data contained "inside" a given body without resorting to a distance (Kuri & Aldana,2008). Therefore, we replace the idea of nearness by one of membership. Gielis superformula (GSF) generalizes the equation of a hyper-ellipse by introducing some parameters which increase the degrees of freedom of the resulting figures when geometrically interpreted. It is given by:

$$r(\rho) = \left[\left| \frac{cos(\frac{m\rho}{4})}{a} \right|^{n_2} + \left| \frac{sin(\frac{m\rho}{4})}{b} \right|^{n_3} \right]^{n_1} \tag{8}$$

Where r is the radius and ρ is the angle. In Fig. 6 we show some forms generated from $a = b = 1$ and several values assigned to m, n_1, n_2, n_3. It is possible to generalize the formula to three or more dimensions. In Fig. 7 we show some forms obtained for a 3-dimensional space. The parameters of the superformula are encoded in the chromosome of the genetic algorithm (GA) (one set per cluster). The GA maximizes the number of elements enclosed in arbitrary figures defined by Gielis' formula. The variables to optimize are m, $n1$, $n2$, $n3$, a, b for each of the clusters. Variables cx, cy, cz which correspond to the centers of the clusters are also introduced. These variables place the locus in a definite point in space. Therefore, the encoding of one cluster for the GA is as shown in Fig. 8.

The full chromosome, assuming there are $four$ clusters, is shown in Fig. 9.

Clearly, this approach is not hampered by distance considerations. A point to be made is that the generalization of Gielis' formula has not been achieved. However, the same approach may be attempted in a way that yields arbitrary shapes in N-space. This is still a matter of open research.

3. Clustering as an optimization problem

The problem of finding an appropriate set of centroids may be seen, in general, as an optimization problem. This is clear from equations (2), (3), (4) and (1) (in the case of Euclidean based SOMs). In all of these cases we wish to minimize a distance. In fact, the method is defined by the minimizing algorithm. Were we able to find an optimization algorithm suitable to all the cases, then the difference between the various methods would almost fundamentally rely on the definition of the distance. Several such general methods exist. Before describing one of particular interest for our purpose we make a brief mention of classical optimization schemes and their inherent limitations.

3.1 Classical optimization

In classical optimization the search for the solution usually depends on iterating along the direction of the negative steepest slope of the function under study. When there is a single variable the slope is found by differentiating with respect to the independent variable. If there are more variables then gradient based methods are used.

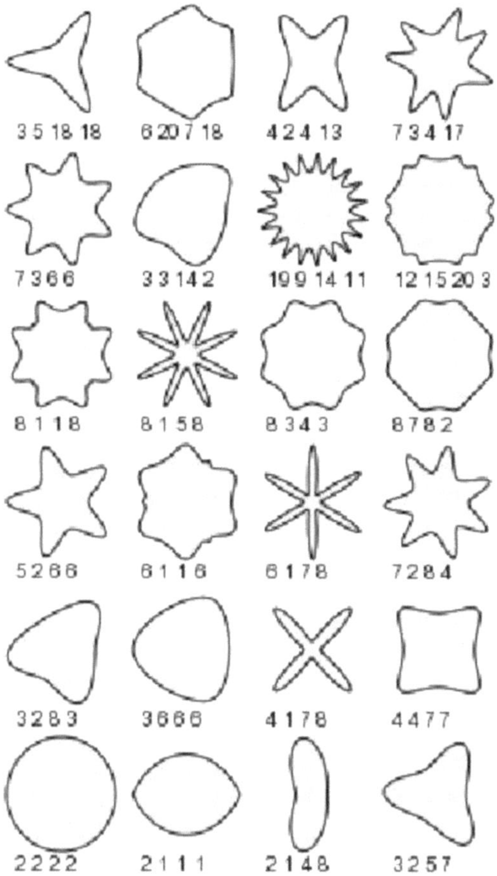

Fig. 6. Shapes in 2D generated by the Gielis equation

3.1.1 Convexity

In order for these methods to work it is stipulated that the function be convex. A real-valued function $f(x)$ defined on an interval is called convex if for any two points x_1 and x_2 in its domain X and any $t \in [0,1]$,

$$f(tx_1 + (1-t)x_2) \leq tf(x_1) + (1-t)f(x_2) \tag{9}$$

This implies that when moving on the optimization path, no point will map out of the space of the function. In other words, and this is the point we want to stress, in classical optimization the function has to be well defined and convex. If either of these two conditions is not met, then the process collapses and we are unable to tackle the problem.

3.1.2 Differentiability

Clearly, if the purportedly optimizable function is not amenable to differentiation, then the problem (which, precisely, depends on the existence of the gradient) is intractable. This too, constitutes a serious limitation. Many functions exhibit discontinuities and/or poles and none of these functions is optimizable (in general) via the classical optimization methods. During the last few decades, given that the computational costs have decreased dramatically, there has been a tendency to consider computationally intensive methods. Such methods were not practical before the advent of low cost computers. Among the many methods which have recently arisen, we may mention: tabu search, simulated annealing, ant colony optimization, particle swarm optimization and evolutionary computation. Some of the variations of evolutionary computation are: evolutionary strategies, evolutionary programming, genetic programming and genetic algorithms. GAs have been extensively used in otherwise difficult or intractable optimization problems. In our case, GAs turn out to be the key to generalize most of the clustering techniques to be discussed in what follows. For this reason we make a brief digression and discuss the basic tenets of GAs.

3.2 Genetic algorithms

Genetic Algorithms (an interesting introduction to GAs and other evolutionary algorithms may be found in (Bäck,1996)) are optimization algorithms which are frequently cited as "partially simulating the process of natural evolution". Although this a suggestive analogy behind which, indeed, lies the original motivation for their inception, it is better to understand them as a kind of algorithms which take advantage of the implicit (indeed, unavoidable) granularity of the search space which is induced by the use of the finite binary representation in a digital computer.

In such finite space, numbers originally conceived as existing in R^n actually map into B^m space. Thereafter it is simple to establish that a genetic algorithmic process is a finite Markov chain (MC) whose states are the populations arising from the so called genetic operators: (typically) selection, crossover and mutation (Rudolph,1994). As such they display all of the properties of a MC. From this fact one may prove the following mathematical properties of a GA:

(1) The results of the evolutionary process are independent of the initial population and

(2) A GA preserving the best individual arising during the process will converge to the global optimum (albeit the convergence process is not bounded in time).

Fig. 7. Shapes in 3D generated by the Gielis equation

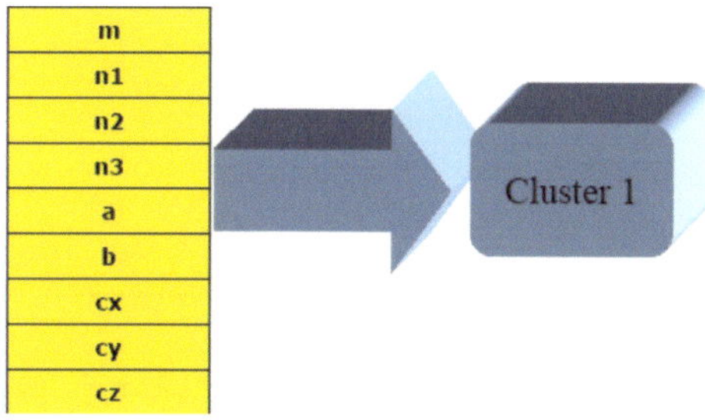

Fig. 8. Part of the chromosome encoding a cluster.

Their most outstanding feature is that, as opposed to other more traditional optimization techniques, the GA iterates simultaneously over several possible solutions. Then, other plausible solutions are obtained by combining (crossing over) the codes of these solutions to obtain hopefully better ones. The solution space (SS) is, therefore, traversed stochastically searching for increasingly better plausible solutions. In order to guarantee that the SS will be globally explored some bits of the encoded solution are randomly selected and changed (a process called mutation). The main concern of GA-practitioners (given the fact that well designed GAs, in general, will find the best solution) is to make the convergence as efficient

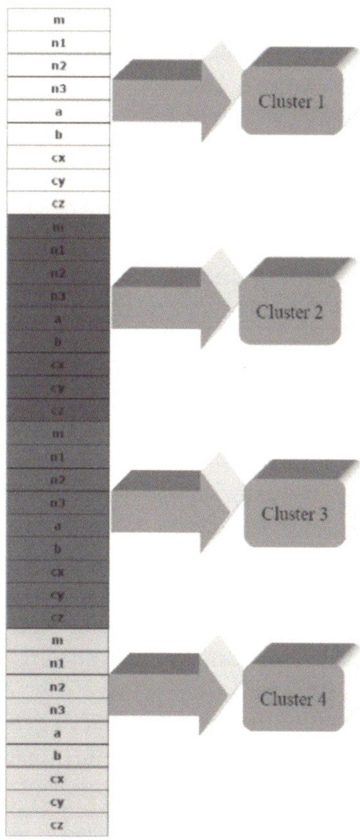

Fig. 9. Full chromosome

Algorithm	Relative Performance	Number of Optimized Functions
VGA	1.000	2,736
EGA	1.039	2,484
TGA	1.233	2,628
SGA	1.236	2,772
CGA	1.267	3,132
RHC	3.830	3,600

Table 1. Relative Performance of Different Breeds of Genetic Algorithms

as possible. The work of Forrest et al. has determined the characteristics of the so-called Idealized GA (IGA) which is impervious to GA-hard problems (Forrest,1993).

3.2.1 Vasconcelos' genetic algorithms

The implementation of the IGA is unattainable in practice. However, a practical approximation called the Vasconcelos' GA (VGA) has been repeatedly tested and proven to be highly efficient (Kuri,2002). The VGA, therefore, turns out to be an optimization algorithm of broad scope of application and demonstrably high efficiency. A statistical analysis was done by minimizing a large number of functions and comparing the relative performance of six optimization methods[1] of which five are GAs. The ratio of every GA's absolute minimum (with probability $p = 0.95$) relative to the best GA's absolute minimum may be found in Table 1 under the column "Relative Performance". The number of functions which were minimized to guarantee the mentioned confidence level is shown under "Number of Optimized Functions". It may be seen that VGA, in this study, was the best of all the analyzed variations. Interestingly the CGA (the classical or "canonical" genetic algorithm) comes at the bottom of the list with the exception of the random mutation hill climber (RHC) which is not an evolutionary algorithm. According to these results, the minima found with VGA are, in the worst case, more than 25% better than those found with the CGA. Due to its tested efficiency, we now describe in more detail VGA.

As opposed to the CGA, VGA selects the candidate individuals deterministically picking the two extreme (ordered according to their respective fitness) performers of the generation for crossover. This would seem to fragrantly violate the survival-of-the-fittest strategy behind evolutionary processes since the genes of the more apt individuals are mixed with those of the least apt ones. However, VGA also retains the best n individuals out of the $2n$ previous ones. The net effect of this dual strategy is to give variety to the genetic pool (the lack of which is a cause for slow convergence) while still retaining a high degree of elitism. This sort of elitism, of course, guarantees that the best solutions are not lost. On the other hand, the admixture of apparently counterpointed plausible solutions is aimed at avoiding the proliferation of similar genes in the pool. In nature as well as in GAs variety is needed in order to ensure the efficient exploration of the space of solutions[2]. As stated before, all elitist GAs will eventually converge to a global optimum. The VGA does so in less generations. Alternatively we may say that VGA will outperform other GAs given the same number of generations. Besides, it is easier to program because we need not to simulate a probabilistic process. Finally, VGA is impervious

[1]VGA: Vasconcelos' GA; EGA: Eclectic GA; TGA: Elitist GA; SGA: Statistical GA; CGA: Canonical (or Simple) GA; RMH: Random Mutation Hill Climber.

[2]The Latin American philosopher José Vasconcelos proposed that the admixture of all races would eventually give rise to a better one he called the "cosmic" race; hence the algorithm's name.

Algorithm 1 Vasconcelos Genetic Algorithm (VGA)

```
Require: p_c, p_m, n, G {Crossover probability, mutation probability, number of individuals and
    number of generations}
Ensure: After G iterations the best individual is the best solution.
population ⇐ generatePopulation(n) {Generate random population of n individuals}
l ⇐ getIndividualLength() {Determine the genome length}
bitsToMutate ⇐ n * l * p_m {Calculate the number of bits that will be mutated}
for all individual ∈ population do
  calculateFitness()
end for
population ⇐ orderByFitness(population) {Order population by fitness value}
numIteration ⇐ 0
repeat
  for i = 1 to n/2 do
    individual_1 ⇐ selectIndividual(i)
    individual_2 ⇐ selectIndividual(n − i + 1)
    if p_c ≥ random() then
      crossover(individual_1, individual_2)
    end if
    newPopulation ⇐ newPopulation ∪ {individual_1, individual_2}
  end for
  population ⇐ population ∪ newPopulation {Merge new individuals and previous
  population}
  for i = 1 to bitsToMutate do
    indexIndividual ⇐ selectIndividualToMutate()
    mutate(indexIndividual)
  end for
  for all individual ∈ population do
    calculateFitness()
  end for
  population ⇐ orderByFitness(population) {Order population by fitness value}
  population ⇐ retainTopN(population) {Retain the best n individuals and discard the
  worst n individuals}
  numIteration ⇐ numIteration + 1
until numIteration < G
```

to negative fitness's values. We, thus, have a tool which allows us to identify the best values for a set of predefined metrics possibly reflecting complementary goals. For these reasons we use in our work VGA as the optimization method. In what follows we explain our proposal based in the concepts mentioned above

3.2.2 Application of genetic algorithms to clustering

We are now in the position of suggesting an immediate application of a general optimization method to achieve non-traditional clustering. The clear advantage of the utilization of this tool is that we are in the position of selecting arbitrary metrics as a vehicle for clustering. As mentioned above, some of the traditional clustering methods rely on a specific optimization algorithm to operate. A case in point is Kohonen's algorithm which aims at finding a set of centroids (one per neuron) such that similar neurons (and the corresponding centroids) share neighboring positions in the typical 2D space. This is done by a set of consecutive contests between the neurons in the network whereupon the victorious neuron acts as an attractor for the rest of the neurons. Since different neurons are apt to emerge as winners in every iteration, this brilliant approach resembles a competition whose tide comes and goes and ends up with a self-organized configuration. A similar purpose may be attempted by simply specifying a function which minimizes the distance between the neurons in 2D space while, simultaneously, finding a cluster (as per Euclidean distance, for example) for every neuron. When the SOM algorithm was developed, GAs had not yet consolidated as general optimization techniques. As far as we know this approach has not been attempted and here we simply wish to stress the generality of the genetic optimization.

4. Optimization in non-traditional methods

4.1 The data sets

In order to illustrate the performance of non-traditional clustering methods, three types of data sets are analyzed in this work. We shall call them "A", "B" and "C" respectively. Every set is composed of vectors (in a $3D$ space) that belong to three different spheres which we call sphere 1, 2 and 3 respectively. There are 10,000 vectors in each one of the spheres. They were generated from.

$$x = x_0 + r\sin\theta\,\cos\varphi \tag{10}$$

$$y = y_0 + r\sin\theta\,\sin\varphi \tag{11}$$

$$z = z_0 + r\cos\theta \tag{12}$$

from uniformly distributed values for $r \subset [0,1)$, $(0 \le \varphi \le 2\pi$ and $0 \le \theta \le \pi)$. For set A the three centers of the spheres were chosen so that the spheres would not intersect (see Fig.3). In set B, the chosen centers yield partially overlapping data (see Fig. 4(a)). Finally, in set C, the spheres shared a common center (see Fig.4(b)). However, in the last set for sphere 1 $r \in [0,1)$; for sphere 2 $r \in [0,0.666)$; for sphere 3 $r \in [0,0.333)$. In this case, then, spheres 1, 2 and 3 share the same space where the density of 2 is larger than that of 1 and the density of 3 is larger than the other two. Our intent is to choose vectors in set A, B and C whose distribution is not uniform but Gaussian. To achieve this, we determined to divide the space of probabilities of a Gaussian curve in 20 equally spaced intervals. The area under the curve for a normal distribution with $\mu = 0$ and $\sigma = 1$ between -4 and +4 is very closely equal to one. Therefore, it is easy to see that 5%, of the observations will be between -4 and -1.654; 5%, will be between -1.654 and -1.280, etc. The required normal behavior may be approximated by selecting 50 of the uniformly distributed values from the interval $[-4,-1{,}654)$; another 50 from the

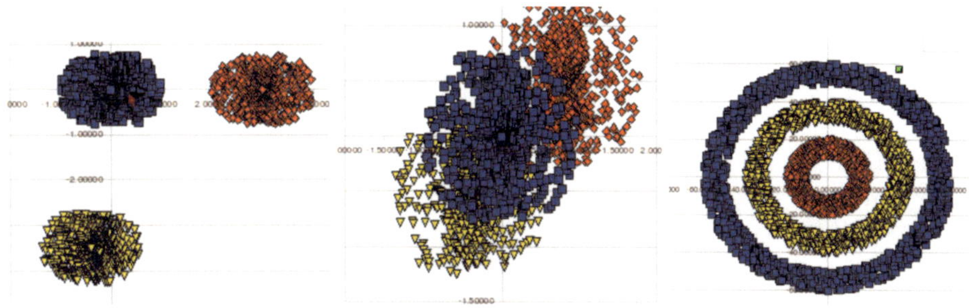

(a) Disjoint data set (b) Overlapped data set (c) Overlapped data set

Fig. 10. Spatial distribution of the test data set

interval $[-1.654, -1.280)$, etc. In all we will end up with 1000 vectors for every sphere. These vectors will now be very closely Gaussian. When data is normally distributed, a Bayesian classifier is optimal. The behavior of one such classifier will serve as a base point. To stress: when the distribution of the data set to classify is Gaussian, a Bayesian classifier yields the best theoretical results (by minimizing the probability of classification error independently of the degree of overlap between the distributions of the clusters) (Haykin,1994). Hence, we resorted to Gaussian distributed data in order to establish a behavior relative to the best theoretical one when measuring the performance of non-traditional methods. Our claim is that, if the methods perform satisfactorily when faced with Gaussian data, they will also perform reasonably well when faced with other possible distributions. That is, we wish to show that the results obtained with non-traditional methods are close to those obtained with a Bayesian classifier for the same data set. This would mean that these results correspond to an efficient algorithm. The data sets are ilustrated in Fig. 10.

4.2 Validity index based

There are some methods that consist in finding certain models for clusters and attempting to optimize the fit between the data and the model. There are many ways to attempt the suggested modeling. In particular, one may try to optimize a validity index. Validity indices are used to compare the performance of the clustering results obtained through some given method. If we work "backwards" and optimize the purported index, we should come up with a "good" clustering. The following indices are used with this purpose.

4.2.1 Dunn and Dunn-like validity indices

A cluster validity index for clustering proposed in (Dunn,1973), attempts to identify "compact and well separated clusters". The index is defined by following equation for a specific number of clusters.

$$D_{nc} = min_{nc} \left\{ min_{j=i+1,\ldots,nc} \left\{ \frac{d(c_i, c_j)}{max_{k=1,\ldots,nc} diam(c_k)} \right\} \right\} \tag{13}$$

where nc is the number of clusters, $d(c_i, c_j)$ is the dissimilarity function between two clusters c_i and cj defined as

$$d(c_i, c_j) = min_{x \in c_i, y \in c_j} d(x, y) \tag{14}$$

and $diam(c_k)$ is the cluster diameter which may be considered as a measure of dispersion of the clusters. The diameter of a cluster C can be defined as follows:

$$diam(C) = max_{x,y \in C} \{d(x, y)\} \tag{15}$$

If the data set contains well-separated clusters, the distance between clusters is usually large and the diameter of the clusters is expected to be small. Therefore a large value is indicative of a better clustering result.

4.2.2 Davies-Bouldin validity index

A similarity measure R_{ij} between the clusters C_i and C_j is defined based on a measure of dispersion of a cluster s_i and a dissimilarity measure between two clusters d_{ij}. The Rij index is defined to satisfy the following conditions (DaviesBouldin,2009):

1. $R_{ij} \geq 0$
2. $R_{ij} = R_{ji}$
3. if $s_i = 0$ and $s_j = 0$ then $R_{ij} = 0$
4. if $s_j > s_k$ and $d_{ij} = d_{ik}$ then $R_{ij} > R_{ik}$
5. if $s_j = s_k$ and $d_{ij} < d_{ik}$ then $R_{ij} > R_{ik}$

These conditions imply that R_{ij} is nonnegative and symmetric. The usual definition of similarity measure is:

$$R_{ij} = \frac{s_i + s_j}{d_{ij}} \tag{16}$$

$$d_{ij} = d(v_i, v_j) \tag{17}$$

$$s_i = \frac{1}{\|c_i\|} \sum_{x \in c_i} d(x, v_i) \tag{18}$$

The Davies-Bouldin index measures the average of similarity between each cluster an its most similar one (Kovacs,2006) The value of the index is calculated as follows:

$$DB = \frac{1}{nc} \sum_{i=1}^{nc} R_i \tag{19}$$

The lower value of this index means better clustering result due to the clusters have to be compact and separated.

4.2.3 SD validity index

The SD validity index is based on the concepts of the average scattering for clusters and total separation between clusters (Halkidi et al.,2001). The average scattering is defined as:

$$Scat(nc) = \frac{1}{nc} \sum_{i=1}^{nc} \frac{\|\sigma(v_i)\|}{\|\sigma(X)\|} \tag{20}$$

The total separation between clusters is given by following equation:

$$Dis(nc) = \frac{D_{max}}{D_{min}} \sum_{k=1}^{nc} \left[\sum_{z=1}^{nc} \|v_k - v_z\| \right]^{-1} \tag{21}$$

where $D_{max} = max(\|vi - vj\|)\ \forall i, j \in \{1,2,3,\ldots,nc\}$ is the maximum distance between cluster centers. The $D_{min} = min(\|vi - vj\|)\ \forall i, j \in \{1,2,3,\ldots,nc\}$ is the minimum distance between cluster centers. Now, we can define a validity index based on equations above, as follows

$$SD(nc) = \alpha Scat(nc) + Dis(nc) \tag{22}$$

where α is a weighting factor equal to $Dis(c_{max})$ where c_{max} is the maximum number of input clusters. Lower value of SD index means better clustering results.

4.2.4 Variance of the nearest neighbor (VNN)

This validity index is based on the study of the local environment of a data elements. Formally the deviation of the nearest neighbor distances is determined in every cluster. It is defined as follows:

$$d_{min}(x_i) = min_{y \in C_i}\{d(x_i, y)\} \tag{23}$$

$$d_{min}(C_i) = \frac{\sum_{x_i \in C_i} d_{min}(x_i)}{\|C_i\|} \tag{24}$$

$$V(C_i) = \frac{1}{\|C_i\|^{-1}} \sum_{x_i \in C_i} d_{min}(x_i) - d_{min}(C_i) \tag{25}$$

Based on above equations it is posible to define the validity index called Variance of the Nearest Neighbor Distance (VNND) (Kovacs,2006)

$$VNND = \sum_{i=1}^{nc} V(C_i) \tag{26}$$

This index measures the homogeneity of the clusters. Lower index value means more homogenous clustering. The principal advantage is that this index does not use global references points to calculate its value. The VNND index is based on local information of each point. Therefore, it can measure arbitrary shaped clusters.

4.2.5 Validity index optimization (VIO)

Clearly, the problem of obtaining the best value of a Validity Index is an optimization problem. To this purpose we use a VGA. The individuals of the algorithm have been encoded as follows:

1. The length of the genome is equal to $nc * N$, where nc is the number of clusters and N is the number of dimensions of the data set.
2. To the gene i is assigned a value in $\mathbb{R}$ that represents one coordinate of the center of the $k - th$ cluster.
3. The center of the $k - th$ cluster is given by a sequence of adjacent genes. The length of this sequence is N.

Fig. 11 exemplifies a genome for $nc = 3$ and $N = 3$. The fitness function is given by a particular Validity Index, so that the best individual will be one whose centers values allow to obtain the optimal value of the index. The following tests were performed:

1. VGA was run 20 times (with different seeds of the pseudo random number generator) with three disjoint clusters. The same data set was tested with the Bayesian Classifier. The results obtained are shown in Table 2.

Fig. 11. Genome of the individual ($nc = 3$ and $N = 3$)

Index	Type of Optimization	Average Effectiveness
Dunn and Dunn	Maximize	99.00
SD Validity Index	Minimize	99.00
Davies-Boulding	Minimize	99.00
Nearest Neighbor Distance	Minimize	99.00
Bayesian Classifier Efectiveness		99.00

Table 2. Results obtained with VIO for different index and disjoint clusters

2. VGA was run 20 times (with different seeds of the pseudo random number generator) with three overlapping clusters. The same data set was tested with the Bayesian Classifier. The results obtained are shown in Table 3.
3. VGA was run 20 times (with different seeds of the pseudo random number generator) with three concentric clusters. The same data set was tested with the Bayesian Classifier. The results obtained are shown in Table 4.

The following results (Table 2) correspond to the data set with disjoint clusters. We can see that all methods show similar trends. We believe that this fact is due to the spatial distribution of the clusters. In Table 3 and Table 4 are shown the results obtained with the data set with overlapping clusters. We can see that the effectiveness is reduced substantially. However the SD Validity index yields better results with respect to other indices and close results relative to a Bayesian Classifier.
The results obtained show that the best index is SD for the data set used. We can see that the proposed method yields "good" results relative to a Bayesian classifier.

4.3 Entropy based

The Entropic Evolutionary Clustering is a method based on the measurement of the information contained in data set D. This approach is based on maximizing density in terms of the entropy of the area of the space that represents a cluster.

4.3.1 ENCLUS

Cheng et al (Cheng,1999), developed an algorithm called ENCLUS (Entropic Clustering) in which they link the entropy with two concepts that the authors call *coverage* and *density*. These are determined by the space's segmentation. Segmentation is made iteratively. Thereafter, several conditions have to be satisfied for every iteration of the algorithm. The space segmentation is a partition on non-overlapping rectangular units based on CLIQUE (Clustering in Quest) algorithm where a unit is dense if the fraction of the elements contained

Index	Type of Optimization	Average Effectiveness	Ratio
Dunn and Dunn	Maximize	67.00	0.77
SD Validity Index	Minimize	71.00	0.82
Davies-Boulding	Minimize	43.00	0.49
Nearest Neighbor Distance	Minimize	67.00	0.77
Bayesian Classifier Efectiveness		87.00	

Table 3. Results obtained with VIO for different index and overlapping clusters

Index	Type of Optimization	Average Effectiveness	Ratio
Dunn and Dunn	Maximize	43.00	0.63
SD Validity Index	Minimize	59.00	0.87
Davies-Boulding	Minimize	41.00	0.60
Nearest Neighbor Distance	Minimize	57.00	0.84
Bayesian Classifier Efectiveness		68.00	

Table 4. Results obtained with VIO for different index and concentric clusters

in the unit is greater than a certain threshold. A cluster is the maximum set of connected dense units.

4.3.2 COOLCAT

Another similar work is the so-called COOLCAT algorithm (Barbara,2002) which also approaches the clustering problem on entropic considerations but is mainly focused on categorical sets of data.

4.3.3 Fixed grid evolutionary entropic algorithm (FGEEA)

The Fixed Grid Evolutionary Entropic Algorithm is a clustering method based on the measurement of the information contained in data set D. This is based on the assumption that the areas of space with more information represent a cluster. This fact is illustrated in Fig. 12. The steps of the algorithm are:

(1) The metric space D is transformed to a metric space D' where its elements are partitions of the space D such that each contains zero or more elements of D. (see example in Fig. 13)

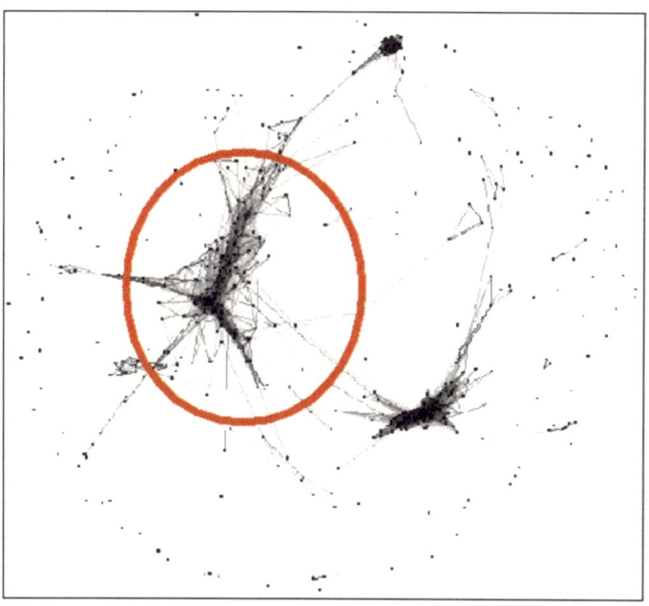

Fig. 12. Example of a high density area (with less information

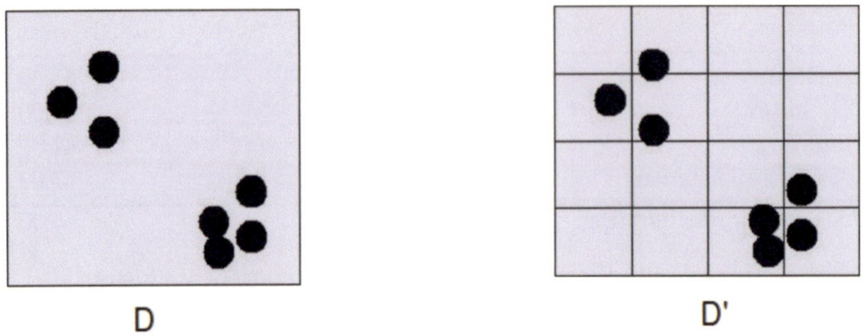

Fig. 13. Transformation of D to D'. The elements on D' are represented as cells

(2) The amount of information of an element(cell) of D' is given by the number of elements (of the original space D) that belong to it. Here each partition or cell of D' is equivalent to a symbol s and the space D' is equivalent to the source S.

(3) In general for a n-dimensional space D, its transformation D' is denominated Hypercube Wrapper (HW). In Fig. 14 is shown a HW in 3D.

(4) Each partition or cell of HW is called a "voxel".

(5) The entropy of HW is:

$$H(HW) = \sum_{i=1}^{n} p(s_i)I(s_i) = -\sum_{i=1}^{n} p(s_i)log_2(p(s_i)) \tag{27}$$

where s_i is a voxel and $HW = S$.

(6) Our hypothesis is that areas with high density have minimum entropy with respect to areas with low density. Therefore the areas with minimum entropy correspond to a cluster. To determine the entropy of a cluster we introduce a concept we call intracluster entropy, defined as:

$$H(c_i) = \sum p(s_j)log_2(s_j) \qquad \forall s_j \in c_i \tag{28}$$

Where $H(c_i)$ is the intracluster entropy of $i-th$ cluster. In order to determine that s_j belongs to c_i we use a genetic algorithm, as discussed in what follows.

Fig. 14. Hypercubic Wrapper in a *tri*-dimensional space where the points represent elements of the data set and the subdivisions are voxels

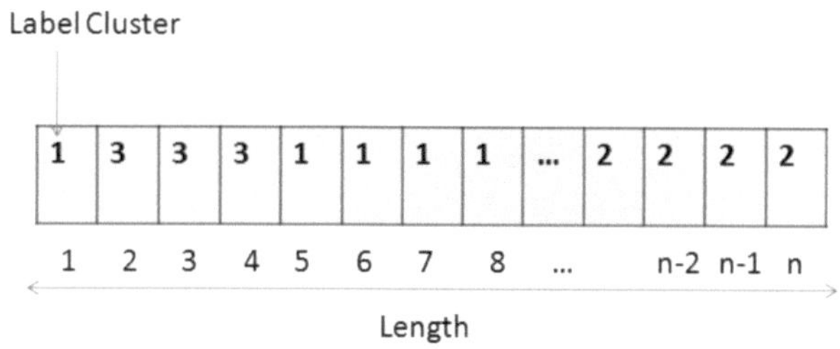

Fig. 15. Genome of the individual (k=3)

4.3.3.1 Application of VGA

Our aim is to find the areas of the subspace HW where the entropy is minimal. We find groups of voxels such that each group has minimal entropy (intracluster entropy). Clearly this is an optimization problem which we tackle with VGA. The individuals of the algorithm have been encoded as follows:

a. The length of the genome is equal to $|HW|$. It is composed by all symbols (or voxels).
b. Each gene is assigned a label that represents the cluster to which it belongs.
c. It has a sequential index. Such index will allow mapping all symbols to subspace HW. Fig. 15 exemplifies a genome for $k = 3$.

Now, we define the fitness function as:

$$f(individual_i) = min \sum_{j=0}^{k} H(c_j) \qquad for \quad i \leq N \tag{29}$$

Subject to:

$$\sum_{j=0}^{k} H(c_j) \geq H(S) \tag{30}$$

$$\left| \sum_{j=0}^{k} H(c_j) - H(S) \right| > \Delta_1 \tag{31}$$

Where N is the size of the population and Δ_1 is a parameter that represents a threshold of the difference between the sum of intracluster entropies and the entropy of source S. Additionally we have introduced a constraint called "intracluster density" defined as:

$$dc_i \leq \epsilon \tag{32}$$

where ϵ is the threshold density. One last constraint is the intracluster density (dc_i). It is the number of elements of data set X which belong to the symbols of $i - th$ cluster:

$$dc_i = \frac{\alpha}{\beta} \tag{33}$$

where α is the number the elements that belong to the data set X and β is the number of symbols within cluster i. This constraint ensures that entropy is minimal within any given cluster. The algorithm yields a best individual which represents a set of clusters of symbols that are map into sets of voxels in HW, as shown in Fig. 16

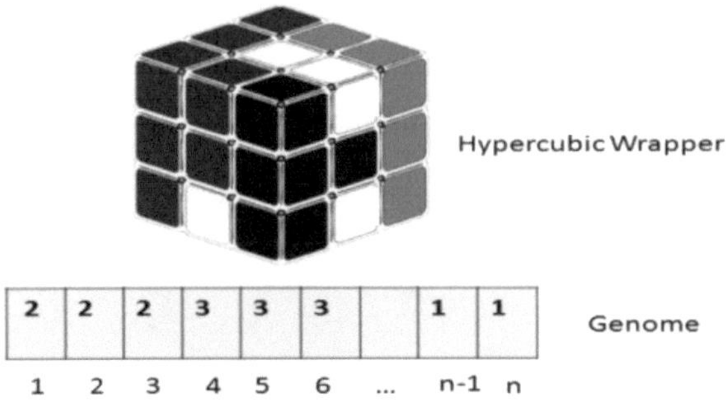

Fig. 16. Possible clustering delivered by VGA. Different intensities in the cube represent a different cluster. (Empty voxels are white).

4.3.3.2 Experimental results

Our algorithm was tested with three synthetic data sets that were described above. The values of the parameters of FGEEA are given in Table 5. This values were determined experimentally. The VGA was run 20 times (with different seeds of the pseudo random number generator) per data set. The same data sets was tested with other algorithms such as K-Means, Kohonen Maps and Fuzzy C-Means. As in the VIO method all tests include a test with the Bayesian Classifier. The results obtained with disjoint clusters are shown in Table 6. This allows us to see that the results of FGEEA are similar to those given by some alternative algorithms. The high effectiveness in all cases is due to the spatial distribution of data set.
The results obtained with overlapping clusters are shown in Table 7 where we can see that the effectiveness decreases significantly in general. However FGEEA showed better results than traditional methods and close results to Bayesian Classifier.
The results obtained in the two last cases (overlapping and concentric clusters) are due to the fact that it is not possible to find a simple separable boundary. Therefore, the boundary decision is unclear and the vast majority of the clustering methods yield poor solutions. The closeness of the results obtained so far (from VIO and FGEEA) relative to a Bayesian Classifier, tells us that both of these approaches are quite efficient. In future works we will report on experiments encompassing a wider range of data sets. We expect them to further support our hypothesis.

4.4 Membership based

As stated, when we approach the clustering problem as the search for the elements in a cluster which belong to a locus we are actually looking for membership functions. There is one

Parameter	Value
N (Number of Individuals)	500
G(Generations)	1000
p_m (Mutation probability)	0.001
p_c(Crossover Probability)	0.99
ϵ	5
δ_1	$3.5 \leq 3.6$

Table 5. Parameters test

Algorithm	Average Effectiveness
FGEEA	0.98
K-Means	0.99
Kohonen Maps	0.99
Fuzzy C-Means	0.98
Bayesian Classifier Efectiveness	0.99

Table 6. Results obtained with disjoint clusters data set

membership function for every cluster and we wish to find:

a. The position of the locus in N-space and

b. The precise definition of parameters the function

The initial work of Gielis had to do with the generalization of the formula of an ellipsoid. By enriching the set of defining parameters, he was able to find complex and somewhat irregular bodies in 2D and 3D. Our aim is to take advantage of this approach when trying to encompass the elements of the data set in a way such that no elements are left out of the "bodies" while, simultaneously, the density of the clusters is appropriate. In this sense, every membership function is determined by a core family of functions. Every core defines a different approach to the problem. We say that any plausible approach represents a kernel function. Gielis' formula represents only one of these kernels. Other kernels are possible, for which see section 4.4.2

4.4.1 Clustering with an n-dimensional extension of Gielis superformula

It is possible to apply Gielis' "superformula" to tackle the problem of clustering in an n-Dimensional space. The formula was originally developed to tackle data in $2D$. Later it was extended to $3D$. According to Gielis, it is possible to extend the formula to 3, 4, or n dimensions, by means of spherical product of superformulas. However, the problem of finding these products is non-trivial and difficult to undertake as n grows.

4.4.1.1 Gielis' formula

Gielis superformula (GSF) generalizes the equation of a hyper-ellipse by introducing some parameters which increase the degrees of freedom of the resulting figures when geometrically interpreted, as remarked when discussing equation (8). By using this approach we were able to find the parameters and positions of the locus (i.e the membership functions) in practical 3D problems. The solution we describe assumes that the number of clusters is already known. To illustrate our method we consistently assumed, without loss of generality, that there are 4 clusters and we are working on 3D. Firstly, we generate 4 n-dimensional object (in what

Algorithm	Average Effectiveness	Ratio
FGEEA	0.72	0.83
K-Means	0.51	0.59
Kohonen Maps	0.66	0.76
Fuzzy C-Means	0.15	0.17
Bayesian Classifier Efectiveness	0.87	

Table 7. Results obtained with overlapping clusters data set

Algorithm	Average Effectiveness	Ratio
FGEEA	0.53	0.78
K-Means	0.36	0.53
Kohonen Maps	0.47	0.69
Fuzzy C-Means	0.23	0.34
Bayesian Classifier Efectiveness	0.68	

Table 8. Results obtained with concentric clusters data set

follows NDO). In this case each NDO corresponds to a $3D$ cluster. These are shown in Fig. 17 For every cluster we calculated 2,500 coordinates. Therefore we got a data set ($3D$ coordinates) of size 10,000. Hence, there are 10,000 elements that we know, a priori, belong to the 4 clusters defined by the NDOs. The goal was to use this set as an input for VGA in a way such that we may verify that the values of the parameters in GSF correspond to those of Fig. 17

4.4.1.2 Encoding the problem for the genetic algorithm

The variables to optimize are m, n_1, n_2, n_3, a, b for each of the clusters. The encoding of one cluster for VGA was discussed in section 2.5. We have introduced variables cx, cy, cz which correspond to the centers of the clusters. For illustration purposes we found the initial coordinates for these centers by applying a fuzzy-c means algorithm. This allows us to compare the results obtained from VGA and those used to define the clusters we used. Fig. 18 shows the $3D$ positions of the centers. The encoding chromosome was shown in Fig. 8 and Fig. 9

4.4.1.3 Fitness function

The fitness for the individuals in the population is given by the correct membership assignment of every vector in the data set to the NDOs given the parameters encoded in the individual. For instance, in a set of size N assumed to lie within 4 clusters a "good" individual is one in which the parameters in GSF yield 4 NDOs which include all N vectors. Hence, the fitness of an individual is given by the number of vectors lying within the clusters encoded in the individual's chromosome. In Fig. 19(a) we may see an individual whose genome corresponds to 4 NDOs which include 5 vectors out of 10. Hence, its fitness is 5. It may happen that an individual includes all vectors in a single NDO as shown in Fig. 19(b). In such case, even if the inclusion is total, the individual is less than optimal and this representation must be penalized. To this effect we introduced an index given by the ratio of the number of clusters induced by the individual and the target number of clusters. In the example these quotient would evaluate to $1/4$ or 0.25. If we now multiply this index times the included number of vectors the individual induces we get which is the proposed fitness function. The following equation generalizes this criterion.

$$f(individual_i) = N * \frac{nc_{vga}}{nc} \tag{34}$$

where nc_{vga} is the number of clusters induced by an individual (or induced by VGA) and nc is the desired number of clusters.

4.4.1.4 Cluster membership for an NDO

A very basic subproblem one has to cope with is how to determine whether a given vector lies inside a given NDO. To this effect we first generate a grid over the surface of the NDO.

We applied a triangulation algorithm called "ear clipping" which, for every 3 non-consecutive points, generates a triangle belonging to the grid. In the end the algorithm yields a number of triangles leading to a body's characterization as shown in Fig. 20. To test whether a point lies within the NDO we make, for every triangle, a projection which has an angle of spread. This defines an orthogonal cone on the grid. One then tests algebraically whether the point under analysis is within the cone.

4.4.1.5 Experimental results

Here the data set differs the previous methods. A synthetic data set (in *tri*-dimensional space) was generated through the 'superformula'. The data set is composed by four clusters (NDOs)

(a) NDOs projected into (x,y)

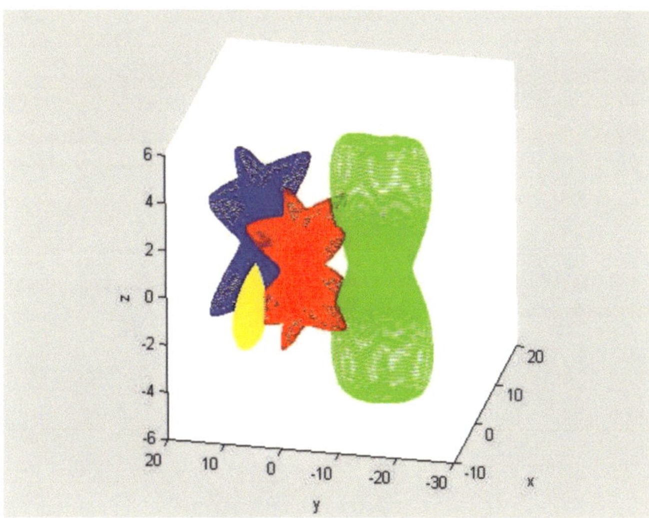

(b) NDOs represented in (x,y,z)

Fig. 17. Two views of the NDOs

Algorithm	Average Effectiveness
Gielis-VGA	0.97
K-Means	0.89
Kohonen Maps	0.91
Fuzzy C-Means	0.96
Bayesian Classifier Efectiveness	0.98

Table 9. Results obtained with clusters data set generated through the Superformula

with some overlapping degree. Our goal was to find through method described the "Gielis Bodies" that encompass the data set. Thus, this bodies should be similar to the NDO generated a priori to construct the data set. The VGA was executed 20 times with a sample of size 10,000 whose memberships are known for 4 clusters. The results gotten so far are preliminary (see Table 9). It is necessary to confirm the effectiveness of the method with data sets as those used in the methods described above. Although we have achieved reasonable clustering for synthetic data where traditional clustering techniques perform poorly, several issues remain to be solved.

4.4.1.6 Considerations

The method is unique in the sense that it is the only one in which there are strictly no metric considerations involved. Therefore, it the only one guaranteed (in principle) to find an acceptable solution to problems such as the one corresponding to data set "C". However, several issues require attention in order for the method to attain practical generality.

a. The fitness function has to be refined. It is not clear whether a simple strategy as outlined above will be adequate in most cases.

b. The computation involved in the determination of the membership of the vectors to an NDO has to be improved, given the computationally intensive nature of the evolutionary algorithm.

Fig. 18. Centers of the NDO's projected in *bi*-dimensional plane.

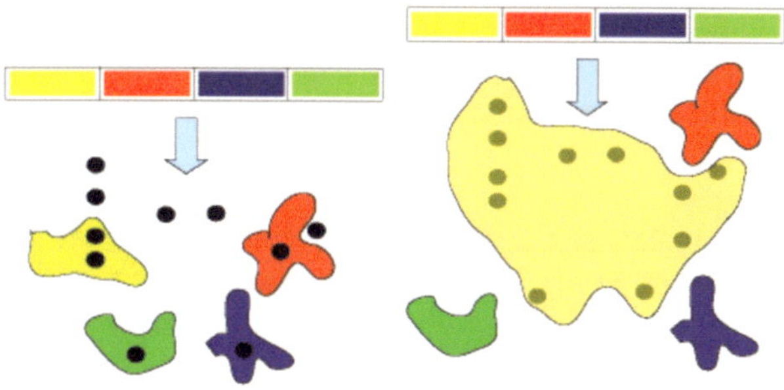

(a) Individual whose genome achieves partial inclusion for a data set (b) Full inclusion in a single set

Fig. 19. Clustering proposal by the different chromosomes

c. The best spread angle has to be determined a priori. We would like to relieve the user from this task.

d. As the number of clusters increases so does the number of parameters. This leads to an even higher computational cost. Some initial attempts at parallelizing the algorithms involved are under way (Guadarrama,2010). Fortunately, this fact is relatively natural because GAs are, by their nature, easily parallelizable. When working in highly parallel computers, therefore, the problem becomes more easily tractable. And, since the technological tendency is to increase the processors both in computer clusters as in the individual chips, this approach seems promising.

e. Most importantly, Gielis' formula, as it stands, is extremely difficult to generalize to n-dimensional spaces. In data mining, clearly, higher dimensional spaces are most common. And these spaces are not amenable to the application of the method as of today. Nonetheless, there are many applications (for example, in robotics, medical applications and image processing, in general) which may greatly benefit form this approach.

All in all we know, from initial experiments, that this method will perform adequately where others simply will not do because of conceptual constraints, as stressed in the introduction. In the past it has been customary to verify the goodness of the clusters gotten by a given method through tests which emphasize one or several criteria. In this method the goodness of the cluster is a necessary condition for the clusters to be found. Therefore, there is no need

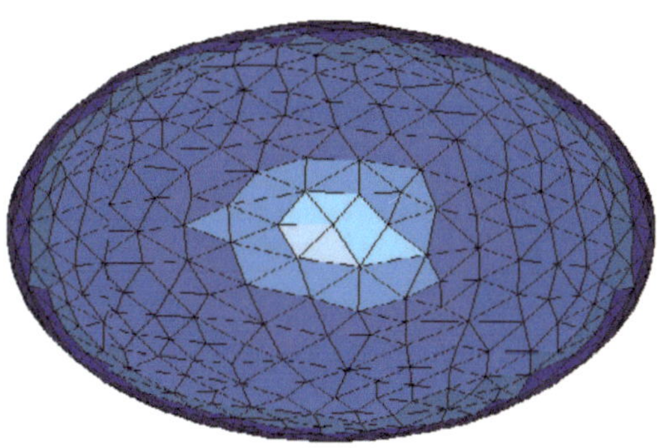

Fig. 20. Surface grid on a 3D NDO

for "outside" validity measures. In fact, the method may be seen as a dynamic measure of such validity, which is another interesting issue. That is, the validity is defined as the one maximizing the set of vectors lying in the NDOs.

4.4.2 Alternative methods

Since Gielis' formula is an extension of a hyper-ellipse, it displays some of the limitations of the resulting locus. In other words, there is no absolute freedom of choice of the possible forms of the locus involved. It is relatively simple to envision alternative choices for the generating kernels. For example, one might try rational functions (Hazewinkel,2001), in general; Padé approximants (Baker & Graves,1996); radial basis functions (Buhmann,2003) and combinations of these. The application of the mathematical formulations of different kernels allows to generalize to n-dimensional spaces. And this generalization is relatively simple. Furthermore, it allows us to find richer sets of n-dimensional locus (or, equivalently, richer sets of membership functions). The promise of this approach is well worth exploring

5. Conclusions

We have analyzed three ways to avoid the limitations of hyper-spherical clusters. We have shown that there is interesting experimental evidence that these methods yield satisfactory approximations. This is true even in the case where the original groups are definitely non-spherical. Of the three approaches, the optimization of validity indices may be considered a reasoned alternative to the usual practice of defining a metric; then testing the results casuistically to determine their usefulness. The density based approach, although (strictly speaking) is based on a distance, relies on the idea of defining an n-dimensional mesh a priori and then determining the amount of information. It differs from other density based methods in that the characteristics of the mesh are a parameter, rather than the result of the search. Finally, the methods based on membership functions seem to hold the greater promise. They also present the greatest challenge on two accounts. First, the computational cost is very high. Second, the systematic generalization to N-space is problematic. In all three cases, in general, the methods are guaranteed to yield better results than typical clustering algorithms because they will uncover the patterns underlying the elements of a cluster regardless of its shape.

6. References

[Agrawal et al.,1998] Agrawal, Rakesh, Gehrke, Johannes, Gunopulos, Dimitrios, and Raghavan, Prabhakar: Automatic subspace clustering of high dimensional data for data mining applications, SIGMOD '98: Proceedings of the 1998 ACM SIGMOD international conference on Management of data, ACM, 94–105, 1998

[Agresti,2002] Agresti A.: Categorical Data Analysis. Wiley Series in Probability and Statistics. Wiley-Interscience, 2nd edition, 2002.

[Bhattacharyya,1943] Bhattacharyya A.: On a measure of divergence between two statistical populations defined by their probability distributions, Math. Soc 35, volume 35, 99–109, 1943

[Bäck,1996] Bäck, Th.: Evolutionary Algorithms in Theory and Practice, Oxford University Press, 1996

[Baker & Graves,1996] Baker , G. A., Jr. and Graves-Morris, P.: Padé Approximants. Cambridge U.P., 1996.

[Barbara,2002] Barbara, Daniel, Li, Yi, and Couto, Julia: COOLCAT: an entropy-based algorithm for categorical clustering, CIKM, ACM, 582–589, 2002

[Buhmann,2003] Buhmann, Martin D.: Radial Basis Functions: Theory and Implementations, Cambridge University Press,2003

[Cha,2008] Cha, Sung-Hyuk: Taxonomy of nominal type histogram distance measures, MATH'08: Proceedings of the American Conference on Applied Mathematics, World Scientific and Engineering Academy and Society (WSEAS), 325–330, 2008

[Chandola et al.,2009] Chandola V., Boriah S., and Kumar V.: A framework for exploring categorical data. In SDM, pages 185-196, 2009.

[Chang & Ding,2005] Chang C. and Ding Z.: Categorical data visualization and clustering using subjective factors. Data Knowl. Eng., 53(3):243-262, 2005.

[Cheng,1999] Cheng, Chun Hung, Fu, Ada Wai-Chee, and Zhang, Yi: Entropy-based Subspace Clustering for Mining Numerical Data, KDD, 84–93, 1999

[DaviesBouldin,2009] Davies, David L., and Bouldin, Donald W.: A Cluster Separation Measure, Pattern Analysis and Machine Intelligence, IEEE Transactions on, Pattern Analysis and Machine Intelligence, IEEE Transactions on PAMI-1(2), volume PAMI-1, 224–227, January 2009

[Dunn,1973] Dunn, J. C.: A Fuzzy Relative of the ISODATA Process and Its Use in Detecting Compact Well-Separated Clusters, Journal of Cybernetics 3, volume 3, 32–57, 1973

[Ester,1996] Ester, Martin, Kriegel, Hans-peter, Jörg, S, and Xu, Xiaowei: A density-based algorithm for discovering clusters in large spatial databases with noise, , AAAI Press, 226–231, 1996

[Forrest,1993] Forrest, and Mitchell: What Makes a Problem Hard for a Genetic Algorithm? Some Anomalous Results and Their Explanation, MACHLEARN: Machine Learning 13, volume 13, 1993

[Gibson,2000] Gibson D., Kleinberg J., and Raghavan P.: Clustering categorical data: an approach based on dynamical systems. The VLDB Journal,8(3-4):222-236, 2000.

[Gielis,2003] Gielis, Johan: A generic geometric transformation that unifies a wide range of natral and abstract shapes, American Journal of Botany 90(3), volume 90, 333–338, 2003

[Guadarrama,2010] Guadarrama, C.:Data Compression through Pattern Recognition, Master's Thesis, IIMAS UNAM, 2010, to be published.

[Guha,1998] Guha, Sudipto, Rastogi, Rajeev, and Shim, Kyuseok: CURE: an efficient clustering algorithm for large databases, SIGMOD '98: Proceedings of the 1998 ACM SIGMOD international conference on Management of data, ACM, 73–84, 1998

[Halkidi et al.,2001] Halkidi, Maria, Batistakis, Yannis, and Vazirgiannis, Michalis: On Clustering Validation Techniques, J. Intell. Inf. Syst. 17(2-3), volume 17, 107–145, 2001

[Hazewinkel,2001] Hazewinkel, Michiel: Rational function, Encyclopaedia of Mathematics, Springer, 2001

[Haykin,1994] Haykin, Simon: Neural networks: A comprehensive foundation, MacMillan, 1994

[Hinneburg et al,1998] Hinneburg, Alexander, Hinneburg, Er, and Keim, Daniel A.: An Efficient Approach to Clustering in Large Multimedia Databases with Noise, , AAAI Press, 58–65, 1998

[Kohonen,1997] Kohonen, Teuvo: Self-organizing maps, Springer-Verlag New York, Inc., 1997

[Kovacs,2006] Kovacs, Ferenc, and Ivancsy, Renata: A novel cluster validity index: variance of the nearest neighbor distance., WSEAS Transactions on Computers, volume 3,

477–483, March 2006

[Kuri & Aldana,2008] Kuri-Morales, Angel, and Bobadilla, Edwin Aldana: Clustering with an N-dimensional extension of Gielis superformula, AIKED'08: Proceedings of the 7th WSEAS International Conference on Artificial intelligence, knowledge engineering and data bases, World Scientific and Engineering Academy and Society (WSEAS), 343–350, 2008

[Kuri,2002] Kuri-Morales, Angel Fernando: A Methodology for the Statistical Characterization of Genetic Algorithms, MICAI, volume 2313, Springer, 79–88, Eds: Coello, Carlos A. Coello, de Albornoz, Alvaro, Sucar, Luis Enrique, and Battistutti, Osvaldo Cairó, 2002

[Kuri & Aldana,2010] Kuri-Morales, Ángel Fernando, and Aldana-Bobadilla, Edwin: Finding Irregularly Shaped Clusters Based on Entropy, ICDM, volume 6171, Springer, 57–70, Eds: Perner, Petra, 2010

[Kuri & Garcia,2010] Kuri-Morales, Ángel Fernando, and Garcia-Garcia, Javier: Encoding Categorical Variables for Unsupervised Clustering in Large Databases, 2010, to be published.

[Yang et al.,2000] Le Cam, Lucien, and Lo Yang, Grace: Asymptotics in Statistics Some Basic Concepts , volume XIII, 2nd edition, Springer Series in Statistics, 2000

[Li,1999] Li, Xin, Mak, Man-Wai, and Li, Chi-Kwong: Determining the Optimal Number of Clusters by an Extended RPCL Algorithm, JACIII 3(6), volume 3, 467–473, 1999

[Mahalanobis,1936] Mahalanobis, P. C: On the generalised distance in statistics, In Proceedings National Institute of Science, World Scientific and Engineering Academy and Society (WSEAS), 49–55, 1936

[MacQueen,1967] McQueen, J. B.: Some Methods of Classification and Analysis of Multivariate Observations, Proceedings of Fifth Berkeley Symposium on Mathematical Statistics and Probability, 281–297, Eds: Cam, L. M. Le, and Neyman, J., 1967, first publication about K-Means algorithm?

[Ng,1994] Ng, Raymond T., and Han, Jiawei: Efficient and Effective Clustering Methods for Spatial Data Mining, Department of Computer Science, University of British Columbia No. TR-94-13, May 1994.

[Pollard,2002] Pollard, David: A User's Guide to Measure Theoretic Probability, Cambridge University Press, Cambridge, 2002

[Rudolph,1994] Rudolph, G.: Convergence Analysis of Canonical Genetic Algorithms, IEEE Transactions on Neural Networks 5(1), volume 5, 96–101, January 1994

[Shannon,1949] Shannon, C. E., and Weaver, W.: The Mathematical Theory of Communication, Scientific American, July 1949

[Sheikholeslami et al.,1998] Sheikholeslami, Gholamhosein, Chatterjee, Surojit, and Zhang, Aidong: WaveCluster: A Multi-Resolution Clustering Approach for Very Large Spatial Databases, VLDB, Morgan Kaufmann, 428–439, Eds: Gupta, Ashish, Shmueli, Oded, and Widom, Jennifer, 1998

[Wang,2000] Wang, W., Yang, J., and Muntz, R. R.: An Approach to Active Spatial Data Mining Based on Statistical Information, IEEE Transactions on Knowledge and Data Engineering 12(5), volume 12, 715–728, 2000

[Zhang,1996] Zhang, T., Ramakrishnan, R., and Livny, M.: BIRCH: an efficient data clustering method for very large databases, Proceedings of ACM-SIGMOD International Conference of Management of Data, 103–114, June 1996

18

A General Model for Relational Clustering

Bo Long[1] and Zhongfei (Mark) Zhang[2]
[1]*Yahoo! Labs, Sunnyvale, CA 94043*
[2]*Computer Science Dept., SUNY Binghamton, Binghamton, NY 13902*
U.S.A.

1. Introduction

Most clustering approaches in the literature focus on "flat" data in which each data object is represented as a fixed-length feature vector (R.O.Duda et al., 2000). However, many real-world data sets are much richer in structure, involving objects of multiple types that are related to each other, such as Web pages, search queries and Web users in a Web search system, and papers, key words, authors and conferences in a scientific publication domain. In such scenarios, using traditional methods to cluster each type of objects independently may not work well due to the following reasons.

First, to make use of relation information under the traditional clustering framework, the relation information needs to be transformed into features. In general, this transformation causes information loss and/or very high dimensional and sparse data. For example, if we represent the relations between Web pages and Web users as well as search queries as the features for the Web pages, this leads to a huge number of features with sparse values for each Web page. Second, traditional clustering approaches are unable to tackle the interactions among the hidden structures of different types of objects, since they cluster data of single type based on static features. Note that the interactions could pass along the relations, i.e., there exists influence propagation in multi-type relational data. Third, in some machine learning applications, users are not only interested in the hidden structure for each type of objects, but also the global structure involving multi-types of objects. For example, in document clustering, in addition to document clusters and word clusters, the relationship between document clusters and word clusters is also useful information. It is difficult to discover such global structures by clustering each type of objects individually.

Therefore, multi-type relational data has presented a great challenge for traditional clustering approaches. In this study, first, we propose a general model, the collective factorization on related matrices, to discover the hidden structures of multi-types of objects based on both feature information and relation information. By clustering the multi-types of objects simultaneously, the model performs adaptive dimensionality reduction for each type of data. Through the related factorizations which share factors, the hidden structures of different types of objects could interact under the model. In addition to the cluster structures for each type of data, the model also provides information about the relation between clusters of different types of objects.

Under this model, we derive a novel spectral clustering algorithm, the spectral relational clustering, to cluster multi-type interrelated data objects simultaneously. By iteratively embedding each type of data objects into low dimensional spaces, the algorithm benefits from the interactions among the hidden structures of different types of data objects. The algorithm has the simplicity of spectral clustering approaches but at the same time also applicable to relational data with various structures. Theoretic analysis and experimental results demonstrate the promise and effectiveness of the algorithm.

2. Related work

Clustering on a special case of multi-type relational data, bi-type relational data, such as the word-document data, is called co-clustering or bi-clustering. Several previous efforts related to co-clustering are model based. PLSA (Hofmann, 1999) is a method based on a mixture decomposition derived from a latent class model. A two-sided clustering model is proposed for collaborative filtering by (Hofmann & Puzicha, 1999).

Spectral graph partitioning has also been applied to bi-type relational data (Dhillon, 2001; H.Zha & H.Simon, 2001). These algorithms formulate the data matrix as a bipartite graph and seek to find the optimal normalized cut for the graph. Due to the nature of a bipartite graph, these algorithms have the restriction that the clusters from different types of objects must have one-to-one associations.

Information-theory based co-clustering has also attracted attention in the literature. (El-Yaniv & Souroujon, 2001) extend the information bottleneck (IB) framework (Tishby et al., 1999) to repeatedly cluster documents and then words. (Dhillon et al., 2003) propose a co-clustering algorithm to maximize the mutual information between the clustered random variables subject to the constraints on the number of row and column clusters. A more generalized co-clustering framework is presented by (Banerjee et al., 2004) wherein any Bregman divergence can be used in the objective function.

Recently, co-clustering has been addressed based on matrix factorization. Both (Long et al., 2005) and (Li, 2005) model the co-clustering as an optimization problem involving a triple matrix factorization. (Long et al., 2005) propose an EM-like algorithm based on multiplicative updating rules and (Li, 2005) proposes a hard clustering algorithm for binary data. (Ding et al., 2005) extend the non-negative matrix factorization to symmetric matrices and show that it is equvilent to the Kernel K-means and the Laplacian-based spectral clustering.

Compared with co-clustering, clustering on general relational data, which may consist of more than two types of data objects, has not been well studied in the literature. Several noticeable efforts are discussed as follows. (Taskar et al., 2001) extend the the probabilistic relational model to the clustering scenario by introducing latent variables into the model. (Gao et al., 2005) formulate star-structured relational data as a star-structured m-partite graph and develop an algorithm based on semi-definite programming to partition the graph. Like bipartite graph partitioning, it has limitations that the clusters from different types of objects must have one-to-one associations and it fails to consider the feature information.

An intuitive idea for clustering multi-type interrelated objects is the mutual reinforcement clustering. The idea works as follows: start with initial cluster structures of the data; derive the new reduced features from the clusters of the related objects for each type of objects; based on the new features, cluster each type of objects with a traditional clustering algorithm; go back to the second step until the algorithm converges. Base on this idea, (Zeng et al., 2002) propose a framework for clustering heterogeneous Web objects and (Wang et al., 2003) present an approach to improve the cluster quality of interrelated data objects through an iterative reinforcement clustering process. However, there are no sound objective function and theoretical proof on the effectiveness and correctness (convergence) of the mutual reinforcement clustering. (Long et al., 2006) formulate multi-type relational data as

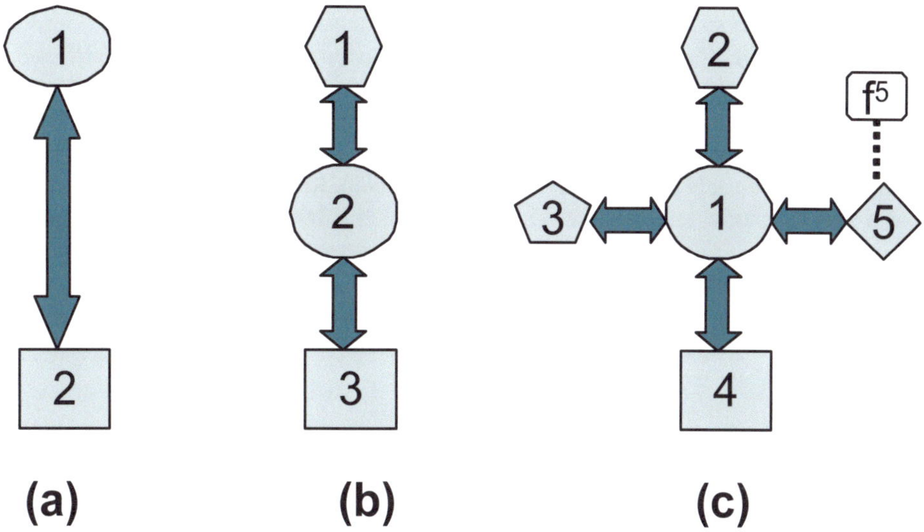

Fig. 1. Examples of the structures of multi-type relational data.

K-partite graphs and propose a novel algorithm to identify the hidden structures of a k-partite graph by constructing a relation summary network to approximate the original k-partite graph under a broad range of distortion measures.

To summarize, the research on multi-type relational data clustering has attracted substantial attention, especially in the special cases of relational data. However, there is still limited and preliminary work on the general relational data. This paper attempts to derive a theoretically sounded model and algorithm for general multi-type relational data clustering.

3. Collective factorization on related matrices

In this section, we propose a general model for clustering multi-type relational data based on factorizing multiple related matrices.

Given m sets of data objects, $\mathcal{X}_1 = \{x_{11}, \ldots, x_{1n_1}\}, \ldots, \mathcal{X}_m = \{x_{m1}, \ldots, x_{mn_m}\}$, which refer to m different types of objects relating to each other, we are interested in simultaneously clustering $\mathcal{X}_1$ into k_1 disjoint clusters, …, and $\mathcal{X}_m$ into k_m disjoint clusters. We call this task as *collective clustering on multi-type relational data*.

To derive a general model for collective clustering, we first formulate Multi-Type Relational Data (MTRD) as a set of related matrices, in which two matrices are related in the sense that their row indices or column indices refer to the same set of objects. First, if there exist relations between $\mathcal{X}_i$ and $\mathcal{X}_j$ (denoted as $\mathcal{X}_i \sim \mathcal{X}_j$), we represent them as a relation matrix $R^{(ij)} \in \mathbb{R}^{n_i \times n_j}$, where an element $R^{(ij)}_{pq}$ denotes the relation between x_{ip} and x_{jq}. Second, a set of objects $\mathcal{X}_i$ may have its own features, which could be denoted by a feature matrix $F^{(i)} \in \mathbb{R}^{n_i \times f_i}$, where an element $F^{(i)}_{pq}$ denotes the qth feature values for the object x_{ip} and f_i is the number of features for $\mathcal{X}_i$.

Figure 1 shows three examples of the structures of MTRD. Example (a) refers to a basic bi-type of relational data denoted by a relation matrix $R^{(12)}$, such as word-document data. Example (b) represents a tri-type of star-structured data, such as Web pages, Web users and search queries in Web search systems, which are denoted by two relation matrices $R^{(12)}$ and $R^{(23)}$. Example (c) represents the data consisting of shops, customers, suppliers, shareholders and advertisement media, in which customers (type 5) have features. The data are denoted by four relation matrices $R^{(12)}$, $R^{(13)}$, $R^{(14)}$ and $R^{(15)}$, and one feature matrix $F^{(5)}$.

It has been shown that the hidden structure of a data matrix can be explored by its factorization (D.D.Lee & H.S.Seung, 1999; Long et al., 2005). Motivated by this observation, we propose a general model for collective clustering, which is based on factorizing the multiple related matrices. In MTRD, the cluster structure for a type of objects $\mathcal{X}_i$ may be embedded in multiple related matrices; hence it can be exploited in multiple related factorizations. First, if $\mathcal{X}_i \sim \mathcal{X}_j$, then the cluster structures of both $\mathcal{X}_i$ and $\mathcal{X}_j$ are reflected in the triple factorization of their relation matrix $R^{(ij)}$ such that $R^{(ij)} \approx C^{(i)} A^{(ij)} (C^{(j)})^T$ (Long et al., 2005), where $C^{(i)} \in \{0,1\}^{n_i \times k_i}$ is a *cluster indicator matrix* for $\mathcal{X}_i$ such that $\sum_{q=1}^{k_i} C_{pq}^{(i)} = 1$ and $C_{pq}^{(i)} = 1$ denotes that the pth object in $\mathcal{X}_i$ is associated with the qth cluster. Similarly $C^{(j)} \in \{0,1\}^{n_j \times k_j}$. $A^{(ij)} \in \mathbb{R}^{k_i \times k_j}$ is the *cluster association matrix* such that A_{pq}^{ij} denotes the association between cluster p of $\mathcal{X}_i$ and cluster q of $\mathcal{X}_j$. Second, if $\mathcal{X}_i$ has a feature matrix $F^{(i)} \in \mathbb{R}^{n_i \times f_i}$, the cluster structure is reflected in the factorization of $F^{(i)}$ such that $F^{(i)} \approx C^{(i)} B^{(i)}$, where $C^{(i)} \in \{0,1\}^{n_i \times k_i}$ is a cluster indicator matrix, and $B^{(i)} \in \mathbb{R}^{k_i \times f_i}$ is the feature basis matrix which consists of k_i basis (cluster center) vectors in the feature space.

Based on the above discussions, formally we formulate the task of collective clustering on MTRD as the following optimization problem. Considering the most general case, we assume that in MTRD, every pair of $\mathcal{X}_i$ and $\mathcal{X}_j$ is related to each other and every $\mathcal{X}_i$ has a feature matrix $F^{(i)}$.

Definition 3.1 *Given a distance function $\mathcal{D}$, m positive numbers $\{k_i\}_{1 \le i \le m}$ and MTRD $\{\mathcal{X}_1, \ldots, \mathcal{X}_m\}$, which is described by a set of relation matrices $\{R^{(ij)} \in \mathbb{R}^{n_i \times n_j}\}_{1 \le i < j \le m}$, a set of feature matrices $\{F^{(i)} \in \mathbb{R}^{n_i \times f_i}\}_{1 \le i \le m}$, as well as a set of weights $w_a^{(ij)}, w_b^{(i)} \in R_+$ for different types of relations and features, the task of the collective clustering on the MTRD is to minimize*

$$
\begin{aligned}
L = & \sum_{1 \le i < j \le m} w_a^{(ij)} \mathcal{D}(R^{(ij)}, C^{(i)} A^{(ij)} (C^{(j)})^T) \\
& + \sum_{1 \le i \le m} w_b^{(i)} \mathcal{D}(F^{(i)}, C^{(i)} B^{(i)}) \qquad (1)
\end{aligned}
$$

w.r.t. $C^{(i)} \in \{0,1\}^{n_i \times k_i}$, $A^{(ij)} \in \mathbb{R}^{k_i \times k_j}$, and $B^{(i)} \in \mathbb{R}^{k_i \times f_i}$ subject to the constraints: $\sum_{q=1}^{k_i} C_{pq}^{(i)} = 1$, where $1 \le p \le n_i$, $1 \le i < j \le m$.

We call the model proposed in Definition 3.1 as the Collective Factorization on Related Matrices (CFRM).

The CFRM model clusters multi-type interrelated data objects simultaneously based on both relation and feature information. The model exploits the interactions between the hidden structures of different types of objects through the related factorizations which share matrix factors, i.e., cluster indicator matrices. Hence, the interactions between hidden structures work in two ways. First, if $\mathcal{X}_i \sim \mathcal{X}_j$, the interactions are reflected as the duality of row clustering and column clustering in $R^{(ij)}$. Second, if two types of objects are indirectly related, the interactions pass along the relation "chains" by a series of related factorizations, i.e., the model is capable of dealing with influence propagation. In addition to local cluster structure for each type of objects, the model also provides the global structure information by the cluster association matrices, which represent the relations among the clusters of different types of objects.

CFRM is a general model for relational clustering, since it is applicable to MTRD with various structures. Moreover, by adopting different distance functions, various algorithms based on various distribution assumptions for a given data can be derived under the CFRM model. To demonstrate the potential of CFRM, in the rest of paper we adopt CFRM with Euclidean distance function to derive a novel spectral clustering algorithm for MTRD. For convenience, we re-define the CFRM model under Euclidean distance function as follows.

Definition 3.2 *Given m positive numbers* $\{k_i\}_{1\leq i\leq m}$ *and MTRD* $\{\mathcal{X}_1,\ldots,\mathcal{X}_m\}$*, which is described by a set of relation matrices* $\{R^{(ij)} \in \mathbb{R}^{n_i\times n_j}\}_{1\leq i<j\leq m}$*, a set of feature matrices* $\{F^{(i)} \in \mathbb{R}^{n_i\times f_i}\}_{1\leq i\leq m}$*, as well as a set of weights* $w_a^{(ij)}, w_b^{(i)} \in R_+$ *for different types of relations and features, the task of the collective clustering on the MTRD is to minimize*

$$\begin{aligned} L &= \sum_{1\leq i<j\leq m} w_a^{(ij)} \|R^{(ij)} - C^{(i)}A^{(ij)}(C^{(j)})^T\|^2 \\ &+ \sum_{1\leq i\leq m} w_b^{(i)} \|F^{(i)} - C^{(i)}B^{(i)}\|^2 \end{aligned} \tag{2}$$

w.r.t. $C^{(i)} \in \{0,1\}^{n_i\times k_i}$, $A^{(ij)} \in \mathbb{R}^{k_i\times k_j}$, *and* $B^{(i)} \in \mathbb{R}^{k_i\times f_i}$ *subject to the constraints:* $\sum_{q=1}^{k_i} C_{pq}^{(i)} = 1$, *where* $1 \leq p \leq n_i$, $1 \leq i < j \leq m$, *and* $\|\cdot\|$ *denotes the Frobenius norm for a matrix.*

4. Spectral relational clustering

Spectral clustering (Ng et al., 2001; Bach & Jordan, 2004) has been well studied in the literature. The spectral clustering methods based on the graph partitioning theory focus on finding the best cuts of a graph that optimize certain predefined criterion functions. The optimization of the criterion functions usually leads to the computation of singular vectors or eigenvectors of certain graph affinity matrices. Many criterion functions, such as the average cut (Chan et al., 1993), the average association (Shi & Malik, 2000), the normalized cut (Shi & Malik, 2000), and the min-max cut (Ding et al., 2001), have been proposed.

Traditional spectral clustering focuses on the single type data. As we discussed before, if we apply traditional spectral clustering to each type of data objects individually, there are a number of limitations. To our best knowledge, there is little research on spectral clustering for general MTRD. In this section, we derive a novel spectral clustering algorithm for MTRD under the CFRM model with Euclidean distance function.

First, without loss of generality, we re-define the cluster indicator matric $C^{(i)}$ as the following vigorous cluster indicator matrix,

$$C_{pq}^{(i)} = \begin{cases} \frac{1}{|\pi_q^{(i)}|^{\frac{1}{2}}} & \text{if } x_{ip} \in \pi_q^{(i)} \\ 0 & \text{otherwise} \end{cases}$$

where $|\pi_q^{(i)}|$ denotes the number of objects in the qth cluster of $\mathcal{X}^{(i)}$. Clearly $C^{(i)}$ still captures the disjoint cluster memberships and $(C^{(i)})^T C^{(i)} = I_{k_i}$ where I_{k_i} denotes $k_i \times k_i$ identity matrix. Hence our task is the minimization:

$$\min_{\substack{\{(C^{(i)})^T C^{(i)}=I_{k_i}\}_{1\leq i\leq m} \\ \{A^{(ij)}\in\mathbb{R}^{k_i\times k_j}\}_{1\leq i<j\leq m} \\ \{B^{(i)}\in\mathbb{R}^{k_i\times f_i}\}_{1\leq i\leq m}}} L \tag{3}$$

where L is the same as in Eq. (2).
Then, we prove the following lemma, which is useful in proving our main theorem.

Lemma 4.1 *If $\{C^{(i)}\}_{1\leq i\leq m}$, $\{A^{(ij)}\}_{1\leq i<j\leq m}$, and $\{B^{(i)}\}_{1\leq i\leq m}$ are the optimal solution to Eq. (3), then*

$$A^{(ij)} = (C^{(i)})^T R^{(ij)} C^{(j)} \tag{4}$$

$$B^{(i)} = (C^{(i)})^T F^{(i)} \tag{5}$$

for $1 \leq i \leq m$.

Proof 4.2 *The objective function in Eq. (3) can be expanded as follows.*

$$\begin{aligned} L = & \sum_{1\leq i<j\leq m} w_a^{(ij)} tr((R^{(ij)} - C^{(i)}A^{(ij)}(C^{(j)})^T) \\ & (R^{(ij)} - C^{(i)}A^{(ij)}(C^{(j)})^T)^T) + \\ & \sum_{1\leq i\leq m} w_b^{(i)} tr((F^{(i)} - C^{(i)}B^{(i)})(F^{(i)} - C^{(i)}B^{(i)})^T) \\ = & \sum_{1\leq i<j\leq m} w_a^{(ij)} (tr(R^{(ij)}(R^{(ij)})^T) + \\ & tr(A^{(ij)}(A^{(ij)})^T) - 2tr(C^{(i)}A^{(ij)}(C^{(i)})^T(R^{(ij)})^T)) \\ & + \sum_{1\leq i\leq m} w_b^{(i)} (tr(F^{(i)}(F^{(i)})^T) + tr(B^{(i)}(B^{(i)})^T) \\ & -2tr(C^{(i)}B^{(i)}(F^{(i)})^T)) \end{aligned} \tag{6}$$

where tr denotes the trace of a matrix; the terms $tr(A^{(ij)}(A^{(ij)})^T)$ and $tr(B^{(i)}(B^{(i)})^T)$ result from the communicative property of the trace and $(C^{(i)})^T(C^{(i)}) = I_{k_i}$. Based on Eq. (6), solving $\frac{\partial L}{\partial A^{(ij)}} = 0$ and $\frac{\partial L}{\partial B^{(i)}} = 0$ leads to Eq. (4) and Eq. (5). This completes the proof of the lemma.

Lemma 4.1 implies that the objective function in Eq. (2) can be simplified to the function of only $C^{(i)}$. This leads to the following theorem, which is the basis of our algorithm.

Theorem 4.3 *The minimization problem in Eq. (3) is equivalent to the following maximization problem:*

$$\begin{aligned} \max_{\substack{\{(C^{(i)})^T C^{(i)} \\ =I_{k_i}\}_{1\leq i\leq m}}} & \sum_{1\leq i\leq m} w_b^{(i)} tr((C^{(i)})^T F^{(i)}(F^{(i)})^T C^{(i)}) + \\ & \sum_{1\leq i<j\leq m} w_a^{(ij)} tr((C^{(i)})^T R^{(ij)} C^{(j)} (C^{(j)})^T (R^{(ij)})^T C^{(i)}) \end{aligned} \tag{7}$$

Proof 4.4 *From Lemma 4.1, we have Eq.* (4) *and* (5). *Plugging them into Eq.* (6), *we obtain*

$$\begin{aligned}L = \sum_{1\leq i\leq m} & w_b^{(i)}(tr(F^{(i)}(F^{(i)})^T) - \\ & tr((C^{(i)})^T F^{(i)}(F^{(i)})^T C^{(i)})) + \\ & \sum_{1\leq i<j\leq m} w_a^{(ij)}(tr(R^{(ij)}(R^{(ij)})^T) - \\ & tr((C^{(i)})^T R^{(ij)} C^{(j)}(C^{(j)})^T (R^{(ij)})^T C^{(i)})). \end{aligned} \tag{8}$$

Since in Eq. (8), $tr(F^{(i)}(F^{(i)})^T)$ *and* $tr(R^{(ij)}(R^{(ij)})^T)$ *are constants, the minimization of L in Eq.* (3) *is equivalent to the maximization in Eq.* (7). *This completes the proof of the theorem.*

We propose an iterative algorithm to determine the optimal (local) solution to the maximization problem in Theorem 4.3, i.e., at each iterative step we maximize the objective function in Eq. (7) w.r.t. only one matrix $C^{(p)}$ and fix other $C^{(j)}$ for $j \neq p$ where $1 \leq p, j \leq m$. Based on Eq. (7), after a little algebraic manipulation, the task at each iterative step is equivalent to the following maximization,

$$\max_{(C^{(p)})^T C^{(p)} = I_{k_p}} \quad \mathrm{tr}((C^{(p)})^T M^{(p)} C^{(p)}) \tag{9}$$

where

$$\begin{aligned}M^{(p)} = & w_b^{(p)}(F^{(p)}(F^{(p)})^T) + \\ & \sum_{p<j\leq m} w_a^{(pj)}(R^{(pj)} C^{(j)}(C^{(j)})^T (R^{(pj)})^T) + \\ & \sum_{1\leq j<p} w_a^{(jp)}((R^{(jp)})^T C^{(j)}(C^{(j)})^T (R^{(jp)})). \end{aligned} \tag{10}$$

Clearly $M^{(p)}$ is a symmetric matrix. Since $C^{(p)}$ is a vigorous cluster indicator matrix, the maximization problem in Eq. (9) is still NP-hard. However, as in the spectral graph partitioning, if we apply real relaxation to $C^{(p)}$ to let $C^{(p)}$ be an arbitrary orthonormal matrix, it turns out that the maximization in Eq. (9) has a closed-form solution.

Theorem 4.5 *(Ky-Fan thorem) Let M be a symmetric matrix with eigenvalues* $\lambda_1 \geq \lambda_2 \geq \ldots \geq \lambda_k$, *and the corresponding eigenvectors* $U = [u_1, \ldots, u_k]$. *Then* $\sum_{i=1}^{k} \lambda_i = \max_{X^T X = I_k} tr(X^T M X)$. *Moreover, the optimal X is given by* $[u_1, \ldots, u_k]Q$ *where Q is an arbitrary orthogonal matrix.*

Based on Theorem 4.5 (Bhatia, 1997), at each iterative step we update $C^{(p)}$ as the leading k_p eigenvectors of the matix $M^{(p)}$. After the iteration procedure converges, since the resulting eigen-matrices are not indicator matrices, we need to transform them into cluster indicator matrices by postprocessing (Bach & Jordan, 2004; Zha et al., 2002; Ding & He, 2004). In this paper, we simply adopt the k-means for the postprocessing.
The algorithm, called Spectral Relational Clustering (SRC), is summarized in Algorithm 1. By iteratively updating $C^{(p)}$ as the leading k_p eigenvectors of $M^{(p)}$, SRC makes use of the interactions among the hidden structures of different type of objects. After the iteration

procedure converges, the hidden structure for each type of objects is embedded in an eigen-matrix. Finally, we postprocess each eigen-matrix to extract the cluster structure.

To illustrate the SRC algorithm, we describe the specific update rules for the tri-type relational data as shown in Figure 1(b): update $C^{(1)}$ as the leading k_1 eigenvectors of $w_a^{(12)}R^{(12)}C^{(2)}(C^{(2)})^T(R^{(12)})^T$; update $C^{(2)}$ as the leading k_2 eigenvectors of $w_a^{(12)}(R^{(12)})^TC^{(1)}(C^{(1)})^TR^{(12)} + w_a^{(23)}R^{(23)}C^{(3)}(C^{(3)})^T(R^{(23)})^T$; update $C^{(3)}$ as the leading k_3 eigenvectors of $w_a^{(23)}(R^{(23)})^TC^{(2)}(C^{(2)})^TR^{(23)}$.

the computational complexity of SRC can be shown to be $O(tmn^2k)$ where t denotes the number of iterations, $n = \Theta(n_i)$ and $k = \Theta(k_i)$. For sparse data, it could be reduced to $O(tmzk)$ where z denotes the number of non-zero elements.

The convergence of SRC algorithm can be proved. We describe the main idea as follows. Theorem 4.3 and Eq. (9) imply that the updates of the matrices in Line 5 of Algorithm 1 increase the objective function in Eq. (7), and hence equivalently decrease the objective function in Eq.(3). Since the objective function in Eq. (3) has the lower bound 0, the convergence of SRC is guaranteed.

5. Experimental results

In this section, we evaluate the effectiveness of the SRC algorithm on two types of MTRD, bi-type relational data and tri-type star-structured data as shown in Figure 1(a) and Figure 1(b), which represent two basic structures of MTRD and arise frequently in real applications. The data sets used in the experiments are mainly based on the 20-Newsgroup data (Lang, 1995) which contains about 20,000 articles from 20 newsgroups. We pre-process the data by removing stop words and file headers and selecting the top 2000 words by the mutual information. The word-document matrix R is based on *tf.idf* and each document vector is normalized to the unit norm vector. In the experiments the classic k-means is used for initialization and the final performance score for each algorithm is the average of the 20 test runs unless stated otherwise.

Algorithm 1 Spectral Relational Clustering

Input: Relation matrices $\{R^{(ij)} \in \mathbb{R}^{n_i \times n_j}\}_{1 \le i < j \le m}$, feature matrices $\{F^{(i)} \in \mathbb{R}^{n_i \times f_i}\}_{1 \le i \le m}$, numbers of clusters $\{k_i\}_{1 \le i \le m}$, weights $\{w_a^{(ij)}, w_b^{(i)} \in R_+\}_{1 \le i < j \le m}$. **Output:** Cluster indicator matrices $\{C^{(p)}\}_{1 \le p \le m}$. **Method:**

1: Initialize $\{C^{(p)}\}_{1 \le p \le m}$ with othonormal matrices.
2: **repeat**
3:    **for** $p = 1$ to m **do**
4:       Compute the matrix $M^{(p)}$ as in Eq. (10).
5:       Update $C^{(p)}$ by the leading k_p eigenvectors of $M^{(p)}$.
6:    **end for**
7: **until** convergence
8: **for** $p = 1$ to m **do**
9:    transform $C^{(p)}$ into a cluster indicator matrix by the k-means.
10: **end for**

Data set	SRC	NC	BSGP
multi2	0.4979	0.1036	0.1500
multi3	0.5763	0.4314	0.4897
multi5	0.7242	0.6706	0.6118
multi8	0.6958	0.6192	0.5096
multi10	0.7158	0.6292	0.5071

Table 1. NMI comparisons of SRC, NC and BSGP algorithms

5.1 Clustering on bi-type relational data

In this section we conduct experiments on a bi-type relational data, word-document data, to demonstrate the effectiveness of SRC as a novel co-clustering algorithm. A representative spectral clustering algorithm, Normalized-Cut (NC) spectral clustering (Ng et al., 2001; Shi & Malik, 2000), and BSGP (Dhillon, 2001), are used as comparisons.

The graph affinity matrix for NC is $R^T R$, i.e., the cosine similarity matrix. In NC and SRC, the leading k eigenvectors are used to extract the cluster structure, where k is the number of document clusters. For BSGP, the second to the $(\lceil \log_2 k \rceil + 1)$th leading singular vectors are used (Dhillon, 2001). K-means is adopted to postprocess the eigenvectors. Before postprocessing, the eigenvectors from NC and SRC are normalized to the unit norm vector and the eigenvectors from BSGP are normalized as described by (Dhillon, 2001). Since all the algorithms have random components resulting from k-means or itself, at each test we conduct three trials with random initializations for each algorithm and the optimal one provides the performance score for that test run. To evaluate the quality of document clusters, we elect to use the Normalized Mutual Information (NMI) (Strehl & Ghosh, 2002), which is a standard way to measure the cluster quality.

At each test run, five data sets, multi2 (NG 10, 11), multi3(NG 1,10,20), multi5 (NG 3, 6, 9, 12, 15), multi8 (NG 3, 6, 7, 9, 12, 15, 18, 20) and multi10 (NG 2, 4, 6, 8, 10, 12 ,14 ,16 ,18,20), are generated by randomly sampling 100 documents from each newsgroup. Here NG i means the ith newsgroup in the original order. For the numbers of document clusters, we use the numbers of the true document classes. For the numbers of word clusters, there are no options for BSGP, since they are restricted to equal to the numbers of document clusters. For SRC, it is flexible to use any number of word clusters. Since how to choose the optimal number of word clusters is beyond the scope of this paper, we simply choose one more word clusters than the corresponding document clusters, i.e., 3,4, 6, 9, and 11. This may not be the best choice but it is good enough to demonstrate the flexibility and effectiveness of SRC.

In Figure 2, (a), (b) and (c) show three document embeddings of a multi2 sample, which is sampled from two close newsgroups, *rec.sports.baseball* and *rec.sports.hockey*. In this example, when NC and BSGP fail to separate the document classes, SRC still provides a satisfactory separation. The possible explanation is that the adaptive interactions among the hidden structures of word clusters and document clusters remove the noise to lead to better embeddings. (d) shows a typical run of the SRC algorithm. The objective value is the trace value in Theorem 4.3.

Table 1 shows NMI scores on all the data sets. We observe that SRC performs better than NC and BSGP on all data sets. This verifies the hypothesis that benefiting from the interactions among the hidden structures of different types of objects, the SRC's adaptive dimensionality reduction has advantages over the dimensionality reduction of the existing spectral clustering algorithms.

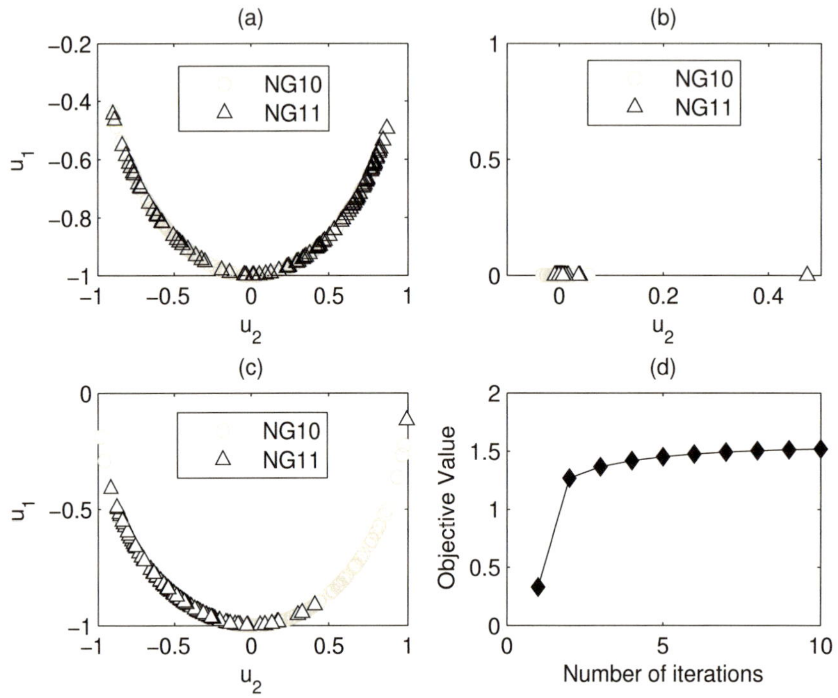

Fig. 2. (a), (b) and (c) are document embeddings of multi2 data set produced by NC, BSGP and SRC, respectively (u_1 and u_2 denote first and second eigenvectors, respectively). (d) is an iteration curve for SRC.

5.2 Clustering on tri-type relational data

In this section, we conduct experiments on tri-type star-structured relational data to evaluate the effectiveness of SRC in comparison with other two algorithms for MTRD clustering. One is based on m-partite graph partitioning, Consistent Bipartite Graph Co-partitioning (CBGC) (Gao et al., 2005) (we thank the authors for providing the executable program of CBGC). The other is Mutual Reinforcement K-means (MRK), which is implemented based on the idea of mutual reinforcement clustering as discussed in Section 2.

The first data set is synthetic data, in which two relation matrices, $R^{(12)}$ with 80-by-100 dimension and $R^{(23)}$ with 100-by-80 dimension, are binary matrices with 2-by-2 block structures. $R^{(12)}$ is generated based on the block structure $\begin{bmatrix} 0.9 & 0.7 \\ 0.8 & 0.9 \end{bmatrix}$, i.e., the objects in cluster 1 of $\mathcal{X}^{(1)}$ is related to the objects in cluster 1 of $\mathcal{X}^{(2)}$ with probability 0.9, and so on so forth. $R^{(23)}$ is generated based on the block structure $\begin{bmatrix} 0.6 & 0.7 \\ 0.7 & 0.6 \end{bmatrix}$. Each type of objects has two equal size clusters. It is not a trivial task to identify the cluster structure of this data set, since the block structures are subtle. We denote this data set as Binary Relation Matrices (BRM) data.

Other three data sets are built based on the 20-newsgroups data for hierarchical taxonomy mining and document clustering. In the field of text categorization, hierarchical taxonomy classification is widely used to obtain a better trade-off between effectiveness and efficiency than flat taxonomy classification. To take advantage of hierarchical classification, one must mine a hierarchical taxonomy from the data set. We can see that words, documents and

Data set	Taxonomy structure
TM1	{NG10, NG11}, {NG17, NG18, NG19}
TM2	{NG2, NG3}, {NG8, NG9}, {NG12, NG13}
TM3	{NG4, NG5}, {NG8, NG9}, {NG14, NG15}, {NG17, NG18}

Table 2. Taxonomy structures for three data sets

categories formulate a tri-type relational data, which consists of two relation matrices, a word-document matrix $R^{(12)}$ and a document-category matrix $R^{(23)}$ (Gao et al., 2005).
The true taxonomy structures for three data sets, TM1, TM2 and TM3, are listed in Table 2. For example, TM1 data set is sampled from five categories, in which NG10 and NG11 belong to the same high level category *res.sports* and NG17, NG18 and NG19 belong to the same high level category *talk.politics*. Therefore, for the TM1 data set, the expected clustering result on categories should be {NG10, NG11} and {NG17, NG18, NG19} and the documents should be clustered into two clusters according to their categories. The documents in each data set are generated by sampling 100 documents from each category.
The number of clusters used for documents and categories are 2, 3 and 4 for TM1, TM2 and TM3, respectively. For the number of word clusters, we adopt the number of categories, i.e., 5, 6 and 8. For the weights $w_a^{(12)}$ and $w_a^{(23)}$, we simply use equal weight, i.e., $w_a^{(12)} = w_a^{(23)} = 1$. Figure 3 illustrates the effects of different weights on embeddings of documents

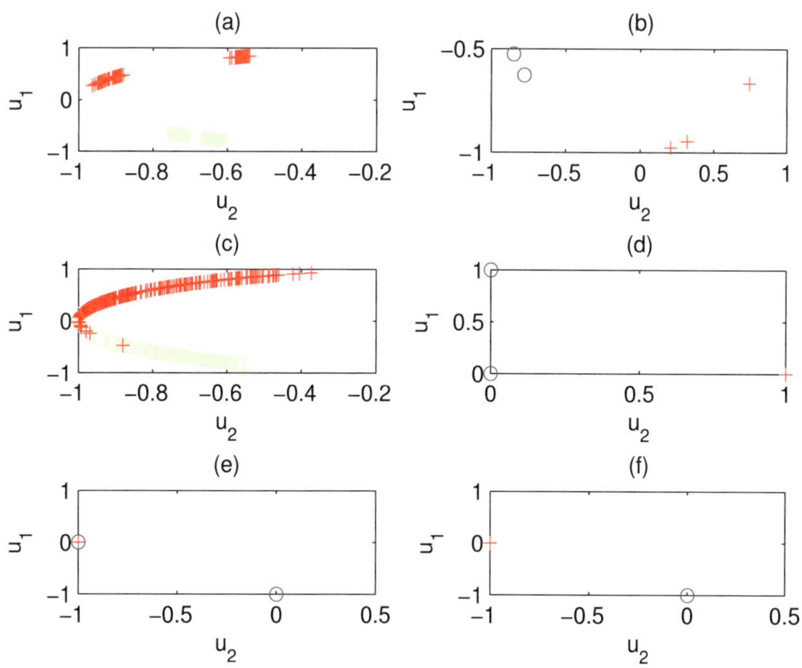

Fig. 3. Three pairs of embeddings of documents and categories for the TM1 data set produced by SRC with different weights: (a) and (b) with $w_a^{(12)} = 1, w_a^{(23)} = 1$; (c) and (d) with $w_a^{(12)} = 1, w_a^{(23)} = 0$; (e) and (f) with $w_a^{(12)} = 0, w_a^{(23)} = 1$.

Data set	SRC	MRK	CBGC
BRM	0.6718	0.6470	0.4694
TM1	1	0.5243	–
TM2	0.7179	0.6277	–
TM3	0.6505	0.5719	–

Table 3. NMI comparisons of SRC, MRK and CBGC algorithms

and categories. When $w_a^{(12)} = w_a^{(23)} = 1$, i.e., SRC makes use of both word-document relations and document-category relations, both documents and categories are separated into two clusters very well as in (a) and (b) of Figure 3, respectively; when SRC makes use of only the word-document relations, the documents are separated with partial overlapping as in (c) and the categories are randomly mapped to a couple of points as in (d); when SRC makes use of only the document-category relations, both documents and categories are incorrectly overlapped as in (e) and (f), respectively, since the document-category matrix itself does not provide any useful information for the taxonomy structure.

The performance comparison is based on the cluster quality of documents, since the better it is, the more accurate we can identify the taxonomy structures. Table 3 shows NMI comparisons of the three algorithms on the four data sets. The NMI score of CBGC is available only for BRM data set because the CBGC program provided by the authors only works for the case of two clusters and small size matrices. We observe that SRC performs better than MRK and CBGC on all data sets. The comparison shows that among the limited efforts in the literature attempting to cluster multi-type interrelated objects simultaneously, SRC is an effective one to identify the cluster structures of MTRD.

6. Conclusions and future work

In this paper, we propose a general model CFRM for clustering MTRD. The model is applicable to relational data with various structures. Under this model, we derive a novel algorithm SRC to cluster multi-type interrelated data objects simultaneously. SRC iteratively embeds each type of data objects into low dimensional spaces. Benefiting from the interactions among the hidden structures of different types of data objects, the iterative procedure amounts to adaptive dimensionality reduction and noise removal leading to better embeddings. Extensive experiments demonstrate the promise and effectiveness of the CFRM model and SRC algorithm. There are a number of interesting potential directions for future research in the CFRM model and SRC algorithm, such as extending CFRM to more general cases with soft clustering, deriving new algorithms under other distance functions and exploring more applications for SRC.

7. References

Bach, F. R. & Jordan, M. I. (2004). Learning spectral clustering, *in* S. Thrun, L. Saul & B. Schölkopf (eds), *Advances in Neural Information Processing Systems 16*.

Banerjee, A., Dhillon, I. S., Ghosh, J., Merugu, S. & Modha, D. S. (2004). A generalized maximum entropy approach to bregman co-clustering and matrix approximation., *KDD*, pp. 509–514.

Bhatia, R. (1997). *Matrix analysis*, Springeer-Cerlag, New York.

Chan, P. K., Schlag, M. D. F. & Zien, J. Y. (1993). Spectral k-way ratio-cut partitioning and clustering, *DAC '93*, pp. 749–754.

D.D.Lee & H.S.Seung (1999). Learning the parts of objects by non-negative matrix factorization, *Nature* 401: 788–791.

Dhillon, I. S. (2001). Co-clustering documents and words using bipartite spectral graph partitioning, *KDD*, pp. 269–274.
URL: *citeseer.ist.psu.edu/dhillon01coclustering.html*

Dhillon, I. S., Mallela, S. & Modha, D. S. (2003). Information-theoretic co-clustering, *KDD'03*, pp. 89–98.
URL: *citeseer.ist.psu.edu/dhillon03informationtheoretic.html*

Ding, C. H. Q. & He, X. (2004). Linearized cluster assignment via spectral ordering., *ICML*.

Ding, C. H. Q., He, X., Zha, H., Gu, M. & Simon, H. D. (2001). A min-max cut algorithm for graph partitioning and data clustering, *Proceedings of ICDM 2001*, pp. 107–114.
URL: *citeseer.ist.psu.edu/ding01minmax.html*

Ding, C., He, X. & Simon, H. (2005). On the equivalence of nonnegative matrix factorization and spectral clustering, *SDM'05*.

El-Yaniv, R. & Souroujon, O. (2001). Iterative double clustering for unsupervised and semi-supervised learning., *ECML*, pp. 121–132.

Gao, B., Liu, T.-Y., Zheng, X., Cheng, Q.-S. & Ma, W.-Y. (2005). Consistent bipartite graph co-partitioning for star-structured high-order heterogeneous data co-clustering, *KDD '05*, pp. 41–50.

Hofmann, T. (1999). Probabilistic latent semantic analysis, *Proc. of Uncertainty in Artificial Intelligence, UAI'99*, Stockholm.
URL: *citeseer.ist.psu.edu/hofmann99probabilistic.html*

Hofmann, T. & Puzicha, J. (1999). Latent class models for collaborative filtering, *IJCAI'99*, Stockholm.
URL: *citeseer.ist.psu.edu/hofmann99probabilistic.html*

H.Zha, C. M. X. & H.Simon (2001). Bi-partite graph partitioning and data clustering, *ACM CIKM'01*.

Lang, K. (1995). News weeder: Learning to filter netnews, *ICML*.

Li, T. (2005). A general model for clustering binary data, *KDD'05*.

Long, B., Wu, X., (mark) zhang, Z. & Yu, P. S. (2006). Unsupervised learning on k-partite graphs, *KDD '06*.

Long, B., Zhang, Z. M. & Yu, P. S. (2005). Co-clustering by block value decomposition, *KDD'05*.

Ng, A., Jordan, M. & Weiss, Y. (2001). On spectral clustering: Analysis and an algorithm, *Advances in Neural Information Processing Systems 14*.
URL: *citeseer.ist.psu.edu/ng01spectral.html*

R.O.Duda, P.E.Hart & D.G.Stork. (2000). *Pattern Classification*, John Wiley & Sons, New York.

Shi, J. & Malik, J. (2000). Normalized cuts and image segmentation, *IEEE Transactions on Pattern Analysis and Machine Intelligence* 22(8): 888–905.
URL: *citeseer.ist.psu.edu/shi97normalized.html*

Strehl, A. & Ghosh, J. (2002). Cluster ensembles – a knowledge reuse framework for combining partitionings, *AAAI 2002*, AAAI/MIT Press, pp. 93–98.
URL: *http://strehl.com/download/strehl-aaai02.pdf*

Taskar, B., Segal, E. & Koller, D. (2001). Probabilistic classification and clustering in relational data, *Proceeding of IJCAI-01*.
URL: *citeseer.ist.psu.edu/taskar01probabilistic.html*

Tishby, N., Pereira, F. & Bialek, W. (1999). The information bottleneck method, *Proceedings of the 37-th Annual Allerton Conference on Communication, Control and Computing*,

pp. 368–377.
URL: *citeseer.ist.psu.edu/tishby99information.html*

Wang, J., Zeng, H., Chen, Z., Lu, H., Tao, L. & Ma, W.-Y. (2003). Recom: reinforcement clustering of multi-type interrelated data objects, *SIGIR '03*, pp. 274–281.

Zeng, H.-J., Chen, Z. & Ma, W.-Y. (2002). A unified framework for clustering heterogeneous web objects, *WISE '02*, pp. 161–172.

Zha, H., Ding, C., Gu, M., He, X. & Simon, H. (2002). Spectral relaxation for k-means clustering, *Advances in Neural Information Processing Systems* 14.
URL: *citeseer.ist.psu.edu/article/zha01spectral.html*

19

Classifiers Based on Inverted Distances

Marcel Jirina and Marcel Jirina, Jr.
Institute of Computer Science AS CR,
Faculty of Biomedical Engineering,
Czech Technical University in Prague,
Czech Republic

1. Introduction

In this chapter we describe an elaborated yet simple classification method (IINC) that can outperform a range of standard classification methods of data mining, e.g. k-nearest neighbors, Naïve Bayes Classifiers' as well as SVM. In any case the method is an alternative to well-known and widely used classification methods.

There is a lot of classification methods, simpler or very sophisticated. Some standard methods of probability density estimate for classification are based on the nearest neighbors method which uses ratio k/V, where k is the number of points of a given class from the training set in a suitable ball of volume V with center at point x (Silverman, 1990; Duda et al., 2000; Cháves et al., 2001) sometimes denoted as query point. For probability density estimation by the k-nearest-neighbor (k-NN) method in E_n, the best value of k must be carefully tuned to find optimal results. Often used role of thumb is that k equals to square root of number of samples of the learning set. Nearest neighbors methods exhibit sometimes surprisingly good results see e.g. (Merz, 2010; Kim & Ghahramani, 2006). Bayesian methods form the other class of most reputable non-parametric methods (Duda et al., 2000; Kim & Ghahramani, 2006). Random trees or random forest approach belong among complex, but the best classification methods as well as neural networks of different types (Bock, 2004). The disadvantage of many these methods is the necessity to find proper set of internal parameters of the system. This problem is often solved by the use of genetic optimization as in the case of complex neural networks see e.g. (Hakl et al., 2002).

First, we will provide a shot overview of the basic idea of the IINC and its features and show a simple demonstative example of a pragmatic approach to a simple classification task. Second, we give a deeper mathematical insight into the method and finally we will demonstrate the power of the IINC on data sets from two well-known repository real-life tasks.

2. Classifier background - idea and motivation

In general, if we have estimates of the probability that a given sample (query point) belongs to a given class, we can easily construct a classifier. We just compare the individual probabilities and select the class with the highest probability. The presented IINC works in the same way, but the probabilities are estimated in a special way that is based on summing up the inverted indexes of neighbors.

We show a practical approach to the classification of data into two classes (extending the classifier to be able to classify to more than two classes will be then straightforward).
Let all samples of the learning set regardless of the class be sorted according to their distances from the query point x. Let indexes be assigned to these points so that index 1 is assigned to the nearest neighbor, index 2 to the second nearest neighbor etc.

Let us compute sums $S_0(x) = \frac{1}{N_0} \sum_{i=1\,(c=0)}^{N} 1/i$ and $S_1(x) = \frac{1}{N_1} \sum_{i=1\,(c=1)}^{N} 1/i$, i.e. the sums of the reciprocals of the indexes of samples from class c = 0 and from class c = 1. N_0 and N_1 are the numbers of samples of class 0 and class 1, respectively, $N_0 + N_1 = N$, N is the total number of samples available.
The probability that point x belongs to class 0 is

$$p(c=0\,|\,x) \cong \frac{S_0(x)}{S_0(x)+S_1(x)}$$

and similarly the probability that point x belongs to class 1 is

$$p(c=1\,|\,x) \cong \frac{S_1(x)}{S_0(x)+S_1(x)}.$$

When a discriminant threshold θ is chosen (e.g. θ = 0.5), then if p(c = 1 | x) ≥ θ point x is of class 1 else it is of class 0. This is the same procedure as in other classification approaches where the output is the estimation of probability (naïve Bayes) or any real valued variable (neural networks). The value of the threshold can be optimized with regard to the minimum classification error.

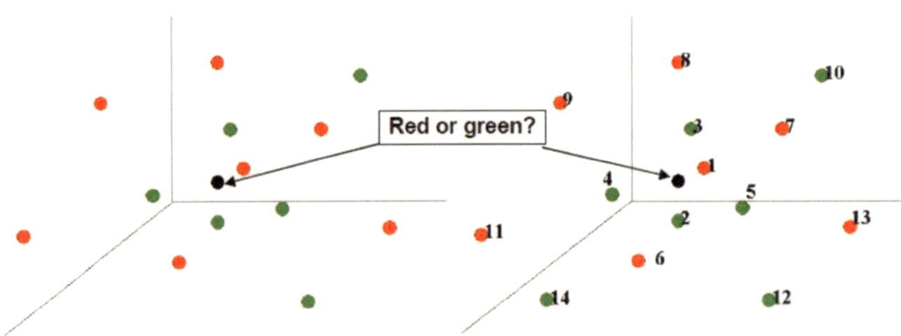

sorted points according to their distance from the black query point (just order not real distance)

1	2	3	4	5	6	7	8	9	10	11	12	13	14	S or S_c	p(r/g|x)
1	0.5	0.33	0.25	0.20	0.17	0.14	0.13	0.11	0.10	0.09	0.08	0.08	0.07	3.251562	
1					0.17	0.14	0.13	0.11		0.09		0.08		1.713467	0.526967
	0.5	0.33	0.25	0.20					0.10		0.08		0.07	1.538095	0.473033

reciprocal values of order for the class of red points
reciprocal values of order (without resp. to class - color)

sums of corresponding rows

probability that the point belongs to the red class

$$0.526967 = \frac{1.713467}{3.251562}$$

Fig. 1. Example of a classification task for a two-class problem of spatial data

As shown, the IINC is very simple. It is based only on the sum of inverted indexes of the nearest neighbors. It opens the question whether it is as powerful as stated above.
In the above formulas the actual data do not appear directly, but are hidden behind the indexes that express their distance from a given sample (query point). To be able to get the indexes we have to sort the original data according to their distances from a particular sample. The only information we work with is their order, not the real distance! To compare distances we need proper metrics (just the L_1 (absolute) metrics yields the best results). And so on. In other words, there are many assumptions that have to be fulfilled (and fortunately they are fulfilled in standard classification tasks) to concentrate them into a simple presented classification algorithm IINC. To vindicate the correctness of the algorithm we offer a deeper mathematical insight into the IINC and demonstrate the IINC on real-life classification tasks.

3. Mathematical background of IINC

Let us consider partial influences of individual points on the probability that point x is of class c. Each point of class c in the neighborhood of point x adds a little to the probability that point x is of class c, where $c \in \{0, 1\}$ is the class mark. This influence grows larger the closer the point considered is to point x and vice versa. This observation is based on the finding of (Cover & Hart, 1967) that the nearest neighbor has the largest influence on the proper estimation to what class point x belongs. Let us assume - for proof see (Jirina & Jirina, 2008) - that the influence to the probability that point x is of class c (the nearest neighbor of class c) is 1, the influence of the second nearest neighbor is 1/2, the influence of the third nearest neighbor is 1/3, etc. We show further that just these values of influence lead to improved classification. Let $p_1(c\,|\,x, r_i)$ be the probability that query point x is of class c if neighbor point number i is of the same class as point x, K is a constant that is used to normalize the probability that point x belongs to any class to 1:

For the first (nearest) point i = 1 $\quad p_1(c\,|\,x,r_1) = K.1$,

for the second point i = 2 $\quad p_1(c\,|\,x,r_2) = K\frac{1}{2}$,

and so on, generally for point No. i $\quad p_1(c\,|\,x,r_i) = K\frac{1}{i}$.

Individual points are independent and then we can sum up these probabilities. Thus we add the partial influences of k individual points together by summing up

$$p(c\,|\,x,r_k) = \sum_{i=1(c)}^{k} p_1(c\,|\,x,r_i) = K \sum_{i=1(c)}^{k} 1/i \,.$$

The sum goes over indexes i for which the corresponding samples of the learning set are of class c. Let

$$S_c = \sum_{i=1(c)}^{k} 1/i$$

and let

$$S = \sum_{i=1}^{N} 1/i$$

(This is, in fact, so-called harmonic number HN, the sum of truncated harmonic series.) The estimation of the probability that query point x belongs to class c is

$$p(x \mid c) = \frac{S_c}{S} \, .$$

The approach is based on the hypothesis that the influence, the weight of a neighbor, is proportional to the reciprocal of its order number just as it is to its distance from the query point.
The hypothesis above is equivalent to the assumption that the influence of individual points of the learning set is governed by Zipfian distribution (Zipf's law), (Zipf, 1968).
It is also possible to show that the use of 1/i has a close connection to the correlation integral and correlation dimension and thus to the dynamics and true data dimensionality of processes that generate the data we wish to separate. It generally leads to better classification.

3.1 Data and the learning set

Let us consider only two classes for a classification task. Let the learning set U of total N samples be given in the form of a matrix X^T with N rows and n columns. Each sample corresponds to one row of X^T and, at the same time, corresponds to a point in n-dimensional space R_n, where n is the sample space dimension. The learning set consists of points (rows, samples) of two classes $c \in \{0, 1\}$, i.e. each row (point or sample) belongs to one of these two classes. Then, the learning set can be formally described as $U = U_0 \cup U_1$, $U_0 \cap U_1 = \emptyset$, $U_c = \{x_{cs}\}$, $s = 1, 2, \ldots N_c$, $c \in \{0, 1\}$. Nc is the number of samples of class c, $N_0 + N_1 = N$, and $x_{cs}=\{x_{cs1}, x_{cs2}, \ldots x_{csn}\}$ is the data sample of class c.
As we need to express which sample is closer to or further from a given point x, we can bind the index of the point of the learning set with its distance from point x. Therefore, let U be a learning set composed of points (patterns, samples) x_i, where i is the index of a point regardless of the class to which it belongs; x_i is the i-th nearest neighbor of point x. By the symbol i(c), we denote those indexes i for which point $x_i(c)$ belongs to class c.
As we need to work with metrics space we have to transform general data space to metric space. Therefore, we use normalized data, i.e. each variable x_{csj} (j fixed, s = 1, 2, ... N, c = 0 or 1 corresponds to the j-th column of matrix X^T) has zero mean and unit variance. The empirical means and variances of individual variables are computed from the whole learning set, i.e. regardless of the classes. Later they are used for the normalization of testing samples. We use Euclidean (L_2) and absolute (L_1) metrics here.

3.2 Mapping the distribution

First we introduce two important notions, the probability distribution mapping function and the distribution density mapping function. It is interesting that there is a close connection between the probability distribution mapping function and the correlation integral by Grassberger and Procaccia (Grassberger & Procaccia, 1983).
Let us have an example of a ball in an n-dimensional space containing uniformly distributed points over its volume. Let us divide the ball into concentric "peels" of the same volume.

Using the formula $r_i = \sqrt[n]{V_i / S(n)}$, which is, in fact, inverted formula for volume V_i of an n-dimensional ball of radius r_i, we obtain a quite interesting succession of radii corresponding to the individual volumes - peels. The symbol S(n) denotes the volume of a ball with unit radius in E_n; note $S(3) = 4/3\pi$. A mapping between the mean density ρ_i in an i-th peel and its radius r_i is $\rho_i = p(r_i)$; $p(r_i)$ is the mean probability density in the i-th ball peel with radius r_i. The probability distribution of points in the neighborhood of a query point x is thus simplified to the function $p(r_i)$ of a scalar variable r_i. We call this function a probability distribution mapping function D(x, r) and its partial differentiation with respect to r the distribution density mapping function d(x, r). Functions D(x, r) and d(x, r) for x fixed are, in fact, the probability distribution function and the probability density function of variable r, i.e. of distances of all points from the query point x. More exact definitions follow.

Definition 1. Probability distribution mapping function D(x, r) of the query point x is function $D(x,r) = \int_{B(x,r)} p(z)dz$, where r is the distance from the query point and B(x, r) is a ball with center x and radius r.

Definition 2. Distribution density mapping function d(x, r) of the query point x is function $d(x,r) = \frac{\partial}{\partial r} D(x,r)$, where D(x, r) is a probability distribution mapping function of the query point x and radius r.

Note. When it is necessary to differentiate the class of a point in distance r from point x, we write D(x, r, c) or d(x, r, c).

3.3 Zipfian distribution (Zipf's law)

The Zipfian distribution (Zipf's law) (Zipf, 1968; Zipf-Mandelbrot, 2009) predicts that out of a population of N elements, the frequency of elements of rank k, f(i;s,N), is

$$f(i;s,N) = \frac{1/i^s}{\sum_{t=1}^{N} 1/t^s},$$

where N is the number of elements, i is their rank, s is the value of the exponent characterizing the distribution.

The law may also be written:

$$f(i;s,N) = \frac{1}{i^s H_{N,s}},$$

where HN, s is the N-th generalized harmonic number.

The simplest case of Zipf's law is a "1/f function". Given a set of Zipfian distributed frequencies of the occurrence of some objects, sorted from the most common to the least common, the second most common frequency will occur 1/2 as often as the first. The third most common frequency will occur 1/3 as often as the first. The n-th most common frequency will occur 1/i as often as the first. However, this cannot hold exactly, because items must occur an integer number of times: there cannot be 2.5 occurrences of anything. Nevertheless, over fairly wide ranges, and to a fairly good approximation, many natural phenomena obey Zipf's law. Note that in the case of a "1/f function", i.e. s = 1, N must be finite; otherwise the denominator is a sum of harmonic series, which is divergent. This is not true if exponent s exceeds 1, s > 1, then

$$\zeta(s) = \sum_{t=1}^{\infty} \frac{1}{t^s} < \infty \ ,$$

where ζ is Riemann's zeta function.

The original motivation of Zipf's law was a corpus of natural language utterances. The frequency of any word is inversely proportional to its rank in the frequency table. Thus the most frequent word will occur approximately twice as often as the second most frequent word, which occurs twice as often as the fourth most frequent word, etc. In this example of the frequency of words in the English language, N is the number of words in the English language and, if we use the classic version of Zipf's law, the exponent s is 1. f(i; s,N) will then be the fraction of the time the i-th most common word occurs. It is easily seen that the distribution is normalized, i.e., the predicted frequencies sum to 1:

$$\sum_{i=1}^{N} f(i;s,N) = 1 \ .$$

3.4 Probability density estimation

As we mentioned above the classification method presented is based on estimation of a probability to which class point x of the data space belongs. The sum of inverted neighbors' indexes can be utilized for the probability estimation with advantage. In this section we give a deeper mathemeatical insight into the probability density estimation and and thus vindication of the method presented.

Let us assume that the best case for the distribution density estimation is the case of uniform distribution. This conjecture follows from generally accepted meaning (often implicit only) that best results are usually obtained in cases which are not too far from uniform distribution. For both classes distributed uniformly the probability that point x belongs to a class is given exactly by apriori probability. Then we are looking for a transformation by which we get the probability distribution mapping function linear and its derivative, the distribution density mapping function, constant.

Let indexes i be assigned to points (samples) of the learning set without respect to a given class so that i = 1 is assigned to the nearest neighbor of point x, i = 2 to the second nearest neighbor etc. We have finite learning set of size N samples and N_c samples of each class. The same number of samples of both classes is assumed without loss of generality in the theorem and proof as follows.

Theorem. Let the task of classification into two classes be given and let the best case for the distribution density estimation is the case of uniform distribution holds. Let the size of the learning set be N and let both classes have the same number of samples. Let i be the index of the i-th nearest neighbor of point x (without considering neighbor's class) and r_i be its distance from the point x. Then

$$p(c \mid x) = \lim_{N \to \infty} \frac{\sum_{i=1(c)}^{N} 1/i}{\sum_{i=1}^{N} 1/i} \qquad (1)$$

(the upper sum goes over indexes i for which the corresponding samples are of class c) is probability that point x belongs to class c.

Proof. For each query point x one can state the probability distribution mapping function $D(x, r_i, c)$. We approximate this function so that it holds (K is a constant)

$$D(x,r_i^q,c) = Kr_i^q$$

in the neighborhood of point x. Using derivation, according to variable $z = r_i^q$, we get $d(x,r_i^q,c) = K$. By the use of $z = r_i^q$, the space is mapped ("distorted") so that the distribution density mapping function is constant in the neighborhood of point x for any particular distribution. The particular distribution is characterized by particular value of the distribution mapping exponent q in point x. In this mapping the distribution of points of class c is uniform.

Let us consider sum $\sum_{i=2}^{N} d(x,r_i^q,c) / r_i^q$. For this sum we have

$$\lim_{N\to\infty}\sum_{i=2}^{N} d(x,r_i^q,c) / r_i^q = p(c\,|\,x) \lim_{N\to\infty}\sum_{i=2}^{N} 1 / r_i^q$$

because $d(x, r_i^q, c) = d(x, z, c) = p(c\,|\,x)$ for all i (uniform distribution has a constant density). By the use of $z_i = r_i^q$, the space is distorted so that the distribution density mapping function $d(x,z_i,c)$ is constant in the neighborhood of point x for any particular distribution. This local property we extend to wider neighborhood to have $d(x,r_i^q,c) = d(x,z_i,c)$ constant in the whole data space. For it the exponent q need not be a constant but can be a function $q = q(i, c)$. Let $r_i^{q(i,c)} = k_1 i$ for all i of class c; k_1 is a constant. (From the last formula one could derive the q(i, c), but we need not it.) We rewrite the equation above in form

$$\lim_{N\to\infty}\sum_{i=2}^{N} d(x,r_i^{q(i,c)},c) / r_i^{q(i,c)} = p(c\,|\,x) \lim_{N\to\infty}\sum_{i=2}^{N} 1 / r_i^{q(i,c)}$$

and then in form

$$\lim_{N\to\infty}\sum_{i=2}^{N} d(x,r_i^q,c) / i = p(c\,|\,x) \lim_{N\to\infty}\sum_{i=2}^{N} 1 / i \,.$$

Given the learning set, we have the space around point x "sampled" by individual points of the learning set. Let $p_c(r_i)$ be an a-posteriori probability point i in distance r_i from the query point x is of the class c. Then $p_c(r_i)$ is equal to 1 if point i is of class c and $p_c(r_i)$ is equal to zero, if the point is of the other class. Then the particular realization of $p(c\,|\,x)\sum_{i=2}^{N} 1/i$ is sum $\sum_{i=2(c)}^{N} 1/i$. Using this sum we can write

$$p(c\,|\,x) \lim_{N\to\infty}\sum_{i=2}^{N} 1 / i = \lim_{N\to\infty}\sum_{i=2(c)}^{N} 1 / i \,.$$

Dividing this equation by the limit of sum on the left hand side we get

$$p(c \mid x) = \frac{\lim\limits_{N\to\infty} \sum\limits_{i=2(c)}^{N} 1/i}{\lim\limits_{N\to\infty} \sum\limits_{i=2}^{N} 1/i}$$

and due to the same limit transition in numerator and in the denominator we can rewrite it in form (1). □

3.5. Generalization of the classifier

Here we generalize the classifier to cases of learning sets of different sizes for each class and for case of more than two classes. For different number of samples of one and the other class formula (1) has form

$$p(c \mid x) = \lim_{N\to\infty} \frac{\frac{1}{N_c} \sum\limits_{i=1(c)}^{N} 1/i}{\frac{1}{N_0} \sum\limits_{i=1(0)}^{N} 1/i + \frac{1}{N_1} \sum\limits_{i=1(1)}^{N} 1/i} \tag{2}$$

It is only recalculation of the relative representation of different numbers of samples of one and the other class. For C classes there is

$$p(c \mid x) = \lim_{N\to\infty} \frac{\frac{1}{N_c} \sum\limits_{i=2(c)}^{N} 1/r_i^q}{\sum\limits_{k=1}^{C} \frac{1}{N_k} \sum\limits_{i=2(c)}^{N} 1/r_i^q}.$$

It is interesting that formula (1) expresses Zipfian distribution (Zipf´s law) (Zipf, 1968) with Zipf´s exponent $s = 1$ (or eventually Zipf-Mandelbrot's law with zero additive parameter (Zipf, Mandelbrot, 2008)). It is easily seen that

$$\sum_{c=1}^{C} p(c \mid x) = \sum_{c=1}^{C} \lim_{N\to\infty} \frac{\sum\limits_{i=1(c)}^{N} 1/i}{\sum\limits_{i=1}^{N} 1/i} = 1$$

and $p(c \mid x)$ is a "sum of relative frequencies of occurrence" of points of a given class c. A "relative frequencies of occurrence" of point i, i.e. of the i-th neighbor of query point x, is just

$$f(i;1,N) = \frac{1/i}{\sum\limits_{j=1}^{N} 1/j}.$$

In fact, $f(i; s, N)$ is a probability mass function of Zipfian distribution. In our case $p(c \mid x)$ is a sum of probability mass functions for all appearances of class c. We could discuss optimal value of Zipf´s exponent s, but as seen above $s = 1$ is just optimal value. In the context of our findings this discrete distribution gets much broader role than its use in linguistics and psychology.

Example. Let us show a practical approach to construction a classifier that classifies to more than two classes and moreover it manages different numbers of patterns in the individual classes. In this example we use the well-know iris data by (Fischer, 1936). The task is to classify irises to three possible classes: Virginic, Versicolor and Setosa on the basis of their sepal and petal leaf width and length. There are totally 150 patterns (irises).

Let us chose one sample from the set as an unknown (test) pattern, say

Sepal Length	Sepal Width	Petal Length	Petal Width	Iris Type
5.9	3	5.1	1.8	Virginic

As we excluded one pattern from the available set of irises we have 149 (49, 50 and 50) patterns to our disposal for classifier construction.

The first step in our classifier construction is a normalization of the data (each individual feature is normalized independently) to zero mean and unit variance and consequently a normalization of the test pattern. Second, we calculate all (Euclidean) distances of the test pattern to all given patterns (149) and sort all the patterns in ascending order according to this distance. Further, a reciprocal value of order index is assigned to each pattern. In other words, 1 is assigned to the nearest pattern from our given pattern, ½ to the second nearest pattern and so on ... Finally, the 1/149 is assigned to the furthest pattern. As a further step we split the patterns with the assigned reciprocal indexes according to their class identifier and sum the particular values of the reciprocal indexes for the corresponding classes. We get the values

Virginic	Versicolor	Setosa
3.11377202	2.062620008	0.408121893

The sum of reciprocal values of indexes of all 149 patterns is 5.584513922. The ratios of these individual values to the number of patterns in the corresponding class is

Virginic	Versicolor	Setosa
3.11377202/49 = 0.063546368	2.062620008/50 = 0.0412524	0.408121893/50 = 0.008162438

After simple recalculation we finally get the probabilities in percentual representation

Virginic	Versicolor	Setosa
56.2550 %	36.5191 %	7.2259 %

On the basis of these results we can conclude that the given test pattern belongs to class 'Virginic' what has been assumed at the begining.

Partial cumulative sums for individual classes are depicted in Fig. 2. It is obvious that the lines do not overlap in this example. It means that it does not matter how many nearest neighbors will be used for the pattern classification (probability determination to which class the pattern belongs). The only difference would take effect in the different values of the probabilities of the individual classes not in their order.

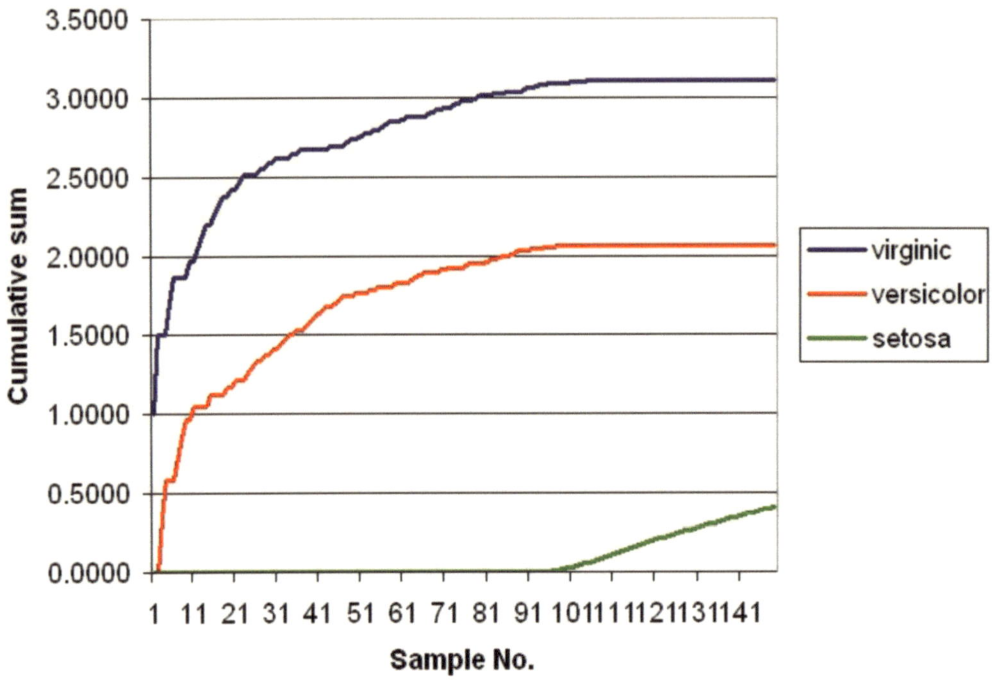

Fig. 2. Partial cumulative sums for individual classes

3.6 Measuring the distance

Usually distances are measured in Euclidean metric. On the experimental observation is seems that L_1 (absolute) metrics gives better results. At the same time, the larger p of L_p metric, the worse. The question arises why? We have no exact proof but point of view only, as follows.

Let us consider a metric written in a standard form

$$\lambda_i(a,b) = \sqrt[i]{\sum_{j=1}^{n} |b_i - a_i|^i} \ .$$

Let us formally rewrite this formula in form of scalar product using a vector which we will call weights

$$\lambda_i(a,b) = \sqrt[i]{(|b_1 - a_1|, |b_2 - a_2|, \dots, |b_n - a_n|).(w_1, w_2, \dots, w_n)} \ .$$

In our case, input arguments for the metric are coordinate differences $\delta_j = b_j - a_j$, j = 1, 2,..., n. Corresponding weight let be w_j. In Table 1 it can be seen that weights depend on the size of coordinate differences, and for L_1 metric only the weights are equal one to another. In other cases the larger the coordinate difference, the larger it's weight. There is also dependence on p of L_p and differences in the weights are the larger the larger p. The limit case is L_{max} metric.

Norm	Weights	distance
		$\sqrt[i]{\sum_{j=1}^{n} \lvert d_j \rvert w_j}$
L_1	$w_j = 1$	$\sqrt[1]{\sum_{j=1}^{n} \lvert d_j \rvert}$
L_2	$w_j = d_j$	$\sqrt[2]{\sum_{j=1}^{n} d_j^2}$
L_3	$w_j = d_{j2}$	$\sqrt[3]{\sum_{j=1}^{n} \lvert d_j^3 \rvert}$
etc.	etc.	etc.
Lmax	$w_j = 1$ for maximal d_j $w_j = 0$ otherwise	$\max(\lvert d_j \rvert)$

Table 1. Metrics as Weighted Sum of Coordinate Differences.

It seems to hold that the only "fair" metric is L_1 as it gives to all coordinate differences the equal "chance" to influence the distances of neighbors and, in the end, their final relative positions and thus their ordering which influences the sums of reciprocals of neighbor's indexes for one and the other class.

3.7 Correspondence of the distribution mapping exponent to correlation dimension

It can be seen that for a fixed x the function D(x, r), r > 0 is monotonously non-decreasing from zero to one. Functions D(x, r) and d(x, r) for fixed x are one-dimensional analogs to the probability distribution function and the probability density function, respectively. In fact, D(x, r) is the distribution function of distances of points from the query point x and d(x, r) is the corresponding probability density function. So we can write $p(c \mid x, r) = d(x, r, c)$. Moreover, D(x, r) resembles the correlation integral (Grassberger & Procaccia, 1983; Camastra & Vinciarelli, 2001). The correlation integral

$$C(r) = \lim_{N \to \infty} \frac{1}{N^2} \sum_{i,j=1}^{N} h(r - \lvert x_{.i} - x_{.j} \rvert),$$

where $x_{.i}$ and $x_{.j}$ are points of the learning set without regard to class and h(.) is the Heaviside's step function, can be written in form (Camastra & Vinciarelli, 2001; Camastra, 2003)

$$C(r) = \lim_{N \to \infty} \frac{1}{N(N-1)} \sum_{i=1}^{N-1} \sum_{j=i+1}^{N} h(r - \lvert x_{.i} - x_{.j} \rvert).$$

It can be seen (Camastra & Vinciarelli, 2001; Camastra, 2003) that correlation integral is a distribution function of all binate distances among the given data points. The probability distribution mapping function is a distribution function of distances from one fixed point. In the case of a finite number of points N, there is N(N - 1)/2 binate distances and from them one can construct the empirical correlation integral. Similarly, for each point there are N - 1 distances and from these N - 1 distances one can construct the empirical probability distribution mapping function. There are exactly N such functions and the mean of these functions gives the correlation integral. This applies also for the limit for the number of points N going to infinity.

On the other hand there are essential differences. The probability distribution mapping function is a local feature dependent on the position of point x. It also includes the boundary effects (Arya et al., 1996) of a true data set. The correlation integral is a feature of a fractal or data generated process and should not depend on the position of a particular point considered or on the size of the data set at hand.

In a log-log graph of the correlation integral, i.e. the graph of dependence of C on r, the slope gives the correlation dimension ν. In the log-log graph of the probability distribution mapping function D(x, r) the curve is also close to a monotonously and nearly linearly growing function. The slope (derivative) is given by a constant parameter. Let us denote this parameter q and call it the distribution mapping exponent. This parameter is rather close but generally different from ν.

The linear part of the log-log graph means

$$\log C(r) = a + \log \nu$$

where a is a constant, and then $C(r) = ar^{\nu}$. Thus C(r) grows linearly with variable r^{ν}.

Similarly the probability distribution mapping function grows linearly with r_q at least in the neighborhood of point x. Its derivative, the distribution density mapping function, is constant there. We will use this finding in the next section.

4. Demonstrations of the IINC on real-life tasks

4.1 Tasks from UCI machine learning repository

The classification ability of the IINC presented here was tested using real-life tasks from UCI Machine Learning Repository (Asuncion & Newman, 2007). Four tasks of classification into two classes for which data from previous tests were known were selected: "German", "Heart", "Adult", and "Ionosphere".

The task "German" decides whether a client is good or bad to be lent money to. In this data errors are weighted so that not to lend money to good a client means error weight 1, and lending money to a bad client means error weight 5.

The task "Heart" indicates the absence or presence of a heart disease in a patient.

The task "Adult" determines whether a person earns over $ 50000 a year.

For the task "Ionosphere" the targets were free electrons in the ionosphere. "Good" radar returns are those showing evidence of some type of structure in the ionosphere. "Bad" returns are those that do not show this; their signals pass through the ionosphere.

We do not describe these tasks in detail here as all can be found in (Asuncion & Newman, 2007). For each task the same approach to testing and evaluation was used as described in (Asuncion & Newman, 2007). Especially splitting the data set into two disjoint subsets, the learning set and the testing set, and the use of cross validation were the same as in (Asuncion & Newman, 2007). For our method the discriminant threshold was tuned accordingly.

The testing should show the classification ability of IINC method for some tasks and also show its classification ability relatively to other published methods and results for the same data sets.

In Table 2 the results are shown together with the results of other methods as given in (Asuncion & Newman, 2007). For each task the methods were sorted according to the classification error, the method with the best - the smallest - error first.

"German"		"Heart"	
Algorithm	Error	Algorithm	Error
IINC	0.1580	**IINC**	0.1519
SVM	0.297	Bayes	0.374
Discrim	0.535	Discrim	0.393
LogDisc	0.538	LogDisc	0.396
Castle	0.583	Alloc80	0.407
Alloc80	0.584	SVM	0.411
Dipol92	0.599	QuaDisc	0.422
Smart	0.601	Castle	0.441
Cal	0.603	Cal5	0.444
Cart	0.613	Cart	0.452
QuaDisc	0.619	Cascade	0.467
KNN	0.694	KNN	0.478
Default	0.700	Smart	0.478
Bayes	0.703	Dipol92	0.507
IndCart	0.761	Itrule	0.515
Back Prop	0.772	Bay Tree	0.526
BayTree	0.778	Default	0.560
Cn2	0.856	BackProp	0.574
"Adult"		**"Ionosphere"**	
Algorithm	Error	Algorithm	Error
FSS Naive Bayes	0.1405	IB3	0.0330
NBTree	0.1410	**IINC**	0.0331
C4.5-auto	0.1446	backprop	0.0400
IDTM (Decision table)	0.1446	Ross Quinlan's C4	0.0600
HOODG	0.1482	nearest neighbor	0.0790
C4.5 rules	0.1494	"non-linear" perceptron	0.0800
OC1	0.1504	"linear" perceptron	0.0930
C4.5	0.1554	SVM	0.1400
Voted ID3 (0.6)	0.1564		
SVM	0.1590		
CN2	0.1600		
Naïve-Bayes	0.1612		
IINC	0.1617		
Voted ID3 (0.8)	0.1647		
T2	0.1684		
1R	0.1954		
Nearest-neighbor (4)	0.2035		
Nearest-neighbor (2)	0.2142		

Table 2. Comparison of the classification error of IINC method for different tasks with results of other classifiers as given in (Asuncion & Newman, 2007).

4.2 Comprehensive tests

Data sets ready for a run with a classifier were prepared by Paredes and Vidal and are available on the net (Lucas & Algoval, 2008). We used all data sets in this corpus. Each task consists of 50 pairs of training and testing sets corresponding to 50-fold cross validation. For DNA data (Paredes, 2008), Letter data (Letter recognition (Asuncion & Newman, 2007)), and Satimage (Statlog Landsat Satellite (Asuncion & Newman, 2007)) the single partition into training and testing sets according to specification in (Asuncion & Newman, 2007) was used. We also added the popular Iris data set (Asuncion & Newman, 2007) with ten-fold cross validation. In Table 3 the results obtained by different methods are summarized. The methods are as follows:

L_2	The nearest neighbor method, data by (Paredes & Vidal, 2006)
1-NN L_2	The nearest neighbor method computed by authors
sqrt-NN L_2	The k-NN method witt k equal to square root of the number of samples of the learning set computed by authors
Bayes 10	The Bayes naive method with ten bins histograms, computed by authors
CDM	The learning weighted metrics method with class dependent Mahalanobis, data by (Paredes & Vidal, 2006)
CW	The learning weighted metrics method with class dependent weighting by (Paredes & Vidal, 2006), data by (Paredes & Vidal, 2006)
PW	The learning weighted metrics method with prototype dependent weighting by (Paredes & Vidal, 2006), data by (Paredes & Vidal, 2006)
CPW	The learning weighted metrics method with class and prototype - dependent weighting by (Paredes & Vidal, 2006), data by (Paredes & Vidal, 2006)
posit. L_1	The learning weighted metrics method (Jirina & Jirina, 2008) with positions weighting and Manhattan L_1 metrics
posit. L_2	The learning weighted metrics method (Jirina & Jirina, 2008) with positions weighting and Euclidean L_2 metrics
diff. L_1	The learning weighted metrics method (Jirina & Jirina, 2008) with coordinate differences weighting and Manhattan L_1 metrics
diff. L_2	The learning weighted metrics method (Jirina & Jirina, 2008) with coordinate differences weighting and Euclidean L_2 metrics
IINC L_1	The method presented here with Manhattan L_1 metrics
IINC L_2	The method presented here with Euclidean L_2 metrics

In Table 3 in each row the best result is denoted by bold numerals. Furthermore, in the last column, the values for IINC better with L_2 metrics than with L_1 metrics are shown in italics. There are 6 such cases out of a total of 24.

Task\Method Dataset \	L_2	1-NN L_2	sqrt-NN L2	Bayes 10	SVM	CDM	CW	PW	CPW	posit. L_1	posit. L_2	diff. L_1	diff. L_2	**IINC L_1**	**IINC L_2**
Australian	34.37	20.73	15.50	13.88	35.99	18.19	17.37	16.95	16.83	17.64	19.00	17.86	21.51	**13.31**	14.75
Balance	25.26	23.61	32.06	15.17	45.48	35.15	17.98	13.44	17.6	17.85	**16.17**	34.48	37.74	32.58	*30.80*
Cancer	4.75	5.07	3.25	2.68	16..34	8.76	3.69	3.32	3.53	17.70	**3.18**	26.46	26.49	3.28	3.48
Diabetes	32.25	29.48	26.46	**24.19**	29.64	32.47	30.23	27.39	27.33	34.90	26.49	34.90	34.90	26.21	*25.52*
Dna	23.4	25.72	34.06	6.66		15	4.72	6.49	**4.21**	20.83	24.37	42.24	41.57	27.82	31.03
German	33.85	32.76	30.90	24.97	27.25	32.15	27.99	28.32	**27.29**	29.02	29.23	29.87	30.00	30.91	31.13
Glass	**27.23**	32.72	42.10	47.37		32.9	28.52	26.28	27.48	43.43	30.29	46.89	43.77	33.01	35.18
Heart	42.18	25.11	16.89	17.44	38.89	22.55	22.34	18.94	19.82	19.04	21.56	21.37	22.52	17.96	***17.93***
Ionosphere	*19.03*	14.05	14.70	**9.26**						29.39	17.58	29.70	30.03	10.82	14.81
Iris	*6.91*	5.91	7.91	9.82	6.55					**4.91**	6.91	25.82	11.82	7.91	***4.91***
Led17	*20.5*	11.50	**0.12**	0.00						7.64	2.67	24.78	37.72	0.46	*0.45*
Letter	4.35	4.80	18.70	28.98	40.53	6.3	3.15	4.6	**4.2**	6.23	5.90	7.95	8.05	4.85	4.98
Liver	37.7	39.59	41.48	39.42	37.68	39.32	40.22	**36.22**	36.95	40.96	42.00	40.70	40.43	38.29	39.13
Monkey1	*2.01*	2.01	9.27	28.01	23.54					2.01	2.82	**1.45**	1.47	4.79	4.79
Phoneme	*18.01*	11.83	20.71	21.47	21.71					14.72	**14.61**	29.27	29.27	17.55	18.06
Satimage	10.6	10.65	15.20	19.15	44.85	14.7	11.7	**8.8**	9.05	11.40	11.70	76.95	75.90	11.00	11.55
Segmen	*11.81*	3.81	11.41	9.85						5.18	5.35	9.96	10.62	**4.12**	5.05
Sonar	*31.4*	18.37	32.51	31.46						21.11	21.89	46.63	46.63	**19.89**	22.85
Vehicle	35.52	30.51	31.51	38.40		32.11	29.38	**29.31**	28.09	30.48	31.01	36.83	34.96	29.40	*29.34*
Vote	8.79	8.74	9.60	9.70		6.97	6.61	5.51	**5.26**	7.97	7.45	7.17	11.98	8.52	8.89
Vowel	1.52	**1.19**	46.68	26.64		1.67	1.36	1.68	1.24	3.52	3.89	5.55	6.17	2.73	2.74
Waveform 21	24.1	23.73	**14.71**	19.26						18.50	18.63	25.56	25.19	16.15	16.38
Waveform 40	31.66	28.22	**16.24**	20.31						20.50	22.61	32.25	32.78	17.59	18.08
Wine	24.14	5.42	6.15	4.50		2.6	1.44	1.35	**1.24**	5.27	6.06	72.04	67.42	4.24	5.66

Table 3. Classification error rates for different datasets and different approaches. Empty cells denote not available data. For legend see text above

5. Conclusion

The IINC seems to provide better classification then other classifiers in most tasks even though it is not the best all the time. This could make it a welcome alternative to standard classification methods.

The method of classification based on probability estimation proposed here consists in finding that each point of class c in the neighborhood of the query point x adds a little to the probability that point x is of class c, where c is the class mark. We proved that the influence to the probability that point x is of class c if the nearest neighbor of class c is 1, the influence of the second nearest neighbor is ½, the influence of the third nearest neighbor is 1/3 etc. We sum up these influences so that the sum goes over indexes i for which the corresponding samples of the learning set are of class c. In the case of two classes we get two numbers S_0 and S_1 which together give the sum of N first elements of harmonic series S = 1 + ½ + 1/3 + ¼ + … + 1/N. The estimation of the probability that the query point x belongs to class c is then $p(x \mid c) = \frac{S_c}{S}$.

The proof that ratio of sums mentioned gives just probability that the query point is of that class uses the notion of distance but no explicit metrics is specified. It was also found experimentally that it is usually better to measure distance by L_1 rather than standard L_2 metrics.

There is no problem with convergence of the method and the curse of dimensionality. The computational complexity grows at most linearly with dimensionality and quadratically or less with the learning set size depending on the sorting algorithm used.

6. Acknowledgements

This work was supported by the Ministry of Education of the Czech Republic under the project Center of Applied Cybernetics No. 1M0567, and No. MSM6840770012 Transdisciplinary Research in the Field of Biomedical Engineering II.

7. References

Arya, S., Mount, D. M., Narayan, O. (1996), Accounting for boundary effects in nearest neighbor searching, *Discrete and Computational Geometry*, Vol. 16, pp. 155-176.

Asuncion, A., Newman, D. J., (2007). UCI Machine Learning Repository [http://www.ics.uci.edu/~mlearn/MLRepository.html]. Irvine, CA: University of California, School of Information and Computer Science

Bock, R. K. (2004). Methods for multidimensional event classification: a case study using images from a Cherenkov gamma-ray telescope. *Nuclear Instruments and Methods in Physics Research*, Vol. A 516, pp. 511-528

Camastra, F. (2003), Data dimensionality estimation methods: a survey. *Pattern recognition* Vol. 36, pp. 2945-2954.

Camastra, P., Vinciarelli, A. (2001), Intristic Dimension Estimation of Data: An Approach based on Grassberger-Procaccia's Algorithm. *Neural Processing Letters*, Vol. 14, No. 1, pp. 27-34.

Cháves, E., Figueroa, K., Navarro, G. (2001). A Fast Algorithm for the all k Nearest Neighbors Problem in General Metric Spaces. Escuela da Ciencias Fisicas y Matematicas, Universidad Michacana, Morelia, Michoacan, Mexico, 2001. Available: http://garota.fismat.umich.mx/~elchavez/publica/.

Cover, T. M., Hart, P. E. (1967). Nearest neighbor Pattern Classification. *IEEE Transactions in Information Theory*, pp. 23-27, Vol. IT-13, No. 1

Duda, R. O., Hart, P. E., Stork, D. G. (2000). Pattern classification, Second Edition, John Wiley and Sons, Inc., New York.

Fisher, R.A. (1936). The Use of Multiple Measurements in Taxonomic Problems. *Annals of Eugenics* , 7: 179–188.

Grassberger, P., Procaccia, I. (1983), Measuring the Strangeness of Strange Attractors. *Physica*, Vol. 9D, pp. 189-208.

Hakl, F., Hlaváček, M., Kalous, R. (2002). Application of Neural Networks Optimized by Genetic Algorithms to Higgs Boson Search. The 6th World Multi-Conference on Systemics, Cybernetics and Informatics. Proceedings. (Ed.: Callaos N., Margenstern M., Sanchez B.) Vol. : 11. Computer Science II. - Orlando, IIIS 2002, pp. 55-59

Hakl, F., Jirina, M., Richter-Was, E. (2005). Hadronic tau's identification using artificial neural network. *ATLAS Physics Communication*, ATL-COM-PHYS-2005-044, CERN, Geneve, Switzerland

Jiřina, M. and Jiřina, M., Jr. (2008). Classifier Based on Inverted Indexes of Neighbors II – Theory and Appendix, *Technical Report*, Institute of Computer Science AS CR, No. V-1041, Prague, Czech Republic

Jiřina, M., Jiřina, M., Jr. (2008). Learning Weighted Metrics Method with a Nonsmooth Learning Process. *Technical report*, V-1026, Institute of Computer Science AS CR, 15pp, Prague, Czech Republic

Kim, H. C., Ghahramani, Z. (2006). Bayesian Gaussian Process Classification with the EM-EP Algorithm. IEEE Trans. on pattern analysis and machine intelligence, pp. 1948-1959, Vol. 28, No. 12

Lucas, S. M., Algoval (2008). Algorithm Evaluation over the Web, [online], 2008, [cited November 23, 2008]. Available: <http://algoval.essex.ac.uk/data/vector/UCI/>

Merz, C. J., Murphy, P. M., Aha, D. W. (2010). UCI Repository of Machine Learning Databases. Dept. of Information and Computer Science, Univ. of California, Irvine, http://www.ics.uci.edu/~mlearn/MLSummary.html

Paredes, R. (2008). CPW: Class and Prototype Weights learning, [online], 2008, [cited November 23, 2008]. Available: <http://www.dsic.upv.es/~rparedes/research/CPW/index.html>

Paredes, R., Vidal, E. (2006). Learning Weighted Metrics to Minimize Nearest Neighbor Classification Error. *IEEE Transactions on Pattern Analysis and Machine Intelligence*, pp. 1100-1110, Vol. 20, No. 7

Silverman, B. W. (1990). Density estimation for statistics and data analysis, Chapman and Hall, London.

Zipf, G. K. (1968), The Psycho-Biology of Language. An Introduction to Dynamic Philology. The MIT Press. (Eventually: http://en.wikipedia.org/wiki/Zipf's_law)

Zipf-Mandelbrot law, [online], 2009, [cited January 28, 2009]. Available: http://en.wikipedia.org/wiki/Zipf-Mandelbrot_law

20

2D Figure Pattern Mining

Keiji Gyohten, Hiroaki Kizu and Naomichi Sueda
Oita University,
Japan

1. Introduction

1.1 Background

With the recent enhancement of desktop design environments, it has become easy for personal users to design graphical documents such as posters, flyers, slides, drawings, etc. These kinds of documents are usually produced by the applications like drawing softwares, which have the advantage that they can store and retrieve the drawing data electronically. By reusing parts of the stored drawing data, the users can design the graphical documents much more easily.

However, generally, the stored data of many users is not shared, although this can be achieved by putting a drawing database. One reason is that it is difficult to retrieve desired figures from large amounts of drawing data in the database. Unlike in text search, the figure search will require enormous amounts of computation time because matching of the geometric primitives in the drawing data will cause their combinatorial explosion in 2D space.

To address this problem, many approaches have been proposed recently. When users search the drawing database, they should conjure up the desired figures and design their 2D sketches as the keys. In case of retrieving general figures, such as electrical symbols and map symbols, there would be little difference between sketches of them drawn by different users, but it is impractical to make them visualize various objects and things and use the sketches as the keys. For example, in case of retrieving human figures, since the sketches of humans differ according to the users, not all of figures of humans will be able to be obtained from the drawing database. To cope with this problem, we need a technique that enables the applications to automatically present users with the list of figures considered to have any meaning. Users can specify a figure of the desired object or thing simply by selecting it from the list and then retrieve the desired figures from the database using it as the key.

1.2 Figure pattern mining

Since the parts appearing many times in many graphical documents would illustrate something significant, the application should analyze all of the data in the drawing database and mine frequent figure patterns automatically so that it can obtain figures which represent some meanings. We call the frequent parts having similar figure patterns semantic figure patterns, which might well be the general figures like symbols. By presenting users with the list of the obtained semantic figure patterns, users can retrieve desired data from the drawing database without sketching. This will lead to sharing of the drawing data stored by many users.

In this chapter, we discuss a data mining approach for 2D drawing data designed by the drawing softwares and propose a method of 2D figure pattern mining. Usually, a variety of symbols registered in drawing softwares are placed on the drawing area through various kinds of 2D affine transformations such as rotation, scaling and translation. In order to mine such drawing data, including symbols placed in a complex manner, it should be represented in the form independent of these affine transformations. Since topology of geometric primitives is invariant to the affine transformations, our method first obtains interim results by mining topology data of the drawing data. After that, the final results are sorted out from the interim ones with the verification of their geometric validity.

In our approach, the topology data of the drawing data is represented by graphs where nodes and edges correspond to the geometric primitives and the spatial relations between them, respectively. We call this graph topology graph, where labels on the nodes denote the kinds of the geometric primitives and those on the edges the types of the spatial arrangements of two primitives. Even if the 2D affine transformation is applied to a partial set of the geometric primitives, its corresponding subgraph in the topology graph will be unchanged. Our method generates these topology graphs from all of the drawing data and mines them to extract the frequent subgraphs as the interim results. These subgraphs represent sets of the geometric primitives having frequent topological figure patterns, but the similarity of their appearance is not guaranteed.

Next, our method checks if the sets of the geometric primitives obtained in the previous step fit each other by inferring the affine transformations between them. If valid transformations can be estimated between the primitive sets, it can be said that they have the same topology and appearance. They can be interpreted as the final result, that is, which are the desired semantic figure patterns appearing frequently in the drawing database.

2. Related works

The analysis of figures has been studied by many researchers. In recent years, interesting study has been carried out not only on 2D figures but on 3D figures. However, the most important point is how to represent their shapes no matter what dimension they are in.

In the studies of the 3D shape matching, one general approach is to represent the 3D shapes with set of points. Barequet and Sharir presented a partial surface and volume matching method, which represents objects to be matched as a set of points and estimates a transformation of one object to the other (Barequet & Sharir, 1997). Aiger et al. proposed a fast and robust alignment scheme for surface registration of 3D point sets (Aiger et al., 2008). Some approaches dealt with not set of points but salient points and achieved advanced matching like partial matching (Novotni et al., 2005) and matching over several views of an object (Castellani et al., 2008).

There is also an approach where the 3D shapes are represented with skeleton graphs. Brennecke and Isenberg used the skeleton graph to calculate a similarity measure for 3D geometry models (Brennecke & Isenberg, 2004). Sundar et al. used graph matching techniques and proposed a method of part-matching of 3D objects. This method is intended to be used for retrieval of the shapes from an indexed database (Sundar et al., 2003). Tung and Schmitt proposed the multiresolution Reeb graph and tried to improve a shape matching method applied to content-based search in database of 3D objects (Tung & Schmitt, 2005). Iyer et al. proposed a shape representation which has multiple levels of detail and preserves geometry and topology of 3D models using a hierarchical skeleton graph.

This is also used for similar 3D shape retrieval. Schnabel et al. used not only graph representation but 3D point-clouds and presented a flexible framework for the rapid detection of semantic shapes (Schnabel et al., 2007).
In order to develop a fast retrieval system of 3D objects, it is important to represent features of the shapes simply and plainly for the reduction of the computation time (Bustos et al., 2004). In this case, many methods retrieve desired objects without considering detailed correspondence between 3D shapes and exploit only the 3D shape features like Krawtchouk moment (Mademlis et al., 2006), Bag-of-Words representation (Li & Godil, 2009) and Bag-of-features SIFT (Ohbuchi et al., 2008).
The 2D shape matching technique has been studied actively in the field of data retrieval where 2D shape is used as a search key. Kim and Grauman presented an asymmetric region-to-image matching method which identifies corresponding points for each region and compares images by considering geometric consistency and appearance similarity (Kim & Grauman, 2010). Liu et al. proposed a sketch-based approach to find matching source images for image composition. The system asks users to draws a rough sketch to identify the desired object and finds a set of matching images (Liu et al., 2009). This sketch-based approach is also used in searching 3D objects. Funkhouser et al. proposed a shape descriptor for boundary contours and used it as the shape-based query. This descriptor is invariant to rotation and is represented with a set of the amplitudes of constituent trigonometrics (Funkhouser et al., 2003). Pu et al. proposed 2D sketch-based user interface for 3D CAD model retrieval, where 2D shapes are compared with each other by matching a large amount of sample points on their edges and calculating the Euclidean distance distribution between the sample points (Pu et al., 2005).
In all cases, most of the techniques for analyzing shapes of figures have been used mainly for matching and data retrieval. There does not appear to be any data mining methods in this field. However, some interesting approaches have been proposed. They analyze shapes without any prior knowledge about the desired objects. Lovett et al. proposed an incremental learning technique for the generalization of object categories based upon the sketches of those objects. The generalized categories are used to classify new sketches (Lovett et al., 2007). Hou et al. proposed a clustering method based on Support Vector Machines to organize the 3D models semantically. The resultant clusters are used to classify the unknown data (Hou et al., 2005). Pauly et al. presented an approach for discovering regular or repeated geometric structures in 3D shapes, which are represented in point or mesh based models (Pauly et al., 2008). Ovsjanikov et al. proposed an approach for computing intrinsic symmetries of a 3D shape (Ovsjanikov et al., 2008).
Since figures are drawn in a multi-dimensional space, it can be said that a shape of a figure is a kind of spatial data. In the field of data mining, spatial data mining is becoming popular and has been studied by many researchers recently (Ng and Han, 1994). Sheikholeslami et al. proposed a multi-resolution clustering method which can effectively identify arbitrary shape clusters at different degrees of accuracy in spatial databases using wavelet transformation (Sheikholeslami et al., 1998). Jiang proposed a spatial hierarchical clustering technique for generalization processes in GIS (Jiang 2004). Visual data mining proposed by Brecheisen et al. is a very interesting approach, where the hierarchical clustering structure of a 3D object database is visualized (Brecheisen et al., 2004).

3. Topology graph mining

Our method represents spatial relations between the geometric primitives as the topology graph, which is invariant to the 2D affine transformations such as rotation, scaling and translation. Sets of the geometric primitives having frequent topological figure patterns can be obtained by generating the topology graphs from large amounts of 2D drawing data and applying a graph mining method to them. The desired semantic figure patterns will be included in these geometric primitive sets.

3.1 Topology graph

In the topology graph, a node corresponds to a geometric primitive, which is denoted as f_h. There exists an edge between the nodes if their corresponding geometric primitives, denoted as (f_h, f_k), touch or intersect with each other. From the above, the topology graph can be denoted as $\mathbf{G}=(\{f_h\}, \{(f_h, f_k)\})$.

Now we consider the topology of the geometric primitives and define the labels on the nodes and edges to deal with their spatial arrangements. Since each geometric primitive in the 2D drawing data generally has its type (line segment, circle, etc.) and the control points (start point, end point, center, etc.) specifying its shape, it can be expressed as $(t^{fh}, \{\mathbf{p}^{fh}_i\})$, where t^{fh} and $\{\mathbf{p}^{fh}_i\}$ is the type and the set of control points of the geometric primitive f_h, respectively. It should be noted that the coordinates of the control points vary according to the 2D affine transformation applied to the geometric primitives. Since the topology graph should be invariant to the 2D affine transformation, the node labels show only the types of the geometric primitives with a digit as shown in Fig. 1. The control points will be considered for the analysis of the spatial relations between the geometric primitives and for the estimation of the affine transformations between the sets of the geometric primitives, as described later.

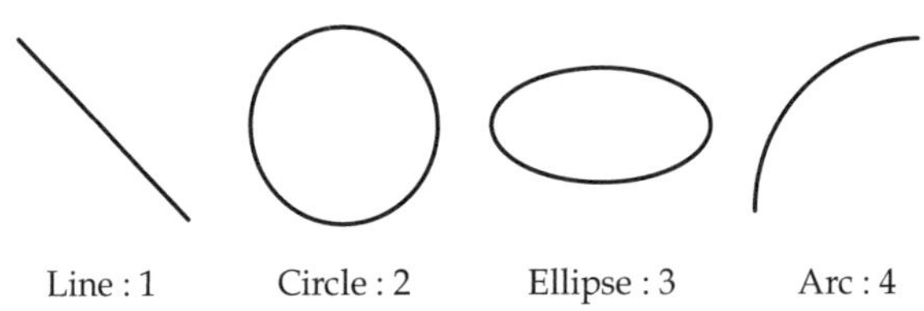

Fig. 1. Digits assigned to geometric primitives

The edge labels represent the spatial relations between the geometric primitives touching or intersecting each other. The spatial relations must be able to be defined for any types of geometric primitives. Therefore, we suppose that each geometric primitive consists of three components: area, boundary and set of end points as shown in Fig. 2 and define five digits as the edge label by considering form of overlapping between these components as shown in Fig. 3. The first digit represents spatial relation between areas of geometric primitives. If these areas overlap partially, the first digit is set to be 1. If an area is entirely included in the other, it is set to be 2. The second digit represents the relationship between the boundaries. It is the number of their intersections. If there is infinite set of the intersections, let the second digit be 9. The third digit is the number of end points which are included in the area of the other geometric primitive. This represents the relationships between the area and the end points. The fourth digit is the number of the end points which are on the boundary of the other geometric primitive. This represents the relationships between the boundary and the end points. The fifth digit is the number of end points that are shared with the other geometric primitive. This represents relationships between the end points. Examples of the edge labels are shown in Fig. 4. These edge labels are unchanged even if their relevant

geometric primitives are moved by the affine transformation. Naturally, the ways of calculating the edge labels differ according to the combination of the geometric primitive types. The an edge label calculation between two line segments is totally different from that between an line segment and a circle. Our method assumes that all of the ways of the edge label calculation are given for any combination of possible geometric primitive types.
Our method generates the topology graphs for all 2D drawing data in the drawing database to represent topological figure patterns. The node labels, the edge labels, and the connections between the nodes are invariant to the 2D affine transformations.

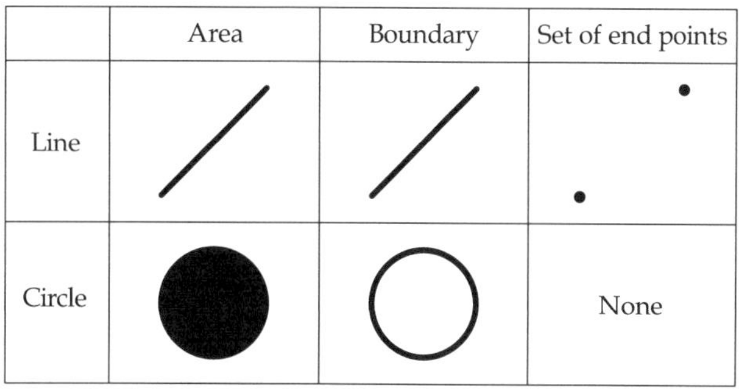

Fig. 2. Area, Boundary and Set of end points of geometric primitives

	Area	Boundary	Set of end points
Area	1		3
Boundary		2	4
Set of end points			5

Fig. 3. Places of digits for edge label

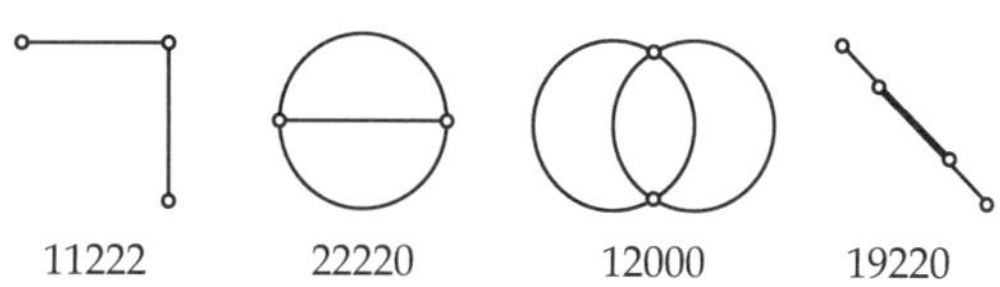

Fig. 4. Examples of edge label

3.2 Mining of topology graph

By mining the topology graphs, our method extracts subgraphs corresponding to the frequent topological figure patterns, which could be the desired semantic figure patterns. In the field of graph mining, various methods have been proposed to obtain frequent subgraphs fast and correctly. Our method uses GASTON graph mining algorithm, which works efficiently, especially for sparse undirected graphs (Nijssen & Kok, 2004). Since the edges in the topology graphs correspond to spatial relations between geometric primitives adjacent to each other, the number of the edges is generally much less than the possible number of edges. Therefore, GASTON will works efficiently for the topology graphs.
Although the extracted subgraphs represent the frequent topological figure patterns, their appearances are not always the same. As shown in Fig. 5, the same topology subgraphs do not always show the same configurations of the geometric primitives. Our method overlays

one of the extracted sets of the geometric primitives onto the other to check the similarity of their appearances. This is done by verifying that a valid 2D affine transformation can be obtained between the primitive sets.

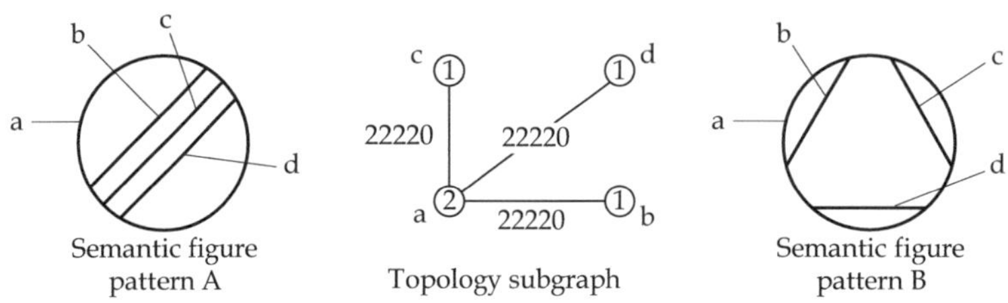

Fig. 5. Same topology subgraph of different semantic figure patterns

4. Check of geometric validity

In order to verify the geometric validity of the sets of the geometric primitives obtained by the topology graph mining, our method tries to overlay one of the sets onto the other and checks the similarity of their appearances. This can be done by taking the following two steps: First, the 2D affine transformation is estimated between the primitive sets. Then their appearances are compared by fitting them with each other using the estimated transformation. If it is judged that they have the same appearance, they can be considered as the final results, that is, frequent figure patterns representing the desired semantic figure patterns.
If coordinates of 2D points are represented as augmented vectors, a 2D affine transform can be expressed as follows:

$$\begin{bmatrix} x' \\ y' \\ 1 \end{bmatrix} = \begin{bmatrix} a_1 & b_1 & d_1 \\ a_2 & b_2 & d_2 \\ 0 & 0 & e \end{bmatrix} \begin{bmatrix} x \\ y \\ 1 \end{bmatrix} \tag{1}$$

where $[x\ y\ 1]^t$ and $[x'\ y'\ 1]^t$ are the coordinates of an original point and of the point after the transformation in the homogeneous coordinate system. a_1, a_2, b_1, b_2, d_1, d_2 are the affine parameters. e is a parameter due to the use of augmented vectors. If n correspondences of the points between two sets of the geometric primitives are obtained by topology graph mining, the following equation is derived:

$$\begin{bmatrix} x_1 & y_1 & 1 & 0 & 0 & 0 & -x_1' \\ 0 & 0 & 0 & x_1 & y_1 & 1 & -y_1' \\ x_2 & y_2 & 1 & 0 & 0 & 0 & -x_2' \\ 0 & 0 & 0 & x_2 & y_2 & 1 & -y_2' \\ \vdots & \vdots & \vdots & \vdots & \vdots & \vdots & - \\ x_n & y_n & 1 & 0 & 0 & 0 & -x_n' \\ 0 & 0 & 0 & x_n & y_n & 1 & -y_n' \end{bmatrix} \begin{bmatrix} a_1 \\ b_1 \\ d_1 \\ a_2 \\ b_2 \\ d_2 \\ e \end{bmatrix} = \begin{bmatrix} 0 \\ 0 \\ 0 \\ 0 \\ 0 \\ 0 \\ 0 \end{bmatrix} \tag{2}$$

where $\mathbf{p}_i=[x_i\ y_i\ 1]^t$ and $\mathbf{p}_i'=[x_i'\ y_i'\ 1]^t$ (i=1, ..., n) are the coordinates of n corresponding points. Eq. (2) can be represented as follows:

$$R_a = 0\ . \tag{3}$$

In practice, Eq. (3) is usually an over-determined system of equations because the number of the control point coordinates is usually more than the number of unknown parameters, that is, affine parameters and e.

Our method obtains the least square solution of Eq.(3) using the Lagrange multiplier method. The value to be minimized is the sum square of the residuals between the corresponding control points as shown in Fig. 6. This value can be represented as follows:

$$C = a^t R^t R a \,. \tag{4}$$

Here one solution to Eq.(4) is $\mathbf{a} = \mathbf{0}$, which is meaningless for the purpose of this approach. To avoid this problem, we set the constraint

$$a^t a = 1 \tag{5}$$

on the unknown parameters and set up the objective function as follows:

$$C = a^t R^t R a + \lambda(a^t a - 1)\,, \tag{6}$$

where λ is a Lagrange multiplier. Since the partial differentiation of Eq.(6) is

$$\frac{\partial C}{\partial a} = 2R^t Ra + 2\lambda a\,, \tag{7}$$

the desired solution is the eigenvector of $\mathbf{R}^t\mathbf{R}$ which corresponds to the minimum eigenvalue.

It should be noted that our method cannot determine a unique correspondence between the control points in the frequent topological figure patterns obtained by the topology graph mining as shown in Fig. 7. Our method obtains all of the combination, estimates affine parameters for each of them, and selects the most valid affine transformation. As shown in Fig. 8, we denote by $\mathbf{S}^F$ the sets of all possible combination of geometric primitives obtained from the results of the topology graph mining. For a geometric primitive combination $g \in \mathbf{S}^F$, the sets of combination of control points are denoted by $\mathbf{S}^P{}_g$. Our method minimizes the standard deviation of the residuals between control points corresponding with each other as follows:

$$d = \min_{g \in S^F} \min_{c \in S_g^P|} (sd(\{|\, t(p_i^c, a^c) - p_i^c{}' \,|\}) \,, \tag{8}$$

where sd({v}) is the standard deviation of the values {v}. $\mathbf{t}(\mathbf{p}, \mathbf{a})$ is the point translated from the point $\mathbf{p}$ through the affine transformation whose parameters are $\mathbf{a}$. Points $\mathbf{p}_i{}^c$ and $\mathbf{p}_i{}^{c'}$ are the i-th corresponding points in the control point combination c. $\mathbf{a}^c$ is the estimated parameters in the combination c using the Lagrange multiplier method as described above. If d is smaller than a threshold, we can state that the set of geometric primitives evaluated with (6) have the same topology and that one of them can be mapped to the other through an affine transformation as shown in Fig. 6. This implies that they represent the same semantic figure pattern.

In this appearance evaluation process, thresholding d starts from the pairs of geometric primitive sets corresponding to the largest topology subgraph. If they are judged to have the same semantic figure pattern, the geometric primitives in them are excluded from this process to avoid extracting their substructures as other semantic figure patterns.

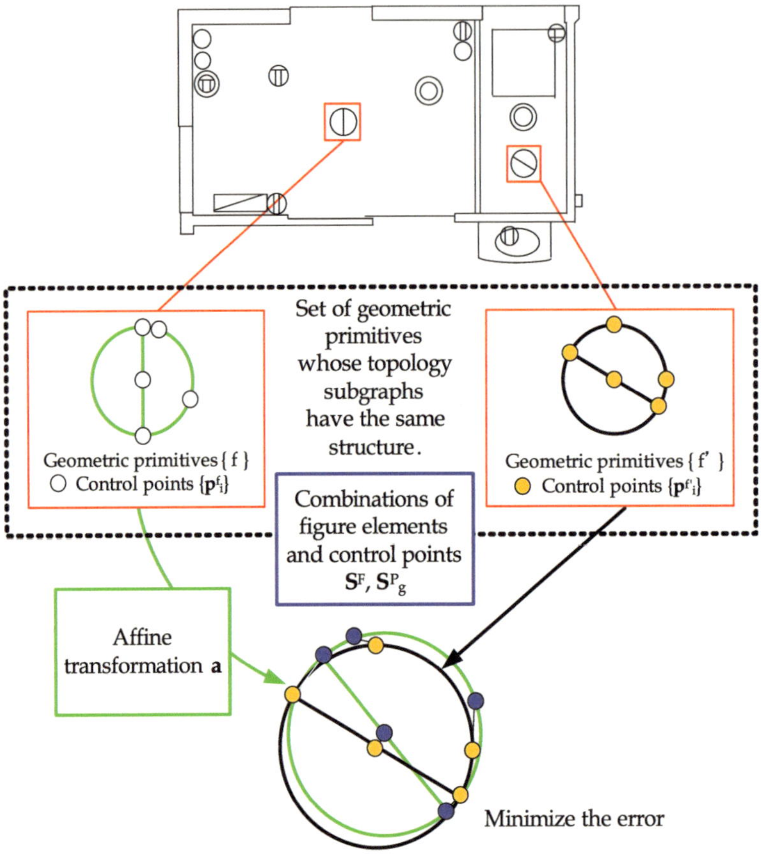

Fig. 6. Estimation of affine transformation

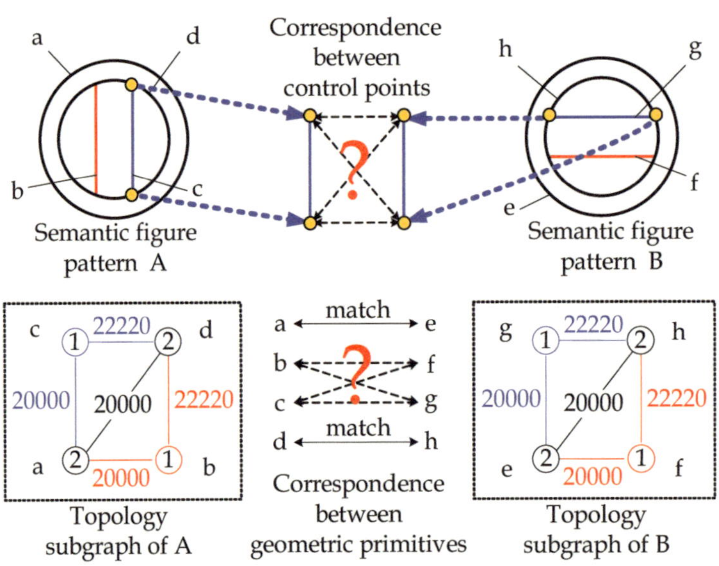

Fig. 7. Ambiguity of correspondence between semantic figure patterns

5. Experiments

We implemented the proposed method on a PC with Intel Core 2 Duo CPU, 2.13GHz, and 4GB RAM using the C++ language and applied it to some 2D drawing data to confirm its validity. As the 2D drawing data for this experiment, we used CAD data of 42 floor plans where there are 8 electrical symbols, which are shown in Fig. 8. These floor plans were drawn by 6 users with Microsoft Office Visio.

Fig. 8. Electrical symbols

In the experiment, we evaluated precision and recall to evaluate the performance of the proposed method. They are computed as follows:

$$\text{Precision} = \frac{N_{tp}}{N_{tp} + N_{fp}}, \tag{9}$$

$$\text{Recall} = \frac{N_{tp}}{N_{tp} + N_{fn}}, \tag{10}$$

where N_{tp} is the number of the semantic figure patterns extracted correctly. N_{fp} is the number of the extracted figure patterns which are not true semantic figure patterns. N_{fn} is the number of the semantic figure patterns not extracted in this experiment.
First, we built topology graphs of all floor plans and applied the topology graph mining to them with the support 1.0. Here the support is defined as follows:

$$\text{Support} = \frac{M_{ff}}{M_{af}}, \tag{11}$$

where M_{ff} is the number of the floor plans where the frequent topology subgraphs appear, and M_{af} is the total number of floor plans. This value can adjust the sensitivity of the mining performance. As the result of the topology graph mining, our method extracts 12 kinds of topology subgraphs, which represent the frequent topological figure patterns and potentially desired semantic figure patterns as illustrated in Fig. 9. These frequent topological figure patterns included 5 out of 8 types of electrical symbols. The remaining 3 types could not be obtained because of the following reasons. First, some of the types did not appear frequently enough to satisfy the support value. The other reason is the error of labelling some edges, where, for example, a geometric primitive did not quite reach to the other one, even though they should touch each other, and vice versa as shown in Fig. 10. In this step, the precision and recall were 66% and 82%, respectively.

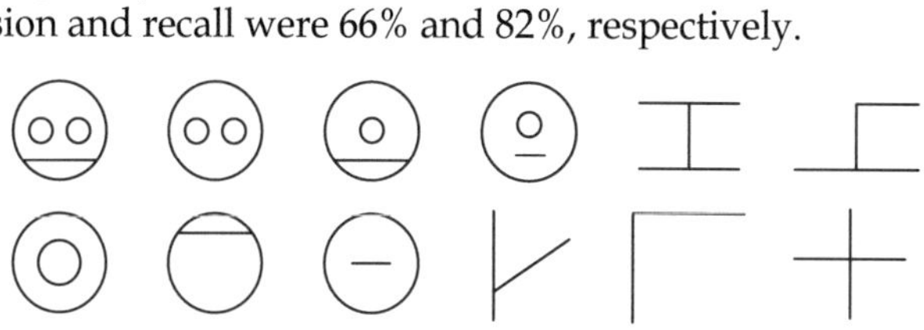

Fig. 9. Result of topology graph mining

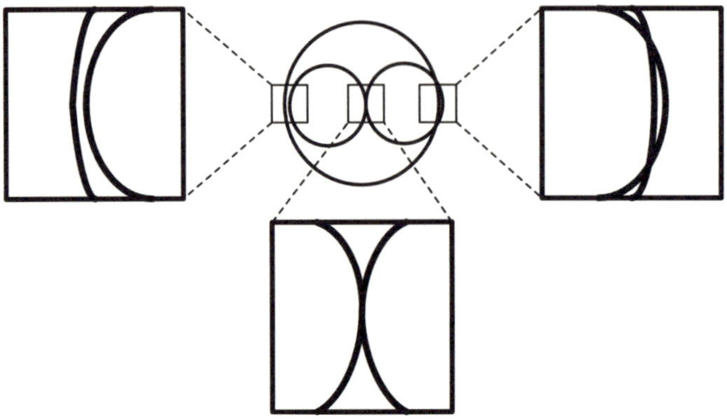

Fig. 10. Example of labeling error

Next, we eliminated wrong semantic figure patterns by checking the appearance similarity between the geometric primitive sets corresponding to the same topological subgraphs. The threshold for d was set to be 1.0 which was determined experimentally. In this step, the precision was improved to be 72%. However, the proposed method has to estimate affine transformations for all of the combinations of geometric primitives and those of control points individually. This will lead to the explosion of the computation time. Moreover, not all of the erroneous semantic figure patterns were eliminated in this step because similar configurations could exist among them. Figure 11 shows an example, where the geometric primitives are arranged similarly, even though they do not represent electrical symbols.

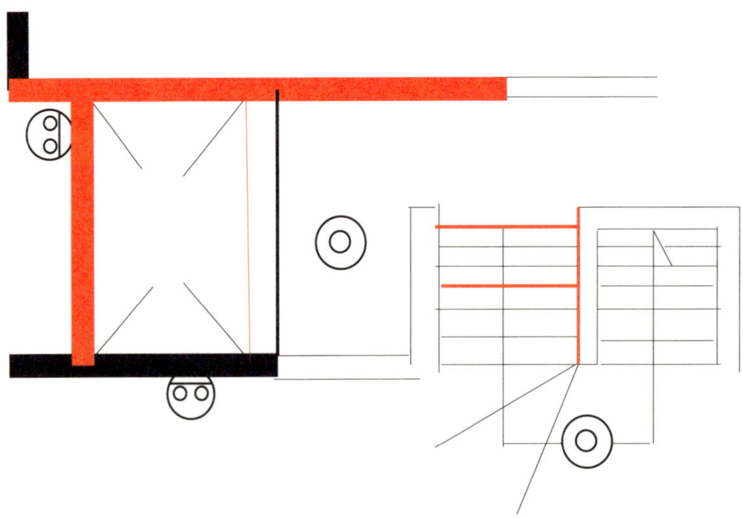

Fig. 11. Example of erroneous figure patterns having similar configuration

In the end, the proposed method shows the obtained results and asks the user to choose correct semantic figure patterns using the GUI shown in Fig. 12. In this step, wrong semantic figure patterns were greatly reduced and the precision rose to 92%. This work is light because the user only selects correct semantic figure patterns. Figura 13 shows one of the resultant floor plans. Table 1 lists the precision and recall at each step.

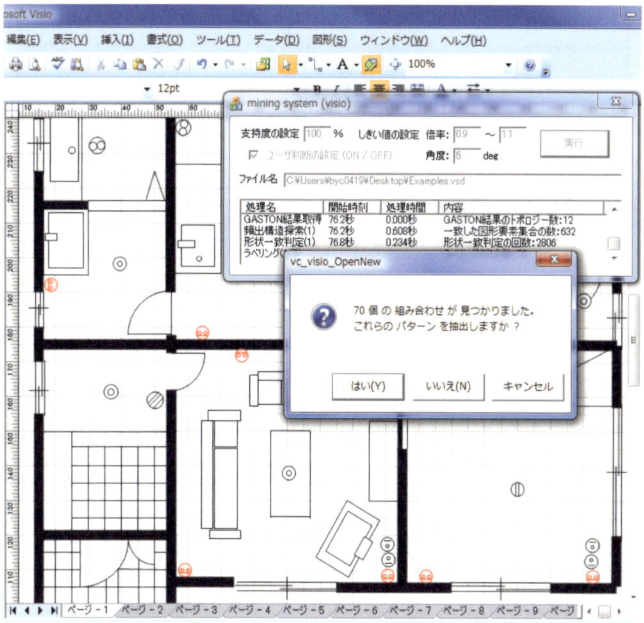

Fig. 12. GUI

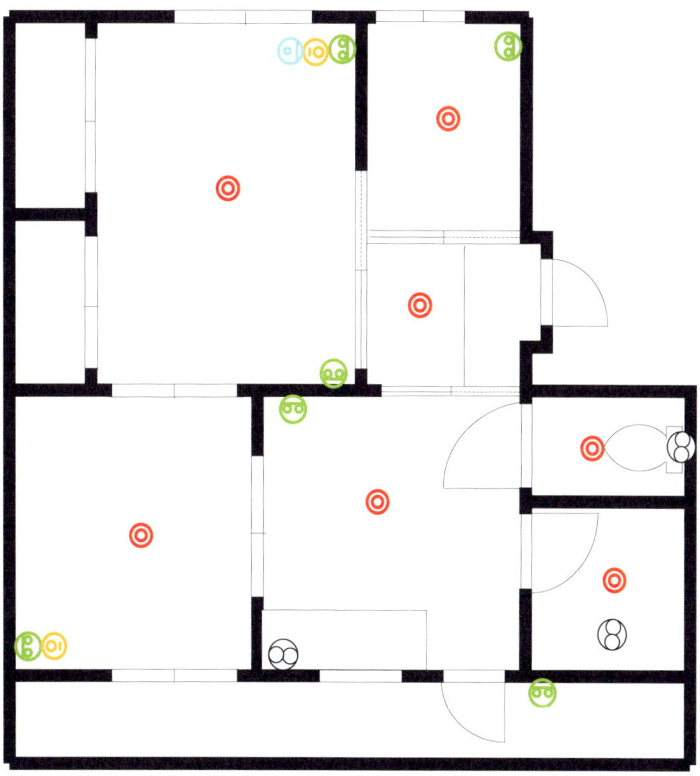

Fig. 13. Example of result

	Precision	Recall
Topology graph mining	66%	82%
Topology graph mining and affine transformation	72%	82%
Topology graph mining and affine transformation and interaction with user	92%	82%

Table 1. Precision and recall at each step

6. Discussion

We now consider the experimental results and future development. One of the serious problems is the explosion of the computation time, especially in the case of dealing with large amounts of the drawing data. In our method, the reduction of the computation time is equivalent to reducing the combinations of geometric primitives and those of control points in the estimation of the affine transformations. This problem is caused by the use of undirected graphs as the topology graphs, which gives rise to the ambiguity of the correspondence between the geometric primitives and that between the control points. This ambiguity increases the combinations of geometric primitives and those of control points. For example, in the case of Fig. 14(a), the proposed method generates the same topology graphs and confuses the correspondence between the geometric primitives and that between the control points. If we can use the directed graphs as the topology graphs, the results obtained in the topology mining step will make the correspondences clear as illustrated in Fig. 14(b). This will lead to a reduction in the number of combinations and the amount of computation time. To actualize this approach, we should develop and use a fast graph mining method for directed graphs.

The failure of the extraction of the desired semantic figure patterns is caused by the change of edge labels that occurs when the corresponding geometric primitives are displaced slightly as illustrated in Fig. 10. Since this failure will lead to poor recall, this is the problem to be solved at present. But this problem is very difficult and leaves room for future studies. The basic approach to this problem is to simplify the description of the edge labels so that their drastic change does not occur in the case of a slight displacement of the geometric primitives. Contrary to this, the precision can be improved using knowledge on the desired object. In the case of dealing with the floor plans, for example, the system can assume that the desired symbols consist of geometric primitives in a large circle. But this will compromise the generality of the proposed method. From this viewpoint, we believe that the objects extracted erroneously should be excluded with the user interaction.

This time we used the drawing data made with Microsoft Office Visio. If the proposed method becomes applicable to the data made with Microsoft Office PowerPoint, the drawing data distributed on the Internet could be sorted and subsequently exploited by many users by incorporating social tagging into the figure pattern mining method (Setz & Snoek, 2009). This is a kind of automatic clipart generation.

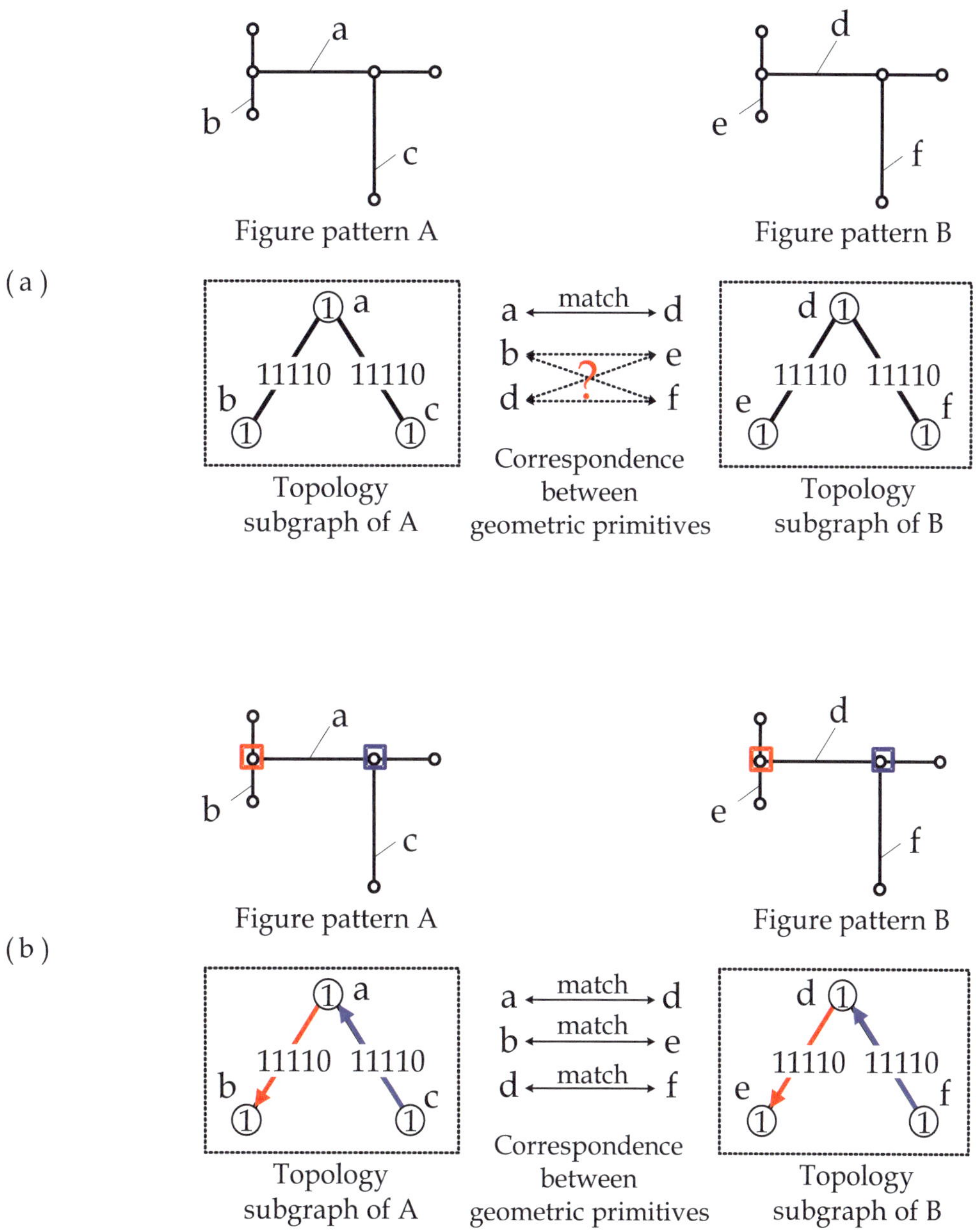

Fig. 14. Undirected and directed topology subgraphs

7. Conclusion

In this chapter, we described a 2D figure pattern mining approach where semantic figure patterns can be obtained from the drawing data without prior knowledge. The proposed method first builds the topology graphs to represent topology of geometric primitives in the drawing data. Then our method extracts frequent topology subgraphs by mining all of the

topology graphs and tries to sort out correct semantic figure patterns from them by inferring affine transformations among the sets of their corresponding geometric primitives.
In the experiment, 82% of electrical symbols placed in floor plans could be extracted through the interaction with the user. However, some electrical symbols were not extracted in the cases where the electrical symbols were placed in few floor plans and where an edge label was changed by the slight error of geometric primitive positions. We hope this kind of study will continue along the lines described in the previous section.

8. References

Aiger, D.; Mitra, N. J. & Cohen-Or, D. (2008). 4-Points Congruent Sets for Robust Pairwise Surface Registration, *ACM Transactions on Graphics*, Vol. 27, No. 3, August 2008, pp. 1-10

Barequet, G. & Sharir, M. (1997). Partial Surface and Volume Matching in Three Dimensions, *IEEE Transactions on Pattern Analysis and Machine Intelligence*, Vol. 19, No. 9, September 1997, pp. 929-948

Brecheisen, S.; Kriegel, H.; Kroger, P. & Pfeifle, M. (2004). Visually Mining Through Cluster Hierarchies, *Proceedings of the 4th SIAM International Conference on Data Mining*, April 2004, pp. 400-412

Brennecke, A. & Isenberg, T. (2004). 3D Shape Matching Using Skeleton Graphs, In: *Simulation and Visualisierung*, pp. 299-310, SCS Europen Publishing House

Bustos, B.; Keim, D.; Saupe, D.; Schreck, T. & Vranic, D. (2004). An Experimental Comparison of Feature-Based 3D Retrieval Methods, *Proceedings of the 2nd International Symposium on 3D Data Processing, Visualization, and Transmission*, September 2004, pp. 215-222

Castellani, U.; Cristani, M.; Fantoni, S. & Murino, V. (2008). Sparse points matching by combining 3D mesh saliency with statistical descriptors, *Computer Graphics Forum* Vol. 27 No. 2, April 2008, pp. 643-652

Funkhouser, T.; Min, P.; Kazhdan, M.; Chen, J.; Halderman, A.; Dobkin, D. & Jacobs, D. (2003). A search engine for 3D models, *ACM Transactions on Graphics*, Vol. 22, No. 1, January 2003, pp. 83-105

Hou, S.; Lou,K. & Raman, K. (2005). SVM-based Semantic Clustering and Retrieval of a 3D Model Database, *Computer-Aided Design & Applications*, Vol. 2, 2005, pp. 155-164

Iyer, N.; Jayanti, S.; Lou, K.; Kalyanaraman, Y. & Ramani, K. (2004). A Multi-Scale Hierarchical 3D Shape Representation for Similar Shape Retrieval, *Proceedings of the International Symposium on Tools and Methods for Competitive Engineering*, April 2004, pp. 1117-1118

Jiang, B. (2004). Spatial Clustering for Mining Knowledge in Support of Generalization Processes in GIS, *ICA Workshop on Generalisation and Multiple representation*, August 2004

Kim, J. & Grauman, K. (2010). Asymmetric Region-to-Image Matching for Comparing Images with Generic Object Categories, *Proceedings of the 23rd IEEE Conference on Computer Vision and Pattern Recognition*, June 2010

Li, X. & Godil, A. (2009). Exploring the Bag-of-Words method for 3D shape retrieval, *Proceedings of the 16th IEEE International Conference on Image Processing*, November 2009, pp.437-440

Liu, Y.; Xu, D.; Wang, J.; Tang, C. K.; Huang, H.; Tong, X. & Guo B. (2009). Sketch and Match: Scene Montage Using a Huge Image Collection, *Tech. Report* MSR-TR-2009-134 Microsoft, September 2009

Lovett, A.; Dehghani, M. & Forbus, K. (2007). Incremental Learning of Perceptual Categories for Open-Domain Sketch Recognition, *Proceedings of the 20th International Joint Conference on Artificial Intelligence*, January 2007, pp. 447-452

Mademlis, A.; Axenopoulos, A.; Daras, P. Tzovaras, D. & Strintzis, M. G. (2006). 3D Content-Based Search Based on 3D Krawtchouk Moments, *Proceedings of the Third International Symposium on 3D Data Processing*, Visualization, and Transmission, June 2006, pp.743-749

Ng, R. T. & Han, J. (1994). Efficient and Effective Clustering Methods for Spatial Data Mining, *Proceedings of the 20th International Conference on Very Large Data Bases*, September 1994, pp. 144-155

Nijssen, S. & Kok, J. (2004). A Quickstart in Frequent Structure Mining Can Make A Difference, *Proceeding of the 2004 ACM SIGKDD International Conference on Knowledge Discovery in Databases*, August 2004, pp. 647-652

Novotni, M.; Degener, P. & Klein, R. (2005). Correspondence Generation and Matching of 3D Shape Subparts, *Technical Reports* CG-2005-2 Universitat Bonn, ISSN 1610-8892

Ohbuchi, R.; Osada, K.; Furuya, T. & Banno, T. (2008). Salient Local Visual Features for Shape-Based 3D Model Retrieval, *Proceedings of IEEE International Conference on Shape Modeling and Applications*, June 2008

Ovsjanikov, M., Sun, J. & Guibas, L. (2008). Global Intrinsic Symmetries of Shapes, *Computer Graphics Forum* (Eurographics Symposium on Geometry Processing), Vol.27, No.5 July 2008, pp. 1341-1348

Pauly, M.; Mitra, N. J.; Wallner, J.; Pottmann, H. & Guibas,L. (2008). Discovering Structural Regularity in 3D Geometry, *ACM Transactions on Graphics*, Vol. 27, No. 3, August 2008, pp.1-11

Pu, J.; Lou, K. & Ramani, K. (2005). A 2D Sketch-Based User Interface for 3D CAD Model Retrieval, *Computer-Aided Design & Applications,* Vol. 2, No. 6, 2005, pp. 717-725

Schnabel, R.; Wahl, R.; Wessel, R. & Klein, R. (2007). Shape Recognition in 3D Point Clouds, *Technical Reports* CG-2007-1 Universitat Bonn, ISSN 1610-8892

Setz, A.T. & Snoek, C.G.M. (2009). Can Social Tagged Images Aid Concept-Based Video Search? *Proceedings of IEEE International Conference on Multimedia and Expo*, June 2009, pp. 1460-1463

Sheikholeslami, G.; Chatterjee, S. & Zhang, A. (1998). WaveCluster: A Multi-Resolution Clustering Approach for Very Large Spatial Databases, *Proceedings of the 24rd International Conference on Very Large Data Bases,* August 1998, pp. 428-439

Sundar, H.; Silver, D.; Gagvani, N. & Dickinson, S. (2003). Skeleton Based Shape Matching and Retrieval, *Proceedings of Shape Modeling International,* May 2003, pp.130-139

Tung, T. & Schmitt, F. (2005). The augmented multiresolution Reeb graph approach for content-based retrieval of 3D shapes, *International Journal of Shape Modeling*, Vol. 11, No. 1, June 2005, pp. 91-120

21

Quality Model based on Object-oriented Metrics and Naive Bayes

Sai Peck Lee and Chuan Ho Loh
University of Malaya
Malaysia

1. Introduction

Software quality engineering is a field in software engineering specializing on improving the approach to software quality on different software artifacts such as object-oriented analysis models, object-oriented design models, and object-oriented implementation models. Software quality is the degree to which a software artifact exhibits a desired combination of quality-carrying attributes (e.g. testability, reliability, reusability, interoperability, and other quality-carrying attributes). This research specializes on improving the code quality of object-oriented systems through a quality model that utilizes a suite of object-oriented metrics and a machine learning technique, namely Naive Bayes. Most of the existing object-oriented metrics and machine learning techniques capture similar dimensions in the data sets, thus reflecting the fact that many of the object-oriented metrics and machine learning techniques are based on similar hypotheses, properties, and principles. Accurate quality models can be built to predict the quality of object-oriented systems by using a subset of the existing object-oriented design metrics and machine learning techniques. This research proposes a software quality model, namely QUAMO to assess the quality of object-oriented code on-the-fly. The primary objective of the model is to make similar studies on software quality more comparable and repeatable. The model is augmented from five quality models, namely Boehm Model, McCall Model, FURPS, ISO 9126, and Dromey Model. The quality model specializes on Bayesian network classifier, Naive Bayes. The Naive Bayes classifier, a simple classifier based Bayes' law with strong independence assumptions among features is comparable to other state-of-the-art classifiers, namely ID3 Decision Tree, J48 Decision Tree, and C4.5 Decision Tree. Naive Bayes is very effective in solving the classification problems addressed in this research, namely the conditional maximum likelihood prediction of faults in object-oriented systems. Most of the metrics proposed by other researchers mainly specialized at the class level such as CK Metrics Suite and MOOD Metrics Suite (Chidamber & Kemerer, 1994). Fewer component level metrics have been proposed such as Rate of Component Observability, Rate of Component Customizability, and Self-Completeness of Component's Return Value. As such, this research also proposes a suite of specialized object-oriented metrics that can be applied at the class and component levels as some insights can be gained by examining the average characteristics of both a class and a component. Each metric quantifies a particular feature of an object-oriented system. In other words, each refers to a structural mechanism of the object-oriented paradigm such as inheritance is expressed as quotient. The numerator in the quotient represents the actual use of a mechanism such as inheritance (M_i) on the object-oriented design (OOD). The denominator, which acts as a normalizer, represents the hypothetical maximum use for the mechanism, M_i on an OOD (i.e. it considers the number of classes and their inheritance relations). The metrics are thus expressed as indexes, ranging from 0 (e.g. indicating no use) to 1 (e.g. indicating maximum use).

2. Motivation

A principal objective of software quality engineering is to improve the quality of software artifacts such as object-oriented analysis models, object-oriented design models, and object-oriented implementation models. Quality in software artifacts is a composite of characteristics such as portability, reliability, testability, reusability, and maintainability, which are collectively known as quality-carrying attributes. The factors that affect software quality can be categorized in two distinctive categories, namely factors that can be directly measured (e.g. number of defects) and factors that can be measured only indirectly (e.g. reusability). Generally, the notion of quality is usually captured in the form of a diagram, function or equation, which is collectively known as a model. There are several types of models, namely software process models, software maturity models, and software quality models. Insights to quality can be gained in two ways: by examining quality-carrying attributes through a software quality model, and by examining software artifacts through software metrics (i.e. formulate a set of meaningful software metrics based on these attributes, and to use the metrics as indicators that will lead to a strategy for software quality improvement) and machine learning techniques (i.e. formulate a set of meaningful machine learning techniques based on these attributes, and to use the machine learning techniques as predictors that will lead to a strategy for software quality improvement). In this research, quality is measured in terms of adherence of a set of metrics to a set of attributes used to distinctively evaluate the quality of object-oriented systems by making quality a quantifiable concept via a software quality model.

3. Related work

A number of software quality models have been proposed to evaluate the quality of a software system. The best known software quality models in chronological order are Boehm Model, McCall Model, FURPS, ISO 9126, and Dromey Model (Boehm et al., 1976; McCall et al., 1977; Dromey, 1995, 1996; Ortega et al., 2003). Existing software quality models can be distinguished based on number of layers (e.g. 2 layers as in Dromey model and 3 layers as in Boehm and McCall models), number of relationships (e.g. 1:n relationship as in ISO 9126 model - every characteristic has its own set of subcharacteristics, and n:m relationship as in Factor-Criteria-Model - every subcharacteristic is linked to one or more characteristics), support for metrics (e.g. no support for metrics as in Dromey model and support for metrics as in McCall model), and approach to software quality measurement (e.g. fixed quality model approach as in Boehm, McCall, and ISO 9126 models, and "define your own quality model" approach as in COQUAMO model) (Ortega et al., 2000, 2002, 2003; Callaos & Callaos, 1996; Bansiya & Davis, 2002; Georgiadou, 2003; Khaddaj & Horgan , 2005; Côté et al., 2007). Supervised learning can be formulated using either a discriminative approach (e.g. Logistic Regression) or a generative approach (e.g. Naive Bayes). A number of supervised learning techniques have been introduced such as Neural Nets, Logistic Regression, Naive Bayes, Decision Tree, and Support Vector Machine. There are three methods to establish a classifier: model a classification rule directly (e.g. Decision Tree), model the probability of class memberships given input data (e.g. Multilayer Perceptron), make a probabilistic model of data within each class (e.g. Naive Bayes). The first and the second methods are examples of discriminative classification. The second and the third methods are both examples of probabilistic classification. The third method is an example of generative classification.

4. Software quality model

4.1 Formulate the software quality model

In the absence of an agreed measure of software quality the number of software defects (e.g. number of software faults and number of software violations) has been a very commonly used surrogate measure. As a result, there have been numerous attempts to build models for predicting the number of software defects. Quality in a typical software artifact is a composite of quality-carrying attributes such as usability, portability, reliability, testability, reusability, and maintainability. As a result, we do not adopt a given model's characterization of quality in QUAMO. We propose a "define your own quality model" approach in QUAMO. In QUAMO, we need to formulate a composition in which we agree specific measures for the lowest-level attributes and specific relationships between the attributes apart from the Key Quality-carrying Attributes (KQA) described in Section 4.2 and Key Quality Metrics (KQM) described in Section 4.3. QUAMO is augmented from five software quality models: Boehm Model, McCall Model, FURPS, ISO 9126, and Dromey Model. In QUAMO, we measure the quality-carrying attributes objectively to investigate if the quality-carrying attributes meet the specified, quantified targets via different object-oriented metrics and Naive Bayes. QUAMO consists of 2 layers: the quality-carrying attribute layer and the object-oriented metrics layer. The upper branches hold important high-level quality-carrying attributes of object-oriented systems. Examples of such quality-carrying attributes are flexibility (i.e. to evaluate the effort required in modifying an operational class or component in an object-oriented system), maintainability (i.e. to evaluate the effort required in maintaining an operational class or component in an object-oriented system), reliability (i.e. to evaluate the extent to which an operational class or component performs its intended functional requirements in an object-oriented system), reusability (i.e. to evaluate the effort required in reusing an operational class or component in an object-oriented system), testability (i.e. to evaluate the effort required in testing an operational class or component in an object-oriented system), usability (i.e. to evaluate the effort required in learning and operating an operational class or component in an object-oriented system), and traceability (i.e. to evaluate the effort required in tracing an operational class or component in an object-oriented system). Each quality attribute is composed of lower-level criteria, namely object-oriented metrics (e.g. depth of inheritance tree, class size, and number of children). QUAMO generally resembles a tree that illustrates the important relationships between quality and its dependent criteria (i.e. quality-carrying attributes) so that quality in terms of the dependent criteria can be measured. Table 1 depicts a typical organization of input attributes, output attributes, and quality-carrying attributes in QUAMO. IA, IAV, OA, IAOAV, QCA, and IAQCAV collectively denotes input attribute, input attribute value (discrete value), output attribute, input attribute/output attribute value (discrete value), quality-carrying attribute, input attribute/quality-carrying attribute value (discrete value). Examples of input attributes (i.e. effect/evidence) include KQM such as class inherited index and lack of class inherited index, and other object-oriented metrics. Examples of output attribute (i.e. cause) are number of software violations (i.e. compile-time defects) and number of software faults (i.e. run-time defects). Examples of quality-carrying attributes include KQA such as efficiency and reliability, and other quality-carrying attributes.

		OA_1	OA_2	...	OA_n	QCA_1	QCA_2	...	QCA_n
IA_1	IAV_1	IA_1OAV_1	IA_1OAV_2	...	IA_1OAV_n	IA_1QCAV_1	IA_1QCAV_2	...	IA_1QCAV_n
IA_2	IAV_2	IA_2OAV_2	IA_2OAV_2	...	IA_2OAV_n	IA_2QCAV_1	IA_2QCAV_2	...	IA_2QCAV_n
IA_3	IAV_3	IA_3OAV_3	IA_3OAV_2	...	IA_3OAV_n	IA_3QCAV_1	IA_3QCAV_2	...	IA_3QCAV_n
IA_4	IAV_4	IA_4OAV_4	IA_4OAV_2	...	IA_4OAV_n	IA_4QCAV_1	IA_4QCAV_2	...	IA_4QCAV_n
....	...	...	...	...	...	...	...	...	...
IA_n	IAV_n	IA_nOAV_n	IA_nOAV_2	...	IA_nOAV_n	IA_nQCAV_1	IA_nQCAV_2	...	IA_nQCAV_n

Table 1. Input attributes, output atributes, and quality-carrying attributes in QUAMO

4.2 Formulate the key quality-carrying attributes

KQA are quality-carrying attributes that present in all the five models studied in this research: Boehm Model, McCall Model, FURPS, ISO 9126, and Dromey Model. Table 2 depicts a comparison of the quality-carrying attributes in Boehm, McCall, FURPS, ISO 9126, and Dromey models. Since efficiency, reliability, and maintainability quality-carrying attributes present in all the models, they are considered essential in QUAMO. They are collectively referred to as KQA in QUAMO, which are mandatory attributes in QUAMO.

4.3 Formulate the key quality metrics

We propose eight KQM to measure the quality of object-oriented systems through QUAMO, namely Class Cohesion Index (CsCohI), Lack of Class Cohesion Index (LCsCohI), Component Cohesion Average (CoCohA), Lack of Component Cohesion Average (LCoCohA), Class Inherited Index (CsII), Lack of Class Inherited Index (LCsII), Component Inherited Average (CoIA), and Lack of Component Inherited Average (LCoIA). Table 3 and Table 4 depict the notations of CsCohI, CoCohA, LCsCohI, and LCoCohA, and the properties of CsCohI, CoCohA, LCsCohI, and LCoCohA, respectively. Similarly, Table 5 and Table 6 depict the notations of CsII, CoIA, LCsII, and LCoIA, and the properties of of CsII, CoIA, LCsII, and LCoIA, respectively.

4.3.1 Class-based cohesion metrics

We propose two class-based cohesion metrics, namely Class Cohesion Index (CsCohI) and Lack of Class Cohesion Index (LCsCohI) to measure the overall density of similarity and dissimilarity of methods in a class. CsCohI measures the degree of similarity of methods in a class. The CsCohI within a class Cs is expressed as:

$$\text{CsCohI(Cs)}=\begin{cases}\dfrac{\text{TCohM}}{\text{TM}}, \text{TCohM>0 and TM} > 0\\ 0, \text{otherwise}\end{cases}$$

Each method within a class accesses one or more attributes (i.e. instance variables). CsCohI is the number of methods that access one or more of the same attributes. If no methods access at least one attribute, then CsCohI = 0. In general, low values for CsCohI imply that the class might be better designed by breaking it into two or more separate classes. Although there are cases in which a low value for CsCohI is justifiable, it is desirable to keep CsCohI high (i.e. keep cohesion high). CsCohI < 1 indicates that the class is not quite cohesive and may need to be refactored into two or more classes. Classes with a low CsCohI can be fault-prone. A low CsCohI value indicates scatter in the functionality provided by the class. CsCohI is expressed as a nondimensional value in the range of 0 ≤ CsCohI ≤ 1. Similarly, the overall degree of dissimilarity of methods within a class Cs, LCsCohI(Cs), is expressed as:

$$\text{LCsCohI(Cs)}=\begin{cases}1-\dfrac{\text{TCohM}}{\text{TM}}, \text{TCohM>0 and TM} > 0\\ 0, \text{otherwise}\end{cases}$$

4.3.2 Component-based cohesion metrics

We propose two component-based cohesion metrics, namely Component Cohesion Average (CoCohA) and Lack of Component Cohesion Average (LCoCohA) to measure the overall density of similarity and dissimilarity of methods in the classes within a component. CoCohA measures the degree of class cohesion indexes in a component. The CoCohA within a component Co is expressed as:

$$\text{CoCohA(Co)}=\begin{cases}\dfrac{\text{TCsCohI}}{\text{TC}}, \text{TCsCohI>0 and TC} > 0\\ 0, \text{otherwise}\end{cases}$$

CoCohA is defined in an analogous manner and provides an indication of the overall degree of similarity of methods in the classes within a component. CoCohA is based on the notation that methods in the classes are similar if they share common instance variables. The larger the number of similar methods in the classes within a component, the more cohesive the component. Hence, CoCohA is a measure of the relatively disparate nature of the methods in the classes within a component. The CoCohA numerator is the sum of class cohesion indexes in a component, TCsCohI. The CoCohA denominator is the total classes in a component. The CoCohA numerator represents the maximum number of similarity of method situations in the classes for a component. CoCohA is expressed as a nondimensional value in the range of 0 ≤ CoCohA ≤ 1. In general, a low value for CoCohA indicates a low proportion of class cohesion indexes in a component, and a high value for CoIA indicates a high proportion of class cohesion indexes in a component. A low value for CoCohA is undesirable. Similarly, the overall degree of dissimilarity of methods in the classes within a component Co, LCoCohA(Co), is expressed as:

$$\text{LCoCohA(Co)}=\begin{cases}1-\dfrac{\text{TCsCohI}}{\text{TC}}, \text{TCsCohI} > 0 \text{ and TC} > 0\\ 0, \text{otherwise}\end{cases}$$

Quality-carrying Attributes	Software Quality Models				
	Boehm Model (1978)	McCall Model (1977)	FURPS (1987)	ISO 9126 (1991)	Dromey Model (1995)
Testability	x	x		x	
Correctness		x			
Efficiency	x	x	x	x	x
Understandability	x			x	
Reliability	x	x	x	x	x
Flexibility		x	x		
Functionality			x	x	x
Human Engineering	x				
Integrity		x		x	
Interoperability		x		x	
Process Maturity					x
Maintainability	x	x	x	x	x
Changeability	x				
Portability	x	x		x	x
Reusability		x			x

Table 2. Quality-carrying attributes in Boehm model, McCall model, FURPS, ISO 9126, and Dromey model

4.3.3 Discussions

LCsCohI and LCoCohA are inverse metrics of CsCohI and CoCohA respectively. A high value of CsCohI, and CoCohA, and a low value of LCsCohI and LCoCohA indicate high cohesion and well-designed class and component. Similarly, a low value of CsCohI, and CoCohA, and a high value of LCsCohI and LCoCohA indicate low cohesion and poorly designed class and component. It is likely that the class and component have good subdivision. A cohesive class tends to provide a high degree of encapsulation. A lower value of CsCohI and CoCohA indicate decreased encapsulation, thereby increasing the likelihood of errors. Similarly, a lower value of LCsCohI and LCoCohA indicate increased encapsulation, thereby decreasing the likelihood of errors.

4.3.4 Class-based inheritance metrics

We propose two class-based inheritance metrics, namely Class Inherited Index (CsII) and Lack of Class Inherited Index (LCsII) to measure the overall inheritance density in a class.

CsII measures the degree of inherited attributes and methods in a class. The CsII within a class Cs is expressed as:

$$\mathrm{CsII(Cs)}=\begin{cases}\dfrac{\mathrm{TIA+TIM}}{\mathrm{TM+TA}}, & \mathrm{TIA+TIM}>0 \text{ and } \mathrm{TM}+\mathrm{TA}>0\\ 0, & \text{otherwise}\end{cases}$$

CsII is defined in an analogous manner and provides an indication of the impact of inheritance at the class level. The CsII numerator is the sum of inherited attributes and methods in a class. The CsII demoninator is the total number of attributes and methods in a class. The CsII numerator represents the maximum number of possible distinct inheritance situations for a class. CsII is expressed as a nondimensional value in the range of $0 \le \mathrm{CsII} \le 1$. In general, a low value for CsII indicates a low proportion of inherited attributes and methods in a class, and a high value for CsII indicates a high proportion of inherited attributes and methods in a class. A high value of CsII is undesirable. As the number of inherited attributes and methods increases, the value of CsII also increases. Similarly, the overall degree of non-inherited attributes and non-inherited methods within a class Cs, LCsII(Cs), is expressed as:

$$\mathrm{LCsII(Cs)}=\begin{cases}1-\dfrac{\mathrm{TIA+TIM}}{\mathrm{TM+TA}}, & \mathrm{TIA+TIM}>0 \text{ and } \mathrm{TM+TA}>0\\ 0, & \text{otherwise}\end{cases}$$

4.3.5 Component-based inheritance metrics

We propose two component-based inheritance metrics, namely Component Inherited Average (CoIA) and Lack of Component Inherited Average (LCoIA) to measure the overall inheritance density in the classes of within a component. CoIA measures the degree of class inherited indexes in a component. The CoIA within a component Co is expressed as:

$$\mathrm{CoIA(Co)}=\begin{cases}\dfrac{\mathrm{TCsII}}{\mathrm{TC}}, & \mathrm{TCsCII}>0 \text{ and } \mathrm{TC}>0\\ 0, & \text{otherwise}\end{cases}$$

CoIA is defined in an analogous manner and provides an indication of the impact of inheritance at the component level. The CoIA numerator is the sum of class inherited indexes in a component. The CoIA denominator is the total classes in a component. The CoIA numerator represents the maximum number of possible distinct inheritance situations for a component. CoIA is expressed as a nondimensional value in the range of $0 \le \mathrm{CoIA} \le 1$. In general, a low value for CoIA indicates a low proportion of class inherited indexes in a component, and a high value for CoIA indicates a high proportion of class inherited indexes in a component. A high value for CoIA is undesirable. As the class inherited indexes increases, the value of CoIA also increases. Similarly, the overall degree of non-inherited attributes and non-inherited methods in the classes within a component Co, LCoIA(Co), is expressed as:

$$\mathrm{LCoIA(Co)}=\begin{cases}1-\dfrac{\mathrm{TCsII}}{\mathrm{TC}}, & \mathrm{TCsCII}>0 \text{ and } \mathrm{TC}>0\\ 0, & \text{otherwise}\end{cases}$$

Notation	Description	C++	Java
CsCohI	class cohesion index within a class	-	-
CoCohA	component cohesion average within a component	-	-
LCsCohI	lack of class cohesion index within a class	-	-
LCoCohA	lack of component cohesion average within a component	-	-
TC	total number of classes in a component	total number of classes in a directive	total number of classes in a package
TCsCohI	total of class cohesion indexes in a component	-	-
TCohM	methods declared and inherited in a class assessing at least one instance variable	all function members declared and inherited in a class excluding virtual (deferred) ones assessing at least one instance variable	all methods declared and inherited in a class excluding abstract (deferred) ones assessing at least one instance variable
TM	methods declared and inherited in a class	all function members declared and inherited in a class excluding virtual (deferred) ones	all methods declared and inherited in a class excluding abstract (deferred) ones

Table 3. Notations of CsCohI, CoCohA, LCsCohI, and LCoCohA

4.3.6 Discussions

LCsII and LCoIA are inverse metrics of CsII and CoIA respectively. A high value of CsII, and CoIA, and a low value of LCsII and LCoIA indicate high inheritance. Similarly, a low value of CsII, and CoIA, and a high value of LCsII and LCoIA indicate low inheritance. A lower value of CsII and CoIA indicate decreased inheritance and complexity, thereby decreasing the likelihood of errors. Similarly, a higher value of LCsII and LCoIA indicate increased inheritance and complexity, thereby increasing the likelihood of errors.

4.4 Formulate the software quality prediction model

This research adopts supervised learning through Naive Bayes to formulate the software quality prediction model. The primary objective of adopting supervised learning in QUAMO is to infer a functional mapping based on a set of training examples to assess the quality of object-oriented code. More specifically, the supervised learning in QUAMO can be formulated as the problem of inferring a function $y = f(x)$ based on a training set $D = \{(x_1,$

y_1), {(x_2, y_2), {(x_3, y_3), {(x_4, y_4),…, (x_n, y_n)}. The obtained function is evaluated by how well it generalizes. This research uses Naive Bayes as the primary method to predict software quality. Naive Bayes classifiers can be trained very efficiently in a supervised learning.

Properties for CsCohI and LCsCohI	
Property 1	If n is a non-negative number, then there is only a finite number of cohesive methods (i.e. number of methods assessing at least one instance variable) TCohM for which TCohM = n.
Property 2	If n is a non-negative number, then there is only a finite number of attributes declared and inherited in a class TCsA for which TCsA = n.
Property 3	If n is a non-negative number, then there is only a finite number of methods declared and inherited in a class TCsM for which TCsM = n.
Property 4	There are distinct classes Cs1 and Cs2 for which Cs1 is the superclass of Cs2.
Property 5	There are inherited attributes, IA1, IA2, IA3,…, IAn, for which IA1 ≠ IA2 ≠ IA3 … ≠ IAn
Property 6	There are inherited methods, IM1, IM2, IM3,…, IMn, for which IM1 ≠ IM2 ≠ IM3 … ≠ IMn
Properties for CoCohA and LCoCohA	
Property 1	If n is a non-negative number, then there is only a finite number of classes TCs for which TCs = n.
Property 2	If n is a decimal number, then there are total class inherited indexes TCsCohI for which TCsCohI = n.

Table 4. Properties of CsCohI, CoCohA, LCsCohI, and LCoCohA

Naive Bayes also generally gives better test accuracy than any other know machine learning techniques such as ID3 Decision Tree, C4.5 Decision Tree, and J48 Decision Tree. We can greatly simplify learning in software quality prediction by assuming that quality-carrying features are independent of each other through Naive Bayes. Naive Bayes assumes that the presence or absence of a particular feature of a class is unrelated to the presence or absence of any other feature. Naive Bayes learning gives better test set accuracy than any other known method, including Backpropagation and Decision Trees. Naive Bayes classifier can also be learned very efficiently. We have selected Naive Bayes as the primary technique to assess software quality in object-oriented code through a 2-layer "define your own quality model" based on a suite of object-oriented metrics.

The Naive Bayes classifier in QUAMO learns the conditional probability of each quality-carrying attribute QA_i given the class label C (i.e. a discretized value of an object-oriented metric). Classification is performed by applying Bayes rule to compute the probability of C given the particular instance of QA_1, QA_2, QA_3, QA_4, QA_5, …, QA_n, and then predicting the class with the highest posterior probability. This computation is possible by making a strong independence assumption that all the quality attributes QA_i are conditionally independent given the value of the class C. We refer independence as probabilistic independence (i.e. X is independent of Y given Z when P(X | Y, Z) = P(X | Z) for all possible values of X, Y, and Z when P(Z) > 0. When X is a vector of discrete-valued object-oriented metrics (e.g. binary, X ∈ {low, high}), we adopt a 2-step approach: learn

Notation	Description	C++	Java
CsII	class inherited index	-	-
LCsII	lack of class inherited index	-	-
CoIA	component inherited average	-	-
LCoIA	lack of component inherited average	-	-
TC	total classes	total number of classes in a directive	total number of classes in a package
TCsII	total class inherited indexes	-	-
TM	Methods declared and inherited	all function members declared and inherited in a class including virtual (deferred) ones	all methods declared and inherited in a class including abstract (deferred) ones
TA	attributes declared and inherited	all data members declared and inherited in a class	all attributes declared and inherited in a class
TIM	methods inherited	all function members inherited and not overridden	all methods inherited in a class and not overridden
TIA	attributes inherited	all data members inherited in the class	all attributes inherited in a class

Table 5. Notations of CsII, CoIA, LCsII, and LcoIA

and test. When X is a vector of continuous-valued object-oriented metrics, we adopt a 3-step approach: discretize, learn, and test. Figure 1 depicts a typical Naive Bayes classifier in QUAMO. We can view the function approximation learning algorithm adopted in QUAMO as statistical estimators of conditional distributions P(Y | X) or of functions that estimate P(Y

| X) from a sample of training data in QUAMO. Naive Bayes uses Bayes' Theorem to predict the value of a target (i.e. output in QUAMO), from evidence given by one or more predictor (i.e. input in QUAMO) fields. Table 7, Table 8, and Table 9 depict the discretize, learn, and test algorithms.

Properties for CsII and LcsII	
Property 1	If n is a non-negative number, then there is only a finite number of inherited attributes TCsIA for which TCsIA = n.
Property 2	If n is a non-negative number, then there is only a finite number of inherited methods TCsIM for which TCsIM = n.
Property 3	If n is a non-negative number, then there is only a finite number of attributes TCsA for which TCsA = n.
Property 4	If n is a non-negative number, then there is only a finite number of methods TCsM for which TCsM = n.
Property 5	There are distinct classes Cs1 and Cs2 for which Cs1 is the superclass of Cs2.
Property 6	There are inherited attributes, IA1, IA2, IA3,…, IAn, for which IA1 $\neq$ IA2 $\neq$ IA3 … $\neq$ IAn
Property 7	There are inherited methods, IM1, IM2, IM3,…, IMn, for which IM1 $\neq$ IM2 $\neq$ IM3 … $\neq$ IMn
Properties for CoIA and LCoIA	
Property 1	If n is a non-negative number, then there is only a finite number of classes TCs for which TCs = n.
Property 2	If n is a decimal number, then there are total class inherited indexes TCsII for which TCsII = n.

Table 6. Properties of CsII, CoIA, LCsII, and LcoIA

5. Conclusion

The primary objective of this research is to propose the characteristics of a quality model through a comparative evaluation of existing software quality models. Based on the comparative evaluation, an improved hierarchical model, QUAMO for the assessment of high-level quality attributes in object-oriented systems specializing on object-oriented code based on object-oriented metrics and Naive Bayes is proposed. In this model, the structural properties of classes and their relationships are evaluated using Naive Bayes and a suite of object-oriented metrics. A key attribute of QUAMO is that the model can be augmented to include different object-oriented metrics and quality-carrying attributes, thus providing a practical quality assessment instrument adaptable to a variety of object-oriented systems. QUAMO relates code properties (also referred to as object-oriented constructs) such as encapsulation, information hiding, and inheritance to high-level quality carrying attributes such as reusability, flexibility, maintainability, and complexity via Naive Bayes and a suite of object-oriented metrics.

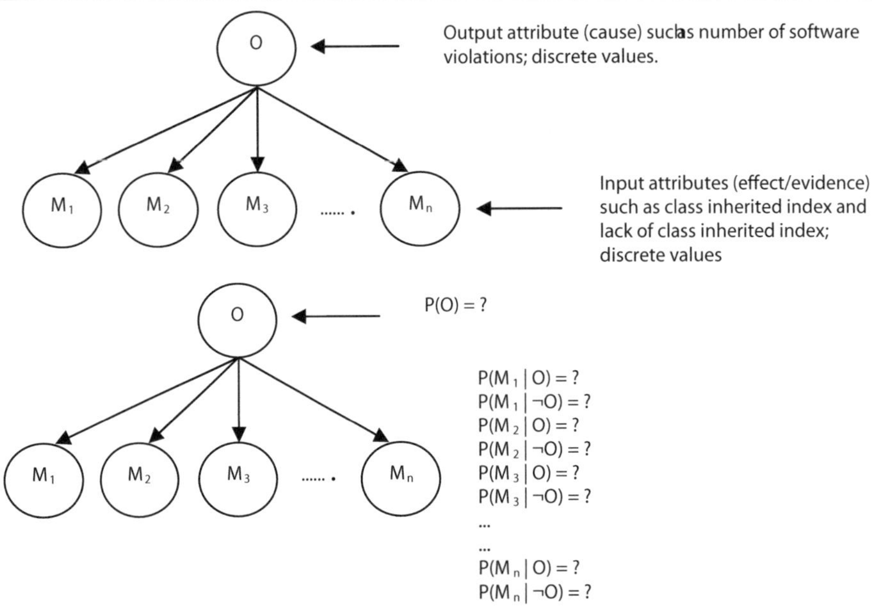

Fig. 1. QUAMO Naive Bayes Classifier

Precondition: There are n training instances for which the value of a numeric attribute (e.g. KQM and other object-oriented metrics, and outputs such as number of software violations and number of software bugs) x_i is known. The minimum and maximum values are v_{min} and v_{max} respectively.
Postcondition: There are k intervals for which the width $w = (v_{max} - v_{min} / k)$.
Rule: The values of the metrics are continuous values.

Algorithm:
Given a numeric attribute x_i
Sort the values of v_i ($v_i = v_1, ..., v_n$) in ascending order
Divide the sorted values of v_i between v_{min} and v_{max} into intervals of equal width

Table 7. Discretize Algorithm

Postcondition: Conditional probability tables for x_j, N_j x L elements.
Rule: The values of the attrtibutes values are discrete values and the values of target values are continuous values.

Algorithm:
Given a training set S
For each target value of c_i ($c_i = c_1, \ldots, c_L$)
$P'(C = c_i) \leftarrow$ estimate $P(C = c_i)$
For every attribute value a_{jk} of each attribute x_j ($j = 1, \ldots, n$; $k = 1, \ldots, N_j$)
$P'(X_j = a_{jk} \mid C = c_i) \leftarrow$ estimate $P(X_j = a_{jk} \mid C = c_i)$

Table 8. Learn Algorithm

Precondition: Conditional probability tables for for x_j, N_j x L elements.
Postcondition: c or c^* is labelled to X'.
Rule: None.

Algorithm:
Given an unknown instance $X' = (a'_1, \ldots, a'_n)$
Look up conditional probability tables to assign the label c^* to X'
Compute $[P'(a'_1 \mid c^*) \ldots P'(a'_n \mid c^*)]P'(c^*)$
Compute $[P'(a'_1 \mid c^*) \ldots P'(a'_n \mid c^*)]P'(c)$
If $[P'(a'_1 \mid c^*) \ldots P'(a'_n \mid c^*)]P'(c^*) > [P'(a'_1 \mid c^*) \ldots P'(a'_n \mid c^*)]P'(c)$,
$c \neq c^*$, $c = c_1, \ldots, c_L$ then
Label X' to be c^*
Else
Label X' to be c

Table 9. Test Algorithm

6. References

Bansiya, J. & Davis, C.G. (2002). A hierarchical model for object-oriented design quality assessment. *IEEE Transactions on Software Engineering*, Vol.28, No.1, pp. 4-17.

Boehm, B. W.; Brownm, J. R. & Lipow M. (1976). Quantitative evaluation of software quality, *Proceedings of the 2nd International Conference on Software engineering*, pp. 592-605, San Francisco, California, United States.

Callaos, N. & Callaos, B. (1996) . Designing with a systemic total quality, *Proceedings of the International Conference on Information Systems Analysis and Synthesis*, pp. 15-23, Orlando, Florida, United States.

Chidamber S.R. & Kemerer C.F. (1994). A metrcs suite for object-oriented design. *IEEE Transactions on Software Engineering*, Vol.20, No.6, pp. 476-493.Côté, M.A.; Suryn, W. & Georgiadou, E. (2007). In search for a widely applicable and accepted software quality model for software quality engineering. *Software Quality Journal*, Vol.15, No.4, pp. 401-416.

Dromey, R.G. (1995). A model for software product quality. *IEEE Transactions on Software Engineering*, Vol.21, No.1, pp. 146-162.

Dromey, R.G. (1996). Concerning the Chimera [software quality]. *IEEE Transactions on Software Engineering*, Vol.13, No.1, pp. 33-43.

Georgiadou, E. (2003). GEQUAMO - A generic, multilayered, customizable, software quality model. *Software Quality Control*, Vol.11, No.4, pp. 313-323.

Khaddaj, S. & Horgan, G. (2005). A proposed adaptable quality model for software quality assurance, *Journal of Computer Science*, Vol.1, No.4, pp. 482-487.

McCall, J.A., Richards, P.K. & Walters, G.F. (1977). Factors in software quality. *National Technical Information Service*, Vol.1-3.

Ortega, M.; Pérez, M. & Rojas, T. (2000). A model for software quality with a systemic focus, *Proceedings of the 4th World Multiconference on Systemics, Cybernetics and Informatics*, pp. 464-469, Orlando, Florida, United States.

Ortega, M.; Pérez, M. & Rojas, T. (2002). A systemic quality model for evaluating software products, *Proceedings of the 6th World Multiconference on Systemics, Cybernetics and Informatics*, pp. 371-376, Orlando, Florida, United States.

Ortega, M.; Pérez, M. & Rojas, T. (2003). Construction of a systemic quality model for evaluating a software product. *Software Quality Journal*, Vol.11, No.3, pp. 219-242.

22

Extraction of Embedded Image Segment Data Using Data Mining with Reduced Neurofuzzy Systems

Deok Hee Nam
Engineering and Computing Science
Wilberforce University
1055 N. Bickett Road, OH 45384
USA

1. Introduction

To realize or implement the large dimensional image data, it may be taking a longer search time to detect the desired target. Recently, for the large amount of data and information in engineering or biomedical applications, various techniques including soft-computing techniques such as neural networks, fuzzy logic, or genetic algorithms, and multivariate analysis techniques like factor analysis, principal component analysis, or clustering analysis, are developed to extract the reduced meaningful information or knowledge from the original raw data.

In this paper, for mining or diminishing the large dimension of the given raw image data, factor analysis, principal component analysis, and clustering analysis are used to make a model using fuzzy logic or neurofuzzy systems, which are applied to predict the characteristics of the images with reduced dimensions. Generally the procedure can produce more precise and reasonable results with reduced dimensions in order to predict the desired images. In addition, all those techniques are useful for searching and saving time for the desired images. Thus, the proposed techniques intend to propose hybrid systems with integrating various multivariate analysis techniques together to establish neurofuzzy or fuzzy logic systems to construct a reasoning system with more accurate and efficient.

2. Literature review

2.1 Multivariate analysis

There are a lot of different kinds of data mining techniques to reduce the large and imprecise raw data into the reduced and precise raw data. Most frequently used techniques are multivariate analyses like factor analysis, principal component analysis, and various

[1] This paper is a revised version with the partial modification from the paper, "Data mining of image segments data with reduced neurofuzzy system" in the Proceedings (LNCS 5620) of 2nd International Conference Digital Human Modeling (ICDHM 2009) in 2009 at San Diego, CA. for the publication of Intech.

clustering analysis. Factor analyses (Gorsuch, 1983) concerns the study of the embedded relationships among the given variables to find or extract new variable sets, which are hidden and fewer in number than the original number of variables from the given data. In general, factor analysis attempts to reduce the complexity and diversity among the interrelationships of the applied data that exist in a set of observed variables by exposuring hidden common dimensions or factors. Therefore, those newly extracted factors (or variables) after factor analysis can reform more precise and independent variables with less common dimensions among newly extracted variables, and the more precise information about the embedded structure of the data can be provided by factor analysis.

Principal component analysis (Kendall, 1980) and factor analysis usually produce very similar estimates. However, principal component analysis is often preferred as a method for data reduction, while factor analysis is often preferred when the goal of the analysis is to detect the embedded structure. One of the goals of principal component analysis is to reduce the dimension of the variables, such as transforming a multidimensional space into another dimension (i.e., same or less number of axes or variables), depending upon the given data. Hence, the principal component analysis converts the normalized data to the new data, called **principal component scores**, which represent the original data with a new pattern using the new variables that describe the major pattern of variation among data.

Finally, clustering analysis (Duda et al., 2001) is a method for grouping objects or observations of similar kinds into respective categories. In other words, cluster analysis is an exploratory data analysis tool which aims at sorting or separating different observations into the similar kinds of groups in a way that the degree of association between two observations or objects is maximal if they belong to the same group and minimal otherwise. In addition, cluster analysis can be used to recognize the structures in data without providing an explanation or interpretation.

2.2 Fuzzy logic and neurofuzzy system

Fuzzy logic was originally identified and set forth by Professor Lotfi A. Zadeh.

In general, fuzzy logic (Lin & Lee, 1996) is applied to the system control or the design analysis, since applying fuzzy logic technique is able to reduce the time to develop engineering applications and especially, in the case of highly complicated systems, fuzzy logic may be the only way to solve the problem. As the complexity of a system increases, it becomes more difficult and eventually impossible to make a precise statement about its behavior. Occasionally, it arrives at a point where it cannot be implemented due to its ambiguity or high complexities.

The neurofuzzy system (Yager & Filev, 1994) consists of the combined concepts from neural network and fuzzy logic. To implement the neurofuzzy systems, Adaptive-Network-Based Fuzzy Inference System (ANFIS) (Jang, 1993) is used by implementing the reduced data sets and the actual data set. ANFIS is originally from the integration of TSK fuzzy model (Yager & Filev, 1994), developed by Takagi, Sugeno, and Kang (TSK), using the backpropagation learning algorithm (Duda et al., 2001) with least square estimation from neural networks. TSK fuzzy model proposed to formalize a systematic approach to generating fuzzy rules from and to input-output data set.

3. Data structure

To perform the proposed technique, the selected image segment data provided by Vision Group of University of Massachusetts are used. The instances were drawn randomly from a database of seven outdoor images. The images were hand segmented to create a classification for every pixel. The selected image segment data are consist of seven different measurement fields such as region centroid column, region centroid row, vedge-mean, hedge-mean, raw red mean, raw blue mean, and raw green mean, and four image classes like brickface, foliage, cement, and grass. The following describes each measurement field and the part of the image segment data.

1. Region centroid column: the column of the center pixel of the region.
2. Region centroid row: the row of the center pixel of the region.
3. Vedge-mean: measure the contrast of horizontally adjacent pixels in the region. There are 6, the mean and standard deviation are given. This attribute is used as a vertical edge detector.
4. Hedge-mean: measures the contrast of vertically adjacent pixels. Used for horizontal line detection.
5. Raw red mean: the average over the region of the R value.
6. Raw blue mean: the average over the region of the B value.
7. Raw green mean: the average over the region of the G value.

	Region centroid column	Region centroid row	Vedge-mean	Hedge-mean	Raw red mean	Raw blue mean	Raw green mean
CEMENT	191	119	1.294	0.77	48.222	35.111	-10.8889
BRICKFACE	140	125	0.063	0.31	7.667	3.556	3.4444
GRASS	204	156	0.279	0.56	25.444	28.333	-19.1111
FOLIAGE	101	121	0.843	0.89	6	3.111	-6.8889
CEMENT	219	80	0.33	0.93	48.222	34.556	-10.1111
BRICKFACE	188	133	0.267	0.08	7.778	3.889	5
GRASS	71	180	0.563	1.87	21.444	27.222	-12
FOLIAGE	21	122	0.404	0.4	1.222	0.444	-1.6667
CEMENT	136	45	1.544	1.53	63.778	47.333	-14.8889
BRICKFACE	105	139	0.107	0.52	7.222	3.556	4.3333
GRASS	60	181	1.2	2.09	17.889	23.889	-7.5556
	......	...	...	...	...	....	...

Table 1. Image segment data (http://www.cs.toronto.edu/~delve/data/datasets.html)

4. Proposed algorithm (Nam & Asikele, 2009)

Among implemented algorithms, the preprocessing of principal components analysis (Kendall, 1980) followed by Fuzzy C-means (FCM) clustering analysis (Duda et al., 2001) is shown as a selected algorithm to present in this paper. The following steps summarize the proposed algorithm to implement the reduced image segment data from the original image segment data.

Step 1. Read the original data set as a matrix format.
Step 2. Normalize the original data from Step 1.
Step 3. Find the correlation matrix of the normalized data from Step 2.
Step 4. Find eigenvalues and eigenvectors of the correlation matrix from Step 3 using characteristic equation.
Step 5. Define a matrix that is the eigenvectors from Step 4 as the coefficients of principal components using the criteria for extracting components.
Step 6. Multiply the standardized matrix from Step 2 and the coefficients of principal components from Step 5.
Step 7. Using the implemented data from Step 6, find the centers of clusters.
Step 8. Initialize the partition matrix, or membership matrix randomly such that $U^{(0)} \in M_{fcn}$.
Step 9. Calculate the cluster centers, v_i, using the equation, $v_i = \dfrac{\sum_{k=1}^{n} (u_{ik})^m x_k}{\sum_{k=1}^{n} (u_{ik})^m}$.
Step 10. Compute the distance, d_{ik}.
Step 11. Update the partition matrix $U^{(new)}$ using the equation $u_{ik} = \dfrac{1}{\sum_{j=1}^{c} \left(\dfrac{d_{ik}}{d_{jk}} \right)^{\frac{2}{m-1}}}$ for u_{ik}.

If $d_{ik} > 0$, for $1 \le i \le c$, and $1 \le k \le n$, then get the new u_{ik}.

Otherwise if $d_{ik} > 0$, and $u_{ik} = [0, 1]$ with $\sum_{i=1}^{c} u_{ik}^{(new)} = 1$, then $u_{ik}^{(new)} = 0$.

Step 12. Until $|| U^{(new)} - U^{(old)} || < \varepsilon$ where ε is the termination tolerance $\varepsilon > 0$.
If this condition is not satisfied, then go back to step 9.

5. Analysis and results

Before the proposed data reduction algorithms are applied into the image segment data, the image segment data need to be examined whether the data can be diminished by the redundancy among its original variables with the highly correlated interrelationship. To examine the redundancy, the correlations between the variables of the image segment data set are calculated. As shown in the Table 2, the correlations of the "Brickface" image segment data are presented. The bolded numbers are showing the relatively higher correlation so that there is a possibility to be extracted as a new factor between those measurements.

In addition, there are different criterions to select the reduced dimension for the new reduced variables after extracting new variables from the original data. For this example, two combined criteria are applied. One is the eigenvalues-greater-than-one rule by Cliff (Cliff, 1988) and the second criterion is the accumulated variance that is more than 0.9 from the reduced system.

Using two conditions, the new reduced system with three newly extracted variables is considered. From Table 3, the evaluated analyses of the performance using the proposed algorithms through the neurofuzzy systems (Lin & Lee, 1996) are shown. In the system with three factors, the best result is from the method using the factor analysis with applying the

FCM analysis from the original data. Based upon the results of three newly extracted variables, the proposed algorithm can show the better result from the conventional methods such as factor analysis and principal component analysis.
Comparing to the three newly extracted factors, the four newly extracted variables are also considered among seven different measurement variables. The evaluated analyses of the performance using the proposed algorithms through the neurofuzzy systems are shown with comparing the statistical categories in Table 4. Even though the 4th newly extracted variable did not meet the applied criteria above. But it covers more variance of the original data than the three newly reduced variables. From the results of Table 4, the result from the method, using factor analysis (Gorsuch, 1983) and FCM clustering analysis, shows a relatively better result than other methods including the combinations of principal component analysis and FCM clustering analysis.

	Region centroid column	**Region centroid row**	**Vedge-mean**	**Hedge-mean**	**Raw red mean**	**Raw blue mean**	**Raw green mean**
Region centroid column	1						
Region centroid row	0.333	1					
Vedge-mean	-0.165	-0.266	1				
Hedge-mean	-0.015	-0.194	0.351	1			
Raw red mean	0.008	**-0.729**	0.33	0.412	1		
Raw blue mean	0.004	-0.691	0.334	0.408	**0.993**	1	
Raw green mean	-0.017	0.675	-0.248	-0.388	**-0.808**	**-0.747**	1

Table 2. Pearson's correlation values for the "Brickface" image segment data (Nam & Asikele, 2009)

	CORR	**TRMS**	**STD**	**MAD**	**EWI**
fa	0.3096	0.9049	0.6064	0.8973	3.0991
pca	0.2628	1.4611	1.0579	1.4489	4.7051
fc	0.5386	0.7693	0.86	0.7597	2.8504
pc	-0.2757	1.2729	1.2195	1.257	4.4737

Table 3. Analysis of performance using proposal algorithm and conventional factor analysis and principal component analysis with three newly extracted factors

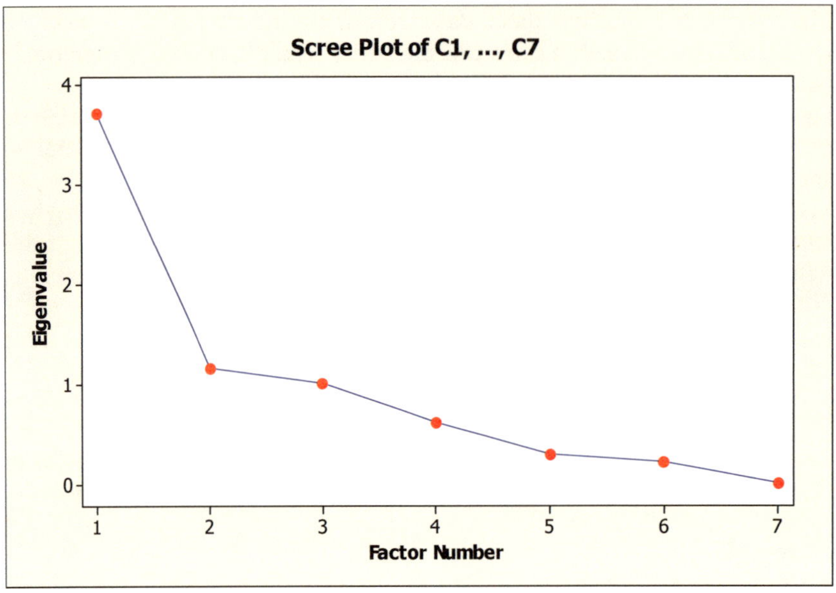

Fig. 1. Scree plot for the newly extracted components for "Brickface" image segment data (Nam & Asikele, 2009)

	CORR	TRMS	STD	MAD	EWI
fa	0.3984	0.8901	0.6664	0.8826	3.0407
pca	0.109	1.5185	1.1062	1.5059	5.0215
fc	0.3652	0.8807	1.3249	0.8697	3.7101
pc	-0.2541	1.2676	1.2878	1.2517	4.5529

Table 4. Analyses of Performance using proposed algorithm and conventional factor analysis and principal component analysis with four newly extracted factors (Nam & Asikele, 2009)

6. Conclusion

The pattern recognition of image segment data is presented and implemented through the neurofuzzy systems using the reduced dimensional data in variables and observations. For the implementation, three and four newly extracted embedded variables from seven original measurements variables are compared. The proposed algorithm performs the relatively better results than using the conventional multivariable techniques alone.

As described in Table 3 and 4, using the combination of factor analysis and FCM clustering analysis, the prediction of the patterns for the image segment data shows the relatively better results than other presented methods. The prediction results using the conventional principal component analyses show relatively worse than using other proposed algorithms.

This result may lead to the conclusion that for a limited number of input-output training data, the proposed algorithm can offer the better performance in comparison with the performance of the other techniques for image segment data.

7. Acknowledgments

This material is based upon the previous work supported by Clarkson Aerospace Corporation.

8. References

Cliff, N. (1988). The Eigenvalues-Greater-Than-One Rule and the Reliability of Components, *Psychological Bulletin*, Vol. 103, No. 2, pp. 276–279.

Duda, R.; Hart, P., & Stork, D. (2001). *Pattern Classification*, 2nd ed., John Wiley & Sons, ISBN 0-471-05669-3, New York, NY.

Gorsuch, R. (1983). *Factor Analysis*, 2nd Ed., Lawrence Erlbaum Associates Inc., ISBN 089859202X, Hillsdale, NJ.

Jang, J. (1993). ANFIS: Adaptive Network Based Fuzzy Inference System, *IEEE Trans. Systems, Man and Cybernetics*, Vol. 23, No. 3, pp.665–684.

Kendall, M. (1980). *Multivariate Analysis*, MacMillan Publishing Co. INC., New York, NY.

Lin, C. & Lee, C. (1996). *Neural Fuzzy Systems: A neuro-fuzzy synergism to intelligent systems*, Prentice Hall, ISBN 0-13-235169-2, Englewood Cliffs, NJ.

Nam, D. & Singh, H. (2006). Material processing for ADI data using multivariate analysis with neuro fuzzy systems, *Proceedings of the ISCA 19th International Conference on Computer Applications in Industry and Engineering, Nov.13–15, Las Vegas, Nevada*, pp.151–156.

Nam, D. & Asikele, E.(2009) Data mining of image segments data with reduced neurofuzzy system, *Proceedings (LNCS 5620) of 2nd International Conference Digital Human Modeling (ICDHM 2009)*, held as Part of *the 13th International Conference on Human-Computer Interaction, July 19 - 24, 2009, Town and Country Resort & Convention Center, San Diego, CA*, pp. 710 - 716.

Yager, R.& Filev, D. (1994). *Essentials of Fuzzy Modeling and Control*, John Wiley & Sons, ISBN 0-471-01761-2, New York, NY.

Appendix

Abbreviations

CORR: Correlation

TRMS: Total Root Mean Square $TRMS = \frac{\sum_{i=1}^{n} \sqrt{(x_i - y_i)^2}}{n-1}$

where x_i is the estimated value and y_i is the original output value.

STD: Standard Deviation

MAD: Mean of the absolute

EWI (Nam & Singh, 2006): Equally Weighted Index, the index value from the summation of the values with multiplying the statistical estimation value by its

equally
weighted potential value for each field
fa: Factor Analysis
pca: Principal Component Analysis
FCM: Fuzzy C-means Clustering Analysis
fc: preprocessing FA and SUBCLUST
pc: preprocessing PCA and SUBCLUST

23

On Ranking Discovered Rules of Data Mining by Data Envelopment Analysis: Some New Models with Applications

Mehdi Toloo[1] and Soroosh Nalchigar[2]
[1]*Department of Mathematics, Islamic Azad University of Central Tehran Branch, Tehran*
[2]*University of Pierre and Marie Curie, Paris*
[1]*Iran*
[2]*France*

1. Introduction

The convergence of computing and communication has resulted in a society that feeds on information. There is exponentially increasing huge amount of information locked up in databases—information that is potentially important but has not yet been discovered or articulated (Whitten & Frank, 2005). Data mining, the extraction of implicit, previously unknown, and potentially useful information from data, can be viewed as a result of the natural evolution of Information Technology (IT). An evolutionary path has been passed in database field from data collection and database creation to data management, data analysis and understanding. According to Han & Camber (2001) the major reason that data mining has attracted a great deal of attention in information industry in recent years is due to the wide availability of huge amounts of data and the imminent need for turning such data into useful information and knowledge. The information and knowledge gained can be used for applications ranging from business management, production control, and market analysis, to engineering design and science exploration. In other words, in today's business environment, it is essential to mine vast volumes of data for extracting patterns in order to support superior decision-making. Therefore, the importance of data mining is becoming increasingly obvious. Many data mining techniques have also been presented in various applications, such as association rule mining, sequential pattern mining, classification, clustering, and other statistical methods (Chen & Weng, 2008).

Association rule mining is a widely recognized data mining method that determines consumer purchasing patterns in transaction databases. Many applications have used association rule mining techniques to discover useful information, including market basket analysis, product recommendation, web page pre-fetch, gene regulation pathways identification, medical record analysis, and so on (Chen & Weng, 2009).

Extracting association rules has received considerable research attention and there are several efficient algorithms that cope with popular and computationally expensive task of association rule mining (Hipp et al., 2000). Using these algorithms, various rules may be obtained and only a small number of these rules may be selected for implementation due, at least in part, to limitations of budget and resources (Chen, 2007). According to Liu et al. (2000) the interestingness issue has long been identified as an important problem in data mining. It refers to finding rules that are interesting/useful to the user, not just any possible rule. Indeed, there exist some situations that make necessary the prioritization of rules for selecting and concentrating on more valuable rules due to the number of qualified rules (Tan & Kumar, 2000) and limited business resources (Choi et al., 2005). The purpose of this chapter, briefly, is to propose a new methodology for prioritizing association rules resulted from the data mining, while considering their business values incorporating the conflicting criteria of business values. Toward this end, a decision analysis method, Data Envelopment Analysis (DEA) is applied.

Recent years have seen a great variety of applications of DEA for use in evaluating the performances of many different kinds of entities engaged in many different activities in many different contexts in many different countries (Cooper et al., 2007). Selection of best vendors (Weber et al., 1998 & Liu et al., 2000), ranking data mining rules (Chen, 2007 & Toloo et al., 2009), evaluation of data warehouse operations (Mannino et al., 2008), selection of flexible manufacturing system (Liu, 2008), assessment of bank branch performance (Camanho & Dyson, 2005), examining bank efficiency (Chen et al., 2005), analyzing firm's financial statements (Edirisinghe & Zhan, 2007), measuring the efficiency of higher education institutions (Johnes, 2006), solving Facility Layout Design (FLD) problem (Ertay et al., 2006) and measuring the efficiency of organizational investments in information technology (Shafer & Byrd, 2000) are samples of using DEA in various areas.

The rest of this chapter is organized as follows: Section 2 provides readers with basic concepts of DEA. Moreover, this section reviews DEA models for finding most efficient DMUs. Section 3 describes data mining association rules, their applications and algorithm. In Section 4, the problem which is addressed by this chapter is expressed. Section 5 provides a review of related studies for solving the problem. Section 6 presents a new methodology for the problem of chapter. Section 7 shows applicability of proposed method. Finally, this chapter closes with some concluding remark in Section 8.

2. Data envelopment analysis

2.1 Basic models

Data envelopment analysis (DEA) is a mathematical optimization technique that measures the relative efficiency of decision making units (DMUs) with multiple input-output. Based on Farrell's pioneering work, Charnes et al. (1978) first proposed DEA as an evaluation tool to measure and compare a DMU's relative efficiency. During last three decades, DEA has been widely recognized and discussed from the methodological as well as practical side in measuring the relative efficiency of units that utilize the same inputs to produce the same outputs. One advantage of DEA is that these inputs and outputs can remain in their natural physical units without reducing or transforming them into some common metric such as dollars. Indeed, DEA defines relative efficiency as the ratio of the sum of weighted outputs to the sum of weighted inputs:

$$\text{DEA efficiency} = \frac{\text{Sum of weighted outputs}}{\text{Sum of weighted inputs}}$$

The more output produced for a given amount of resources, the more efficient is the unit. The problem is how to weight each of the individual input and output variables, expressed in their natural units; solving for these weights is the fundamental essence of DEA. For each DMU, the DEA procedure finds the set of weights that makes the efficiency of that DMU as large as possible. The values the weights any DMU can obtain is restricted through the evaluation of those weights in the input/output vectors for all the other comparable DMUs, where the resultant ratio of the sum of weighted outputs to the sum of weighted inputs is constrained to be no larger than 1. The procedure is repeated for all other DMUs to obtain their weights and associated relative efficiency score; ultimately providing decision makers with a listing of comparable DMUs ranked by their relative efficiencies.

Assume that there are n DMUs, $(\text{DMU}_j : j = 1,2,...,n)$. Some common input and output items for each of these n DMUs are selected as follows (Cooper et al., 2007):

1. Numerical data are available for each input and output, with the data assumed to be positive for all DMUs.
2. The items (inputs, outputs and choice of DMUs) should reflect an analyst's or a manager's interest in the components that will enter into the relative efficiency evaluations of the DMUs.
3. In principle, smaller input amounts are preferable and larger output amounts are preferable so the efficiency scores should reflect these principles.
4. The measurement units of the different inputs and outputs need not be congruent. Some may involve number of persons, or areas of floor space, money expended, etc.

Suppose each DMU consume m inputs $(\mathbf{x}_i : i = 1,2,\ldots,m)$ to produce s outputs $(\mathbf{y}_r : r = 1,2,\ldots,s)$. The CCR input oriented (CCR-I) model (Charnes et al., 1978) evaluates the efficiency of DMU_o, DMU under consideration, by solving the following linear program:

$$
\begin{aligned}
& \max \sum_{r=1}^{s} u_r y_{rj} \\
& \text{s.t.} \\
& \qquad \sum_{i=1}^{m} w_i x_{io} = 1 \\
& \qquad \sum_{r=1}^{s} u_r y_{rj} - \sum_{i=1}^{m} w_i x_{ij} \le 0 \qquad j = 1,2,...,n \\
& \qquad w_i \ge \varepsilon \qquad i = 1,2,...,m \\
& \qquad u_r \ge \varepsilon \qquad r = 1,2,...,s
\end{aligned}
\tag{1}
$$

where x_{ij} and y_{rj} (all nonnegative) are the inputs and outputs of the DMUj, w_i and u_r are the input and output weights (also referred to as multipliers). x_{io} and y_{ro} are the inputs and outputs of DMU_o. Also, ε is non-Archimedean infinitesimal value for forestalling weights to be equal to zero. To find a suitable value for ε, there exists a polynomial time algorithm, Epsilon algorithm, which introduced by Amin & Toloo (2004). The CCR-I model must be run n times, once for each unit, to get the relative efficiency of all DMUs.

It should be noted that Model (1) assumes that the production function exhibits constant returns-to-scale. As a theoretical extension, Banker et al. (1984) developed a variable returns to scale variation of Model (1). The BCC model (Banker et al., 1984) adds an additional constant variable in order to permit variable returns-to-scale. The BCC input oriented (BCC-I) model evaluates the efficiency of DMU_o, DMU under consideration, by solving the following linear program:

$$
\begin{aligned}
&\max \sum_{r=1}^{s} u_r y_{rj} - u_0 \\
&\text{s.t.} \\
&\quad \sum_{i=1}^{m} w_i x_{io} = 1 \\
&\quad \sum_{r=1}^{s} u_r y_{rj} - u_0 - \sum_{i=1}^{m} w_i x_{ij} \le 0 \qquad j = 1,2,\ldots,n \\
&\quad w_i \ge \varepsilon \qquad i = 1,2,\ldots,m \\
&\quad u_r \ge \varepsilon \qquad r = 1,2,\ldots,s \\
&\quad u_0 \ \text{free}
\end{aligned}
\tag{2}
$$

The structure and variables of this model are similar to Model (1). It is clear that a difference between the CCR and BCC models is present in the free variable u_0, which is used to measure the return to scale of DMU_o.

New applications and extensions with more variables and more complicated models are being introduced (Emrouznejad et al., 2007). In many applications of DEA, finding the most efficient DMU is desirable. The next section of this chapter introduces readers with some new DEA model for finding the most efficient DUMS. It is noteworthy to mention that Cook & Seiford (2009) provide a sketch of some of the major research thrusts in DEA over the three decades. Interested readers can refer to this paper of for further discussion on DEA, and a comprehensive review on it.

2.2 DEA model for finding the most efficient DMU

By applying basic DEA models (CCR and BCC), DMUs are grouped into two sets: efficient and inefficient DMUs. On the other hand, often decision-makers are interested in a complete ranking, beyond the dichotomized classification, in order to refine the evaluation of the units and find most efficient DMUs. Recently, the problem of finding most efficient DMUs in DEA has gained attention between researchers. For instance Ertay et al. (2006) integrated DEA and Analytic Hierarchy Process (AHP) and presented a decision-making methodology for evaluating Facility Layout Designes (FLDs). In the last step of their methodology, they extended minimax DEA model to identify single most efficient DMU. Amin & Toloo (2007) extended their work and proposed an integrated DEA model in order to detect the most CCR-efficient DMU. It was able to find the most CCR-efficient DMU without solving the model n times (one Linear Programming (LP) for each DMU) and therefore allowed the user to get faster results. Amin & Toloo (2007)'s model is as follows:

$$
\begin{aligned}
&\min M \\
&\text{s.t.} \\
&\quad M - d_j \ge 0 \qquad j = 1,2,\ldots,n \\
&\quad \sum_{i=1}^{m} w_i x_{ij} \le 1 \qquad j = 1,2,\ldots,n \\
&\quad \sum_{r=1}^{s} u_r y_{rj} - \sum_{i=1}^{m} w_i x_{ij} + d_j - \beta_j = 0 \qquad j = 1,2,\ldots,n
\end{aligned}
\tag{3}
$$

$$
\begin{aligned}
&\sum_{j=1}^{n} d_j = n-1 \\
&0 \le \beta_j \le 1 && j=1,2,\dots,n \\
&d_j \in \{0,1\} && j=1,2,\dots,n \\
&w_i \ge \varepsilon && i=1,2,\dots,m \\
&u_r \ge \varepsilon && r=1,2,\dots,s \\
&M \ \text{free}
\end{aligned}
\tag{3}
$$

where d_j as a binary variable represents the deviation variable of DMU_j. β_j is considered in the Model (3) because of discrete nature of d_j and M represents maximum inefficiency which should be minimized. DMU_j is most efficient if and only if $d_j^*=0$.

First constraint of Model (3) implies that M is equal to maximum inefficiency. Second constraint shows input-oriented nature of the Model (2). Third constraint causes efficiency of all units to be less that 1. The last one implies among all the DMUs for only most efficient unit, say DMU_p, which has $d_p^*=0$ in any optimal solution. In addition, to determine the non-Archimedean epsilon, Amin & Toloo (2007) developed an epsilon model.

It should be noted that Model (3) is based on CCR model and identify most CCR-efficient DMU. Indeed, Model (3) is not applicable for situations in which DMUs operating in variable return to scale. To overcome this drawback, Toloo & Nalchigar (2009) proposed an integrated model which is able to find most BCC-efficient DMU. They developed Model (3) as a new integrated model for finding the most BCC-efficient DMU.

$$
\begin{aligned}
&\min M \\
&\text{s.t.} \\
&\quad M - d_j \ge 0 && j=1,2,\dots,n \\
&\quad \sum_{i=1}^{m} w_i x_{ij} \le 1 && j=1,2,\dots,n \\
&\quad \sum_{r=1}^{s} u_r y_{rj} - u_0 - \sum_{i=1}^{m} w_i x_{ij} + d_j - \beta_j = 0 && j=1,2,\dots,n \\
&\quad \sum_{j=1}^{n} d_j = n-1 \\
&\quad 0 \le \beta_j \le 1 && j=1,2,\dots,n \\
&\quad d_j \in \{0,1\} && j=1,2,\dots,n \\
&\quad w_i \ge \varepsilon && i=1,2,\dots,m \\
&\quad u_r \ge \varepsilon && r=1,2,\dots,s \\
&\quad M, u_0 && \text{free}
\end{aligned}
\tag{4}
$$

Model (4) is computationally efficient and also has wider range of application than models which find most CCR-efficient DMU (Model (3)), because is capable for situation in which return to scale is variable. They illustrated the applicability of their model on a real case data.

Recently, Amin (2009) extended the work of Amin & Toloo (2007) and indicated the problem of using the Model (3). He indicated that Model (3) may identify more than one efficient DMU in a given data set. Then, he presented an improved Mixed Integer Non-Linear Programming (MINLP) integrated DEA model for determining the best CCR-efficient unit, as follows:

$$
\begin{aligned}
&\min M \\
&\text{s.t.} \\
&\quad M - d_j \geq 0 && j = 1,2,\dots,n \\
&\quad \sum_{i=1}^{m} w_i x_{ij} \leq 1 && j = 1,2,\dots,n \\
&\quad \sum_{r=1}^{s} u_r y_{rj} - \sum_{i=1}^{m} w_i x_{ij} + d_j = 0 && j = 1,2,\dots,n \\
&\quad \sum_{j=1}^{n} \theta_j = n-1 \\
&\quad \theta_j - d_j \beta_j = 0 && j = 1,2,\dots,n \\
&\quad \beta_j \geq 1 && j = 1,2,\dots,n \\
&\quad d_j \geq 0 && j = 1,2,\dots,n \\
&\quad \theta_j \in \{0,1\} && j = 1,2,\dots,n \\
&\quad w_i \geq \varepsilon && i = 1,2,\dots,m \\
&\quad u_r \geq \varepsilon && r = 1,2,\dots,s \\
&\quad M && \text{free}
\end{aligned}
\tag{5}
$$

Obviously, variables β_j (j = 1, ... ,n) are eliminated from the third type constraints of Model (3) and new binary variables θ_j (j = 1, ... ,n) are added in Model (5). Also the constraints $0 \leq \beta_j \leq 1$ are changed to $\beta_j \geq 1$ (j = 1, ... ,n). Moreover, the nonlinear constraints $\theta_j - d_j\beta_j = 0$ (j = 1, ... ,n) beside the constraint $\sum_{j=1}^{n} \theta_j = n-1$ implies for one and only one of the deviation variables d_j can be vanished, meaning that only one CCR-efficient DMU can be achieved, as the most CCR-efficient DMU, by Model (5). It should be noted that Model (5) is computationally difficult to be used since it is MINLP in nature.

In order to overcome this drawback, Toloo (2010) proposed a new Mixed Integer Linear Programming (MILP) as follows:

$$
\begin{aligned}
&\min M \\
&\text{s.t.} \\
&\quad M - d_j \geq 0 && j = 1,2,\dots,n \\
&\quad \sum_{i=1}^{m} w_i x_{ij} \leq 1 && j = 1,2,\dots,n \\
&\quad \sum_{r=1}^{s} u_r y_{rj} - \sum_{i=1}^{m} w_i x_{ij} + d_j = 0 && j = 1,2,\dots,n
\end{aligned}
\tag{6}
$$

$$\begin{aligned} & \sum_{j=1}^{n} \theta_j = n-1 \\ & m\theta_j \le d_j \le \theta_j && j=1,2,\dots,n \\ & d_j \ge 0,\ \theta_j \in \{0,1\} && j=1,2,\dots,n \\ & w_i \ge \varepsilon && i=1,2,\dots,m \\ & u_r \ge \varepsilon && r=1,2,\dots,s \\ & M && \text{free} \end{aligned} \tag{6}$$

In this model, if $\theta_j = 0$, then constraint $d_j \le \theta_j$ forces that $d_j = 0$ and if $\theta_j = 1$, then constraint $m\theta_j \le d_j$ forces that $d_j > 0$. Hence:

$$d_j \begin{cases} = 0 & \text{if } \theta_j = 0 \\ > 0 & \text{if } \theta_j = 1 \end{cases}$$

These constraints added to the constraint $\sum_{j=1}^{n} \theta_j = n-1$ imply for one and only one of the deviation variables d_j can be vanished. According to Toloo (2010) there exists a basic model that conceptually underlies Models (3) to (6) as follows:

$$\begin{aligned} & \min M \\ & \text{s.t.} \\ & \quad M - d_j \ge 0 && j=1,2,\dots,n \\ & \quad \sum_{i=1}^{m} w_i x_{ij} \le 1 && j=1,2,\dots,n \\ & \quad \sum_{r=1}^{s} u_r y_{rj} - \sum_{i=1}^{m} w_i x_{ij} + d_j = 0 && j=1,2,\dots,n \\ & \quad d_j \ge 0 && j=1,2,\dots,n \\ & \quad w_i \ge \varepsilon && i=1,2,\dots,m \\ & \quad u_r \ge \varepsilon && r=1,2,\dots,s \\ & \quad M && \text{free} \end{aligned} \tag{7}$$

Model (7) determines efficient unit(s) with a common set of optimal weighs $(\mathbf{u}^*, \mathbf{w}^*)$, i.e. all DMUs are evaluated by a common set of weights. Indeed, in Model (7) DMU_k is an efficient unit iff $\mathbf{u}^*\mathbf{y}_k - \mathbf{w}^*\mathbf{x}_k = 0$ (or equivalently $d_k^* = 0$). Let J be a set of indexes of efficient DMU(s) mathematically, $J = \{j \mid d_j^* = 0\, j = 1,\dots,n\}$. Clearly, if $|J|=1$, then definitely DMU_k is unique efficient DMU and hence is the best efficient DMU with the common set of optimal weights, $(\mathbf{u}^*, \mathbf{w}^*)$, iff $k \in J$. In this case, the best efficient unit can be easily determined by model (7) and no more models are needed. Otherwise, if $|J|>1$, then Model (7) cannot be used to find a single CCR-efficient unit. As he mentioned, to encounter this situation, some suitable constraints can be added to force this model to find only a single efficient unit. In other words, by restricting the feasible region of Model (7) only one efficient DMU can be achieved. Toward this end, Amin (2009) added the following constraints to the basic model (Model (7)):

$$\begin{aligned} &\sum_{j=1}^{n} \theta_j = n-1 \\ &\theta_j - d_j\beta_j = 0 \quad j=1,2,\ldots,n \\ &\beta_j \geq 1 \quad j=1,2,\ldots,n \\ &\theta_j \in \{0,1\} \quad j=1,2,\ldots,n \end{aligned} \tag{8}$$

and clearly, as mentioned before, the resulting model is a MINLP. Toloo (2010), instead of mixed integer non-linear constraints (8) , adjoined the following mixed integer linear constraints:

$$\begin{aligned} &\sum_{j=1}^{n} \theta_j = n-1 \\ &m\theta_j \leq d_j \leq \theta_j \quad j=1,2,\ldots,n \\ &d_j \geq 0,\ \theta_j \in \{0,1\} \quad j=1,2,\ldots,n \end{aligned}$$

where, $0 < m \ll 1$ is a positive parameter. Briefly, Model (6) is resulted from adding these equations to the basic model. Toloo (2010) mathematically proved that in Model (6) there exist only a single efficient DMU. Due to advantages of Model (6), this model is used to propose a new methodology for ranking data mining association rules. The next section introduces readers with these rules, their applications, and algorithms.

3. Data mining association rules

Association rules are valuable patterns that can be derived from large databases. Conceptually, an association rule indicates that the presence of a set of items (itemset) in a transaction would imply the occurrence of other items in the same transaction. The problem was first introduced by Agrawal et al. (1993), who defined it as finding all rules from transaction data satisfying the minimum support and the minimum confidence constraints. In brief, the association rule discovery problem could be divided into two separate tasks: (1) to discover all itemsets having support above a user-defined threshold, and (2) to generate rules from the frequent itemsets (Tan & Kumar, 2000).

Since introduction of association rules, this branch of data mining has gained great deal of attention by both researchers and practitioners. Today, the mining of such rules is still one of the most popular pattern discovery methods (Hipp et al., 2000). Nowadays, many applications have used association rule mining to discover useful information, including market basket analysis (Agrawal et al., 1993), web personalization (Mobasher et al., 2000 and Mulvenna et al., 2000) product recommendation (Adomavicius & Tuzhilin, 2005), soil quality assessment (Ju et al., 2010), extraction of failure patterns and forecast failure sequences of aircrafts (Han et al., 2009), credit card fraud detection (Sanchez et al., 2009), evaluation of agility in supply chains (Jain et al., 2008), exploration of cause-effect relationships in occupational accidents (Cheng et al., 2010), etc. In addition, due to its great

success and widespread application, many algorithms have been proposed for association rule mining. Based on data types which are handled by algorithm, they can be classified into three categories: nominal/Boolean data, ordinal data, and quantitative data. First, according to Agrawal et al.'s definition, transaction data is merely a set of items bought in that transaction. In other words, we can view transaction data as a set of Boolean variables, each of which corresponds to whether an item is purchased or not. The algorithms in this category find association rules from Boolean data. Second, since many data in the real world are nominal, such as hair color, grade, and birthplace, a natural extension is to modify the algorithms in the first category so that they can find association rules from nominal data. Usually, the algorithms in the first category can be easily adapted to handle nominal data. Therefore, from the algorithm's point of view, these two categories can be merged into a single category. Finally, the third category extends the algorithms so that they can find association rules from quantitative data, such as salary, height, humidity, and so on (Chen & Weng, 2008).
According to Agrawal & Sirkant (1994), given an item set $I=\{i_1,i_2,\ldots,i_m\}$ and given D represent a set of transaction, where each transaction T is a subset of I, $T\subset I$. A unique identifier, namely TID, is associated with each transaction. A transaction T is said to contain X, a set of items in I, if $X\subseteq T$. An association rule is said to be an implication of the form $X\Rightarrow Y$ denoting the presence of Itemset X and Y in some of the T transactions, assuming that $X,Y\subset I, X\cap Y=\varphi$ and $X,Y\neq\varphi$. The rule $X\Rightarrow Y$ holds in the transaction set D with *confidence, c,* where c% of transactions in D that contain X also contain Y. The rule has *support, s,* in the transaction set D if s% of transactions in D contain $X\cup Y$. It is noteworthy to mention that the idea of mining association rules originates from the analysis of market-basket data where rules like "A customer who buys product x_1 and x_2 will also buy product y with probability c%." are found. Their direct applicability to business problems together with their inherent understandability - even for non data mining experts - made association rules a popular mining method. In addition, it became clear that association rules are not restricted to dependency analysis in the context of retail applications, but are successfully applicable to a wide range of business problems (Hipp et al., 2000). In order to extract these rules, an efficient algorithm is needed that restrict the search space and checks only a subset of all association rules, yet does not miss important rules. The Apriori algorithm developed by Agrawal et al. (1993) is such an algorithm. However, the interestingness of rule is only based on support and confidence. The Apriori algorithm is as follows:

$$
\begin{array}{ll}
(1) & L_1 = \text{find\_large\_1} - \text{itemsets;} \\
(2) & \text{for}(k=2; L_{k-1}\neq\varphi; k++)\,\text{do begin} \\
(3) & \quad C_k = \text{apriori\_gen}(L_{k-1});\ //\text{new candidates} \\
(4) & \quad \text{forall TID}\,T\in \text{D do begin} \\
(5) & \qquad C_T = \text{subset}(C_k, T);//\text{candidates contained in } T \\
(6) & \qquad \text{forall candidates } C\in C_T \text{ do} \\
(7) & \qquad C.count++; \\
(8) & \quad \text{end} \\
(9) & L_k = \{C\in C_k \mid C.count/no\_of\_data \geq \text{minimum support threshold}\} \\
(10) & \text{end} \\
(11) & \text{Return } L = \bigcup_k Lk.
\end{array}
\tag{9}
$$

In the above Apriori algorithm, the aprioir_gen procedure generates candidates of itemset and then uses the minimum support criterion to eliminate infrequent itemsets. The aprioir_gen procedure performs two actions, namely, join and prune, which are discussed in Han & Kamber (2001). In join step, L_{k-1} is joined with $L_{k-1}$to generate potential candidates of itemset. The prune step uses the minimum support criterion to remove candidates of itemset that are not frequent. In fact, expanding an itemset reduces its support. A k-itemset can only be frequent if and only if its (k-1) -subsets are also frequent; consequently aprioir_gen only generates candidates with this property, a situation easily achievable given the set L_{k-1} (Chen, 2007).

Generally, support and confidence are considered as two main criteria to evaluate the usefulness of association rules (Agrawal et al., 1993; Srikant & Agrawal, 1997). Association rules are regarded as interesting if their support and confidence are more than minimum support and minimum confidence, defined by user. In data mining, it is important but difficult to appropriately determine these two thresholds of interestingness.

4. The problem

According to Hipp et al. (2000), when mining association rules there are mainly two problems to deal with: First of all there is the algorithmic complexity. The number of rules grows exponentially with the number of items. It is to be noted that new algorithms are able to prune this immense search space based on minimal thresholds for quality measures on the rules. Second, interesting rules must be picked from the set of generated rules. This is important and costly because applying association rule algorithms on datasets results in quite large number of rules and in contrast the percentage of useful rules in typically only a very small fraction. This chapter generally addresses the second problem.

In existing data mining techniques, there exist some situations that make necessary the prioritization of rules for selecting and concentrating on more valuable rules due to the number of qualified rules (Tan & Kumar, 2000) and limited business resources. In other words, one main problem of association rule induction is that there are so many possible rules. Obviously such a vast amount of rules cannot be processed by inspecting each one in turn (Tajbakhsh et al., 2009). Even though the purpose of data mining is rule (pattern) extraction that is valuable for decision making, patterns are deemed 'interesting' just on the basis of passing certain statistical tests such as support/confidence in data mining. To the enterprise, however, it remains unclear how such patterns can be used to maximize business values. Choi et al. (2005) believe that the major obstacle lies in the gap between statistic-based summaries (the statistic-based pattern extraction) extracted by traditional rule mining and a profit-driven action (the value-based decision making) required by business decision making which is characterized by explicit consideration of conflicts of business objectives and by multiple decision makers' involvement for corporate decision making.

It is to be noted that confidence and support of the rules are not sufficient measures to select "interesting" rules (Tajbakhsh et al., 2009). An association rule which is advantageous and profitable to sellers may not be discovered by setting constraints of minimum support and minimum confidence in the mining process because high value products are relatively uncommonly bought by customers, (Chen, 2007). Consider the following case, entitled the Ketel vodka and Beluga caviar in the market basket problem: Although, most customers infrequently buy either of these two products, and they rarely appear in frequent itemsets, their profits may be potentially higher than many lower value products that are more frequently bought. Another example regarding the interesting infrequent itemsets is described in Tao et al. (2003). The association rule of [wine$\Rightarrow$salmon, 1%, 80%] may be more interesting to analysts than [bread $\Rightarrow$milk, 3%, 80%] despite the first rule having lower support. The items in the first rule typically are associated with more profit per unit sale. This chapter proposes a new method for estimating and ranking the efficiency (interestingness or usefulness) of association rules with multiple criteria by using a non-parametric approach, DEA. The interestingness of association rules is measured by considering multiple criteria involving support, confidence and domain related measures. This paper uses DEA as a post-processing approach. After the rules have been discovered from the association rule mining algorithms, DEA is used to rank those discovered rules based on the specified criteria.

5. Previous related studies

The problem of ranking discovered rules of data mining has gained attention by some researchers. Sirkant et al. (1997) presented three integrated algorithms for mining association rules with item constraint. Moreover, Lakshmanan et al. (1998) extended the approach presented by Srikant et al. to consider much more complicated constraints, including domain, class, and SQL-style aggregate constraints. Liu et al. (2000) presents an Interestingness Analysis System (IAS) to help the user identify interesting association rules. In their proposed method, they consider two main subjective interestingness measures, unexpectedness and actionability. The degree of unexpectedness of rules can be measured by the extent to which they surprise the analyst. Meanwhile, the degree of actionability can be measured by the extent to which analysts can use the discovered rules to their advantage. Choi et al. (2005), using Analytic Hierarchy Process (AHP) presented a method for association rules prioritization which considers the business values which are comprised of objective metric or managers' subjective judgments. They believed that proposed method makes synergy with decision analysis techniques for solving problems in the domain of data mining. Nevertheless this method requires large number of human interaction to obtain weights of criteria by aggregating the opinions of various managers. Chen (2007) developed their work and proposed a Data Envelopment Analysis (DEA) based methodology for ranking association rules while considering multiple criteria. During his ranking procedure, he uses a DEA model, proposed by Cook & Kress (1990), to identify efficient association rules.

In fact, his proposed method uses a DEA model, proposed by Cook & Kress (1990), for identifying efficient association rules. This model is as follows:

$$
\begin{aligned}
&\max \sum_{j=1}^{k} \mathrm{w}_j v_{oj} \\
&\text{s.t.} \\
&\qquad \sum_{j=1}^{k} \mathrm{w}_j v_{ij} \le 1 \qquad\qquad i = 1,2,\ldots,m \\
&\qquad w_j - w_{j+1} \ge d(j,\varepsilon) \qquad j = 1,2,\ldots,k-1 \\
&\qquad w_k \ge d(k,\varepsilon)
\end{aligned}
\tag{10}
$$

where w_j denotes the weight of the jth place; v_{ij} represents the number of jth place votes of candidate $i\,(i=1,2,...,m,\ j=1,2,...,k)$ and $d(\bullet,\varepsilon)$, known as the discrimination intensify function, is nonnegative and nondecreasing in ε and satisfies $d(\bullet,\varepsilon)=0$.
Model (3) should be resolved for each candidate $o, o=1,2,...,m$. The resulting objective value is the preference score of candidate o. Because of the fact that DEA frequently generates several efficient candidates (Obata & Ishii, 2003), Chen's proposed method uses another DEA model, proposed by Obata & Ishii (2003), for discriminating efficient association rules. This model is as follows:

$$\begin{aligned} &\max \sum_{j=1}^{k} w_j \\ &\text{s.t.} \\ &\quad \sum_{j=1}^{k} w_i v_{oj} = 1 \\ &\quad \sum_{j=1}^{k} w_j v_{ij} \le 1 \quad \text{for all efficient } i \ne o \\ &\quad w_j - w_{j+1} \ge d(j,\varepsilon) \qquad j=1,2,...,k-1 \\ &\quad w_j \ge d(j,\varepsilon) \end{aligned} \tag{11}$$

It should be noted that this model does not employ any information about inefficient candidates and should be solved only for efficient association rules. It should be noted that his proposed method requires the first model to be solved for all DMUs and the second model to be solved for efficient DMUs. As a drawback, this approach requires considerable number of Linear Programming (LP) models to be solved. Toloo et al. (2009) mentioned following problems in using Chen's proposed method:

- Chen's method requires computing v_{ij} from y_{ij} (j^{th} outputs of ith association rule). Although, the algorithm of computing v_{ij} from y_{ij} is polynomial, it is time consuming. Identifying efficient association rules can be done through a more simple and efficient way. Interested readers are referred to Toloo et al. (2009) for further explanations.
- Result of Chen's method is immensely dependent on discrimination intensify function.
- Suppose that there are e efficient association rules which are obtained from Model (10). To rank e efficient units, Chen's method includes solving $(n+e)$ LPs.
- To overcome above problems, Toloo et al. (2009) improved the work of Chen (2007) and proposed a methodology which ranked association rules by solving less numbers of LP models. Their methodology was based on Model (3) and include following steps:

Step 0. Let $T=\phi$ and $e=$ number of association rules to be ranked.

Step 1. Solve following model:

$$\begin{aligned} &\min M \\ &\text{s.t.} \\ &\quad M - d_j \ge 0 \qquad\qquad j=1,2,...,n \\ &\quad \sum_{r=1}^{s} u_r y_{rj} + d_j - \beta_j = 1 \qquad j=1,2,...,n \end{aligned} \tag{12}$$

$$\begin{aligned}
&\sum_{j=1}^{n} d_j = n-1 && \\
&d_j = 1 && \forall j \in \mathrm{T} \\
&0 \le \beta_j \le 1 && j = 1,2,\ldots,n \\
&d_j \in \{0,1\} && j = 1,2,\ldots,n \\
&w_i \ge \varepsilon && i = 1,2,\ldots,m \\
&u_r \ge \varepsilon && r = 1,2,\ldots,s \\
&M && \text{free}
\end{aligned} \tag{12}$$

Suppose in optimal solution $d_p^* = 0$.

Step 2. Let $\mathrm{T} = \mathrm{T} \cup \{p\}$.

Step 3. If $|\mathrm{T}| = e$, then stop; otherwise go to Step 1.

Indeed, in Step 1 of Toloo et al.'s algorithm, an association rule is identified as best efficient rule. It is noteworthy to mention that Model (12) is based on Model (3) and the only difference is that Model (12) considers a single input with equal value for all association rules. This is because of the fact that all evaluation criteria of association rules are output in nature. Clearly using DEA models (e.g. Model (3)) requires input data of DMUs and consequently Model (12) were developed by Toloo et al. (2009) to handle this situation and be applicable for ranking association rules. In Step 2, the best efficient association rule identified in Step 1 is added to T. Next, in step 3, if all rules are ranked, the algorithm finishes, else it goes to next iteration; finally, after e iterations all association rules are ranked. Although they improved Chen's method, their methodology was based on Model (3) which suffers from some drawbacks, as mentioned in Section 2.2. In the next section we propose a new methodology based on the latest developments by Toloo (2010).

6. Proposed method

This section proposes a new DEA-based methodology for ranking units. Previously, various methodologies have been proposed to rank DMUs, most of which are reviewed by Adler (2002). Interested readers can refer to this reference for further discussion on ranking methods. DEA is able to compare DMUs using different criteria as the basis for comparison, while utilizing all inputs and outputs simultaneously. Generally, in DEA applications, the criteria that should be maximized are considered as outputs and ones that should be minimized are treated as inputs. In case of ranking data mining association rules, previous studies such as Chen (2007) and Toloo et al. (2009) considered criteria that are outputs in nature. In other words, the more value of those criteria the more interesting association rule for business. In this section, a new DEA model is presented which identifies the best efficient unit by considering only output data of DMUs. The model proposed as:

$$\begin{aligned}
&\min M \\
&\text{s.t.} \\
&\quad M - d_j \ge 0 \qquad j = 1,2,\ldots,n
\end{aligned} \tag{13}$$

$$
\begin{aligned}
&\min M \\
&\text{s.t.} \\
&\quad M - d_j \geq 0 && j = 1,2,\ldots,n \\
&\quad \sum_{r=1}^{s} u_r y_{rj} + d_j = 1 && j = 1,2,\ldots,n \\
&\quad \sum_{j=1}^{n} \theta_j = n-1 \\
&\quad m\theta_j \leq d_j \leq \theta_j && j = 1,2,\ldots,n \\
&\quad d_j \geq 0 && j = 1,2,\ldots,n \\
&\quad \theta_j \in \{0,1\} && j = 1,2,\ldots,n \\
&\quad w_i \geq \varepsilon && i = 1,2,\ldots,m \\
&\quad u_r \geq \varepsilon && r = 1,2,\ldots,s \\
&\quad M && \text{free}
\end{aligned} \tag{13}
$$

The structure of Model (13) is similar to Model (6) and the main idea is trying to find only one most efficient DMU. However, Model (6) considers various criteria as inputs and outputs and Model (13) considers only output data of DMUs. In other words, Model (13) is applicable for situations in which all evaluation criteria are output in nature (e.g. association rules). In simple words, Model (13) is a customized version of Model (6). Using Model (13), in this section Toloo et al.'s methodology is improved as follows:

Step 0. Let $T = \varphi$ and $e =$ number of association rules to be ranked.

Step 1. Solve following model:

$$
\begin{aligned}
&\min M \\
&\text{s.t.} \\
&\quad M - d_j \geq 0 && j = 1,2,\ldots,n \\
&\quad \sum_{r=1}^{s} u_r y_{rj} + d_j = 1 && j = 1,2,\ldots,n \\
&\quad \sum_{j=1}^{n} \theta_j = n-1 \\
&\quad m\theta_j \leq d_j \leq \theta_j && j = 1,2,\ldots,n \\
&\quad \theta_j = 1 && j \in T \\
&\quad d_j \geq 0 && j = 1,2,\ldots,n \\
&\quad \theta_j \in \{0,1\} && j = 1,2,\ldots,n \\
&\quad w_i \geq \varepsilon && i = 1,2,\ldots,m \\
&\quad u_r \geq \varepsilon && r = 1,2,\ldots,s \\
&\quad M && \text{free}
\end{aligned} \tag{14}
$$

Suppose in optimal solution $d_p^* = 0$.

Step 2. Let $T = T \cup \{p\}$.

Step 3. If $|T| = e$, then stop; otherwise go to Step 1.

Step 1 ensures that one and only one DMU is selected as the best efficient unit. Step 2 adds this DMU to *T* and Step 3 ensures that all DMUs are ranked. Although the proposed methodology is similar to Toloo et al.'s methodology in structure, it overcomes the former drawbacks. In other words, as contribution, proposed methodology is based on latest development in DEA and overcome the problems of previous DEA models.

7. Illustrative example

In this section, to indicate the application of proposed method and compare its results with previous methods, an example of market basket data is adopted from Chen (2007). Association rules first are discovered by the Apriori algorithm, in which minimum support and minimum confidence are set to 1.0% and 10.0%, respectively. Forty-six rules then are identified and presented in Table (1).

By applying Model (14) to data presented in Table (1), DMU_{12} is identified as the most efficient association rule (considering m=0.001). In Step 2, 12 is added to *T* and in Step 3, methodology enters second iteration. Based on the methodology, in second iteration the constraint $\theta_{12} = 1$ is added to model. Solving Model (14) in second iteration resulted in ($\theta_{18}^* = 0,\ \theta_{j \neq 18}^* = 1$) implies that DMU_{18} is second efficient association rule. Table (2) presents results of ranking efficient rules in comparison to Chen's method and Toloo et al.'s method. Table 2 shows that the results of proposed method are different from results of previous methods. In order to provide readers with further insight, basic model has been applied to data set of Table.1[1]. As mentioned in Section 2.2, basic model determines DMU(s) which are candidate to be the best efficient DMU with considering common set of weights. The results show that $d_{12}^* = 0$ meaning that DMU_{12} should be the highest ranked DMU, since there is no other candidate to be the best efficient DMU. It is notable that this DMU is ranked 10th by Chen's method and 4th by Toloo et al.'s method. Obviously, proposed method provides decision maker with more accurate results as its main advantage to previous methods.

Association Rule Number (DMU)	Support (%)	Confidence (%)	Itemset value	Cross-selling profit
1	3.87	40.09	337.00	25.66
2	1.42	18.17	501.00	11.63
3	2.83	17.64	345.00	11.29
4	2.34	30.83	163.00	19.73
5	2.63	23.90	325.00	15.30
6	1.19	55.65	436.00	35.61
7	1.19	47.42	598.00	30.35
8	1.19	15.70	436.00	52.91

[1] Appendix A indicates GAMS program of basic model.

Association Rule Number (DMU)	Support (%)	Confidence (%)	Itemset value	Cross-selling profit
9	1.19	10.82	598.00	36.45
10	1.19	12.32	436.00	20.08
11	1.19	12.32	598.00	40.04
12	3.87	38.08	337.00	103.97
13	1.18	15.09	710.00	41.19
14	2.44	15.22	554.00	41.56
15	2.14	28.21	372.00	77.02
16	2.51	22.81	534.00	62.26
17	1.19	50.92	436.00	139.02
18	1.19	45.25	598.00	123.52
19	1.19	11.70	436.00	43.54
20	1.19	11.70	598.00	62.50
21	1.42	13.99	501.00	61.16
22	1.18	12.23	710.00	53.45
23	1.50	13.64	698.00	59.59
24	2.83	27.82	345.00	78.17
25	2.44	25.27	554.00	71.00
26	1.25	15.97	718.00	44.87
27	1.22	34.89	339.00	98.04
28	1.30	35.12	435.00	98.68
29	1.42	33.81	534.00	95.01
30	1.91	25.26	380.00	70.97
31	1.43	37.14	618.00	104.35
32	2.38	21.63	542.00	60.78
33	1.18	30.24	366.00	84.98
34	1.23	29.36	626.00	82.51
35	1.58	22.65	354.00	63.64
36	2.34	22.99	163.00	22.76
37	2.14	22.14	372.00	21.92
38	1.91	11.94	380.00	11.82
39	2.03	18.42	360.00	18.23
40	1.19	30.73	436.00	30.43
41	2.63	25.87	325.00	67.52
42	2.51	25.98	534.00	67.81
43	1.50	19.16	698.00	50.02
44	2.38	14.85	542.00	38.75
45	2.03	26.73	360.00	69.78
46	1.19	30.73	598.00	80.22

Table 1. Data of Association Rules

Ranking	Association Rule Number (DMU)		
	Chen's Method	Toloo et al.'s Method	Proposed Method
1	26	18	12
2	22	23	18
3	18	26	26
4	17	12	43
5	7	31	23
6	23	43	31
7	6	22	1
8	43	6	7
9	31	17	6
10	12	1	17
11	1	7	22

Table 2. Ranking of Proposed Method in Comparison to Chen's method and Toloo et al.'s method

8. Conclusion

Association rule discover is one of widely recognized data mining techniques which has gained great deal of attention recently. Association rules are valuable patterns because they offer useful insight into the types of dependencies that exist between attributes of a data set. By applying association rules algorithms, there exist some situations that make necessary the prioritization of rules for selecting and concentrating on more valuable rules due to the number of qualified rules and limited business resources. In other words, one main problem of association rule induction is that there are so many possible rules. Hence, evaluating the interestingness or usefulness of association rules and ranking them is a critical task in data mining applications. Indeed, selecting the more valuable rules for implementation increases the possibility of success in data mining. In this chapter, a new methodology proposed for ranking association rules of data mining. This method uses a non-parametric linear programming technique, DEA, for ranking the units. As an advantage, the proposed method utilizes the latest developments in DEA models and finds the best efficient association rule by solving only one MILP. The applicability of proposed method is indicated and its results are compared with the results of previous methods. Using basic model presented in this chapter, it is shown that results of new proposed method is more advantageous than previous ones since it results in more accurate results.

As directions for further researches, extending the applicability of proposed method to imprecise/fuzzy situations is suggested. Obviously, in many real world business applications of data mining, data of association rules is imprecise/fuzzy. Besides, future researchers could extend the applicability of proposed method to solve other business decision problems such as supplier selection, ranking of projects, and etc.

9. References

Adler, N., Friedman, L., Sinuany-stern, Z. (2002). Review of ranking methods in data envelopment analysis context. *European Journal of Operational Research*, 140, 249-265.

Adomavicius, G., Tuzhilin, A. (2005). Toward the next generation of recommender systems: a survey of the state-of-the-art and possible extensions. *IEEE Trans. Knowledge Data Engrg.* 17, 734–749.

Agrawal, R., Imielinski, T., Swami, A. (1993). Mining association between sets of items in massive database. *International proceedings of the ACM-SIGMOD international conference on management of data*, 207–216.

Agrawal, R., Srikant, R. (1994). Fast algorithms for mining association rules. *Proceedings of the international conference on very large data bases*, 407–419.

Amin, Gholam R., Toloo, M. (2004). A polynomial-time algorithm for finding Epsilon in DEA models, *Computers and Operations Research*, 31, 803–805.

Amin, Gholam R., Toloo, M. (2007). Finding the most efficient DMUs in DEA: An improved integrated model. *Computers & Industrial Engineering*, 52, 71-77.

Amin, Gholam R., (2009). Comments on finding the most efficient DMUs in DEA: An improved integrated model. *Computers & Industrial Engineering*, 56, 1701-1702.

Banker, R. D., Charnes, A., Cooper, W. W. (1984). Some models for estimating technical and scale inefficiency in data envelopment analysis. *Management Science*, 30, 1078–1092.

Camanho, A. S., Dyson, R.G. (2005). Cost efficiency measurement with price uncertainty: a DEA application to bank branch assessments. *European Journal of Operational Research*, 161, 432-446.

Charnes, A., Cooper, W. W., Rhodes, E. (1978). Measuring the efficiency of decision-making units. *European Journal of Operational Research*, 2, 429–444.

Chen, M. C. (2007). Ranking discovered rules from data mining with multiple criteria by data envelopment analysis. *Expert Systems with Applications*, 33, 1110-1116.

Chen, X., Skully M., Brown, K. (2005). Banking efficiency in China: Application of DEA to pre- and post-deregulation eras: 1993-2000. *China Economic Review*, 16, 229-245.

Chen, Y.L., Weng, C.H. (2008). Mining association rules from imprecise ordinal data. *Fuzzy Sets and Systems*, 159, 460-474.

Chen, Y.L., Weng, C.H. (2009). Mining fuzzy association rules from questionnaire data. *Knowledge-Based Systems*. 22, 46–56.

Cheng, C.W., Lin, C.C., Leu, S.S. (2010). Use of association rules to explore cause–effect relationships in occupational accidents in the Taiwan construction industry. *Safety Science*, 48, 436–444.

Choi, D.H., Ahn, B.S., Kim, S.H. (2005). Prioritization of association rules in data mining: Multiple criteria decision approach. *Expert Systems with Applications*, 29, 867-878.

Cook, W.D., Seiford, L.M. (2009). Data Envelopment Analysis (DEA): Thirty years on. *European Journal of Operational Research*, 192, 1-17.

Cook, W. D., Kress, M. (1990). A data envelopment model for aggregating preference rankings. *Management Science*, 36, 1302–1310.

Cooper, W.W., Seiford,L.M., Tone, K. (2007). Data Envelopment Analysis: A Comprehensive text with Models, Applications, References and DEA-Solver Software. Springer, 978-0387-45283-8.

Edirisinghe, N.C.P., Zhang, X. (2007). Generalized DEA model of fundamental analysis and its application to portfolio optimization. *Journal of Banking & Finance*, 31, 3311-3335.

Emrouznejad, A., Tavares, G., Parker, B. (2007). A bibliography of data envelopment analysis (1978–2003). *Socio-Economic Planning Sciences*, 38, 159-229.

Ertay, T., Ruan, D., Tuzkaya, U. R. (2006). Integrating data envelopment analysis and analytic hierarchy for the facility layout design in manufacturing systems. *Information Sciences*, 176, 237-262.

Han, J.W., Kamber, M. (2001). Data Mining: Concepts and Techniques, *MORGAN KAUFMANN PUBLIOSHERS*, San Francisco.

Han, H.K., Kim, H.S., Sohn, S.Y. (2009). Sequential association rules for forecasting failure patterns of aircrafts in Korean airforce. *Expert Systems with Applications*, 36, 1129-1133.

Hipp, J., Guntzer, U., Nakhaeizadeh, G. (2000). Algorithms for Association Rule Mining - A General Survey and Comparison. *SIGKDD Explorations*, 2, 58-64.

Jain, V., Benyoucef, L., Deshmukh, S.G. (2008). A new approach for evaluating agility in supply chains using

Fuzzy Association Rules Mining. *Engineering Applications of Artificial Intelligence*. 21, 367-385.

Johnes, J. (2006). Measuring teaching efficiency in higher education: An application of data envelopment analysis to economics graduates from UK Universities 1993. *European Journal of Operational Research*, 174, 443-456.

Liu, J., Ding, F.Y., Lall, V. (2000). Using data envelopment analysis to compare suppliers for supplier selection and performance improvement, *Supply Chain Management*, 5, 143-150.

Liu, B., Hsu, W., Chen, S., Ma, Y. (2000). Analyzing the subjective interestingness of association rules. *IEEE Intelligent Systems*, 15, 47-55.

Liu, S.T. (2008). A fuzzy DEA/AR approach to the selection of flexible manufacturing systems. *Computers & Industrial Engineering*, 54, 66-76.

Mannino, M., Hong, S.N., Choi, I.J. (2008). Efficiency evaluation of data warehouse operations. *Decision Support Systems*, 44, 883-898.

Mobasher, B., Cooley, R., Srivastava, J. (2000). Automatic personalization based on web usage mining. *Communications of the ACM*, 43, 142-151.

Mulvenna, M. D., Anand, S. S., Bu¨chner, A. G. (2000). Personalization on the net using Web mining. *Communications of the ACM*, 43, 123-125.

Ng. R. T., Lakshmanan, L. V. S., Han, J., Pang, A. (1998). Exploratory mining and pruning optimizations of constrained association rules. *In Proceedings of the ACM SIGMOD international conference on management of data, SIGMOD-98*, 13-24.

Obata, T., Ishii, H. (2003). A method for discriminating efficient candidates with ranked voting data. *European Journal of Operational Research*, 151, 233-237.

Sanchez, D., Vila, M.A., Cerda, L., Serrano, J.M. (2009). Association rules applied to credit card fraud detection. *Expert Systems with Applications*, 36, 3630-3640.

Shafer, S.M., Byrd, T.A. (2000). A framework for measuring the efficiency of organizational investments in information technology using data envelopment analysis. *Omega*, 28, 125-141.

Srikant, R., Vu, Q., Agrawal, R. (1997). Mining association rules with item constraints. *In Proceedings of the third international conference on knowledge discovery and data mining, KDD-97*, 67-73.

Tajbakhsh, A., Rahmati, M., Mirzaei, A. (2009). Intrusion detection using fuzzy association rules. *Applied Soft Computing*, 9, 462-469.

Tan, P. N., Kumar, V. (2000). Interestingness measures for association patterns: A perspective, *KDD 2000 workshop on postprocessing in machine learning and data mining*, Boston, MA, August.

Tao, F., Murtagh, F., Farid, M. (2003). Weighted association rule mining using weighted support and significance framework. *In Proceedings of the ACM SIGMOD international conference on management of data*, Sigmod-03, 661–666.

Toloo, M. (2010). A new mixed integer linear programming integrated model for finding the most efficient unit in data envelopment analysis. *Computers & Industrial Engineering* (Submitted Manuscript Number: CAIE-D-10-00438.

Toloo, M., Nalchigar, S. (2009). A new integrated DEA model for finding most BCC-efficient DMU. *Applied Mathematical Modelling*, 33, 597-604.

Toloo, M., Sohrabi. B., Nalchigar, S. (2009). A new method for ranking discovered rules from data mining by DEA. *Expert Systems with Applications*, 36, 8503-8508.

Weber, C.A., Current, J.R., Desai, A. (1998). Non-cooperative negotiation strategies for vendor selection. *European Journal of Operational Research*, 108, 208-223.

Whitten, I.H., Frank, E. (2005). Data Mining: Practical Machine Learning Tools and Techniques. *MORGAN KAUFMAN PUBLISHERS*. 0-12-088407-0

Xue, Y. J., Liu, S. G., Hu, Y. M. and Yang, J. F. (2010). Soil quality assessment using weighted fuzzy association rules. *Pedosphere*. 20, 334–341.

Appendix A

Basic Model in GAMS

```
$title Basic Model
$ontext
This program is written as a part of a book chapter with following specifications. In brief, this
program shows applicability of a mathematical model which is proposed by Toloo (2010) for finding
the best data mining association rule.

Authors: Mehdi Toloo & Soroosh Nalchigar
Book Name: Data Mining
Chapter Name:
On Ranking Discovered Rules of Data Mining by Data Envelopment Analysis: Some New Models
with Applications
Publisher: INTECH
2011

$offtext
SETS
  J  "Number of DMUs"     /01*46/
  O  "Number of outputs"  /1*4/

ALIAS (J,L);

PARAMETERS
  Yo(O)     "Output vector of DMUo"
  ep;
```

ep=0.0001;

TABLE Y(J,O) "Output vectors of all DMUs"

	1	2	3	4
01	3.87	40.09	337	25.66
02	1.42	18.17	501	11.63
03	2.83	17.64	345	11.29
04	2.34	30.83	163	19.73
05	2.63	23.9	325	15.3
06	1.19	55.65	436	35.61
07	1.19	47.42	598	30.35
08	1.19	15.7	436	52.91
09	1.19	10.82	598	36.45
10	1.19	12.32	436	20.08
11	1.19	12.32	598	40.04
12	3.87	38.08	337	103.97
13	1.18	15.09	710	41.19
14	2.44	15.22	554	41.56
15	2.14	28.21	372	77.02
16	2.51	22.81	534	62.26
17	1.19	50.92	436	139.02
18	1.19	45.25	598	123.52
19	1.19	11.7	436	43.54
20	1.19	11.7	598	62.5
21	1.42	13.99	501	61.16
22	1.18	12.23	710	53.45
23	1.5	13.64	698	59.59
24	2.83	27.82	345	78.17
25	2.44	25.27	554	71
26	1.25	15.97	718	44.87
27	1.22	34.89	339	98.04
28	1.3	35.12	435	98.68
29	1.42	33.81	534	95.01
30	1.91	25.26	380	70.97
31	1.43	37.14	618	104.35
32	2.38	21.63	542	60.78
33	1.18	30.24	366	84.98
34	1.23	29.36	626	82.51
35	1.58	22.65	354	63.64
36	2.34	22.99	163	22.76
37	2.14	22.14	372	21.92
38	1.91	11.94	380	11.82
39	2.03	18.42	360	18.23
40	1.19	30.73	436	30.43
41	2.63	25.87	325	67.52

```
42    2.51    25.98    534    67.81
43    1.5     19.16    698    50.02
44    2.38    14.85    542    38.75
45    2.03    26.73    360    69.78
46    1.19    30.73    598    80.22;

VARIABLES
Mstar
M
 POSITIVE VARIABLES
 u(O)
 d(j)

EQUATIONS
obj
const1
const2
const3;
   obj..          Mstar =e=M ;
   const1(j)..  M-d(j)=g=0;
   const2(j)..  sum(o,u(o)*y(j,o))+d(j)=e= 1 ;
   const3(o)..  u(o)=g=ep;

FILE  result/Basic_Model_Results.txt/;

MODEL Basic_Model /all/ ;

SOLVE Basic_Model using LP minimizing Mstar ;
PUT result ;
PUT "M*=", PUT Mstar.L:9:6,"  ", PUT /;
LOOP (j, PUT "d*_", PUT  j.tl, PUT@7 "= " PUT d.l(j):10:8, PUT /);
```

24

Temporal Rules Over Time Structures with Different Granularities - a Stochastic Approach

Paul Cotofrei and Kilian Stoffel
Information Management Institute, University of Neuchâtel
Switzerland

1. Introduction

The domain of temporal data mining focuses on the discovery of causal relationships among events that are ordered in time and may be causally related. The contributions in this domain encompass the discovery of temporal rule, of sequences and of patterns. However, in many respects this is just a terminological heterogeneity among researchers that are, nevertheless, addressing the same problem, albeit from different starting points and domains.
It is obvious that there is an implicit relationship between the characteristics of the knowledge extracted from data with temporal dimension and the time scale of the same data. Therefore, a natural question is how (or when) an information discovered based on a given level of time granularity may be reused if this granularity changes. For example, a temporal rule ($\mathbb{T}$) expressed as "If the sales **increase** *today* by 10% and *tomorrow* by 5% then the *day after tomorrow* they will **increase** only by 1%" may be used to make predictions if its degree of confidence remains stable along a time scale using days as basic time granules. But what can we say about the confidence of the rule ($\mathbb{T}_{new}$) obtained by replacing *"today"*, *"tomorrow"* and *"day after tomorrow"* with *"this week"*, *"next week"* and *"the week after next"*, when applied on a time scale using weeks as granules? Is this confidence still well-defined? And if the answer is yes, can its degree be deduced from the confidence of $\mathbb{T}$?
There are at least two important issues related to the conversion of $\mathbb{T}$ into $\mathbb{T}_{new}$ that must be emphasized. First, if the event "**increase**" is in fact the elementary event "**daily increase**" (denoted e), it is quite simple (if daily sales are available) to check the truth of the proposition "e by p% during day n" and, consequently, the truth of the implication/implicated clause of $\mathbb{T}$ for a given day (or time granule). But if we consider the week as the new time granule, we cannot interpret as true or false the proposition "e by p% during week n" and, consequently, not the truth of the implication/implicated clause of $\mathbb{T}_{new}$ either. So the classical definition of confidence for a rule is no more effective for this new time scale and a new, more appropriate definition of confidence must be introduced. Second, if we consider, in the context of week as time granule, the new event "**weekly increase**" (denoted e^*), then we may retrieve the classical definition of confidence for the rule ($\mathbb{T}_{new}$) if it were possible to check the truth of the proposition "e^* by p% during week n". As a remark, the value of truth for this proposition cannot be checked in the initial context (day as time granule) simply because e^* does not exist here. The new event may be seen as an *aggregation* of basic events of type e (considering, for example, the rate of the weekly increase as the mean of all daily increase rates, during the week). Therefore, a formula linking the truth values of the basic events with the truth value of the aggregated event must be introduced. And it is also clear that proposing either a new

definition for the confidence measure or formulae linking the truth value of the same event in worlds with different granularities cannot be made outside of a coherent, logical framework.

1.1 Previous work

Although there is a rich literature concerning the formalism for temporal databases, there are few articles on this topic for temporal data mining. In Al-Naemi (1994); Chen & Petrounias (1998); Malerba et al. (2001), general frameworks for temporal mining are proposed, but usually the research on causal and temporal rules is more concentrated on the methodological/algorithmic aspect and less on the formal aspect. An innovative formalism based on first-order temporal logic, which permits an abstract view on temporal rules, was proposed in Cotofrei & Stoffel (2005). The central concept defined in this formalism is the property of *consistency* for a linear time structure M, which guarantees the preservation over time of the confidence/support of a temporal rule (defined as the limit of a given sequence). The formalism was developed around a time model in which the events are those that describe system evolution.

But the real world systems are systems whose components (events) have dynamic behavior regulated by very different – even by magnitude – time granularities. Analyzing such systems (hereinafter, granular systems) means approaching theories and methodologies that make use of granules (or groups, clusters of a universe) in the process of problem solving. Granular computing (the label which covers this approach) is a way of thinking that relies on our ability to perceive the real world under various grain sizes, to abstract and to consider only those things that serve our present interest, and to switch among different granularities. By focusing on different levels of granularities, we can obtain various levels of knowledge, as well as inherent knowledge structure. Granular computing is essential to human problem solving, and hence has a very significant impact on the design and implementation of intelligent systems, as in Yao & Zhong (1999); Zadeh (1998); Lin & Louie (2002).

The notions of granularity and abstraction are used in many subfields of artificial intelligence. The granulation of time and space leads naturally to temporal and spatial granularities. They play an important role in temporal and spatial reasoning (Euzenat, 1995; Hornsby, 2001; Combi et al., 2004). Based on granularity and abstraction, many authors studied fundamental topics in artificial intelligence, such as knowledge representation (Zhang & Zhang, 1992), search (Zhang & Zhang, 2003), natural language understanding (Mani, 1998) or machine learning (Saitta & Zucker, 1998). Concerning data mining tasks, Bettini et al. (Bettini, Wang, Jajodia & Lin, 1998; Bettini, Wang & Jajodia, 1998a;b) investigated the formal relationships among event structures having temporal constraints, defined the pattern-discovery problem with these structures and studied effective algorithms to solve it.

To include the concept of time granularity in the initial formalism, we defined (Cotofrei & Stoffel, 2009) a process by which a given structure of time granules μ (called temporal type) induces a first-order linear time structure M_μ (called granular world) on the basic (or absolute) linear time structure M. The major change for the temporal logic based on M_μ is at the semantic level: for a formula p, the interpretation does no more assign a meaning of truth (one of the values $\{true, false\}$), but a degree of truth (a real value from $[0,1]$). By an extension at the syntactic and semantic level, we were able to define an aggregation mechanism for events reflecting the following intuitive phenomenon: in a coarser world, not all events inherited from a finer world are satisfied, but in exchange, there are new events which become satisfiable.

A deeper analysis of how these results may be applied to make predictions (i.e., the issues related to temporal rules evolution due to changes in data time scale) shows the limitation of the pure logical approach to solve some open questions. One of these questions is to what extent is it possible to guarantee the existence of the support for an aggregated event, and consequently, the consistency of a given granular world? A second question is linked to the way in which a temporal rule implying aggregated events can be used to make predictions in a granular world.

Unfortunately, the answers to these questions cannot be given inside the granular temporal logic formalism we developed, because the existence of the limit cannot be proven. The solution we propose in this paper consists of adding a probabilistic dimension to the granular formalism using the stochastic approach introduced in Cotofrei & Stoffel (2007). This extension was put forward in response to the difficulty of checking the consistency property for a linear time structure M (which involves verifying the existence of the support for *each* well-defined formula). By providing a probability system to the set of states S, we could define a stochastic linear time structure such that for each realization of the stochastic sequence $\psi(\omega)$ obtained by randomly drawing a point ω in $S^{\mathbb{N}}$, there is a corresponding (ordinary) linear time structure M_ω. The key answer to the consistency question is the equivalence, as we proved, between the existence of the support for a given formula p and the property of a particular stochastic sequence to obey the strong law of large numbers (SLLN). The sequence corresponding to p (*characteristic sequence*) is constructed, using appropriate transformations, from the stochastic sequence ψ.

This stochastic layer added to the temporal granular logic allows us to define a unified framework (the *stochastic granular time formalism*) in which many of the initially defined concepts become consequences of the properties of a fundamental stochastic structure. Among the results we will prove in the paper based on this formalism we may cite the theorems concerning the existence of the consistency property for any granular time structure induced from a stochastic structure $\mathbb{M}$ under the hypothesis that the random process ψ contains a certain amount of dependence (i.i.d, α-mixing or L_2-NED). These results are stronger than those obtained in the framework of the classical temporal granular logic, due to the fact that in a probabilistic framework we may apply fundamental results which go beyond a simple algebraic manipulation. Furthermore, we could prove the consistency property based only on the requirement that the function giving the interpretation of a temporal formula is a Borel transformation. Concerning the support of an aggregate event, we could establish that the characteristic sequence for this type of event is obtained by applying a particular type of transformation, which asks certain restrictions for the temporal type. Beside these theoretical results, the rationale we followed to prove them emphasizes the main advantage of the stochastic approach: the possibility of inferring, from specific properties of a stochastic process, the existence of different types of consistency, defined based on user necessity.

The structure of the chapter is as follows. In the next section, the main terms (*temporal event, temporal rule*) and concepts (*support, consistency, confidence*) of the first-order temporal logic formalism are described. The definitions and theorems concerning the extension of the formalism towards a temporal granular logic are presented in Sec. 3, whereas the limits of these results from a practical viewpoint and the proposed solution to overcome these issues (the stochastic extension) are described in the following section. Finally, the last section summarizes the work and proposes some promising future developments.

2. Logical formalism of temporal rules

Time is ubiquitous in information systems, but the mode of representation/perception varies in function of the purpose of the analysis (Chomicki & Toman, 1997; Emerson, 1990). The temporal ontology, on which the logical formalism introduced in Cotofrei & Stoffel (2004; 2005) was constructed, is represented by linearly ordered discrete instants. Syntactically, all the terms and formulae are defined over a restricted first-order temporal language $\mathbb{L}$ containing constant symbols, n-ary function symbols, variable symbols $\{y_1, y_2, ...\}$, n-ary predicate symbols ($n \geq 1$), the set of relational symbols $\{=, <, \leq, >, \geq\}$, the logical connective $\wedge$ and a temporal connective of the form ∇_k, $k \in \mathbb{Z}$, where k strictly positive means *after k time instants*, k strictly negative means *before k time instant* and $k = 0$ means *now*.
A Horn clause cannot be expressed in $\mathbb{L}$ because the logical connective $\rightarrow$ is not included. However, to allow the description of rules, which formally look like Horn clauses, a new logical connective, $\mapsto$, was introduced (in practical terms, it is a rewrite of the connective $\wedge$). The next definitions introduce the main types of formulae (based on known concepts from temporal data mining) and the conditions allowing the use of the new connective.

Definition 1 *An event (or temporal atom) is an atom formed by the predicate symbol E followed by a bracketed n-tuple of terms ($n \geq 1$) $E(t_1, t_2, \ldots, t_n)$. The first term of the tuple, t_1, is a constant symbol representing the name of the event, and all others terms are expressed according to the rule $t_i = f(t_{i1}, \ldots, t_{ik_i})$.*

Definition 2 *A constraint formula for the event $E(t_1, \ldots t_n)$ is a conjunctive compound formula, $E(t_1, t_2, \ldots t_n) \wedge C_1 \wedge \cdots \wedge C_k$. Each C_j is a relational atom $t \rho c$, where the term t is one of the terms $t_i, i = 1 \ldots n$, the term c is a constant symbol and ρ a relational symbol.*

Definition 3 *A temporal rule in standard form is a formula of the form $H_1 \wedge \cdots \wedge H_m \mapsto H_{m+1}$, where H_{m+1} is a constraint formula prefixed by ∇_0 and $H_i, i = 1..m$ are constraint formulae, prefixed by the temporal connectives ∇_{-k}, $k > 0$. The maximum value of the index k is called the time window of the temporal rule.*

Remark. The reason for which the implication connective was not included in $\mathbb{L}$ is related to the truth table for a formula $p \rightarrow q$: even if p is false, the formula is still true, which is unacceptable for a temporal rationing of the form *cause$\rightarrow$ effect*.
If all the terms $t_i, i = 1 \ldots n$, from the expression of a temporal atom, constraint formula or temporal rule are represented by variable symbols (and not by constant symbols), then the new formula is denoted a temporal atom template $E(y_1, \ldots, y_n)$ (respectively, a constraint formula template or temporal rule template). These templates are considered as general patterns for events or temporal rules. Practically, the only formulae constructed in $\mathbb{L}$ are temporal atoms, constraint formulae, temporal rules and the corresponding templates.
The semantics of $\mathbb{L}$ is provided by an interpretation **I** over a domain **D**. The interpretation assigns an appropriate meaning over **D** to the (non-logical) symbols of $\mathbb{L}$. Based on Definition 1, an event can be seen as a labelled (constant symbol t_1) sequence of points extracted from raw data and characterized by a finite set of features (terms $t_2, \cdots, t_n$). Consequently, the domain **D** is the union $\mathbf{D}_e \cup \mathbf{D}_f$, where the set $\mathbf{D}_e$ contains all the strings used as event names and the set $\mathbf{D}_f$ represents the union of all domains corresponding to chosen features. But a temporal logic cannot be defined without a structure having a temporal dimension and capable of capturing the relationship between a time moment and the interpretation **I** at this moment.

Definition 4 *Given $\mathbb{L}$ and a domain $\mathbf{D}$, a (first order) linear time structure is a triple $M = (S, x, \mathbf{I})$, where S is a set of states, $x : \mathbb{N} \rightarrow S$ is an infinite sequence of states $(s_1, s_2, \ldots, s_n, \ldots)$ and $\mathbf{I}$ is a function that associates with each state s an interpretation $\mathbf{I}_s$ of all symbols from $\mathbb{L}$.*

In the framework of a linear temporal logic, the set of symbols is divided into two classes: the class of global symbols (having the same interpretation in each state) and the class of local symbols (the interpretation depends on the state in which they are evaluated). The formalism of temporal rules assumes that all function symbols (including constants) and all relational symbols are global, whereas the predicate symbols and variable symbols are local. Consequently, the meaning of truth for any temporal atom, constraint formula, temporal rule or corresponding template depends on the state at which they are evaluated. Given a first order time structure M and a formula p, the instant i (or equivalently, the state s_i) for which $\mathbf{I}_{s_i}(p) = true$ is denoted by $i \models p$. Therefore, $i \models E(t_1, \ldots, t_n)$ means that at time i an event with the name $\mathbf{I}(t_1)$ and characterized by the global features $\mathbf{I}(t_2), \ldots, \mathbf{I}(t_n)$ occurs. Concerning the event template $E(y_1, \ldots, y_n)$, the interpretation of the variable symbols y_j at the state s_i, $\mathbf{I}_{s_i}(y_j)$, is chosen such that $i \models E(y_1, \ldots, y_n)$ for each time moment i. Finally, $i \models \nabla_k p$ if and only if $i + k \models p$, whereas a temporal rule (template) is true at time i if and only if $i \models H_{m+1}$ and $i \models (H_1 \wedge \cdots \wedge H_m)$.
The connection between the restricted first-order temporal logic and the temporal data mining task this logic tries to formalize (temporal rules extraction) is given by the following assumptions:

A. For each formula p in $\mathbb{L}$, there is an algorithm that calculates the value of the interpretation $\mathbf{I}_s(p)$, for each state s, in a finite number of steps.

B. There are states (called incomplete states) that do not contain enough information to calculate the interpretation for all formulae defined at these states.

C. It is possible to establish a measure (called *general interpretation*) about the degree of truth of a compound formula along the entire sequence of states $(s_0, s_1, .., s_n, .)$.

The first assumption expresses the calculability of the interpretation **I**. The second assumption expresses the situation (e.g., due to missing data) when only the body of a temporal rule can be evaluated at a time moment i, but not the head of the rule. Therefore, for the state s_i, the interpretation of the temporal rule cannot be calculated, and the only solution (expressed by the third assumption) is to estimate it using a general interpretation. However, to ensure that this general interpretation is well-defined, the linear time structure must present some property of consistency. In practical terms, this means that the conclusions inferred from a sufficiently large subset of time instants are sufficiently close to those inferred from the entire set of time instants. Therefore,

Definition 5 *A structure M is called* ***consistent linear time structure*** *for $\mathbb{L}$ if, for every formula p, the limit $supp(p) = \lim_{n \rightarrow \infty} n^{-1} \# A$ exists, where # means "cardinality" and $A = \{i = 1..n \mid i \models p\}$. The notation $supp(p)$ denotes the support (of truth) of p.*

Consequently, if M is a consistent time structure, the general interpretation - seen as a function taking values in $[0,1]$ - is well-defined for any formula p defined in $\mathbb{L}$, by the relation $I_G(p) = \text{supp}(p)$. There is another useful measure, called *confidence*, but available only for temporal rules (templates). This measure is calculated as a limit ratio between the number of certain applications (time instants where both the body and the head of the rule are evaluated

as true) and the number of potential applications (time instants where only the body of the rule is evaluated as true). Furthermore, it can be proved that, for a consistent structure, the confidence is the ratio between the support of the entire rule and the support, not null, of its body.
If, for different reasons (e.g., the states the user has access to are incomplete or are missing), the support measure cannot be calculated, then a possible solution is to estimate $\text{supp}(p)$ using a finite linear time structure, i.e. a model.

Definition 6 *Given L and a consistent time structure $M = (S, x, \mathbf{I})$, a model for M is a structure $\tilde{M} = (\tilde{T}, \tilde{x})$ where $\tilde{T}$ is a finite temporal domain $\{i_1, \ldots, i_n\}$, $\tilde{x}$ is the subsequence of states $\{x_{i_1}, \ldots, x_{i_n}\}$ (the restriction of x to the temporal domain $\tilde{T}$) and for each $i_j, j = 1, \ldots, n$, the state x_{i_j} is a complete state.*

This particular structure can be used to obtain an estimator for the support measure ($\text{supp}(p, \tilde{M}) = \#\tilde{T}^{-1}\#\{i \in \tilde{T} \mid i \models p\}$) or for the confidence measure ($\text{conf}(H, \tilde{M}) = \#B^{-1}\#A$, where $A = \{i \in \tilde{T} \mid i \models H_1 \wedge \cdots \wedge H_m \wedge H_{m+1}\}$ and $B = \{i \in \tilde{T} \mid i \models H_1 \wedge \cdots \wedge H_m\}$).
EXAMPLE 1. Consider raw data representing the price variations (six daily records) of a given stock and suppose that a particular methodology for event detection reveals two types of potentially useful events. The output of the methodology is a database of events, where each tuple (v_1, v_2) with record index i expresses the event occurring at time moment i, labeled (v_1 value) with one of the strings $\{increse, decrease\}$ and characterized (v_2 value) by the feature given by the mean of the daily records. In the frame of the temporal logic formalism, the language $\mathbb{L}$ will contain a 2-ary predicate symbol E, two variable symbols y_1, y_2, a 6-ary function symbol f, two sets of constant symbols – $\{d_1, d_2\}$ and $\{c_1, \ldots, c_n\}$ – and the usual set of relational symbols and logical (temporal) connectives. According to the syntactic rules of $\mathbb{L}$, a temporal atom is defined as $E(d_i, f(c_{j_1}, .., c_{j_6}))$, an event template as $E(y_1, y_2)$, whereas a possible temporal rule ($\mathcal{H}$) is

$$E(t_1, t_2) \wedge (t_1 = increase) \wedge (t_2 \leq 5) \mapsto \nabla_1(E(t_1, t_2) \wedge (t_1 = decrease) \wedge (t_2 \geq 3))$$

("translated" in a natural language as "IF at time t the price increases in average with at most five units THEN at time $t+1$ the price decreases in average with at least 3 units"). A linear time structure $M = (S, x, \mathbf{I})$ may be defined by considering the set S as the set of all distinct tuples from the event database and the sequence x as the ordered sequence of tuples in the database (see Table 1). At this stage the interpretation of all symbols (global and local) can be defined. For the global symbols, the interpretation is quite intuitive: the meaning $\mathbf{I}(d_1)$ is *increase*, $\mathbf{I}(d_2)$ is *decrease* and $\mathbf{I}(f)$ is the function $f : R^6 \mapsto R, f(x_1, \ldots x_6) = 1/6 \sum_{i=1}^{6} x_i$. For the predicate symbol E, the function $\mathbf{I}_{s_i}(E(t_1, t_2)) : D \to \{true, false\}$ is provided by a finite algorithm, receiving as input the state $s_i = (v_1, v_2)$ and providing as output the value *true* if $\mathbf{I}_{s_i}(t_j) = v_j$ for all $j = 1..2$ and *false* otherwise. If M is a consistent linear time structure having a model $\tilde{M}$ given by the first n states from the sequence x, then the finite structure $\tilde{M}$ can be used to estimate the confidence of the temporal rule $\mathcal{H}$ (based on the first ten states, this estimation is 2/5). And, due to the consistency property, this degree of confidence is reliable information about the prediction power of this rule when applied to future data.

v_1	increase	increase	decrease	increase	increase	increase	decrease	increase	decrease	decrease
v_2	3	5	5	1	8	4	2	4	3	2

Table 1. The first ten states of the linear time structure M

3. The granularity model

The inherent granularity of time implies necessary granular-dependent structure of knowledge extracted by any general temporal data mining methodology. Once the framework in which temporal data is analyzed accepts the dynamic of time scale change, natural questions arise, such as how temporal rule interpretations related to different levels of granularities are connected, or when the consistency property is preserved under time scale changes. In order to find answers to these issues, we extended the initial "static" formalism to include the concept of time granularity (Cotofrei & Stoffel, 2009) by defining a process from which a given structure of time granules μ (called temporal type) induces a first-order linear time structure M_μ (called granular world) on the basic (or absolute) linear time structure M. The concept of a temporal type, formalizing the notion of time granularity, was introduced by Bettini, Wang & Jajodia (1998a).

Definition 7 *Let $(\mathcal{T},<)$ (index) be a linearly ordered temporal domain isomorphic to a subset of integers with the usual order relation, and let $(\mathcal{A},<)$ (absolute time) be a linearly ordered set. Then a temporal type on $(\mathcal{T},\mathcal{A})$ is a mapping μ from $\mathcal{T}$ to $2^{\mathcal{A}}$ such that*

1. *$\mu(i) \neq \emptyset$ and $\mu(j) \neq \emptyset$, where $i<j$, imply that each element in $\mu(i)$ is less than all the elements in $\mu(j)$,*
2. *for all $i<j$, if $\mu(i) \neq \emptyset$ and $\mu(j) \neq \emptyset$, then $\forall k, i<k<j$ implies $\mu(k) \neq \emptyset$.*

Each set $\mu(i)$, if non-empty, is called a granule of μ. Property (1) says that granules do not overlap and that the order on indexes follows the order on the corresponding granules. Property (2) disallows an empty set to be the value of a mapping for a certain index value if a lower index and a higher index are mapped to non-empty sets.
When considering a particular application or formal context, we can specialize this very general model along in different directions, as the choice of the sets $\mathcal{T}$ or $\mathcal{A}$, or the restrictions on the structure of granules. We call the resulting formalization a *temporal type system*. Also following Bettini, Wang & Jajodia (1998a), a number of interesting relationships between two temporal types, μ and ν, on $(\mathcal{T},\mathcal{A})$, are defined.

A. *Finer-than*: μ is said to be finer than ν, denoted $\mu \preccurlyeq \nu$, if $\forall i \in \mathcal{T}, \exists j \in \mathcal{T}$ such that $\mu(i) \subseteq \nu(j)$.
B. *Groups-into*: μ is said to group into ν, denoted $\mu \trianglelefteq \nu$, if $\forall \nu(j) \neq \emptyset, \exists S \subset \mathcal{T}$ such that $\nu(j) = \bigcup_{i \in S} \mu(i)$.
C. *Shifting*: μ and ν are said to be shifting equivalent, denoted $\mu_1 \rightleftharpoons \mu_2$, if there is a bijective function $h : \mathcal{T} \rightarrow \mathcal{T}$ such that $\mu(i) = \nu(h(i))$, for all $i \in \mathcal{T}$.

When a temporal type μ is finer than a temporal type ν, we also say that ν is *coarser* than μ. The *finer-than* relationship formalizes the notion of finer partitions of the absolute time. This relation is reflexive, transitive, but if no restrictions are given, it is not antisymmetric, and hence it is not a partial order. Considering the *groups-into* relation, $\mu \trianglelefteq \nu$ ensures that for each granule of μ there exists a set of granules of ν covering exactly the same span of time. The *groups-into* relation has the same properties as the *finer-than* relation, but generally $\mu \preccurlyeq \nu$ does not imply $\mu \trianglelefteq \nu$ or vice-versa. Finally, *shifting* is clearly an equivalence relation. But by considering only temporal type systems satisfying the restriction that no pair of different types can be shifting equivalent, we obtain a class of systems for which the relationships $\preccurlyeq$ and $\trianglelefteq$ are partial order, i.e, are reflexive, transitive and antisymmetric.

Let $\mathcal{G}_0$ denote the set of temporal types for which the index set and the absolute time set are isomorphic with the set of positive natural numbers, i.e. $\mathcal{A} = \mathcal{T} = \mathbb{N}$. Consider now the following particular subsets of $\mathcal{G}_0$, represented by temporal types with a) non-empty granules, b) with granules covering all the absolute time and c) with constant size granules:

$$\mathcal{G}_1 = \{\mu \in \mathcal{G}_0 \,|\, \forall i \in \mathbb{N}, 0 < \#\mu(i)\} \tag{1}$$

$$\mathcal{G}_2 = \{\mu \in \mathcal{G}_1 \,|\, \forall i \in \mathbb{N}, \mu(i)^{-1} \neq 0\} \tag{2}$$

$$\mathcal{G}_3 = \{\mu \in \mathcal{G}_2 \,|\, \forall i \in \mathbb{N}, \mu(i) = c_\mu\} \tag{3}$$

The membership of a temporal type defined by one of these subsets implies very useful properties, the most important being:

$$\mu, \nu \in \mathcal{G}_2 \Longrightarrow \mu \preccurlyeq \nu \Leftrightarrow \mu \trianglelefteq \nu. \tag{4}$$

If $M = (S, x, \mathbf{I})$ is a first-order linear time structure, then let the absolute time $\mathcal{A}$ be given by the sequence x, by identifying the time moment i with the state $s_{(i)}$ (on the ith position in the sequence). If μ is a temporal type from $\mathcal{G}_2$, then the temporal granule $\mu(i)$ may be identified with the set $\{s_j \in S \,|\, j \in \mu(i)\}$. Therefore, the temporal type μ induces a new sequence, x_μ, defined as $x_\mu : \mathbb{N} \to 2^S$, $x_\mu(i) = \mu(i)$. Consider now the linear time structure derived from M, $M_\mu = (2^S, x_\mu, \mathbf{I}^\mu)$. To be well-defined, we must give the interpretation $\mathbf{I}^\mu_{\mu(i)}$ for each $i \in \mathbb{N}$. Because for a fixed i the set $\mu(i)$ is a finite sequence of states, it defines (if all the states are complete states) a model $\tilde{M}_{\mu(i)}$ for M. Therefore, the estimated support measure exists, and we consider, by definition, that for a temporal free formula (which does not contains any ∇ operator, e.g. a temporal atom) p in $\mathbb{L}$

$$\mathbf{I}^\mu_{\mu(i)}(p) = \text{supp}(p, \tilde{M}_{\mu(i)}) \tag{5}$$

This interpretation is extended to any temporal formula in $\mathbb{L}$ according to the rule:

$$\mathbf{I}^\mu_{\mu(i)}(\nabla_{k_1} p_1 \wedge \ldots \wedge \nabla_{k_n} p_n) = \frac{1}{n} \sum_{j=1}^{n} \mathbf{I}^\mu_{\mu(i+k_j)}(p_j) \tag{6}$$

where p_i are temporal free formulae and $k_i \in \mathbb{Z}, i = 1 \ldots n$.

Definition 8 *If $M = (S, x, \mathbf{I})$ is a first-order linear time structure and μ is a temporal type from $\mathcal{G}_2$, then the linear granular time structure induced by μ on M is the triple $M_\mu = (2^S, x_\mu, \mathbf{I}^\mu)$, where $x_\mu : \mathbb{N} \to 2^S$, $x_\mu(i) = \mu(i)$ and $\mathbf{I}^\mu$ is a function that associates with almost each set of states $\mu(i)$ an interpretation $\mathbf{I}^\mu_{\mu(i)}$ according to rules (5)-(6).*

3.1 Linking two granular structures

All the granular time structures induced by a temporal type have in common interpretations which take values in [0,1] if applied to formulae in $\mathbb{L}$. This observation allows us to establish relationships linking the interpretations $\mathbf{I}^\mu$ and $\mathbf{I}^\nu$, from two linear granular time structures induced by μ and ν, when there exists a relationship *finer-than* ($\mu \preccurlyeq \nu$) between these two temporal types. The key for establishing such a relation is given by property 4, which guarantees that for each $i \in \mathbb{N}$ there is a subset $N_i \subset \mathbb{N}$ such that $\nu(i) = \bigcup_{j \in N_i} \mu(j)$. As we proved in Cotofrei & Stoffel (2009), the capacity to "transfer" information (here, formula interpretation) from a finer world to a coarser one depends strictly on the nature of information.

- The **time independent** part of information may be "transferred" between two granular worlds, i.e. knowing the interpretation of an event in a finer structure allows the calculation of its interpretation (degree of truth) in each coarser structure (see Theorem 1).
- The **time dependent** part of information can't be "transferred" without loss between two granular worlds, and concerns especially the interpretation of temporal rules (see Theorem 2). One consequence of this theorem is that all the information related to temporal formulae having a time window less than k (where k is the coefficient of conversion between the two worlds) is lost during the transition to the coarser world.

Theorem 1 *If μ, ν are temporal types from $\mathcal{G}_2$ such that $\mu \preccurlyeq \nu$, and $\boldsymbol{I}^\mu, \boldsymbol{I}^\nu$ are the interpretations from the induced linear time structures M_μ and M_ν on M, then $\forall i \in \mathbb{N}$,*

$$\boldsymbol{I}^\nu_{\nu(i)}(p) = \frac{1}{\#\nu(i)} \sum_{j \in N_i} \#\mu(j) \boldsymbol{I}^\mu_{\mu(j)}(p), \tag{7}$$

where N_i is the subset of $\mathbb{N}$ satisfying $\nu(i) = \bigcup_{j \in N_i} \mu(j)$ and p is a temporal free formula in $\mathbb{L}$.

Theorem 2 *If M_μ, M_ν are granular time structures induced by $\mu, \nu \in \mathcal{G}_3$ (constant size granular worlds), $\mu \preccurlyeq \nu$, then $\forall i \in \mathbb{N}$,*

$$\boldsymbol{I}^\nu_{\nu(i)}(\nabla_{k_1} p_1 \wedge ... \nabla_{k_n} p_n) = \frac{1}{k} \sum_{j \in N_i} \boldsymbol{I}^\mu_{\mu(j)} \mathbb{Z}_k(\nabla_{k_1} p_1 \wedge ... \nabla_{k_n} p_n)) \tag{8}$$

where $k = c_\nu / c_\mu$, $\nu(i) = \bigcup_{j \in N_i} \mu(j)$, p_i, $i = 1..n$, are temporal free formulae in $\mathbb{L}$ and $\mathbb{Z}_k$ is the operator defined over the set of formulae in $\mathbb{L}$, as $\mathbb{Z}_k(\nabla_{k_1} p_1 \wedge \ldots \wedge \nabla_{k_n} p_n) = \nabla_{k \cdot k_1} p_1 \wedge \ldots \wedge \nabla_{k \cdot k_n} p_n$.

3.2 The consistency problem

The importance of the concepts of consistency, support and confidence (see Sec. 2) for the process of information transfer between worlds with different granularity may be highlighted by analyzing the analogous expressions for a linear granular time structure M_μ.

Definition 9 *Given $\mathbb{L}$ and a linear granular time structure M_μ on M, we say that M_μ is a consistent granular time structure if, for every formula p, the limit $supp(p, M_\mu) = \lim_{n \to \infty} \frac{1}{n} \sum_{i=1}^{n} \boldsymbol{I}^\mu_{\mu(i)}(p)$ exists. The notation $supp(p, M_\mu)$ denotes the support (degree of truth) of p under M_μ.*

A natural question concerns the inheritance of the consistency property from the basic linear time structure M by the induced time structure M_μ. The answer is formalized in the following theorem (see (Cotofrei & Stoffel, 2009) for proof).

Theorem 3 *If M is a consistent time structure and $\mu \in \mathcal{G}_3$ then the granular time structure M_μ is also consistent.*

The implications of Theorem 3 are extremely important, because by defining the confidence of a temporal rule $\mathcal{H}$, $H_1 \wedge \ldots \wedge H_m \mapsto H_{m+1}$ over a consistent granular time structure M_μ as:

$$\text{conf}(\mathcal{H}, M_\mu) = \frac{\text{supp}(H_1 \wedge \ldots \wedge H_m \wedge H_{m+1}, M_\mu)}{\text{supp}(H_1 \wedge \ldots \wedge H_m, M_\mu)} \tag{9}$$

we could prove the corollary that the confidence of $\mathcal{H}$, over any granular time structure M_μ induced on a consistent time structure M by a temporal type $\mu \in \mathcal{G}_3$, **exists and is independent of** μ. In other words, the property of consistency is a sufficient condition for the independence of the measure of support/confidence, during the process of information transfer between worlds with different granularities, all derived from an absolute world using constant conversion factors. In practice, this means that even if we are not able to establish, for a given granule $\mu(i)$ in a given world M_μ, the degree of truth for the temporal rule $\mathcal{H}$, we are sure that the confidence of $\mathcal{H}$, given by (9), is the same in each world $M_\mu, \forall \mu \in \mathcal{G}_3$.

3.3 Events aggregation

Another inherent phenomenon accompanying the process of transition between two real worlds with different time granularities is related to the creation of new kinds of significant events. Intuitively, a new event is obtained by applying a kind of "aggregation" mechanism on a set of "similar" events. Formally we need to define the syntax and semantics of these concepts.

We introduce the notion of event type (denoted $E[t]$) as the set of all temporal atoms from $\mathbb{L}$ having the same name (or head). Consider $E(t,t_2,\ldots,t_n) \in E[t]$. According to Definition 1, a term $t_i, i \in \{2,..,n\}$ has the form $t_i = f(t_{i1},\ldots,t_{ik_i})$. Suppose now that for each index i the function symbol f from the expression of t_i belongs to a family of function symbols with different arities, denoted $\mathcal{F}_i[t]$ (so different sets for different event types $E[t]$ and different index i). $\mathcal{F}_i[t]$ has the property that the interpretation for each of its members is given by a real function which is applied to a variable number of arguments, and is invariant in the order of arguments. A good example of a such real function is a statistical function, e.g. $\text{mean}(x_1,..,x_n)$. Let $T_i[t]$ be the set of terms expressed as $f_k(c_1,\ldots,c_k)$, where f_k is a function symbol from $\mathcal{F}_i[t]$ and c_j are constant symbols. Consider now the following two operators, $\oplus : T_i[t] \times T_i[t] \to T_i[t]$ and $\boxplus : E[t] \times E[t] \to E[t]$ such that:

$$f_n(c_1,..,c_n) \oplus f_m(d_1,..,d_m) = f_{n+m}(c_1,..,c_n,d_1,..,d_m)$$
$$E(t,t_2,..,t_n) \boxplus E(t,t'_2,..,t'_n) = E(t,t_2 \oplus t'_2,..,t_n \oplus t'_n)$$

Obviously the operators $\oplus$ and $\boxplus$ are commutative and associative. Therefore, we can apply the operator $\boxplus$ on a subset $\mathcal{E}$ of temporal atoms from $E[t]$ and denote the result as $\boxplus_{e_i \in \mathcal{E}} e_i$.

By definition, a formula p is satisfied by a linear time structure $M = (S,x,\mathbf{I})$ (or by a model $\tilde{M}$ of M) if there is at least a state $s_i \in x$ (respectively in $\tilde{x}$) such that $\mathbf{I}_{s_i}(p) = true$. Therefore, the set of events of type t satisfied by M is given by $E[t]_M = \{e \in E[t] \mid \exists s_i \in x, \mathbf{I}_{s_i}(e) = true\}$. Similarly, the set of events of type t satisfied by M_μ (the structure induced by μ on M) is defined as $E[t]_{M_\mu} = \{e \in E[t] \mid \exists \mu_i \in x_\mu, \mathbf{I}^{\mu}_{\mu(i)}(e) = 1\}$. Generally $E[t]_M \supset E[t]_{M_\mu} \supset E[t]_{M_\nu}$, for $\mu \preccurlyeq \nu$, which is a consequence of the fact that a coarser world satisfies less temporal events than a finer one. At the same time a coarser world may satisfy new events, representing a kind of aggregation of local, "finer" events.

Definition 10 *If $\mu \in \mathcal{G}_2$ then the aggregate event of type t induced by the subset of satisfied events $\mathcal{A} \subset E[t]_M$ (denoted $e[t]_\mathcal{A}$) is the event obtained by applying the operator $\boxplus$ on the set of events from $\mathcal{A}$, i.e.*

$$e[t]_\mathcal{A} = \boxplus_{e_i \in \mathcal{A}} e_i \tag{10}$$

Of a practical interest is the aggregate event induced by the subset $\mathcal{A}$ containing all the events of type t satisfied by a model $\tilde{M}_{\mu(i)}$ (for a given i) denoted $e[t]_{\mu(i)}$. According to (5), the interpretation of an event e in any world M_μ depends on the interpretation of the same event in M. Therefore, if e is not satisfied by M it is obvious that $\mathbf{I}^{\mu}_{\mu(i)}(e) = 0$, for all μ and all $i \in \mathbb{N}$. Because an aggregate event (conceived as a new, "federative" event) is not usually satisfied by M, the relation (5) is not appropriate to give the degree of truth for $e[t]_{\mu(i)}$. By restricting to linear time structures M satisfying the condition that two different events of type t cannot be evaluated as *true* at the same state $s \in S$, the formula expressing the interpretation for an aggregate temporal atom is given by the following definition:

Definition 11 *If M_μ is a linear granular time structure ($\mu \in \mathcal{G}_2$) and $e[t]_{\mathcal{A}}$ is an aggregate event, then the interpretation of $e[t]_{\mathcal{A}}$ in the state $\mu(i)$ is defined as:*

$$\mathbf{I}^{\mu}_{\mu(i)}(e[t]_{\mathcal{A}}) = \frac{\#(\mathcal{E}_i \cap \mathcal{A})}{\#\mathcal{A}} \sum_{e_j \in \mathcal{A}} \mathbf{I}^{\mu}_{\mu(i)}(e_j) \tag{11}$$

where $\mathcal{E}_i = E[t]_{\tilde{M}_{\mu(i)}}$.

The restriction is necessary to assure that the interpretation of an aggregate event is well-defined, i.e. $\mathbf{I}^{\mu}_{\mu(i)}(e[t]_{\mathcal{A}}) \leq 1$. Furthermore, the interpretation is equal one if and only if all (and only these) satisfied events of type t from $\mathcal{A}$ are also satisfied by $\tilde{M}_{\mu_i}$.

4. Temporal rules in a granular world: toward a stochastic approach

The theoretical framework used to define a linear granular time structure allowed us to prove some nice mathematical results, as the heritage of the consistency property by the worlds with constant granule size, or the independence regarding μ of the confidence measure for a temporal rule over a world M_μ. But if we return to the "real world" and reflect on how these results could be practically applied, we found a number of issues which cannot be avoided. To start our reasoning, let's consider another more simple temporal rule $\mathcal{H}$, defined in the context of Example 1 (according to the described context, the absolute unit time of the linear time structure M is "day"). Suppose that the confidence of this rule (in a natural language, it says that *"IF today there is a daily increase in average of five percent THEN tomorrow will be a daily decrease in average of three percent"*) is 0.6. Consider now the granular time structure M_μ, induced on M by $\mu(i) =$ week i (constant granule size equals five).

- **First issue: the temporal rule meaning.** The rule in the new context M_μ (translated as *"IF this week there is a **daily** increase in average of five percent THEN the next week will be a **daily** decrease in average of three percents"*) is lacking utility, due to the fact that the events $E(t_1, t_2)$, even if formally theorem 1 permits them to calculate their interpretation for each week granule, reflects well the system behavior only for a time scale using days as basic granules. A *"**daily** increase in average of five percent during a week"* has no meaning, except the particular case where in *each* day of the week there is an increase in average of five percent. On the other hand, if during a given week there are three daily *increase* events in average of 5, 8 and 11 percent (and two daily *decrease* events in average of 3 and 1 percents), a natural way to define a meaningful event of type *increase* for a week granule is to consider a "weekly increase" with an average of $(5 + 8 + 11)/3 = 8$ percent (the feature is the mean function), with a degree of truth for this week equal to 3/5 (respectively a "weekly decrease" event with an average of $(3+1)/2 = 4$ percent). This is exactly the approach "events aggregation", introduced in Subsec. 3.3, which allows us to consider the new (now meaningful) rule $\mathcal{H}_{new}$: *"IF this week there is a **weekly** increase in average of eight percent THEN the next week will be a **weekly** decrease in average of two percent"*.

- **Second issue: predictive power.** If events aggregation (when applicable) represents a solution to obtain meaningful events for a given granular time structure, let's analyse how a temporal rule implying such events can be used to make predictions. In the world M, if the implication clause of $\mathcal{H}$ is true for a particular day, then we expect, with a confidence (probability) of 0.6, that the implicated clause will also be true the next day. The corollary of Theorem 3 assures us that the confidence – defined in (9) as a ratio of the degree of truth for all rule clauses/all implication clauses – of the rule $\mathcal{H}$ over the world M_μ exists. But the fact that in a particular week the implication clauses of $\mathcal{H}_{new}$ have a degree of truth equal to (lets say) 0.4 and that the confidence is (lets say) 0.8 does not allow us to infer any information about the degree of truth for the implicated clause. A useful way to employ the rule would be a rationing of type *"If the degree of truth for the implication clauses of $\mathcal{H}_{new}$ is at least (lets say) 0.7 for a particular week then we expect, with a confidence of 0.8, that the degree of truth of the implicated clause to be at least (lets say) 0.6 the next week"*. In order to be able to apply this inference schema we need a new definition for the confidence measure over a granular world, seen as the limit ratio between the number of granules where both the implication clauses and the implicated clause have a degree of truth greater than some chosen constants and the number of granules where only the implication clauses have a degree of truth greater than the chosen constant.

Definition 12 *Given M_μ a linear time structure on M and $\mathcal{H}$ a temporal rule $H_1 \wedge .. \wedge H_m \mapsto H_{m+1}$, the confidence (α,β) of $\mathcal{H}$, denoted $conf_{\alpha,\beta}(\mathcal{H},M_\mu)$, is the limit (if exists) $\lim_{n\to\infty}(\#B)^{-1}\#A$, where $A = \{i \le n | \mathbf{I}^{\mu}_{\mu(i)}(H_1 \wedge .. \wedge H_m) \ge \alpha, \mathbf{I}^{\mu}_{\mu(i)} H_{m+1} \ge \beta\}$ and $B = \{i \le n | \mathbf{I}^{\mu}_{\mu(i)}(H_1 \wedge .. \wedge H_m) \ge \alpha\}$, where $\alpha,\beta \in (0,1]$.*

At this moment two questions naturally arise: (1) If M_μ is consistent, does the support of an aggregate event exist? (2) If M_μ is consistent, does the confidence (α,β) for a temporal rule exist? Unfortunately, the answers to these questions cannot be given inside the granular temporal logic formalism we developed because the existence of the limits can't be proved. A possible solution is to extend this pure logical formalism using the stochastic approach introduced in Cotofrei & Stoffel (2007). This extension was proposed in response to the difficulty of checking the consistency property for a linear time structure M (which involves verifying the existence of the support for *each* well-defined formula), by deriving the consistency as an objective consequence of a specific property of a stochastic process.

4.1 The stochastic model

The key of the stochastic extension for a first order time structure $M = (S, x, \mathbf{I})$ is given by the observation that the sequence x may be considered as a particular realization of a stochastic process. Technically, this can be done by providing a probability system $(S, \sigma(S), P)$ for the set of states S. Indeed, if $S = \{s_0, s_1, \ldots\}$ is a countable set of states, consider $\sigma(S)$ the $\sigma-$algebra generated by S. The probability measure P on $\sigma(S)$ is defined such that $P(s_i) = p_i > 0, \forall i \in \mathbb{N}$. Consider now a random variable $\mathbb{X} : S \to \mathbb{R}$ such that the probability $P(\mathbb{X} = s_i) = p_i$ for all $i \in \mathbb{N}$. If $S^{\mathbb{N}} = \{\omega | \omega = (\omega_1, \omega_2, \ldots, \omega_t, \ldots), \omega_t \in S, t \in \mathbb{N}\}$, then the variable $\mathbb{X}$ induces the stochastic sequence $\psi : S^{\mathbb{N}} \to \mathbb{R}^{\mathbb{N}}$, where $\psi(\omega) = \{\mathbb{X}_t(\omega), t \in \mathbb{N}\}$ and $\mathbb{X}_t(\omega) = \mathbb{X}(\omega_t)$ for all

$t \in \mathbb{N}$. The fact that each $\omega \in S^{\mathbb{N}}$ may be uniquely identified with a function $x : \mathbb{N} \to S$ and that $\mathbb{X}$ is a bijection between S and $\mathbb{X}(S)$ allows us to uniquely identify the function x with a single realization of the stochastic sequence. In other words, the sequence $x = (s_{(1)}, s_{(2)}, \ldots, s_{(i)}, \ldots)$ from the structure M can be seen as one of the outcomes of an infinite sequence of experiments, each experiment being modelled by the probabilistic system $(S, \sigma(S), P)$.

Definition 13 *Given $\mathbb{L}$ and a domain D, a stochastic (first order) linear time structure is a quintuple $\mathbb{M} = (S, P, \mathbb{X}, \psi, \boldsymbol{I})$, where*

- *$S = \{s_1, s_2, \ldots\}$ is a (countable) set of states,*
- *P is a probability measure on the $\sigma-$algebra $\sigma(S)$ such that $P(s_i) = p_i > 0, i \in \mathbb{N}$*
- *$\mathbb{X}$ is a random variable such that $P(\mathbb{X} = s_i) = p_i$,*
- *ψ is a random sequence, $\psi(\omega) = \{\mathbb{X}(\omega_i)\}_1^\infty$ where $\omega \in S^{\mathbb{N}}$,*
- ***I** is a function that associates with each state s an interpretation $\boldsymbol{I}_s$ for all symbols from $\mathbb{L}$.*

To each realization of the stochastic sequence ψ, obtained by random drawing of a point in $\mathbb{R}^\infty$ (or equivalently, of a point ω in $S^{\mathbb{N}}$), corresponds a realization of the stochastic structure $\mathbb{M}$. This realization is given by the (ordinary) linear time structure $M_\omega = (S, \omega, \mathbf{I})$, which implies that the semantics attached to the symbols of $\mathbb{L}$, described in Section 2, is totally effective. Moreover, if p is a formula defined in language $\mathbb{L}$ and A_p the event[1] "the interpretation of the formula p is true", then

$$\overline{\mathbf{1}_{A_p n}}(\omega) = \frac{\sum_{t=1}^{n} \mathbf{1}_{A_p}(\omega_i)}{n} = \frac{\#\{i \leq n \mid \mathbf{1}_{A_p}(\omega_i) = 1\}}{n} = \frac{\#\{i \leq n \mid \mathbf{I}_{s_{(i)}}(p) = true\}}{n} \tag{12}$$

where the last term is exactly the expression which gives, at the limit, the support of p. Consequently, ***supp(p) exists (almost sure) if the stochastic sequence $\{\mathbf{1}_{A_p}\}_1^\infty$ satisfies the strong law of large numbers***.

To obey the law of large numbers, a sequence must satisfy regularity conditions relating to two distinct factors: the probability of extreme values (limited by bounding absolute moments) and the degree of dependence between coordinates. The necessity of a set of regularity conditions is usually hard to prove (except if the sequences are independent), but various configurations of dependency and boundedness conditions can be shown to be sufficient. The characteristic sequences, which are derived from the stochastic process ψ using appropriate Borel transformation (depending on p), have all absolute moments bounded by 0 and 1. Therefore, the only regularity condition which may vary (and which is inherited from ψ) is the degree of dependence. After a deeper analysis of the various types of dependence restrictions a stochastic process may contain, we proved (Cotofrei & Stoffel, 2007) the following results:

- **Independence and Consistency.** *If the random process ψ from the stochastic first-order linear time structure $\mathbb{M} = (S, P, \mathbb{X}, \psi, \boldsymbol{I})$ is i.i.d., then almost all linear time structures $M_\omega = (S, \omega, \boldsymbol{I}_s)$ are consistent.* But the independence condition represents a serious drawback for any temporal rule extraction methodology, because it implies a null correlation between the body and the head of a rule, i.e. not at all meaningful temporal rules.

[1] In this context, an event is a set of possible outcomes of a random experiment

- **Dependence and Consistency.** *If the random process ψ from the stochastic first-order linear time structure $\mathbb{M} = (S, P, \mathbb{X}, \psi, \mathbf{I})$ is α-mixing[2] or is $L_2 - NED$[3], then almost all linear time structures $M_\omega = (S, \omega, \mathbf{I}_s)$ are consistent.* Therefore, with up to a certain amount of dependence between events (that makes the rules meaningful), it is possible to guarantee the "correctness" of the temporal rules (expressed by the confidence measure) when applied to future data.

4.2 The granularity stochastic model

If we apply the stochastic approach, as developed in the previous subsection, to the granularity model, we obtain what we call a stochastic granular time formalism. Let $\psi = \{\mathbb{X}_i\}_1^\infty$ be a stochastic process and μ a temporal type. If we denote $\mathbf{X}_{\mu(i)}$ the random vector $(\mathbb{X}_{j_1}, \ldots, \mathbb{X}_{j_k})$, where $j_i, i = 1..k$ are all the indices from $\mu(i)$, then the random sequence induced by μ on ψ is simply $\mu[\psi] = \{\mathbf{X}_{\mu(i)}\}_{i=1}^\infty$. Similarly, if $\omega \in S^{\mathbb{N}}$ then $\omega_{\mu(i)} = (\omega_{j_1}, \ldots, \omega_{j_k})$ and $\mu[\omega] = \{\omega_{\mu(i)}\}_1^\infty$. Therefore, we define a stochastic granular time structure as:

Definition 14 *If $\mathbb{M} = (S, P, \mathbb{X}, \psi, \mathbf{I})$ is a stochastic (first-order) linear time structure and μ is a temporal type from $\mathcal{G}_1$, then the stochastic granular time structure induced by μ on $\mathbb{M}$ is the quintuple $\mathbb{M}_\mu = (2^S, P, \mathbb{X}, \mu[\psi], \mathbf{I}^\mu)$, where $\mathbf{I}^\mu$ is given by (5)-(6).*

Practically, the random process $\mu[\psi]$ from the stochastic granular time structure M_μ is a sequence of random vectors obtained by grouping the coordinates of the process ψ according to the mapping μ. To each realization of the stochastic sequence ψ, obtained by a random drawing of a point ω in $S^{\mathbb{N}}$, corresponds to a realization of the stochastic structure $\mathbb{M}$ (i.e., the time structure $M_\omega = (S, \omega, \mathbf{I}_\omega)$) and a corresponding realization of the stochastic structure $\mathbb{M}_\mu$ (i.e., the granular time structure $M_{\mu[\omega]} = (2^S, \mu[\omega], \mathbf{I}_\omega^\mu)$).
In the following we establish the expression linking the interpretation $\mathbf{I}^\mu$ of a given formula in $\mathbb{L}$ with the random process $\mu[\psi]$. For this we introduce the function $\overline{\mathcal{S}}$ defined by $\overline{\mathcal{S}}(\mathbf{X}_{\mu(i)}) = (\#\mu(i))^{-1} \sum_{j \in \mu(i)} \mathbb{X}_j$. If $\{\mathbb{X}_i\}$ are identical distributed, with $E(\mathbb{X}_i) = \gamma$, then it is evident that $E(\overline{\mathcal{S}}(\mathbf{X}_{\mu(i)})) = \gamma$, for all $i \in \mathbb{N}$. Consider the following two situations:

- *Temporal free formula*: According to (5) and to (12),

$$\mathbf{I}^\mu_{\mu[\omega](i)}(p) = \text{supp}(p, \tilde{M}_{\mu[\omega](i)}) = \overline{\mathcal{S}}\left((\mathbf{1}_{A_p})_{\mu[\omega](i)}\right). \tag{13}$$

- *Temporal formula*: According to (6) and (13), for a temporal formula $\nabla_{k_1} p_1 \wedge \ldots \wedge \nabla_{k_n} p_n$

$$\mathbf{I}^\mu_{\mu[\omega](i)}(\nabla_{k_1} p_1 \wedge \ldots \wedge \nabla_{k_n} p_n) = \frac{1}{n}\sum_{j=1}^{n} \mathbf{I}^\mu_{\mu[\omega](i+k_j)}(p_j) = \frac{1}{n}\sum_{j=1}^{n} \overline{\mathcal{S}}\left((\mathbf{1}_{A_{p_j}})_{\mu[\omega](i+k_j)}\right). \tag{14}$$

The consequence of these relations is that ***the support of any formula p under $M_{\mu[\omega]}$ exists if and only if the characteristic sequence $\{\overline{\mathcal{S}}(\mathbf{1}_{A_p})_{\mu[\omega]}\}$ satisfies the strong law of large numbers***. The sequence corresponding to p is constructed by applying a mapping μ and a particular Borel transformation on the stochastic sequence ψ. By analyzing the sufficient conditions (the dependence degree) for ψ which assure, through the transformation function, the applicability of SLLN for any characteristic sequence, we arrived at the following results:

[2]the degree of dependence converges to zero if the distance between coordinates converges to ∞
[3]a function of a mixing sequence with an infinite number of parameters

Theorem 4 ***(Independence and Consistency)*** *If the random process ψ from the stochastic first-order linear time structure $\mathbb{M} = (S,P,\mathbb{X},\psi,\boldsymbol{I})$ is i.i.d., then almost all granular time structures induced by a temporal type $\mu \in \mathcal{G}_1$, $M_{\mu[\omega]} = (2^S,\mu[\omega],\boldsymbol{I}^{\mu})$, are consistent.*

(For proof see Appendix). This result is stronger than those obtained in Theorem 3, where the temporal type has to satisfy a more restrictive condition, i.e. $\mu \in \mathcal{G}_3$. This is explained by the fact that in a probabilistic framework we can apply fundamental results which go beyond a simple algebraic manipulation. Furthermore, we can prove that the consistency is preserved even if we replace the function giving the interpretation of a temporal formula (the arithmetic mean, see (6)) with any t-norm transformation.

Theorem 5 ***($\alpha-$Mixing and Consistency)*** *If the random process ψ from the stochastic first-order linear time structure $\mathbb{M} = (S,P,\mathbb{X},\psi,\boldsymbol{I})$ is $\alpha-$mixing, then almost all granular time structures induced by a temporal type $\mu \in \mathcal{G}_2$, $M_{\mu[\omega]} = (2^S,\mu[\omega],\boldsymbol{I}^{\mu})$, are consistent.*

(For proof see Appendix). This result is, once again, stronger than those obtained in the pure granular logical formalism, but we must remark on the supplementary condition imposed on μ (now in $\mathcal{G}_2$) compared with the independence case.

Theorem 6 ***(Near-Epoch Dependence and Consistency)*** *If the random process ψ from the stochastic first-order linear time structure $\mathbb{M} = (S,P,\mathbb{X},\psi,\boldsymbol{I})$ is L_2-NED on an $\alpha-$mixing sequence, then almost all granular time structures induced by a temporal type $\mu \in \mathcal{G}_3$, $M_{\mu[\omega]} = (2^S,\mu[\omega],\boldsymbol{I}^{\mu})$, are consistent.*

(For proof see Appendix). For the near-epoch dependence case we were forced to impose the stronger restriction to the temporal type μ (constant size and total coverage) to compensate the higher degree of dependence of the stochastic process ψ. This type of dependence is, according to the stochastic limit theory (Davidson, 1994; Davidson & de Jong, 1997), the highest degree of dependence for which theorems concerning SLLN still hold.

4.2.1 Aggregated event support and (α,β) confidence

All these results were obtained by analyzing the characteristic sequences for the formulae constructed in $\mathbb{L}$, for which the interpretation is given by the expressions (5)-(6). The transformations applied to the process ψ to generate characteristic sequences belong to a family of Borel functions $\mathcal{G}$,

$$g_p(\mathbb{X}_{i+k}(\omega)) = (g_p \circ \mathbb{X}_{i+k})(\omega) = \begin{cases} 1 & \text{if } \omega_{i+k} \in A_p, \\ 0 & \text{if not} \end{cases} \quad \text{for all } k \geq 0 \tag{15}$$

(for independence and $\alpha-$mixing dependence) and to a slightly different family $\tilde{\mathcal{G}}$, satisfying *i)* $\tilde{g}_p(\mathbb{X}_i(\omega)) = g_p(\mathbb{X}_i(\omega))$, *ii)* $\tilde{g}_p$ continuous and iii) $|\tilde{g}(\boldsymbol{X}^1) - \tilde{g}(\boldsymbol{X}^2)| \leq M\sum_{i=1}^{n} |x_i^1 - x_i^2|$ a.s., where $\boldsymbol{X}^1$, $\boldsymbol{X}^2$ are random vectors from $\mathbb{R}^n$ (for near-epoch dependence).
The degree of truth of an aggregate event is given by a different rule (11), implying that a particular type of transformation $(\mathcal{T})$ must be applied to ψ to obtain the corresponding characteristic sequence. To start the rationale, let ω be a sequence of states generated by the process ψ and $e[t]_{\mathcal{A}}$ an aggregate event induced by the set $\mathcal{A}$. The expression given at the limit

the support of $e[t]_\mathcal{A}$ in the granular time structure M_μ is

$$\frac{1}{n}\sum_{i=1}^{n}\mathbf{I}^{\mu}_{\mu[\omega](i)}(e[t]_\mathcal{A}) = \frac{1}{n}\sum_{i=1}^{n}\left(\frac{\#(\mathcal{E}_i \cap \mathcal{A})}{\#\mathcal{A}}\sum_{e_j\in\mathcal{A}}\mathbf{I}^{\mu}_{\mu[\omega](i)}(e_j)\right) = \frac{1}{\#\mathcal{A}}\sum_{e_j\in\mathcal{A}}\left(\frac{1}{n}\sum_{i=1}^{n}\#(\mathcal{E}_i\cap\mathcal{A})\mathbf{I}^{\mu}_{\mu[\omega](i)}(e_j)\right)$$

For a fixed j and according to (13), $\mathbf{I}^{\mu}_{\mu[\omega](i)}(e_j) = \overline{\mathcal{S}}\left((\mathbf{1}_{A_{e_j}})_{\mu[\omega](i)}\right)$, which represents the ith coordinate of a random sequence $(X_i^j)_1^\infty$ of variables obtained from ψ by applying a Borel transformation (an application of the mean function on functions from family $\mathcal{G}$). Consider now the sequence $(\mathbf{1}_{A_{e_j}})_1^\infty$, $N_i^j = \sum_{k\in\mu[\omega](i)}\mathbf{1}_{A_{e_j}}(\omega_k)$ (the variable counting the number of times e_j is satisfied in $\mu[\omega](i)$) and $gt(\cdot)$ a function defined as

$$gt(N_i^j) = \begin{cases} 1 & \text{if } N_i^j \geq 1, \\ 0 & \text{if not} \end{cases}$$

Consequently we have $\#(\mathcal{E}_i\cap\mathcal{A}) = \sum_{k\in\mu[\omega](i)} gt(N_i^k)$, which represents the ith coordinate of a second random sequence $(Y_i)_1^\infty$, obtained again from ψ by applying a Borel transformation. The variables Y_i^j are identical distributed if and only if $\#\mu[\omega](i)$ is a constant, which implies $\mu \in \mathcal{G}_3$. Under this restriction, the characteristic sequence for the aggregate event $e[t]_\mathcal{A}$ (which is $\left(\frac{1}{\#\mathcal{A}}\sum_{e_j\in\mathcal{A}} Y_i \cdot X_i^j\right)_1^\infty$ and is obtained from ψ by applying a particular Borel transformation) inherits the dependence degree of ψ. Therefore, the answer to our first question is given by the following theorem:

Theorem 7 *If the random process ψ from the stochastic first-order linear time structure $\mathbb{M} = (S, P, \mathbb{X}, \psi, \mathbf{I})$ is i.i.d or α-mixing or L_2-NED on an $\alpha-$mixing sequence, then in almost all granular time structures induced by a temporal type $\mu \in \mathcal{G}_3$, an aggregated event has a support.*

Concerning the confidence (α,β) for a temporal rule, let introduces a particular type of measure, the (α)support for a formula p under M_μ, denoted $\text{supp}_\alpha(p, M_\mu)$ and defined as $\lim_{n\to\infty} n^{-1}\#\{i \leq n \,|\, \mathbf{I}^{\mu}_{\mu(i)}(p) \geq \alpha\}$. Furthermore, following a similar rationing used in the proofs of theorems 4-6 and treating the two cases (p temporal free formula and p temporal rule), we can prove the possibility of constructing a specific characteristic sequence - denoted $\left((X_p^\alpha)_i\right)_1^\infty$ - derived from ψ by applying a specific Borel transformation, such that the existence of $\text{supp}_\alpha(p)$ is guaranteed by the capacity of the specific sequence to obey SLLN. Because this capacity is assured only if $\mu \in \mathcal{G}_3$, we can assert that

Theorem 8 *If the random process ψ from the stochastic first-order linear time structure $\mathbb{M} = (S, P, \mathbb{X}, \psi, \mathbf{I})$ is i.i.d or α-mixing or L_2-NED on an $\alpha-$mixing sequence, then in almost all granular time structures induced by a temporal type $\mu \in \mathcal{G}_3$, an aggregated event has an (α)support, for any $\alpha \in (0,1]$*

The expression given $\text{conf}_{\alpha,\beta}(\mathcal{H}, M_\mu)$ may be rewritten as:

$$\lim_{n\to\infty}\frac{\#\{i\leq n|\mathbf{I}^{\mu}_{\mu(i)}(H_1\wedge..\wedge H_m)\geq\alpha, \mathbf{I}^{\mu}_{\mu(i)}H_{m+1}\geq\beta\}}{\#\{i\leq n|\mathbf{I}^{\mu}_{\mu(i)}(H_1\wedge..\wedge H_m)\geq\alpha\}} = \lim_{n\to\infty}\frac{\left(\overline{X^{\alpha}_{H_1\wedge..\wedge H_m}\cdot X^{\beta}_{H_{m+1}}}\right)_n}{\left(\overline{X^{\alpha}_{H_1\wedge..\wedge H_m}}\right)_n}$$

so the existence of the confidence(α,β) is directly related to the existence of a non null $\text{supp}_\alpha(H_1 \wedge .. \wedge H_m)$ and of the property of the sequence $\left((X^\alpha_{H_1\wedge..\wedge H_m} \cdot X^\beta_{H_{m+1}})_i\right)_1^\infty$ to obey SSLN (which is assured by Theorem 8). In conclusion, the answer to our second question is:

Theorem 9 *If the random process ψ from the stochastic first-order linear time structure $\mathbb{M} = (S,P,\mathbb{X},\psi,\mathbf{I})$ is i.i.d or α-mixing or L_2-NED on an $\alpha-$mixing sequence then in almost all granular time structures induced by a temporal type $\mu \in \mathcal{G}_3$, a temporal rule $(\mathcal{H})$, $H_1 \wedge .. \wedge H_m \mapsto H_{m+1}$ for which $\text{supp}_\alpha(H_1 \wedge .. \wedge H_m) \neq 0$ has a well-defined confidence $conf_{(\alpha,\beta)}(\mathcal{H},M_\mu)$, $\forall \alpha,\beta \in (0,1]$.*

The rationale we followed to prove the existence of the confidence (α,β) for a temporal rule emphasizes the main advantage of the stochastic approach: the possibility to infer, from specific properties of a stochastic process, the existence of *different types of consistency*, defined based on user necessity. For a temporal granular structure M_μ, as an example, the consistency may be defined either in the classical way (Definition 9) or as the existence, for any formula p, of $\text{supp}_\alpha(p,M_\mu)$. And depending on the user's needs for other types of confidence measures, other concepts of consistency may be defined (of course, under the hypothesis that SLLN still implies these new concepts). Therefore, by considering all the consistency concepts introduced in this chapter we could prove that:

Theorem 10 *If the random process ψ from the stochastic linear time structure $\mathbb{M} = (S,P,\mathbb{X},\psi,\mathbf{I})$ is i.i.d, α-mixing or L_2-NED, then almost all granular time structures induced by a temporal type $\mu \in \mathcal{G}_3$, are consistent.*

From a practical point of view, after testing (see Cotofrei & Stoffel (2007) for a discussion about possible statistical tests) that the sequence ω of states, derived from raw data, contains a certain amount of dependence, this theorem assures us that any temporal rule $H_1 \wedge .. \wedge H_m \mapsto H_{m+1}$ (implying *any* type of defined temporal events - aggregated events included), for which the support of $H_1 \wedge .. \wedge H_m$ is not null, has a well-defined (but not μ independent) confidence over any M_μ with $\mu \in \mathcal{G}_3$.

5. Conclusions

Starting from the inherent behavior of temporal systems - the perception of events and of their interactions is determined, in a large measure, by the temporal scale - the question about the mechanisms of transferring (transforming) discovered knowledge from a finer time scale to a coarser one is naturally imposed. We approached this question using a theoretical framework based on first-order temporal logic and extended to "capture" the concept of time granularity. The introduced formalism allows us to define main notions such as *event, temporal rule, support and confidence* in a formal way, based on the fundamental concept of consistency for a linear time structure M.

To keep a unitary viewpoint on the semantics of the same formula at different scales of time, the usual definition of the interpretation $\mathbf{I}^\mu$ for a formula was changed: now it returns the degree of truth (a real value between zero and one) and not only the meaning of truth (*true* or *false*). Based on the concept of consistency extended to granular time structures, we could prove that this property is inherited from the basic time structure M if the temporal type μ is of type $\mathcal{G}_3$ (granules with constant size). The major consequence of this theorem is that a given form of confidence, expressed by (9), is preserved in all granular time structures derived from the same consistent time structure.

By reflecting on how the changes of the time scale affect the meaning (in the "real world") of the temporal rules, we could emphasize an intrinsic connection between the significance of an event for a user and the granularity of the time. Indeed, any methodology which extracts events from raw temporal data acts based on an implicit granularity (usually given by the time scale of raw data). Therefore, all the generated temporal events have a specific meaning *only* for this initial time scale, and any change in the time granularity implies the "loss" of this meaning. Our solution to this problem was the introduction of the concept of "event aggregation", a mechanism generating new events with an appropriate significance and satisfied in a coarser world. To achieve this we extended the syntax and the semantics of the language $\mathbb{L}$ by allowing "families" of function symbols and by adding two new operators. Due to the limitations in proving the existence of the support for aggregate events and of the new introduced confidence (α, β) (allowing the use of temporal rules for prediction purposes under a granular world), we extended our formalism by a stochastic dimension. In this framework, using the relation between the capacity of a stochastic process to obey the strong law of large numbers and the consistency property, we proved that under a given amount of dependency (which implies meaningful rules), the existence of the confidence for any temporal rule is guaranteed (which implies preserving the predictive power of the rule on any future data sets).

In our opinion, the conclusion of our analysis may be summarized as follows: *only the fundamental properties (knowledge) concerning the time structures conceived as a whole may be transferred (preserved) during a granularity time change process. On the other hand, the information linked to a granule, seen as "local knowledge" cannot be transferred during the same process (or if it can, it's a meaningless transfer).*

6. Appendix

6.1 Proof of theorem 4

If ψ is an i.i.d. process, then for p a temporal free formula the sequence $\{\mathbf{1}_{A_p}\}_1^\infty$ is also i.i.d. By applying Pfeiffer (1989, page 255) Theorem , the vectors $(\mathbf{1}_{A_p})_{\mu(i)}$ are independent, and consequently, according to the Theorem (Pfeiffer, 1989, page 254) and to the fact that the function $\overline{S}$ is a Borel transformation, the sequence $\left\{\overline{S}\left((\mathbf{1}_{A_p})_{\mu[\omega](i)}\right)\right\}_{i=1}^{\infty}$ is independent. Therefore, the classical Kolmogorov theorem may be applied, and so the support of the formula p, under the granular time structure $M_{\mu[\omega]}$, exists almost sure. For the temporal formula $\nabla_{k_1} p_1 \wedge \ldots \wedge \nabla_{k_n} p_n$, similar considerations assure that, for a fixed i, the random variables $\overline{S}\left((\mathbf{1}_{A_{p_1}})_{\mu[\omega](i+k_1)}\right), \ldots, \overline{S}\left((\mathbf{1}_{A_{p_n}})_{\mu[\omega](i+k_n)}\right)$ are independent. The sequence corresponding to the temporal formula (see 14) is not independent, but k_n-dependent, and so the conditions of the Theorem (Hall & Heyde, 1980, page 40) are satisfied. As a consequence, this sequence obeys the law of large numbers, i.e. the support of the temporal formula exists.

6.2 Proof of theorem 5

If ψ is α-mixing then it is evident that any subsequence of ψ is also α-mixing. The following result, necessary for our rationale, is a consequence of the fact that mixing is a property of σ-fields generated by $\{\mathbb{X}_i\}$.

Lemma 1 *Consider $\mathbb{X}_i$ an α-mixing sequence of size $-\varphi$ and let be k sequences ${}_j\mathbb{Y}_i$ obtained by applying on $\{\mathbb{X}_i\}$ the measurable functions $g_j(\mathbb{X}_t, \ldots, \mathbb{X}_{t-\tau_j})$, $j = 1 \ldots k$. Then the sequence*

$_1\mathbb{Y}_{i_1}, {_2}\mathbb{Y}_{i_2}, \ldots, {_k}\mathbb{Y}_{i_k}, {_1}\mathbb{Y}_{i_{k+1}}, \ldots$, obtained by tacking successively from each sequence $_j\mathbb{Y}_i$ coordinates with indices in an increasing order, is also α-mixing of size $-\varphi$.

The utility of this lemma is due to the fact that the granules of a temporal type from $\mathcal{G}_2$ have a variable size, and so we cannot apply a single measurable function $g(\cdot)$, with a fixed number of parameters, on $\{\mathbf{1}_{A_p}\}$. By considering for each effective size $k \in \mathbb{N}$ the function $mean_k(x_1, \ldots, x_k) = k^{-1}\sum x_i$ and applying Lemma 1 on $\{\mathbf{1}_{A_p}\}$ we obtain that $\overline{\mathcal{S}}\left((\mathbf{1}_{A_p})_{\mu[\omega](i)}\right)$, p a temporal free formula, is $\alpha-$mixing. Concerning a temporal formula $\nabla_{k_1} p_1 \wedge \ldots \wedge \nabla_{k_n} p_n$, by applying n times Lemma 1 for the $\alpha-$mixing sequences $\{\mathbf{1}_{A_{p_j}}\}$, $j = 1 \ldots n$, we obtain the $\alpha-$mixing sequences $\overline{\mathcal{S}}\left((\mathbf{1}_{A_{p_j}})_{\mu[\omega](i)}\right)$, $j = 1 \ldots n$. From these sequences we extract the subsequence $\overline{\mathcal{S}}\left((\mathbf{1}_{A_{p_1}})_{\mu[\omega](i+k_1)}\right), \ldots, \overline{\mathcal{S}}\left((\mathbf{1}_{A_{p_n}})_{\mu[\omega](i+k_n)}\right)$, $i \in \mathbb{N}$ (which is $\alpha-$mixing, according to the same Lemma), on which we apply the function $g_n(\cdot)$. The resulting sequence is again $\alpha-$mixing, according to the Theorem (Davidson, 1994, page 210). Finally, the corresponding sequence for any formula in L is $\alpha-$mixing, bounded by the interval $[0,1]$, thus fulfilling the conditions of Theorem (Hall & Heyde, 1980, page 40).

6.3 Proof of theorem 6

According to a corollary proved in Cotofrei & Stoffel (2007), any sequence $\{\mathbf{1}_{A_p}\}$ is also L_2-NED on the same sequence $\{\mathbb{V}_i\}$. If $\#\mu(i) = k$ then it is easy to show that the function $mean_k(\cdot)$ is continuous and satisfies the uniform Lipschitz condition. Therefore, according to the Theorem (Davidson, 1994, page 269), the sequence corresponding to the temporal free formula p, $\mathcal{S}\left((\mathbf{1}_{A_p})_{\mu[\omega](i)}\right)$, is also L_2-NED on $\{\mathbb{V}_i\}$. The same theorem, applied to the sequence of vectors $\left(\mathcal{S}\left((\mathbf{1}_{A_{p_1}})_{\mu[\omega](i+k_1)},\right) \ldots, \mathcal{S}\left((\mathbf{1}_{A_{p_n}})_{\mu[\omega](i+k_n)}\right)\right)$, all L_2-NED on $\{\mathbb{V}_i\}$, and for the Lipschitz function $mean_n(\cdot)$, assures that the sequence $\frac{1}{n}\sum_{j=1}^{n} \mathcal{S}\left((\mathbf{1}_{A_{p_j}})_{\mu[\omega](i+k_j)}\right)$ is L_2-NED on $\{\mathbb{V}_i\}$. Therefore, for any formula in L the corresponding sequence is L_2-NED on the α-mixing sequence $\{\mathbb{V}_i\}$. Furthermore, these sequences fulfil the conditions of the Theorem (Davidson & de Jong, 1997, page 258) for $q = 2$ and so obey the strong law of large numbers.

7. References

Al-Naemi, S. (1994). A theoretical framework for temporal knowledge discovery, *Proc. of Int. Workshop on Spatio-Temporal Databases*, Spain, pp. 23–33.

Bettini, C., Wang, X. S. & Jajodia, S. (1998a). A general framework for time granularity and its application to temporal reasoning., *Ann. Math. Artif. Intell.* 22(1-2): 29–58.

Bettini, C., Wang, X. S. & Jajodia, S. (1998b). Mining temporal relationships with multiple granularities in time sequences, *Data Engineering Bulletin* 21(1): 32–38.

Bettini, C., Wang, X. S., Jajodia, S. & Lin, J.-L. (1998). Discovering frequent event patterns with multiple granularities in time sequences, *IEEE Trans. Knowl. Data Eng.* 10(2): 222–237.

Chen, X. & Petrounias, I. (1998). A Framework for Temporal Data Mining, *Lecture Notes in Computer Science* 1460: 796–805.

Chomicki, J. & Toman, D. (1997). Temporal Logic in Information Systems, *BRICS Lecture Series* LS-97-1: 1–42.

Combi, C., Franceschet, M. & Peron, A. (2004). Representing and reasoning about temporal granularities, *J. Log. Comput.* 14(1): 51–77.

Cotofrei, P. & Stoffel, K. (2004). From temporal rules to temporal meta-rules, *LNCS, vol 3181*, pp. 169–178.

Cotofrei, P. & Stoffel, K. (2005). First-order logic based formalism for temporal data mining, *Fundation of Data Mining and Knowledge Extraction*, Vol. 6 of *Studies in Computational Intelligence*, pp. 185–210.

Cotofrei, P. & Stoffel, K. (2007). Stochastic processes and temporal data mining, *Proceedings of the 13th KDD*, San Jose, USA, pp. 183–190.

Cotofrei, P. & Stoffel, K. (2009). *Foundations in Computational Intelligence*, Springer Verlang, chapter Time Granularity in Temporal Data Mining, pp. 67–96.

Davidson, J. (1994). *Stochastic Limit Theory*, Oxford University Press.

Davidson, J. & de Jong, R. (1997). Strong law of large numbers for dependent and heterogenous processes: a synthesis of new and recent results, *Econometric Reviews* 16: 251–279.

Emerson, E. A. (1990). Temporal and Modal Logic, *Handbook of Theoretical Computer Science* pp. 995–1072.

Euzenat, J. (1995). An algebraic approach to granularity in qualitative time and space representation., *IJCAI (1)*, pp. 894–900.

Hall, P. & Heyde, C. (1980). *Martingale Limit Theory and Its Application*, Academic Press.

Hornsby, K. (2001). Temporal zooming, *Transactions in GIS* 5: 255–272.

Lin, T. Y. & Louie, E. (2002). Data mining using granular computing: fast algorithms for finding association rules, *Data mining, rough sets and granular computing*, Physica-Verlag GmbH, pp. 23–45.

Malerba, D., Esposito, F. & Lisi, F. (2001). A logical framework for frequent pattern discovery in spatial data, *Proceedings of FLAIRS*, pp. 557 – 561.

Mani, I. (1998). A theory of granularity and its application to problems of polysemy and underspecification of meaning, *Proceedings of the Sixth International Conference Principles of Knowledge Representation and Reasoning*, pp. 245–255.

Pfeiffer, P. (1989). *Probability for Applications*, Springer-verlag.

Saitta, L. & Zucker, J.-D. (1998). Semantic abstraction for concept representation and learning., *Proc. of the Symp. on Abstraction, Reformulation and Approximation*, pp. 103–120.

Yao, Y. & Zhong, N. (1999). Potential applications of granular computing in knowledge discovery and data mining, *Proceedings of WMSCI*, Orlando, pp. 573–580.

Zadeh, L. A. (1998). Information granulation and its centrality in human and machine intelligence., *Rough Sets and Current Trends in Computing*, pp. 35–36.

Zhang, B. & Zhang, L. (1992). *Theory and Applications of Problem Solving,*, North-Holland, Amsterdam.

Zhang, L. & Zhang, B. (2003). The quotient space theory of problem solving, *Proceedings of International Conference on Rough Sets, Fuzzy Set, Data Mining and Granular Computing*, pp. 11–15.

25

Data Mining for Problem Discovery

Donald E. Brown
University of Virginia
U.S.A.

1. Introduction

Data mining typically focuses on knowledge discovery. This means the identification or recognition of persistent patterns or relationships in data. Data mining can also support problem discovery or the identification of patterns or relationships in data that represent either causal mechanisms or association mechanisms. Association mechanisms fall short of causality but can provide useful insights for the design of solutions in the problem domain. A common goal of problem discovery is to identify the causal or association mechanisms behind metrics that measure system performance or behavior. Depending on the domain these metrics can be quantitative, e.g., cost of operation, or qualitative, e.g., acceptable or unacceptable behavior.

Data mining contains many approaches that can support problem discovery. This chapter reviews some significant examples and shows how their combination provides useful results. Before reviewing these approaches we note that problem discovery places four key requirements on the data mining approaches. The first is for unsupervised learning techniques for data association. Data association derives from unsupervised learning techniques that find structure in data. As such, data association seeks patterns of domain specific similarity among observations and uses a variety of similarity measures to find these patterns.

A second and closely related requirement for data association for problem discovery is the need for text association. Much of problem discovery concerns finding relationships in free text as well as fixed field data. Free text presents many challenges and a number of data mining techniques have been proposed to group documents and identify similarities. Problem discovery can exploit these methods but requires that they work closely with data association discoveries made using the fixed field data. The combination of free text and fixed field data can provide considerable information about the underlying causal or association mechanisms at the heart of problem discovery.

A third requirement for problem discovery methods applies to the use of supervised learning techniques. Specifically these techniques must produce interpretable results. This means that the discovery methods must reveal insights into causal or association mechanisms that contribute to the problem. So, unlike traditional data mining, problem discovery focuses more on interpretability at the possible expense of accuracy.

Finally, problem discovery requires the integration of methods from both supervised and unsupervised learning. By definition the exact nature of the problem is unknown so the application of, say, supervised learning tends to provide a narrow focus that misses important aspects of the problem. In contrast, unsupervised learning provides too broad a perspective in the presence of known instances of problematic behavior. Hence, problem discovery requires integrated strategies that combine results from supervised and unsupervised learning approaches.

The organization of this chapter provides a pathway for showing how we can meet these four requirements for problem discovery methods. The chapter begins with two sections dedicated to the current data mining techniques with most direct applicability to problem discovery. The next section, Section 2, reviews relevant results from unsupervised learning and the section following that, Section 3, provides the background in supervised learning techniques. Both sections show the strengths and weaknesses of these techniques for the specific issues in problem discovery. After this foundation, Section 4 shows how we can extend existing methods and integrate them into an approach for problem discovery. Finally, Section 5 provides an example of the use of the problem discovery methods for uncovering factors to guide strategies to reduce the number and severity train accidents.

2. Unsupervised learning methods for problem discovery

Problem discovery typically begins with the application of methods from unsupervised learning. Unsupervised learning techniques find patterns in data where the variables in the data do not include any response or output variables. Even in data sets that have output variables, the use unsupervised methods provides insight into the relationships among the variables needed to discover lurking or hidden problems not visible by simply apply supervised learning techniques.

A major difficulty with unsupervised learning follows from the lack of one or more output variables; namely, these methods do not have strong evaluation metrics. The presence of one or more output variables in the case of supervised learning means that we can measure the deviation from the actual to the predicted output and score the methods the accordingly. Since the data for unsupervised learning techniques do not contain output variables, we do not have the same straightforward measure of effectiveness. Hence, we typically judge unsupervised learning with a variety of subjective measures. This has led to a wide variety of methods and this section cannot possibly provide coverage of them all. Instead, we focus on those methods with the most direct applicability to problem discovery: association methods. Subsection 2.1 describes association rules, Subsection 2.2 overviews methods for associating variables, and Subsection2.3 gives an introduction to clustering. Lastly, Section 2.4 describes current methods for text mining that have applicability to problem discovery.

2.1 Association rules

Association rules are actually part of a collection of data mining techniques known as market basket analysis. Market basket analysis seeks to organize data on customer purchase behavior. Consider, for example, data on the purchase of items by customers at a store over a recent period of time. Do these customers frequently buy the same groups of items? So, for example, when they purchase cheese, do they also purchase wine? Understanding these associations may help store managers to better inventory, display, and manage their marketable items. Despite the name, market basket analysis provides useful methods for domains outside of retail sales. For instance, in health care, market basket analysis can provide an understanding of associations among patients with demands for similar services and treatments. In this sense the market basket contains a group of services purchased or requested by the customer.

Consider the set of all possible items or services that can be placed in a customer's market basket. Then each item has value associated with it which represents the quantity purchased by that customer. The goal of market basket analysis is to find those values of items for which their joint probability of occurrence is high. Unfortunately, for even modest sized businesses this problem is intractable.

Instead, analysts typically simplify the problem to allow only binary values for the items or services. These values reflect a yes or no decision for that item and not the quantity. Each basket then is represented as a vector of binary valued variables. These vectors show the associations among the items. The results are typically formed into association rules. For example, 'customers who buy cheese (c) and bread (b) also buy wine (w)' is converted to the rule,

$$c, b \Rightarrow w \tag{1}$$

These rules are augmented by the data to show the support and the confidence in the rule. Support for a rule means the proportion of observations or transactions in which both items occurred together. In the example in 1 the support for rule indicates the proportion of purchases in which cheese, bread, and wine appear together. The confidence for a rule shows the proportion of times the consequent of the rule occurs within the set of transactions containing the antecedent. In the above example, the confidence for the rule would be proportion of times that wine was purchased among those customers who also purchased cheese and bread.

A number of algorithms have been developed to find rules of this sort. One of the earliest and most commonly used of these algorithms is the Apriori algorithm Agrawal et al. (1996). Other algorithms for association rules have been developed and Zheng et al. (2001) provides comparison of several of these algorithms. For purposes of this chapter the Apriori algorithm provides a good illustration of the usefulness of association rule techniques for problem discovery.

The Apriori algorithm operates on sets of items in baskets, i.e., those with value one in binary formulation. These sets are called itemsets. The algorithm begins with the most frequently observed single itemsets. This means those items most often purchased by themselves. The algorithm uses these sets to find the most commonly purchased 2 item itemsets. At each iteration it prunes itemsets that do not pass a threshold on support or the frequency with which the itemset appears in the transactions. Once the common 2 item itemsets are found that pass this threshold, the algorithm uses these to consider 3 item itemsets. These are again pruned based on the support threshold. The algorithm proceeds in this way and stops when the threshold test is not satisfied by any itemset.

The Apriori algorithm and other association rule algorithms produce rules of the type shown in 1 with both confidence and support values. For problem discovery these results can provide some insight into association and causal mechanisms. For instance, in trying to determine the problems underlying train accidents we would be interested in association rules that show relationships between potential causes of accidents and measures of accident severity. Unfortunately, current versions of these algorithms cannot handle non-binary variables. This severely restricts the usefulness of association rules for problem discovery.

2.2 Variable association

Like association rules, variable association methods look for patterns among the variables in the data set. However, unlike association rules, the more general methods of variable association attempt to find simple, typically linear, relationships among the variables without the additional requirement of finding a rule that represents that relationship. By relaxing this

latter requirement variable association can work with the non-binary data typically found in problem discovery.
A common and effective method for associating variables is principal components. Principal components provide linear combinations of the variables that can approximate the original data with fewer dimensions. The linear combinations found by principal components satisfy the following properties:

1. The variance of each principal component is maximized;
2. The principal components are pairwise orthogonal; and
3. Each component is normalized to unit length.

The first property follows from a desire to maintain as much of the spread of the original data set as possible. The second property is for convenience. Orthogonality means that the projection into the of the principal components is a projection of the original basis functions. The final property is also for convenience. In this case it enables obtainment of a bounded solution to the optimization problem.
With these properties it is straightforward to find the linear combinations of the variables that produce the principal components. Let X be the data matrix with N rows and p columns or variables. Let S be the $p \times p$ variance-covariance matrix for this data matrix. For principal components these variables must be in Euclidean space. Now consider U the matrix of principal components with p rows and q columns, where $q \leq p$. For the first principal component, u_1, the properties above mean that we want to find the

$$\underset{u_1,\lambda_1}{\text{argmax}}\{u_1^T S u_1 + \lambda_1(1 - u_1^T u_1)\}. \tag{2}$$

The solution to 2 is given by

$$S u_1 = \lambda_1 u_1. \tag{3}$$

The solution in 3 implies that the first principal component is the eigenvector of the variance-covariance matrix, S with the largest eigenvalue, λ_1. The remaining principal are similarly defined and are orthogonal to all preceding principal components. Hence, U is the matrix of eigenvectors for S and $\lambda_1, \ldots, \lambda_q$ are the eigenvectors. The eigenvalues also provide the variance of the data in the projection of respective principal component.
In data mining we typically look for solutions in which the number of principal components is less than the number of variables in the data set, i.e., $q < p$. The proportion of variance in the data in a subset of the principal components is found from the appropriate ratio of eigenvalues. For example, the variance of the data projected into the first two principal components is $(\lambda_1 + \lambda_2)/(\lambda_1 + \lambda_2 + \ldots + \lambda_K)$.
Since data mining looks for associations among variables, the results are particularly interesting when a small number of principal components explains a large amount of the variance in the database. It is unrealistic to expect a small number of variables to explain nearly all of the variance; however, it is often possible to find a small number of principal components that explain as much as half of the original variance. As the number of variables gets larger it can become harder to achieve this goal.
A method closely related to principal components is singular valued decomposition (SVD). To see the relationship, again consider a data set, X, with N observations and p variables. We can decompose X, into 2 orthogonal matrices and a diagonal matrix Golub & Loan (1983) defined as follows:

$$X = UDT^T \tag{4}$$

In 4 U is an $N \times p$ matrix called the left singular vectors and T is $p \times p$ matrix called the right singular vectors. Also $U^T U = I$ and $T^T T = I$. D is diagonal matrix with dimensions and $p \times p$ and whose elements are the singular values. The major advantage to this decomposition is that it enables variable association for problems in which $N < p$.

Principal components has seen a number of important extensions. Among these are variational Bishop (1999b) and Bayesian Bishop (1999a) methods for principal components. In addition to principal components many other methods exist for associating variables. Some representative methods include partial least squares Wold (1975), ridge regression Hoerl & Kennard (1964), and independent components Comon (1994). A discussion and comparison of methods can be found in Copas (1983).

While these variable association methods provide a mechanism to link variables for problem discovery, they work only on quantitative variables. Much of the data in problem discovery consists of categorical variables and text. Hence, these methods cannot effectively provide complete solutions for problem discovery.

2.3 Clustering

Clustering is another class of unsupervised learning techniques with applicability to problem discovery. Quite simply the goal of clustering is to organize or group items based on the properties of those items. This goal has been of practical concern for a long time; hence, there exists a large number of approaches to this problem. Modern clustering techniques have their roots in statistics and taxonomy and these areas provide the foundation for many of the data mining techniques.

Clustering begins with a distance, similarity, or dissimilarity score for pairs of observations. The most common distances are Euclidean, Manhattan (or city block), and Max. Suppose we have observations x_i, x_j each consisting vectors of quantitative values over p variables. Then the Euclidean, Manhattan, and Max distances are defined as follows:

$$\begin{aligned} d_{\text{Euclid}} &= \left[\sum_{k=1}^{p} (x_{ik} - x_{jk})^2 \right]^{\frac{1}{2}} \\ d_{\text{Man}} &= \sum_{k=1}^{p} |x_{ik} - x_{jk}| \\ d_{\text{Max}} &= \operatorname*{Max}_k \{ |x_{ik} - x_{jk}| \}. \end{aligned}$$

A commonly used similarity is cosine, defined as $x_i \cdot x_j$.

Clustering algorithms employ the distance, similarity, or dissimilarity scores to group observations. For convenience researchers often categorize clustering algorithms as hierarchical, partitioning, or model-based, although these categories are neither inclusive nor mutually exclusive. We briefly describe these approaches to show their applicability to problem discovery.

As the name implies hierarchical clustering provides a level that shows the point of formation of different clusters. This allows for viewing of the data set in two dimensions: one (typically the abscissa) showing the cluster labels and the other (the ordinate) showing the level of

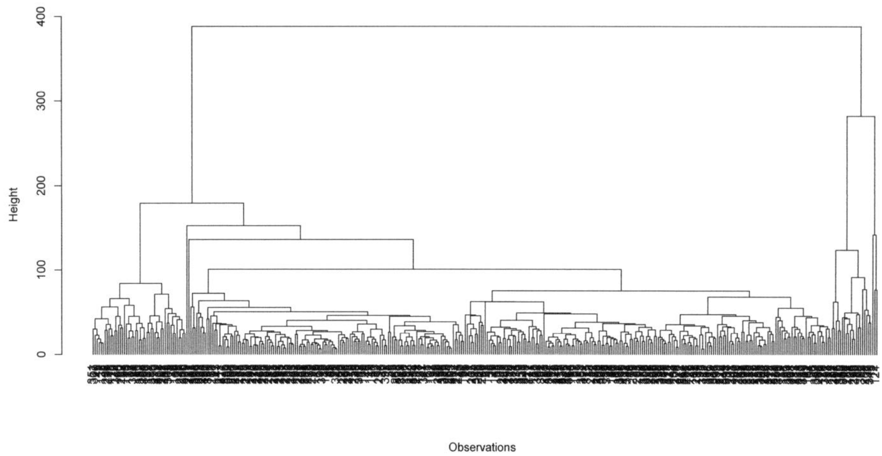

Fig. 1. Dendrogram of average link clustering

cluster formation. This plot is called a dendrogram (illustrated in Figures 1). The combination of labels and levels provides an indication of the patterns and structures in the database.

Partitioning methods group the observations based on their distance, similarity, or dissimilarity scores with each other. K-means is a typical and commonly used partitioning method. K-means requires the a-priori choice of the number of clusters and then randomly assigns observations to clusters. The algorithm next calculates the cluster centroids from this initial clustering. In the subsequent step the algorithm moves observations that have smaller dissimilarity or greater similarity with other centroids than they have to their assigned centroid. New centroids are calculated after this reassignment step. Once again observations are moved if their minimum dissimilarity or maximum similarity is with a centroid different from their assigned centroid. The process stops when no reassignments are made. It is easy to show this algorithm converges in a finite number of steps.

A number of researchers have extended the basic K-means formulation to improve its performance over a wide range of problems. A major disadvantage to K-means and its extensions for problem discovery is that it produces clusters of roughly the same size. Problem discovery tends to have unbalanced clusters with widely different sizes. Also, K-means requires knowledge of the number of clusters which requires the further use of various forward and backward search strategies.

A simple partitioning approach variously called the leader algorithm or nearest neighbor clustering starts by putting the first observation in the first cluster. The algorithm next finds the similarity or dissimilarity of the second observation with the first cluster, $s(x_2, c_1)$ or $s(x_2, c_1)$, respectively. If $s(x_2, c_1) > \tau$ or $d(x_2, c_1) < \tau$ then the second observation is added to the first cluster. Otherwise a new cluster is formed out the second observation. This logic is used to cluster the remaining observations. Typically the similarity or distance between the new observation and the clusters are found from the maximum similarity or minimum distance between the new observation and all observations assigned to the cluster. However, the similarity or distance could also be the maximum or the average of the points in the cluster, or another suitable choice function.

This algorithm is very efficient ($o(N)$), but is also order dependent. While it does not require

the explicit delineation of the number of clusters it does require specification of the threshold, τ and that indirectly specifies the number of clusters.
Model-based clustering uses a probabilistic model for the data. This model assumes the data come from draws against a mixture distribution with k components. One popular choice uses mixtures of Gaussians so the distribution of an observation x_j is found as

$$p(x_j) = \sum_{i=1}^{k} \pi_i \phi(x_j|\mu_i,\Sigma_i) \tag{5}$$

where $\phi(x|\mu,\Sigma)$ is a Gaussian distribution with parameters μ and Σ, and π_i are mixing coefficients with $\pi_i \in [0,1]$ and $\sum_{i=1}^{k} \pi_i = 1$. Unlike partitioning methods model-based clustering makes probabilistic assignments of observations to clusters.
Model-based clustering uses the expectation-maximization (EM) algorithm to find the parameters, μ_i,Σ_i,π_i and k for $i = 1,\ldots,k$. This algorithm proceeds in a fashion similar to k-means. The EM algorithm's first step initializes all the parameters (either randomly or according to some specified values). Next the algorithm finds $Pr(x_j \in C_i)$, the probability, x_i was drawn from cluster C_i for all observations, $j = 1,\ldots,N$ and clusters, $j = 1,\ldots,k$. The EM algorithm next re-estimates the parameters that maximize the likelihood of the current cluster assignments. The $Pr(x_j \in C_i)$ are calculated again for these new parameter estimates. The algorithm proceeds in this way and stops when no new assignments are made.

2.4 Text mining

Text mining does not fit entirely within unsupervised learning. However, as indicated in Section 1 text association is a critical component of problem discovery and methods from text mining or text data mining provide a foundation for meeting this requirement. At its most general level, text mining is a process of deriving consistent patterns from text. Text mining first structures the input text by parsing narrative data, then derives patterns within the structured data, and finally evaluates and interprets the output. The first step in text mining is similar to transforming free text into feature vectors in information retrieval. However, text mining usually applies more techniques on the structured data to derive useful information and speed this process. Typically, text mining tasks include information extraction, text categorization, summarization, and clustering Konchady (2006).
Information extraction techniques extract interesting information from the text. For example, they can extract peoples names, locations, vehicle types, and accidents from a passage. Information extraction techniques can be rule-based Ciravegna et al. (1999) and Krupka & Hausman (1998), statistics-based Witten et al. (1999), or use machine learning Baluja et al. (1999). Text categorization and clustering are like categorization and clustering performed in data mining, but performed on narratives or text. Applications of text categorization are described by Fall et al. (2003) and Gentili et al. (2001) and text clustering algorithms are described by Deerwester et al. (1990) and Hotho et al. (2001). Text summarization techniques seek to automatically summarize passages or narratives. These techniques can be based on linguistic rules, statistics, or both. Text summarization algorithms are described by Mani & Maybury (1999).
Other text mining techniques are developed to process text for specific applications. Yetisgen-Yildiz and Pratt Yetisgen-Yildiz & Pratt (2006) developed a literature-based discovery system called LitLinker to mine the biomedical literature for new, potentially interesting connections between biomedical terms. To reduce the dimensions of word vectors, they used Medical Subject Headings (MeSH) keywords assigned to the documents to capture the

content of the documents. The system uses a MeSH dictionary which is manual built by experts and the resulting text mining system can process narrative information quickly. Corley and Mihalcea Corley & Mihalcea (2005) presented a knowledge-based method for measuring the semantic-similarity of texts. They introduced a text-to-text semantic similarity metric by combining metrics of word-to-word similarity and language models. The word-to-word similarity metrics measure the semantic similarity of words using semantic networks or distributional similarity learned from large text collections. The language models provide the specificity of words. In their method, they determined the specificity of a word using the inverse document frequency as discussed in section 2.2. The specificity of each word is derived from the British National Corpus. Similarity between texts is determined by word-to-word similarities between all the words in the texts and specificity of each word. Experiments show their method outperforms the traditional text similarity metrics based on lexical matching. Hoang Hoang (2004) presented a method using the principal components to reduce dimensions of word vectors to reduce the time of text mining. paper discussed how the principal components method is used in information retrieval and how the latent semantic indexing is related to the principal component method. With word vectors from texts, the proposed method computes the principal components for these vectors and uses the reduced dimension vectors to represent the texts. Experiments showed the method works efficiently as well as effectively.

3. Supervised learning methods for problem discovery

Problem discovery requires techniques that go beyond discovering relationships between variables and observations through unsupervised learning. We also require techniques that can further characterize relationships between variables and can indicate the importance of the variables in these relationships. Supervised learning provides a set of techniques for accomplishing these tasks.

The inputs to supervised learning contain a further segmentation of the variable types into predictors and response. The goal of supervised learning is to find the relationships between the predictor variables and the response variables that will enable accurate and ideally fast estimation of the response values.

Predictor variables are further decomposed into control and environmental variables. The values of control variables can be set by the users or systems operating in the problem domain. Environmental variables are exogenous to these users and systems and hence cannot be set by them. Response variables are the outputs of the processes or systems in the problem domain. If an unsupervised learning technique works well it will produce a function that accurately maps the heretofore unseen predictor variable inputs to accurate estimates of the response variables.

As with unsupervised learning, the area of supervised learning encompasses a large number of techniques. Again we focus on the major techniques applicable to problem discovery. Also, to keep the notation manageable we describe these techniques using only a single response variable. The extension to the multi-variate case is conceptually straightforward once the univariate case is understood. The section begins with numeric response, since this builds directly on commonly used regression or least squares techniques. From there the discussion moves to the categorical response variables. Most data mining methods can handle both types of response, although the actual mechanics of the methods change with changing response type.

Unlike unsupervised learning, supervised learning has direct methods for measuring and evaluating performance or accuracy. Section 3.3 describes the fundamentals of evaluating the accuracy of supervised learning techniques.

While accuracy is important in may applications of supervised learning for problem discovery, interpretability or understanding the contribution of the variables to the response is also important. Not all data mining methods are easily interpretable. Among the most interpretable are tree-based methods. Among the least interpretable are support vector machines and other kernel methods. Since problem discovery depends on interpretability this section will describe only those methods with good interpretability that have application to problem discovery.

3.1 Regression

As noted the mechanics of supervised learning methods changes with the response variable . Numeric response variables have values over a continuum or a reasonably large set of integers. Categorical response variables have values that are unordered labels, such as names. Some response values are simply ordered which means they do not fit neatly into either of the previous categories. For the purposes of this chapter, the methods that can handle categorical response can also handle ordered response, although not necessarily in a manner that fully exploits the ordering.

For numeric response variables the field of statistics provides a rich set of techniques that fall under the rubric regression. Many of these regression methods find a linear function of the predictor variables that minimizes the sum of square differences with the response values. Let y_i be the response value and x_i be the vector of predictor values for observation i, $i = 1, \ldots, n$. Also let f be the function that estimates the response and θ be the vector of parameters in this function. For a given functional form, least squares chooses the parameters that minimize the sum of square distances to each observed response value. So, the estimated parameters, $\hat{\theta}$ are given by

$$\hat{\theta} = argmin\{\sum_{i=1}^{n}(y_i - f(\theta, x_n))^2\}. \tag{6}$$

A convenient choice for f in equation (6) is a linear form and for p predictor variables this gives the following:

$$f(\theta, x_n) = \theta_0 + \theta_1 x_1 + \cdots + \theta_p x_p. \tag{7}$$

The linear form show in equation (7) is useful for interpretation. Each coefficients on variables, $\theta_i, i = 1, \ldots, p$, provides an easy interpretation as the change in response for a one unit change the variable while holding all other variables constant. Of course, holding all other variables constant is typically a mental exercise, since only in controlled experiments can we meet this condition. Also, as the relationship becomes nonlinear the coefficients provide less easily understood interpretations.

Other measures of interpretability provided by regression models are the statistics obtained for the model and for each coefficient in the model. For the model the statistic is a value for the F distribution and for the individual coefficients the statistic is a value from the t distribution, although the F distribution can also be used. These distributions follow directly from the sum of squares errors where the errors measure the absolute difference between the regression predictions and the actual values. Details of this can be found in Seber (1984). These F and t values allow tests of hypotheses, such as, $\theta_1 = \theta_2 = \ldots = \theta_p = 0$ for the model and $\theta_i = 0$ for the

coefficients, $i = 1,\ldots,p$. The F statistic can also test hypotheses about groups of coefficients, e.g., $\theta_i = \theta_j = \theta_k = 0$ These tests provide a measure of variable importance in the model.
Least squares regression as described here is the topic of a vast literature, for example, see Seber (1984). It has also extended numerous ways to include handling of correlation among variables Hoerl & Kennard (1964) and correlation among observations Kedem & Fokianos (2003).
While least squares regression models data mining problems with numeric response variables, to find patterns with categorical response variables requires a different approach to regression. Consider the simplest case where the categorical variable is binary, e.g., the accident had deaths or no deaths. Least squares regression would not be appropriate for this problem since it would provide predictions that would lie outside the binary response values.
An extension to the regression approach is accomplished by modeling the probability of a binary response. With n independent observations then the probability of k occurrences of an event is given a binomial distribution. Let π be the parameter for this binomial distribution which is simply the probability of an event in any observation. A convenient, but by no means unique model, assumes this probability, π is a logistic function of the predictors with parametric vector θ. This yields the following:

$$log[\frac{\pi}{1-\pi}] = \theta^T x \tag{8}$$

where $x^T = (x_0, x_1, \ldots, x_k)$ and $\theta^T = (\theta_0, \theta_1, \ldots, \theta_k)$.
As with linear regression, logistic regression provides insight into influence of the predictors on the response. Now instead of using the F and t distributions, we use a χ^2 distribution as a large sample distribution for the likelihood ratio. This allows for the same hypotheses tests as we used for interpretability in linear regression, i.e., $\theta_1 = \theta_2 = \ldots = \theta_p = 0$ for the model and $\theta_i = 0$ for the coefficients, $i = 1,\ldots,p$. The coefficients themselves show the factor by which the odds ratio in equation (8) changes as the result of a one unit change in the variable while holding all other variables constant. Again, this interpretation is easy for linear models, such as equation (8), but not easy for nonlinear models. The motivates interest in other techniques that provide interpretability across more complex relationships.

3.2 Tree-based methods

Tree-based methods provide models for both numeric and categorical response variables. The advantage tree-based methods have over other supervised learning approaches is their interpretability. At the foundation all tree-based methods is the construction of a tree that represents a partition of the data set into regions for which a particular response value is prominent. The partitioning is accomplished through a series of questions. For example, at the time of the accident was the vehicle traveling at a speed in excess of posted maximum? Observations with affirmative answers to this question are separated from those with negative answers. Additional questions continue the partitioning until regions are found that primarily contain a single response value for categorical response variables or are near a value for a numeric response.
To see how this partitioning can be viewed as a tree, let each node represent a question that partitions the data. The answer to one question, leads to another question (the branch of the tree) until we finally arrive at the leaf. The leaf nodes give the estimated classification for a categorical response or value for a numeric response. This combination of questions or nodes and questions that follow questions can be represented as a tree (although one that is growing down rather than up).

The resulting tree is easily interpretable since it is simply a set of linked questions. This reasoning is familiar to most people and hence the output tree-based methods can be implemented in virtually all settings with little explanation. For problem discovery this interpretability means uncovering relations that might not otherwise be exposed amidst. Unlike regression methods, trees can display nonlinear relationships in a form that is easy to interpret. Obviously a large tree with many variables becomes less easily understood, but even in these cases it is possible to view the tree in segments or branches. These branches can aid in understanding and problem discovery.

We can construct tree classifiers and regression trees with a variety of algorithms. One of the most effective of these, known as recursive partitioning (RP), was developed by Breiman et al. (1984). This algorithm constructs trees by providing answers to three tree construction questions: (1) When to stop growing the tree; (2) What label to put on a leaf node; and (3) How to choose a question at a node.

The question, when to stop growing the tree, they answered simply by not stopping. Instead the RP algorithm grows the tree out to its maximum size (e.g., each observation in its own terminal node). RP then prunes the tree back to a size that best predicts a set of hold-out samples (the actual approach used is discussed in Section 3.3). This pruning approach avoids generating trees that are not effective because they did not consider a sufficiently large and cooperative set of nodes.

The second question, what label to put on a leaf node, has an easy answer: for categorical response choose the category with the most members in the node; and for numeric response take the average or median. Ties among categories are simply reported. This approach means that the algorithm provides a quick estimate of the probabilities for each category in the leaf nodes. It also provides an empirical distribution for numeric values in the leaf nodes.

The third question, How to choose a question at a node, has a more involved answer. RP develops a question for a node by considering the values of every variable for every observation in a node as possible question. For numeric variables the questions considered ask if the variable has a value less than the mid point between two adjacent values of that variable for the observations in the node. For categorical variables, the questions ask if the value of the variable is a member of one of the proper subsets of the values observed for that variable in the node's observations. The algorithm chooses from this large set the question that best partitions the data. Best is measured by purity of the results (see Breiman et al. (1984) for definitions of purity). So, for example, a question that partitions the data into nodes with dominant class labels is preferred to one that has the labels in roughly equal proportions. Similarly, a regression tree that partitions the data into nodes whose response values have low variance is preferred to one one high variance.

Other approaches exist to building classification trees and use different answers to the questions on tree construction (e.g., Kass (1980)). For example, it is possible to build trees with more than pairwise partitions at the nodes and to consider trees that ask more complicated questions involving more than one variable Brown & Pittard (1993).

Although trees have obvious interpretability advantages over other methods, they often suffer from less accuracy. Two of the more important recent extensions are boosting Freund & Schapire (1997) and random forests Breiman (2001). Boosting provides a method for trees to improve in accuracy by adapting to the errors they make in classification.

Random forests provides a mechanism for combining results from multiple classification trees to produce more accurate predictions. The random forests (RF) algorithm grows a group of classification trees (a forest). The RF algorithm constructs each tree in the forest using a modified version of the recursive partitioning algorithm. One modification the RF algorithm makes is that it construct the trees using a subset of the data drawn from the original data set by sampling with replacement. This is known as "bagging".

The RF algorithm also modified the choice of questions procedure. For each question the RF algorithm considers only a subset of the available variables. The RF algorithm chooses this subset at the begging of the tree growing process and keeps it constant throughout tree growing.

Finally, RF has modifies the labeling or estimation of the response. Since we now have a forest rather than a single tree the label provided by a leaf node containing an observation in one tree may differ from the leaf node containing that same observation in another tree. For a categorical response the RF algorithm labels a new observation by a vote among the leaf nodes containing the observation in all trees. For a numeric response the RF algorithm estimates the value as the mean or median of the values produced by the respective leaf nodes in all trees.

Random forests sacrifices the interpretability of a single tree for the improved accuracy provided by an involved sampling and merging scheme. The RF approach recovers some of the interpretability by constructing forests with changes to the original data set. These changes involve sampling without replacement the values of a single variable using data not used in the original forest construction (i.e., the "out-of-bag" data). The difference in performance of the forest with the newly sampled variable and the original variable values gives a measure of importance for that variable. However, we do not recover the relationships among variables. The RF algorithm does provide a rough measure of interactions by finding the number trees with commonly paired variables and comparing this to random pairing. Comments on this procedure are in Breiman (2001).

3.3 Evaluation

Unlike unsupervised learning techniques, we can and should evaluate results from supervised learning techniques. Evaluation requires testing procedures and metrics. The goal of testing procedures is to provide an objective view of the performance of the unsupervised learning technique on future observations. For many reasons it is best not to rely on the observations in the database that were used to parameterize a technique to assess its performance on future values. The major reason for this caveat is because each technique can be made to perform perfectly on a set of observations. However, this perfect performance on a known data set would not translate into perfect performance on newly obtained observations. In fact, the performance on these would be quite poor because we *overfit* the technique to the existing data set.

Testing procedures provide a way to avoid overfitting. The simplest testing procedure is to divide the database into two parts. One part, the training set, is used to build and parameterize the data mining technique. The second part is used to test the technique. For reasonably sized databases the division is normally two thirds for training and one third for testing. In addition, the choice of observations for each set is randomly made. It may be useful to use stratified sampling for either of both of the training and test sets if the distributions of groups within a target population is known.

Cross validation is another testing procedure that is used when the database is small or when concerns exist about the representativeness of a test set. Cross validation begins by dividing the data into M roughly equal sized parts. For each part, $i = 1, \ldots, M$ the model is fit using the data in the other $M - 1$ parts. The metric is then computed using the data in the remaining part. This is done M times giving M separate estimates of the metric. The final estimate for

the metric is simply the average over all M estimates.
Cross validation has the advantage that it uses all the data for both training and testing. This means that the analyst does not have to form a separate test set. Recursive partitioning, discussed in Section 3.2 uses cross validation to determine the final size of the tree. In this way cross validation is frequently used to find parameter values for the different data mining techniques. For those methods that do not use it for parameter estimation it provides a convenient testing approach to assess a data mining technique.
In addition to testing procedures, the analyst must also select a metric or metrics to use to evaluate the techniques. For numeric response problems, common metrics are functions of sums of squares or sums of absolute deviations. Both measures weight performance by distance to the correct response, but the former measure tends to penalize extreme errors more than measures that use absolute deviation.
For categorical response, metrics that count the number of errors are typically used. However, in many applications the type of error is also important. This is particularly true in diagnostic applications. In these cases it is convenient to separate the errors into false positives and false negatives. False positives occur when the data mining technique predicts an outcome and the outcome does not occur. False negatives happen when the data mining technique fails to predict an outcome that occurred. The diabetes example illustrates a case where these two errors are not equally weighted. In this a case a false negative typically is worse than a false positive since the latter error can be caught by subsequent testing. On the other hand, it would be disastrous if only false positives occurred since this would quickly overwhelm the available testing resources. Hence, in performing evaluations on classifiers both types of errors need to measured and trade-offs made between their predicted values.
A useful display that allows for viewing of both metrics is the Receiver Operating Characteristic (ROC) curve. The name for this graphic derives from its origin in WWII where it was used by the allies to assess the performance of early radar systems. The ROC curse shows the trade-offs between false positives and false negatives by plotting true positives (1-false negatives) versus false positives. This means that the ideal performance is in the upper left hand corner of the plot. The worst performance is in the lower right hand corner. Random performance is shown by a diagonal line at 45°.
ROC curves often show there is no one, clear winner among the techniques. This happens frequently because the lines in the ROC curve cross (this will be illustrated in Figure 4 in Section 5). The choice in these cases become a matter of trade-offs between false positives and false negatives.

4. Integrated learning for problem discovery

Returning to the requirements for problem discovery we described in Section 1, we noted the need for techniques that provide

1. Data association;
2. Outlier identification and exploitation;
3. Interpretable relationships; and
4. Integrate operation.

The elements of this section provide for each of these capabilities by filling in the gaps in existing techniques noted in the previous two sections. Subsection 4.1 describes unsupervised learning methods for data association. Subsection 3 describes the use of supervised learning methods with the interpretability needed for problem discovery. We combine all of these methods into a useful package for problem discovery in Subsection 4.3.

4.1 Data association

Data association refers to techniques that can find patterns that represent consistent causal or association mechanisms among the observations given evidence in the measured variables. To accomplish this goal data association uses and extends clustering and variable association to help uncover the mechanisms behind the problems in the domain of interest.

As with clustering (see Section 2.3) data association begins with measures of distance, similarity, or dissimilarity. To simplify our discussion here we consider only similarity. However, unlike general clustering algorithms, data association uses similarity measures tailored to the problem domain. Our approach to data association computes a problem tailored measure called a total similarity measure (TSM) between observations, $x_j, x_k, j,k \in \{1,\ldots,N\}$. The TSM is tailored to the domain through as a weighted composition of individual variable similarities or

$$\text{TSM}(x_j, x_k) = \frac{\sum_{i=1}^{p} w_i \alpha_i(x_{ji}, x_{ki})}{\sum_{i=1}^{p} w_i} \tag{9}$$

where $w_i, i \in \{1,\ldots,p\}$ are the weighting coefficients and $\alpha(x_{ji}, x_{ki})$ are similarity scores for each variable,$i \in \{1,\ldots,p\}$. Both the weights and the variable similarities are scaled between zero and one, so for $i \in \{1,\ldots,p\}, j,k \in \{1,\ldots,N\}$

$$\begin{aligned} w_i &\in [0,1] \\ \sum_{i=1}^{p} w_i &= 1 \\ \alpha(x_{ji}, x_{ki}) &\in [0,1] \end{aligned} \tag{10}$$

The similarity measures are typically scaled differences for quantitative variables and partial match scores for binary variables. Details are in (Brown & Hagen (2003)).

To tailor the TSM to the problem domain the weights are adjusted based on the observed values. Values common across all observation do not provide as much information for problem discovery as those with greater diversity. Greater diversity means that the occurrence of the same values in multiple observations gives greater confidence that these observations have common causal or association mechanisms. We formalize this idea using information theory. Let $\mathcal{I}(x_j \sim x_k; x_{ji}, x_{ki})$ represent the information that observations x_i and x_j have the same causal or association mechanism given the values of variable k for both observations. Now consider the following axioms from information theory as applied to this data association problem.

1. $\mathcal{I}(x_j \sim x_k; x_{ji}, x_{ki})$ should be a function only of the prior probability of causality or association before the values of the variable k are obtained and only of the posterior probability after their measurement.
2. If the values of two variable are statistically independent evidence of the causality or association of the observations then the combined information in their measurement should be the sum of the information provided by their separate, sequential measurement. Formally,

$$\mathcal{I}(x_j \sim x_k; x_{ji}, x_{ki}, x_{j\ell}, x_{k\ell}) = \mathcal{I}(x_j \sim x_k; x_{ji}, x_{ki}) + \mathcal{I}(x_j \sim x_k, i; x_{j\ell}, x_{k\ell}). \tag{11}$$

The left hand quantity is the information about the causality or association of the observations when we get the values of both variables simultaneously. The first term on the right is the information we would get from first obtaining the values on one variable (i). The second term on the right is the information we would get from now updating the information we had from variable i with the arrival of the values of variable ℓ.

3. Finally we require the evidence for causality or association in multiple instances to be additive. For example, suppose we have four observations, $a,b,c,$ and d. Then the information that x_a and x_b associate given the evidence in variable i plus the information that x_c and x_d associate given the evidence in variable ℓ should equal the information that they associate given the simultaneous presence of the information. Formally,

$$\mathcal{I}(x_a \sim x_b, x_c \sim x_d; x_{ai}, x_{bi}, x_{c\ell}, x_{d\ell}) = \mathcal{I}(x_a \sim x_b; x_{ai}, x_{bi}) + \mathcal{I}(x_c \sim x_d; x_{c\ell}, x_{d\ell}) \quad (12)$$

Taken together these axioms imply (see Feinstein (n.d.)) that information for causality or association given in the values of variable i for records j and k should be measured by

$$\mathcal{I}(x_j \sim x_k; x_{ji}, x_{ki}) = \mathcal{K} log\left(\frac{Pr(x_j \sim x_k; x_{ji}, x_{ki})}{Pr(x_j \sim x_k)}\right) \quad (13)$$

where $\mathcal{K}$ is a constant, the numerator is the posterior probability of mutual causality or association given the evidence in variable i, and the denominator is the prior probability of mutual causality or association.

Now since the observations may or may not have common causality or association, we want to measure the expected value of the information given the values measured for variable i. We take the expectation under the distribution for the posterior which gives a measure known as the Kullback-Leibler divergence or relative entropy (see, Brown & Smith (1990)):

$$\begin{aligned} \mathfrak{I}_i(x_j, x_k) &= Pr(x_j \sim x_k; x_{ji}, x_{ki}) log\left(\frac{Pr(x_j \sim x_k; x_{ji}, x_{ki})}{Pr(x_j \sim x_k)}\right) \\ &+ Pr(x_j \nsim x_k; x_{ji}, x_{ki}) log\left(\frac{Pr(x_j \nsim x_k; x_{ji}, x_{ki})}{Pr(x_j \nsim x_k)}\right) \end{aligned} \quad (14)$$

where $x_j \nsim x_k$ indicates that the observations do not have a common causal or association mechanism. Notice that this measure treats variables that give negative evidence about causality or association in the same way as positive evidence. Taken together equations 13 and 14 provide metrics for the information found in the value of a variable. In other words, a metric that dynamically adapts to the specifics of data association for problem discovery. This dynamic metric defines the weights, $w_i, i = 1, \ldots, p$ for the variables in equation 9

To use this metric we need to estimate the prior and posterior probabilities. These can be found from the observed frequencies in the data (see Brown & Hagen (2003)). The new Total Similarity Measure (TSM) with the information theoretic based weights is

$$\text{TSM}(x_j, x_k) = \frac{\sum_{i=1}^{p} \mathfrak{I}_i(x_j, x_k) v_i \alpha_i(x_{ji}, x_{ki})}{\sum_{i=1}^{p} \mathfrak{I}_i(x_j, x_k) v_i} \quad (15)$$

where the $v_i, i = 1, \ldots, p$ ensure satisfaction of the conditions in (10).

When used with clustering algorithms, such as those described in Section 2.3, the TSM in (15) provides us with a way to identify groups of observations with possible common causal or association mechanisms. However, the approach described in this section applies only to fixed field data or variables with defined levels. For free text or narrative variables we need results from text mining. The next section explores our approach to incorporating free text for problem discovery.

4.2 Text association

As discussed in Section 1 text association is a critical component of problem discovery. This follows from the common occurrence of text in domains that have interesting but complex causal and association relationships. For example, understanding the causal or association factors behind accidents, medical conditions, and even customer behavior requires the incorporation of evidence from text to fully understand the complex relationships in these domains.

As indicated in Section 2.4 A major problem with existing text mining and natural language processing is the computational complexity of the methods. This limits their usefulness for problem discovery where the amount text can overwhelm many current techniques. Additionally, methods from information retrieval require query specification to get the documents related to the query. Also information retrieval techniques compute the similarities between documents based only on the similarities between terms in the query and terms in the documents. Hence, high similarity scores between terms do not imply causation or association if the query was not well chosen.

To measure the similarities between narratives, we describe the use of High Information Content Words (HICW) to represent the narratives. We compute similarities between HICW as surrogates for similarities between narratives. We begin our description with a brief introduction to HICW and follow this with our method for using HICW for computing similarities between text and narratives.

High Information Content Words are a set of words selected from an observation's narrative that provide important information for distinguishing the observation and determining its similarity to other observations with possibly identical causal or association mechanisms. HICW have two features: the ability to represent the narrative and the ability to distinguish the observation.

HICW is not the same as the keywords of the observational narratives. Keywords are a set of words which can summarize the narratives. Although keywords can represent narratives, they may lose important information about the observations needed to understand causal or association mechanisms. For example, suppose we have a collection of narratives about accidents. One of the narratives states "An derailment occurred when a southbound passenger train struck a maintenance vehicle on the track." Another narrative states "A head-on collision and subsequent derailment occurred when an eastbound freight train failed to change tracks and struck a westbound freight train. The engineer of the eastbound train tested positive for drug use." A keyword for both narratives would be "derailment", because both narratives describe derailment accidents and this one word provides a nice summary. However, these two observations have different HICW. Derailments may occur with sufficient frequency that this word would not distinguish these observations from other observations. More importantly this word does not help capture the causal or association mechanisms. For this we need words like "maintenance vehicle on track" and "drug use." Hence, using HICW we seek to find these factors that can help with problem discovery.

HICW also provide a computational advantageous approach to measuring similarities between narratives. Rather than compute the similarities using all words in the narrative, the HICW approach focuses on a small but informative set of words. Perhaps more importantly, HICW excludes words with limited information values.

In order to use HICW for text association, we first generate a word dictionary. This word dictionary derives from the corpus of all narratives within the observations. The word dictionary lists words and their Inverse Document Frequency (IDF). IDF for word i is calculated as

$$\mathrm{IDF}_i = log_2\left(\frac{N}{n_i}\right) \tag{16}$$

where N is again the number of observations but also the number of narratives and n_i is the number of narrative that contain word i. Importantly, only content words are included in the word dictionary. Content words include nouns, verbs, adjectives, and adverbs, but exclude articles, conjunctions, and pronouns.

To generate HICW from a narrative, we first measure the importance of each word in the narrative. The importance of a word is decided by two criteria: the ability to represent the narrative and the ability to distinguish the observation. To paraphrase (Salton (n.d.)), the more times a word occurs in a narrative, the more likely the narrative is about this word and the greater the number of narratives containing the word, the less distinctively the word describes any of those narratives. Therefore, we can measure the importance or weight, w_{ij}, of a word i in narrative j by

$$w_{ij} = \mathrm{TF}_{ij} \times \mathrm{IDF}_i \tag{17}$$

where IDF_i is given in equation (16) and TF_{ij} is the term frequency of word i in narrative j defined as follows:

$$\mathrm{TF}_{ij} = \frac{\mathrm{tf}_{ij}}{\max_j\{\mathrm{tf}_{ij}\}}. \tag{18}$$

To generate the HICW from a narrative, the importance of each word in the narrative is computed using equation (17). Next the words are ranked based on these importance scores. A specified number of words with the highest importance are the HICW. Clearly if the number is too small we do not capture possibly important characteristics of the observation. On the other hand, if the number is too large we increase computation time and risk including insignificant words. We have found using test sets or cross-validation (see Section 3.3) provide good selection criteria for this number.

Once we have the HICW we can compute the similarities between narratives, and hence, the observations that contain those narratives. The simplest method to measure this similarity, S_{ij}, between narratives i and j is to compute

$$S_{ij} = \frac{2M_{ij}}{m_i + m_j} \tag{19}$$

where m_i and m_j are the number of words narratives i and j, respectively. M_{ij} is the number of words they have in common.

We can also measure this similarity using a synonym dictionary. This gives the following similarity measure

$$S_{ij} = \min \left\{ \frac{2\sum_{k=1}^{m_i} \sum_{\ell=1}^{m_j} \text{Sy}(W_{ki}, W_{\ell j})}{m_i + m_j}, 1 \right\} \tag{20}$$

where W_{ki} and $W_{\ell j}$ are the kth and ℓ^{th} HICW in narratives i and j, respectively. Sy() is the synonym dictionary function which returns a value for the synonym match between the words given as inputs. At its simplest this is a binary function that indicates whether the words are synonyms. A more sophisticated synonym function returns a value between zero and one indicating the quality of the synonymy.

4.3 Supervised learning for problem discovery

Recalling the goal for problem discovery we want to find patterns or relationships that indicate causal or association mechanisms. As canonical examples of problem discovery we have used the discovery of factors causing or contributing to accidents or disease states. As we noted in Sections 2 and Section 3 data mining techniques provide a foundation for this work, but they cannot answer the problem questions in isolation from each other.

We have found an integrated approach to problem discovery that marries the results from unsupervised learning with supervised learning works well. This approach has the following steps:

1. Calculate the similarity between observations using the adaptive techniques described in Sections 4.1 and 4.2;
2. Cluster the observations using one or more the clustering techniques described in Section 2.3;
3. Use interpretable supervised learning techniques, such as those described in Section 3 to validate the cluster solution or solutions; and
4. If validated, use the insights provided by the interpretable supervised learning techniques combined with the structure identified by the clustering procedures to identify causal or association mechanisms.

The previous sections have provided an overview to the conduct of steps 1 – 2. In this section we turn to the final steps, 3 – 4 in our integrated method.

The results from the unsupervised learning step will yield a clustering solution that we can represent as a probability density function over the space of variables. For example, equation (5) shows this density function as a mixture of Gaussian densities. Using the insightful approach of Breiman (Breiman (2001)) we can apply supervised learning to help validate the cluster solution.

To apply this approach, let $f_(x)$ represent the density given by the original data. It is this density that our cluster solution has estimated. We now take independent draws from each variable in the data set and call this new distribution $f_I(x)$. Notice that if the original data set contains structure in $f(x)$ which we approximated with our cluster solution, then the independent variable distribution, $f_I(x)$ contains none of this structure. Thus, we can treat the observations in the original data set as coming from class 1 and the observations created by the independently sampled data set as class 2. This formulation enables the use of supervised learning to indicate the separability of the observations from the two classes. The greater the accuracy of supervised learning methods on test sets drawn from these two distributions the more confident we are in the clustering solution, and hence, the patterns this solutions provides. The lower accuracy reduces our confidence in the clustering solution.

This use of supervised learning can provide more general comparisons as indicated in Hastie et al. (2001). Instead of forming the distribution $f_I(x)$ using independent and uniform draws on each of the variables, we can instead create the new distribution according to any appropriate reference distribution. This enables a richer set of comparisons with the distribution observed in the original data set. To this we again apply supervised learning to classify observations from $f(x)$ and $f_I(x)$. Again we are interested in using the supervised learning methods to give us measures of departure of the original distribution from the reference distribution.

If the application of supervised learning shows significant departure from the reference distribution (say, with classification accuracy of better than 70%) then we can proceed to further understand the characteristics and relationships in the problem domain. For instance, in addition to providing a validation measure of the clustering solution, when this supervised learning approach is implemented with the methods described in Section 3 it can reveal variable importance, the presence of outliers, and variable interactions and nonlinearities. These characteristics can help narrow the focus of the problem discovery and allow for variable reductions or shrinkage (using the methods in Section 2.2). Once the number of variables is reduced or the variables are transformed using principal components or singular value decomposition, we can find a new clustering solution. Again we apply supervised learning to this clustering solution and repeat this process until the change is minimal (below some predefined threshold).

The previous two sections have provided us with the similarity measures that can be directly tailored to the specifics of the problem discovery domain of interest. Section 4.1 showed an information theoretic formulation for adaptively weighting and then scoring the similarities of values from fixed field variables. Section 4.2 showed how we can get adaptive weights and similarity scores for free-text variables. Once we have these similarity scores we can use any of the clustering techniques.

A third requirement for problem discovery methods applies to the use of supervised learning techniques. Specifically these techniques must produce interpretable results. This means that the discovery methods must reveal insights into causal or association mechanisms that contribute to the problem. So, unlike traditional data mining, problem discovery focuses more on interpretability at the possible expense of accuracy.

Finally, problem discovery requires the integration of methods from both supervised and unsupervised learning. By definition the exact nature of the problem is unknown so the application of, say, supervised learning tends to provide a narrow focus that misses important aspects of the problem. In contrast, unsupervised learning provides too broad a perspective in the presence of known instances of problematic behavior. Hence, problem discovery requires integrated strategies that combine results from supervised and unsupervised learning approaches.

5. Problem discovery example

As an example of the of the method described in the previous sections for the problem discovery, consider the rail operations in the U.S. In particular, the U.S. wants to reduce the number and severity of train accidents. Positive Train Control (PTC) has been advocated as an approach to enabling the desired reduction. PTC consists of a suite of technologies, e.g., accelerometers, controllers, temperature, humidity, and other environmental sensors, and GPS. The Federal Railroad Administration (FRA) has spent more than 15 years in development of PTC and expects to deploy this technology later this decade Administration

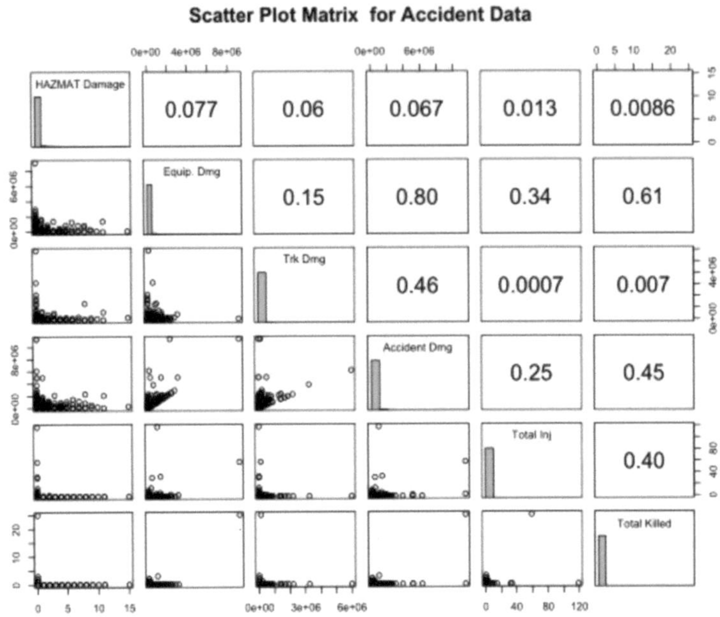

Fig. 2. Scatter plot and correlations for accident outcome variables.

(2009b). "The National Transportation Safety Board (NTSB) has named PTC as one of its "most-wanted" initiatives for national transportation safety" Administration (2009b). Beginning in 2001 the railroads deployed components of PTC on small sections of track to test and validate its usefulness. A complete list of these deployments is in Administration (2009b).

Despite the development and incremental deployment of this technology, rail operators in the U.S. do not fully understand the causes or associated mechanisms behind train accidents. They specifically do not know how the number and severity of these accidents will be affected by the deployment of PTC.

To apply problem discovery methods to train accidents we use the data available on accidents for the last decade Administration (2009a). The data consist of yearly reports of accidents and each yearly set has has 141 variables. The variables are a combination of numeric, e.g., accident speed, categorical, e.g., equipment type, and free text. The free text is contained in narrative fields that describe the accident. We can divide the fixed field variables into three categories: control, exogenous, and outcome. The control variables, such as, speed can be set by the engineer or train operator. The exogenous variables like weather provide uncontrollable conditions at the time of the accident. Outcome variables measure the results of the accident. Examples of these results are the cost of damage and the number of people injured or killed.

The train accident data are typical of other types of accident data in that they are highly skewed. Figure 2 shows pairwise scatter plots and linear correlations among the outcome variables. This figure shows that most accidents have little damage or loss of life. Extreme events do occur, however. The question for problem discovery methods is to find patterns in these events that may guide solutions.

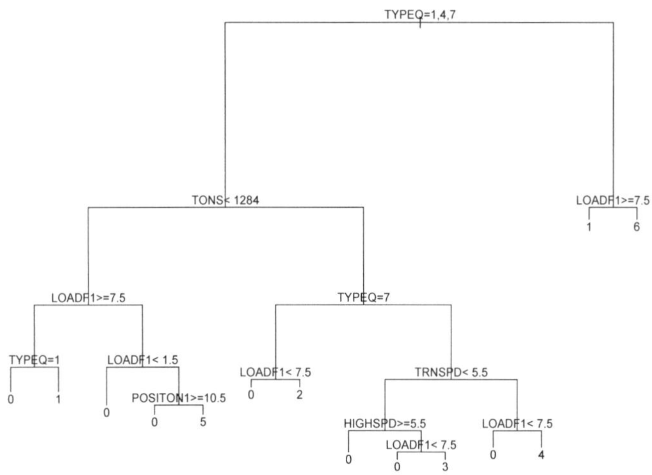

Fig. 3. Tree representation of clusters found by data association.

Applying the methods discussed in Section 4 we first apply clustering techniques. In this case we applied the data association and the text mining methods from Sections 4.1 and 4.2. We used both nearest neighbor and model-based clustering algorithms with the similarity scores computed as those sections describe. The results can be viewed in several ways. Figure 3 shows a classification tree representation of the clusters found with just the fixed field variables. This representation is convenient, but somewhat misleading since other variables become important to the relationship as we include the high information content words (HICW) from the narratives. Nonetheless, it does show the use of data association to uncover patterns in the data.

Before proceeding with additional problem discovery we need to validate that the data contain enough structure to justify the clustering results. Figure 4 shows the ROC curves from applying both random forests and recursive partitioning to the data and to two data sets randomly created with the variables and values given in the original data. These two new data sets are random permutations of the original values. Then using the method described in Section 4.3 we sought to discover if the original data could be accurately discriminated from the random sets. To make this comparison we built the models using approximately two thirds of the data and tested with the remaining one third. As this figure shows, both random forests and recursive partitioning provide highly accurate models on these out-of-sample data. This suggests that the data do contain relationships susceptible to problem discovery.

With those results we applied the combined data and text association techniques described in Sections 4.1 and 4.2. Figure 5 shows the four cluster solution projected into the first two principal components of the outcome variables. Principal components are described in Section 2.2. This solution suggests that there are some causes that have particular relevance to the outcome variables. As an illustration of high information words, the HICW found that accompany cluster 1 are "drugs", "alcohol", and "positive."

Also of interest are indicators of variable importance. Figure 6 shows the variable importance

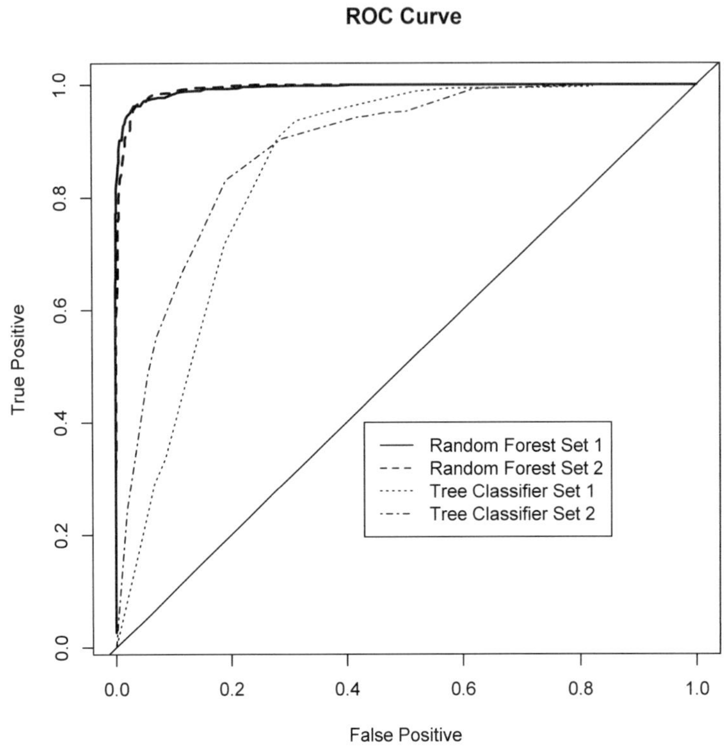

Fig. 4. ROC validation plots for cluster structure in the data.

plot found by apply random forests to the discovered types of accidents. The variables suggest the components that contribute to each of the different types of accidents discovered in the data and text association. This variable importance applies only to the fixed field variables.

The results from this problem discovery exercise suggest that most accidents will not be affected by the use of PTC. Further the most extreme accident was a head-on collision with an HICW of "drugs". This incident had a total cost of $11M, 25 killed, and 62 injured. It clustered with others accidents that were not as costly but nonetheless were more damaging the median. While the potential for head-on collisions can be detected by PTC it is not clear that PTC would matter given mental state train operator. The largest cluster of accidents had little cost and very low speeds. An HICW for accidents in this large cluster is "fouling," and this will continue to occur with the same regularity and cost even if PTC is fully implemented. Another cluster that had deaths or injuries greater than zero concerned crossing and intersection accidents. These would not be affected significantly by PTC. However, there are a small number of accidents at speeds and conditions that suggest that PTC could have an influence. Unfortunately removing them will not greatly impact the overall severity of accidents.

Clearly this exercise suggests that investment in other strategies may produce more significant results for reducing the number and severity than PTC. For instance, warning systems for equipment on the tracks or at grade crossing will have the most effect on reducing the number of those killed by trains.

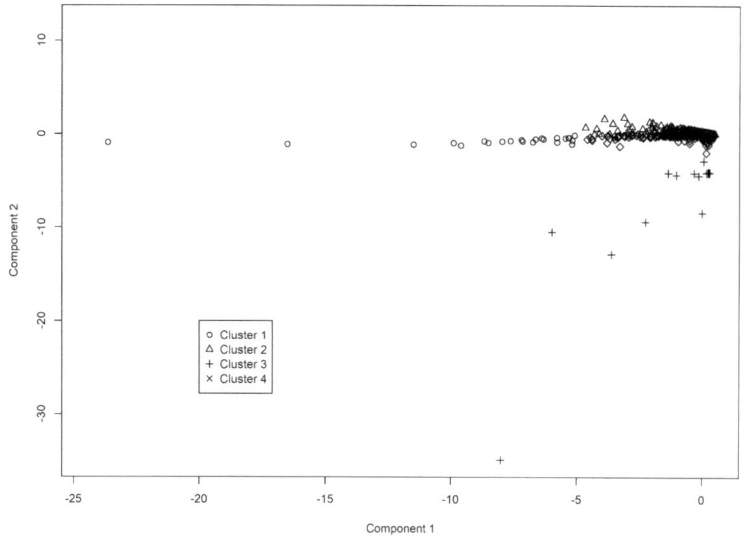

Fig. 5. Clusters showing types of accidents as projected into the first two principal components.

From the perspective of this chapter, this exercise shows the effectiveness of combined methods from unsupervised and supervised learning.

6. Conclusion and future work

Problem discovery represents a major application for data mining techniques. The goal of problem discovery is to find causal or association mechanisms and the discovery processes in data mining can contribute greatly the achievement of this goal. However, to make this happen requires that data mining techniques address the four key requirements of problem discovery: data association; text association; supervised learning for structural characterization; and integration of methods.

While unsupervised learning has techniques and methods similar to those need in the areas of data and text association, we note that there are gaps. The methods described in Sections 4.1 and 4.2 show ways to fill these gaps. For data association Section 4.1 describes the use of information theory to obtain similarity measures tailored for problem discovery. Section 4.2 illustrates how high information content words relevant to the causal and association mechanisms can be found and exploited.

Once we have the initial clustering structure evident in the data, we can apply supervised learning to provide greater insights into the nature of this structure. As Section {subsec:int shows, supervised learning also provides the means for validating the structures found by the unsupervised learning methods. These results then lead to another round of unsupervised learning and closer inspection of the variables indicated as important by the supervised learning techniques. Section 4.3 also show the general integration methodology for coupling the supervised and unsupervised techniques.

Finally, Section 5 provides an example of the use of these techniques to understand the problems at the foundation train accidents in the U.S. In so doing, it provides an critique of the

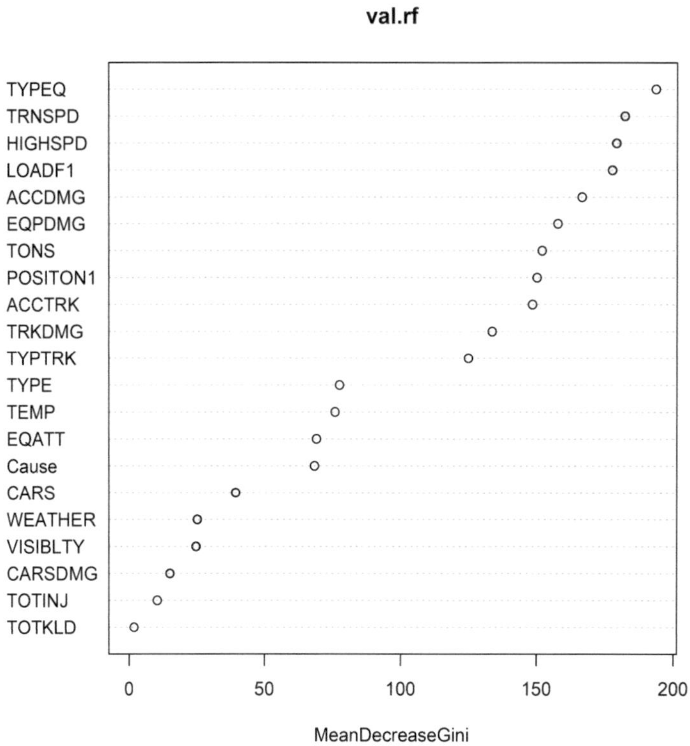

Fig. 6. Variable importance in classifying the types of accidents

pursuit of technologies such as Positive Train Control as the means to reduce the extent and severity of accidents. The section shows the results from the data and text association. It also shows the structures discovered by supervised learning. Finally, it shows how this integrated approach to problem discovery can guide designs for addressing the factors most relevant to accomplishing the goal of the rail operators to diminish the number and costs of accidents.

The methods presented here show promise for improving problem discovery. However, many important challenges remain to extend methods such as these across a wider range of applications. First, methods are needed to incorporate the temporal characteristics. Temporal data are correlated and this correlation structure needs to be well-modeled if we are to understand the problem mechanisms related to time versus other causes.

Similarly, spatial characteristics should be specifically modeled as part of the problem discovery toolkit of techniques. As with time, spatial variables have special correlation structures. These structures require methods more directed than the overarching approaches currently used, particularly in unsupervised learning.

Finally, the integration of supervised and unsupervised learning methods for areas like problem discovery is not well studied. Unlike the combination of supervised learning techniques, which has received considerable attention, the integration of methods from both general areas remains a matter of folklore rather than rigorous investigation. This has to change. Problem discovery requires richer integration of these methodological areas to provide techniques for improving our understanding of the possibly complex relationships

among variables at the heart of causal and association mechanisms. This is true for more than problem understanding where the need is particularly evident.
Overall problem discovery will grow in importance as the challenges of dealing with complex issues in health care, energy, transportation, and other areas become evident and pressing. The methods described in this chapter introduce the critical use of ideas from data mining to aid in the problem discovery process. If we are successful the next decade will witness major advances in this important field.

7. References

Administration, F. R. (2009a). Office of safety analysis. http://safetydata.fra.dot.gov/officeofsafety/.

Administration, F. R. (2009b). Positive train control (ptc). http://www.fra.dot.gov/us/content/784.

Agrawal, R., Mannila, H., Srikant, R., Toivonen, H. & Verkamo, A. (1996). Fast discovery of association rules, *in* U. Fayyad, G. Pietsky-Shapiro, P. Smyth & R. Uthurusamy (eds), *Advances in Knowledge Discovery and Data Mining*, AAAI/MIT Press, Cambridge, MA, pp. 307–328.

Baluja, S., Mittal, V. & Sukthankar, R. (1999). Applying machine learning for high performance named-entity extraction, *Proceedings of the Conference of the Pacific Association for Computational Linguistics*, Pacific Association for Computational Linguistics, Watterloo, Canada.

Bishop, C. (1999a). Bayesian pca, *in* M. Kearns, S. Solla & D. Cohn (eds), *Advances in Neural Information Processing Systems, Volume 11*, MIT Press, Cambridge, MA, pp. 382–388.

Bishop, C. (1999b). Variational methods in principal components, *Proceedings of the Ninth International Conference on Artificial Neural Networks, ICANN*, Vol. 1, IEE, pp. 509–514.

Breiman, L. (2001). Random forests, *Machine Learning* 45: 5–32.

Breiman, L., Friedman, J., Olshen, R. & Stone, C. (1984). *Classification and Regression Trees*, Wadsworth, Belmont, CA.

Brown, D. E. & Hagen, S. (2003). Data association methods with application to law enforcement, *Decision Support Systems* 34: 369–378.

Brown, D. E. & Smith, R. L. (1990). A correspondence principle for relative entropy minimization, *Naval Research Logistics* 37: 191–202.

Brown, D. & Pittard, C. (1993). Classification trees with optimal multi-variate splits, pp. 475–478. Proceedings of the IEEE International Conference on Systems, Man, and Cybernetics, Le Touquet, France.

Ciravegna, F., Lavelli, A., Mana, N., Matiasek, J., Gilardoni, L., Mazza, S., Black, W. & Rinaldi, F. (1999). Facile: Classifying texts integrating pattern matching and information extraction, *Proceedings of 16th International Joint Conference on Artificial Intelligence (IJCAI-99)*, AAAI, San Francisco, CA, pp. 890–895.

Comon, P. (1994). Independent component analsysis, a new concept?, *Technometrics* 36: 287–314.

Copas, J. (1983). Regression, prediction and shrikage (with discussion), *Journal of the Royal Statistical Society, Series B Methodological* 45: 31–354.

Corley, C. & Mihalcea, R. (2005). Measuring the semantic similarity of texts, *Proceeding of the ACL Workshop on Empirical Modeling of Semantic Equivalence and Entailment*, Ann Arbor, MI, pp. 13–18.

Deerwester, S., Dumais, S., Furnas, G., Landauer, T. & Harshman, R. (1990). Indexing by latent semantic analysis, *Journal of the American Society of Information Science* 41: 391–407.

Fall, C., Torcsvari, A., Benzineb, K. & Karetka, G. (2003). Automated categorization in the international patent classification, *ACM SIGIR Forum* 37: 10–25.

Feinstein, A. (n.d.). *Foundations of Information Theory*, McGraw-Hill, New York.

Freund, Y. & Schapire, R. (1997). A decision theoretic generalization of online learning and an application to boosting, *Journal of Computer and System Sciences* 55: 119–139.

Gentili, G., Marinilli, M., Micarelli, A. & Sciarrone, F. (2001). Text categorization in an intelligent agent for filtering information on the web, *International Journal of Pattern Recognition and Artificial Intelligence* 15: 527–549.

Golub, G. & Loan, C. V. (1983). *Matrix Computations*, Johns Hopkins University Press, Baltimore, MD.

Hastie, T., Tibshirani, R. & Friedman, J. (2001). *The elements of statistical learning*, Springer Verlag, New York, NY.

Hoang, A. (2004). Information retrieval with principal components, *Proceeding of the International Conference on Information Technology: Coding and Computing (ITCC'04)*, Vol. 1, IEEE Computer Society, Las Vegas, NV, p. 262.

Hoerl, A. & Kennard, R. (1964). Ridge regression: Biased estimation for nonorthogonal problems, *Technometrics* 12: 55–67.

Hotho, A., Staab, S. & Maedche, A. (2001). Onthology-based text clustering, *Proceedings of the IJCAI-2001 Workshop Text Mining: Beyond Supervision*, Springer-Verlag, Seattle, WA, pp. 264–278.

Kass, G. (1980). An exploratory technique for investigating large quantities of categorical data, *Applied Statistics* 29: 119–127.

Kedem, B. & Fokianos, K. (2003). *Regression Models for Time Series Analysis*, John Wiley and Sons, Inc., Hoboken, NJ.

Konchady, M. (2006). *Text Mining Application Programming*, Charles River Media, Boston, MA.

Krupka, G. R. & Hausman, K. (1998). Isoquest inc.: Description of the netowltm extractor system as used for muc-7, *Proceedings of the Seventh Message Understanding Conference (MUC-7)*, Science Applications International Corporation, 10260 Campus Pt. Dr., San Diego, CA.

Mani, I. & Maybury, M. (1999). *Advances in Automatic Text Summarization*, The MIT Press, Cambridge, MA.

Salton, G. (n.d.). *Automatic Text Processing: The Transformation, Analysis and Retrieval of Information by Computer*, Addison-Wesley, Massachusetts.

Seber, G. (1984). *Multivariate Observations*, John Wiley and Sons, Inc., New York.

Witten, I. H., Bray, Z., Mahoui, M. & Teahan, W. (1999). Using language models for generic entity extraction, *Proceedings of the International Conference on Machine Learning (ICML 1999), Workshop on Text Mining*, Morgan Kaufmann, Bled, Slovenia.

Wold, H. (1975). Soft modeling by latent variables: The nonlinear iterative partial least squares (nipals) approach, *Perspectives in Probability and Statistics, In Honor of M.S. Bartlett* pp. 117–144.

Yetisgen-Yildiz, M. & Pratt, W. (2006). Using statistical and knowledge-based approaches for literature-based discovery, *Journal of Biomedical Informatics* 39: 600–611.

Zheng, Z., Kohavi, R. & Mason, L. (2001). Real world performance of association rule algorithms, *in* F. Provost & R. Srikant (eds), *Proceedings of the ACM SIGKDD Intentional Conference on Knowledge Discovery in Databases and Data Mining (KDD-01)*, ACM Press, pp. 401–406.

26

Development of a Classification Rule Mining Framwork by Using Temporal Pattern Extraction

Hidenao Abe
Department of Medical Informatics, Shimane University
Japan

1. Introduction

In recent years, KDD (Knowledge Discovery in Databases) (Fayyad et al., 1996) has been widely known as a process to extract useful knowledge from databases. In the research field of KDD, 'Temporal (Time-Series) Data Mining' is one of important issues to mine useful knowledge such as patterns, rules, and structured descriptions for a domain expert. However, huge numerical temporal data such as stock market data, medical test data, and sensor data have been only stored to databases. Besides, many temporal mining schemes such as temporal pattern extraction methods and frequent itemset mining methods have been proposed to find out useful knowledge from numerical temporal databases. Although each method can find out partly knowledge of each suggested domains, there is no systematic framework to utilize each given numerical temporal data through whole of the KDD process.

To above problems, we have developed an integrated temporal data mining environment, which can apply numerical temporal data to find out valuable knowledge systematically. The environment consists of temporal pattern extraction, mining, mining result evaluation support system to attempt numerical temporal data from various domains.

In this chapter, we describe a classification rule mining framework by combining temporal pattern extraction and rule mining. This framework has been developed for mining if-then rules consisting of temporal patterns in left hand side of the rules. The right hand side of the rules is indicated to predict both of important events and temporal patterns of important index. In order to show the effectiveness of the framework, we implemented this framework for a medical sequential data of laboratory test results for chronic hepatitis patients and a sequential data consisting of technical indexes for Japanese stocks. By using the implementations and experimental results, we present the following merits achieved by the classification rules with considering temporal patterns of the target attributes:

- Finding different interesting aspects of the decisions/results
- Finding important temporal patterns and attributes for the decision at the same time

In the remaining of this chapter, we describe the related works of this framework in Section 2. In Section 3, we present the framework to mine classification rules that are consisting of temporal patterns and decisions[1]. After implementing this framework, an experiment about Japanese stock trading is performed in Section 4. Finally, we summarize the experimental results in Section 6.

---

[1]'decision' means just a cross-sectional decision making, and also means important future situations in this framework.

2. Related work

Many efforts have been done to analyze temporal data at the field of pattern recognitions. Statistical methods such as autoregressive model (Akaike, 1969) and ARMA(Auto Regressive Integrated Moving Average) model have been developed to analyze temporal data, which have linearity, periodicity, and equalized sampling rate. As signal processing methods, Fourier transform, Wavelet (Mallat, 1989), and fractal analysis method have been also developed to analyze such well formed temporal data. These methods based on mathematic models restrict input data, which are well sampled.

However, temporal data include ill-formed data such as clinical test data of chronic disease patients, purchase data of identified customers, and financial data based on social events. To analyze these ill-formed temporal data, we take another temporal data analysis method such as DTW (Dynamic Time Wrapping) (Berndt & Clifford, 1996), temporal clustering with multiscale matching (Hirano & Tsumoto, 2002), and finding Motif based on PAA (Piecewise Approximation Aggregation) (Keogh et al., 2003).

For finding out useful knowledge to decide orders for stock market trading, many studies have done. For example, temporal rule induction methods such as Das's framework (Das et al., 1998) have been developed. Frequent itemset mining methods are also often attempt to the domain (Wong & Fu, 2006). Although they analyze the trend of price movement, many trend analysis indices such as moving average values, Bolinger band signals, MACD signals, RSI and signals based on balance table are often never considered.

In addition, these studies aim not to find out decision support knowledge, which directly indicates orders for stock market trading, but useful patterns to think better decision by a domain expert. Therefore, the decision support of trading order is still costly task even if a domain expert uses some temporal data analysis methods. The reason of this problem is that decision criteria of trading called anomaly are obtained from very complex combination of many kinds of indices related to the market by domain experts.

3. An integrated framework for temporal rule mining by using automatic temporal pattern extraction

Our temporal data mining environment needs temporal data as input. Output rules are if-then rules, which have temporal patterns or/and ordinal clauses, represented in $A = x$, $A \leq y$, and $A > z$. Combinations of extracted patterns and/or ordinal clauses can be obtained as if-then rules by a rule induction algorithm.

To implement the environment, we have analyzed temporal data mining frameworks (Das et al., 1998; Ohsaki et al., 2004). Then, we have identified procedures for pattern extraction as data pre-processing, rule induction as mining, and evaluation of rules with visualized rule as post-processing of mined result. The system provides these procedures as commands for users. At the same time, we have designed a graphical interface, which include data processing, validation for patterns on elemental sequences, and rule visualization as charts.

Our integrated time-series data mining environment combines the following major functional components: time-series data pre-processing, mining, post-processing for mined results, and other database operators to validate data and results of every phase.

With this environment, we aim the following efforts for each agent:

1. Developing and improving time-series data mining procedures for system developers
2. Collaborative data processing and rule induction for data miners

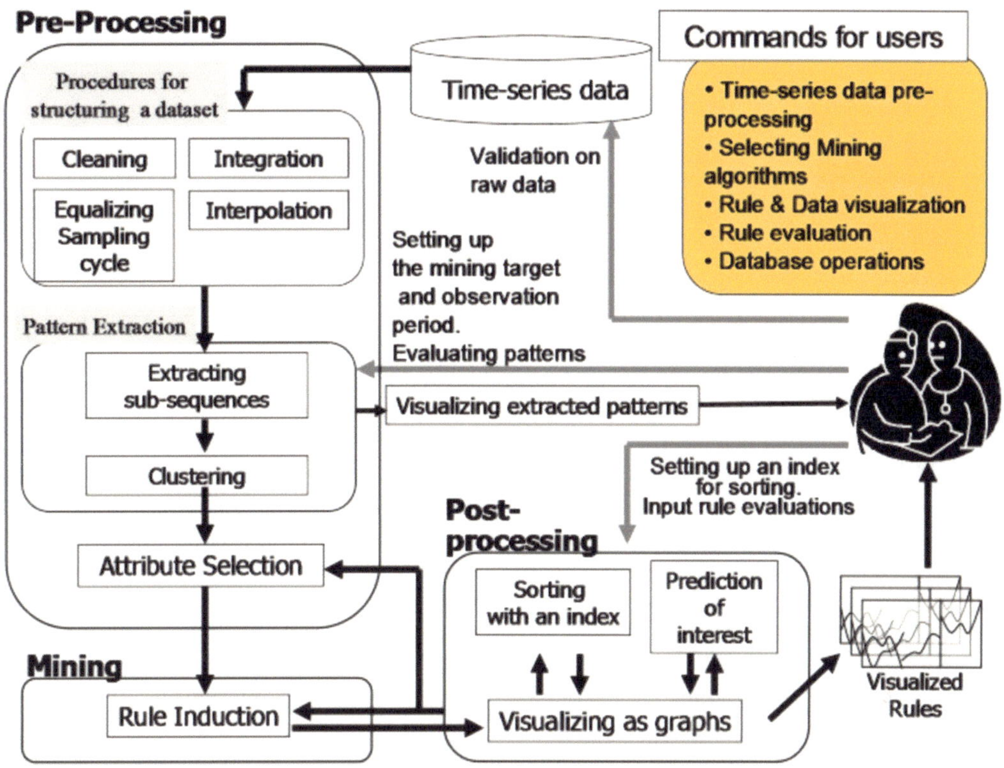

Fig. 1. A system flow view of the integrated time-series data mining environment.

3. Active evaluation and interaction for domain experts

Since we have standardized input/output data formats, data miners and domain experts can execute different algorithms/methods in each procedure seamlessly. They can execute these procedures on graphical human-system interfaces, discussing each other. Beside, system developers can connect new or improved method for a procedure separately. Only following input/output data formats, system developers can also connect a complex sub-system, which selects a proper algorithm/method to the procedure before executing it. If an algorithm/method lacks for a procedure, they are only needed to develop its wrapper to connect the procedure, because each procedure assumes plug-in modules in this environment. To implement the environment, we have analyzed time-series data mining frameworks. Then we have identified procedures for pattern extraction as data pre-processing, rule induction as mining, and evaluation of rules with visualized rule as post-processing of mined result. The system provides these procedures as commands for users. At the same time, we have designed graphical interfaces, which include data processing, validation for patterns on elemental sequences, and rule visualization as graphs. Fig. 1 shows us a typical system flow of this time-series data mining environment.

3.1 Mining classification rules consisting of temporal patterns

In order to obtain classification rules with temporal patterns in their consequents, we firstly collect temporal data for the objective problem. For the temporal data, we have identified procedures for temporal data mining as follows:

- Data pre-processing
  - pre-processing for data construction
  - temporal pattern extraction
  - attribute selection
- Mining
  - classification rule induction
- Other database procedures
  - selection with conditions
  - join

As data pre-processing procedures, pre-processing for data construction procedures include data cleaning, equalizing sampling rate, interpolation, and filtering irrelevant data. Since these procedures are almost manual procedures, they strongly depend on given temporal data and a purpose of the mining process. Temporal pattern extraction procedures include determining the period of sub-sequences and finding representative sequences with a clustering algorithm such as K-Means, EM clustering (Liao, 2005) and the temporal pattern extraction method developed by Ohsaki et al. (Ohsaki, Abe & Yamaguchi, 2007). Attribute selection procedures are done by selecting relevant attributes manually or using attribute selection algorithms (Liu & Motoda, 1998). At mining phase, we should choose a proper rule induction algorithm with some criterion. There are so many classification rule induction algorithms such as Version Space (Mitchell, 1982), AQ15 citepMichalski86, C4.5 rule (Quinlan, 1993), and any other algorithm. To support this choice, we have developed a tool to construct a proper mining application based on constructive meta-learning called CAMLET (Abe & Yamaguchi, 2004). However, we have taken PART (Frank et al., 1998) implemented in Weka (Witten & Frank, 2000) in the case study to evaluate improvement of our pattern extraction algorithm.

3.2 Prediction for test data with classifying temporal patterns and evaluation with visualizing rules

- Post-processing of mined results
  - predicting classes of test(unknown) data
  - visualizing mined rule
  - rule selection
  - supporting rule evaluation

In order to predict class of a test dataset with learned a classification model, the system should formally predict pattern symbols of the test dataset using some accurate classification learning method L^2 based on the training dataset as shown in Fig. 2.

[2]Since this classification learning algorithm is not required understandability of the learning model, we can use more complicate but accurate learning algorithms such as neural network and ensemble learning scheme in this process.

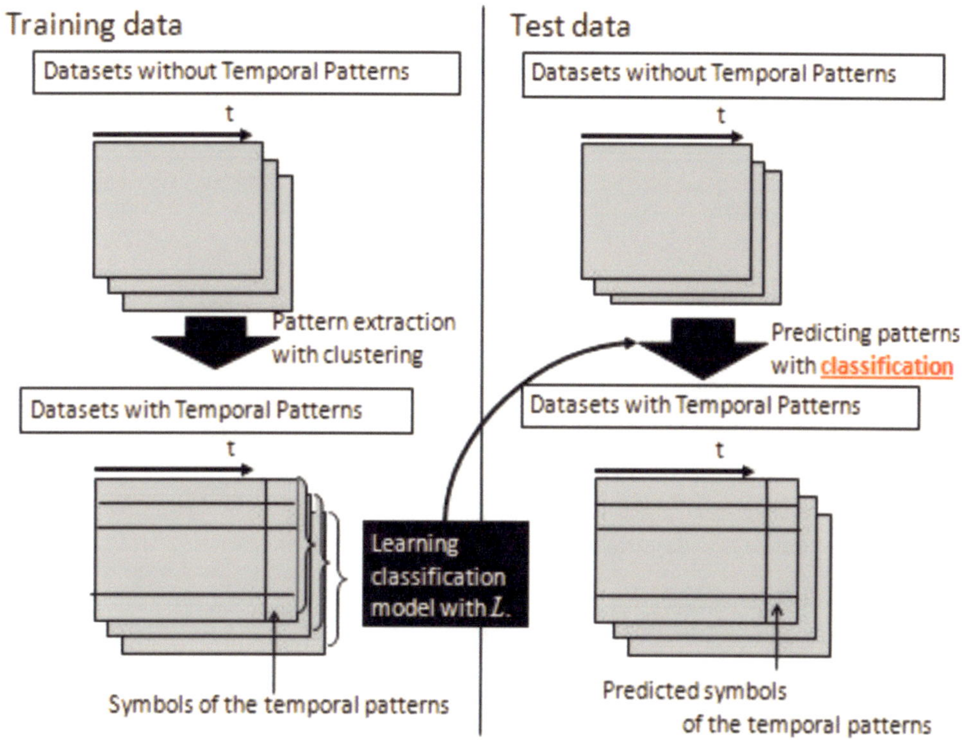

Fig. 2. Temporal pattern prediction phase for test data to predict by using the mined classification rules with temporal patterns.

To validate mined rules correctly, users need readability and ease for understand about mined results. We have taken 39 objective rule evaluation indexes to select mined rules (Ohsaki, Abe, Tsumoto, Yokoi & Yamaguchi, 2007), visualizing and sorting them depended on usersf interest. Although these two procedures are passive support from a viewpoint of the system, we have also identified active system reaction with prediction of user evaluation based on objective rule evaluation indexes and human evaluations.
Other database procedures are used to make target data for a data mining process. Since the environment has been designed based on open architecture, these procedures have been able to develop separately. To connect each procedure, we have only defined input/output data format by using the comma separated value style.

4. Temporal rule mining for japanese stock trading

After implementing the integrated temporal data mining environment described in Section 3, we have done a case study on Japanese stock market database. In this case study, we firstly gathered temporal price data and its trend index values through Kaburobo SDK (*Kaburobo*, 2004). Then, using the environment, we evaluated the performance of if-then rules based on temporal patterns. Finally, with regarding to the results, we discuss about the availability of our temporal rule mining based on temporal pattern extraction.

Attribute name		Description
RAW	opening	opening price of the day (O_t)
	high	Highest price of the day (H_t)
	low	Lowest price of the day (L_t)
	closing	Closing price of the day (C_t)
	Volume	Volume of the day (V_t)
TREND INDICES	Moving Average	Buy: if $SMA_t - LMA_t < 0 \cap SMA_{t-1} - LMA_{t-1} > 0$,Sell: if $SMA_t - LMA_t > 0 \cap SMA_{t-1} - LMA_{t-1} < 0$ Where $SMA_t = (C_t + C_{t-1} + \ldots + C_{t-12})/13$, and $LMA_t = (C_t + C_{t-1} + \ldots + C_{t-25})/26$
	Bolinger Band	Buy: if $C_t \geq (MA_t + 2\sigma) \times 0.05$, Sell: if $C_t \leq (MA_t - 2\sigma) \times 0.05$ where $MA_t = (C_t + C_{t-1} + \ldots + C_{t-24})/25$
	Envelope	Buy: if $C_t \geq MA_t + (MA_t \times 0.05)$, Sell: if $C_t \leq MA_t - (MA_t \times 0.05)$
	HLband	Buy: if $C_t < LowLine_{t-10days}$, Sell: if $C_t > HighLine_{t-10days}$
	MACD	Buy: if $MACD_t - AvgMACD_{t-9days} > 0 \cap MACD_{t-1} - AvgMACD_{(t-1)-9days} < 0$ Sell: if $MACD_t - AvgMACD_{t-9days} < 0 \cap MACD_{t-1} - AvgMACD_{(t-1)-9days} > 0$ Where $MACD_t = EMA_{t-12days} - EMA_{t-26days}$, $EMA_t = EMA_{t-1} + (2/range+1)(C_{t-1} - EMA_{t-1})$
	DMI	Buy: if $PDI_t - MDI_t > 0 \cap PDI_{t-1} - MDI_{t-1} < 0$, Sell: if $PDI_t - MDI_t < 0 \cap PDI_{t-1} - MDI_{t-1} > 0$ Where $PDI = \sum_{i=t-n}^{t}(H_i - H_{i-1}) \div \sum_{i=t-n}^{t} TR_i \times 100$, $MDI = \sum_{i=t-n}^{t}(L_i - L_{i-1}) \div \sum_{i=t-n}^{t} TR_i \times 100$ $\cdot TR_t = \max\{(H_t - C_{t-1}), (C_{t-1} - L_t), (H_t - L_t)\}$
	volumeRatio	$VR_t = \{(\sum_{i=t-25, H_i > L_i}^{t} V_i + \sum_{i=t-25, H_i = L_i}^{t} V_i)/(\sum_{i=t-25, H_i < L_i}^{t} V_i + \sum_{i=t-25, H_i = L_i}^{t} V_i)\} \times 100$
	RSI	$RSI_t = 100 - 100/\{\sum_{i=t-13, C_{i-1} < C_i}^{t}(C_{i-1} - C_i) / \sum_{i=t-13, C_{i-1} > C_i}^{t}(C_{i-1} - C_i) + 1\}$
	Momentum	$M_t = C_t - C_{t-10}$
	Ichimoku1	Buy: if $C_{t-1} < RL_{t-9days} \cap C_t > RL_{t-9days}$, Sell: if $C_{t-1} > RL_{t-9days} \cap C_t < RL_{t-9days}$ Where $RL_{t-9days} = average\ (\max(H_i) + \min(L_i))$ $(i = t-8, t-7, \ldots t)$
	Ichimoku2	Buy: if $C_{t-1} < RL_{t-26days} \cap C_t > RL_{t-26days}$, Sell: if $C_{t-1} > RL_{t-26days} \cap C_t < RL_{t-26days}$ Where $RL_{t-26days} = average\ (\max(H_i) + \min(L_i))$ $(i = t-25, t-24, \ldots t)$
	Ichimoku3	Buy: if $RL_{(t-2)-26days} < RL_{(t-2)-9days} \cap RL_{(t-1)-26days} > RL_{(t-1)-9days} \cap RL_{(t-1)-26days} < RL_{t-26days}$ Sell: if $RL_{(t-2)-26days} > RL_{(t-2)-9days} \cap RL_{(t-1)-26days} < RL_{(t-1)-9days} \cap RL_{(t-1)-26days} > RL_{t-26days}$
	Ichimoku4	Buy: if $C_t > AS1_{t-26} \cap C_t > AS2_{t-26}$, Sell: if $C_t < AS1_{t-26} \cap C_t < AS2_{t-26}$ Where $AS1_t = median\ (RL_{t-9days} - RL_{t-26days})$, $AS2_t = (\max(H_i) - \min(L_i))/2$ $(i = t-51, t-50, \ldots t)$

Table 1. The description about attributes from Kaburobo SDK.

4.1 Description about temporal datasets

Using Kaburobo SDK, we got four price values, trading volume, and 13 trend index values as shown in Table 1. The daily four price volumes and daily trading volume of each stock are gathered from the Kaburobo SDK as raw values. Then, we set up 13 days as short term range and 26 days as long term range for calculating technical indexes that consider both of short and long terms. Excepting DMI, volume ratio, and momentum, the trend indices are defined as trading signals: buy and sell. The attribute values of these indices are converted from 1.0 to -1.0. Thus, 0 means nothing to do (or hold on the stock) for these attributes.

We obtained temporal data consists of the above mentioned attributes about five financial companies and four telecommunication companies as follows: Credit Saison (Saison), Orix, Mitsubishi Tokyo UFJ Financial Group (MUFJFG), Mitsui Sumitomo Financial Group (MSFG), Mizuho Financial Group (MizuhoFG), NTT, KDDI, NTT Docomo (NTTdocomo), and Softbank. The period, which we have collected from the temporal stock data, is from 5th January 2006 to 31st May 2006. For each day, we have made decisions as the following: the decision is if the closing value rises 5% within 20 days then 'buy', otherwise if the closing value falls 5% within 20 days then 'sell', otherwise 'hold'.

We set these decisions as the class attribute to each target instance. Table 2 shows the class distributions about the nine stocks for the period.

For each gathered temporal data of the nine stocks, the system extracted temporal patterns for each attribute. To extract temporal patterns, we have used K-Means and Gaussian Mixture Model (GMM) clustering optimized with EM algorithm[3], which are implemented in Weka. As for the number of extracted patterns for K-Means as k, we set up $k = 4$ for being easy to

[3]Hereafter, we call this clustering algorithm as "GMM with EM algorithm."

Finance	buy	sell	Telecom	buy	sell
Saison	37	53	NTT	27	32
Orix	43	40	KDDI	42	39
MUFJFG	0	50	NTTdocomo	19	29
MSFG	6	27	Softbank	23	69
MizuhoFG	38	31			

Table 2. The class distributions of the nine stocks during the five months.

understand the extracted patterns on each technical indexes and their combinations. Then, the symbols of each pattern and the decision of each day joined as each instance of the target dataset.

5. Evaluating temporal pattern prediction by boosted C4.5

In order to predict temporal pattern of each test dataset, we have used Boosted C4.5 (Quinlan, 1996), which is also implemented in Weka. Table 3 and Table 4 show accuracies of temporal pattern prediction using Boosted C4.5 on patterns obtained by each clustering algorithm. These accuracies are averages of 100 times repeated 10-fold cross validation on the 18 datasets of the technical indexes as the attribute of each target dataset.

5.1 Mining results of the nine temporal stock data

In this section, we show accuracies of temporal rule mining with PART on each datasets themselves and cross-stocks.

As shown in Table 5, each rule set predicts the class labels of training dataset itself on each stock. The accuracies of the nine dataset are satisfactory high scores as a classification task.

As for evaluating the accuracy and efficiency of the classification rules with real value temporal patterns, we performed a cross-stock evaluation. In this evaluation, we obtained a rule set from one stock, and apply it to the other stock for predicting class labels; sell, buy, or hold. Table 6 and Table 6 show accuracies (The cross stock evaluation uses different stocks as training dataset and test dataset. Stocks in rows mean training datasets, and columns mean test datasets. As shown in these tables, emphasized numbers go beyond 50%, which means that the mined rules work better than just predicting sell or buy. The result shows the performance of our temporal rules depends on the similarity of trend values rather than the field of each stock.

5.2 Detailed result of the obtained classification rules with temporal patterns

As shown in Table 6 and Table 6, some rule sets predict significant decisions compared to the random prediction. In order to describe the rules more clearly, we present the representative rules in this section.

Fig. 3 shows an example of the classification rules with temporal patterns. These rules are obtained from the training dataset obtained by GMM with EM algorithm temporal pattern extraction for Saison. As shown in Table 6, the rule set of Saison works the best to KDDI as the test dataset.

With regarding Fig. 3, our temporal rule mining system can find out adequate combinations of trend index patterns for each stock. To learn adequate trend index pattern combinations is very costly work for trading beginners. Thus, our temporal rule mining can support traders who want to know the adequate combinations of trend indexes for each stock.

IndexName	Saison	MUFJFG	MSFG	MizuhoFG	Orix	KDDI	NTT	NTTdocomo	Softbank	AVERAGE
opening	88.0	83.0	86.0	89.0	83.0	93.0	92.0	91.0	93.0	88.7
high	84.0	88.0	94.0	87.0	83.0	93.0	91.0	90.0	95.0	89.4
low	85.0	92.0	90.0	92.0	81.0	93.0	91.0	92.0	91.0	89.7
closing	86.0	86.0	93.0	91.0	74.0	93.0	92.0	89.0	95.0	88.8
volume	70.0	79.0	86.0	72.0	71.0	79.0	80.0	69.0	85.0	76.8
MovingAvg.	96.0	94.9	84.8	88.9	81.8	91.9	62.6	94.9	62.6	84.3
BollingerBand	94.9	90.9	79.8	93.9	94.9	80.8	100.0	86.9	100.0	91.4
Envelope	89.9	89.9	93.9	89.9	89.9	85.9	82.8	100.0	80.8	89.2
HLband	91.9	83.8	90.9	89.9	83.8	87.9	76.8	72.7	91.9	85.5
MACD	84.8	91.9	77.8	81.8	91.9	76.8	90.9	71.7	61.6	81.0
DMI	76.8	84.8	88.9	82.8	90.9	85.9	85.9	90.9	77.8	85.0
volumeRatio	87.9	87.9	91.9	88.9	90.9	91.9	91.9	92.9	84.8	89.9
RSI	85.9	88.9	85.9	88.9	83.8	87.9	83.8	89.9	86.9	86.9
Momentum	82.8	85.9	76.8	81.8	86.9	85.9	82.8	85.9	89.9	84.3
Ichimoku1	67.7	92.9	90.9	86.9	74.7	48.5	87.9	57.6	79.8	76.3
Ichimoku2	58.6	87.9	77.8	82.8	83.8	58.6	73.7	86.9	68.7	75.4
Ichimoku3	97.0	97.0	94.9	74.7	100.0	100.0	100.0	75.8	90.9	92.3
Ichimoku4	78.8	84.8	93.9	89.9	91.9	73.7	93.9	81.8	93.9	87.0

Table 3. Accuracies (%) of temporal pattern prediction by Boosted C4.5 on the patterns obtained by K-Means.

IndexName	Saison	MUFJFG	MSFG	MizuhoFG	Orix	KDDI	NTT	NTTdocomo	Softbank	AVERAGE
opening	88.0	93.0	86.0	89.0	99.0	90.0	90.0	93.0	94.0	91.3
high	90.0	88.0	85.0	96.0	93.0	90.0	91.0	93.0	91.0	90.8
low	94.0	91.0	92.0	90.0	94.0	92.0	80.0	95.0	90.0	90.9
closing	87.0	95.0	83.0	92.0	97.0	93.0	84.0	93.0	89.0	90.3
volume	72.0	58.0	77.0	64.0	64.0	71.0	81.0	60.0	86.0	70.3
MovingAvg.	49.5	63.6	65.7	54.5	63.6	43.4	42.4	54.5	46.5	53.8
BollingerBand	74.7	82.8	80.8	59.6	86.9	48.5	100.0	74.7	100.0	78.7
Envelope	85.9	90.9	85.9	60.6	74.7	78.8	57.6	100.0	87.9	80.2
HLband	71.7	89.9	84.8	87.9	79.8	68.7	58.6	57.6	77.8	75.2
MACD	63.6	51.5	49.5	49.5	58.6	64.6	44.4	58.6	40.4	53.4
DMI	55.6	62.6	69.7	45.5	80.8	57.6	38.4	57.6	59.6	58.6
volumeRatio	89.9	81.8	92.9	93.9	81.8	84.8	85.9	92.9	92.9	88.6
RSI	85.9	88.9	92.9	86.9	80.8	89.9	81.8	80.8	84.8	85.9
Momentum	84.8	87.9	81.8	88.9	89.9	85.9	78.8	84.8	88.9	85.7
Ichimoku1	47.5	39.4	45.5	47.5	54.5	56.6	60.6	54.5	47.5	50.4
Ichimoku2	50.5	46.5	51.5	63.6	58.6	54.5	53.5	41.4	65.7	54.0
Ichimoku3	72.7	80.8	75.8	97.0	100.0	100.0	100.0	85.9	97.0	89.9
Ichimoku4	82.8	82.8	87.9	94.9	62.6	76.8	78.8	85.9	97.0	83.3

Table 4. Accuracies (%) of temporal pattern prediction by Boosted C4.5 on the patterns obtained by GMM with EM algorithm.

Stock Name	K-Means	EM	Stock Name	K-Means	EM
Saison	90.1	88.9	NTT	84.8	90.9
Orix	88.9	84.8	KDDI	86.9	78.8
MUFJFG	90.9	93.9	NTTdocomo	80.8	85.9
MSFG	96.0	90.9	Softbank	93.9	89.9
MizuhoFG	92.9	83.8			

Table 5. Re-substitution accuracies (%) of the rule sets obtained with the two temporal pattern extraction with K-Means and GMM with EM algorithm.

The shapes of the visualized temporal patterns and their combination are also useful for supporting knowledge discovery in medical data. As described in (Abe et al., 2007), a physician could found interesting temporal patterns of ALT (alanine transaminase) and RBC (Red Blood-cell Count) related to the good result of the INF (interferon) treatment.

6. Conclusion

In this chapter, we described the temporal classification rule mining framework that combines time-series data pre-processing, mining, post-processing for mined results, and other database operators to validate data and results of every phase.
By using the implementations and experimental results, we present the following merits achieved by the classification rules with considering temporal patterns of the target attributes:

- Finding different interesting aspects of the decisions/results
- Finding important temporal patterns and attributes for the decision at the same time

In order to utilize this framework with proper methods in each step, we expect that the readers may construct their own temporal classification rule mining systems for their sequential data by combining other temporal pattern extraction methods and classification rules.

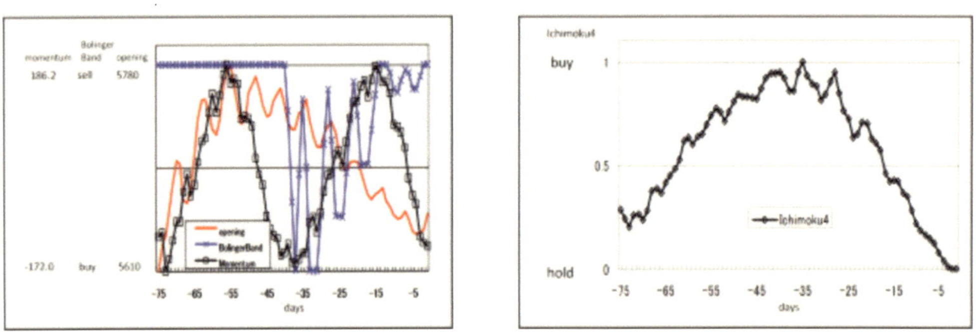

(a)Example for 'buy' (b) Example for 'sell'

Fig. 3. An example of rule for 'buy' and rule for 'sell'.

(a)

Training\Test	Saison	MUFJFG	MSFG	MizuhoFG	Orix	NTT	KDDI	NTTdocomo	Softbank
Saison		44.4	28.3	31.3	40.4	29.3	35.4	22.2	49.5
MUFJFG	46.5		44.4	30.3	42.4	32.3	39.4	29.3	55.6
MSFG	44.4	24.2		38.4	31.3	28.3	27.3	29.3	22.2
MizuhoFG	46.5	31.3	33.3		29.3	22.2	20.2	22.2	58.6
Orix	38.4	50.5	27.3	31.3		32.3	39.4	19.2	30.3
NTT	14.1	50.5	27.3	31.3	14.1		39.4	37.4	6.1
KDDI	12.1	44.4	56.6	27.3	31.3	41.4		55.6	16.2
NTTdocomo	26.3	40.4	52.5	33.3	23.2	30.3	20.2		8.1
Softbank	44.4	28.3	18.2	45.5	34.3	40.4	30.3	26.3	

(b)

Training\Test	Saison	MUFJFG	MSFG	MizuhoFG	Orix	NTT	KDDI	NTTdocomo	Softbank
Saison		46.5	28.3	31.3	38.4	51.5	65.7	21.2	32.3
MUFJFG	31.3		51.5	31.3	38.4	29.3	41.4	22.2	46.5
MSFG	23.2	58.6		34.3	31.3	43.4	32.3	30.3	29.3
MizuhoFG	35.4	31.3	34.3		31.3	42.4	38.4	43.4	20.2
Orix	41.4	29.3	39.4	34.3		37.4	21.2	28.3	25.3
NTT	41.4	21.2	20.2	42.4	44.4		33.3	23.2	39.4
KDDI	61.6	59.6	50.5	28.3	27.3	42.4		28.3	37.4
NTTdocomo	27.3	42.4	29.3	52.5	25.3	30.3	19.2		28.3
Softbank	52.5	45.5	27.3	31.3	41.4	33.3	43.4	19.2	

Table 6. a) Accuracies (%) of cross stock evaluation with the temporal patterns obtained by K-Means. b)Accuracies (%) of cross stock evaluation with the temporal patterns obtained by GMM with EM algorithm.

7. References

Abe, H. & Yamaguchi, T. (2004). Constructive meta-learning with machine learning method repositories, *Proc. of the 17th International Conference on Industrial and Engineering Applications of Artificial Intelligence and Expert Systems IEA/AIE 2004, LNAI 3029*, pp. 502–511.

Abe, H., Yokoi, H., Ohsaki, M. & Yamaguchi, T. (2007). Developing an integrated time-series data mining environment for medical data mining, *ICDMW '07: Proceedings of the Seventh IEEE International Conference on Data Mining Workshops*, IEEE Computer Society, Washington, DC, USA, pp. 127–132.

Akaike, H. (1969). Fitting autoregressive models for prediction, 21(1): 243–247.

Berndt, D. J. & Clifford, J. (1996). Finding patterns in time series: a dynamic programming approach, pp. 229–248.

Das, G., King-Ip, L., Heikki, M., Renganathan, G. & Smyth, P. (1998). Rule discovery from time series, *Proc. of International Conference on Knowledge Discovery and Data Mining*, pp. 16–22.

Fayyad, U. M., Piatetsky-Shapiro, G. & Smyth, P. (1996). From data mining to knowledge discovery: an overview, pp. 1–34.

Frank, E., Wang, Y., Inglis, S., Holmes, G. & Witten, I. H. (1998). Using model trees for classification, *Machine Learning* 32(1): 63–76.

Hirano, S. & Tsumoto, S. (2002). Multiscale comparison of temporal patternsin time-series medical databases, *PKDD '02: Proceedings of the 6th European Conference on Principles of Data Mining and Knowledge Discovery*, Springer-Verlag, London, UK, pp. 188–199.

Kaburobo (2004). `http://www.kaburobo.jp/`.

Keogh, E., Chu, S., Hart, D. & Pazzani, M. (2003). Segmenting time series: A survey and novel approach, *an Edited Volume, Data mining in Time Series Databases.*, World Scientific, pp. 1–22.

Liao, T. W. (2005). Clustering of time series data: a survey, *Pattern Recognition* 38: 1857–1874.

Liu, H. & Motoda, H. (1998). *Feature Selection for Knowledge Discovery and Data Mining*, Kluwer Academic Publishers, Norwell, MA, USA.

Mallat, S. G. (1989). A theory for multiresolution signal decomposition: The wavelet representation, *IEEE Trans. Pattern Anal. Mach. Intell.* 11(7): 674–693.

Mitchell, T. M. (1982). Generalization as search, *Artificial Intelligence* 18(2): 203–226.

Ohsaki, M., Abe, H., Tsumoto, S., Yokoi, H. & Yamaguchi, T. (2007). Evaluation of rule interestingness measures in medical knowledge discovery in databases, *Artif. Intell. Med.* 41(3): 177–196.

Ohsaki, M., Abe, H. & Yamaguchi, T. (2007). Numerical time-series pattern extraction based on irregular piecewise aggregate approximation and gradient specification, *New Gen. Comput.* 25(3): 213–222.

Ohsaki, M., Kitaguchi, S., Kume, S., Yokoi, H. & Yamaguchi, T. (2004). Evaluation of rule interestingness measures with a clinical dataset on hepatitis, *Proceedings of ECML/PKDD 2004, LNAI3202*, pp. 362–373.

Quinlan, J. R. (1993). *Programs for Machine Learning*, Morgan Kaufmann Publishers.

Quinlan, J. R. (1996). Bagging, boosting, and c4.5, *Proceedings of the Thirteenth National Conference on Artificial Intelligence*, AAAI Press, pp. 725–730.

Witten, I. H. & Frank, E. (2000). *Data Mining: Practical Machine Learning Tools and Techniques with Java Implementations*, Morgan Kaufmann.

Wong, R. C.-W. & Fu, A. W.-C. (2006). Mining top-k frequent itemsets from data streams, *Data Min. Knowl. Discov.* 13(2): 193–217.

27

Evolutionary-Based Classification Techniques

Rasha Shaker Abdul-Wahab
Ahlia University,
Bahrain

1. Introduction

Recently data mining has attracted a great attention in the information industry due to the need for turning data into useful information [Freitas]. In fact, Data Mining comes with two different directions depending mainly on the application domain and the user interest. The first direction attempts to classify some target filed whereas the second direction attempts to find similarities among groups of data. However, one of the most common Data Mining tasks is Classification. Classification belongs to the first flavor of Data Mining directions which is used to assign objects to one of several predefined categories. The input data for classification task is a collection of records. Each record, also known an instance or example, is characterized by a typle (x,y), where x is the attributes set and y is a special attributes, designated the class label [Falco, Dasgupta]. In the literature several methods have been proposed to solve classification problem which are [Falco, Dasgupta] statistical methods, trees, neural-networks, rule induction method, evolutionary algorithms methods, etc. The choice of a particular method depends, however, on factors like the kind of problem to be solved, the resources available, etc. Classification is applied with different major types of EAs algorithms which are: Genetic Algorithms (GAs), Genetic Programming (GPs), Evolutions Strategies (ES), and Evolutionary Programming (EP).). All of them share the same basic concepts, but differ in the way they encode the solutions and in the operators they use. However, this work aims to use another type of EAs to solve classification problems.

EAs are very flexible search techniques, they can be used to solve many different kinds of problems and have been used in a wide variety of fields and applications [Langdon]. EAs are randomized search procedures inspired by the mechanics of genetics and natural selection. Most of data mining applications seek to reach optimality in their solutions which is considering the goal of most EAs algorithms. EAs work on a population of individuals that represent possible solutions to a problem in their chromosomes. Each individual can be as simple as a string of zeroes and ones, or as complex as a computer program [Langdon, Norman].

The aim of this chapter is to investigate the effect of using an alternative form of EAs to solve classification problem, for which a new System MRule is developed. This technique is an aggregation of different proposal; the first is based on GAPBNF [Abdul-Wahab] (Genetic Algorithm for developing Program using Backus Naur form) to discover comprehensible If Then rules. The second proposal is to integrate the syntax of Structured Query Language (SQL) language with GAPBNF.

The subsequent sections are organized as follows. Section 2 gives the definition of the classification problem. The objective of this chapter presented in section 3. MRule algorithm is described in section 4 with its major characteristic. The main units of MRule are illustrated in section 5. Section 6 contains the performance of the proposed system compared with that achieved by other methods. In last section, final remarks and future work are outline.

2. Problem definition

Given a dataset $X = \{x_1, x_2, \ldots, x_n\}$ of tuples (items, records, variable) and a set of classes $C = \{C_1, \ldots\ldots, C_m\}$, the classification problem is to define a mapping $f : X \rightarrow C$ where each x_i is assigned to one class. A class C_j contains precisely those tuples mapped to it. That is

$C_j = \{ x_i \mid f(x_i) = C_j,\ 1 \le i \le n,\ \text{ and } x_i \in X \}$ [Dunham].

3. Objective

This aims of this chapter is to investigate the effect of using an alternative form of EAs to solve the problem of one of the DM tasks, classification, for which a new technique to mine set of rules (MRule) is developed. The second objective tries to design new form which avoiding the time consuming through the frequent evaluation of candidates (rules) against the dataset. In addition try on focusing to deliver understandable rules and easy expressed them later in a database access language such as SQL to retrieve raw data in a particular category.

4. MRule system

MRule is a technique based on GAPBNF (Genetic Algorithm for Developing Program using Backus Naur Form) to perform the task of classification that has the ability to discover comprehensible If-Then rules. The reason for performing classification task with GAPBNF is that GAPBNF uses the GA engine and works on simpler structure, thus it expect some changes in the performance of the proposed technique for developing classification rules.
MRule has the ability to learn one disjunct at a time, and then all the discovered disjuncts together form the target concept description. It follows the standard strategy (also called covering strategy) in separate-and-conquer rule learning algorithms: learn a rule that covers part of the training set, remove the covered examples from training set and then recursively learn the remaining examples until all are covered [Pang_Ning]. Figure (1) describes the components of MRule system.

5. GAPBNF with classification problem

This section describes how to incorporate GAPBNF with classification problem, namely the phenotype language, ontogentic mapping, phenotype and genotype generator, genetic operators, and fitness function are explained in this section.

5.1 The phenotype language

The phenotype language is the language in which the phenotypes produced by GAPBNF are written. The Phenotype language in this work is the syntax of SQL language. Integrating the syntax of SQL in MRule system avoids the drawbacks of evaluation of rules against data.

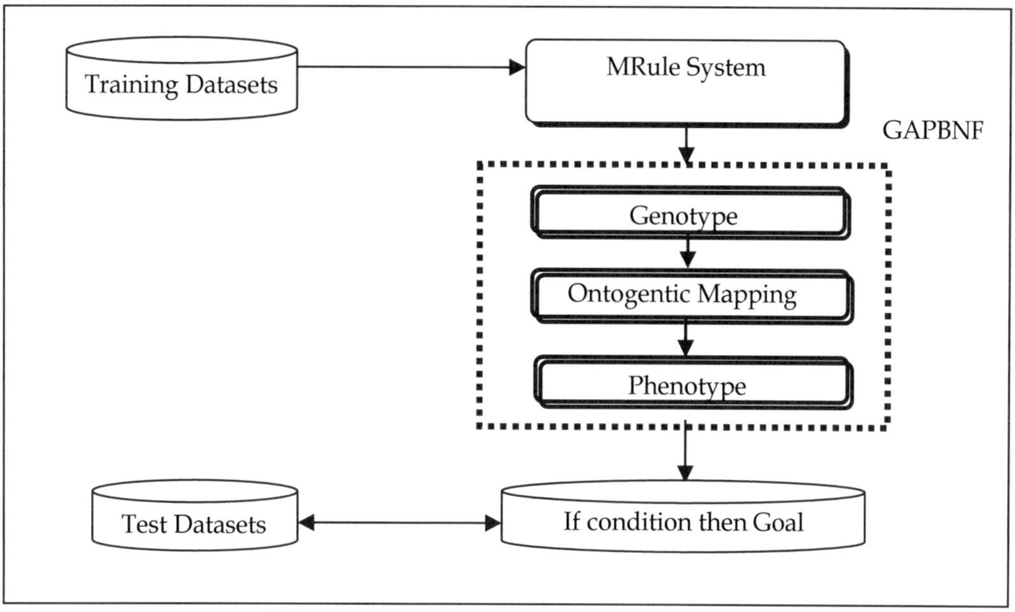

Fig. 1. General Description of MRule System

5.2 The ontogenic mapping

Genotype in GAPBNF is distinct from the phenotype. However, to convert the genotype to phenotype, the ontogenic mapping is needed. Ontogenic mapping uses the BNF definition of SQL language. The diagram to represent the engine of ontogentic mapping is illustrated in figure (2).

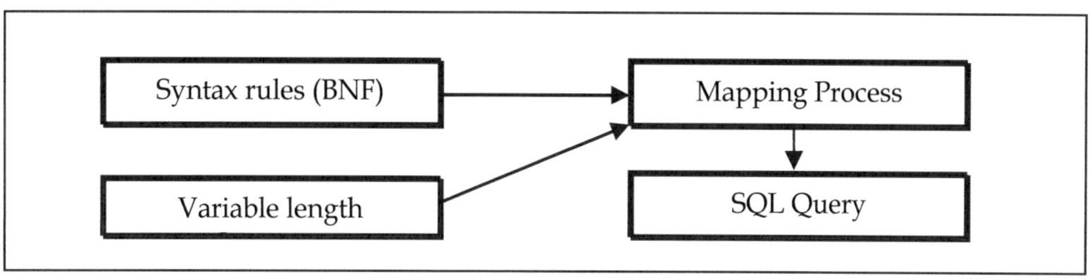

Fig. 2. The Engine of Ontogentic Mapping in MRule Sysyem

5.3 Genotype generator

The GAPBNF genotype is a list of genes encoded as an integer values. The generator used to generate variable length genotypes employs a controlled randomization based on some constraints which are represented as a context free grammar. These constraints help this generator to generate a valuable individual. These constraints are a set of rules that put some restriction on how the gene of GAPBNF should be arranged.

For instance, if $a_1, a_2,\ldots a_L$ is the genotype, the selection of a_2 is not generated randomly, instead the selection is done depending on a_1 and a_L is dependent on L-1, where L is the maximum length of the genotype which was generated randomly. In addition, using these constraints leads to reduce the search space. Consider an individual made up of the following genes: 11 30 10 21 41 50 10 22 40 60 51 52. These numbers represent the production rules number of the syntax language which is represented as table. The syntax which is consider the base to generate genotypes is presented in figure (3). To generate genotypes, two production numbers are fixed for all individuals which are (depending on Table 1) 11 and 30. These numbers represent the first and the second genes of individuals. The remaining genes will be generated depending on the identified constraints for the corresponding problem.

<table>
<tr><th>Rule</th><th colspan="2">Production rule number</th><th>Number for each choice</th></tr>
<tr><td>Condition → <input>
|<application></td><td>1</td><td>0
1</td><td>10
11</td></tr>
<tr><td>Input → <att > = <var>
|<att> < = <var>
|<att> between <exp></td><td>2</td><td>0
1
2</td><td>20
21
22</td></tr>
<tr><td>Application → <condition> and <condition></td><td>3</td><td>0</td><td>30</td></tr>
<tr><td>Att → <A₁> |<A₂>
|<A₃></td><td>4</td><td>0
1
2</td><td>40
41
42</td></tr>
<tr><td>Var → <r></td><td>5</td><td></td><td>5 [index]</td></tr>
<tr><td>Exp → <var> and <var></td><td>6</td><td>0</td><td>60</td></tr>
</table>

Fig. 3. The required syntax rules of MRule System

To build these constraints, a number will be assign to each production rule as follows:

$$S_1 \rightarrow 10, \mathrm{A} \rightarrow 11, \mathrm{B}_1 \rightarrow 20, \mathrm{B}_2 \rightarrow 21, \mathrm{B}_3 \rightarrow 22, \mathrm{C} \rightarrow 30, \mathrm{D}_1 = 40, \mathrm{D}_2 = 41, \mathrm{D}_3 = 42,$$
$$E \rightarrow 5[INDEX], \mathrm{F} \rightarrow 60$$

thus the constraints depending on figure (3) are shown in figure (4).

$$\begin{array}{l}
S \rightarrow A_1 \mid \lambda \\
A_1 \rightarrow AC_1 \mid \lambda \\
C_1 \rightarrow \mathrm{CS}_1 \mid \lambda \\
S_1 \rightarrow \mathrm{BD} \\
D \rightarrow D_1 I \mid D_{2I} \mid D_3 I \mid \mathrm{D}_1 F \mid D_2 F \mid \mathrm{D}_3 F \\
I \rightarrow ES \mid EI \\
B \rightarrow B_1 \mid B_2 \mid B_3 \\
F \rightarrow I
\end{array}$$

Fig. 4. The CFG of fig. 3.

As shown in figure (3), for production rule 5 there is no number associated with this rule, but through the creation process of the genotype, this rule is presented as 50, 51, 52 or 53 and so on. These associated numbers represent the index of the local memory which contains the intermediate values for the corresponding genotype. GAPBNF genotype needs these local values to give its corresponding phenotype the data upon which to operate.

Generating local memory values for each genotype is done as follows: grouping all examples that belong to the same class, then for each attribute in these examples compute its maximum and minimum values. These values are considered the ranges from which the corresponding value of the selected attribute in the genotype will be chosen. This technique tries to generate rules which have high consistency and coverage. Through the creation process the uniqueness of the attributes selection must be considered, i.e., it means genotype creation must be stopped when all attributes are chosen. The pseudo-code for creating the initial population is presented in algorithm (1)

Algorithm 1 Initial population Processer

Input *: Popsize which represents the number of individuals in a population, Maxlenrule which represents the maximum length of the generated genotype.*

Output : *Set of individual (genotypes)*

While P < = Popsize **do**
  L = uniform (0, Maxlenrule)
  For i = 1 to L **do**
  Create geni using the identify constraints of the corresponding problem
    If (geni is equal to the number of attribute rule) **then**
      Check the selected geni is not chosen before
    Else
      Exit if there is no more attributes that construct the genotype
    End if
    If (geni is equal to the number of l.m rule) **then**
      Stored the selected value in its local memory
    End if
    $rule_{(genotype)} = rule_{(genotype)} \cup \{geni\}$
  End for
  Individual-set= Individual-set $\cup$ $rule_{(genotype)}$
End while

5.4 Rule generator

At the beginning of the process of converting the genotype to the corresponding phenotype, an initial value is needed. The initial value of the phenotype is usually the start symbol of the syntax of the problem language. In this work, "Condition" symbol is identified as an initial value for the converter process.

The Phenotype is generated as Abstract Syntax Tree (AST). Consider the following individual (genotype): 11 30 10 21 41 50 10 22 40 60 51 52. Each gene in the above genotype is used to map into the corresponding production rule, this is done by reading each one alone and an appropriate production rule will be used to build one node of the AST (phenotype).

To build the AST of the above genotype, the first gene is read and will be used to generate the root node of this tree which is 11 in this case. This number matches production rule 1 (based on figure (1)). So to create the root node, the right hand side of this rule will be taken which has number 1 in this case. The created root node is presented in figure(5).

Null	Application	Nu11

Fig. 5. The root of the Abstract Syntax Tree.

The process is continuing by reading the second gene, which is 30 in this case. The left hand side matches the above root node, and then the right hand side of this rule will be taken and will be linked to the root node. The created AST at this step is presented in Figure (6).

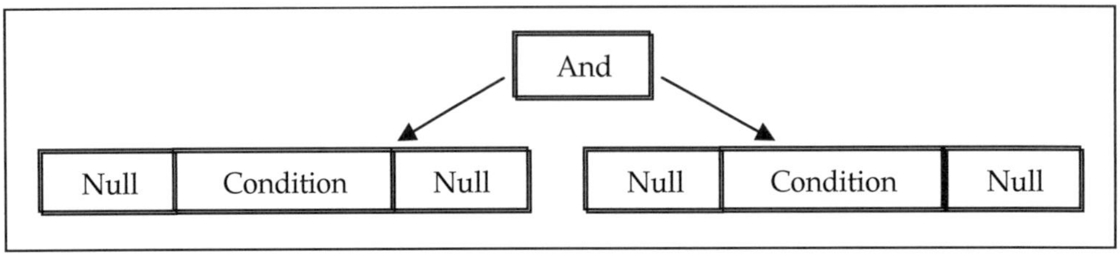

Fig. 6. The Abstract Syntax Tree (AST)

Then, the generator continues to process other genes in that genotype until the AST creation is complete. The AST of the above genotype after processing all its genes is presented in Figure (7), which represents the expression (A1 ≤ 128 and A2 between 3 and 7). The generated AST represents the condition part of the discovered rule which will be converted as a SQL statement through the evaluation process and will be discarded after computing the fitness value of this individual.

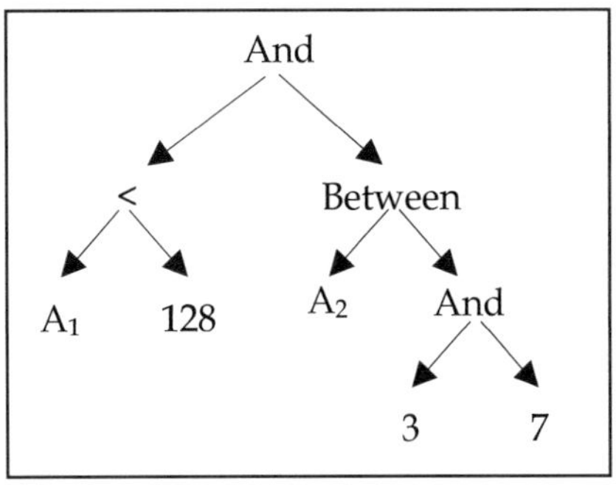

Fig. 7. The completed AST

Example: if we have the following genotype: 11 30 10 22 47 60 50 51 10 21 42 52 10 20 45 53 11 30 10 20 40 54 11 30. Based on the BNF of figure (3), the AST which represents the condition part of the rule is presented in figure (8).

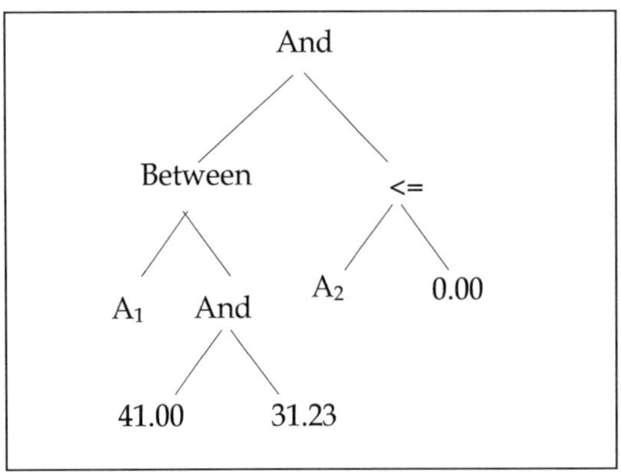

Fig. 8. The completed AST of the example

The corresponding expression of the above tree is:

$$A_1 \text{ between } 41.00 \text{ and } 31.23 \text{ and } A_2 <= 0.00$$

the SQL statement to evaluate the above condition is:

Select * from Tabledataset where A_1 between 41.00 and 31,23 and A_2 <= 0.00

5.5 The modification operators

According to the fitness value, individuals are selected to reproduce with modification, creating the necessary genetic diversification that allows evolution in the long run. The following subsections proceed with the detailed description of the necessary GAPBNF operators.

a. Crossover operator

The crossover operator used in this work uses two parent genotypes (Parent1, Parent2) producing two offspring (Offspring1, Offspring2). This operator follows the principles of one-point crossover. Two parents (genotype) of different lengths are aligned with each other and two crossover points are chosen at random but one must consider the specified constraint, whereas if the two selected points conform to the CFG, then these two points are taken otherwise select other points until the correct points are found. The steps of doing the conformation process are presented in algorithm (2). The first point (Pc1) is randomly selected according to the length of the first parent; the second point is selected randomly according to the length of the second parent (Pc2). The tails of the second parent from the onward point are switched to create the first Offspring1, while the tails of the first parent from the point Pc1 are switched to create the second child Offspring2.

Through the job of this operator, one must consider the uniqueness of the attribute in Offspring1 and Offspring2, i.e., each attribute can occur only once. This is implemented to avoid the inconsistent genotype which leads to avoiding the inconsistence of the generated rule. The pseudo-code version of this operator is presented in algorithm (3).

Algorithm 2 The validation process

Input : Two point $gene_{pc1}$ and $gene_{pc2}$, and the previous gene of pc1
Output : True or false

If ($gene_{pc1}$ =30) and ($gene_{pc2}$ =10 or $gene_{pc1}$= 11) return true
Else
If ($gene_{pc1}$ represent the number of l.m rule) and ((previous of $gene_{pc1}$= represent the number of l.m rule) and ($gene_{pc2}$ =10 or $gene_{pc2}$ =11) return true
Else
If ($gene_{pc1}$ = represent the number of l.m rule) and ((previous of $gene_{pc1}$ = represent the number of attribute rule) and ($gene_{pc2}$ =10 or $gene_{pc2}$ =11)) then return true
Else
If ($gene_{pc1}$ =10) and ($gene_{pc2}$ =20 or $gene_{pc2}$ =21 or $gene_{pc1}$ =22) then return true
Else
If ($gene_{pc1}$ =11) and ($gene_{pc2}$ =30) then return true
Else
return false
End algorithm

b. The improvement operator

This operator is applied to modify the values that have been stored in the local memory of the individual. The dummy groups which correspond for each class is created in this operator. The centroids of the dummy groups for classi are denoted by the mean vector of all the data points for this class. Then the distance value is computed between the values that are stored in the local memory which were selected randomly and the corresponding values stored in the dummy groups. For instance, if local memory (l.m) = {lm1, lm3} which represents the values of attribute one and three that have been created during the generation process, and the dummy group of the corresponding class which is in the learning process is equal to = {D1, D2,….., DM}, where M is the number of attributes, this operator works as follows: in the beginning, if the value of the attribute stored in the local memory (let be lm3) is selected randomly, then the distance between lm3 and D3 (the centroid of the corresponding selected attribute) is computed (let it be d3). Then the stored value in l.m will be either increased or decreased depending on the d=(r*d3)/2 (the increased or decreased process is done randomly). After that the competition is done between the new created individual with its new local memory value and the current individual with the old local memory, the best one is chosen and the processing of this operator will be repeated until the specified condition is reached.

Algorithm 3 Crossover operator

Input: *Local memory of parent$_1$ (l.m.p$_1$), local memory of parent$_2$ (l.m.p$_2$), pc$_1$= crossover point of parent$_1$, pc$_2$ =crossover point of parent$_2$, p$_1$_length, p$_2$_length which represents the length of parent$_1$ and parent$_2$ respectively.*

Output: *New individual (offspring)*

```
Index=1
For i=1 to pc1 do
    If gen_i of parent_1 represent production rule 5 then
       l.m.offspring=l.m.offpring □ l.m.p_1[index]
       Increment the value of index
    End if
    offspring_genotype=offspring_genotype □ geni
End for
For i=pc2 to p_2_length do
    If gen_i of parent_2 represents production rule 5 then
      l.m.offspring=l.m.offspring □ l.m.p_2[index]
      increment the value of index
    Endif
    If gen_i of parent_2 represents the production rule 4 then
      check the consistency of attribute
    Else
       Exit if there is no more attribute that constructs the genotype
    End if
    offspring_genotype=offspring_genotype □ gen_i
End for
```

c. **Other operators**

The selection operator assigns to each chromosome a real number which is the target sampling rate that indicates the expected number of offspring to be generated from that chromosome, and gives the probability offspring to be generated from that chromosome, and gives the probability of the chromosome to be selected in the following sampling process.

The 2-tournament selection is chosen in this work. It works by randomly choosing 2 individual from the population and copying the best one of these 2 individuals to the new population.

An elitist reproduction strategy, where the best individual of each generation passes unaltered to the next generation is used.

The relational operator mutation is used. This operator modifies the relational operator currently being used in condition of the rule by replacing it with another one generated randomly.

Some extracted rules are removed if they are noisy or redundant rules [Han]. Noisy rules mean the rules that cover more examples from the other classes than from its own and redundant rules means the rules cover the same examples that covered by another rules which exist in the rule list.

5.6 The fitness function

The fitness function evaluates the quality of each rule (individual). Let tp, fp, fn denote respectively the number of true positive, false positives, and false negative observed when a rule is used to classify a set of examples. The fitness function combines two indicators, namely the confidence measures and coverage measures which is defined as follows:

$$Confidence = \frac{\mathrm{tp}}{\mathrm{tp} + \mathrm{fp}}, \tag{1}$$

$$\text{Coverage} = \frac{\mathrm{tp}}{\mathrm{tp} + \mathrm{fn}} \tag{2}$$

Computing the value of tp and fp is very simple task because all it needs is to send the query to the training dataset and return the number of examples that match correctly the condition which belongs to classes C (let be Count(c)) and not C. While fn is calculated by using the following formula:

$$fn = Count(C) - tp \tag{3}$$

Finally, the fitness function used by MRule technique is defined as follows:

$$Fitness = 0.5 * Confidenc + 0.5 * Coverage \tag{4}$$

Each run of GAPBNFR solves a two class classification problem. Therefore, the GAPBNFR is run at least one for each class. Hence, the above formulas can be applied to the problem with any number of classes [Takač]. Therefore, GAPBNFR is not necessary to encode class in the chromosome represenation.

6. Experimental results

In this section, the results on applying the proposed method to a number of benchmark problems are presented. For the comparison reasons, the same datasets that have been used with other based evolutionary approaches: Iris, Hearts, Breast, and Pima are adopted. These datasets form UCI machine learning datasets repository [Blake].

The proposed method is evaluated using 10_fold cross validation where the performance is the average accuracies over 10_fold. Comparison is made between the proposed method and ESIA[June] and clustering GP[Falco]. The results for ESIA and clustering GP reported here are taken directly from the above mentioned papers. Both algorithms also use 10-folds cross validation. This comparison is made in terms of predictive accuracy of the discovered rules. Table 2 shows the results of these three methods; N/A indicates that no results are available. As can be seen in table 2, the proposed method outperforms ESIA and Clustering GP in pima and breast data. The proposed method gives the same accuracy rate in heart data while outperforming ESIA. For iris datasets, the proposed method gives the same accuracy rate. As a result, we consider these results very promising, bearing in mind that, unlike ESIA and Clustering GP algorithms, the structure adopted in the proposed method is much simpler than the ESIA and clustering GP. Like most evolutionary algorithms, this method needs a substantial amount of computational time to run.

Datasets	GAPBNFR	ESIA	Clustering GP
Breast	94.5	80.5	N/A
Heart	80.4	80.4	80.1
Pima	80.7	78.1	73.7
iris	94.5	95.33	N/A

Table 2. Accuracy rate on test data of GAPBNFR, ESIA, Clustering GP

7. Discussions and conclusion

A new method for rule discovery has been developed for numerical datasets. This technique uses GAPBNF to perform this task. GAPBNF is an evolutionary algorithm that distinguishes between the genotype and the phenotype. The genotype is a list of integers representing productions in a defined syntax while phenotype is based on SQL operations in order to produce an SQL query. The most important points of the proposed method are: it performs global search of solutions space s and copes well with attribute interaction and producing a comprehensible classification rules. Its effectiveness through the evaluation process of individuals is inherent from one of the facilities provided by GAPBNF technique. The type of a representation scheme obtains efficient results and allows a compact representation of complex conditions using liner chromosomes. Our method incorporates innovative ideas with respect to the encoding of individuals which afterwards converted into the corresponding rules. This facilities the work of crossover and mutation operators in which the GA engine can be used without any modification.

The proposed method is evaluated against four numerical public datasets and compared with two other evolutionary systems ESIA and GP clustering techniques. The results can be considered promising and allow us to conclude that the type of representation that is used in this work to discover a set of rules is efficient. In addition the good predictive accuracy that is obtained by our method stems from its ability to correctly predict the class label of previously unseen data. The performance of GAPBNF in the proposed technique is good enough to confirm its feasibility and is an important direction that further research should follow.

8. References

R. Sh. Abdul-Wahab, “Genetic Algorithm for Developing Program Using Backus Naur Form(GAPBNF), Engineering and Technology Journla, Vol 24, no. 6, 2005.

C. L. Blake and C.J. Merz. UCI Repository of Machine Learning Databases, University of California, Irvine, Dept. of Information and Computer Sciences, http://www.ics.uci.edu/simmlearn/MLRepository. html.1998

C. C. Bojarczuk, H. S. Lopes, A. A. Freitas. Discovering Comprehensible Classification Rules Using Genetic Programming: a case study in a medical domain.

E. Cantu-Paz, C. Kamath. "On the Use of Evolutionary Algorithms in Data Mining,in Data Mining". In Data Mining: A heuristic Approach, 2001.

D. Dasgupta, F. A. González. " Evolving Complex Fuzzy Classifier Rules Using a Linear Genetic Representation". In the proceedings of the International Conference Genetic and Evolutionary Computation (GECCO), San Francisco, California, July 7-11, 2001.

M. H. Dunham. Data Mining Techniques and Algorithms, Prentice Hall.2000.

D. Falco, A. Della Cioppa, A. Lassetta, E. Tarantino, Evolutionary Approach for Automatically Extracting Intelligible Classification Rules, Knowledge and Information System. Springer Verlag London Lid, pp 179-201, 2004.

A. A. Freitas. "Genetic Programming Framework for Two Data Mining Tasks: Classification and Generalized Rule Induction". In John R. Koza and Kalyanmoy Deb and Marco Dorigo and David B. Fogel and Max Garzon and Hitoshi Iba and Rick L. Riolo (Eds.) Genetic Programming 1997: Proceedings of the Second Annual Conference. Morgan Kaufmann. pp 96-101.1997

A. A. Freitas. Data Mining and Knowledge Discovery with Evolutionary Algorithms (Natural Computing Series). Springer,2002.

J. Han, M. Kamber. Data Mining: Concepts and Techniques, Academic press. 2001.

J. June, J. T. Kwok. "An Extended Genetic Rule Induction Algorithm". In Proceedings of the 2000 Congress on Evolutionary Computation CECoo,pp 458-463.2000.

W. B. Langdon, R. Poli. Foundation of Genetic Programming, Springers, 2004.

Norman R. Paterson, Mike Livesey, “Distinguishing Genotype and Phenotype in Genetic Programming”, in Koza, J.R. (Ed.), Late breaking papers at the genetic programming 1996 Conf. Stanford Univ., July, pp141-150. 1996.

Pang_Ning Tan, M. Steinbach, V. Kumar, Introduction to Data Mining, Pearson Education, 2006.

A. Takač. Genetic Programming in Data Mining: Cellular Approach. Institute of Informatics Faculty of Mathematics, Physics and Informatics Comenius University, Bratislava, Slovakia. MS.cThesis. 2003.

28

Multiobjective Design Exploration in Space Engineering

Akira Oyama and Kozo Fujii
Institute of Space and Astronautical Science, Japan Aerospace Exploration Agency
Japan

1. Introduction

Most of real world design optimization problems in space engineering are multiobjective design optimization problems that simultaneously involve several competing objectives (Oyama et al., 2002) (Tani et al., 2008) (Oyama et al., 2009) (Oyama et al., 2010). For example, design of a turbopump for liquid rocket engine involves maximization of total head, minimization of input power, minimization of weight, minimization of manufacturing cost, and so on. Another example is trajectory design of a spacecraft where payload weight should be maximized, time required to reach the target point should be minimized, distance from the sun should be maximized (or minimized), and manufacturing cost should be minimized. Many other multiobjective design optimization problems can be easily found, such as reusable space transportation system design, spacecraft design, and Mars airplane design.

While a single objective design optimization problem may have a unique optimal solution, multiobjective design optimization problems present a set of compromised solutions, largely known as Pareto-optimal solutions or non-dominated solutions. Each of these solutions is optimal in the sense that no other solutions in the search space are superior to it when all objectives are considered (Fig. 1). Therefore, the goal of multiobjective design optimization problems is to find as many non-dominated solutions as possible to provide useful information of the problem to the designers.

Recently, idea of multiobjective design exploration (MODE) (Obayashi et al., 2005) is proposed as a framework to extract essential knowledge of a multiobjective design optimization problem such as trade-off information between contradicting objectives and the effect of each design parameter on the objectives. In the framework of MODE, non-dominated solutions are obtained by multiobjective optimization using, for example, a multiobjective evolutionary computation (Deb, 2001), and then design knowledge is extracted by analysing the values of objective functions and design parameters of the obtained non-dominated solutions. There, data mining approaches such as the self-organizing map (SOM) (Kohonen, 1998) and analysis of variance (ANOVA) (Donald, 1998) are used. Recently, MODE framework has been applied to a wide variety of design optimization problems including multidisciplinary design of a regional-jet wing (Chiba et al., 2007a) (Chiba et al., 2007b), aerodynamic design of multi-element airfoil (Kanazaki et al., 2007), and car tire design (Shimoyama, 2009).

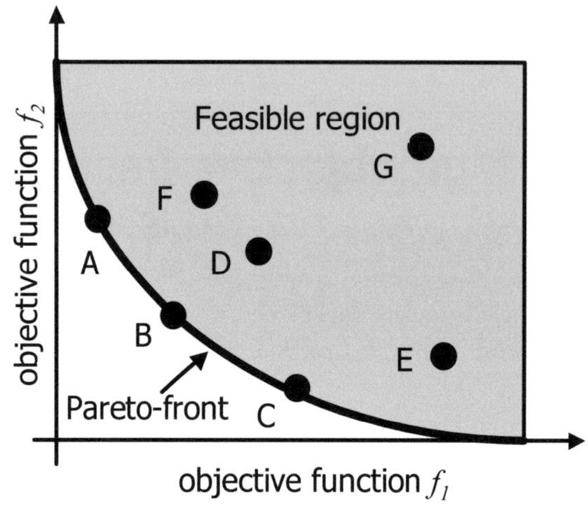

Fig. 1. The concept of Pareto-optimality. This is an example of multiobjective design optimization problems, which minimizes two conflicting objectives f_1 and f_2. Gray-colored area is feasible region where solutions can exit. This problem has innumerable compromised non-dominated solutions such as solutions A, B, and C on the edge of the feasible region (Pareto-front). These solutions are optimal in the sense that there is no better solution in both objectives. One cannot say which is better among these non-dominated solutions because improvement in one objective degrades another.

Although the MODE framework is useful for real-world designs, analysis of design parameters and objective functions values of the non-dominated solutions is not sufficient for design exploration in space engineering. For example, for a wing shape design optimization problem, design knowledge one can obtain depends on how the shape is parameterized. If an airfoil (i.e., wing profile) shape is represented by B-spline curves and the coordinates of the B-spline curves are considered as the design parameters, it is difficult to obtain design knowledge related to leading edge radius, maximum thickness, or trailing edge angle (Fig. 2). Another reason is that data mining of the objective function and design parameter values does not lead to understanding of the physics behind the design problem. For example, if only the design parameter and objective function values of non-dominated airfoils were analysed, it would not be possible to clarify the relation between shock wave generation and aerodynamic characteristics of an airfoil.

To solve such problems, it is necessary to analyse shape data and flow data of the obtained non-dominated solutions. Fortunately, in the process of objective function value evaluation for aerodynamic optimization, such data is computed for each design candidate. For example, in an aerodynamic airfoil shape optimization, evaluation of objective function values requires 1) shape construction from the design parameter values, 2) computational grid generation around the shape, 3) flow computation using computational fluid dynamics, and 4) surface pressure and friction distribution on the shape (Fig.3). Therefore, analysis of the shape and flow data does not require any additional computation. What we should do is not to discard such data for data mining process after the optimization.

However, analysis of shape and flow data is not straightforward because the data set can be very large. The number of the obtained non-dominated solutions is typically 100-10,000 while each non-dominated solution has large data set (Table.1). Therefore, traditional approach such as analysis with SOM or ANOVA is not adequate any more.

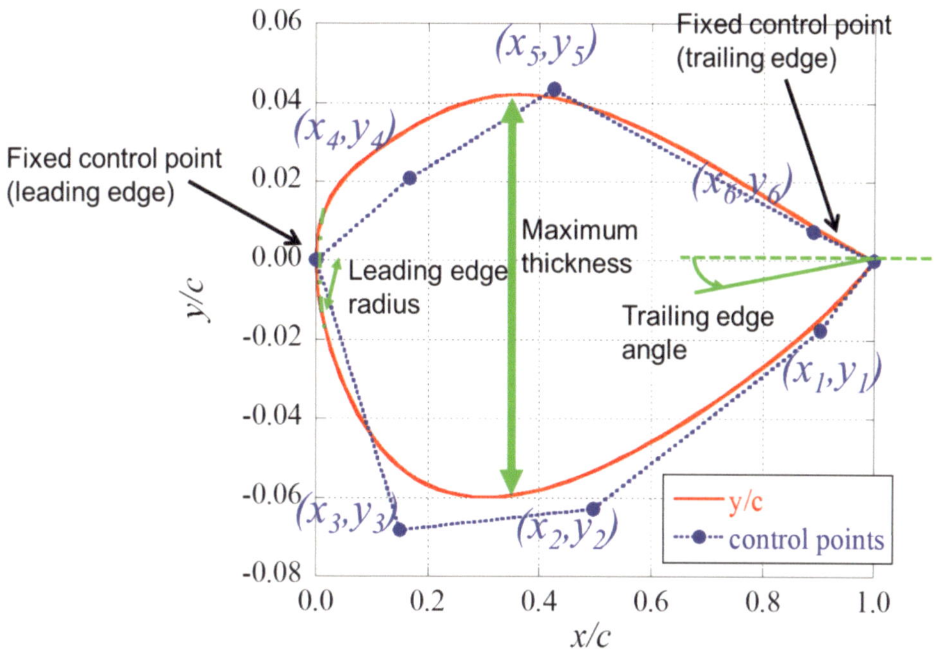

Fig. 2. An example of airfoil shape parameterization

Type of data	Typical data set size that each non-dominated solution has
two-dimensional shape data (such as airfoil)	200-2,000 (x-y coordinates of 100 to 1000 points that define the shape)
three-dimensional shape data (such as wing)	30,000-300,000 (x-y-z coordinates of 10,000 to 100,000 points that define the shape)
Two-dimensional flow data	10,000-100,000(several types of flow property (density, velocity, pressure, etc.) at the points distributed in the x-y space)
Three-dimensional flow data	500,000-5,000,000(several types of flow property (density, velocity, pressure, etc.) at the points distributed in the x-y-y space)

Table 1. Typical data set size that each non-dominated solutions has for an aerodynamic design

This chapter introduces a new approach that enables analysis of large data such set as the shape and flow data of all non-dominated solutions. This approach bases on proper orthogonal decomposition, which decomposes large data into principal modes and eigenvectors. Feasibility of this method is shown though knowledge extraction from principal modes and eigenvectors of the shape data and flow data of non-dominated solutions of an aerodynamic transonic airfoil shape optimization problem.

In section 3, characteristics of the non-dominated solutions are shown. Section 4 presents the POD-based data mining approach for analysis of non-dominated solutions. In section 5, an application for analysis of airfoil shape data of the non-dominated solutions is presented. In section 6, flow data of the non-dominated solutions is analysed with POD.

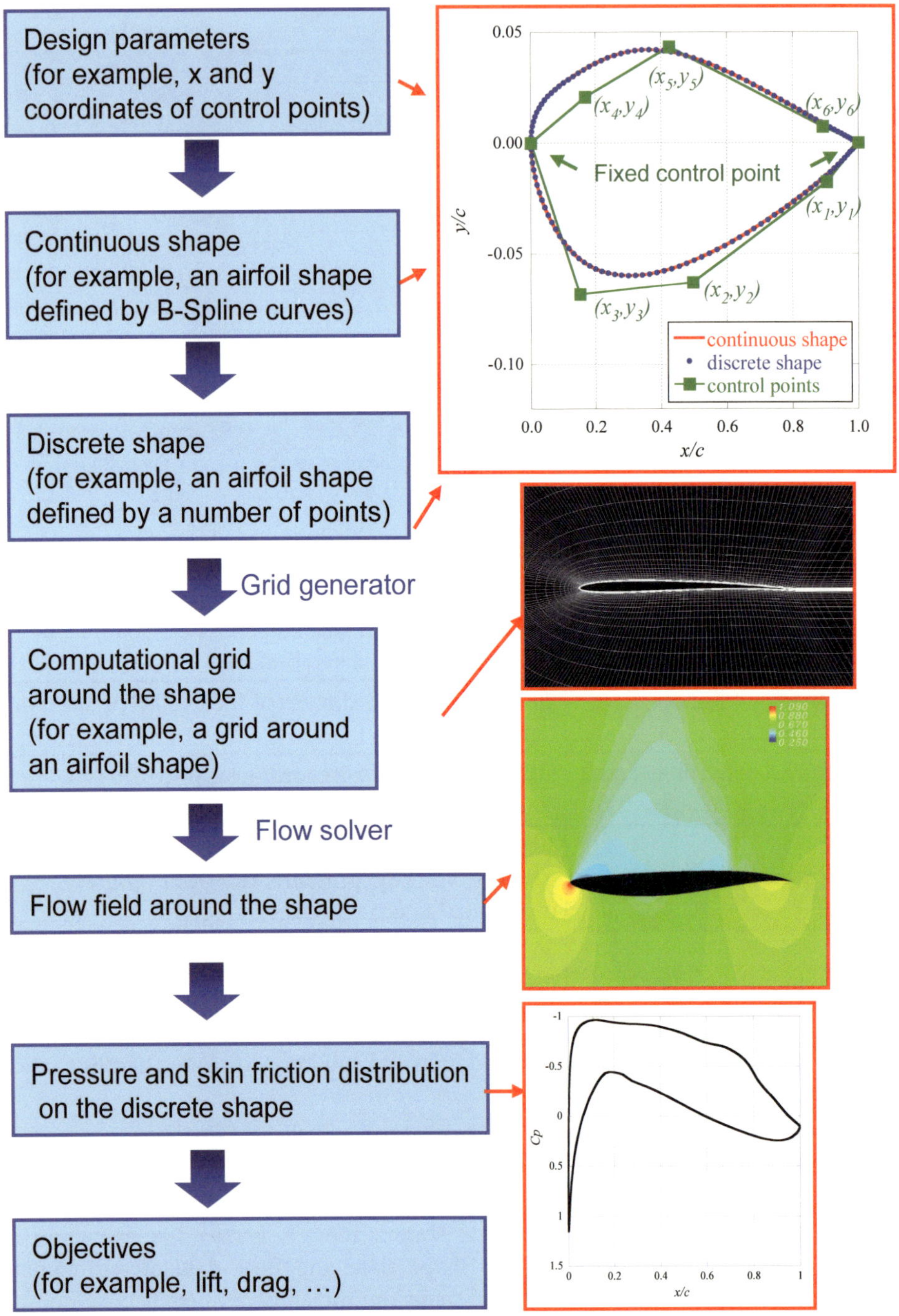

Fig. 3. Objective function value evaluation process for aerodynamic airfoil design optimization problem

2. Nomenclature

$a_m(n)$	=	eigenvector of mode m of non-dominated solution n
c	=	airfoil chord length
C_d	=	drag coefficient
C_l	=	lift coefficient
j	=	index of grid points
$jmax$	=	number of grid points
l/d	=	lift-to-drag ratio ($=C_l/C_d$)
m	=	index of modes
$mmax$	=	number of modes ($mmax$=$nmax$)
n	=	index of non-dominated solutions
$nmax$	=	number of non-dominated solutions
$p(j,n)$	=	pressure of non-dominated solution n at grid point j
$q(j,n)$	=	data of non-dominated solution n at grid point j
$q_{l/d\_max}(j)$	=	data of maximum-lift-to-drag-ratio design at grid point j
$q'(j,n)$	=	fluctuation of data $q(j,n)$ of non-dominated solution n at grid point j
$q'_{base}(j,m)$	=	orthogonal base vector of mode m
$S_{m1,m2}$	=	covariance of orthogonal base vectors of mode $m1$ and mode $m2$
$x(j,n)$	=	coordinate in chordwise direction of non-dominated solution n at grid point j
$y(j,n)$	=	coordinate in normal direction of non-dominated solution n at grid point j

3. Non-dominated solutions

The non-dominated solutions of the design optimization problem below are considered.

Objective functions:	lift coefficient (maximization)
	drag coefficient (minimization)
Constraints:	lift coefficient must be greater than 0
	maximum thickness must be greater than 0.10 chord length
Design parameters:	coordinates of 6 control points of the B-Spline curves
	representing an airfoil shape (Fig. 4)
Flow conditions:	free stream Mach number of 0.8
	Reynolds number of 10^6 (based on the chord length)
	angle of attack of 2 degrees.

The non-dominated solutions are obtained by a multiobjective evolutionary algorithm (MOEA) used in (Oyama et al., 2009). The present MOEA adopts real number coding, which enables efficient search in real number optimizations compared with binary or gray coding. The population size is maintained at 64 and the maximum number of generations is set to 60. The initial population is generated randomly so that the initial population covers the entire design space presented in Table 2. The fitness of each design candidate is computed according to Pareto-ranking, fitness sharing, and Pareto-based constraint handling (Oyama et al., 2007) based on its objective function and constraint function values. Here, Fonseca and Fleming's Pareto-based ranking method (Foncesa et al., 1993) and the fitness sharing method of Goldberg and Richardson (Goldberg et al., 1987) are used for Pareto-ranking where each individual is assigned a rank according to the number of individuals dominating it. In Pareto-based constraint handling, the rank of feasible designs is determined by the Pareto-ranking based on the objective function values, whereas the rank

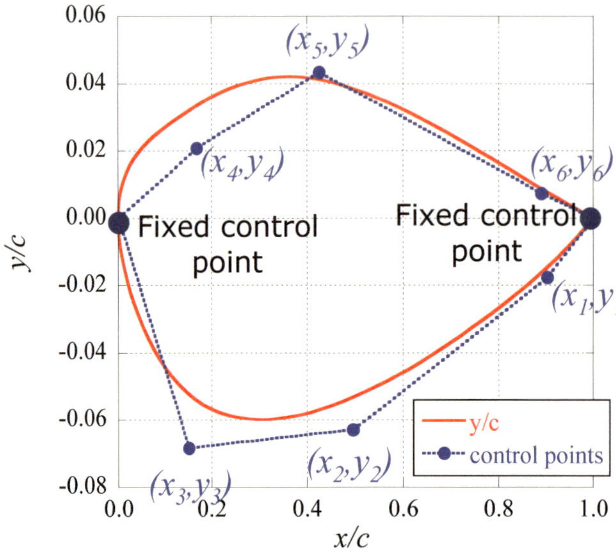

Fig. 4. Parameterization of the airfoil shape. The coordinates of six control points of the B-Spline curves representing an airfoil shape are considered as design parameters.

Design parameter	Lower bound	Upper bound
x_1	0.66	0.99
x_2	0.33	0.66
x_3	0.01	0.33
x_4	0.01	0.33
x_5	0.33	0.66
x_6	0.66	0.99
y_1	-0.10	0.10
y_2	-0.10	0.10
y_3	-0.10	0.10
y_4	0.00	0.20
y_5	0.00	0.20
y_6	0.00	0.20

Table 2. Search range of each design parameter

of infeasible designs is determined by the Pareto-ranking based on the constraint function values. The parents of the new generation are selected through roulette selection (Goldberg, 1989) from the best 64 individuals among the present generation and the best 64 individuals in the previous generation. A new generation is reproduced through crossover and mutation operators. The term "crossover" refers to an operator that combines the genotype of the selected parents and produces new individuals with the intent of improving the fitness value of the next generation. Here, the blended crossover (Eshlman et al., 1993), where the value of α is 0.5, is used for crossover between the selected solutions. Mutation is applied to the design parameters of the new generation to maintain diversity. Here, the probability of mutation taking place is 20%; this adds a random disturbance to the corresponding gene of up to 10% of the given range of each design parameter. Present MOEA used to find quasi-optimal solutions has been well validated (Obayashi et al., 2004) (Oyama et al., 2002).

Lift and drag coefficients of each design candidate are evaluated using a two-dimensional Reynolds-averaged Navier-Stokes solver. This code employs total variation diminishing type upwind differencing (Obayashi et al., 1994), the lower-upper symmetric Gauss-Seidel scheme (Obayashi et al., 1995), the turbulence model of Baldwin and Lomax (Baldwin et al., 1985) and the multigrid method (Brant, 1977) for the steady-state problems.

All the design candidates and non-dominated solutions are plotted in Fig. 5. The number of non-dominated solutions obtained is 85. A strong trade-off between lift maximization and drag minimization is observed. This figure also indicates that there are two groups in the obtained non-dominated solutions; low drag design group (roughly, C_l <0.75) and high lift design group (roughly, C_l > 0.75).

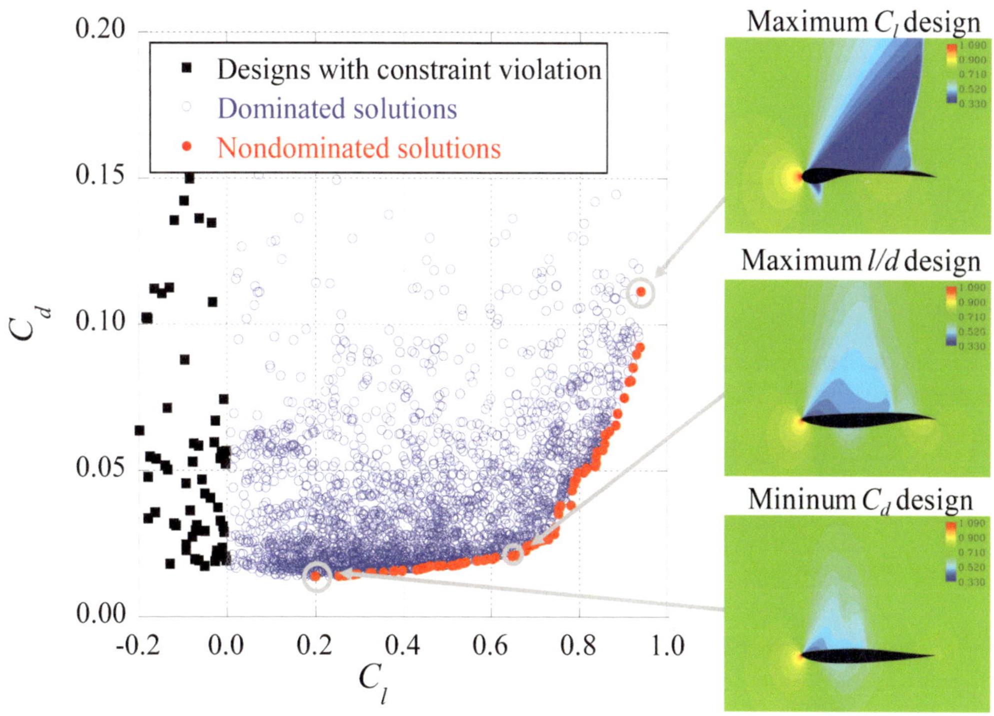

Fig. 5. Distribution of the non-dominated solutions and other design candidates with the pressure distribution around the minimum-drag, maximum-lift-to-drag-ratio, and maximum-lift airfoils.

4. Data mining approach based on POD

Proper orthogonal decomposition (POD, known as the Karhunen-Loeve expansion in pattern recognition, and principal component analysis in the statistical literature) is a statistical approach that can extract dominant features in data by decomposing the data into a set of optimal orthogonal base vectors of decreasing importance. These base vectors are optimal in the sense that any other set of orthogonal base vectors cannot capture more information than the orthogonal base vectors obtained by POD as long as the number of base vectors is limited. The POD has also been extensively used in image processing, structural vibration, analysis of unsteady flow data and so on.

In this study, airfoil shape and flow data of the non-dominated solutions are analyzed using the snapshot POD proposed by Sirovich (Sirovich, 1987). The non-dominated solutions from the minimum drag design to the maximum-lift design are numbered as shown in Fig. 6. Each non-dominated solution has large scale data such as shape and flow defined on all grid points (Fig.7).

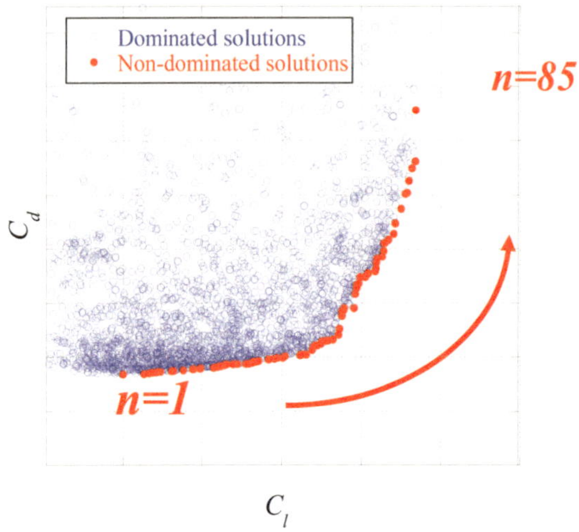

Fig. 6. Index of the non-dominated solutions. For the minimum-drag design, n=1; for the maximum-lift design, n=$nmax$=85.

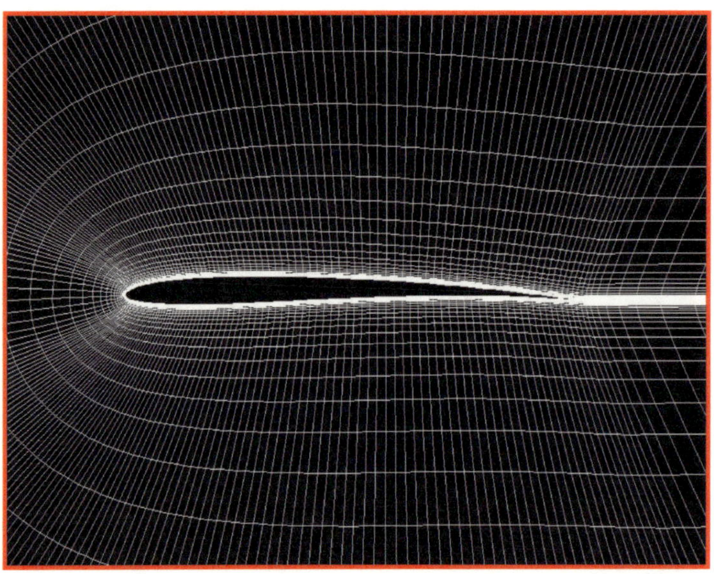

Fig. 7. Computational grid around an airfoil shape. The number of grid points is 9,849 (201x49)

In the original snapshot POD, the data to be analyzed are decomposed into the mean vector and the fluctuation vector, which is defined from the mean vector. It is known that analysis of the fluctuation from the mean vector maximizes variance of the data. However, for analysis of non-dominated solutions, it would be reasonable to define the fluctuation from one representative design, for example, the median design. Here, the fluctuation from the *l/d*-maximum design is analyzed. The data of the non-dominated solutions are decomposed into the data of the maximum-lift-to-drag-ratio design and fluctuation data as follows:

$$\begin{bmatrix} q(1,n) \\ q(2,n) \\ \vdots \\ q(j\max-1,n) \\ q(j\max,n) \end{bmatrix} = \begin{bmatrix} q_{l/d\_\max}(1) \\ q_{l/d\_\max}(2) \\ \vdots \\ q_{l/d\_\max}(j\max-1) \\ q_{l/d\_\max}(j\max) \end{bmatrix} + \begin{bmatrix} q'(1,n) \\ q'(2,n) \\ \vdots \\ q'(j\max-1,n) \\ q'(j\max,n) \end{bmatrix} \tag{1}$$

The fluctuation vector is then expressed by the linear sum of normalized eigenvectors and orthogonal base vectors as follows:

$$\begin{bmatrix} q'(1,n) \\ q'(2,n) \\ \vdots \\ q'(j\max-1,n) \\ q'(j\max,n) \end{bmatrix} = a_1(n) \begin{bmatrix} q'_{base}(1,1) \\ q'_{base}(2,1) \\ \vdots \\ q'_{base}(j\max-1,1) \\ q'_{base}(j\max,1) \end{bmatrix} + \cdots + a_{m\max}(n) \begin{bmatrix} q'_{base}(1,m\max) \\ q'_{base}(2,m\max) \\ \vdots \\ q'_{base}(j\max-1,m\max) \\ q'_{base}(j\max,m\max) \end{bmatrix} \tag{2}$$

where each eigenvector is determined so that the energy defined by Eq. (3) is maximized:

$$\sum_{j=1}^{j\max} q'^{2}_{base}(j,m), \quad m = 1, 2, \ldots, mmax \tag{3}$$

The eigenvectors that maximize the energy defined by Eq. (3) can be obtained by solving the eigenvalue problem of the following covariance matrix:

$$\begin{pmatrix} S_{1,1} & \cdots & S_{m1,1} & \cdots & S_{m\max,1} \\ \vdots & \ddots & \vdots & & \vdots \\ S_{1,m2} & \cdots & S_{m1,m2} & \cdots & S_{m\max,m2} \\ \vdots & & \vdots & \ddots & \vdots \\ S_{1,m\max} & \cdots & S_{m1,m\max} & \cdots & S_{m\max,m\max} \end{pmatrix} \tag{4}$$

where

$$S_{m1,m2} = \sum_{j=1}^{j\max} q'(j,m1)q'(j,m2) \tag{5}$$

5. Data mining of airfoil shape data

The shape data analysed here are the y coordinates defined on the grid points along the airfoil surface as shown in Fig. 8 where the number of grid points is 137. The energy ratios of

10 principal orthogonal base vectors (principal POD modes) to the total energy are shown in Fig. 9. While the fluctuation from the airfoil shape data of the *l/d* maximum design is analysed, principal modes are successfully extracted. The first mode is dominant (more than 83%) and the first two modes represent more than 94% of the total energy.

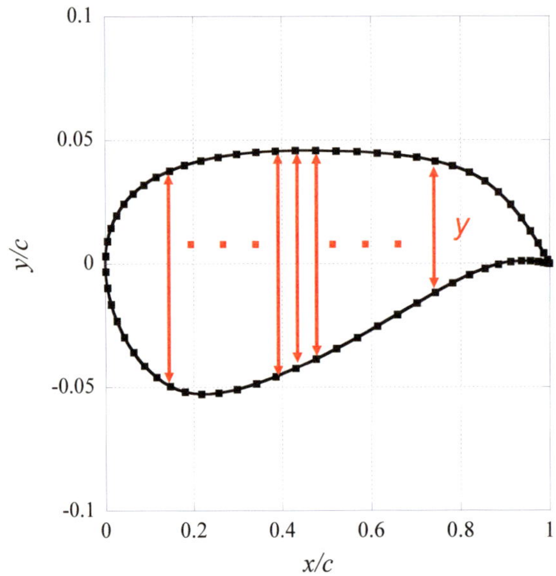

Fig. 8. Definition of the shape data. Shape data analyzed here are *y* coordinates defined on grid points along the airfoil surface.

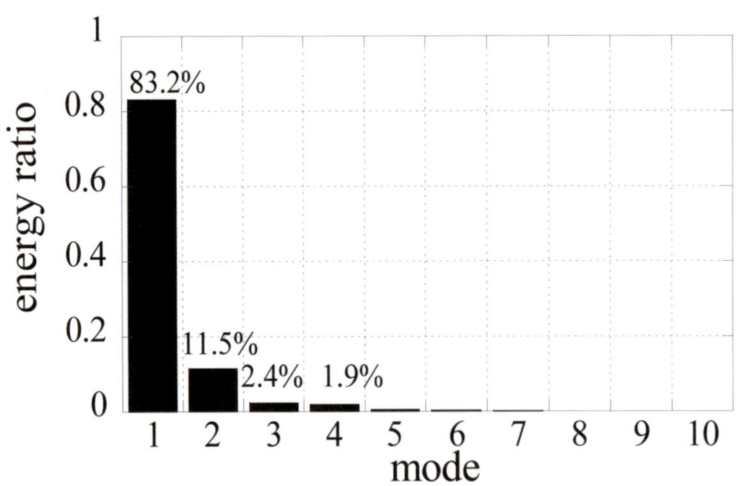

Fig. 9. Energy ratio of the top ten principal modes of the airfoil shape.

Figure 10 shows the components of the eigenvectors of the first and second modes with respect to the index of the non-dominated solutions *n* (left) and the lift coefficient $C_l(n)$ (right), respectively. Obtained non-dominated airfoil shapes are categorized into three groups, i.e., low drag design group (roughly $1 \le n \le 39$ and $C_l < 0.65$), high l/d design group ($40 \le n \le 52$ and $0.65 < C_l < 0.75$), and high lift design group ($53 \le n \le 85$ and $C_l > 0.75$). As for the low drag design group, the second mode is dominant and the eigenvector of the first mode is approximately zero. Among the high lift design group, the first mode is dominant and the eigenvector of the second mode is small. The non-dominated solutions in the high l/d design group have no significant difference in the shape. A large jump in the first mode is observed between n=52 and n=53. This jump indicates a significant change in the shape between the high l/d designs and high lift designs.

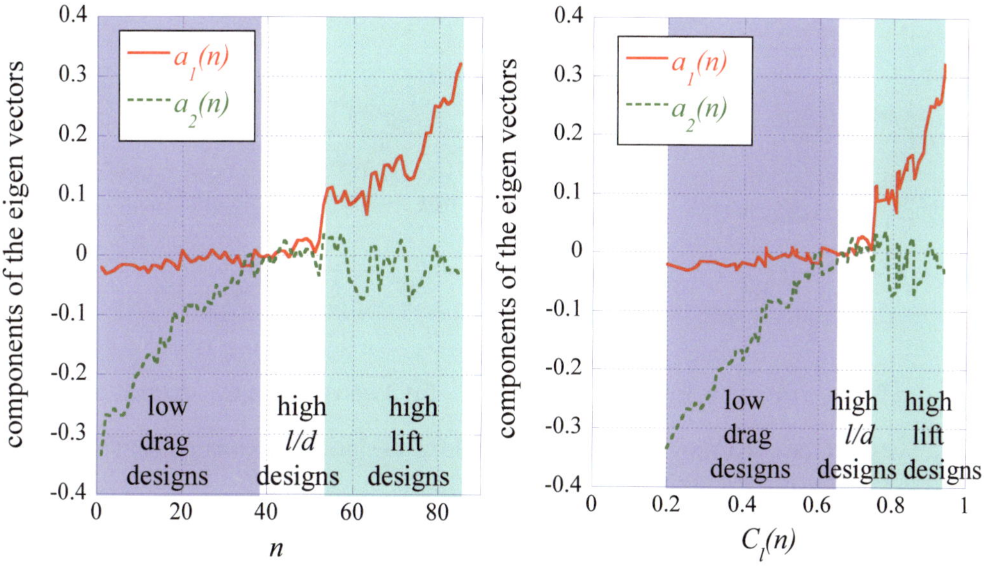

(a) Components of the eigenvectors with respect to n

(b) Components of the eigenvectors with respect to $C_l(n)$

Fig. 10. Components of the eigenvectors of the first and second modes.

Figure 11 presents the l/d-maximum airfoil shape and orthogonal base vectors of the first and second modes. This figure indicates that the mode 1 mainly contributes to the most part of the lower surface change. The base vector of the mode 1 also indicates that thickness near the leading edge should be increased as the camber is increased. This comes from the constraint on the maximum thickness imposed on the design optimization problem. The base vector of the second mode indicates that the second mode mainly contributes to the camber near the trailing edge.

Recalling the shapes of the non-dominated solutions are represented by equations (1) and (2), Figures 10 and 11 indicate that the low drag design group increase lift by changing the camber near the trailing edge while the other part of the airfoil shape is almost fixed. As for the high lift design group, lift is increased by moving the lower surface upward without significant change in the trailing edge angle. This movement of the lower surface corresponds to camber increase. The thickness near the leading edge is increased as the lower surface moves upward to satisfy the constraint applied to the airfoil maximum thickness near the leading edge.

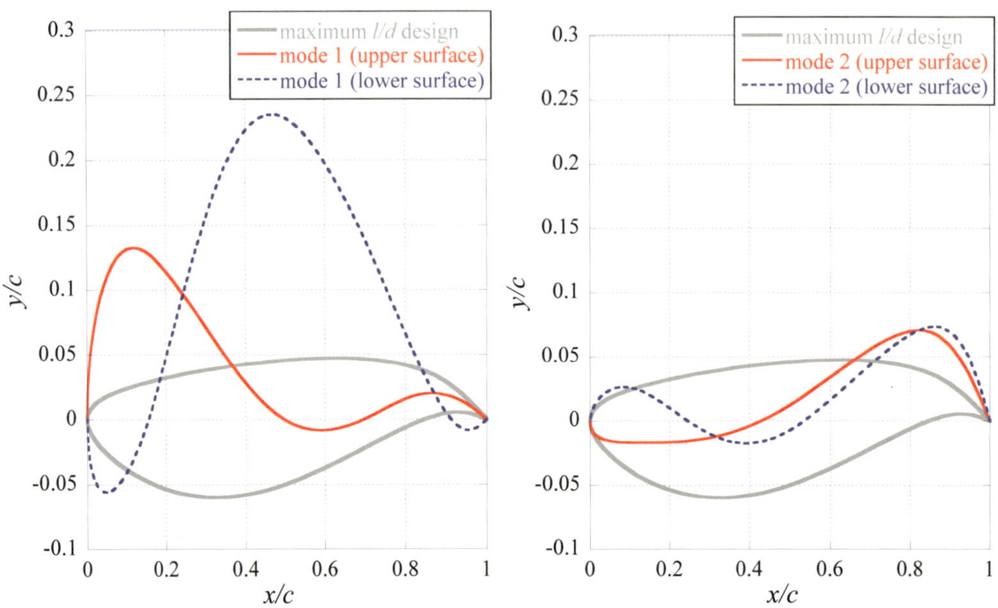

(a) Base vector of the first mode (b) Base vector of the second mode

Fig. 11. Shape of the maximum-lift-to-drag-ratio airfoil design and the orthogonal base vectors of the first and second modes.

To identify the advantage of the present approach over the conventional approach, design parameters of the non-dominated designs are analysed. Figure 12 presents scatter plots of the design parameters of the non-dominated solutions against the lift coefficient (upper) and the drag coefficient (lower). These plots give us some ideas such as 1) the non-dominated solutions may be categorized into two groups (see for example C_l against y_2 or y_4), and 2) airfoil camber increases as the lift increases. However, analysis of this figure hardly leads to the design knowledge we obtained in this section such as 1) the non-dominated solutions can be categorized into three groups, 2) Among the low drag designs, lift is increased by changing the camber near the trailing edge and 3) Among the high lift designs, the lift is increased by moving the lower surface upward. The reason for that is these features are represented by multiple design parameters. For example, camber near the trailing edge is mainly represented by x_1, y_1, x_6, and y_6.

6. Data mining of flow data

Here, as an example of flow data, static pressure data defined on all grid points of the non-dominated solutions are analysed, where the number of the grid points is 9,849 (201x49) (Fig.7). The energy ratios of the 10 principal orthogonal base vectors are presented in Fig. 13. The first mode is dominant (more than 79%) and the first two modes represent more than 92% of the total energy. These results are qualitatively the same as the airfoil shape data mining results.

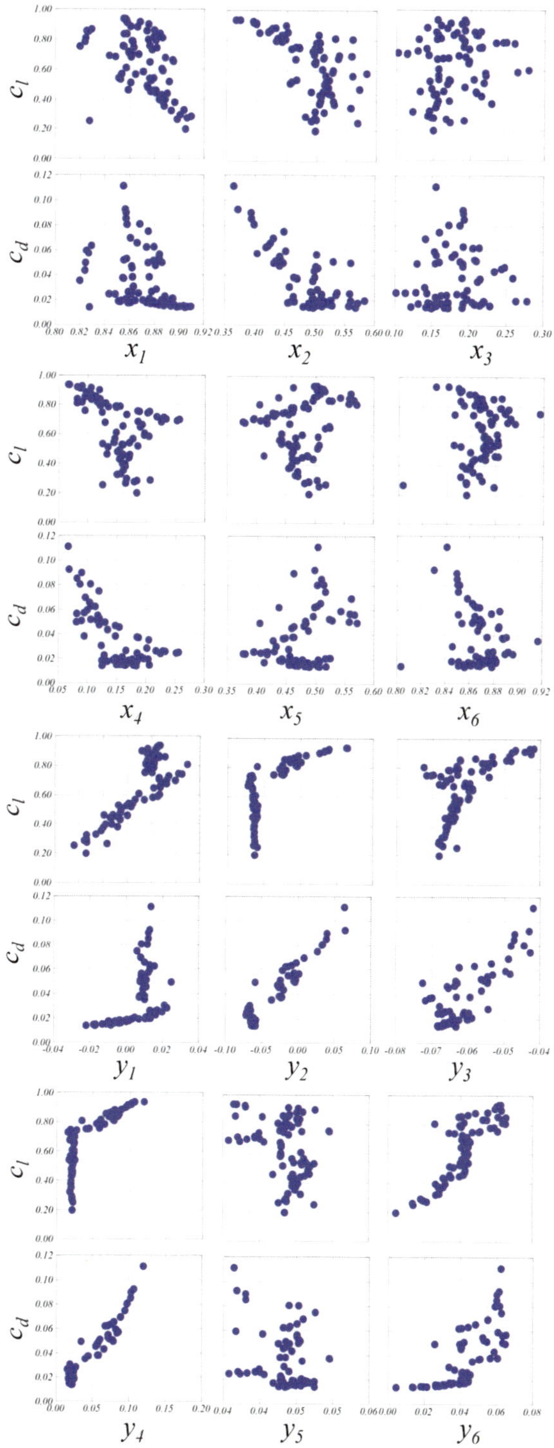

Fig. 12. Scatter plot matrix of the design parameters with respect to the lift or drag coefficients.

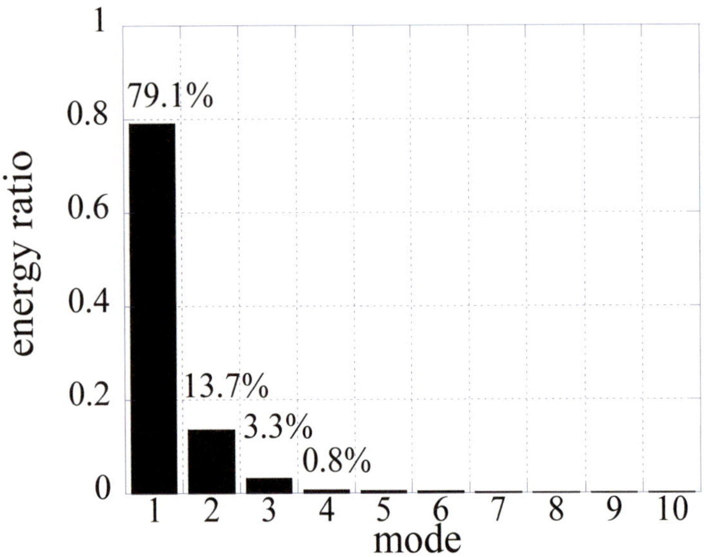

Fig. 13. Energy ratio of the top 10 principal modes of the pressure field distribution.

Figure 14 plots the components of the eigenvector of the first four modes with respect to the index of the non-dominated solutions (left) and the lift coefficient (right). This figure indicates that the pressure field of the non-dominated solutions can be categorized into three groups as the result of the shape data mining, namely, low-drag designs ($1 \leq n \leq 39$), high-lift-to-drag-ratio designs ($40 \leq n \leq 52$), and high-lift designs ($53 \leq n \leq 85$). Among the low-drag designs, the components of the first and second modes increase monotonically to zero as n or $C_l\ (n)$ increases. Among the high-lift-to-drag-ratio designs, the first mode increases monotonically as n or $C_l\ (n)$ increases, whereas the second mode is approximately

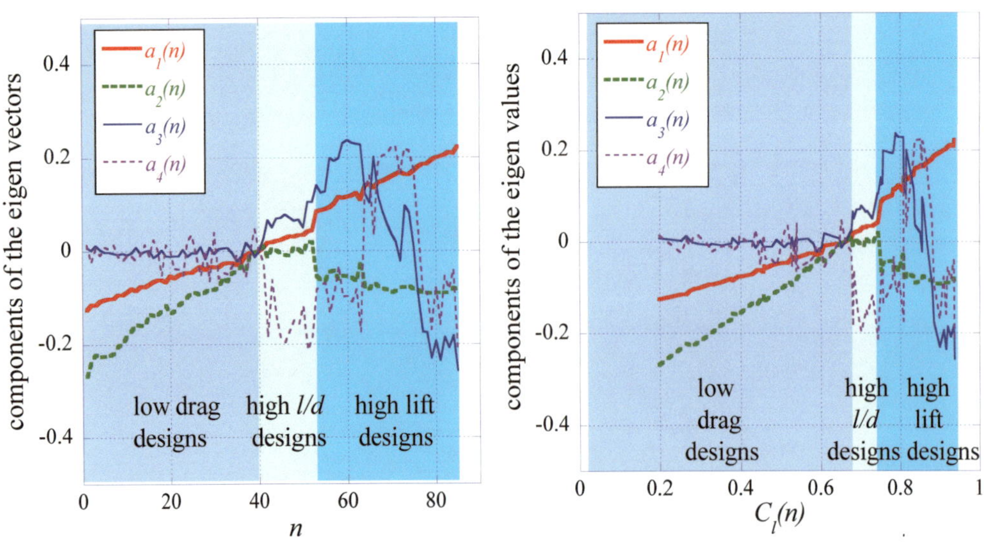

Fig. 14. Eigenvectors of the first four modes of the pressure field distribution.

zero. Among the high-lift designs, the first mode increases monotonically as n or C_l (n) increases, whereas the second mode decreases monotonically as n or C_l (n) increases. In this figure, a large jump in the components of the eigenvectors is also observed between n = 52 and n = 53. This jump indicates a significant change in the flow field between the high-lift-to-drag-ratio designs and high-lift designs.

The orthogonal base vectors of the first and second modes are shown in Fig. 15. These vectors indicate that the major changes among the pressure fields of the non-dominated solutions are 1) on the lower surface side near the trailing edge (region 1), 2) on the lower surface side near the leading edge (region 2), and 3) on the upper surface (region 3). These vectors also indicate that the pressure on the lower surface side near the leading and trailing edges decreases as the pressure on the upper surface side decreases.

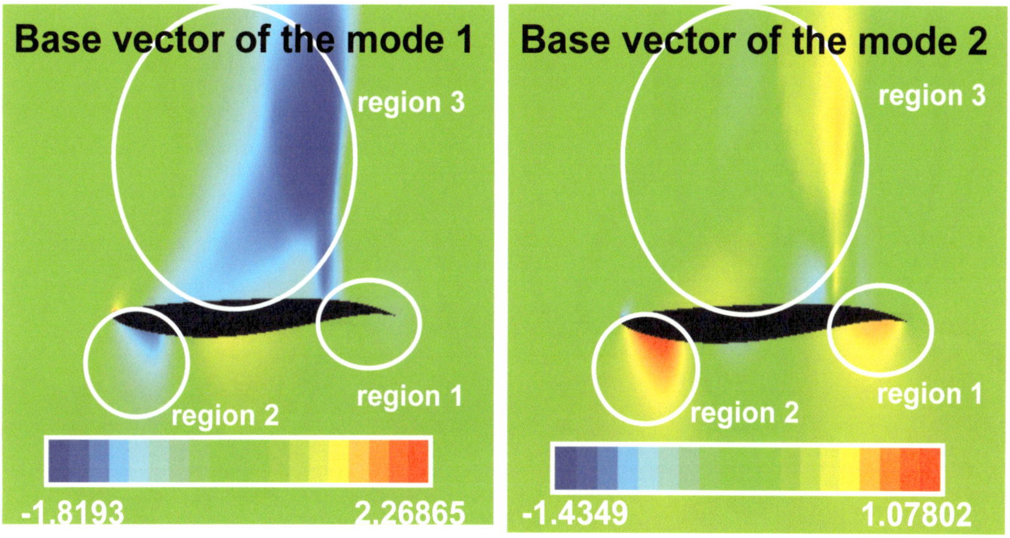

Fig. 15. Orthogonal base vectors of the first and second modes of the pressure field.

Recalling that the pressure fields of the non-dominated solutions are represented by Eqs. (1) and (2) and that the first and second modes are dominant (more than 92%), the eigenvectors (Fig. 14) and base vectors (Fig. 15) of the first and second modes and the pressure field of the maximum-lift-to-drag-ratio design (Fig. 16) provide the following observations:

1. In region 1, the second mode is dominant because the base vector of the first mode is approximately zero. Since the base vector of the second mode in region 1 is positive, the eigenvector of the second mode indicates that the high-lift-to-drag-ratio designs have the highest pressure near the trailing edge on the lower surface and that the pressure in region 1 increases monotonically as n (or lift) increases among the low-drag designs.
2. In region 2, the base vector of the first mode is negative, whereas that of the second mode is positive. The absolute value of the second mode is approximately half that of the first mode. Among the low-drag designs, the eigenvectors of the first and second modes increases monotonically as n (or lift) increases, and the absolute value of the second mode is approximately double that of the first mode. These facts indicate that the pressure field in region 2 does not change much among the low-drag designs because the first and second modes cancel out. Among the high-lift-to-drag-ratio

designs, the eigenvector of the first mode increases monotonically, whereas that of the second mode is approximately zero, which indicates that pressure in this region decreases as n (or lift) increases. Among the high-lift designs, the pressure in this region decreases drastically as n (or lift) increases.

3. In region 3, as in region 2, the pressure field does not change much among the low-drag designs because the first and second modes (the first and second terms of the right-hand side of Eq. (2)) approximately cancel out. Among the high-lift-to-drag-ratio designs and high-lift designs, the pressure in region 3 increases as n (or lift) increases. The jump in the components of the eigenvectors of the first and second modes is due to strong shock wave generation on the upper surface.

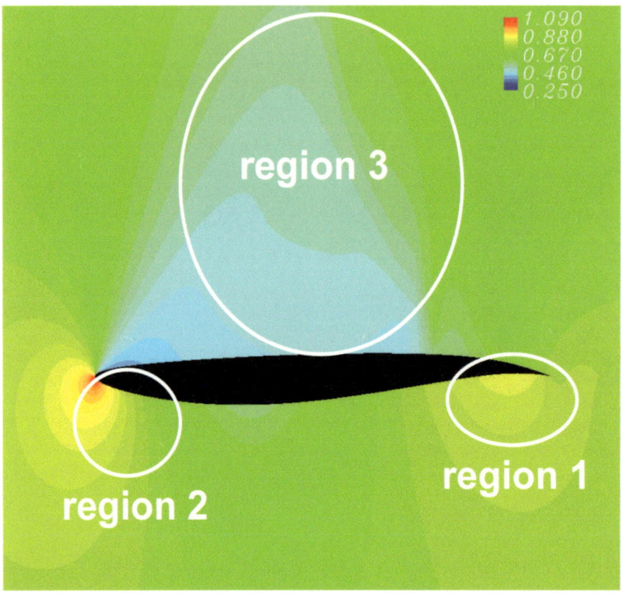

Fig. 16. Pressure field of the maximum-lift-to-drag-ratio design

7. Conclusion

A new approach for knowledge extraction from large data set of the non-dominated solutions is presented and applied to the non-dominated solutions of an aerodynamic transonic airfoil shape optimization. This approach decomposes the data of all non-dominated solutions into principal modes and base vectors using POD. One can discover knowledge from large data set of the non-dominated solutions by analysing the principal modes and base vectors. One of the advantages of this method is that the knowledge one can obtain does not depend on how the shape is parameterized for design optimization. Another advantage is that data mining of flow data leads to understanding of the physics behind the design problem.

This chapter demonstrated knowledge extraction from shape and static pressure data of non-dominated solutions of an aerodynamic transonic airfoil shape design optimization problem. The present result showed feasibility and benefit of data mining of such data.

Though the application of the POD-based data mining method was limited to the non-dominated solutions of a two-objective aerodynamic shape optimization problem in this chapter, its application is not limited to two-objective aerodynamic optimization problems. Application of this method to design optimization problem in other research field such as structure and heat transfer is straightforward. Application to non-dominated solution of a three or more objective design optimization problem is also possible if it is coupled with other visualization methods and/or data mining methods such as scatter plot matrix and SOM. The POD-based data mining method has strong potential for innovation in design in space engineering.

8. Acknowledgements

The present research is supported in part by KAKENHI (20760552) and KAKENHI (20246122).

9. References

Baldwin, B. S. & Lomax, H. (1985). Thin-Layer Approximation and Algebraic Model for Separated Turbulent Flows, *Proceedings of the 16th Aerospace Sciences Meeting*, 78-257, Huntsville, Alabama, January 1978, American Institute of Aeronautics and Astronautics, Reston, Virginia

Brant, A. (1977). Multi-Level Adaptive Solutions to Boundary Value Problems. *Mathematics of Computation*, Vol. 31, No. 138, 333-390, ISSN 0025-5718

Chiba, K.; Oyama, A.; Obayashi, S. & Nakahashi, K. (2007a). Multidisciplinary Design Optimization and Data Mining for Transonic Regional-Jet Wing. *Journal of Aircraft*, Vol. 44, No. 4, 110-1112, ISSN 0021-8669

Chiba, K. & Obayashi, S. (2007b). Data Mining for Multidisciplinary Design Space of Regional-Jet Wing. *Journal of Aerospace Computing, Information, and Communication*, Vol. 4, No. 11, 1019-1036, ISSN 1542-9423

Deb, K. (2001). *Multiobjective Optimization Using Evolutionary Algorithms*, John Wiley & Sons, Ltd., ISBN 047187339X, Chichester, UK

Donald, R. J.; Matthias, S. & William, J. W. (1998). Efficient Global Optimization of Expensive Black-Box Function. *Journal of Global Optimization*, Vol. 13, 455-492, ISSN 0925-5001

Eshelman, L. J. & Schaffer, J. D. (1993). Real-Coded Genetic Algorithms and Interval Schemata, In: *Foundations of Genetic Algorithms 2*, Whitley, L. D., (Ed.), 187-202, Morgan Kaufmann Publishers, Inc., ISBN 1558602631, San Mateo, CA

Fonseca, C. M. & Fleming, P. J. (1993). Genetic Algorithms for Multiobjective Optimization: Formulation, Discussion and Generalization, *Proceedings of the 5th International Conference on Genetic Algorithms*, pp. 416-423, ISBN 1-55860-299-2, Champaign, Illinois, July 1993, Morgan Kaufmann Publishers, Inc., San Mateo

Goldberg, D. E. & Richardson, J. (1987). Genetic Algorithms with Sharing for Multimodal Function Optimization, *Proceedings of the Second International Conference on Genetic Algorithms*, pp. 41-49, ISBN 0-8058-0158-8, Cambridge, Massachusetts, October 1987, Lawrence Erlbaum Associates, Inc., Mahwah

Goldberg, D. E. (1989). *Genetic Algorithms in Search, Optimization and Machine Learning*, Addison-Wesley Publishing Company, Inc., ISBN 0201157675, Reading, MA

Kanazaki, M.; Tanaka, K.; Jeong, S. & Yamamoto, K. (2007). Multi-Objective Aerodynamic Exploration of Elements' Setting for High-Lift Airfoil Using Kriging Model. *Journal of Aircraft*, Vol.44, No.3, 858-864, ISSN 0021-8669

Kohonen, T. (1998). *Self-Organizing Maps, 2nd edition*, Springer, ISBN 3540679219, Heidelberg, Germany

Obayashi, S. & Wada, Y. (1994). Practical Formulation of a Positively Conservative Scheme. *AIAA Journal*, Vol. 32, No. 5, 1093-1095, ISSN 0001-1452

Obayashi, S. & Guruswamy, G. P. (1995). Convergence Acceleration of an Aeroelastic Navier-Stokes Solver. *AIAA Journal*, Vol. 33, No. 6, 1134-1141, ISSN 0001-1452

Obayashi, S.; Sasaki, D. & Oyama, A. (2004). Finding Tradeoffs by Using Multiobjective Optimization Algorithms. *Transactions of the Japanese Society for Aeronautical and Space Sciences*, Vol. 27, 51-58, ISSN 0549-3811

Obayashi, S.; Jeong, S. & Chiba, K. (2005). Multi-Objective Design Exploration for Aerodynamic Configurations, *Proceedings of the 35th AIAA Fluid Dynamics Conference and Exhibit*, CD-ROM, Toronto, Ontario, June 2005, AIAA, Reston, Virginia

Obayashi, S. & Chiba, K. (2008). Knowledge Discovery for Flyback-Booster Aerodynamic Wing Using Data Mining. *Journal of Spacecraft and Rockets*, Vol. 45, No. 5, 975-987, ISSN 0022-4650

Oyama, A. & Liou, M. S. (2002). Multiobjective Optimization of Rocket Engine Pumps Using Evolutionary Algorithm. *Journal of Propulsion and Power*, Vol. 18, No. 3, 528-535, ISSN 0748-4658

Oyama, A.; Shimoyama, K. & Fujii, K. (2007). New Constraint-Handling Method for Multi-objective Multi-Constraint Evolutionary Optimization. *Transactions of the Japan Society for Aeronautical and Space Sciences*, Vol. 50, No. 167, 56-62, ISSN 0549-3811

Oyama, A.; Okabe, Y.; Shimoyama, K. and Fujii, K. (2009). Aerodynamic Multiobjective Design Exploration of a Flapping Airfoil Using a Navier-Stokes Solver. *Journal of Aerospace Computing, Information, and Communication*, Vol. 6, No. 3, 256-270, ISSN 1542-9423

Oyama, A.; Kawakatsu, Y. & Hagiwara, K. (2010). Application of Multiobjective Design Exploration to SOLAR-C Orbit Design, Proceedings of the 20th workshop on JAXA Astrodynamics and Flight Mechanics, Sagamihara, Japan, July 2010, ISAS/JAXA, Sagamihara (to be appeared)

Shimoyama, K.; Lim, J. N.; Jeong, S.; Obayashi, S. & Koishi, M. (2009). Practical Implementation of Robust Design Assisted by Response Surface Approximation and Visual Data-Mining. Journal of Mechanical Design, Vol.131, No.6, 061007-1-11, ISSN 1050-0472

Sirovich, L. (1987). Turbulence and Dynamics of Coherent Structures Part 1: Coherent Structures. *Quarterly of Applied Mathematics*, Vol. 45, No. 3, 561-571, ISSN 1552-4485

Tani, N.; Oyama, A. & Yamanishi, N. (2008). Multiobjective Design Optimization of Rocket Engine Turbopump Turbine, *Proceedings of the 5th International Spacecraft Propulsion Conference* (CDROM)

29

Privacy Preserving Data Mining

Xinjing Ge and Jianming Zhu
School of Information, Central University of Finance and Economics
Beijing, China

1. Introduction

With the development of network, data collection and storage technology, the use and sharing of large amounts of data has become possible. Once the data and information accumulated , it will become the wealth of information. Data mining, otherwise known as *knowledge discovery*, can extracted "meaningful information" or "knowledge" from the large amounts of data, so supports people's decision-making (Han & Kamber, 2006). However, traditional data mining techniques and algorithms directedly opreated on the original data set, which will cause the leakage of privacy data. At the same time, large amounts of data implicates the sensitive knowledge that their disclosure can not be ingored to the competitiveness of enterprise. These problems challenge the traditional data mining, so privacy-preserving data mining (PPDM) has become one of the newest trends in privacy and security and data mining research.

In privacy-preserving data mining (PPDM), data mining algorithms are analyzed for the side-effects they incur in data privacy, and the main objective in privacy preserving data mining is to develop algorithms for modifying the original data in some way, so that the private data and private knowledge remain private even after the mining process (Verykios et al., 2004a). A number of techniques such as Trust Third Party, Data perturbation technique, Secure Multiparty Computation and game theoretic approach, have been suggested in recent years in order to perform privacy preserving data mining.

However, most of these privacy preserving data mining algorithms such as the Secure Multiparty Computation technique, were based on the assumption of a semi-honest environment, where the participating parties always follow the protocol and never try to collude. As mentioned in previous works on privacy-preserving distributed mining (Lindell & Pinkas, 2002), it is rational for distributed data mining that the participants are assumed to be semi-honest, but the collusion of parties for gain additional benefits can not be avoided. So there has been a tendency for privacy preserving data mining to devise the collusion resistant protocols or algorithms, recent research have addressed this issue, and protocols or algorithms based on penalty function mechanism, the Secret Sharing Technique, and the Homomorphic Threshold Cryptography are given (Kargupta et al.,2007 ; Jiang et al., 2008; Emekci et al., 2007).

This chapter is organized as follows. In Section 2, we introduce the related concepts of the PPDM problem. In Section 3, we describe some techniques for privacy preserving data mining In Section 4, we discuss the collussion behaviors in Privacy Preserving Data Mining. Finally, Section 5 presents our conclusions.

2. The related concepts of PPDM

The concept of privacy is often more complex, In particular, in data mining, the definition of privacy preservation is refered to "getting valid data mining results without learning the underlying data values."(Clifton et al., 2002a), and (Stanley et al., 2004) also indicated PPDM encompasses the dual goal of meeting privacy requirements and providing valid data mining results, so the definition emphasizes the dilemma of balancing privacy preservation and knowledge disclosure.

2.1 Defining privacy preservation in data mining

Privacy-preserving data mining considers the problem of running data mining algorithms on confidential data that is not supposed to be revealed even to the party running the algorithm. The main consideration of PPDM is two fold (Verykios et al., 2004a). First, sensitive raw data like identifiers,names, addresses and so on, should be modified or trimmed out from the original database, in order for the recipient of the data not to be able to compromise another person's privacy. Second, sensitive knowledge which can be mined from a database by using data mining algorithms, should also be excluded, because such a knowledge can equally well compromise data privacy. So, privacy preservation occurs in two major dimensions: users' personal information and information concerning their collective activity. the former is referred to individual privacy preservation and the latter is refferred to collective privacy preservation (Stanley et al., 2004).

- **Individual privacy preservation:** The primary goal of data privacy is the protection of personally identifiable information. In general, information is considered personally identifiable if it can be linked, directly or indirectly, to an individual person. Thus, when personal data are subjected to mining, the attribute values associated with individuals are private and must be protected from disclosure. Miners are then able to learn from global models rather than from the characteristics of a particular individual.
- **Collective privacy preservation:** Protecting personal data may not be enough. Sometimes, we may need to protect against learning sensitive knowledge representing the activities of a group. We refer to the protection of sensitive knowledge as collective privacy preservation. The goal here is quite similar to that one for statistical databases, in which security control mechanisms provide aggregate information about groups and, at the same time, should prevent disclosure of confidential information about individuals. However, unlike as is the case for statistical databases, another objective of collective privacy preservation is to preserve strategic pattern that are paramount for strategic decisions, rather than minimizing the distortion of all statistics. In other words, the goal here is not only to protect personally identifiable information but also some patterns and trends that are not supposed to be discovered.

Privacy Preservation in Data Mining has some limitations: Privacy Preservation Data Mining techniques do not mean pefect privacy, for example, The SMC computation won't reveal the sensitive data, but the data mining result will enable all parties to estimate the value of the sensitive data. It isn't that the SMC was "broken", but that the result itself violates privacy.

2.2 Data distribution

In PPDM, How are the data available for mining: are they centralized or distributed across many sites? With distributed data, the way the data is distributed also plays an important

role in defining the problem. The different partitioning poses different problems and can lead to different algorithms for privacy-preserving data mining.
Distributed data scenarios can be classified as horizontal data distribution and vertical data distribution (Verykios et al., 2004a). **Horizontal distribution** refers to these cases where different database records reside in different places, while **vertical data distribution**, refers to the cases where all the values for different attributes reside in different places.

2.3 Models of PPDM

In the study of privacy-preserving data mining (PPDM), there are mainly four models as follows:
1. Trust Third Party Model

The goal standard for security is the assumption that we have a trusted third party to whom we can give all data. The third party performs the computation and delivers only the results - except for the third party, it is clear that nobody learns anything not inferable from its own input and the results. The goal of secure protocols is to reach this same level of privacy preservation, without the problem of finding a third party that everyone trusts.
2. Semi-honest Model

In the semi-honest model, every party follows the rules of the protocol using its correct input, but after the protocol is free to use whatever it sees during execution of the protocol to compromise security.
3. Malicious Model

In the malicious model, no restrictions are placed on any of the participants. Thus any party is completely free to indulge in whatever actions it pleases. In general, it is quite difficult to develop efficient protocols that are still valid under the malicious model. However, the semi-honest model does not provide sufficient protection for many applications.
4. Other Models - Incentive Compatibility

While the semi-honest and malicious models have been well researched in the cryptographic community, other models outside the purview of cryptography are possible. One example is the interesting economic notion of incentive compatibility. A protocol is incentive compatible if it can be shown that a cheating party is either caught or else suffers an economic loss. Under the rational model of economics, this would serve to ensure that parties do not have any advantage by cheating. Of course, in an irrational model, this would not work.
We remark, in the "real world", there is no external party that can be trusted by all parties, so the Trust Third Party Model is a ideal model.

2.4 Evaluation of privacy preserving algorithms

An important aspect in the development and assessment of algorithms and tools, for privacy preserving data mining is the identification of suitable evaluation criteria and the development of related benchmarks. It is often the case that no privacy preserving algorithm exists that outperforms all the others on all possible criteria. Rather, an algorithm may perform better that another one on specific criteria, such as performance and/or data utility. It is thus important to provide users with a set of metrics which will enable them to select the most appropriate privacy preserving technique for the data at hand, with respect to some specific parameters they are interested in optimizing.

A preliminary list of evaluation parameters to be used for assessing the quality of privacy preserving data mining algorithms, is given below: (Verykios et al., 2004a)

- the ***performance*** of theney, proposed algorithms in terms of time requirements, that is the time needed by each algorithm to hide a specified set of sensitive information;
- the ***data utility*** after the application of the privacy preserving technique, which is equivalent with the minimization of the information loss or else the loss in the functionality of the data;
- the ***level of uncertainty*** with which the sensitive information that have been hidden can still be predicted;
- the ***resistance*** accomplished by the privacy algorithms, to different data mining techniques.

3. Privacy preserving data mining techniques

Data mining includes various algorithms such as classification, association rule mining, and clustering. In recent years, a number of techniques have been proposed to preserve privacy. Privacy preserving data mining techniques can be classified by different assumptions or domain knowledge.for example, data distribution, data modification, data mining algorithm, data or rule hiding, privacy preservation (Verykios et al., 2004a). In this section, we will introduce some mainly privacy preserving data mining techniques, which include the Trust Party tehnique, randomization technique, Secure Multiparty Computation and anonymity techniques.

3.1 The trust party tehnique

The typical approach to data mining of distributed privacy preserving data is to build a data warehouse containing all the data, then mine the warehouse. This requires that the warehouse be trusted to maintain the privacy of all parties - since it knows the source of data, it learns site specific information as well as global results. For privacy preserving data mining, if we can find a fully trusted third party, then all parties give their input to the trust third party, and the trust third party computes the output and returns it to the parties. For example, current e-commerce transactions have a trusted (central) third party with access to all the information. The "trust" is governed by legal contracts enjoining the improper release of information. In some cases, the third party is dispensed with and contracts exist between the interested parties themselves. This is obviously insecure from the technical perspective.
Trusted third parties are, however, difficult to find, especially when the number of participants increases. Though SMC enables this *without* the trusted third party, but the computation and/or communication required may be high. so the protocols obtained by this general construction are inefficient and useless in the case of a large number of participants. Other factors, such as the need for continual online availability of the parties, create further restrictions and problems in realworld settings such as a web-based survey. So we need to extend the fully trusted party technique. For example, refernce (Gilburd et al., 2004) proposed a new privacy model: *k*-privacy --by means of an innovative, yet natural generalization of the accepted trusted third party model. This allows implementing cryptographically secure efficient primitives for real-world large scale distributed systems. As an example for the usefulness of the proposed model, we employ *k*-privacy to introduce a technique for obtaining knowledge --by way of an association-rule mining algorithm from large-scale data basement, while ensuring that the privacy is cryptographically secure.

3.2 Data perturbation technique

Data perturbation technique, first proposed in (Agrawal & Srikant, 2000), represents one common approach in privacy preserving data mining, where the original (private) dataset is perturbed and the result is released for data analysis. Data perturbation includes a wide variety of techniques including (but not limited to): additive, multiplicative (Kim & Winkler, 2003), matrix multiplicative, k-anonymization (Sweeney, 2002), micro-aggregation (Li & Sarkar, 2006), categorical data perturbation (Verykios, 2004b), data swapping (Fienberg & McIntyre, 2004), resampling (Liew, 1985), data shuffling (Muralidhar & Sarathy, 2006). Now we mostly focus on two types of data perturbation that apply to continuous data: additive and matrix multiplicative, other detailed data perturbation techniques can refer to the related literatures.

3.2.1 Additive perturbation

The additive perturbation is a technique for privacy-preserving data mining in which noise is added to the data in order to mask the attribute values of records (Agrawal & Srikant, 2000). The noise added is sufficiently large so that individual record values cannot be recovered. Therefore, techniques are designed to derive aggregate distributions from the perturbed records. Subsequently, data mining techniques can be developed in order to work with these aggregate distributions. The method of randomization can be described as follows.

Consider a set of data records denoted by $X=\{x_1,x_2,\cdots,x_N\}$. For record $x_i \in X$, we add a noise component which is drawn fromthe probability distribution $f_Y(y)$. These noise components are drawn independently, and are denoted $Y=\{y_1,y_2,\cdots y_N\}$. Thus, the new set of distorted records are denoted by $x_1+y_1,\cdots x_N+y_N$. We denote this new set of records by $Z=\{z_1,\cdots z_N\}$. So the data owner replaces the original dataset X with $Z=X+Y$. where Y is a noise matrix with each column generated independently from a n-dimensional random vector Y with mean vector zero. As is commonly done, we assume throughout that Σ_Y equals $\sigma^2 I$, *i.e.*, the entries of Y were generated independently from some distribution with mean zero and variance σ^2 (typical choices for this distribution include Gaussian and uniform). In this case, Y is sometimes referred to as *additive white noise*. Thus, the original records cannot be recovered, but the distribution of the original records can be recovered.

3.2.2 Matrix multiplicative perturbation

The most common method of data perturbation is that of additive perturbations. However, matrix multiplicative perturbations can also be used to good effect for privacy-preserving data mining.

The data owner replaces the original data X with $Y=MX$ where M is an $n'\times n$ matrix chosen to have certain useful properties. If M is orthogonal ($n'=n$ n and $M^TM=I$), then the perturbation exactly preserves Euclidean distances, *i.e.*, for any columns x_1,x_2 in X ,their corresponding columns y_1,y_2 in Y satisfy $\|x_1-x_2\|=\|y_1-y_2\|$. If each entry of M is generated independently from the same distribution with mean zero and variance σ^2 (n' not necessarily equal to n), then the perturbation approximately preserves Euclidean distances on expectation up to constant factor $\sigma^2 n'$. If M is the product of a discrete cosine transformation matrix and a truncated perturbation matrix, then the perturbation approximately preserves Euclidean distances.

3.2.3 Evaluation of data perturbation technique

The data perturbation technique have the benefits of efficiency, and does not require knowledge of the distribution of other records in the data. This is not true of other methods such as k-anonymity which require the knowledge of other records in the data. this technique does not require the use of a trusted server containing all the original records in order to perform the anonymization process. While this is a strength of the data perturbation technique, it also leads to some weaknesses, since it treats all records equally irrespective of their local density. Therefore, outlier records are more susceptible to adversarial attacks as compared to records in more dense regions in the data. In order to guard against this, one may need to be needlessly more aggressive in adding noise to all the records in the data. This reduces the utility of the data for mining purposes.

Reference (Liu et al., 2006) provides a detailed survey of attack techniques on the data perturbation, especially additive and matrix multiplicative perturbation. These attacks offer insights into vulnerabilities data perturbation techniques under certain circumstances. In summary, the following information could lead to disclosure of private information from the perturbed data.

1. **Attribute Correlation:** Many real world data has strong correlated attributes, and this correlation can be used to filter off additive white noise.
2. **Known Sample:** Sometimes, the attacker has certain background knowledge about the data such as the *p.d.f.* or a collection of independent samples which may or may not overlap with the original data.
3. **Known Inputs/Outputs:** Sometimes, the attacker knows a small set of private data and their perturbed counterparts. This correspondence can help the attacker to estimate other private data.
4. **Data Mining Results:** The underlying pattern discovered by data mining also provides a certain level of knowledgewhich can be used to guess the private data to a higher level of accuracy.
5. **SampleDependency:** Most of the attacks assume the data as independent samples from some unknown distribution. This assumption may not hold true for all real applications. For certain types of data, such as the time series data, there exists auto correlation/dependency among the samples. How this dependency can help the attacker to estimate the original data is still an open problem.

At the same time, a "privacy/accuracy" trade-off is faced for the data perturbation technique. On the one hand, perturbation must not allow the original data records to be adequately recovered. On the other, it must allow "patterns" in the original data to be mined.

Data perturbation technique is needed for situations where accessing the original form of the data attributes is mandatory. It happens when, for instance, some conventional off-the-shelf data analysis techniques are to be applied. While this approach is more generic, some inaccuracy in the analysis result is to be expected.

3.2.4 Application of the data perturbation technique

The randomization method has been extended to a variety of data mining problems. Refercence (Agrawal & Srikant, 2000) firstly discussed how to use the approach for solving the privacy preserving classification problem classification. Refercence (Zhang et al. 2005; Zhu & Liu, 2004) have also proposed a number of other techniques which seem to work well over a variety of different classifiers.

There has been research considering preserving privacy for other type of data mining. For instance, reference (Evfimievski et al., 2002) proposed a solution to the privacy preserving distributed association mining problem.The problem of association rules is especially challenging because of the discrete nature of the attributes corresponding to presence or absence of items. In order to deal with this issue, the randomization technique needs to be modified slightly. Instead of adding quantitative noise, random items are dropped or included with a certain probability. The perturbed transactions are then used for aggregate association rule mining. The randomization approach has also been extended to other applications, for example, SVD based collaborative filtering (Polat & Du, 2005).

3.3 Secure multiparty computation technique

3.3.1 Background

In privacy preserving distributed data mining, two or more parties owning confidential databases wish to run a data mining algorithm on the union of their databases without revealing any unnecessary information. For example, consider separate medical institutions that wish to conduct a joint research while preserving the privacy of their patients. One way to view this is to imagine a trusted third party-- everyone gives their input to the trusted party, who performs the computation and sends the results to the participants. However, this is exactly what we don't want to do, for example, hospitals are not allowed to hand their raw data out, security agencies cannot afford the risk, and governments risk citizen outcry if they do. Thus, the question is how to compute the results without having a trusted party, and in a way that reveals nothing but the final results of the data mining computation. Secure Multiparty Computation enables this *without* the trusted third party. The concept of Secure Multiparty Computation was introduced in (Yao, 1986) and has been proved that there is a secure multi-party computation solution for any polynomial function (Goldreich,1998). The basic idea of Secure Multiparty Computation is that a computation is secure if at the end of the computation, no party knows anything except its own input and the results. This approach was first introduced to the data mining community by Lindell and Pinkas (Lindell & Pinkas, 2002), with a method that enabled two parties to build a decision tree without either party learning anything about the other party's data, except what might be revealed through the final decision tree. Now this technique have been developed for association rules, clustering, k-nearest neighbor classification, and are working on others.

Allowed adversarial behavior: there are two main types of adversaries. (Lindell & Pinkas, 2002)

a. **Semi-honest adversaries:** In semi-honest adversarial model, it correctly follows the protocol specification, yet attempts to learn additional information by analyzing the transcript of messages received during the execution. This is a ratherweak adversarial model. However, there are some settings where it can realistically modelthe threats to the system. Semi-honest adversaries are also called "honest-but-curious"and "passive".
b. **Malicious adversaries:** In malicious adversarial model , a party may arbitrarily deviate from the protocol specification .In general, providing security in the presence of malicious adversaries is preferred, as it ensures that no adversarial attack can succeed. Malicious adversaries are also called "active".

We remark that although the semi-honest adversarial model is far weaker than the malicious model, it is often a realistic one. This is because deviating from a specified program which may be buried in a complex application is a non-trivial task.

3.3.2 Techniques for building secure multiparty computation protocols

In this section,we describe here some simple protocols that are often used as basic building blocks, or primitives, of secure computation protocols.

Oblivious Transfer: Oblivious transfer is a simple functionality involving two parties. It is a basic building block of many cryptographic protocols for secure computation. The notion of 1-out-2 oblivious transfer was suggested by (Even et al., 1985) (as a variant of a different but equivalent type of oblivious transfer that has been suggested by (Rabin, 1981)). The protocol involves two parties, the sender and the receiver. and its functionality is defined as follows:

- **Input:** The sender's input is a pair of strings (x_0, x_1) and the receiver's input is a bit $\sigma \in \{0,1\}$.
- **Output:** The receiver's output is x_σ (and nothing else), while the sender has no output.

In other words, 1-out-of-2 oblivious transfer implements the function $((x_0, x_1), \sigma) \mapsto (\lambda, x_\sigma)$, where λ denotes the empty string (i.e., no output).

Oblivious transfer protocols have been designed based on virtually all known assumptions which are used to construct specific trapdoor functions (i.e. public key cryptosystems), and also based on generic assumptions such as the existence of enhanced trapdoor permutations. There are simple and eficient protocols for oblivious transfer which are secure only against semi-honest adversaries (Even et al., 1985).

Oblivious Polynomial Evaluation: The problem of "oblivious polynomial evaluation" (OPE) involves a sender and a receiver. The sender's input is a polynomial Q of degree k over some finite field F, namely a polynomial $Q(z) = \sum_{i=0}^{k} a_i z^i$ (the degree k of the polynomial, wis public). The receiver's input is an element . The protocol is such that the receiver obtains $Q(z)$ without learning anything else about the polynomial Q, and the sender learns nothing. That is, the problem considered is the private computation of the function $(Q, z) \mapsto (\lambda, Q(z))$ .where λ is the empty output.

The major motivation for oblivious polynomial evaluation is the fact that the output of a k egree random polynomial is $k+1$ wise independent; this is very useful in the construction of cryptographic protocols. Another motivation is that polynomials can be used for approximating functions that are defined over the Real numbers.

Homomorphic Encryption:A homomorphic encryption scheme is an encryption scheme which allows certain algebraic operations to be carried out on the encrypted plaintext, by applying an eficient operation to the corresponding ciphertext. In particular, we will be interested in additively homomorphic encryption schemes (Paillier ,1999) that is comparable with the encryption process of RSA in terms of the computation cost, while the decryption process of the additive homomorphism is faster than the decryption process of RSA.

An additively homomorphic cryptosystem has the nice property that for two plain text message m_1 and m_2, it holds $e(m_1) \times e(m_2) = e(m_1 + m_2)$,where $\times$ denotes multiplication. This essentially means that we can have the sum of two numbers without knowing what those numbers are. Moreover, because of the property of associativity, $e(m_1 + m_2 + \cdots + m_s) = e(m_1) \times e(m_2) \times \cdots \times e(m_s)$, where $e(m_i) \neq 0$.

And we can easily have the following corollary: $e(m_1)^{m_2} = e(m_2)^{m_1} = e(m_1 \times m_2)$

An eficient implementation of an additive homomorphic encryption scheme with semantic security was given by Paillier (Paillier ,1999).

Threshold decryption: Threshold decryption is an example of a multiparty functionality. The setting includes m parties and an encryption scheme. It is required that any $m' < m$ of the parties are able to decrypt messages, while any coalition of strictly less than m' parties learns nothing about encrypted messages. This functionality can, of course, be implemented using generic constructions, but there are specific constructions implementing it for almost any encryption scheme, and these are far more eficient than applying the generic constructions to compute this function ality. Interestingly, threshold decryption of homomorphic encryption can be used as a primitive for constructing a very eficient generic protocol for secure multiparty computation, with a communication overhead of only $O(mk|c|)$ bits (Franklin & Haber (1996) for a construction secure against semi-honest adversaries, and Cramer et al. (2001) for a construction secure against malicious adversaries).
Other Cryptographic Tools:
Many basic security operations now have been applied to Secure protocols of privacy preserving data mining, such as Secure Sum, Secure Set, Secure Size of Set Intersection Union, Scalar Product (Clifton et al., 2002b)..

3.3.3 Application of the secure multiparty computation technique

Secure Multi-party Computation (SMC) technique is a common approach for distributed privacy preserving data mining, and now has been extended to a variety of data mining problems. For example, Lindell & Pinkas (2002) introduced a secure multi-party computation technique for classification using the ID3 algorithm, over horizontally partitioned data. Specifically, they consider a scenario in which two parties owning confidential databases wish to run a data mining algorithm on the union of their databases, without revealing any unnecessary information. Du & Zhan (2002) proposed a protocol for making the ID3 algorithm privacy-preserving over vertically partitioned data. Vaidya & Clifton (2002) presented the component scalar product protocol for privacy-preserving association rule mining over vertically partitioned data in the case of two parties; Wright & Yang (2004) applied homomorphic encryption to the Bayesian networks induction for the case of *two* parties. Zhan et al., (2007) proposed a cryptographic approach to tackle collaborative association rule mining among multiple parties.

3.3.4 Common errors of the secure multiparty computation

There are common errors which often occur when designing secure protocols, here we would like to use this section to introduce some of these errors briefly, interested reader can refer to (Lindell & Pinkas, 2009).

- **Semi-honest Behavior does not Preclude Collusions:** Assuming that adversaries are semi-honest does not ensure that no two parties collude. The "semi-honest adversary" assumption merely ensures that an adversary follows the protocol, and only tries to learn information from messages it received during protocol execution. It is still possible, however, that the adversary controls more than a single party and might use the information it learns from all the parties it controls.
- **Deterministic Encryption Reveals Information:** A common misconception is that encrypting data, or hashing it, using any encryption system or hash function, keeps the data private. The root of the problem is the use of a deterministic function (be it a hash function or a deterministic encrypting scheme such as textbook RSA). One should therefore never apply a deterministic function to an item and publish the result.

Instead, a semantically secure encryption scheme must be used. Unfortunately, this rules out a number of "simple and eficient" protocols that appear in the literature (indeed, these protocols are not and cannot be proven secure).

- **Input Dependent Flow:** the flow of the protocol (namely, the decision which parts of it to execute), must not depend on the private input of the parties. Otherwise, The protocolis not secure
- **Security Proofs:** It is tempting to prove security by stating what constitutes a "bad behavior" or an "illegitimate gain" by the adversary, and then proving that this behavior is impossible. Any other behavior or gain is considered benign and one need not bother with it. This approach is often easier than the use of simulation based proofs. However , it is hard to predict what type of corrupt behavior an adversary might take and thus dangerous to disregard any other behavior that we have not thought of as useless for the adversary. Indeed, real world attackers often act in ways which were not predicted by the designers of the system they attack. It is also hard to define what constitutes a legitimate gain by the adversary, and allow it while preventing illegitimate or harmful gains. The notion of "harmful" might depend on a specific application or a specific scenario, and even then it might be very hard to define. So the protocol designers must prove security according to the simulation based proof (Lindell & Pinkas, 2009), which prevent any attack which is not possible in an idealized scenario.

3.3.5 Evaluation of the secure multiparty computation technique

Secure Multiparty Computation enables distributed privacy preserving data mining *without* the trusted third party, Moreover, the secure multiparty computation technique make the result of data mining correct without information loss. The shortcoming of the technique is the computation and communication overhead of protocol is very high, esperically for the large database, which hinder its application in practice. So secure multiparty computation, due to its high computational requirement, is most suitable for situations where the number of distributed sources is relatively small and the global analysis to be supported can be derived by the given set of primitives.

3.4 A game theoretic approach to privacy preserving data mining

Game theory has been widely applied in many different domains like economics, finance, etc. Recently, it has also been applied for managing distributed computing environment. Applications of game theory in secure multi-party computation and privacy preserving distributed data mining is relatively new. Kleinberg et al. (1998) proposed a microeconomic view of data mining and illustrated how data clustering for customer segmentation in a market with two players could be modeled as a two-player game so that the segmentation was driven by the objective of deriving best marketing strategies. Kleinberg et al., (2001) tried to justify the fairness of disclosing private information as part of a transaction by the compensation of gaining better services using a game theoretic approach, for applications like marketing survey and collaborative filtering. In addition, there are some recent studies based on game theory to address the collusion problem of privacy preserving data mining that use secure multiparty computation (Abraham et al., 2006; Kargupta et al., 2007). Kargupta et al.(2007) offers a game-theoretic framework for the PPDM problem as a multi-party game where each party tries to maximize its own objectives, and also presents equilibrium-analysis of such PPDM-games and outlines a game-theoretic solution based on the concept of "cheap-talk" borrowed from the economics and the game theory literature.

4. The collussion behaviors in privacy preserving data mining

Based on cryptographic techniques and secure multi-party computations, privacy preserving protocols or algorithms have been designed for Privacy preserving data mining . However, many of these algorithms make strong assumptions about the behavior of the participating entities, such as, they assume that the parties are semi-honest, that is, they always follow the protocol and never not try to collude or sabotage the process.

As mentioned in previous works on privacy-preserving distributed mining (Lindell & Pinkas, 2002), the participants are assumed to be semi-honest that is rational for distributed data mining, but these kind of assumptions fall apart in real life and the collusion of parties happen easily to gain additional benefits. For example (Kargupta et al., 2007), the US Department of Homeland Security funded PURSUIT project involves privacy preserving distributed data integration and analysis of network traffic data from different organizations. However, network traffic is usually privacy sensitive and no organization would be willing to share their network traffic with a third party. PPDM offers one possible solution which would allow comparing and matching multi-party network traffic for detecting common attacks, stealth attacks and computing various statistics for a group of organizations without necessarily sharing the raw data. However, participating organization in a consortium like PURSUIT may not all be ideal. Some may decide to behave like a "leach" exploiting the benefit of the system without contributing much. Some may intentionally try to sabotage the multi-party computation. Some may try to collude with other parties for exposing the private data of a party.

4.1 The collussion analysis of PPDM based on the game theory

Applications of game theory in secure multi-party computation and privacy preserving distributed data mining is relatively new (Abraham et al., 2006 ; Kargupta et al., 2007). Kargupta et al. (2007) argues that large-scale multi-party PPDM can be thought of as a game where each participant tries to maximize its benefit by optimally choosing the strategies during the entire PPDM process. With a game theoretic framework for analyzing the rational behavior of each party, authors present detailed equilibrium analysis of the well known secure sum computation (Clifton et al., 2002b) as an example. A new version of the secure sum is proposed as follows and interested readers can find a detailed anysis in Kargupta et al. (2007).

Secure Sum Computation (Clifton et al., 2002b)**:** Suppose there are n individual nodes organized in a ring topology, each with a value v_j , $j = 1,2,\cdots,n$ .It is known that the sum $v = \sum_{j=1}^{n} v_j$ (to be computed) takes an integer value in the range $[0, \quad N-1]$.

The basic idea of secure sum is as follows. Assuming nodes do not collude, node 1 generates a random number R uniformly distributed in the range $[0, \quad N-1]$, which is independent of its local value v_1 . Then node 1 adds R to its local value v_1 and transmits $(R+v_1) \bmod N$ to node 2. In general, for $i = 2,\cdots n$, node i performs the following operation: receive a value z_{i-1} from previous node $i-1$, add it to its own local value v_i and compute its modulus N. In other words, $z_i = (z_{i-1} + v_i) \bmod N = (R + \sum_{j=1}^{i} v_j) \bmod N$, where z_i is the perturbed version of local value v_i to be sent to the next node i + 1. Node n performs the same step and sends the result z_n to node 1. Then node 1, which knows R, can subtract R from z_n to obtain the actual sum. This sum is further broadcasted to all other sites.

Collusion Analysis (Kargupta et al., 2007): it can be shown that any z_i has an uniform distribution over the interval $[0, \; N-1]$ due to the modulus operation. Further, any z_i and v_i are statistically independent, and hence, a single malicious node may not be able to launch a successful privacy-breaching attack. Then how about collusion?

Assume that there are $k(k \geq 2)$ nodes acting together secretly to achieve a fraudulent purpose. Let v_i be an honest node who is worried about her privacy. We also use v_i to denote the value in that node. Let v_{i-1} be the immediate predecessor of v_i and v_{i+1} be the immediate successor of v_i. The possible collusion that can arise are:

- If $k = n-1$, then the exact value of v_i will be disclosed.
- If $k \geq 2$ and the colluding nodes include both v_{i-1} and v_{i+1}, then the exact value of v_i will be disclosed.
- If $n-1 > k \geq 2$ and the colluding nodes contain neither v_{i-1} nor v_{i+1}, or only one of them, then v_i is disguised by $n-k-1$ other nodes' values.

The first two cases need no explanation. Now let us investigate the third case. Without loss of generality, we can arrange the nodes in an order such that $v_1, v_2 \cdots v_{n-k-1}$ are the honest sites, v_i is the node whose privacy is at stake and $v_{i+1}, \cdots v_{i+k}$ form the colluding group. We have

$$\underbrace{\sum_{j=1}^{n-k-1} v_j}_{denoted\ by\ X} + \underbrace{v_i}_{denoted\ by\ Y} = \underbrace{v - \sum_{j=i+1}^{i+k} v_j}_{denoted\ by\ W}$$

where W is a constant and is known to all the colluding nodes. Now, it is clear that the colluding nodes will know v_i is not greater than W, which is some extra information contributing to the utility of the collusions. To take a further look, the colluding nodes can compute the posteriori probability of v_i and further use that to launch a maximum a posteriori probability (MAP) estimate-based attack. It can be shown that, this posteriori probability is:

$$f_{posterior}(v_i) = \frac{1}{(m+1)(n-k-1)} \times \sum_{j=0}^{r} (-1)^j c_j^{(n-k-1)} \times c_{(n-k-1)+(r-j)(m+1)+t-1}^{(r-j)(m+1)+t}$$

where $v_i \leq W, r = \left\lfloor \frac{W - v_i}{m+1} \right\rfloor$ and $t = W - v_i - \left\lfloor \frac{W - v_i}{m+1} \right\rfloor (m+1)$. When $v_i > W$, $f_{posterior}(v_i) = 0$.

Due to space constraints, we have not included the proof of this result here.

Game Analysis (Kargupta et al., 2007): In a multi-party PPDM environment, each node has certain responsibilities in terms of performing their part of the computations, communicating correct values to other nodes and protecting the privacy of the data. Depending on the characteristics of these nodes and their objectives, they either perform their duties or not, sometimes, they even collude with others to modify the protocol and reveal others' private information. Let M_i denote the overall sequence of computations node *i* has performed, which may or may not be the same as what it is supposed to do defined by the PPDM protocol. Similarly, let R_i be the messages node *i* has received, and S_i he messages it has sent. Let G_i be a subgroup of the nodes that would collude with node *i*. The strategy of each node in the multi-party PPDM game prescribes the actions for such computations, communications, and collusions with other nodes, *i.e.*, $\sigma_i = (M_i, R_i, S_i, G_i)$. Further let $c_{i,m}(M_i)$ be the utility of performing M_i, and similarly we can define $c_{i,r}(R_i), c_{i,s}(S_i), c_{i,g}(G_i)$. Then the overall utility of node *i* will be a linear or nonlinear function of utilities obtained by the choice of strategies in the respective dimensions of computation, communication and collusion. Without loss of generality, we consider an utility function which is a weighted linear combination of all of the above dimensions:

$$u_i(\{\sigma_i, \sigma_{-i}\}) = \omega_{i,m}c_{i,m}(M_i) + \omega_{i,s}c_{i,s}(S_i) + \omega_{i,r}c_{i,r}(R_i) + \omega_{i,g}c_{i,g}(G_i)$$

where $\omega_{i,m}, \omega_{i,s}, \omega_{i,r}, \omega_{i,g}$ represent the weights for the corresponding utilityfactors. Note that we omitted other nodes' strategies in the above expression just for simplicity.
In secure sum computation, the derived posteriori probability can be used to quantify the utility of collusion, *e.g.*,

$$g(v_i) = Posteriori - \Pr ior = f_{posterior}(v_i) - \frac{1}{m+1}$$

We see here that this utility depends on $W - v_i$ and the size of the colluding group *k*. Now we can put together the overall utility function for the game of multi-party secure sum computation:

$$u_i(\{\sigma_i, \sigma_{-i}\}) = \omega_{i,m}c_{i,m}(M_i) + \omega_{i,s}c_{i,s}(S_i) + \omega_{i,r}c_{i,r}(R_i) + \omega_{i,g} \sum_{j \in P - G_i} g(v_j)$$

where *P* is the set of all nodes and G_i is the set of nodes colluding with node *i*.

Now considering a special instance of the overall utility where the node performs all the communication and computation related activities as required by the protocol. This results in a function: $u_i(\{\sigma_i, \sigma_{-i}\}) = \omega_{i,g} \sum_{j \in P - G_i} g(v_j)$, where the utilities due to communication and computation are constant and hence can be neglected for determining the nature of the function. Through studying the plot of the overall utility of multi-party secure sum as a function of the distribution of the random variable $W - v_i$ and the size of the colluding group *k*, it shows that the utility is maximum for a value of *k* that is greater than 1. Since the strategies opted by the nodes are dominant, the optimal solution corresponds to the Nash equilibrium. This implies that in a realistic scenario for multi-party secure sum computation, nodes will have a tendency to collude. Therefore the non-collusion (*k* = 1) assumption of the classical secure multi-party sum is sub-optimal.
From the above analysis we can see, the collusion of parties happen easily to gain additional benefits in multi-party privacy preserving data mining, because the strategies of following protocol is not always optimal. Based on the penalty mechanism without having to detect collusion, a cheap-talk protocol is proposed to offer a more robust process,and the optimal strategy is to following the protocol for secure computation with punishment strategy.
In a word, the semi-honest adversarial model is often a realistic one (Lindell & Pinkas ,2002), but it sometimes deviate from the real-life application of privacy preserving distributed data

mining, so it will a new trend for privacy preserving data mining is to make the collusion resistant protocols or algorithms algorithm work well in real life. Recent research have addressed this issue, and collusion resistant protocols or algorithms based on penalty function mechanism, the Secret Sharing Technique, and the Homomorphic Threshold Cryptography are given.

4.2 Collusion resistant protocols based on penalty function mechanism

For distributed privacy preserving data mining, to achieve a Nash equilibrium with no collusions, the game players can adopt a punishment strategy to threaten potential deviators. Kargupta et al., (2007) design a mechanism to penalize colluding nodes in various ways:

1. **Policy I:** Remove the node from the application environment because of protocol violation. Although it may work in some cases, the penalty may be too harsh since usually the goal is to have everyone participate in the process and faithfully contribute to the data mining process.
2. **Policy II:** Penalize by increasing the cost of computation and communication. For example, if a node suspects a colluding group of size k' (an estimate of k), then it may split the every number used in a secure sum among $\alpha k'$ different parts and demand $\alpha k'$ rounds of secure sum computation one for each of these $\alpha k'$ parts, here $\alpha > 0$ is a constant factor. This increases the computation and communication cost by $\alpha k'$ fold. This linear increase in cost with respect to k', the suspected size of colluding group, may be used to counteract possible benefit that one may receive by joining a team of colluders. The modified utility function is given by $\tilde{u}_i(\{\sigma_i,\sigma_{-i}\}) = u_i(\{\sigma_i,\sigma_{-i}\}) - \omega_{ip} * \alpha k'$ .The last term in the equation accounts for the penalty due to excess computation and communication as a result of collusion.

The new secure sum with penalty (SSP) protocol is as follows (Kargupta et al., 2007):
Consider a network of n nodes where a node can either be *good* (honest) or *bad* (colluding). Before the secure sum protocol starts, the good nodes set their estimate of bad nodes in the network $k' = 0$ and bad nodes send invitations for collusions randomly to nodes in the network. Every time a good node receives such an invitation, it increments its estimate of k'. Bad nodes respond to such collusion invitations and form collusions. If a bad node does not receive any response, it behaves as a good node. To penalize nodes that collude, good nodes split their local data into $\alpha k'$ random shares. This initial phase of communication is cheap talk in our algorithm. The secure sum phase consists of $O(\alpha k')$ rounds of communication for every complete sum computation. This process converges to the correct sum in $O(n\alpha k)$ time. Note that, the SSP protocol does not require detecting all the colluding parties. Raising k' based on a perception of collusion will do. If the threat is real, the parties are expected to behave as long they are acting rationally to optimize their utility.

4.3 Collusion resistant protocols based on the secret sharing technique

Now, we are particularly interested in the mining of association rule in a scenario where the data is vertically distributed among different parties. To mine the association rule, these parties need to collaborate with each other so that they can jointly mine the data and produce results that interest all of them. And we will provide a secure, efficient and collusion resistant distributed association rules mining algorithm based on the Shamir's secret sharing technique (Shamir,1979).

4.3.1 Shamir's secret sharing technique

Shamir's secret sharing method (Shamir,1979) allows a dealer D to distribute a secret value v_s among n peers $P_1, P_2, \cdots P_n$, such that the knowledge of any $k(k \le n)$ peers is required to reconstruct the secret. The method is described in Algorithm 1.

Algorithm 1(Shamir's secret sharing algorithm):

Require: v_s **: Secret value,**

P: Set of parties $P_1, P_2, \cdots P_n$ **to distribute the shares,**

k **: Number of shares required to reconstruct the secret.**

1: Select a random polynomial

$q(x) = a_{k-1}x^{k-1} + \cdots + a_1x^1 + v_s$,where $a_{k-1} \ne 0, q(0) = v_s$.

2: Choose n **publicly known distinct random values** $x_1, \cdots x_n$ **such that** $x_i \ne 0$.

3: Compute the share of each peer, P_i**, where** $share_i = q(x_i)$.

4: for $i = 1$ **to** n **do**

5: Send $share_i$ **to peer** P_i.

6: end for.

Shamir's method is information theoretically secure, in order to construct the secret value v_s, at least k shares are required to determine the random polynomial $q(x)$ of degree $k-1$, so the complete knowledge of up to $k-1$ peers does not reveal any information about the secret.

4.3.2 Privacy-preserving distributed association rule mining problem

Party $P_1, P_2, \cdots P_n$ have private data set $DB_1, DB_2, \cdots, DB_n$ respectively, and $DB_i \cap DB_j = \Phi, for\ \forall\ i, j \in n$. The data set $DB_1, DB_2, \cdots, DB_n$ forms a database DB, namely $DB = DB_1 \cup DB_2 \cup \cdots \cup DB_n$, let N denote the total number of transactions for each data set. The n parties want to conduct association rule mining on $DB = DB_1 \cup DB_2 \cup \cdots \cup DB_n$ and find the association rule with support and confidence being greater than the given thresholds.

During the mining of association rule, we assume all parties follow the protocol, and the object of the paper is to propose a protocol of distributed association rules mining in vertically partitioned data based on the Shamir's secret sharing technique (Shamir,1979), which can prevent effectively the collusion behaviors and conduct the computations across the parties without compromising their data privacy, simultaneously, the security of the protocol refer to semantic security (Goldreich, 2001).

4.3.3 Distributed association rule mining algorithm

In order to learn association rule, one must compute confidence and support of a given candidate itemset, and given the values of the attributes are 1 or 0, to judge whether a particular itemset is frequent, we only need to find out the number of records (denote ***c.count***) where the values for all the attributes in the itemset are 1. if c.count $\ge$ Ns% , then the candidate itemset is the frequent itemset. The following is the algorithm to find frequent itemsets:

Algorithm 2: The algorithm to find frequent itemsets

1. $L_1 = \{ \text{ large } 1\_itemsets \}$
2. **for** $(k = 2; L_{k-1} \neq \Phi; k++)$ **do begin**
3. $C_k = \text{apriori-gen}(L_{k-1})$
4. **for** all candidates $c \in C_k$ **do begin**
5. **if** all the attributes in c are entirely the same party that party independently compute ***c.count***
6. **else** collaboratively compute **c.count** (We will show how to compute it in Section 4.3.)
7. **end**
8. $L_k = L_k \cup \{c | c.count \geq \min \sup\}$
9. end
10. Return $L = \cup_k L_k$

In step 3, the function $C_k = \text{apriori-gen}(L_{k-1})$ can generate the set of candidate itemsets C_k, which is discussed in (Agrawal & Srikant, 1994). Given the counts and frequent itemsets, we can compute all association rules with $\text{support} \geq \text{minsup}$.

In the procedure of association rule mining, step 1, 3, 6 and 8 require sharing information. In step 3 and 8, we use merely attribute names, in step 1, to compute large 1-itemsets, each party elects her own attributes that contribute to large $1\_itemsets$, where only one attribute forms a large 1-itemset, there is no computation involving attributes of other parties, therefore, data disclosure across parties is not necessary. At the same time, since the final result $L = \cup_k L_k$ is known to all parties, step 1, 3 and 8 reveal no extra information to either party. However, to compute *c.count* in step 6, a computation accessing attributes belonging to different parties is necessary. How to conduct these computations across parties without compromising each party's data privacy is the challenge we are faced with. If the attributes belong to different parties, they then construct vectors for themselves attributes, for example, for the some candidate itemset, party P_i have p attributes $a_1, a_2, \cdots, a_p$, then party P_i can construct vector A_i, the jth element denote $A_{ij} = \prod_{k=1}^{p} a_k$ in vector A_i. Subsequently, they can apply our secure algorithm to obtain *c.count*, which will be discussed in Section 4.3.4

4.3.4 Privacy-preserving algorithm to collaboratively compute *c.count*

The fact that the distributed parties jointly compute ***c.count*** without revealing their raw data to each other presents a great challenge. In this section, we show how to privately compute ***c.count*** based on Shamir's secret sharing algorithm (Shamir, 1979) for the case of multiple parties without revealing the secret values to others.

Without loss of generality, assuming party P_1 has a private vector A_1, party P_2, a private vector A_2,..., and party P_n, a private vector A_n, we use A_{ij} to denote the jth element in vector A_i, the value of A_{ij} is the attribute value of the P_i in the jth transaction of the database. Given that the absence or presence of an attribute is represented as 0 or 1, the value of A_{ij} is equal to 0 or 1, for example $A_i = (1, 0, 1, 1 \cdots 0)^T$.

Assuming all parties follow the algorithm and do the computations honestly, the whole process is summarized in Algorithm 3.

Algorithm 3: Privacy-Preserving Algorithm to Collaboratively Compute *c.count*
Require: P: Set of parties $P_1, P_2, \cdots P_n$.
$A_{i\,j}$: Secret value of P_i ,
X : A set of n publicly known random values $x_1, x_2, \cdots x_n$.
k : Degree of the random polynomial $k = n-1$.
1: for each transaction $j = 1$ **to** N **do**
2: for each party P_i **(** $i = 1, \cdots n$ **) do**
3: Select a random polynomial $q_i(x) = a_{n-1}x^{n-1} + \cdots + a_1 x^1 + A_{i\,j}$
4: Compute the share of each party P_t **, where** $sh(A_{i\,j}, P_t) = q_i(x_t)$
5: for $t = 1$ **to n do**
6: Send $sh(A_{i\,j}, P_t)$ **to party** P_t
7: Receive the shares $sh(A_{i\,j}, P_t)$ **from every party** P_t **.**
8: Compute $S(x_i) = q_1(x_i) + q_2(x_i) + \cdots + q_n(x_i)$
9: for $t = 1$ **to n do**
10: Send $S(x_i)$ **to party** P_t
11: Receive the results $S(x_i)$ **from every party** P_i **.**
12: Solve the set of equations to find the sum $\sum_{i=1}^{n} A_{i\,j}$ **of secret values**
13: if the $\sum_{i=1}^{n} A_{i\,j} = n$ **, let** $m_j = 1$ **, otherwise** $m_j = 0$ **.**
14: Each party computes $c.count = \sum_{j=1}^{N} m_j$ **.**

4.3.5 Analysis of the privacy-preserving algorithm to obtain *c.count*

In this section, we give the correctness, complexity and security analysis of the privacy-preserving algorithm 3.

Correctness Analysis: Assuming party P_i has a private vector $\mathrm{A_i}$, so for arbitrary transaction j in database DB, party P_i has a private value $\mathrm{A_{i\,j}}$, according algorithm 3, the sum $\sum_{i=1}^{n} A_{i\,j}$ of secret values is the constant term of the sum polynomial $S(x) = q_1(x) + q_2(x) + \cdots + q_n(x)$, so we need to solve the following liner equations:

$$\begin{cases} b_{n-1}{x_1}^{n-1} + b_{n-2}{x_1}^{n-2} + \cdots + b_1 x_1 + \sum_{i=1}^{n} A_{i\,j} = s(x_1) \\ b_{n-1}{x_2}^{n-1} + b_{n-2}{x_2}^{n-2} + \cdots + b_1 x_2 + \sum_{i=1}^{n} A_{i\,j} = s(x_2) \\ \qquad\qquad\cdots\cdots \\ b_{n-1}{x_n}^{n-1} + b_{n-2}{x_n}^{n-2} + \cdots + b_1 x_n + \sum_{i=1}^{n} A_{i\,j} = s(x_n) \end{cases}$$

Noted that there are n unknown coefficients and n equations, determinant of coefficient $D=\begin{vmatrix} x_1^{n-1} & x_1^{n-2} & \cdots & x_1 & 1 \\ x_2^{n-1} & x_2^{n-2} & \cdots & x_1 & 1 \\ \vdots & \vdots & \cdots & \vdots & \vdots \\ x_n^{n-1} & x_n^{n-2} & \cdots & x_n & 1 \end{vmatrix}$ is the Vander monde determinant, when $D=\prod_{1\le j\le i\le n}(x_i-x_j)\neq 0$, that is $x_i \neq x_j$, the equations has a unique solution, and each party P_i can solve the set of equations and determine the value of $\sum_{i=1}^{n} A_{i\,j}$, however it cannot determine the secret values of the other parties since the individual polynomial coefficients selected by other parties are not known to P_i. If $A_{1\,j}, A_{2\,j}, \cdots, A_{n\,j}$ are all equal to 1, that is $\sum_{i=1}^{n} A_{i\,j}=n$, this means the transaction has the whole attributes and supports the association rule, we let $m_j=1$. Otherwise, if some attributes of $A_{1\,j}, A_{2\,j}, \cdots, A_{n\,j}$ are not equal to 1, that is, $\sum_{i=1}^{n} A_{i\,j}\neq n$, this means the transaction has not the whole attributes and does not support the association rules, we let $m_j=0$. To compute the number of transactions which support the association rule, we only count the number of $m_j=1$, then $c.count=\sum_{j=1}^{N} m_j$, so the algorithm 3 can compute ***c.count*** correctly under the condition of all parties doing the computations honestly during the mining of association rule.

Complexity Analysis: Assuming there are N transactions and n parties, the communication cost is $2n(n-1)$ from step 5,6 and step 9,10 of algorithm 3, so the communication cost of algorithm 3 is $2Nn(n-1)$.

The following contribute to the computational cost of each transaction: (1) the generation of the random polynomial $q_i(x)$, $i=1,\cdots n$ from step 3; (2) the total number of n^2 computations on the share of each party from step 4; (3) the total number of $n(n-1)$ additions from step 8; (4) the computational cost of solving the set of equations to find the sum $\sum_{i=1}^{n} A_{i\,j}$ of secret values from step 12; (5)the computational cost of letting $m_j=1\,or\,0$ according the sum $\sum_{i=1}^{n} A_{i\,j}$ from step 13.

Compared to the other technique, for example, commutative encryption and secure multi-party computations, although these techniques are very secure, the excessive computation and communication cost associated render them impractical for scenarios involving a large number of parties. However the algorithm proposed by our paper is scalable in terms of computation and communication cost, and therefore it can be run even when there is a large number of parties involved. So our algorithm is efficient and practical.

Security Analysis: Proposition 1: Algorithm 3 is semantic security (Goldreich, 2001) for the network attackers.

Proof: A network attackers listening to the network traffic of the parties cannot learn any useful information, such as the private values or the sum of those values, expect for all the shares and the intermediate values, however these values cannot be used to determine the coefficients of the sum polynomial and each party's secretly random polynomial without knowing random values $x_1, x_2, \cdots x_n$ for which the intermediate results are calculated, and it can not be concluded whether the transaction is support the association rule.

Proposition 2: Algorithm 3 is semantic security and can prevent effectively the collusion behaviors for the collaborative parties under the condition of the number of the collusion parties $t < n-1$.

Proof: Firstly, algorithm 3 is semantic security for the collaborative parties. Compared with the network attackers, the collaborative parties know random values $x_1, x_2, \cdots x_n$. At algorithm 3, P_i computes the value of its polynomial at n points as shares, and then keeps one of these shares for itself and sends the remaining $n-1$ shares to other parties, so if the collaborative party gets all other parties shares and intermediate values through listening to the network traffic of the parties, except for the value of the corresponding sum polynomial at n different points, he can get, for example, the value of that party P_i's secretly random polynomial at $n-1$ different point $x_1, \cdots, x_{i-1}, x_{i+1}, \cdots, x_n$. And because the degree of each party P_i's secretly random polynomial is $k = n-1$ and have n unkown coefficients, in order to compute the coefficients of the corresponding party P_i's secretly random polynomial and get the party P_i's private value, the value at n different points are needed, so party P_i's private value can not be achieved.

Secondly, algorithm 3 can prevent effectively the collusion behaviors for the collaborative parties under the condition of the number of the collusion parties $t < n-1$. If there are $n-1$ parties collusion, for example, $P_2, \cdots P_n$, they can get the value $s(x_1)$ of sum polynomial at x_1 and $q_1(x_2), \cdots, q_1(x_n)$ which is the value of party P_1's secretly random polynomial $q_1(x)$ at $n-1$ different points $x_2, \cdots x_n$, note that $S(x_1) = q_1(x_1) + q_2(x_1) + \cdots + q_n(x_1)$, so they can compute $q_1(x_1) = S(x_1) - q_2(x_1) - \cdots - q_n(x_1)$, then can conclude the party P_1's private value through solving the following liner equations:

4.4 Collusion resistant protocols based on the homomorphic threshold cryptography

Now we have known homomorphic encryption and threshold decryption often are used as basic building blocks of secure computation protocols for PPDM. In this section , we will study the privacy preserving distributed association rule mine problem(§4.3.2) base on homomorphic encryption and threshold decryption, where homomorphic encryption and threshold decryption can refer to §3.3.3.

In order to learn association rule, we should find frequent itemsets, Algorithm 2 give how to find frequent itemsets, where the key step is step 6 (compute c.count) . How to conduct these computations across parties without compromising each party's data privacy is the challenge we are faced with. If the attributes belong to different parties, they then construct vectors for themselves attributes, for example, for the some candidate itemset, party P_i have p attributes $a_1, a_2, \cdots, a_p$, then party P_i can construct vector A_i, the jth element denote $A_{ij} = \prod_{k=1}^{p} a_k$ in vector A_i . Subsequently, they can also apply our secure algorithm to obtain *c.count,* which will be discussed in Section 4.4.1.

4.4.1Collusion resistant protocol based on the homomorphic threshold cryptography

The fact that the collaborative parties jointly compute ***c.count*** without revealing their raw data to each other presents a great challenge. In this section, we develop secure protocol to compute ***c.count*** for the case of multiple parties. Without loss of generality, assuming Party P_1 has a private vector A_1, Party P_2 , a private vector A_2 ,..., and Party P_n, a private vector A_n. we use A_{ij} to denote the jth element in vector A_i, so the value of A_{ij} is the attribute value of the P_i in the jth transaction of the database. Given that the absence or presence of an attribute is represented as 0 or 1, the value of A_{ij} is equal to 0 or 1, for example $A_i = (1, 0, 1, 1 \cdots 0)^T$.

1. $P_1, P_2, \cdots P_n$ **perform the following:**

a. $P_1, P_2, \cdots P_t \ (1 \le t \le n)$ jointly generate a threshold cryptographic key pair $(d(d_1, d_2, \cdots, d_t), e)$ of a homomorphic encryption scheme. That is, a secret key associated with a single public key is distributed among a group of parties. For simplicity and without loss of generality, let $t = n$, then only if all parties cooperate, can they decrypt the ciphertext and prevent the collusion of parties. Let $e(\cdot)$ denote encryption and $d_i(\cdot)$ denote party i decryption. Meanwhile, the threshold cryptographic key pair $(d(d_1, d_2, \cdots, d_t), e)$ is semantic security. They also generate the number, X, where X is an integer which is more than n.

b. P_1 generates a set of random integers $R_{11}, R_{12}, \cdots, R_{1N}$ and sends $e(A_{11} + R_{11}X), e(A_{12} + R_{12}X), \cdots, e(A_{1N} + R_{1N}X)$ to P_n; P_2 generates a set of random integers $R_{21}, R_{22}, \cdots, R_{2N}$ and sends $e(A_{21} + R_{21}X), e(A_{22} + R_{22}X), \cdots, e(A_{2N} + R_{2N}X)$ to P_n;... P_{n-1} generates a set of random integers $R_{(n-1)1}, R_{(n-1)2}, \cdots, R_{(n-1)N}$ and sends $e(A_{(n-1)1} + R_{(n-1)1}X), e(A_{(n-1)2} + R_{(n-1)2}X), \cdots, e(A_{(n-1)N} + R_{(n-1)N}X)$ to P_n; P_n generates a set of random integers $R_{n1}, R_{n2}, \cdots, R_{nN}$ and encrypts his private vector

$$e(A_{n1} + R_{n1}X), e(A_{n2} + R_{n2}X), \cdots, e(A_{nN} + R_{nN}X)$$

c. P_n computes:

$$E_1 = e(A_{11} + R_{11}X) \times e(A_{21} + R_{21}X) \times \cdots \times e(A_{n1} + R_{n1}X)$$
$$= e(A_{11} + A_{21} + \cdots A_{n1} + (R_{11} + R_{21} + \cdots R_{n1})X)$$

$$E_2 = e(A_{12} + R_{12}X) \times e(A_{22} + R_{22}X) \times \cdots \times e(A_{n2} + R_{n2}X)$$
$$= e(A_{12} + A_{22} + \cdots A_{n2} + (R_{12} + R_{22} + \cdots R_{n2})X)$$

....

$$E_N = e(A_{1N} + R_{1N}X) \times e(A_{2N} + R_{2N}X) \times \cdots \times e(A_{nN} + R_{nN}X)$$
$$= e(A_{1N} + A_{2N} + \cdots A_{nN} + (R_{1N} + R_{2N} + \cdots R_{nN})X)$$

d. P_n randomly permutes $E_1, E_2, \cdots, E_N$ and obtains the permuted sequence $D_1, D_2, \cdots, D_N$.

e. From computational balance point of view, P_n divides $D_1, D_2, \cdots, D_N$ into n parts with each part having approximately equal number of elements.

f. P_n decrypts using himself private key d_n and sends $d_n(D_1), d_n(D_2), \cdots, d_n(D_{N/n})$ to P_{n-1}; P_{n-1} decrypts $d_{n-1}d_n(D_1), d_{n-1}d_n(D_2), \cdots, d_{n-1}d_n(D_{N/n})$, send it to $P_{n-2}, \ldots, P_1$; P_1 decrypts $d_1 d_2 \cdots d_{n-1} d_n(D_1) = M_1, d_1 d_2 \cdots d_{n-1} d_n(D_2) = M_2, \cdots, d_1 d_2 \cdots d_{n-1} d_n(D_{N/n}) = M_{N/n}$;

g. P_n decrypts using himself private key d_n and sends

$d_n(D_{N/n+1}), d_n(D_{N/n+2}), \cdots, d_n(D_{2N/n})$ to P_{n-1}; P_{n-1} decrypts $d_{n-1}d_n(D_{N/n+1}), d_{n-1}d_n(D_{N/n+2}), \cdots, d_{n-1}d_n(D_{2N/n})$, sends it to $P_{n-2}, \ldots, P_3, P_1, P_2$, P_2 decrypts
$d_2 d_1\ d_3 \cdots d_{n-1} d_n(D_{N/n+1}) = M_{N/n+1}$, $d_2 d_1\ d_3 \cdots d_{n-1} d_n(D_{N/n+2}) = M_{N/n+2}, \cdots,$
$d_2 d_1\ d_3 \cdots d_{n-1} d_n(D_{2N/n}) = M_{2N/n}$;

h. Continue until P_n decrypts using himself private key d_n and sends $d_n(D_{(n-2)N/n}+1), d_n(D_{(n-2)N/n+2}), \cdots, d_n(D_{(n-1)N/n})$ to P_{n-2}, P_{n-2} decrypts and sends it to $P_{n-3}, \ldots, P_2, P_1, P_{n-1}$, P_{n-1} decrypts

$d_{n-1}d_1\ d_2 \cdots d_{n-2} d_n(D_{(n-2)N/n}+1) = M_{(n-2)N/n+1}$, $d_{n-1}d_1\ d_2 \cdots d_{n-2} d_n(D_{(n-2)N/n+2}) = M_{(n-2)N/n+2}, \cdots,$
$d_{n-1}d_1\ d_2 \cdots d_{n-2} d_n(D_{(n-1)N/n}) = M_{(n-1)N/n}$

i. P_n sends $D_{(n-1)N/n+1}, D_{(n-1)N/n+2}, \cdots, D_N$ to P_{n-1}, P_{n-1} decrypts $d_{n-1}(D_{(n-1)N/n+1}), d_{n-1}(D_{(n-1)N/n+2}), \cdots, d_{n-1}(D_N)$, sends it to $P_{n-2}, \ldots, P_2, P_1, P_n$
P_n decrypts
$d_n d_1\ d_2 \cdots d_{n-2} d_{n-1}(D_{(n-1)N/n+1}) = M_{(n-1)N/n+1}, d_n d_1\ d_2 \cdots d_{n-2} d_{n-1}(D_{(n-1)N/n+2}) = M_{(n-1)N/n+2},$
$\cdots, d_n d_1\ d_2 \cdots d_{n-2} d_{n-1}(D_N) = M_N$

2. Compute *c.count*

a. $P_1, P_2, \cdots P_n$ make $M_1, M_2, \cdots M_N$ module X respectively, note that if a decrypted term M_i is equal to $n \bmod X$, it means the values of $P_1, P_2, \cdots P_n$ are all 1, then let $m_i = 1$, otherwise $m_i = 0$ For example, if the transaction j is permuted as position i ,then $M_i \bmod X = (A_{1j} + A_{2j} + \cdots A_{nj} + (R_{1j} + R_{2j} + \cdots R_{nj})X) \bmod X = A_{1j} + A_{2j} + \cdots A_{nj}$

Consequently, compare whether each decrypted term $M_i \bmod X$ is equal to $n \bmod X$. If yes, then let $m_i = 1$, otherwise $m_i = 0$.

b. P_1 computes $c_1 = \sum_{i-1}^{N/n} m_i$, P_2 computes $c_2 = \sum_{i=N/n+1}^{2N/n} m_i$, ..., P_n computes $c_n = \sum_{i=(n-1)N/n+1}^{N} m_i$.

c. all parties $P_i\ (i = 1, 2, \cdots, n-1)$ encrypted $e(c_i)$ and send it to P_n.

d. P_n computes $e(c_1) \times e(c_2) \times \cdots e(c_n) = e(c_1 + c_2 + \cdots c_n)$,then decrypts $d_n(e(c_1 + c_2 + \cdots c_n))$ and sends it to P_{n-1}, P_{n-1} decrypts $d_{n-1}d_n(e(c_1 + c_2 + \cdots c_n))$ and sends it to $P_{n-2}, \ldots,$ P_1 decrypts $d_1 \cdots d_{n-1} d_n(e(c_1 + c_2 + \cdots c_n)) = c_1 + c_2 + \cdots c_n = c.count$.

4.4.2 Analysis of collusion resistant protocol based on the homomorphic threshold cryptography

Correctness Analysis: Assume all of the parties follow the protocol, in which the threshold cryptographic system is a additively homomorphic cryptosystem, which enable us to get

$$E_i = e(A_{1i} + R_{1i}X) \times e(A_{2i} + R_{2i}X) \times \cdots \times e(A_{ni} + R_{ni}X)$$
$$= e(A_{1i} + A_{2i} + \cdots A_{ni} + (R_{1i} + R_{2i} + \cdots R_{ni})X) \quad i = 1,2,\cdots n$$

And given $X > n$, so

$$M_i \bmod X = (A_{1j} + A_{2j} + \cdots A_{nj} + (R_{1j} + R_{2j} + \cdots R_{nj})X) \bmod X = A_{1j} + A_{2j} + \cdots A_{nj}$$

If $A_{1j}, A_{2j}, \cdots, A_{nj}$ are all equal to 1, this means the transaction has the whole attributes and supports the association rule, we let $m_i = 1$. Otherwise, if some attributes of $A_{1j}, A_{2j}, \cdots, A_{nj}$ are not equal to 1, this means the transaction has not the whole attributes and does not support the association rules, we let $m_i = 0$, to compute the number of transactions which support the association rule, we only count the number of $m_i = 1$, then

$$c.count = c_1 + c_2 + \cdots c_n = \sum_{i=1}^{N} m_i .$$

Meanwhile, in the protocol, P_n permutes $E_i, i = 1,2,\cdots N$ before sending them to other parties, permutation does not affect $c.count$, and summation is not affected by a permutation. Therefore, the final $c.count$ is correct.

Complexity Analysis: The bit-wise communication cost of this protocol is upper bounded by $2\alpha[(n-1)N + n]$, where a is the number of bits for each encrypted element. It consist of (1) the maximum cost of $(n-1)N$ from step 1(b); (2) the maximum cost of $(n-1)N$ from step 1(f)-1(i); (3) the maximum cost of $2n$ from step 2(c) and 2(d).

The following contributes to the computational cost: (1) the generation of a threshold cryptographic key pair, the integer X and nN random integers (2) the total number of $nN + n$ encryptions; (3) the total number of $(n-1)(N+1)$ multiplications; (4) the generation of permutation function; (5) the total number of N permutations; (6) the total number of $(n+1)N$ decryptions; (7) the total number of N modulo operations; (8) the total number of $(n+1)N$ additions; (9) dividing N numbers into n parts.

Security Analysis: Given that P_n obtains all the encrypted terms from other parties and the cryptographic system is a semantic security, the ciphertext does not leak any useful information about the plaintext and P_n can not get other useful information of the plaintext from the ciphertext. Meanwhile, since the cryptographic system is a threshold cryptosystem, those parties will not able to decrypt and get the plaintext unless they cooperate. That is, P_n will not have access to the original values of other parties without cooperating with those parties. As a result, the collusion behaviors can be prevented effectively. $P_1, P_2, \cdots P_n$ in our protocol jointly generate a threshold cryptographic key pair $(d(d_1, d_2, \cdots, d_n), e)$ of a homomorphic encryption scheme, which means the protocol is secure under the condition of the number of the collusion parties is less than n. Generally, given $P_1, P_2, \cdots P_t$ $(1 \le t \le n)$ jointly generate a threshold cryptographic key pair $(d(d_1, d_2, \cdots, d_t), e)$ of a homomorphic encryption scheme, which means the protocol is secure under the condition of the number of the collusion parties is less than t.

Meanwhile, Each party of $P_1, P_2, \cdots P_{n-1}$ obtains some plaintexts of all D_i. Since D_i are in permuted form and those n-1 parties don't know the permutation function, so they cannot know which transaction support the association rule. And each party only knows a part of transactions supporting the association rules, which lead to trivial benefit for them.

5. Conclusion

Due to the right to privacy in the information ear, privacy-preserving data mining (PPDM) has become one of the newest trends in privacy and security and data mining research. In this chapter, we intrduced the related concepts of privacy-preserving data mining and some privacy preserving techniques such as Trust Third Party , Data perturbation technique, Secure Multiparty Computation and game theoretic approach. Moreover, we discussed the collussion behaviors in privacy-preserving data mining (PPDM) and gave the collusion resistant protocols or algorithms based on penalty function mechanism, the Secret Sharing Technique, and the Homomorphic Threshold Cryptography.

6. References

Abraham I., Dolev D., Gonen R. &Halpern J. (2006). Distributed computing meets game theory: Robust mechanisms for rational secret sharing and multiparty computation. *Proceedings of the Twenty-fifth Annual ACM Symposium on Principles of Distributed Computing*, pp. 53–62, ISBN:1-59593-384-0, New York, NY, USA,. ACM Press.

Agrawal, R. & Srikant, R. (1994). Fast Algorithms for Mining Association Rules in Large Databases, *Proceedings of 20th International Conference on Very Large Data Bases*, pp.487-499, ISBN 55860-153-8, Santiago, Chile.

Agrawal R. & Srikant R. (2000). Privacy-Preserving Data Mining. *Proceedings of the ACM SIGMOD Conference on Management of Data*, pp.439–450, ISBN 1-58113-217-4.

Clifton C., Kantarcioglu M. &Vaidya J.(2002a). Defining privacy for data mining. *Proceeding of the National Science Foundation Workshop on Next Generation Data Mining*, pp.126-133, Baltimore, MD, USA.

Clifton C., Kantarcioglu M., Vaidya J., Lin X. & Zhu M.Y. (2002b). Tools for Privacy Preserving Distributed Data Mining. *ACM SIGKDD Explorations*, Vol 4, No 2, pp. 28-34, ISSN 1931-0145.

Cramer R., Damgard I. & Nielsen J. B. (2001) . Multiparty Computation from Threshold Homomorphic Encryption. *Proceedings of the International Conference on the Theory and Application of Cryptographic Techniques: Advances in Cryptology*, pp. 280-299, ISBN:3-540-42070-3, Springer-Verlag.

Du W. & Zhan Z. (2002). Building decision tree classifier on private data. *Proceedings of the IEEE international conference on Privacy, security and data mining*, pp. 1-8, ISSN 0-909-92592-5, Maebashi City, Japan.

Emekci F., Sahin O. D., Agrawal D. & Abbadi A. El. (2007). Privacy preserving decision tree learning over multiple parties. *Data and Knowledge Engineering*, Vol.63, No 2, pp.348-361,ISSN 0169-023X.

Even S., Goldreich O. & Lempel A.(1985). A Randomized Protocol for Signing Contracts, *Communications of the ACM,* vol. 28, Issue 6, pp. 637–647, ISSN 0001-0782.

Evfimievski A., Srikant R., Agrawal R. & Gehrke J. (2002). Privacy-Preserving Mining of Association Rules. *Proceedings of the Eighth ACM SIGKDD International Conference on Knowledge Discovery and Data Mining,* pp.217–228, ISBN:1-58113-567-X, Edmonton, Alberta, Canada.

Fienberg S. E. & McIntyre J.(2004). Data Swapping: Variations on a Theme by Dalenius and Reiss. *Privacy in Statistical Databases (PSD),* pp.14-29, Barcelona, Spain.

Franklin M. K & Haber S. (1996). Joint Encryption and Message-Efficient Secure Computation. *Journal of Cryptology,* Vol 9, No 4, pp.217-232, ISSN 0933-2790 .

Gilburd B. ; Schuster A. & Wolff. R. (2004). k-TTP: A New Privacy Model for Largescale Distributed Environments. *Proceedings of the 10th ACM SIGKDD International Conference on Knowledge Discovery and Data Mining,* pp. 563–568, ISBN 1-58113-888-1, Seattle, WA, USA.

Goldreich O. (1998). Secure Multi-party Computation, http://www.wisdom weizmann.ac.il/.

Goldreich, O. (2001). *Foundations of cryptography,* Volume Basic Tools, ISBN 13:978-0521791724, Cambridge Universiy Press.

Han J.& Kamber M.(2006). *Data Mining: Concepts and Techniques.* 2nd edition, San Francisco: Morgan Kaufmann Publishers.

Jiang W., Clifton C. & Kantarcioglu M. (2008). Transforming semi-honest protocols to ensure accountability. *Data and Knowledge Engineering,* Vol.65, pp.57–74, ISSN 0169-023X .

Kargupta H., Das K.& Liu d K.(2007). Multi-party, privacy-preserving distributed data mining using a game theoretic framework. *PKDD,* Vol.4702, pp.523–531, Springer.

Kim J. J. & Winkler W. E.(2003). Multiplicative Noise for Masking Continuous Data. *Technical Report Statistics #2003-01,* Statistical Research Division, U.S. Bureau of the Census, Washington D.C.

Kleinberg J., Papadimitriou C.& Raghavan P. (1998). A microeconomic view of data mining. *Data Mining and Knowledge Discovery,* Vol 2, No 4, pp.311–324, ISSN 1384-5810.

Kleinberg J., Papadimitriou C.& Raghavan P. (2001). On the value of private information. *Proceedings of the Eighth Conference on Theoretical Aspects of Rationality and Knowledge,* pp. 249–257, ISBN:1-55860-791-9, Morgan Kaufmann Publishers Inc. San Francisco, CA, USA.

Li X.B.& Sarkar S.(2006). A Tree-based Data Perturbation Approach for Privacy-Preserving Data Mining. *IEEE Transactions on Knowledge and Data Engineering,* Vol 18, No 9, pp.1278–1283 , ISSN 1041-4347.

Liew C. K., Choi U. J. & Liew C. J.(1985). A Data Distortion by Probability Distribution. *ACM Transactions on Database Systems (TODS),* Vol 10, No 3, pp.395–411. [3] Lindell Y. & Pinkas B.(2002). Privacy preserving data mining. *Journal of Cryptology,* Vol.15, No 3, pp.177–206, ISSN 0933-2790 .

Lindell Y. & Pinkas B.(2009). Secure Multiparty Computation for Privacy-Preserving Data Mining. *Journal of Privacy and Confidentiality*, Vol 1, No 1, pp.59-98.

Liu K., Giannella C. & Kargupta H.(2006) An Attacker's View of Distance Preserving Maps for Privacy-Preserving Data Mining. *PKD 2006*, pp.297-308, LNCS.

Muralidhar K.& Sarathy R.(2006). Data shuffling a new masking approach for numerical data. *Management Science*, Vol 52, No 5, pp.658–670.

Paillier P. (1999). Public-key Cryptosystems based on Composite Degree Residuosity Classes. *Proceedings of the 17th international conference on Theory and application of cryptographic techniques*, pp. 223–238, ISSN 3-540-65889-0, Prague, Czech Republic.

Polat H. & Du W. (2005). SVD-based Collaborative Filtering with Privacy. *Proceedings of the 2005 ACM symposium on Applied computing*, pp.791-795, ISBN1-58113-964-0, Santa Fe, New Mexico.

Rabin M. O. (1981). How to Exchange Secrets by Oblivious Transfer, *Technical Report* TR-81, Aiken Computation Laboratory.

Shamir, A. (1979). How to share a secret. *Communications of the ACM*, Vol 22, No.11, pp 612-613, ISSN:0001-0782.

Stanley R. M. Oliveira and Osmar R. Zaïane. (2004). Toward standardization in privacy-preserving data mining, *ACM SIGKDD 3rd Workshop on Data Mining Standards*, pp. 7–17, Seattle, WA, USA.

Sweeney L.(2002). k-Anonymity: a Model for Protecting Privacy. *International Journal on Uncertainty, Fuzziness and Knowledge-based Systems*, Vol 10, No 5, pp.557–570,

Vaidya J. & Clifton C.W. (2002) . Privacy preserving association rule mining in vertically partitioned data. *Proceedings of the 8th ACM SIGKDD International Conference on Knowledge Discovery and Data Mining*, pp.639-644, ISBN 1-58113-567-X, Edmonton, Alberta, Canada.

Verykios V.S., Bertino E., Fovino I.N., Provenza L.P., Saygin, Y. & Theodoridis Y.(2004a). State-of-the-art in privacy preserving data mining, *SIGMOD Record*, Vol. 33, No. 1, pp.50-57.

Verykios V. S., Elmagarmid A. K., Bertino E., Saygin Y. & Dasseni E.(2004b) . Association Rule Hiding. *IEEE Transactions on Knowledge and Data Engineering*, Vol 16, Issue 4, pp.434–447, ISSN 1041-4347.

Wright R. & Yang Z. (2004). Privacy-preserving bayesian network structure computation on distributed heterogeneous data. *Proceedings of the 10th ACM SIGKDD International Conference on Knowledge Discovery and Data Mining*, pp. 713-718, ISBN:1-58113-888-1. ACM, New York, NY, USA.

Yao A. C. (1986). How to Generate and Exchange Secrets. *Proceedings of the 27th IEEE Symposium on Foundations of Computer Science*, pp. 162-167, ISSN 0-8186-0740-8.

Zhan Z., Matwin S. & Chang L. (2007). Privacy-preserving collaborative association rule mining. *Journal of Network and Computer Applications*, Volume 30, Issue 3, pp. 1216-1227, ISSN:1084-8045.

Zhang P., Tong Y., Tang S.& Yang D.(2005). Privacy-Preserving Naive Bayes Classifier. *Advanced Data Mining and Applications*, Vol 3584， pp. 744-752, LNCS.

Zhu Y.& Liu L. (2004).Optimal Randomization for Privacy-Preserving Data Mining. *ACM KDD Conference*, pp.761-766, ISBN1-58113-888-1, Seattle, WA, USA.

30

Using Markov Models to Mine Temporal and Spatial Data

Jean-François Mari[1], Florence Le Ber[1,2], El Ghali Lazrak[3], Marc Benoît[3]
Catherine Eng[4], Annabelle Thibessard[4] and Pierre Leblond[4]
[1]*LORIA / Inria-Grand Est, Campus scientifique, BP 239, F-54500, Vandœuvre-lès-Nancy*
[2] *ENGEES, 1 Quai Koch, F-67000, Strasbourg*
[3]*INRA, UR 055, SAD-ASTER domaine du Joly, F-88500, Mirecourt*
[4]*Laboratoire de Génétique et de Microbiologie, UHP-INRA, UMR 1128-IFR110, F-54500, Vandœuvre-lès-Nancy*
France

1. Stochastic modelling, temporal and spatial data and graphical models

Markov models represent a powerful way to approach the problem of mining time and spatial signals whose variability is not yet fully understood. Initially developed for pattern matching (Baker, 1974; Geman & Geman, 1984) and information theory (Forney, 1973), they have shown good modelling capabilities in various problems occurring in different areas like Biosciences (Churchill, 1989), Ecology (Li et al., 2001; Mari & Le Ber, 2006; Le Ber et al., 2006), Image (Pieczynski, 2003; Forbes & Pieczynski, 2009) and Signal processing (Rabiner & Juang, 1995). These stochastic models assume that the signals under investigation have a local property –called the Markov property– which states that the signal evolution at a given instant or around a given location is uniquely determined by its neighbouring values. In 1988, Pearl (Pearl, 1988) shown that these models can be viewed as specific dynamic Bayesian models which belong to a more general class called graphical models (Whittaker, 1990; Charniak, 1991).

The graphical models (GM) are the results of the marriage between the theory of probabilities and the theory of graphs. They represent the phenomena under study within graphs where the nodes are some variables that take their values in a discrete or continuous domain. Conditional –or causal– dependencies between the variables are graphically expressed. As an example, the relation between the random variables U, V and W depicted by Fig. 1 expresses that V and W are the reasons –more or less probable– of U. In a Bayesian attitude, the uncertainty about this relation is measured by the conditional probability $P(U/V,W)$ of observing U given V and W.

In graphical models, (see Fig. 2-4), some nodes model the phenomenon's data thanks to adequate distributions of the observations. They are called "observable" variables whereas the others are called "hidden" variables. The observable nodes of the graph give a frozen view of the phenomenon. In the time domain, the temporal changes are modelled by the set of transitions between the nodes. In the space domain, the theory of graphs allows to take into account the neighbourhood relations between the phenomenon's constituents.

The mining of temporal and / or spatial signals by graphical models can have several purposes:

Segmentation : in this task, the GM clusters the signal into stationary (or homogeneous) and transient segments or areas (Jain et al., 1999). The term stationnary means that the signal values are considered as independent outcomes of probability density functions (pdf). These areas are then post-processed to extract some valuable knowledge from the data.

Pattern matching : in this task, the GM measures the *a posteriori* probability $P(model = someLabel/observedData)$. When there are as many GM as labels, the best probability allows the classification of an unknown pattern by the label associated with the highest probability.

Background modelling : in order to make proper use of quantitative data, the GM is used as a background model to simulate an averaged process behavior that corrects for chance variation in the frequency counts (Huang et al., 2004). The domain expert compares the simulated and real data frequencies in order to distinguish if he / she is facing to over- or under-represented data that must be investigated more carefully.

In this chapter, we will present a general methodology to mine different kinds of temporal and spatial signals having contrasting properties: continuous or discrete with few or many modalities.
This methodology is based on a high order Markov modelling as implemented in a free software: CARROTAGE (see section 3). Section 2 gives the theoretical basis of the modelling. Section 3 describes a general flowchart for mining temporal and spatial signals using CARROTAGE. The next section is devoted to the description of three data mining applications following the same flowchart. Finally, we draw some conclusions in section 5.

2 The HMM as a graphical model

The Hidden Markov Model is a graphical model which represents the sequence of observations as a doubly stochastic process: an underlying "hidden" process, called the state sequence of random variables $Q_1, Q_2, ... Q_T$ and an output (observation) process, represented by the sequence $O_1, O_2, ... O_T$ over the same time interval (see Fig. 2-3). The sequence (Q_t) is a Markov chain and represents the different clusters that must be extracted.

2.1 HMM definition

We define a hidden Markov model by giving:

- $\mathbf{S} = \{s_1, s_2, \ldots, s_N\}$, a finite set of N states ;
- $\mathbf{A}$ a matrix defining the transition probabilities between the states:

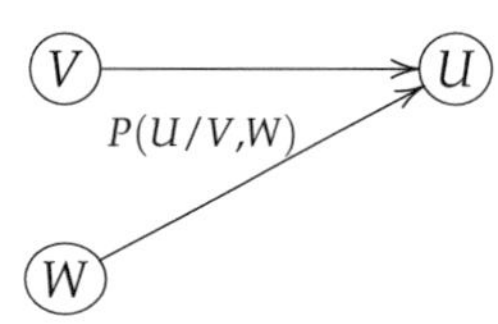

Fig. 1. Conditional dependency of U with V and W in a Bayesian network. The probability measures the confidence of the dependency

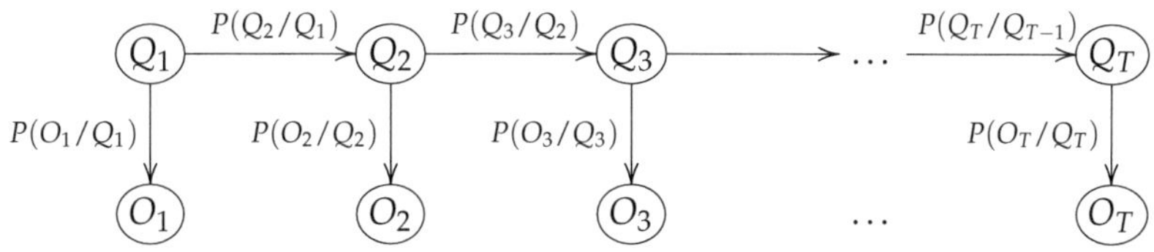

Fig. 2. Conditional dependencies in a HMM1 represented as a Bayesian network. The hidden variables (Q_t) govern the observable variables (O_t)

$\mathbf{A} = \left(a_{ij}\right)$ for a first order HMM (HMM1) (Fig. 2),

$\mathbf{A} = \left(a_{ijk}\right)$ for a second order HMM (HMM2) (Fig. 3);

- $\mathbf{b_i}(.)$ the distributions of observations associated to the states s_i. This distribution may be parametric, non parametric or even given by an HMM in the case of hierarchical HMM (Fine et al., 1998).

As opposite to a Markov chain where the states are unambiguously observed, in a HMM, the observations are not uniquely associated to a state s_i but are drawn from a random variable that has a conditional density $\mathbf{b_i}(.)$ that depends on the actual state s_i (Baker, 1974). There is a doubly stochastic process:

- the former is hidden from the observer, is defined on a set of states and is a Markov chain;
- the latter is visible. It produces an observation at each time slot –or index in the sequence– depending on the probability density function that is defined on the state in which the Markov chain stays at time t. It is often said that the Markov chain governs the latter.

2.2 Modelling the dependencies in the observable process

Defining the observation symbols is the first step of a HMM data processing. In this chapter, we will present our data mining work based on various GM applied on different kinds of signals having contrasting properties:

- genomic data characterized by long sequences (several millions) of the 4 nucleotides A, C, G, T (application 1);
- short temporal discrete sequences (around 10 value long) with a great number (around 50) of modalities like the temporal land use successions (LUS) of agricultural fields whose mosaic defines a 2-D spatial territory (application 2);

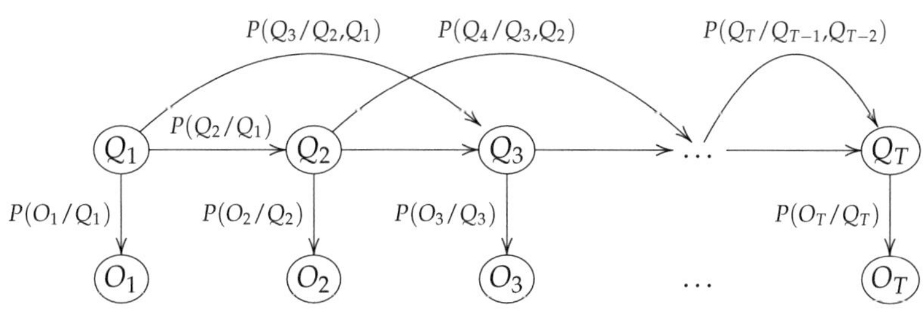

Fig. 3. Conditional dependencies in a HMM2 represented as a Bayesian network. The hidden variables (Q_t) govern the observable variables (O_t)

- continuous data like the values of a river width sampled from the river's source up to its end (application 3).

To take into account the correlations between successive or neighbouring observations, several options are possible.

2.2.1 Continuous observations

The usual way to model continuous random observations is to consider them as Gaussian distributed. When the observations are vectors belonging to $\mathbb{R}^d$, multivariate Gaussian `pdf` are used. The main reason of this consideration is that an unknown `pdf` can be approximated by a mixture of multivariate Gaussian `pdf`. To take into account the correlations between successive observations, first and second order regression coefficients (Furui, 1986) are stacked over the observation vector:

$$R(t) = \frac{\sum_{n=-n_0}^{n_0} nO(t+n)}{\sum_{n=-n_0}^{n_0} n^2} \tag{1}$$

where $O(t+n)$ is the observation (frame) $t+n$. The $2n_0+1$ frames involved in the computation of the regression coefficient $R(t)$ are centered around frame t. By this way, the vector at time t models the shape of the observation variations and incorporates information about the surrounding context.

2.2.2 Categorical observations

When the observations are discrete and belong to a finite set $C = \{c_1, c_2, ...c_M\}$, it is convenient to represent this correlation by adding new dependencies between the current observation and the previous observations. In the particular case shown in Fig. 4, the observation distribution is a conditional `pdf` $\mathbf{b_{iuv}}(o_t)$ that represents the conditional probability of observing o_t assuming the state s_i and the observations u and v that occured respectively at indices $t-1$ and $t-2$:

$$o_{t-1} = u,\ o_{t-2} = v \quad u, v \in C.$$

In the temporal domain, this leads to the definition of a `Mp-Mq HMM` where p is the order of the hidden Markov process and q refers to the dependencies in the observable process.
Another way to take into account the correlations between successive (neighbouring) observations, is to consider composite observations drawn from the n-fold product $C^n = C \times C \ldots C$. The elementary observation (for example, a nucleotide, a land use ...) is considered together with its context. This leads to the definition of *k-mer* (see section 4.1.1) in biology or land use succession in agronomy (see section 4.2.1.3). As a direct consequence, the `pdf` size will be changed from $|C|$ to $|C|^n$ where $|C|$ denotes the cardinality of C. It is

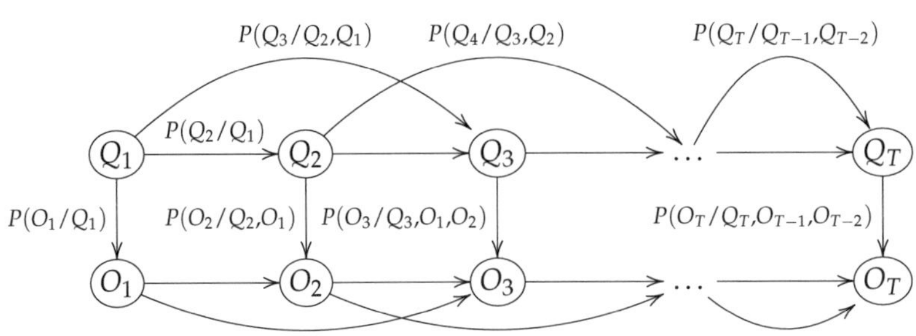

Fig. 4. Conditional dependencies of a `M2-M2 HMM` represented in a Bayesian network

then possible to control the balance between the parameter number assigned to the hidden variables and to the observable ones in the model.

2.3 Automatic estimation of a HMM2

The estimation of an HMM1 is usually done by the forward backward algorithm which is related to the EM algorithm (Dempster et al., 1977). We have shown in (Mari et al., 1997) that an HMM2 can be estimated following the same way. The estimation is an iterative process starting with an initial model and a corpus of sequences of observations that the HMM2 must fit even when the insertions, deletions and substitutions of observations occur in the sequences. The very success of the HMM is based on their robustness: even when the considered data do not suit a given HMM, its use can give interesting results. The initial model has equi-probable transition probabilities and a uniform distribution in each state. At each step, the forward backward algorithm determines a new model in which the likelihood of the sequences of observation increases. Hence this estimation process converges to a local maximum. Interested readers may refer to (Dempster et al., 1977; Mari & Schott, 2001) to find more specific details of the implementation of this algorithm.
If N is the number of states and T the sequence length, the second-order forward backward algorithm has a $N^3 \times T$ complexity for an HMM2.
The choice of the initial model has an influence on the final model obtained by convergence. To assess this last model, we use the Kullback-Leibler distance between the distributions associated to the states (Tou & Gonzales, 1974). Two states that are too close are merged and the resulting model is re-trained. Domain experts do not interfere in the process of designing a specific model, but they have a central role in the interpretation of the results that the final model gives on the data.

3. CARROTAGE a general framework to mine sequences

We have developed a knowledge discovery system based on high-order hidden Markov models for analyzing temporal data bases (Fig. 5). This system, named CARROTAGE[1], takes as input an array of discrete or continuous data –the rows represent the individuals and the columns the time slots– and builds a partition together with its *a posteriori* probability. CARROTAGE is a free software [2] under a Gnu Public License. It is written in C++ and runs under Unix systems. In all applications, the data mining processing based on CARROTAGE is decomposed into four main steps:

Model specification. Even if CARROTAGE may use models of any topology, we mainly use two different graph topologies: linear and ergodic. In a linear model, there is no circuit between the nodes except self loops on some nodes. Whereas in an ergodic model, all the nodes are inter connected; a node can reach all the others. The first HMM2 that CARROTAGE has to estimate is linear with equi-probable transitions from each state and uniform distributions of observations in every states. The only parameter let to the user is the number of states.

[1] CARROTAGE is a retro acronym that comes from the word carrot that can be translated by Markov in Russian and age to refer to the temporal component of the data. It is also a technique which consists in drilling a hole in some material (a tree or the ice of the Antarctic) to withdraw a cylinder that allows to date the process of creation

[2] http://www.loria.fr/~jfmari/App/

Iterative estimate of the model parameters. The parameter estimation of the model is performed by the forward backward algorithm for `M2-Md HMM`. Basically, given a sequence of symbols $(o_1^T) = o_1, o_2, \ldots o_T$ the second-order forward backward algorithm computes the expected count of the state transition $s_{i_1} \to s_{i_2} \to s_{i_3}$

$$\eta_t(i_1, i_2, i_3) = P(Q_{t-2} = s_{i_1}, Q_{t-1} = s_{i_2}, Q_t = s_{i_3} / O_1^T = o_1^T) \tag{2}$$

at index $t-2, t-1, t$.

The first parameter estimate is performed on a linear model to acquire a segmentation of the sequence into as many homogeneous regions than there are states in the specified model.

Linear to ergodic model transform. The estimated linear model is transformed into an ergodic one by keeping the previously estimated `pdf` and interconnecting the states. This allows the stochastic process to re-visit the states and, therefore, segment the data into an unconstrained number of homogeneous regions, each of them associated to a state.

Decoding. The decoding state uses the last iteration of EM algorithm to calculate the *a posteriori* probability of the hidden states. It is possible to compute three types of *a posteriori* probability. In all the following definitions, we assume that the hidden state s_i is attained at time t and that we have a T length observation sequence (o_1^T).

type 0

$$P_0(i, t) = \sum_{i_1, i_2} \eta_t(i_1, i_2, i) \tag{3}$$

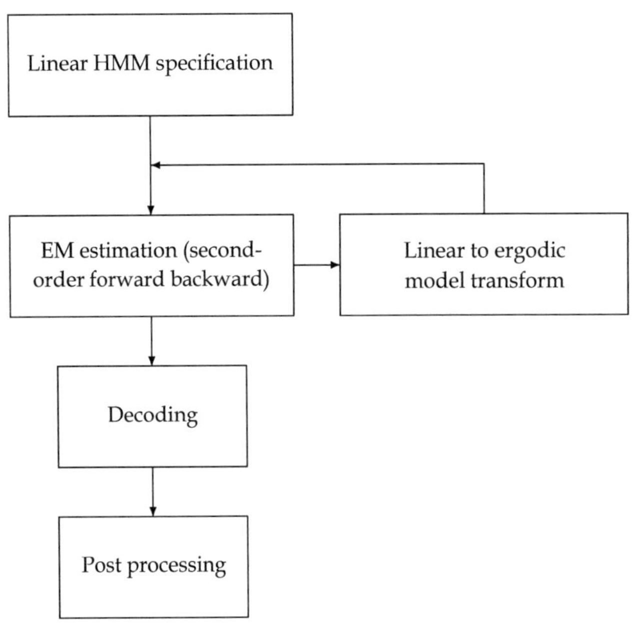

Fig. 5. General flow Chart of the data mining process using CARROTAGE

The *a posteriori* probability of the state s_i at index t assuming the whole sequence (o_1^T).

type 1

$$P_1(i,t) = \sum_{i_1} \eta_t(i_1,i,i) \tag{4}$$

The *a posteriori* probability of the 2 state transition $s_i \rightarrow s_i$ at index t assuming the whole sequence (o_1^T). This probability can be computed either by a `HMM1` or by a `HMM2`.

type 2

$$P_2(i,t) = \eta_t(i,i,i) \tag{5}$$

The *a posteriori* probability of the 3 state transition $s_i \rightarrow s_i \rightarrow s_i$ at index t assuming the whole sequence (o_1^T). This probability is typical of a `HMM2`.

In some applications, as the mining of crop successions (see section 4.2), the *a posteriori* transition probability (type 1) between 2 states can be used and gives an interesting information. In such a case, we use:

$$P_1(i,j,t) = \sum_{i_1} \eta_t(i_1,i,j) \tag{6}$$

Post processing: The post processing is application dependent and involves mostly a classification step of the different segments. Further ad-hoc treatments must be performed in order to extract valuable information as shown in the application section.

4. Applications

4.1 Mining genomic data

In this section, we describe a new data mining method based on second-order HMM and combinatorial methods for Sigma Factor Binding Site (SFBS) prediction (Eng et al., 2009) and Horizontal Gene Transfer (HGT) (Eng et al., 2011) detection that voluntarily implements a minimum amount of knowledge. The original features of the presented methodology include (i) the use of the CARROTAGE framework, (ii) an automatic area extraction algorithm that captures atypical DNA motifs of various size based on the variation of the state *a posteriori* probability, and (iii) a set of post processing algorithms suitable to the biologic interpretation of these segments. On some points, our data mining method is similar to the work of Bize et al. (Bize et al., 1999) and Nicolas et al. (Nicolas et al., 2002). All the methods use one HMM to model the entire genome. The parameter estimation is done in all cases by the EM algorithm. All the methods look for attributing biological characteristics to the states by analyzing the state output *a posteriori* probability. But our method differs on the following points: we use (i) an HMM2 that has proved interesting capabilities in modelling short sequences, and (ii) depending on the modelled dependencies in the genomic sequence, we can locate either short nucleotides sequences that could be part of SFBS (box1 or box2) or more generally regulation sites for gene expression –Transcriptional Factor Binding sites (TFBS)– or even wider areas potentially acquired by HGT. These sequences are post processed to assess the exact nature of the heterogeneities (SFBS, TFBS or HGT).

4.1.1 Data preparation

In this application, the genome is modelled as an ordered nucleotide sequence whose unknown structure is represented by the state Markov chain. The index t in equation (2) refers to the nucleotide index in the ordered sequence of nucleotides. In a genome sequence, two templates must be considered depending upon the strength of the compositional biases. To incorporate the biased base composition of DNA strands relative to the position of the replication origin when a marked GC skew[3] is observed, as in the case of *Streptococcus thermophilus*, a sequence is constructed *in silico* by concatenating the two leading strands from the origin to the terminus of replication. Its reverse complement is also considered. In contrast, when the genome does not show a marked GC skew, as in *Streptomyces coelicolor*, the 5′ to 3′ sequence of the linear chromosome and its reverse complement are considered. In both cases, these two sequences are used for training purposes and specify two HMM2 named HMM2+ and HMM2-. The best decoding state is identified for both models.
We have also investigated the use of *k-mer* (Delcher et al., 1999) as output symbols instead of nucleotides. A *k-mer* may be viewed as a single nucleotide y_t observed at index t with a specific context $y_{t-k+1}, \ldots y_{t-1}$ made of $k-1$ nucleotides that have been observed at index $t-k+1, \ldots, t-1$. Similarly, a DNA sequence can be viewed as a sequence of overlapping *k-mer* that an HMM analyzes with a consecutive shift of one nucleotide. For example, the seven nucleotide sequence `TAGGCTA` can be viewed as a sequence of seven *3-mer*: `##T` - `#TA` - `TAG` - `AGG` - `GGC` - `GCT` - `CTA`, where # represents an empty context.

4.1.2 *a posteriori* decoding

The mining of irregularities follows the general flow chart given in figure 5. The *a posteriori* probability variations look very different depending on the dependencies that are implemented in the genomic sequence. When modelling the *k-mer* sequence using a `M2-M0 HMM`, the decoding stage locates atypical short DNA segments (see Fig. 6) whereas the modelling of the nucleotide sequence using a `M2-M2 HMM` exhibits wider atypical areas (see Fig.7).

4.1.3 Post processing

The atypical regions extracted by the stochastic models must be processed in order to extract valuable information. A specific suite of algorithms has been designed and tuned in the two applications: TFBS and HGT detections.

4.1.3.1 TFBS retrieval

Our bacterial model is the Gram-positive actinomycete *Streptomyces coelicolor* whose genome is 8.7 Mb long. The streptomycetes are filamentous bacteria that undergo complex morphological and biochemical differentiation, both processes being inextricably interlinked. The purpose of the TFBS application is to retrieve composite motifs *box1-spacer-box2* involved in the *Streptomyces coelicolor* regulation. The two boxes can be part of the intergenic peak motifs (see Fig. 6). The spacer ranges from 3 to 25 and is tuned depending on the type of the investigated TFBS. The basic idea of the mining strategy is to cluster the set of intergenic ipeak motifs located by a `M2-M0 HMM` modelling *3-mer*, select a cluster having a well defined consensus, extend all the sequences belonging to this cluster and look for over-represented motifs by appropriate software (Hoebeke & Schbath, 2006). The consensus of the cluster acts

[3]the GC skew is a quantitative feature that measures the relative nucleotide proportion of G *versus* C in the DNA strand

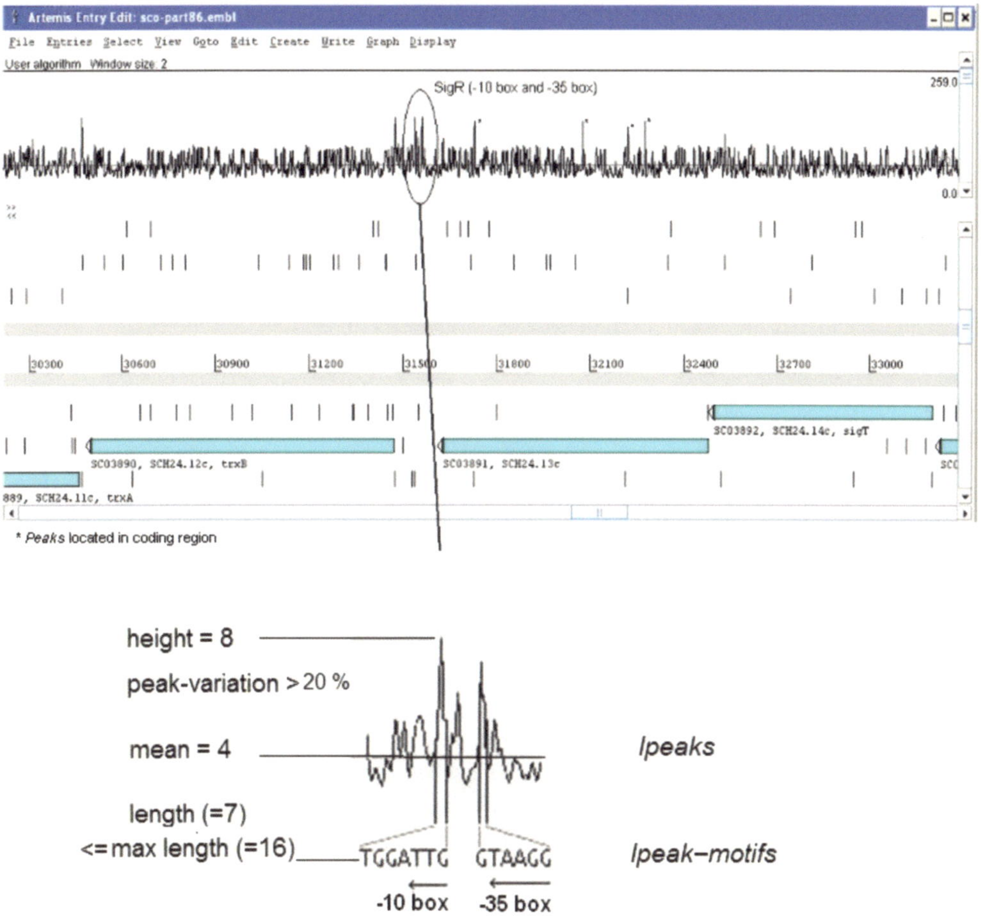

Fig. 6. *A posteriori* probability variation of a `M2-M0 HMM` hidden state as a function of the *3-mer* index in the *Streptomyces coelicolor* genome. The top graph shows the *a posteriori* probability together with the annotated physical sequence (using the EMBL file). As an example, among the intergenic peak motifs, the -35 box (GGAAT) and -10 box (GTT) motifs recognized by the sigma factor SigR are detected. Peak characteristics (peak-variation and length) are marked in the figure. The biological interpretation of the peaks inside the coding regions is not yet fully established (Eng et al., 2009)

for *box1*, the shorter motifs spaced with appropriate spacer value(s) act for *box2*. Interested readers will find in (Eng et al., 2009) an extensive description of this data mining strategy based on stochastic and combinatorial methods.

4.1.3.2 Horizontal gene transfer detection

Our bacterial model is the Gram-positive bacteria *Streptococcus thermophilus* which is a lactic acid bacteria carrying a 1.8 Mb genome and having a considerable economic importance. It is used as starter for the manufacturing of yogurts and cheeses. *Streptococcus thermophilus* is assumed to have derived very recently at the evolutionary time-scale (3,000-30,000 years back: the beginning of the pastoral epoch) from a commensal ancestor which is closely related to

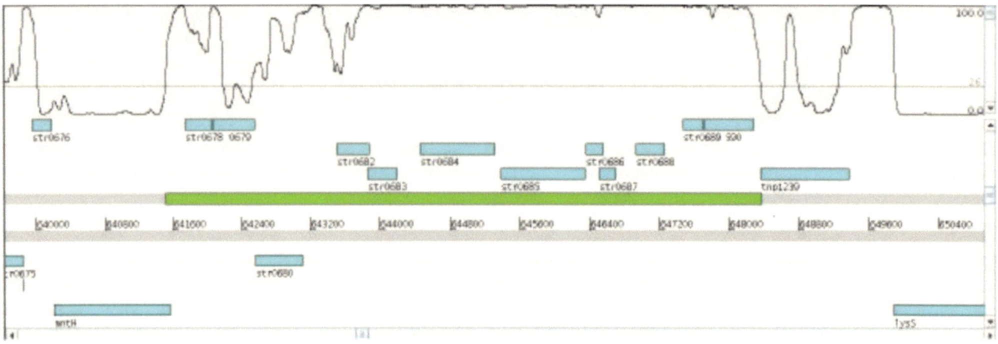

Fig. 7. *A posteriori* probability variation of a `M2-M2 HMM` hidden state as a function of the nucleotide index in the *Streptococcus thermophilus* genome. The additional dependencies in the nucleotide sequence dramatically smooth the state *a posteriori* probability

the contemporary oral bacterium *Streptococcus salivarius* to adapt to its only known ecological niche: the milk. HGT deeply shaped the genome and played a major role in adaptation to its new ecological niche.

In this application, we have observed that the `M2-M2 HMM` modelling nucleotides performs better than `M1-M2 HMM` as implemented in SHOW software [4] (Nicolas et al., 2002) and `M2-M0 HMM` modelling *3-mer* (see section 4.1.3.1).

After tuning the HMM topology, the decoding state that captures the highest heterogeneities is selected by considering the distances between all states according to the Kullback-Leibler distance. The state which is the most far away from the others is selected. On this state, the variations of the *a posteriori* probability as a function of the index in the nucleotide sequence are analyzed. The positions having *a posteriori* probabilities higher than the mean over the whole genome are considered. Regions enriched in these positions through at least 1000 nucleotide length were extracted and named atypical regions. A total of 146 atypical regions were extracted. If a gene were at least half included in these regions then it was considered. A total of 362 genes of 1915 (the whole gene set of the bacterium), called "atypical", were retrieved from these regions. Based on their functional annotation and their sporadic distribution either at the interspecific level (among the other genomes belonging to the same phylum: the Firmicutes) or at the intraspecific level (among a collection of 47 strains of *Streptococcus thermophilus*), a HGT origin can be predicted for a large proportion (about two thirds) (Eng, 2010).

4.2 Mining agricultural landscapes

In agricultural landscapes, land-use (LU) categories are heterogeneously distributed among different agricultural fields managed by farmers. At a first glance, the landscape spatial organization and its temporal evolution seem both random. Nevertheless, they reveal the presence of logical processes and driving forces related to the soil, climate, cropping system, and economical pressure. The mosaic of fields together with their land-use can be seen as a noisy picture generated by these different processes.

Recent studies (Le Ber et al., 2006; Castellazzi et al., 2008) have shown that the ordered sequences of LU in each field can be adequately modelled by a high order Markov process. The LU at time t depends upon the former LU at previous times: $t-1, t-2 \ldots$ depending on

[4] http://genome.jouy.inra.fr/ssb/SHOW/

	Case study	
	Niort Plain	**Yar watershed**
Data source	Land-use surveys	Remote sensing
Surface (sq. km)	350	60
Study period	1996 to 2007	1997 to 2008
Number of LU modalities	47	6
Spatial representation	Vector	Raster (converted to vector)
Elementary spatial entities	Elementary plots (polygons)	Pixels (20 x 20 sq. m)
Data base format	ESRI Shapefile	ESRI Shapefile

Table 1. Comparison between 2 land-use databases coming from two different sources: land-use surveys and remote sensing

the order of the Markov process. In the space domain, the theory of the random Markov fields is an elegant mathematical way for accounting neighbouring dependencies (Geman & Geman, 1984; Julian, 1986). In this section, we present a data mining method based on CARROTAGE to cluster a landscape into patches based on its pluri annual LU organization. Two medium-size agricultural landscapes will be considered coming from different sources: long-term LU surveys or remotely sensed LU data.

4.2.1 Data preparation

For CARROTAGE, the input corpus of LU data is an array in which the columns represent the LU year by year and the rows represent regularly spaced locations in the studied landscape (e.g. 1 point every 20 m). Data preparation aims at reducing the requirement of the memory resources while putting the data in the appropriate format required by CARROTAGE. The data preparation process must tackle several issues: (i) to regroup into LU categories the different LU when there are too many observations, (ii) to define the elementary observation for the HMM, and (iii) to choose the sampling spatial resolution.
The corpus of spatiotemporal LU data is generally built either from long-term LU surveys or from remotely sensed LU data. Depending on the data source, several differences in the LU database may exist. These differences are mostly regarding the number of LU modalities and the representation of the spatial entities: polygons in vector data or pixels in raster data. In the following, the first data source (long-term LU field surveys) is illustrated by the Niort Plain case study (Lazrak et al., 2010), and the second (remotely sensed LU) is illustrated by the Yar watershed case study. Principal characteristics of the two case studies are summarized in table 1.

4.2.1.1 The agricultural landscape mosaic

The agricultural landscape can be seen as an assemblage of polygons of variable size where each polygon holds a given LU. When data derives from LU surveys, the polygons are fields bounded by a road, a path or a limit of a neighbouring field. The polygon boundaries can change every year. To take into account this change, the surveyors update each year the boundaries of fields in the GIS database. For remotely sensed images, the polygons are obtained by grouping similar pixels in the same class and are represented in vector format. In the two cases, the list of the polygon boundaries –that change over the time– led to the definition of the elementary polygon –the plot– as the result of the spatial union of previous polygon boundaries (Figure 8). Each plot holds one LU succession during the study period. There are about 20,000 elementary plots in the Niort study area over the 1996 – 2007 period.

The corpus of land-use data is next sampled and is represented in a matrix in which the columns are related to the time slots and the rows to the different grid locations.
Following Benmiloud and Pieczynski (Pieczynski, 2003), we have approximated the Markov random field (MRF) by sampling the 2-D landscape representation using a regular grid and, next, defining a scan by a Hilbert-Peano curve (figure 9). The Markov field is then represented by a Markov chain. Two successive points in the Markov chain represent two neighbour points in the landscape but the opposite is not true, nevertheless, this rough modelling of the neighbourhood dependencies has shown interesting results compared to an exact Markov random field modelling (Benmiloud & Pieczynski, 1995). To take into account the irregular neighbour system, we can also adjust the fractal depth to the mean plot size. The figure 9 illustrates this concept.

4.2.1.2 LU categories definition

When LU derive from LU surveys, there is often a great number of LU modalities which must be reduced by defining LU categories. For the Niort Plain case study, the 47 LU have been grouped with the help of agricultural experts in 10 categories (see Tab. 2) following an

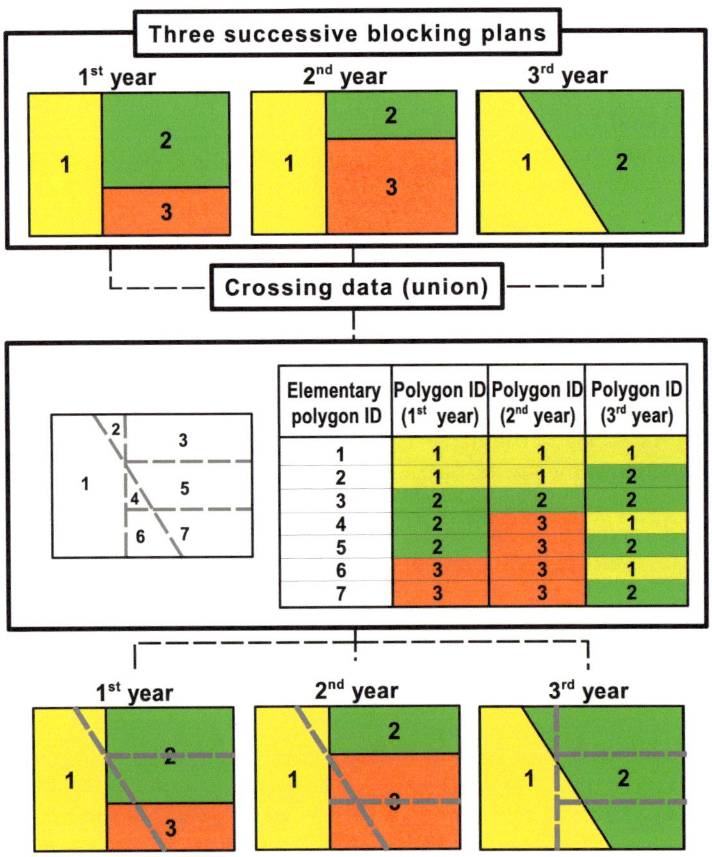

Elementary polygon ID	Polygon ID (1st year)	Polygon ID (2nd year)	Polygon ID (3rd year)
1	1	1	1
2	1	1	2
3	2	2	2
4	2	3	1
5	2	3	2
6	3	3	1
7	3	3	2

Fig. 8. An example of field boundary evolution over three successive years. The union of field boundaries during this period leads to the definition of seven plots

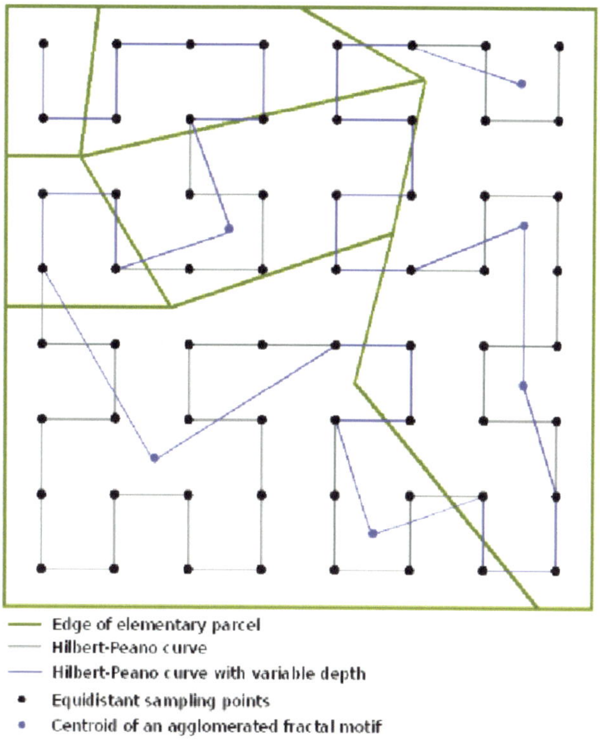

Fig. 9. Variable depth Hilbert-Peano scan to take into account the field size. Two successive merging in the bottom left field yield to the agglomeration of 16 points

approach based on the LU frequency in the spatiotemporal database and the similarity of crop management.
For the Yar watershed case study, only six LU have been distinguished: Urban, Water, Forest, Grassland, Cereal and Maize. There was no need of grouping them into categories.

4.2.1.3 Choice of the elementary observation

An elementary observation can range from a LU (such as Cereal in the Yar watershed case study) or a LU category (such as Wheat in the Niort Plain case study) to a LU succession (LUS) spanning several years. For this latter, the length of the LU succession influences the interpretation of the final model. However, the total number of LUS is a power function of the succession length, and memory resources required during the estimation of HMM2 parameters increase dramatically.
To determine the succession length, we compared the diversity of LUS between field-collected data (the Niort Plain) and randomly generated data for different lengths of successions (Fig. 10(a)). For this case study, 4-year successions begin to clearly differentiate the landscape from a random landscape in which the LU are randomly allocated in the plots. Therefore, 4-year successions appear to be the shortest HMM2 elementary observation symbol suitable for modelling LUS within the Niort Plain landscape. The choice for the elementary observation can also be set by domain specialists based on previous works (Le Ber et al., 2006; Mignolet et al., 2007). This was the case for the Yar watershed where we chose to model the

LU category	LU	Frequency	Cumul
Wheat	Wheat, bearded wheat, cereal	0.337	0.337
Sunflower	Sunflower, ryegrass followed by sunflower	0.139	0.476
Rapeseed	Rapeseed	0.124	0.600
Urban	Built area, peri-village, road	0.096	0.696
Grassland	Grassland of various types, alfalfa,...	0.078	0.774
Maize	Maize, ryegrass followed by maize	0.076	0.850
Forest	Forest or hedge, wasteland	0.034	0.884
Winter barley	Winter barley	0.034	0.918
Ryegrass	Ryegrass, ryegrass followed by ryegrass	0.024	0.942
Pea	Pea	0.022	0.964
Others	Spring barley, grape vine, clover, field bean, ryegrass, cereal-legume mixture, garden/market gardening,...	0.036	1.000

Table 2. Composition and average frequencies of adopted LU categories (Lazrak et al., 2010)

agricultural dynamics through 3-year LUS.

4.2.1.4 Choice of the spatial resolution

For medium-size and large landscapes, a high-resolution sampling generates a large amount of data. With such amount, only rough models can be tested. On the other hand, with a coarse resolution sampling, small fields are omitted. In order to have an objective criterion for choosing the optimal spatial resolution, we can estimate information loss in terms of LUS diversity for increasingly coarse resolution samplings. Figure 10(b) shows the obtained curve for the Niort Plain case study. The tested resolutions were: 10, 20, 40, 80, 160, 320 and 640 m. Irregularity in sampling intervals is dictated by an algorithmic constraint: the resolution must be proportional to a power of 2. The most precise resolution is considered as the reference

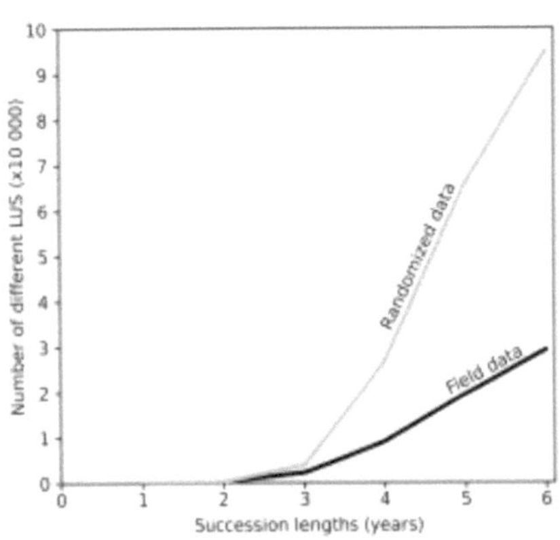

(a) Compared diversity of LUS between field-collected data and 10 random generated data sets for different succession lengths

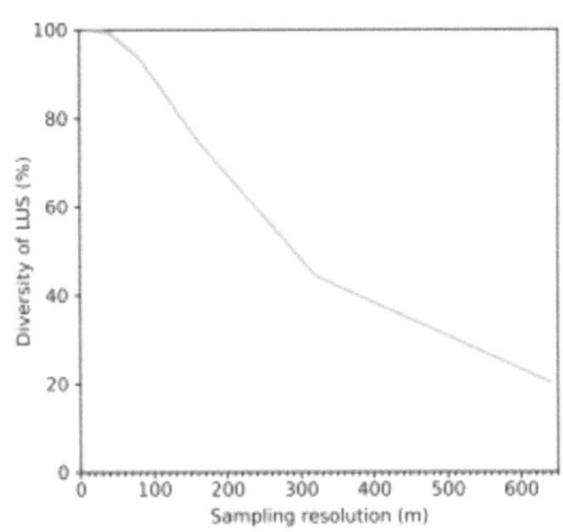

(b) Information loss in terms of LUS diversity in relation to sampling resolutions for 4-year LUS

Fig. 10. Relations between LUS diversity and sampling rates

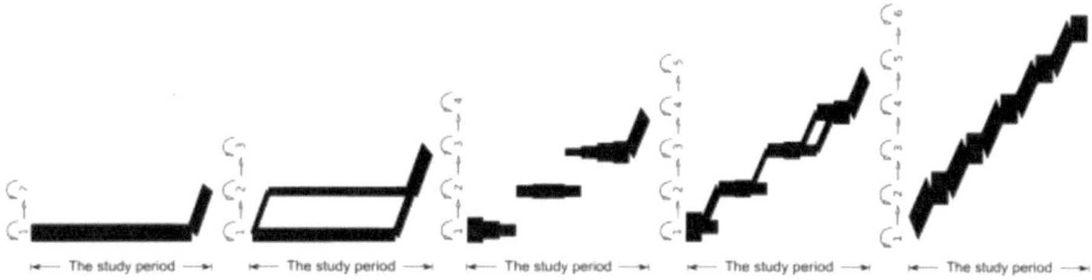

Fig. 11. Seeking the best temporal segmentation of the Yar watershed study period by using 5 growing state number linear HMM2. The line width is proportional to the *a posteriori* transition probability (Eq. 6). The 6 state HMM2 segments the study period into 6 non-overlapping periods

(100%). As a compromise, we chose the 80 m x 80 m resolution that led to a corpus 64 times smaller than the original one, with only a loss of 6% in information diversity.
For the Yar watershed landscape, which has a surface roughly 7 times smaller than the Niort Plain landscape and has few LU modalities, we were not constrained by the corpus size. Thus, we chose a 20 m x 20 m resolution which was the original resolution of satellite images used to identify the LU.

4.2.2 *a posteriori* decoding

We propose to build a time spatial analysis through spatial analysis of crop dynamics. This data mining method is a time x space analysis where a temporal analysis is performed in order to identify temporal regularities before locating these regularities in the landscape by means of a hierarchical HMM2 (HHMM2). The HHMM2 allows segmenting the landscape into patches, each of them being characterized by a temporal HMM2.

4.2.2.1 Mining temporal regularities

Depending on the investigated temporal regularities, we can either use a linear HMM2 or a multi-column ergodic HMM2 (Fig. 12). Linear models allow segmenting the study period into homogeneous sub-periods in terms of LUS distributions (see Figure 11).
Multi-column ergodic models (Mari & Le Ber, 2006; Le Ber et al., 2006) (Fig. 12) have been designed for measuring the probability of a succession of land-use categories. Actually, we have defined a specific state, called the *Dirac state*, whose distribution is zero except on a particular land-use category. Therefore, the transition probabilities between the Dirac states measure the probabilities between the land-use categories. Figure 12 shows the topology of a HMM2 that has two kinds of states: Dirac states associated to the most frequent land-use categories (wheat, sunflower, barley,...) and *container states* associated to uniform distributions over the set of observations. The estimation process usually empties the container state of the land-use categories associated with Dirac states. Therefore this model generalises both hidden Markov models and Markov models.
The model generation follows the same flowchart given in figure 5. When it is needed, the *Dirac states* can be initialized by some search patterns for capturing one or many particular observations.
Agronomists interpret the resulting diagrams to find the LU dynamics. Figure 13 shows a quasi steady agricultural system. The crop rotations involve Rapeseed, Sunflower and Wheat. In order to determine the exact rotations (2-year or 3-year), it is necessary to envisage the

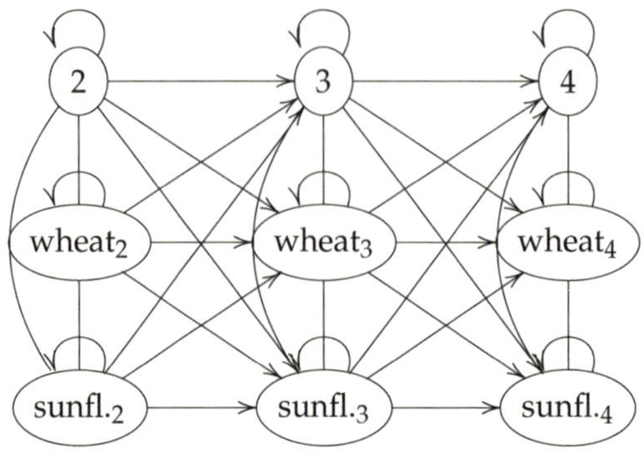

Fig. 12. Multiple column ergodic model: the states denoted 2, 3 and 4 are associated to a distribution of land-use categories, as opposite to the *Dirac* states denoted with a specific land-use category. The number of columns determines the number of time intervals (periods). A connection without arrow means a two directional connection

modelling of 4-year LUS (Lazrak et al., 2010). Note the monoculture of Wheat that starts in 2004.

4.2.2.2 Spatial clustering based on HMM2

We model the spatial structure of the landscape by a MRF whose sites are random LUS. The dynamics of these LUS are modelled by a temporal HMM2. This leads to the definition of

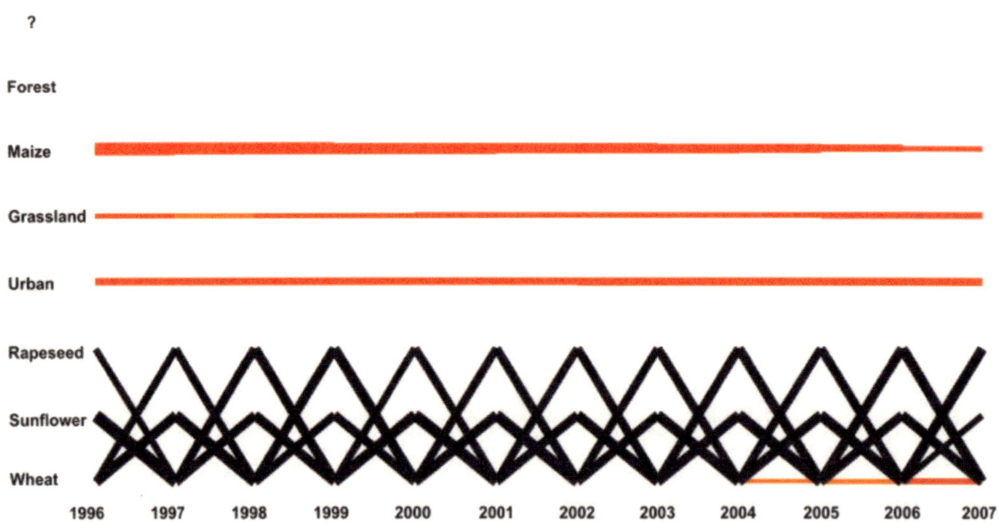

Fig. 13. Markov diagram showing transitions between LU categories in the Niort Plain. The x-axis represents the study period. The y-axis stands for the states of the ergodic one-column HMM2 used for data mining. Each state represents one LU category. The state '?' is the *container* state associated to a `pdf`. Diagonal transitions stand for inter-annual LU changes. Horizontal transitions indicate inter-annual stability. For simplicity, only transitions whose frequencies are greater than 5 % are displayed. The line width reflects the *a posteriori* probability of the transition assuming the observation of the 12-year LU categories (Eq. 6)

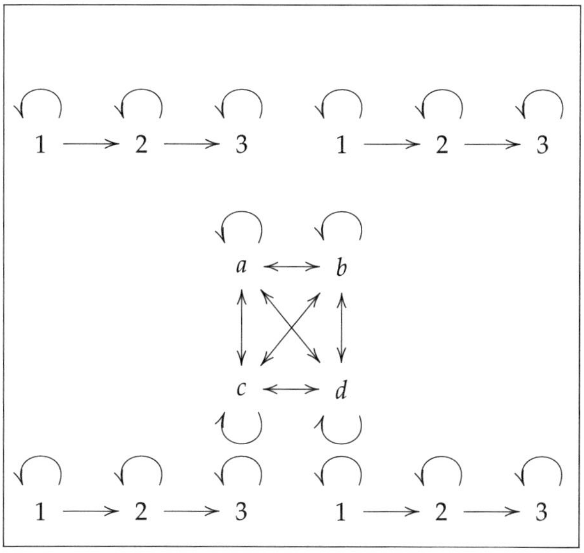

Fig. 14. Example of hierarchical HMM2. Each spatial state a, b, c, d of the master HHMM2 (ergodic model) is a temporal HMM2 (linear model) whose states are 1, 2, 3

a hierarchical HMM2 (Figure 14) where a master HMM2 approximates the MRF. Then, the probability of LUS is given by a temporal HMM2 as fully described in (Fine et al., 1998; Mari & Le Ber, 2006; Lazrak et al., 2010). This hierarchical HMM is used to segment the landscape into patches, each of them being characterized by a temporal HMM2. At each index l in the Hilbert-Peano curve, we look for the best *a posteriori* state in the HHMM2 (Maximum Posterior Mode algorithm). The state labels, together with the geographic coordinates of the indices l, determine a clustered image of the landscape that can be coded within an ESRI shapefile. An example of this segmentation for the Yar watershed case study is given in Figure 15.

4.2.3 Post processing

For the Yar watershed case study, we have performed preliminary temporal segmentation tests with linear models having an increasing number of states (Figure 11). This led us to use a 6-state HMM2 to segment the study period into 6 sub-periods characterized by different `pdf`. Plotting together the 6 sub-periods gives a global view on the LU dynamics (Figure 15).
In figure 15, the Yar watershed is represented by a mosaic of patches of LU evolutions. These patches are associated to a 5-state ergodic HHMM2. States 1 and 2, respectively represent Forest and Urban and are steady during the study period. The Urban state is also populated by less frequent LU that constitute its privileged neighbours. Grassland is the first neighbour of Urban, but it vanishes over the time. The other 3 states exhibit a greater LU diversity and a more pronounced temporal variation. In state 3, Grassland, Maize and Cereal evolve together until the middle of the study period. Next, Grassland and Maize decrease and are replaced by Cereal. This trend shows very likely that a change of cropping system was undertaken in the patches belonging to this state.

4.3 Mining hydro-morphological data

In this section we describe the use of `HMM2` for the segmentation of data describing river channels. Actually, a river channel is considered as a continuum and is characterised

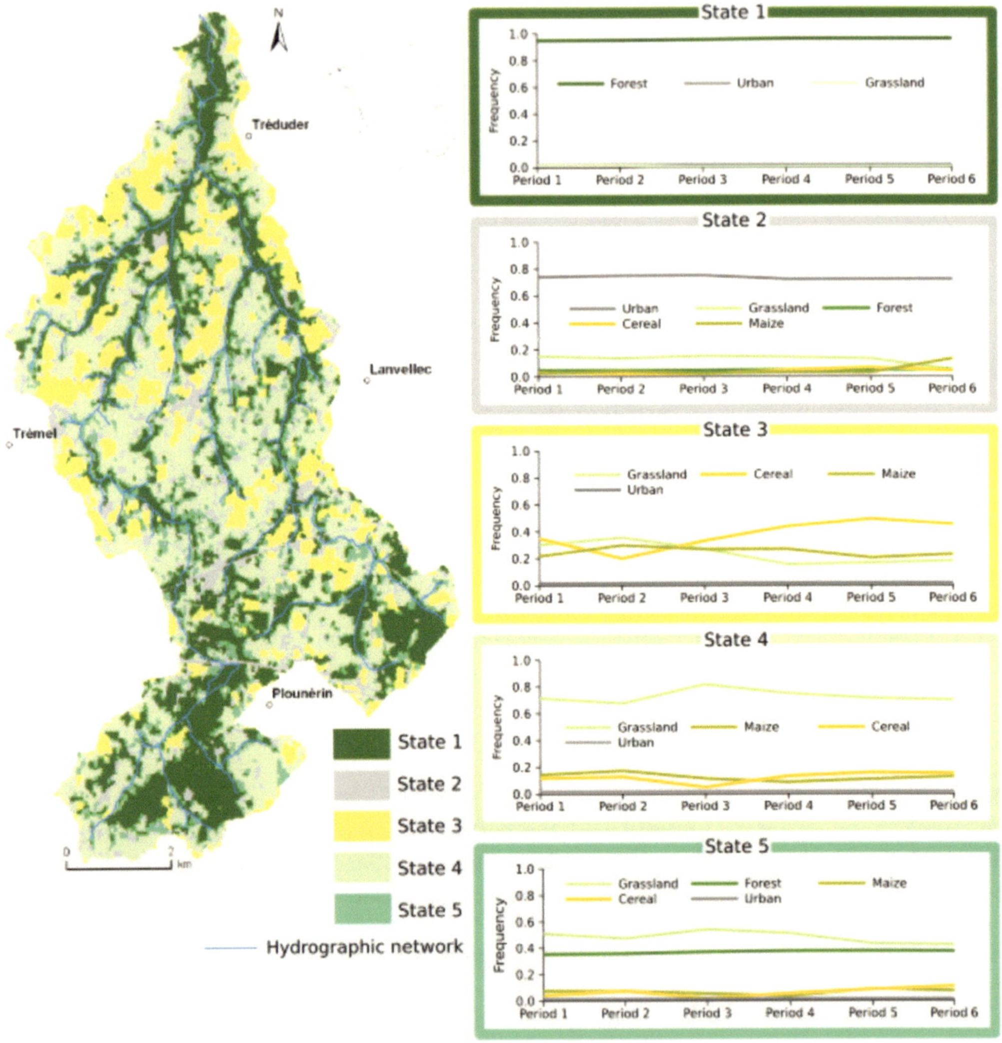

Fig. 15. The Yar watershed seen as patches of LU dynamics. Each map unit stands for a state of the HHMM2 used to achieve the spatial segmentation. Each state is described by a diagram of the LU evolution. The 6 sub-periods are the time slots derived from the temporal segmentation with the 6-state HMM2 describing each state of the HHMM2. Location of the Yar watershed in France is shown by a black spot depicted in the upper middle box

by its width or depth that is increasing downstream whereas its slope and grain size decrease (Schumm, 1977). The segmentation of this continuum with respect to local characteristics is an important issue in order to better manage the river channels (e.g. protection of plant or animal species, prevention of flood or erosion processes, etc.). Several methods have been proposed to perform such a segmentation. Markov chains Grant et al. (1990) and `HMM1` (Kehagias, 2004) are also been used.

4.3.1 Data preparation

The aim is to establish homogeneous units of the river Drome (South-East of France) continuum according to its geomorphological features. First of all, the continuum has been segmented within 406 segments of 250 meters length. Each segment is then described with several variables computed from aerial photographs (years 1980/83 and 1994/96) supplemented with terrain observations. Details about the computing of these variables can be found in (Aubry & Piégay, 2001; Alber & Piégay, 2010; Alber, 2010). In the following, we focus on the variable describing the width of the active channel (i.e. the water channel and shingle banks without vegetation).

4.3.2 *a posteriori* decoding

The stochastic modelling follows the same flow chart given in Fig. 5. Both linear and ergodic models have been used. The `pdf` associated in the `M2-M0 HMM` are univariate Gaussian $\mathcal{N}(\mu_i, \Sigma_i)$.

$$b_i(O_t) = \mathcal{N}(O_t; \mu_i, \Sigma_i) \tag{7}$$

where O_t is the input vector (the frame) at index t and $\mathcal{N}(O_t; \mu, \Sigma)$ the expression of the likelihood of O_t using a gaussian density with mean μ and variance Σ. The maximum likelihood estimates the mean and covariance are given by the formulas using the definition of P_0 (cf. Equ.3):

$$\overline{\mu_i} = \frac{\sum_t P_0(i,t) O_t}{\sum_t P_0(i,t)} \tag{8}$$

$$\overline{\Sigma_i} = \frac{\sum_t P_0(i,t)(O_t - \mu_i)(O_t - \mu_i)^t}{\sum_t P_0(i,t)} \tag{9}$$

Specific user interfaces have been designed, in order to fit the experts' requirements: the original data are plotted, together with the mean value and the standard deviation of the current (most probable) state.

The linear model (Fig. 16) allows to detect a limited number (due to the specified number of states) of high variations, i.e. large and short vs narrow and long sections of the river channel. The ergodic model (Fig. 17) allows to detect an unknown number of small variations and repetitions.

4.3.3 Post processing

The final aim of this study is to build a geomorphical typology based on the river characteristics and to link it to external criteria (e.g. geology, land-use). The clustering is useful to define a relevant scale for this typology. If the typology is limited to the Drome river, the linear `HMM` allows to detect a set of segments that can be characterised by further variables and used as a basis for the typology. Ten segments for 101.5 kilometres appeared to be a good

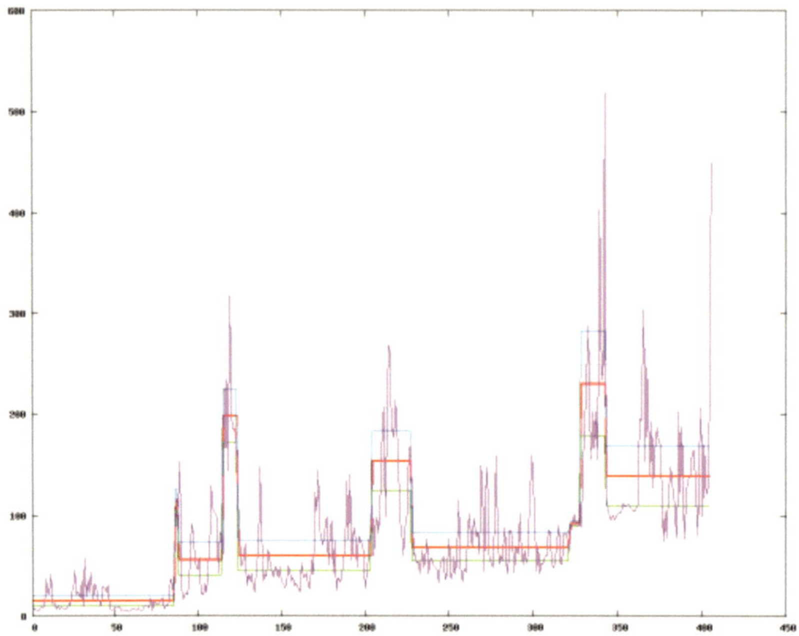

Fig. 16. Clustering the active channel width of the Drome river: linear HMM2 with 10 states

scale. On the contrary, if a whole network is considered -with several rivers and junctions-, the segmentation performed by the ergodic HMM would be more interesting since it allows to segment the data with less states than the linear model and to reveal similar zones (i.e.

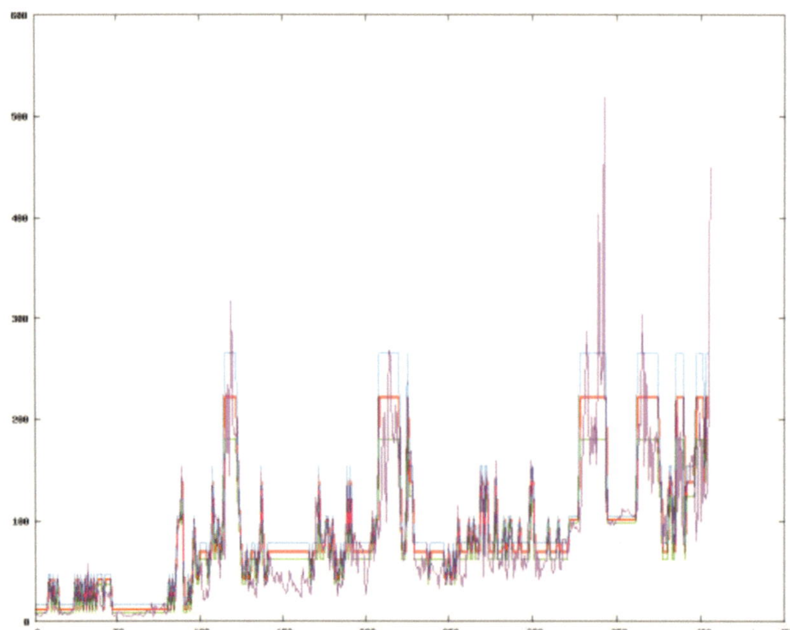

Fig. 17. Clustering the active channel width of the Drome river: ergodic HMM2 with 6 states

belonging to the same state) in the network. The probability transitions between states can also be exploited to reveal similar sequences of states along the network and thus to perform nested segmentations. Furthermore, transition areas appearing as significant mixtures of several states may be dealt with separately or excluded from a typology. Specific algorithms have to be designed and tuned to deal with these last questions.

5. Conclusions

We have described in this chapter a general methodology to mine temporal and spatial data based on a high order Markov modelling as implemented in CARROTAGE. The data mining is basically a clustering process that voluntary implements a minimum amount of knowledge. The HMM maps the observations into a set of states generated by a Markov chain. The classification is performed, both in time domain and spatial domain, by using the *a posteriori* probability that the stochastic process stays in a particular state, assuming a sequence of observations. We have shown that spatial data may be re-ordered using a fractal curve that preserves the neighbouring information. We adopt a Bayesian point of view and measure the temporal and the spatial variability with the *a posteriori* probability of the mapping. Doing so, we have a coherent processing both in temporal and spatial domain. This approach appeared to be valuable for time space data mining.

In the genomic application, two different HMM (`M2-M0 HMM` and `M2-M2 HMM`) have extracted meaningful regularities that are of interest in the area of promoter and HGT detection. The dependencies in the observation sequence smooth dramatically the *a posteriori* probability. We put forward the hypothesis that this smoothing effect is due to the additional normalisation constraints used to transform a 64 bin `pdf` of *3-mer* into 16 `pdf` of nucleotides. This smoothing effect allows the extraction of wider regularities in the genome as it has been shown in the HGT application.

In the agronomic application, the hierarchical HMM produces a time space clustering of agricultural landscapes based on the LU temporal evolution that gives to the agronomist a concise view of the current trends. CARROTAGE is an efficient tool for exploring large land use databases and for revealing the temporal and spatial organization of land use, based on crop sequences (Mari & Le Ber, 2003). Furthermore, this mining strategy can also be used to investigate and visualize the crop sequences of a few specific farms or of a small territory. In a recent work (Schaller et al., 2010) aiming at modelling the agricultural landscape organization at the farm and landscape levels, the stochastic regularities have been combined with farm surveys to validate and explain the individual farmer decision rules. Finally, the results of our analysis can be linked to models of nitrate flow and used for the evaluation of water pollution risks in a watershed (**?**).

In the mining of hydro-morphological data, the HMM have given promising results. They could be used to perform nested segmentations and reveal similar zones in the hydrological network. We are carrying out extensive comparisons with other methods in order to assess the gain given by the high order of the Markov chain modelling.

In all these applications, the extraction of regularities has been achieved following the same flowchart that starts by the estimation of a linear HMM to get initial seeds for the probabilities and, next, a linear to ergodic transform followed by a new estimation by the forward backward algorithm. Even if the data do not suit the model, the HMM can give interesting results allowing the domain specialist to put forward some new hypothesis. Also, we have noticed that the data preparation is a time consuming process that conditions all further steps

of the data mining process. Several ways of encoding elementary observations have been tried in all applications during our interactions with the domain specialists.
A much discussed problem is the automatic design of the HMM topology. So far, CARROTAGE does not implement any tools to achieve this goal. We plan to improve CARROTAGE by providing it with these tools and assess this new feature in the numerous case studies that we have already encountered. Another new trend in the area of artificial intelligence is the clustering of both numerical and symbolic data. Also, based on their transition probabilities and `pdf`, the HMM could be considered as objects that have to be compared and clustered by symbolical methods. The frequent items inside the `pdf` can be analyzed by frequent item set algorithms to achieve a description of the intent of the classes made of the most frequent observations that have been captured in each state in the HMM. These issues must be tackled if we want to deal with different levels of description for large datasets.

6. Acknowledgments

Many organizations had provided us with support and data. The genetic data mining work was supported by INRA, the région Lorraine and the ACI IMP-Bio initiative. Hydro-morphological data were provided by H. Piégay and A. Alber, UMR 5600 CNRS, Lyon. The original idea of this work arose from discussions with T. Leviandier, ENGEES, Strasbourg. The agronomic work was supported by the ANR-ADD-COPT project, the API-ECOGER project, the région Lorraine and the ANR-BiodivAgrim project. We thank the two CNRS teams: UPR CEBC (Chizé) for their data records obtained from the "Niort Plain database" and UMR COSTEL (Rennes) for the "Yar database".

7. References

Alber, A. (2010). PhD thesis, U. Lyon 2, France. to be published.

Alber, A. & Piégay, H. (2010). Disaggregation-aggregation procedure for characterizing spatial structures of fluvial networks: applications to the Rhône basin (France), *Geomorphology* . In press.

Aubry, P. & Piégay, H. (2001). Pratique de l'analyse de l'autocorrélation spatiale en géomorphologie fluviale : définitions opératoires et tests, *Géographie Physique et Quaternaire* 55(2): 115–133.

Baker, J. K. (1974). Stochastic Modeling for Automatic Speech Understanding, *in* D. Reddy (ed.), *Speech Recognition*, Academic Press, New York, New-York, pp. 521 – 542.

Benmiloud, B. & Pieczynski, W. (1995). Estimation des paramètres dans les chaînes de Markov cachées et segmentation d'images, *Traitement du signal* 12(5): 433 – 454.

Bize, L., Muri, F., Samson, F., Rodolphe, F., Ehrlich, S. D., Prum, B. & Bessières, P. (1999). Searching Gene Transfers on *Bacillus subtilis* Using Hidden Markov Models, *RECOMB'99*.

Castellazzi, M., Wood, G., Burgess, P., Morris, J., Conrad, K. & Perry, J. (2008). A systematic representation of crop rotations, *Agricultural Systems* 97: 26–33.

Charniak, E. (1991). Bayesian Network without Tears, *AI magazine* .

Churchill, G. (1989). Stochastic Models for Heterogeneous DNA Sequences, *Bull Math Biol* 51(1): 79 – 94.

Delcher, A., Kasif, S., Fleischann, R., Peterson, J., White, O. & Salzberg, S. (1999). Alignment of whole genomes, *Nucl. Acids Res.* 27(11): 2369 – 2376.

Dempster, A., Laird, N. & Rubin, D. (1977). Maximum-Likelihood From Incomplete Data Via

The EM Algorithm, *Journal of Royal Statistic Society, B (methodological)* 39: 1 – 38.

Eng, C. (2010). *Développement de méthodes de fouille de données fondées sur les modèles de Markov cachés du second ordre pour l'identification d'hétérogénéités dans les génomes bactériens*, PhD thesis, Université Henri Poincaré Nancy 1. http://www.loria.fr/~jfmari/ACI/these_eng.pdf.

Eng, C., Asthana, C., Aigle, B., Hergalant, S., Mari, J.-F. & Leblond, P. (2009). A new data mining approach for the detection of bacterial promoters combining stochastic and combinatorial methods, *Journal of Computational Biology* 16(9): 1211–1225. http://hal.inria.fr/inria-00419969/en/.

Eng, C., Thibessard, A., Danielsen, M., Rasmussen, T., Mari, J.-F. & Leblond, P. (2011). In silico prediction of horizontal gene transfer in *Streptococcus thermophilus*, *Archives of Microbiology* . in preparation.

Fine, S., Singer, Y. & Tishby, N. (1998). The Hierarchical Hidden Markov Model: Analysis and Applications, *Machine Learning* 32: 41 – 62.

Forbes, F. & Pieczynski, W. (2009). New Trends in Markov Models and Related Learning to Restore Data, *IEEE International Workshop on Machine Learning for Signal Processing (MSLP)*, IEEE, Grenoble.

Forney, G. (1973). The Viterbi Algorithm, *IEEE Transactions* 61: 268–278.

Furui, S. (1986). Speaker-independent Isolated Word recognition Using Dynamic Features of Speech Spectrum, *IEEE Transactions on Acoutics, Speech and Signal Processing* .

Geman, S. & Geman, D. (1984). Stochastic Relaxation, Gibbs Distribution, and the Bayesian Restoration of Images, *IEEE Trans. on Pattern Analysis and Machine Intelligence* 6.

Grant, G., Swanson, F. & Wolman, M. (1990). Pattern and origin of stepped-bed morphology in high-gradient streams, Western Cascades, Oregon, *Geological Society of America Bulletin* 102: 340–352.

Hoebeke, M. & Schbath, S. (2006). R'mes: Finding exceptional motifs. user guide, *Technical report*, INRA.
URL: *http://genome.jouy.inra.fr/ssb/rmes*

Huang, H., Kao, M., Zhou, X., Liu, J. & Wong, W. (2004). Determination of local statistical significance of patterns in markov sequences with application to promoter element identification, *Journal of Computational Biology* 11(1).

Jain, A., Murty, M. & Flynn, P. (1999). Data Clustering: A Review, *ACM Computing Surveys* 31(3): 264 – 322.

Julian, B. (1986). On the Statistical Analysis of Dirty Picture, *Journal of the Royal Statistical Society* B(48): 259 – 302.

Kehagias, A. (2004). A hidden Markov model segmentation procedure for hydrological and environmental time series, *Stochastic Environmental Research* 18: 117–130.

Lazrak, E., Mari, J.-F. & Benoît, M. (2010). Landscape regularity modelling for environmental challenges in agriculture, *Landscape Ecology* 25(2): 169 - 183. http://hal.inria.fr/inria-00419952/en/.

Le Ber, F., Benoît, M., Schott, C., Mari, J.-F. & Mignolet, C. (2006). Studying Crop Sequences With CarrotAge, a HMM-Based Data Mining Software, *Ecological Modelling* 191(1): 170 – 185. http://hal.archives-ouvertes.fr/hal-00017169/fr/.

Li, C., Bishas, G., Dale, M. & Dale, P. (2001). *Advances in Intelligent Data Analysis*, Vol. 2189 of *LNCS*, Springer, chapter Building Models of Ecological Dynamics Using HMM Based Temporal Data Clustering – A Preliminary study, pp. 53 – 62.

Mari, J.-F., Haton, J.-P. & Kriouile, A. (1997). Automatic Word Recognition Based on

Second-Order Hidden Markov Models, *IEEE Transactions on Speech and Audio Processing* 5: 22 – 25.

Mari, J.-F. & Le Ber, F. (2003). Temporal and spatial data mining with second-order hidden markov models, *in* M. Nadif, A. Napoli, E. S. Juan & A. Sigayret (eds), *Fourth International Conference on Knowledge Discovery and Discrete Mathematics - Journées de l'informatique Messine - JIM'2003, Metz, France*, IUT de Metz, LITA, INRIA, pp. 247–254.

Mari, J.-F. & Le Ber, F. (2006). Temporal and Spatial Data Mining with Second-Order Hidden Markov Models, *Soft Computing* 10(5): 406 – 414. http://hal.inria.fr/inria-00000197.

Mari, J.-F. & Schott, R. (2001). *Probabilistic and Statistical Methods in Computer Science*, Kluwer Academic Publishers.

Mignolet, C., Schott, C. & Benoît, M. (2007). Spatial dynamics of farming practices in the Seine basin: Methods for agronomic approaches on a regional scale, *Science of The Total Environment* 375(1–3): 13–32. http://www.sciencedirect.com/ science/article/ B6V78-4N3P539-2/2/ 562034987911fb9545be7fda6dd914a8.

Nicolas, P., Bize, L., Muri, F., Hoebeke, M., Rodolphe, F., Ehrlich, S. D., Prum, B. & Bessières, P. (2002). Mining *Bacillus subtilis* Chromosome Heterogeneities Using Hidden Markov Models, *Nucleic Acids Research* 30(6): 1418 – 1426.

Pearl, J. (1988). *Probabilistic Reasoning in Intelligent Systems: Network of Plausible Inference*, Morgan Kaufman.

Pieczynski, W. (2003). Markov models in image processing, *Traitement du signal* 20(3): 255–278.

Rabiner, L. & Juang, B. (1995). *Fundamentals of Speech Recognition*, Prentice Hall.

Schaller, N., Lazrak, E.-G., Martin, P., Mari, J.-F., Aubry, C. & Benoît, M. (2010). Modelling regional land use: articulating the farm and the landscape levels by combining farmers' decision rules and landscape stochastic regularities, Poster session, European Society of Agronomy. Agropolis2010, Montpellier.

Schumm, S. (1977). *The fluvial system*, Wiley, New York. 338p.

Tou, J. T. & Gonzales, R. (1974). *Pattern Recognition Principles*, Addison-Wesley.

Whittaker, J. (1990). *Graphical Models in Applied Multivariate Statistics*, Wiley.